Tibet

Bradley Mayhew
Monique Choy
John Vincent Bellezza
Tony Wheeler

LONELY PLANET PUBLICATIONS
Melbourne • Oakland • London • Paris

MT KAILASH KORA
Four-day pilgrimage trek around Asia's holiest mountain

LAKE MANASAROVAR
Sacred and serene destination for Hindu and Buddhist pilgrims

RONGPHU MONASTERY
Has stunning views of Mt Everest's north face

SAKYA MONASTERY
Fortress-like monastery with the most spectacular assembly hall in Tibet

CHINA

XINJIANG

KUNLUN

RANGE

AKSAI CHIN
Under Chinese Administration
Claimed by India

Ladakh Range

XINJIANG - TIBET HWY

Changtang Nature Preserve

Changtang
(Northern Plateau)

HIMALAYA RANGE

Gangdise Range

NEPAL

The Terai

UTTAR PRADESH

INDIA

KATHMANDU

The external boundaries of India on this map have not been authenticated and may be not be correct.

Ruoqiang
Qiemo
Yecheng
Pishan
Kudi
Mazar
Dahongliutan
Yutian
Minfeng
Manni
Sumzhi
Gozha-tso
Rutok
Dormar
Tse-tso
Lumajiandong-tso
Memar-tso
Jaggang
Rutok Xian
Zapug
Aru-tso
Gomo-tso
Sali
Ali
Nganglong Kangri (6596m)
Qagcaka
Tsaka
Oma-chu
Gertse
Kangro
Xijiakonglong
Tishigang
Gar
Gegye
Dong-tso
Lhazhong
Tagtse-tso
Namru
Pongba
Yagra
Gunmidengli
Lumaxia
Beidaneikechuke
Ombu
Jaido
Tsaparang
Songsha
Daman Zhigon
Gongxianya
Dangra-tso
Zango
Zanda
Moincer
Mt Kailash (6714m)
Denglong
Lunggar
Tsochen
Zhari Nam-tso
Ngangtse-tso
Dongpo
Darchen
Barkha
Hor Qu
Thesum
Tuoya
Moerkesung
Amzhong
Rakshas Tal
Lake Manasarovar
Samsang
Qungtag
Nanda Devi (7817m)
Purang
Saipal (7050m)
Paryang
Xier Zhong
Zhongba
Basaguke
Raka
Sangsang
Gyading
Liasi
Saga
Tase
Lhatse
Rampur
Mahendranagar
Mustang
Tsangpo
Yarlung
Mangup
Gutso
Shegar
Sakya Monastery
Chay
Ganges River
Nepalganj
Dzongka
Siling
Rongphu Monastery
Shahahanpur
Pokhara
Paiku-tso
Zhangmu
Nyalam
Qomolangma NP
Kodari
Mt Everest (Qomolangma) (8848m)
Kanchenjunga (8598m)
Amlekhganj
Faizabad
Gorakhpur

Indus River
Sutlej River

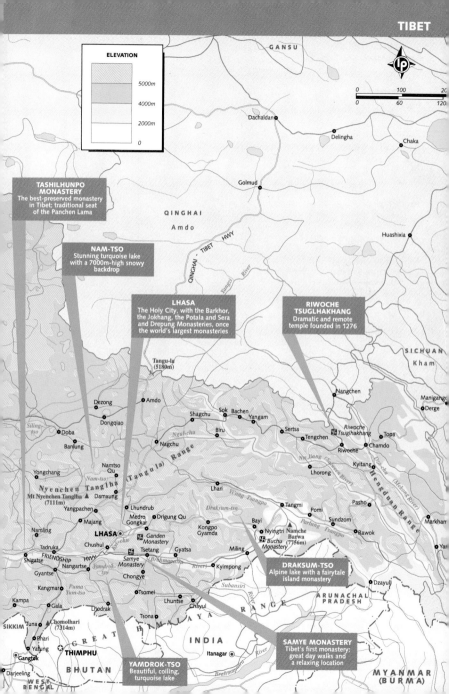

TIBET

ELEVATION

5000m
4000m
2000m
0

TASHILHUNPO MONASTERY
The best-preserved monastery in Tibet; traditional seat of the Panchen Lama

NAM-TSO
Stunning turquoise lake with a 7000m-high snowy backdrop

LHASA
The Holy City, with the Barkhor, the Jokhang, the Potala and Sera and Drepung Monasteries, once the world's largest monasteries

RIWOCHE TSUGLHAKHANG
Dramatic and remote temple founded in 1276

DRAKSUM-TSO
Alpine lake with a fairytale island monastery

SAMYE MONASTERY
Tibet's first monastery; great day walks and a relaxing location

YAMDROK-TSO
Beautiful, coiling, turquoise lake

GANSU

GOLMUD

Dachaldan

Delingha

Chaka

Huashixia

QINGHAI

Amdo

QINGHAI - TIBET HWY

Yangzi River

SICHUAN

Kham

Tangu-la (5180m)

Nangchen

Manigango

Derge

Dezong

Amdo

Shagchu

Sok
Bachen
Yangam

Sertsa

Tengchen

Riwoche Tsuglhakhang

Topa

Chamdo

Dongqiao

Biru

Riwoche

Siling-tso

Doba

Banlung

Nagchu

Ngul-chu

Kyitang

Nu Jiang (Salween River)

Yongchang

Namtso Qu

Nam-tso

Nyenchen Tanglha

(Tangula) Range

Lhari

Nyang-Tsangpo

Lhorong

Pasho

Markham

Mt Nyenchen Tanglha (7111m)

Damxung

Draksum-tso

Tangmi

Pomi

Sundzom

Rawok

Yar

Yangpachen

Lhundrub

Medro Gongkar

Drigung Qu

Kongpo Gyamda

Bayi

Nyingtri

Parlung Tsangpo

Namling

LHASA

Ganden Monastery

Tsetang

Gyatsa

Nyingtri
Namche Barwa (7756m)

Buchu Monastery

Chushul

Miling

Kyimpong

Tadruka

FRIENDSHIP HWY

Samye Monastery

Brahmaputra

Joveri

Subansiri

Dzayul

Shigatse

Nangartse

Yamdrok-tso

Chongye

ARUNACHAL PRADESH

Gyantse

Puma Yum-tso

Tsomei

River

Kangmar

Lhuntse

Chayul

Kampa

Gala

Lhodrak

Tsona

HIMALAYA

RANGE

Hengduan Range

Dza-chu (Mekong River)

Chomolhari (7314m)

SIKKIM

Tuna

Phari

GREAT

INDIA

Itanagar

River

Brahmaputra

MYANMAR (BURMA)

Yatung

THIMPHU

Gangtok

Darjeeling

WEST BENGAL

BHUTAN

Sertsa

Lhasa

Wang-Tsangpo

Tibet
5th edition – May 2002
First published – April 1986

Published by
Lonely Planet Publications Pty Ltd ABN 36 005 607 983
90 Maribyrnong St, Footscray, Victoria 3011, Australia

Lonely Planet offices
Australia Locked Bag 1, Footscray, Victoria 3011
USA 150 Linden St, Oakland, CA 94607
UK 10a Spring Place, London NW5 3BH
France 1 rue du Dahomey, 75011 Paris

Photographs
Many of the images in this guide are available for licensing from
Lonely Planet Images:
W www.lonelyplanetimages.com

Front-cover photograph
Prayer wheels and flags at Palha Lupuk, Lhasa
(Julia Wilkinson)

ISBN 1 86450 162 6

Contents – Text

THE AUTHORS   5

THIS BOOK   7

FOREWORD   8

INTRODUCTION   9

FACTS ABOUT TIBET   11

History 11	Fauna 30	Arts 35
Geography 27	National Preserves 32	Society & Conduct 40
Geology 28	Government & Politics 32	Religion 43
Climate 28	Economy 33	**Important Figures of Tibetan**
Ecology & Environment 28	Population & People 34	**Buddhism** 48
Flora 29	Education 35	Language 58

FACTS FOR THE VISITOR   59

Highlights 59	Newspapers & Magazines 82	Dangers & Annoyances 97
Suggested Itineraries 59	Radio & TV 82	Legal Matters 98
Planning 61	Video Systems 82	Business Hours 98
Responsible Tourism 65	Photography & Video 82	Public Holidays 99
Tourist Offices 65	Laundry 84	Special Events 99
Visas & Documents 65	Toilets 84	Activities 101
Embassies & Consulates 70	Health 84	Courses 101
Customs 71	Women Travellers 95	Work 102
Money 71	Gay & Lesbian Travellers 95	Accommodation 102
Post & Communications 74	Disabled Travellers 96	Food 103
Digital Resources 76	Senior Travellers 96	Drinks 105
Books 76	Travel with Children 96	Entertainment 106
Films 80	Useful Organisations 96	Shopping 106

GETTING THERE & AWAY   108

Air 108	Kathmandu 115	Air 118
Organised Tours 113	Chengdu 117	Land 119
Gateway Cities 115	**Tibet** 118	

GETTING AROUND   124

Bus 124	Car & Motorcycle 125	Local Transport 129
Minibus 124	Hitching 128	Organised Tours 129

LHASA   131

History 131	Drubthub Nunnery &	Tsepak Lhakhang 153
Orientation 132	Palha Lupuk 152	Gyüme 153
Information 134	Chagpo Ri 152	Meru Sarpa Monastery 154
Barkhor Area 138	Parma Ri 152	Karmashar Temple 154
The Potala 140	Lukhang 153	Ani Sangkhung Nunnery 154
The Jokhang 141	Ramoche Temple 153	Lho Rigsum Lhakhang 154

Muslim Quarter 155
The Norbulingka 155
Tibetan Traditional Hospital 157
Tibet Museum 158
Special Events 158
Places to Stay 158

Places to Eat 161
Entertainment 163
Shopping 164
Getting There & Away 166
Getting Around 168
Around Lhasa **169**

Drepung Monastery 169
Nechung Monastery 172
Sera Monastery 173
Pabonka Monastery 176
Ganden Monastery 177
Drölma Lhakhang 180

Ü
182

Northern Ü **182**
Tsurphu Monastery 184
Nam-Tso 186
Drak Yerpa 189
Lhundrub Valley 190
Talung Monastery 192
Reting Monastery 192
Road to Drigung Til Monastery 193

Drigung Til Monastery 194
Tidrum Nunnery 195
Yarlung Tsangpo Valley **196**
Gongkar 196
Dorje Drak Monastery 197
Dranang Monastery &
Valley 197
Mindroling Monastery 198

Samye Monastery 199
Namseling Manor 204
Tsetang 204
Gangpo Ri 206
Yarlung Valley 206
Chongye Valley 209
Lhamo La-Tso 210

TSANG
212

Yamdrok-Tso 212
Gyantse 216
Tsechen Monastery & Fort 222
Yungdrungling Monastery ..222
Shigatse 223

Around Shigatse 233
Sakya 234
Lhatse 238
Around Lhatse 239
Shegar 240

Everest Region 240
Tingri 245
Nyalam 246
Zhangmu 247

NGARI (WESTERN TIBET)
250

Southern Route 255
Northern Route 258
Ali 261
Ali to Mt Kailash 263
Mt Kailash 263

Lake Manasarovar 265
Tirthapuri Hot Springs &
Kora 267
Guge Kingdom 269
Dungkar 274

Rutok 274
Xinjiang to Ali 275
Western Nepal to
Mt Kailash 276

KHAM (EASTERN TIBET)
279

Kongpo Gyamda 283
Draksum-Tso 284
Bayi 286
Around Bayi 287
Nyingtri to Pomi 290
Pomi 291
Rawok-Tso 292
Rawok-Tso to Pasho 292

Pasho 293
Pasho to Chamdo 293
Chamdo 294
Chamdo to Riwoche 296
Riwoche 297
Riwoche Tsuglhakhang 297
Riwoche to Tengchen 298
Tengchen 299

Tengchen to Sok 299
Sok 300
Sok to Nagchu 300
Nagchu 300
Nagchu to Lhasa 301
Northern Route to Sichuan ..301
Southern Route to Sichuan ..307

TREKKING
310

Facts about Trekking **310**
History 310
Geography 310
Climate 310
Ecology & Environment 311
Flora & Fauna 311
People & Society 312
Facts for the Trekker **312**

Planning 312
Trekking Agencies 313
Documents 315
Health 315
Trekking with Children 315
Guides & Pack Animals 315
Routes **318**
Ganden to Samye 319

Tsurphu to Yangpachen 323
Shalu to Nartang 326
Friendship Highway to Everest
Base Camp 329
Everest Base Camp to
Tingri 335
Mt Kailash Kora 338
Lake Manasarovar Kora 345

LANGUAGE 348

Tibetan 348   Chinese 352

GLOSSARY 358

INDEX 366

Text 369   Boxed Text 375

Contents – Maps

INTRODUCTION

Tibet Locator Map 9

LHASA

Lhasa 136-7   Red Palace of the Potala 150   Drepung Monastery 172
Barkhor Area 139   The Norbulingka 155   Sera Monastery 174
The Jokhang 143   Around Lhasa 170   Ganden Monastery 178

Ü

Ü 183   Tsetang 205
Samye Monastery 200   Yarlung & Chongye Valleys ..206

TSANG

Tsang 214-15   Shigatse 224   Nyalam 246
Yamdrok-Tso 216   Tashilhunpo Monastery 226   Zhangmu 248
Gyantse 217   Sakya 235

NGARI (WESTERN TIBET)

Ngari (Western Tibet) 251   Tirthapuri Hot Springs & Kora 267   Tsaparang 272
Ali 262   Zanda & Thöling Monastery 270   Purang 277

KHAM (EASTERN TIBET)

Kham (Eastern Tibet) 280   Bayi 286
Kongpo Region 285   Chamdo 295

TREKKING

Ganden to Samye 320   Shalu to Nartang 328   Mt Kailash Kora 339
Tsurphu to Yangpachen 324   Everest Region Treks 330   Lake Manasarovar Kora 346

MAP LEGEND back page

METRIC CONVERSION inside back cover

MAPS

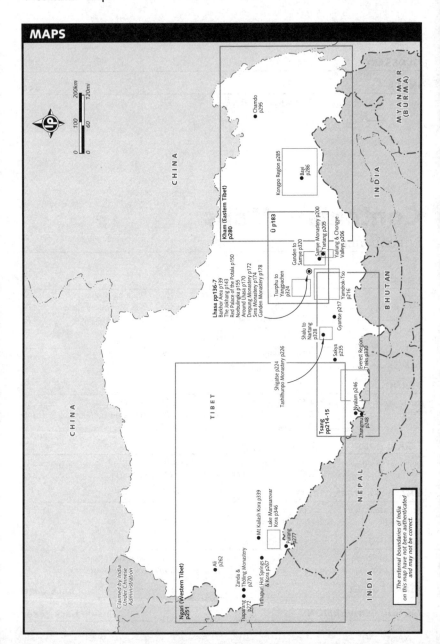

MYANMAR (BURMA)

CHINA

Chamdo p295

Kongpo Region p285

Bayi p286

INDIA

Kham (Eastern Tibet) p280

Ü p183

Samye Monastery p200

Setang p205

Yarlung & Chongye Valleys p206

Ganden to Samye p320

Tsurphu to Yangpachen p224

Lhasa pp136-7
Barkhor Area p139
The Jokhang p143
Red Palace of the Potala p150
Norbulingka p155
Around Lhasa p170
Drepung Monastery p172
Sera Monastery p174
Ganden Monastery p178

CHINA

Yamdrok-Tso p216

Gyantse p217

Shalu to Nartang p328

Shigatse p224
Tashilhunpo Monastery p226

Sakya p235

Everest Region Treks p330

TIBET

Tsang pp214-15

Nyalam p246

Zhangmu p248

BHUTAN

NEPAL

Mt Kailash Kora p339

Lake Manasarovar Kora p346

Purang p277

INDIA

Claimed by India Under Chinese Administration

Ali p262

Zanda & Thöling Monastery p270

Tsaparang p272

Tirthapuri Hot Springs & Kora p267

Ngari (Western Tibet) p251

The external boundaries of India on this map have not been authenticated and may not be correct.

0   100   200km
0   60   120mi

The Authors

Bradley Mayhew

Bradley started travelling in south-west China, Tibet and northern Pakistan while studying Chinese at Oxford University. Upon graduation he fled to Central America for six months to forget his Chinese and now regularly travels to China's borderlands in a futile attempt to get it back. He wrote Lonely Planet's *Mongolia* and *Shanghai* guides, and co-wrote *Pakistan*, *Karakoram Highway* and *Central Asia*, among others. He splits his time between Sevenoaks in south-east England and obscure parts of Montana.

Monique Choy

On Monique's travels she has sipped tea with a Templar knight on the Camino de Santiago in Spain, cast a line for barramundi with Yolngu people in Arnhemland and tussled with an angry ghost on a former island of the banished in the Maldives.

She now lives in the town of Cockatoo, near Melbourne, Australia, where she attempts to keep her organic garden alive between trips overseas. She has contributed to Lonely Planet's *Aboriginal Australia & the Torres Strait Islands*, *Australia*, and *Out to Eat – Melbourne* guides.

John Vincent Bellezza

John Vincent Bellezza was born in New York City. Suffocating in his comfortable suburban American lifestyle, he left to wander around the mountains and jungles of the Americas for several years before realising his childhood dream of visiting the Himalaya. 'Jungly' John has lived in Tibet and adjoining Himalaya regions for the past 19 years and has covered a great deal of ground on foot. Through much legwork and study he has become an expert in the indigenous religious traditions of Tibet. His books include *Divine Dyads: Ancient Civilization in Tibet*; *Antiquities of Northern Tibet*; and *Antiquities of Upper Tibet*.

Tony Wheeler

Tony Wheeler was born in England but grew up in Pakistan, the Bahamas and the USA. He returned to England to do a degree in engineering at Warwick University, worked as an automotive design engineer, returned to London Business School to complete an MBA, then set out on an Asian overland trip with his wife, Maureen. That led to Tony and Maureen founding Lonely Planet Publications in Australia in 1973, and they've been travelling, writing and publishing guidebooks ever since.

FROM THE AUTHORS

From Bradley

Thanks to Andre for yet another fine trip into remotest eastern Tibet and for being a fine trekking partner in western Sichuan. Where to next, compadre? John Ackerly of the International Campaign for Tibet was generous with several maps. Thanks to Eric Woefel and Nicole Graaf in Lhasa for information on studying in Tibet and for Nicole's images of statue casting. Thanks to Clare Mercer for information on shopping in Lhasa and her trip out to western Tibet and Kashgar. Cheers to co-authors John Bellezza for Kathmandu information and Monique Choy for her unflagging help with various parts of the text. Thanks to all at LP for working hard around my tight time frames. Finally, loving thanks to Kelli for creating a home to come back to every time.

From Monique

Special thanks to Miri Sellem, Lisa Ognjanovic, Brett Dalliston and Clint Curé for their humour, flexibility and incomparable company on the road. I'm also indebted to Tsewang, Dobje, Nimasuri, Lavasuri and Dicky for their insights into Tibetan culture. In Hong Kong, thanks to Dad, Aunty Lee and especially Trevor for giving me a roof over my head, and in Chengdu thanks to Paul for the poetry. My deep admiration goes to the people of Tibet for their steely spirit, and my appreciation to the many travellers who told me the stories of their (often incredible) journeys and patiently answered my probing questions, down to the last yuan. I'm grateful also to Clare Mercer and all the readers who wrote in with useful information about their trips.

Finally, a very big thank you to Bradley Mayhew for his wise words and guidance, and to the Lonely Planet team.

From John

I would like to heartily thank Tibetans of all walks of life who helped make my treks successful. Along with the mystic landscape it was the people that made my peregrinations around Tibet one of the highlights of my life. A special thanks is also due to Stan Armington and his staff at Malla Treks for all their support.

This Book

The first edition of this book was researched and written by Michael Buckley and Robert Strauss. Robert Strauss was responsible for the second edition, Chris Taylor for the third, and Bradley Mayhew, Tony Wheeler and John Bellezza for the fourth.

Bradley Mayhew was coordinating author for this edition of *Tibet*, the fifth. Monique Choy updated the Ngari (Western Tibet) and Tsang chapters; John Bellezza updated the Trekking chapter.

FROM THE PUBLISHER

This edition of *Tibet* was coordinated by Kerryn Burgess (editor) and Shahara Ahmed (cartographer and designer) in Lonely Planet's Melbourne office. Rodney Zandbergs designed the colour pages and assisted with layout. Jenny Mullaly, Anne Mulvaney, Nancy Ianni and John Hinman assisted with editing and proofreading, while Anna Judd, Sarah Sloane, Amanda Sierp, Katie Butterworth and Huw Fowles helped with mapping. Emma Koch and Quentin Frayne coordinated the Language chapter, Annie Horner coordinated the images from LPI, and Matt King coordinated the illustrations, which were drawn by Jenny Bowman and Sarah Jolly. Mark Germanchis helped with Quark matters, and Margaret Jung designed the cover. Hilary Ericksen and Adriana Mammarella oversaw the project.

THANKS
Many thanks to the travellers who used the last edition and wrote to us with helpful hints, advice and interesting anecdotes. Your names appear in the back of this book.

Foreword

ABOUT LONELY PLANET GUIDEBOOKS

The story begins with a classic travel adventure: Tony and Maureen Wheeler's 1972 journey across Europe and Asia to Australia. There was no useful information about the overland trail then, so Tony and Maureen published the first Lonely Planet guidebook to meet a growing need.

From a kitchen table, Lonely Planet has grown to become the largest independent travel publisher in the world, with offices in Melbourne (Australia), Oakland (USA), London (UK) and Paris (France).

Today Lonely Planet guidebooks cover the globe. There is an ever-growing list of books and information in a variety of media. Some things haven't changed. The main aim is still to make it possible for adventurous travellers to get out there – to explore and better understand the world.

At Lonely Planet we believe travellers can make a positive contribution to the countries they visit – if they respect their host communities and spend their money wisely. Since 1986 a percentage of the income from each book has been donated to aid projects and human rights campaigns, and, more recently, to wildlife conservation.

> Although inclusion in a guidebook usually implies a recommendation we cannot list every good place. Exclusion does not necessarily imply criticism. In fact there are a number of reasons why we might exclude a place – sometimes it is simply inappropriate to encourage an influx of travellers.

UPDATES & READER FEEDBACK

Things change – prices go up, schedules change, good places go bad and bad places go bankrupt. Nothing stays the same. So, if you find things better or worse, recently opened or long-since closed, please tell us and help make the next edition even more accurate and useful.

Lonely Planet thoroughly updates each guidebook as often as possible – usually every two years, although for some destinations the gap can be longer. Between editions, up-to-date information is available in our free, quarterly *Planet Talk* newsletter and monthly email bulletin *Comet*. The *Upgrades* section of our website (W www.lonelyplanet.com) is also regularly updated by Lonely Planet authors, and the site's *Scoop* section covers news and current affairs relevant to travellers. Lastly, the *Thorn Tree* bulletin board and the *Postcards* section carry unverified, but fascinating, reports from travellers.

Tell us about it! We genuinely value your feedback. A well-travelled team at Lonely Planet reads and acknowledges every email and letter we receive and ensures that every morsel of information finds its way to the relevant authors, editors and cartographers.

Everyone who writes to us will find their name listed in the next edition of the appropriate guide-book, and will receive the latest issue of *Comet* or *Planet Talk*. The very best contributions will be rewarded with a free guidebook.

We may edit, reproduce and incorporate your comments in Lonely Planet products such as guide-books, Web sites and digital products, so let us know if you don't want your comments reproduced or your name acknowledged.

How to contact Lonely Planet:
Online: e talk2us@lonelyplanet.com.au, W www.lonelyplanet.com
Australia: Locked Bag 1, Footscray, Victoria 3011
UK: 10a Spring Place, London NW5 3BH
USA: 150 Linden St, Oakland, CA 94607

Introduction

Shangri-la, the Land of Snows, the roof of the world: For centuries the mysterious Buddhist kingdom of Tibet, locked away in its mountain fastness of the Himalaya, has exercised a unique hold on the imagination of the West. The Jesuits, hearing rumours of Tibet in faraway Goa, believed it to harbour a long-lost community of Christians, the kingdom of Prester John. For adventurers and traders it was a land of treasure and riches. Those on a spiritual quest whispered of a lost land steeped in magic and mystery.

But as Tibetans woke to the sound of foreign travellers prying at the closed doors of their kingdom, they slipped the lock and threw away the keys. Lhasa, the ultimate prize for countless proselytisers, adventurers and dreamers, became the Forbidden City.

Until recently, very few Westerners were privileged to lay eyes on the Holy City.

When the doors were finally flung open in the mid-1980s, Tibet was no longer the hidden hermit kingdom that had so intoxicated early Western travellers. In 1950, the newly established People's Republic of China (PRC) had decided to make good a long-held but dubious Chinese claim on the strategically important plateau between China and the subcontinent. Between 1950 and 1970, the Chinese 'liberated' the Tibetans of their independence, drove their spiritual leader and some 100,000 of Tibet's finest into exile (admittedly a 'side-effect' rather than a goal of Chinese policy), caused some 1.2 million Tibetan deaths (again largely a 'side-effect') and destroyed most of the Tibetan cultural and historical heritage.

When the first tourists were allowed into Tibet in the mid-1980s, they came to a devastated country. Most of Tibet's finest monasteries lay in ruins. Monks who, under a recent thaw in Chinese ethnic chauvinism, were once again donning their vestments, cautiously folded them back to display the scars of 'struggle sessions'. The journalist Harrison Salisbury referred to Tibet as a 'dark and sorrowing land'.

Throughout Tibet, Tibetans are rebuilding their world. Some observers have compared this process to the Tibetan renaissance of the 11th century, when Buddhism returned to the land after two centuries of persecution. Yet early in the new millennium this world is changing faster than at any time in Tibet's history. You can now send emails from Lhasa and get a Pepsi in even the smallest of villages, while modern Chinatowns continue to sprout up around Tibetan settlements.

And still the quintessence of Tibet remains remarkably intact. The Jokhang temple is still full of pilgrims murmuring mantras in the golden light of a thousand yak-butter lamps. Butter tea remains the most popular beverage by far and strangers will continually invite you to share some tea or a bowl of barley beer. A walk around Lhasa's Barkhor pilgrimage circuit is proof enough that all the efforts of the Chinese to build a Brave New (Roof of the) World have foundered on the remarkable faith of the Tibetan people. Tibet can truly claim to be on a higher 'plain'.

Tibet is without doubt one of the most remarkable places to visit in Asia. It offers fabulous monastery sights, breathtaking high-altitude treks, stunning views of the world's highest mountains and one of the most likeable peoples you will ever meet. But you are never far from the reality of politics. For anyone who travels with their eyes open, a visit to Tibet will be a memorable, fascinating, but sobering and at times even saddening experience.

Facts about Tibet

HISTORY
Mythological Beginnings

Little is known of the beginnings of the Tibetan people. They originated from the nomadic, warlike tribes known as the Qiang. Chinese records of these tribes, which harried the borders of the great Chinese empire, date back as far as the 2nd century BC. However, the people of Tibet were not to emerge as a politically united force to be reckoned with until the 7th century AD.

Like all peoples, the Tibetans have a rich corpus of myths concerning the origin of the world and themselves. In the beginning, according to a Tibetan creation myth, the void was filled with a wind that gathered in force until storm clouds brewed and unleashed a torrential rain, forming in time the primeval ocean. After the cessation of the rains, the wind continued to blow over the ocean, churning it like cream, until lands, like butter, came into existence.

According to myth, the Tibetan people owe their existence to the union of an ogress and a monkey on Gangpo Ri at Tsetang (anticipating Darwin by over a millennium!). Another legend tells of how the first Tibetan king descended from heaven on a sky cord. These early myths are no doubt Bön in origin, but have been appropriated by Buddhism, so that the monkey is seen as a manifestation of Chenresig (Avalokiteshvara), the Bodhisattva of Compassion. The ogress and the monkey had six children, who are seen as the ancestors of the six main tribes of Tibet.

Yarlung Valley Dynasty

As early myths of the origin of the Tibetan people suggest, the Yarlung Valley was the cradle of the civilisation of central Tibet. The early Yarlung kings, although glorified in legend, were probably no more than chieftains whose domains extended not much further than the Yarlung Valley area itself. A reconstruction of Tibet's first fortress, Yumbulagang, can still be seen in the Yarlung Valley, and it is here that the 28th king of Tibet is said to have received Tibet's first Buddhist scriptures in the 5th century. According to legend, they fell on the roof of Yumbulagang.

Credible historical records regarding the Yarlung Valley dynasty date only from the time when the fledgling kingdom entered the international arena in the 6th century. By this time the Yarlung kings, through conquest and alliances, had made significant headway in unifying much of central Tibet. Namri Songtsen (c. 570–619), the 32nd Tibetan king, continued this trend and extended Tibetan influence into inner Asia, defeating the Qiang tribes on China's borders. But the true flowering of Tibet as an important regional power came about with the accession to rule of Namri Songtsen's son, Songtsen Gampo (r. 630–49).

Under Songtsen Gampo, central Tibet entered a new era. Tibetan expansion continued unabated. The armies of Tibet ranged as far afield as northern India and emerged as a threat to the Tang dynasty in China. Both Nepal and China reacted to the Tibetan incursions by reluctantly agreeing to alliances through marriage. Princess Wencheng, Songtsen Gampo's Chinese bride, and Princess Bhrikuti, his Nepali bride, became important historical figures for the Tibetans, as it was through their influence that Buddhism first gained royal patronage and a foothold on the Tibetan plateau. The king went as far as passing a law making it illegal *not* to be a Buddhist.

King Songtsen Gampo's reign saw the establishment of the Jokhang and Ramoche temples and the construction of a fort on the site of what much later was to become the Potala palace in Lhasa. Contact with the Chinese led to the introduction of the sciences of astronomy and medicine, and a Tibetan script was developed from Indian sources. It was used in the first translations of Buddhist scriptures, in drafting a code of law and in writing the first histories of Tibet.

For two centuries after the reign of Songtsen Gampo, Tibet continued to grow in power and influence. By the time of King Trisong Detsen (r. 755–97), Tibetan influence extended across Turkestan, northern Pakistan, Nepal and India. In China, Tibetan armies conquered Gansu and Sichuan and controlled the great Buddhist cave complex of Dunhuang. In 763, Tibetan armies overran Chang'an (present-day Xi'an), the Chinese capital, forcing the Chinese to conclude a treaty that recognised new borders incorporating most of the Tibetan conquests.

A further Sino-Tibetan treaty was signed in 821 during the reign of King Tritsug Detsen Ralpachen (r. 817–36). It was immortalised in stone on three steles: one in Lhasa, outside the Jokhang; one in the Chinese capital of Chang'an; and one on the border of Tibet and China. Only the Lhasa stele still stands (see Barkhor Square in the Lhasa chapter). Signatories to the treaty swore that '…the whole region to the east…being the country of Great China and the whole region to the west being assuredly that of the country of Great Tibet, from either side of that frontier there shall be no warfare, no hostile invasions, and no seizure of territory…'. The treaty went on to herald a new era in which 'Tibetans shall be happy in Tibet and Chinese shall be happy in China'.

Introduction of Buddhism

By the time Buddhism first arrived in Tibet during the reign of Songtsen Gampo, it had already flourished for some 1100 years and had become the principal faith of all Tibet's neighbouring countries. Buddhism was initially slow to take hold in Tibet.

Early missionaries, such as Shantarakshita from the Indian Buddhist centre of Nalanda (in modern-day Bihar), faced great hostility from the Bön-dominated court. The influence of Songtsen Gampo's Chinese and Nepali wives was almost certainly limited to the royal court, and priests of the time were probably Indian and Chinese, not Tibetan.

It was not until King Trisong Detsen's reign that Buddhism began to make any real progress. Trisong Detsen was responsible for founding Samye Monastery, the first institution to carry out the systematic translation of Buddhist scriptures and the training of Tibetan monks.

Still, the introduction of Buddhism to Tibet was no simple matter of adopting a prescribed body of precepts. By the 9th century many schools of Buddhism had evolved from the original teachings of Sakyamuni (Sakya Thukpa), and Tibetans were in no way presented with a coherent unified body of beliefs.

Contention over the path that Buddhism was to take in Tibet culminated in the Great Debate of Samye, in which King Trisong Detsen is said to have adjudicated in favour of Indian teachers who advocated a gradual approach to enlightenment, founded in scholastic study and moral precepts. There was, however, much opposition to this institutionalised, clerical Buddhism, largely from supporters of the Bön faith. The next Tibetan king, Tritsug Detsen Ralpachen, fell victim to this opposition and was assassinated by his brother, Langdharma, who launched an attack on Buddhism. In 842,

Sakyamuni (Sakya Thukpa),
the Historical Buddha

Langdharma was himself assassinated – by a Buddhist monk disguised as a Black Hat dancer, during a festival – and the Tibetan state soon collapsed into a number of warring principalities. In the confusion that followed, support for Buddhism dwindled and clerical monastic Buddhism experienced a 150-year hiatus.

Second Diffusion of Buddhism

The collapse of the Tibetan state in 842 put a stop to Tibetan expansion in Asia; Tibet was never again to rise to arms. Overwhelmed initially with local power struggles, Buddhism gradually began to exert its influence again, giving the Tibetan mind a spiritual bent and turning it inward on itself. As the tide of Buddhist faith receded in India, Nepal and China, Tibet slowly emerged as the most devoutly Buddhist nation in the world.

While Tibetan Buddhist tradition holds that the collapse of the Tibetan state corresponds with the systematic persecution of Buddhism, many Western scholar believe that this was probably not the case. It is more likely that Buddhist institutions, such as Samye Monastery, which were brought into being by the state, fell into neglect with the collapse of central power. There is evidence that Buddhism survived in pockets and received the patronage of some noble families in the 150 years that passed before the resurgence of monastic Buddhism.

The so-called second diffusion of Buddhism (also referred to as the dharma) corresponded with two developments. First, Tibetan teachers who had taken refuge in Kham, to the east, returned to central Tibet and established new monasteries in the late 10th century. Second, and not long after, the kingdom of Guge in western Tibet invited the Bengali scholar Atisha (Jowo-je; 982–1054) to Tibet in the mid-11th century. Disciples of Atisha (Jowo-je), chiefly Dromtönpa, were instrumental in establishing the Kadampa order, and monasteries such as Reting in Ü.

This resurgence of Buddhist influence in the 11th century led to many Tibetans travelling to India to study. The new ideas they brought back with them had a revitalising effect on Tibetan thought and produced other new schools of Tibetan Buddhism. Among them was the Kagyupa order, established by Milarepa (1040–1123) who was the disciple of Marpa the translator (1012–93). Meanwhile, in Sakya, the Kön family established a monastery in 1073 that was to emerge as the seat of the Sakyapa order.

Sakyapa Order Ascendancy & Mongol Overlordship

With the collapse of a central Tibetan state, Tibet's contacts with China dwindled. By the time the Tang dynasty reached the end of its days in 907, China had already recovered almost all the territory it had previously lost to the Tibetans. Throughout the Song dynasty (960–1276) the two nations had virtually no contact with each other, and Tibet's sole foreign contacts were with its southern Buddhist neighbours.

This was all set to change when Genghis Khan launched a series of conquests in 1206 that led to Mongol supremacy in the form of a vast empire that straddled central Asia and China. China was not to fall to the Mongols until 1279, but in the meantime the Mongols made short work of central Asia. Preoccupied with other matters, the Mongols did not give Tibet serious attention until 1239, when they sent a number of raiding parties into the country. Numerous monasteries were razed and the Mongols almost reached Lhasa before turning back.

Tibetan accounts have it that returning Mongol troops related the spiritual eminence of the Tibetan lamas to Godan Khan, grandson of Genghis Khan and ruler of the Kokonor region (modern-day Qinghai), and in response Godan summoned Sakya Pandita, the head of Sakya Monastery, to his court. The outcome of this meeting was the beginning of a priest-patron relationship between the deeply religious Tibetans and the militarily adventurous Mongols. Tibetan Buddhism became the state religion of the Mongol empire in east Asia, and the head Sakya lama became its spiritual leader, a position that also entailed temporal authority over Tibet. Many monasteries converted (or were converted) to the Sakya school.

The Sakyapa ascendancy lasted less than 100 years. It was strife-torn from the start. The Sakyapa relationship with the Mongol court and its rule of Tibet aroused the jealousy of other religious orders. Political intrigue, power struggles and violence were the order of the day. By 1350, Changchub Gyaltsen, a monk who had first trained in Sakya and then returned to his home district in the Yarlung Valley as a local official, contrived, through alliances and outright confrontation, to overturn the Sakya hegemony. Just 18 years later, the Mongol Yuan dynasty in China lost its grip on power and the Chinese Ming dynasty was established.

Tibetan Independence

Certain Chinese claims on Tibet have looked to the Mongol Yuan dynasty overlordship of the high plateau, and the priest-patron relationship that existed at the time, as setting a precedent for Chinese sovereignty over Tibet. Pro-independence supporters state that this is like India claiming sovereignty over Myanmar (Burma) because both were ruled by the British.

Reincarnation Lineages

It is not unusual for an important Tibetan lama to be a *trulku* (also spelt *tulku*), or 'incarnate lama'. There are thought to be several thousand of these lamas in contemporary Tibet. The abbots of many monasteries are trulku, and thus abbotship can be traced back through a lineage of rebirths to the original founder of a monastery, or at least to an important figure associated with the founding of the monastery.

Strictly speaking, however, this investiture of power through rebirth is known as *yangsid*, and a trulku is a manifestation of a Tantric deity that repeatedly expresses itself through a series of rebirths. The honorific title *rinpoche*, meaning 'very precious', is a mark of respect and does not necessarily imply that the holder is a trulku.

The most famous manifestation of a deity is of course the Dalai Lama lineage. The Dalai Lamas are manifestations of Chenresig (Avalokiteshvara), the Bodhisattva of Compassion. The Panchen Lama, on the other hand, is a manifestation of Jampelyang (Manjushri), the Bodhisattva of Insight. There is no exclusivity in such a manifestation: Tsongkhapa, founder of the Gelugpa order, was also a manifestation of Jampelyang (Manjushri), as traditionally were the abbots of the Sakya Monastery.

As a general rule, the reincarnations of high-status lamas tend to be found in aristocratic families (as in the early Dalai Lamas) or in families where trulkus have already been identified. The family of the present Dalai Lama, for example, was by no means aristocratic, but his elder brother had already been identified as a trulku and his younger brother was also later recognised as a trulku.

Lamas approaching death often leave behind clues pointing to the location of their reincarnation. The Panchen Lamas have their reincarnation confirmed by lots drawn from a golden urn. Potential candidates are tested by being required to pick out the former lama's possessions from a collection of objects. Disputes over trulku status are not uncommon. A family's fortunes are likely to improve if an incarnate lama is discovered among the children; this creates an incentive for fraud.

It is possible to see in the trulku system a substitute for the system of hereditary power (as in Western royal lineages) in a society where, historically, many of the major players were celibate and unable to produce their own heirs. Not that celibacy was overwhelmingly the case. The abbots of Sakya took wives to produce their own trulku reincarnations, and it is not uncommon for rural trulkus to do the same.

The major flaw with the system is the time needed for the reincarnation to reach adulthood. Regents have traditionally been appointed to run the country but this tradition takes on an added dimension under modern political circumstances. The Dalai Lama has made it clear that he will not be reincarnated in Chinese-occupied Tibet and may even be the last Dalai Lama.

In fact, Tibetan submission was offered to the Mongols before they conquered China and it ended when the Mongols fell from power in that country. When the Mongol empire disintegrated, both China and Tibet regained their independence. Sino-Tibetan relations took on the form of regular exchanges of diplomatic courtesies by two independent governments.

After defeating the Sakyapas, Changchub Gyaltsen undertook to remove all traces of the Mongol administration. In doing this he drew on the tradition of the former Yarlung kings: Officials were required to dress in the manner of the former royal court; a revised version of King Songtsen Gampo's code of law was enacted; a new taxation system was enforced; and scrolls depicting the glories of the Yarlung dynasty were commissioned (although Changchub Gyaltsen claimed they were 'discovered'). The movement was nothing short of a declaration of Tibet's independence from foreign interference and a search for national identity.

Changchub Gyaltsen and his successors ruled Tibet until 1435 from Nedong, near the Yarlung Valley. Their rule was succeeded by the princes of Rinpung, an area south-west of Lhasa. In 1565, the kings of Tsang became secular rulers of Tibet from Shigatse. Spiritual authority at this time was vested in the Karmapa, head of a Kagyupa suborder at Tsurphu Monastery.

Rise of the Gelugpa & the Dalai Lamas

In 1374, a young man named Tsongkhapa set out from his home near Kokonor in eastern Tibet to central Tibet, where he undertook training with all the major schools of Tibetan Buddhism. By the time he was 25 years old, he had already gained a reputation as a teacher and a writer, although he continued to study under eminent lamas of the day.

Tsongkhapa established a monastery at Ganden near Lhasa, and it was here that he had a vision of Atisha (Jowo-je), the 11th-century Bengali scholar who had been instrumental in the second diffusion of Buddhism in Tibet. At Ganden, Tsongkhapa maintained a course of expounding his thinking, steering clear of political intrigue, and espousing doctrinal purity and monastic discipline. Although it seems unlikely that Tsongkhapa intended to found another school of Buddhism, his teachings attracted many disciples, who found his return to the original teachings of Atisha (Jowo-je) an exciting alternative to the politically tainted Sakyapa and Kagyupa orders.

Disciples of Tsongkhapa, determined to propagate their master's teachings, established monasteries at Drepung (1416) and at Sera (1419). In 1447 yet another monastery (Tashilhunpo) was established at Shigatse, and the movement came to be known as the Gelugpa (Virtuous) order. The founder of Tashilhunpo, Genden Drup, was a nephew of Tsongkhapa, and shortly before his death he announced that he would be reincarnated in Tibet and gave his followers signs that would enable them to find him. His reincarnation, Genden Gyatso, served as the head of Drepung Monastery, which was now the largest in Tibet, and further consolidated the prestige of the new Gelugpa order.

By the time of the third reincarnated head of the Gelugpa, Sonam Gyatso (1543–88), the Mongols began to take an interest in Tibet's new and increasingly powerful order. In a move that mirrored the 13th-century Sakyapa entrance into the political arena, Sonam Gyatso accepted an invitation to meet with Altyn Khan near Kokonor in 1578. At the meeting, Sonam Gyatso received the title of *dalai*, meaning 'ocean', and implying 'ocean of wisdom'. The title was retrospectively bestowed on his previous two reincarnations, and Sonam Gyatso became the third Dalai Lama.

The Gelugpa-Mongol relationship marked the Gelugpa's entry into the turbulent waters of worldly affairs. Ties with the Mongols deepened when, at the third Dalai Lama's death in 1588, his next reincarnation was found in a great-grandson of the Mongolian Altyn Khan. The boy was brought to Lhasa with great ceremony under the escort of armed Mongol troops.

It is no surprise that the Tsang kings and the Karmapa of Tsurphu Monastery saw this Gelugpa-Mongol alliance as a direct threat

Tangtong Gyelpo

Tangtong Gyelpo (1385–1464) was Tibet's Renaissance man *par excellence*. Nyingmapa yogi, treasure finder, engineer, medic and inventor of Tibetan opera, Tangtong formed a song-and-dance troop of seven sisters to raise money for his other passion, bridge building. He eventually built 108 bridges in Tibet, the most famous of which was over the Yarlung Tsangpo near modern-day Chushul. Tangtong is often depicted in monastery murals with long white hair and a beard, and is often holding a section of chain links from one of his bridges.

to their power. Bickering broke out, and in 1611 the Tsang king attacked Drepung and Sera Monasteries. The fourth Dalai Lama fled central Tibet and died at the age of 25 (he was probably poisoned) in 1616.

The Great Fifth Dalai Lama

A successor to the fourth Dalai Lama was soon discovered, and the boy was brought to Lhasa, again under Mongol escort. In the meantime, Mongol intervention in Tibetan affairs continued in the guise of support for the embattled Gelugpa order.

In 1621 a Mongolian invasion was turned back at the last minute through mediation by the Panchen Lama of Tashilhunpo Monastery. This suggests that there were probably elements of the Gelugpa order that preferred a truce with the kings of Tsang to outright conflict.

Whatever the case, it seems that proponents of Gelugpa domination had the upper hand, and in 1640, Mongol forces intervened on their behalf, defeating the Tsang forces. The Tsang king was taken captive and later executed, probably at the instigation of Tashilhunpo monks.

Unlike the Sakya-Mongol domination of Tibet, under which the head Sakya lama was required to reside in the Mongol court, the fifth Dalai Lama was able to carry out his rule from within Tibet. With Mongol backing, all of Tibet was pacified by 1656,

and the Dalai Lama's control ranged from the Mt Kailash area in the west to Kham in the east. The fifth Dalai Lama had become both the spiritual and temporal sovereign of a unified Tibet. The Dalai Lamas are shown in wall paintings holding the Wheel of Law (Wheel of Dharma) as a symbol of their new-found political power.

The fifth Dalai Lama is remembered as having ushered in a great new age for Tibet. He made a tour of the monasteries of Tibet, and although he stripped most Kadampa monasteries – his chief rivals for power – of their riches, he allowed them to re-establish afterwards. A new flurry of monastic construction began, the major achievement being Labrang Monastery (in what is now Gansu province). In Lhasa, work began on a fitting residence for the head of the Tibetan state: the Potala. The Dalai Lama also invited Indian scholars to Tibet, and with Mongol financial support saw to the renovation and expansion of many temples and monasteries.

Manchu Intervention

Reincarnation lineages were probably first adopted as a means of maintaining the illusion of a continuous spiritual authority within the various monastic orders of Tibet. With the death of the fifth Dalai Lama in 1682, however, the weakness of such a system became apparent. The Tibetan government was confronted with the prospect of finding his reincarnation and then waiting some 18 years until the boy came of age. The great personal prestige and authority of the fifth Dalai Lama himself had played no small part in holding together a newly unified Tibet. The Dalai Lama's regent decided to shroud the Dalai Lama's death in secrecy, announcing that the fifth lama had entered a long period of meditation (over 10 years!).

In 1695 the secret was leaked and the regent was forced to hastily enthrone the sixth Dalai Lama, a boy of his own choosing. The choice was an unfortunate one. The sixth Dalai Lama soon proved himself to be more interested in wine and women than meditation and study – he would often sneak out of the Potala to visit the brothels at its base. A resident Jesuit monk who met him noted that 'no good-looking person of either sex was safe from his unbridled licentiousness'. The enthronement of an inept head of state chosen by a dubious process requiring the child contender to select specific auspicious tokens could not have come at a worse time.

In China, the Ming dynasty had fallen in 1644 and the Manchus from the north had swiftly moved in to fill the power vacuum, establishing the Manchu Qing dynasty (1644–1912). The events that followed were complicated. Basically, Tibet's ineffectual head of state, the Qing perception of the threat of Tibetan relations with the Mongols, disunity within the ranks of Tibet's Mongol allies and Qing ambitions to extend their power into Tibet led to a Qing intervention that was to have lasting consequences for Tibet.

Tibet's dealings with the new Qing government went awry from the start. Kangxi, the second Qing emperor, took offence when the death of the fifth Dalai Lama was concealed from him. At the same time, an ambitious Mongol prince named Lhabzang Khan came to the conclusion that earlier Mongol leaders had taken too much of a back-seat position in their relations with the Tibetans and appealed to Emperor Kangxi for support. It was granted, and in 1705, Mongol forces descended on Lhasa, killed the Tibetan regent and captured the sixth Dalai Lama with the intention of delivering him to Kangxi in Beijing. The sixth died en route at Litang (he was probably murdered) and Lhabzang Khan installed a new Dalai Lama in Lhasa.

Lhabzang Khan's machinations backfired. The Mongol removal, possible murder and replacement of the sixth Dalai Lama aroused intense hostility in Tibet. Worse still, it created enemies among other Mongol tribes, who saw the Dalai Lama as their spiritual leader.

In 1717 the Dzungar Mongols from central Asia attacked Lhasa, killed Lhabzang Khan and deposed the new Dalai Lama. Not that this solved anything in particular. The seventh Dalai Lama, who had been discovered according to a prophesy by the sixth in Litang (present-day Sichuan), was languishing in Kumbum Monastery under Chinese 'protection'.

The resulting confusion in Tibet was the opportunity for which Emperor Kangxi had been waiting. He responded by sending a military expedition to Lhasa in 1720. The Chinese troops drove out the Dzungar Mongols and were received as liberators by the Tibetans. They were unlikely to have been received any other way: With them they brought the seventh Dalai Lama.

Emperor Kangxi wasted no time in declaring Tibet a protectorate of China. Two Chinese representatives, known as Ambans, were installed at Lhasa along with a garrison of Chinese troops. It was the thin end of the wedge, leading to two centuries of Manchu overlordship and serving as a convenient historical precedent for the Communist takeover nearly 250 years later.

Manchu Overlordship

The Manchu overlordship was characterised by repeated military intervention in reaction to crises rather than a steady hand in governing Tibetan political affairs. Such interventions typically resulted in a reorganisation of the Tibetan government. The Manchus appointed a king at one stage, but temporal rule reverted to the seventh Dalai Lama in 1750.

The seventh Dalai Lama ruled successfully until his death in 1757. However, at this point it became clear that another ruler would have to be appointed until the next Dalai Lama reached his majority. The post of regent was created, and it was decided that it should be held by a lama.

It is perhaps a poor reflection on the spiritual attainment of the lamas appointed as regents that few were willing to relinquish the reins once they were in the saddle. In the 120 years between the death of the seventh Dalai Lama and the majority of the 13th, actual power was wielded by the Dalai Lamas for only seven years. Three of them died very young and under suspicious circumstances. Only the eighth Dalai Lama survived to his majority, living a quiet, contemplative life until the age of 45.

The last Chinese military intervention took place in reaction to a Gurkha invasion from Nepal in 1788. As usual there was an administrative reshuffle with short-lived consequences, and from this time Manchu influence in Tibet receded, although the post of Amban continued to be filled until the fall of the Qing dynasty in 1911. Perhaps the one significant outcome of the 1788 intervention was a ban on foreign contact, imposed because of fears of British collusion in the Gurkha invasion.

Barbarians at the Doorstep

Early contact between Britain and Tibet commenced with a mission to Shigatse headed by a Scotsman, George Bogle, in 1774. Bogle soon ingratiated himself with the Panchen Lama – to the extent of marrying one of his sisters. With the death of the third Panchen Lama in 1780 and the Gurkha invasion of Tibet in 1788, however, Britain lost all official contact with Tibet.

Meanwhile, Britain watched nervously as the Russian empire swallowed up central Asia, pushing the borders of its empire 1000km further towards India. The reported arrival of Russian 'adviser' Agvan Dorjieff in Lhasa exacerbated fears that Russia had military designs on Britain's 'jewel in the crown'.

Dorjieff was a Buryat Buddhist monk from near Lake Baikal who had studied at Drepung Monastery for 15 years before finally becoming one of the spiritual advisers of the 13th Dalai Lama. Dorjieff seems to have convinced both himself and the Dalai Lama that the Russian empire was the home of Shambhala, the mythical kingdom from the north whose king (or tsar) would come to save Tibet from its enemies.

When Dorjieff led embassies from the Dalai Lama to Tsar Nicholas II in 1898, 1900 and 1901, and when British intelligence confirmed that Lhasa had received Russian missions (while similar British advances had been refused), the Raj broke into a cold sweat. There was even wild conjecture that the tsar of Russia was poised to convert to Buddhism.

It was against this background that Lord Curzon, viceroy of India, decided to nip Russian designs in the bud. In late 1903, an expedition led by Colonel Francis

Christian Missionaries in Early Tibet

The West's earliest contact with Tibet was via Jesuit missionaries, some of whom were convinced Tibet was the home of a lost Christian community known as the kingdom of Prester John. Portuguese Jesuits reached the Guge capital of Tsaparang in western Tibet in the 1620s and even managed to set up a church there before it was ransacked by outraged Ladakhis. In 1707 another early Jesuit mission was established in Lhasa. It survived until 1745, when it closed because of lack of funds and local opposition by monks.

One fascinating Western character of this era was the Italian priest Ippolito Desideri, who arrived in Tibet in 1716. Not only was he the first Westerner to set eyes on Mt Kailash, but he also managed to stay five years in Lhasa trying to master the language and customs of Tibet so that he could convert the Tibetans to Catholicism. He even managed to write a refutation of Buddhism in Tibetan, which locals admired and then ignored.

Desideri found that the main obstacle to potential conversion was reincarnation, which he explained away by saying that the Tibetan dead descended into the pit of hell and were then sent back to earth possessed by the devil. During his time in Lhasa he witnessed a Mongol invasion, a massacre of Red Hat monks by Yellow Hats, and then a Manchu invasion, before he was finally ordered home by the Vatican in 1721.

Neither he nor any of the other missionaries really had much luck in Tibet – after a hundred years of intense proselytising they managed to convert only 13 Tibetans. If you look around in Lhasa you'll find them still trying to this day.

Younghusband entered Tibet via Sikkim. After several months waiting for a Tibetan delegation, the British expedition moved on to Lhasa, where it was discovered that the Dalai Lama had fled to Mongolia with Dorjieff. However, an Anglo-Tibetan convention was signed following negotiations with Tri Rinpoche, a lama from Ganden whom the Dalai Lama had appointed as regent in his absence. British forces withdrew after spending just two months in Lhasa. (For more on the story of the British invasion, see the boxed text 'Bayonets to Gyantse' in the Tsang chapter.)

The missing link in the Anglo-Tibetan accord was a Manchu signature. In effect the accord implied that Tibet was a sovereign power and therefore had the right to make treaties of its own. The Manchus objected and in 1906 the British signed a second accord with the Manchus, one that recognised China's suzerainty over Tibet. In 1910, with the Manchu Qing dynasty teetering on the verge of collapse, the Manchus made good on the accord and invaded Tibet, forcing the Dalai Lama once again into flight – this time into the arms of the British in India.

Tibetan Independence Revisited
In 1911 a revolution finally toppled the decadent Qing dynasty in China. The spirit of revolt soon spread to Tibet, which was still under occupation by Manchu troops. In Lhasa, troops mutinied against their officers, and in other parts of the country fighting broke out between Tibetans and Manchu troops. By the end of 1912, the last of the occupying forces were escorted out of Tibet via India and sent back to China. In January 1913 the 13th Dalai Lama returned to Lhasa.

The government of the new Chinese republic, anxious to maintain control of former Qing territories, sent a telegram to the Dalai Lama expressing regret at the actions of the Manchu oppressors and announcing that the Dalai Lama was being formally restored to his former rank. The Dalai Lama replied that he was uninterested in ranks bestowed by the Chinese and that he was hereby assuming temporal and spiritual leadership of his country.

Tibetans have since read this reply as a formal declaration of independence. It certainly was in spirit if not quite in letter. As for the Chinese, they chose to ignore it, reporting that the Dalai Lama had responded with a letter expressing his great love for the motherland. Whatever the case, Tibet was to enjoy 30 years free of interference from China. What is more, Tibet was suddenly presented with an opportunity to create a state that was ready to rise to the challenge of the modern world, and, if needs be, protect itself from the territorial ambitions of China. Sadly, the opportunity foundered on Tibet's entrenched theocratic institutions, and Tibetan independence was a short-lived affair.

Attempts to Modernise
During the period of his flight to India, the 13th Dalai Lama had become intimate friends with Sir Charles Bell, a Tibetan scholar and political officer in Sikkim. The relationship was to initiate a warming in Anglo-Tibetan affairs and to see the British playing an increasingly important role as mediators in problems between Tibet and China.

In 1920 Bell was dispatched on a mission to Lhasa, where he renewed his friendship with the Dalai Lama. It was agreed that the British would supply the Tibetans with modern arms providing they agreed to use them only for self defence. The Dalai Lama readily agreed and a supply of arms and ammunition was set up. Tibetan military officers were trained in Gyantse and India, and a telegraph line was set up linking Lhasa and Shigatse. Other developments included the construction of a small hydroelectric station near Lhasa and the establishment of an English school at Gyantse. Four Tibetan boys were sent to public school at Rugby in England. At the invitation of the Dalai Lama, British experts conducted geological surveys of parts of Tibet with a view to gauging mining potential.

It is highly likely that the 13th Dalai Lama's trips away from his country had made him realise that it was imperative that Tibet begin to modernise. At the same time he must also have been aware that the road to modernisation was fraught with difficulties. The biggest problem was the Tibetan social system itself.

Since the rise of the Gelugpa order, Tibet had been ruled as a theocracy. Monks, particularly those in the huge monastic complexes of Drepung and Sera at Lhasa, were accustomed to a high degree of influence in the Tibetan government. And for the monks of Tibet, the principal focus of government was the maintenance of the religious state. Attempts to modernise were seen as inimical to this aim, and before too long they began to meet intense opposition.

Perhaps as much as anything else, the large monastery complexes of central Tibet feared the increasing empowerment of lay elements in Tibetan society. The establishment of an army, for example, was seen as a direct threat to the monasteries rather than as a means of self defence against external threats to the nation. Most monasteries kept their own small armies of fighting monks, and the presence of a well-equipped state army posed the threat of state intervention in monastic disputes. In fact, such fears proved to be well founded when the Dalai Lama brought the newly established army into action to quell a threatened uprising at Drepung Monastery.

Before too long, the 13th Dalai Lama's innovations fell victim to a conservative backlash. Newly trained Tibetan officers were reassigned to nonmilitary jobs, causing a rapid deterioration of military discipline; a newly established police force was left to its own devices and soon became ineffective; the English school at Gyantse was closed down; and a mail service set up by the British was stopped.

However, Tibet's brief period of independence was troubled by more than just an inability to modernise. Conflict sprang up between the Panchen Lama and the Dalai Lama over the autonomy of Tashilhunpo Monastery and its estates. The Panchen Lama, after appealing to the British to mediate, fled to China, where he was kept for 14 years until his death. In 1933 the 13th Dalai Lama died, leaving the running of the country to the regent of Reting. The present

(14th) Dalai Lama was discovered at the village of Pari Takster near Xining in Amdo, but was brought to Lhasa only after the local Chinese commander had been paid off with a huge 'fee' of 300,000 Chinese dollars. The boy was renamed Tenzin Gyatso and he was installed as the Dalai Lama on 22 February 1940, aged 4½.

In 1947 an attempted coup d'etat, known as the Reting Conspiracy, rocked Lhasa. And in 1949 the Chinese Nationalist government, against all odds, fell to Mao Zedong and his Communist 'bandits'.

Liberation

When the iron bird flies and horses run on wheels, the Tibetan people will be scattered throughout the world and the Dharma will come to the land of red men.

Guru Rinpoche

Unknown to the Tibetans, the Communist takeover of China was to open what is probably the saddest chapter in Tibetan history. The Chinese 'liberation' of Tibet was eventually to lead to 1.2 million Tibetan deaths, a full-on assault on the Tibetan traditional way of life, the flight of the Dalai Lama to India and the large-scale destruction of almost every historical structure on the plateau. The chief culprits were Chinese ethnic chauvinism and an epidemic of social madness known as the Cultural Revolution.

On 7 October 1950, just a year after the Communist takeover of China, 30,000 battle-hardened Chinese troops attacked central Tibet from six different directions. The Tibetan army, a poorly equipped force of some 4000 men, stood little chance of resisting the Chinese, and any attempt at defence soon collapsed before the onslaught. In Lhasa, the Tibetan government reacted by enthroning the 15-year-old 14th Dalai Lama, an action that brought jubilation and dancing on the streets, but did little to protect Tibet from advancing Chinese troops.

An appeal to the United Nations (UN) was equally ineffective. To the shame of all involved, only El Salvador sponsored a motion to condemn Chinese aggression, and Britain and India, traditional friends of

Tibet, actually managed to convince the UN not to debate the issue for fear of incurring Chinese disapproval.

Presented with this seemingly hopeless situation, the Dalai Lama dispatched a mission to Beijing with orders that it refer all decisions to Lhasa. As it turned out there were no decisions to be made. The Chinese had already drafted an agreement. The Tibetans had two choices: Sign on the dotted line or face further Chinese aggression.

The 17-point *Agreement on Measures for the Peaceful Liberation of Tibet* promised a one-country two-systems structure much like that offered later to Hong Kong and Macau, but provided little in the way of guarantees that such a promise would be honoured. The Tibetan delegates protested that they were unauthorised to sign such an agreement and anyway lacked the seal of the Dalai Lama. Thoughtfully, the Chinese had already prepared a forged Dalai Lama seal, and the agreement was ratified.

Initially, the Chinese occupation of central Tibet was carried out in an orderly way, but tensions inevitably mounted. The presence of large numbers of Chinese troops in the Lhasa region soon depleted food stores and gave rise to massive inflation. Rumours of massacres and forced political indoctrination in Kham began to filter through to Lhasa. In 1954 the Dalai Lama was invited to Beijing, where, amid cordial discussions with Mao Zedong, he was told that religion was 'poison'.

In 1956 the Preparatory Committee for the Autonomous Region of Tibet (Pcart) was established. Although headed by the Dalai Lama, a majority of its seats were filled by Chinese puppets. In any case, real power lay in the hands of the committee of the Communist Party in Tibet, which claimed no Tibetan representatives at all.

In the same year, uprisings broke out in eastern Tibet (see History in the Kham (Eastern Tibet) chapter); and in 1957 and 1958, protests and armed revolt spread to central Tibet (with covert CIA assistance). With a heavy heart, the Dalai Lama returned to Lhasa in March 1957 from a trip to India to celebrate the 2500th anniversary of the birth of the Buddha. It seemed inevitable that Tibet would explode in revolt and equally inevitable that it would be ruthlessly suppressed by the Chinese.

1959 Uprising

The Tibetan New Year of 1959, like all the New Year celebrations before it, attracted huge crowds to Lhasa, doubling the usual population of the city. In addition to the usual festival activities, the Chinese had added a highlight of their own – a performance by a Chinese dance group at the Lhasa military base. The invitation to the Dalai Lama came in the form of a thinly veiled command. The Dalai Lama, wishing to avoid offence, accepted.

As preparations for the performance drew near, however, the Dalai Lama's security chief was surprised to hear that the Dalai Lama was expected to attend in secrecy and without his customary contingent of 25 bodyguards. Despite the Dalai Lama's agreement to these conditions, news of them soon leaked, and in no time simmering frustration at Chinese rule came to the boil among the crowds on the streets. It seemed obvious to the Tibetans that the Chinese were about to kidnap the Dalai Lama. Large numbers of people gathered around the Norbulingka (the summer palace of the Dalai Lama) and swore to protect him with their lives.

The Dalai Lama had no choice but to cancel his appointment at the military base. In the meantime the crowds on the streets were swollen by Tibetan soldiers, who changed out of their People's Liberation Army (PLA) uniforms and started to hand out weapons. A group of government ministers announced that the 17-point agreement was null and void, and that Tibet renounced the authority of China.

The Dalai Lama was powerless to intervene, managing only to pen some conciliatory letters to the Chinese as his people prepared for battle on the streets of Lhasa. In a last-ditch effort to prevent bloodshed, the Dalai Lama even offered himself to the Chinese. The reply came in the sound of two mortar shells exploding in the gardens of the Norbulingka. The attack made it obvious that the only option remaining to the Dalai Lama was flight. On 17 March, the Dalai Lama left the Norbulingka disguised as a soldier. Fourteen days later he was in India.

Bloodshed in Lhasa

With both the Chinese and the Tibetans unaware of the Dalai Lama's departure, tensions continued to mount in Lhasa. Early on the morning of 20 March, Chinese troops began to shell the Norbulingka and the crowds surrounding it, killing hundreds of people. Later, as the corpses were searched, it became obvious that the Dalai Lama had escaped – 'abducted by a reactionary clique' went the Chinese reports.

Still the bloodshed continued. Artillery bombed the Potala, Sera Monastery and the medical college on Chagpo Ri. Tibetans armed with petrol bombs were picked off by Chinese snipers, and when a crowd of some 10,000 Tibetans retreated into the sacred precincts of the Jokhang, that too was bombed. It is thought that after three days of violence, 10,000 to 15,000 Tibetans lay dead in the streets of Lhasa.

Socialist Paradise on the Roof of the World

The Chinese quickly consolidated their quelling of the Lhasa uprising by taking control of all the high passes between Tibet and India. Freedom fighters were put out of action by Chinese troops, and able-bodied young men were rounded up, shot, incarcerated or put to work on Chinese work teams. As the Chinese themselves put it, they were liberating Tibet of reactionary forces and ushering in a new socialist society. Naturally they did not bother to ask the Tibetans themselves whether they wanted a socialist paradise.

The Chinese abolished the Tibetan government and set about reordering Tibetan society in accordance with their Marxist principles. The educated and the aristocratic were put to work on menial jobs and subjected to struggle sessions, known as *thamzing*, which sometimes resulted in death. A ferment of class struggle was whipped up and former feudal exploiters – some of whom the poor of Tibet may have harboured genuine resentment for – were subjected to punishments of awful cruelty.

The Chinese also turned their attention to Tibet's more than 6000 'feudal' monasteries. Tibetans were refused permission to donate food to the monasteries, and monks were compelled to join struggle sessions, discard their robes and marry. Monasteries were stripped of their riches, Buddhist scriptures were burnt and used as toilet paper, and the vast wholesale destruction of Tibet's monastic heritage began in earnest.

Notable in this litany of errors was the Chinese decision to alter Tibetan farming practices. Instead of barley, the Tibetan staple, Tibetan farmers were instructed to grow wheat and rice. Tibetans protested that these crops were unsuited to Tibet's high-altitude conditions. They were right, and mass starvation resulted. It is estimated that by late 1961, 70,000 Tibetans had died or were dying of starvation.

By September 1961, even the Chinese-groomed Panchen Lama began to have a change of heart. He presented Mao Zedong with a 70,000-character report on the hardships his people were suffering and also requested, among other things, religious freedom and an end to the sacking of Tibetan monasteries. Four years later he was to disappear into a high-security prison for a 10-year stay. For the Chinese, he was the last obstacle to be cleared away in the lead up to the establishment of the Tibetan Autonomous Region (TAR).

On 1 September 1965 the TAR was formally brought into being with much fanfare and talk of happy Tibetans fighting back tears of gratitude at becoming one with the great motherland. The tears were set to keep on coming. In China, trouble was brewing in the form of a social movement that came to be known as the Cultural Revolution.

The Cultural Revolution

Among the writings of Mao Zedong is a piece entitled 'On Going Too Far'. It is a subject on which he was particularly well qualified to write. What started as a power struggle between Mao and Liu Shaoqi in 1965 had become by August 1966 the Great Proletarian Cultural Revolution, a movement that was to shake China to its core, trample all its traditions underfoot, cause countless deaths and give running of the country over to mobs of Red Guards. All of China suffered in Mao's bold experiment in creating a new socialist paradise, but it was Tibet that suffered most dearly.

The first Red Guards arrived in Lhasa in July 1966. Two months later, the first rally was organised and Chinese-educated Tibetan youths raided the Jokhang, desecrating whatever religious objects they could get their hands on. It was the beginning of the large-scale destruction of virtually every religious monument in Tibet, and was carried out in the spirit of destroying the 'Four Olds': old thinking, old culture, old habits and old customs. The Buddhist *'om mani padme hum'* ('hail to the jewel in the lotus') was replaced by the communist mantra 'long live Chairman Mao'. The Buddha himself was accused of being a 'reactionary'.

For more than three years the Cultural Revolution went about its destructive business of turning the Tibetan world on its head. Tibetan farmers were forced to collectivise into communes and were told what to grow and when to grow it. Merrymaking was declared illegal, women had their jewellery taken from them, and the traditional plaits of Tibetan men were cut off by Red Guards in the street. Anyone who objected was arrested and subjected to thamzing. The Dalai Lama became public enemy number one and Tibetans were forced to denounce him as a parasite and traitor. The list goes on: a harrowing catalogue of crimes against a people whose only fault was to hold aspirations that differed from those of their Chinese masters.

By late 1969, the PLA had the Red Guards under control. Tibet, however, continued to be the site of outbreaks of violence. Tibetan uprisings were brief and subdued brutally. In 1972, restrictions on Tibetans' freedom of worship were lifted with much fanfare but little in the way of results. In 1975, a group of foreign journalists

sympathetic to the Chinese cause were invited to Tibet. The reports they filed gave a sad picture of a land whose people had been battered to their knees by Chinese-imposed policies and atrocities that amounted to nothing less than cultural genocide. In the same year the last CIA-funded Tibetan guerilla bases, in Mustang, northern Nepal, were closed down.

The Post-Mao Years

By the time of Mao's death in 1976 even the Chinese themselves must have begun to realise that their rule in Tibet had taken a wrong turn. Rebellion was ever in the wings, and maintaining order on the high plateau was a constant drain on Beijing's coffers. Mao's chosen successor, Hua Guofeng, decided to soften the government's line on Tibet and called for a revival of Tibetan customs. In mid-1977, China announced that it would welcome the return of the Dalai Lama and other Tibetan refugees, and shortly afterwards the Panchen Lama was released from more than 10 years of imprisonment.

The Tibetan government-in-exile received cautiously the invitation to return to Tibet, and the Dalai Lama suggested that he be allowed to send a fact-finding mission to Tibet first. To the surprise of all involved, the Chinese agreed. As the Dalai Lama himself remarked in his autobiography, *Freedom in Exile*, it seemed that the Chinese were of the opinion that the mission would find such happiness in their homeland that 'they would see no point in remaining in exile'. In fact, the results of the mission were so damning that the Dalai Lama decided not to publish them.

Nevertheless, two more missions followed. Their conclusions were despairing. The missions catalogued 1.2 million deaths, the destruction of 6254 monasteries and nunneries, the absorption of two-thirds of Tibet into China, 100,000 Tibetans in labour camps and extensive deforestation. In a mere 30 years, the Chinese had turned Tibet into a land of nearly unrecognisable desolation.

In China, Hua Guofeng's short-lived political ascendancy had been eclipsed by Deng

Xiaoping's rise to power. In 1980, Deng sent Hu Yaobang on a Chinese fact-finding mission that coincided with the visits of those sent by the Tibetan government-in-exile.

Hu's conclusions, while not as damning as those of the Tibetans, painted a grim picture of life on the roof of the world. A six-point plan to improve the living conditions and freedoms of the Tibetans was drawn up, taxes were dropped for two years and limited private enterprise was allowed. The Jokhang was reopened for two days a month in 1978; the Potala opened in 1980. As was the case in the rest of China, the government embarked on a program of extended personal freedoms in concert with authoritarian one-party rule.

The Deng Years

The early 1980s saw the return of limited religious freedoms. Monasteries that had not been reduced to piles of rubble began to reopen and some religious artefacts were returned to Tibet from China.

Importantly, there was also a relaxation of the Chinese proscription on pilgrimage. Pictures of the Dalai Lama began to reappear on the streets of Lhasa. Not that any of this pointed to a significant reversal in Chinese thinking on the question of religion, which remained an opiate of the masses. Those who exercised their religious freedoms did so at considerable risk.

Talks aimed at bringing the Dalai Lama back into the ambit of Chinese influence continued, but with little in the way of results. A three-person team sent to Beijing from Dharamsala, India, in 1982 heard lectures on how Tibet was part of China and was told in no uncertain terms that the Dalai Lama would be given a desk job in Beijing if he were to return. By 1983 talks had broken down and the Chinese had decided that they did not want the Dalai Lama to return after all. Tibet became the 'front line of the struggle against splittism', according to the Chinese government.

Perhaps most dismaying for Tibetans, however, was the emergence of a Chinese policy of Han immigration to the high plateau. Sinicisation had already been suc-cessfully carried out in Xinjiang, Inner Mongolia and Qinghai, and now Tibet was targeted for mass immigration. Attractive salaries and interest-free loans were made available to Chinese willing to emigrate to Tibet, and, in 1984 alone, more than 100,000 Han Chinese took advantage of the incentives to 'modernise' the backward province of Tibet.

In 1986 a new influx of foreigners arrived in Tibet. The Chinese began to loosen restrictions on tourism, and the trickle of tour groups and individual travellers soon became a flood. For the first time since the Chinese takeover, visitors from the West were given the opportunity to see first hand the results of Chinese rule in Tibet.

For the Chinese, the foreigners were a mixed blessing. The tourist dollars were appreciated, but foreigners had an annoying habit of sympathising with the Tibetans. They also got to see things that the Chinese would rather they did not see.

When in September 1987 a group of 30 monks from Sera Monastery began circum-ambulating the Jokhang and crying out 'Independence for Tibet' and 'Long live his Holiness the Dalai Lama', their ranks were swollen by bystanders and arrests followed. Four days later, another group of monks repeated their actions, this time brandishing Tibetan flags.

The monks were beaten and arrested. With Western tourists looking on, a crowd of some 2000 to 3000 angry Tibetans gathered. Police vehicles were overturned and Chinese police began firing on the crowd.

The Chinese response was swift. Communications with the outside world were broken and foreigners were evicted from Lhasa. It was still too late, however, to prevent eyewitness accounts of what had happened from reaching newspapers around the world. A crackdown followed in Lhasa, but it failed to prevent further protests in the following months.

The Mönlam festival of March 1988 saw shooting in the streets of Lhasa, and in December of the same year a Dutch traveller was shot in the shoulder; 18 Tibetans died and 150 were wounded in the disturbances.

The Dalai Lama & the Search for Settlement

By the mid-1970s, the Dalai Lama had become a prominent international figure, working tirelessly from his government-in-exile in Dharamsala, India, to make the world more aware of the plight of his people. His visits to the USA led to official condemnation of the Chinese occupation of Tibet. In 1987 he addressed the US Congress and outlined a five-point peace plan.

The plan called for Tibet to be established as a 'zone of peace'; for the policy of Han immigration to Tibet to be abandoned; for a return to basic human rights and democratic freedoms; for the protection of Tibet's natural heritage and an end to the dumping of nuclear waste on the high plateau; and for joint discussions between the Chinese and the Tibetans on the future of Tibet. The Chinese denounced the plan as an example of 'splittism'. They gave the same response when, a year later, the Dalai Lama elaborated on the speech before the European parliament at Strasbourg in France, conceding

The 14th Dalai Lama now lives in exile in India.

any demands for full independence and offering the Chinese the right to govern Tibet's foreign and military affairs.

Protests and crackdowns continued in Tibet through 1989, and despairing elements in the exiled Tibetan community began to talk of the need to take up arms. It was an option that the Dalai Lama had consistently opposed. If there was to be any improvement in the situation in Tibet, he reasoned, it could only be achieved through nonviolent means. The Dalai Lama's efforts to achieve peace and freedom for his people were rewarded on 4 October 1989, when he was awarded the Nobel peace prize. It must have seemed a small consolation for the civilised world's notable failure to put any real pressure on China regarding its activities in Tibet.

Tibet Today

Tibetans have won back many religious freedoms, but at great expense. Monks and nuns, who are often the focus of protests and Tibetan aspirations for independence, are regarded suspiciously by the authorities and are often subject to arrest and beatings. Nuns in particular, considering their small numbers, have been very active, and accounted for 55 out of the 126 independence protests in the mid-1990s. Regulations make it impossible for nuns, once arrested and imprisoned, to return to their nunneries.

Religious institutions have recently been the focus of 'patriotic education' and 'civilising atheism' campaigns, and strict quotas have been imposed on the numbers of monasteries and their resident monks and nuns. Monks in Drepung were recently forced to sign a form denouncing the Dalai Lama on pain of imprisonment. Tibetan guides educated in India have been banned from working. Religious crackdowns were continuing at the time of research.

The Chinese officially deny any policy of Han immigration to Tibet, but for visitors who have made repeated trips to Tibet the increased numbers of Han Chinese are staggering. The extent of immigration poses the grave danger that the Tibetans will become a minority in their own country. The Dalai

Lama has described the policy as cultural genocide.

It must be said that great effort has been made to curb the worst excesses of the Chinese administration and that a comparatively softened line on 'minorities' has improved conditions for many Tibetans. There are now over 2000 functioning monasteries in Tibet. But the basic problems remain. Protests and government crackdowns have continued into the new millennium. The Chinese government has in no way relented in regarding Tibet as a province of China and is no closer to reaching an agreement of any kind with the Dalai Lama.

The Dalai Lama continues to be vocal in the Tibetan struggle for independence in some form. He has abandoned any hope of nationhood, but continues to strive for a system of Tibetan cultural, religious and linguistic autonomy within the Chinese state. In Western political circles covert sympathy rarely translates into active support, and foreign governments are careful not to receive the Dalai Lama in any way that recognises his political status as the head of an exiled government. The Chinese government continues to protest regularly against the Dalai Lama's international activities. In February 2000, celebrations were held in Dharamsala for the 60th anniversary of the Dalai Lama's enthronment.

In recent years the Dalai Lama has quietly admitted to a growing sense of failure in his dealings with the Chinese and there is a small but growing split within the Tibetan community on the best way forward. A series of small bombs were detonated at night in Lhasa in 1996 and 2000 (one next to a courthouse near the Banak Shol hotel), suggesting that at least some Tibetans are moving away from the Dalai Lama's overtly pacifist stand.

As the Chinese authorities trumpet rapid advances in industrial and agricultural output, there is a growing feeling among observers that China has switched from systematic persecution to a second, far

Undercover Monks

Frequent travellers to Tibet will tell you that some of the monks in Tibet's larger monasteries are not what they seem. There is no reason to believe that someone in a monk's or nun's habit is actually a monk or a nun. They may in fact be working undercover for the Chinese government. And if this reeks ever so slightly of paranoia, give some thought to a US couple who brought three taped speeches of the Dalai Lama with them to Tibet and handed one to a monk at Tashilhunpo Monastery in Shigatse.

After being tailed by two plain-clothes Chinese police, they were stopped at a checkpoint, where a boy in civilian clothes, whom they recognised as one of the 'monks' from Tashilhunpo, identified them. At the Shigatse police station they were interrogated and then taken back to their hotel room, which was searched; the two remaining cassette tapes and some Dalai Lama pictures were confiscated. They were detained in Shigatse for four days and subject to further interrogations and threats before being made to sign statements to the effect that they were guilty of 'distributing propaganda'. Finally they were escorted to Gongkar airport and deported to Kathmandu.

This story illustrates a number of issues. First, it is unwise to trust anyone, including monks, when it comes to sensitive issues that might be construed as political. Second, even if you get away with it, any incriminating material that you hand to a Tibetan could have serious consequences for the recipient (such as torture or jail) if it is discovered. And third, never forget that Tibet is highly politicised, and even the simple act of handing out a picture of the Dalai Lama is significant to the Chinese authorities.

The safest path is to avoid handing out anything 'political' at all times. In particular be wary of monks who speak English and act as guides at monasteries. Furthermore, do not hand out pictures of the Dalai Lama to those who request them.

more sophisticated phase in assimilating Tibet into the motherland. Foreign investment, Han immigration and an education system that exclusively uses the (Mandarin) Chinese language at higher levels ensures that only Sinicised Tibetans will be able to actively participate in Tibet's economic advances. Chinese economic control, coupled with large numbers of Chinese settlers, makes the Tibetan dream of independence ever harder to realise.

On the positive side, the US government appointed a 'Special Coordinator for Tibet' in 1997, and in 1998 the United Nations human rights commissioner, Mary Robinson, visited Tibet. It is even hoped that talks might begin between the Dalai Lama and Chinese premier Jiang Zemin; the Dalai Lama's brother Gyalo Thondub visited Beijing in October 2000. Don't hold your breath though. In many ways the status quo suits the West: As long as there are no bloody crackdowns in Lhasa, foreign countries can continue to trade with China while quietly criticising its human-rights record well out of China's earshot. The 50th anniversary of the 'liberation' of Tibet in 2001 offered a sobering moment of reflection on half a century of tragedy for the Tibetan people.

GEOGRAPHY

The Tibetan plateau is one of the most isolated regions in the world, bound to the south by the 2500km-long Himalaya, to the west by the Karakoram and to the north by the Kunlun and Altyn Tagh ranges. Four of the world's 10 highest mountains straddle its southern border. The north-west in particular is bound by the most remote and least explored wilderness left on earth, outside the polar regions. With an average altitude of 4000m and large swathes of the country well above 5000m, the Tibetan plateau (nearly the size of Western Europe) deserves the title 'the roof of the world'.

The Tibetan Autonomous Region, with an area of 1.23 million sq km, covers only part of this geographical plateau (the rest is parcelled off into Qinghai and Sichuan provinces). It encompasses the traditional Tibetan provinces of Ü (capital, Lhasa),

Tsang (capital, Shigatse), and Ngari, or western Tibet, as well as parts of Kham. The TAR shares a 3482km international border with India, Bhutan, Nepal and Myanmar (Burma), and is bordered to the north and east by the Chinese provinces of Xinjiang, Qinghai, Sichuan and Yunnan.

Much of Tibet is a harsh and uncompromising landscape best described as a high-altitude desert. Little of the Indian monsoon makes it over the Himalayan watershed, and shifting sand dunes are a common sight along the Samye valley and the road to Mt Kailash.

Regions

Ütsang (the combined provinces of Ü and Tsang, which constitute central Tibet) is the political, historical and agricultural heartland of Tibet. Its relatively fertile valleys enjoy a mild climate and are irrigated by wide rivers such as the Yarlung Tsangpo and the Kyi Chu.

To the north of Ütsang are the harsh, high-altitude plains of the Changtang (northern plateau), the highest and largest plateau in the world, occupying an area of over one million sq km. This area has no river systems, and supports little in the way of life. Dead lakes on the plateau are the brackish remnants of the Tethys Sea that found no run-off when the plateau started its ascent skyward.

Ngari, or western Tibet, is similarly barren, although here river valleys provide grassy tracts that support nomads and their grazing animals. Indeed, the Kailash range in the far west of Tibet is the source of the subcontinent's four greatest rivers: the Ganges, Indus, Sutlej and Brahmaputra. The Ganges, Indus and Sutlej Rivers all cascade out of Tibet in its far west, not far from Mt Kailash itself. The Brahmaputra (known in Tibet as Yarlung Tsangpo), however, meanders along the northern spine of the Himalaya for 2000km searching for a way south, before coiling back on itself in a dramatic U-turn and draining into India not far from the border with Myanmar (Burma).

Kham, which encompasses the eastern TAR, western Sichuan and north-west Yunnan, marks a tempestuous drop in elevations down to the Sichuan plain. The concertina landscape produces some of the most spectacular roller-coaster roads in Asia as Himalayan extensions such as the Hengduan Mountains are sliced by the deep gorges of the Yangzi (Jinsha), Salween (Nu Jiang) and Mekong (Lancang) headwaters. The Yarlung Tsangpo itself crashes through a 5km-deep gorge here as it swings around 7756m-high Namche Barwa. Many parts of this alpine region are lushly forested and support abundant wildlife, largely thanks to the lower altitudes and effects of the Indian monsoon.

Tibet has several thousand lakes (*tso* in Tibetan), of which the largest are Nam-tso, Yamdrok-tso, Manasarovar (Mapham yumtso), Siling-tso and Palgon-tso, the last crossing the Indian border into Ladakh.

GEOLOGY

The high plateau of Tibet is the result of prodigious geological upheaval. The time scale is subject to much debate, but at some point in the last 100 million years the entire region lay beneath the Tethys Sea. And that is where it would have stayed had the mass of land now known as India not broken free from the protocontinent Gondwanaland and drifted off in a collision course with another protocontinent known as Laurasia. The impact of the two land masses sent the Indian plate burrowing under the Laurasian landmass, and two vast parallel ridges, over 3000km in length and in places almost 9km high, piled up. These ridges, the Himalaya and associated ranges, are still rising at around 10cm a year.

You may well find locals near Shegar selling fossils of marine animals – at an altitude of more than 4000m above sea level!

CLIMATE

The high altitudes of the Tibetan plateau make for climatic extremes – temperatures on the Changtang have been known to drop 27°C (80°F) in a single day! At any time of the year, particularly in western Tibet, it is a good idea to be prepared for sudden drops of temperature at night. But, basically, the Tibetan climate is not as harsh as many people imagine it to be.

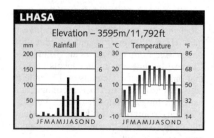

LHASA
Elevation – 3595m/11,792ft

The best time of year to be in Tibet is from May to the beginning of November, after which temperatures start to plummet. However, in May and June there is a wind factor to consider, and dust storms are not unusual. These are not pleasant if you're hitching or trekking but they usually come in squalls and you can see them coming. Lhasa and Shigatse generally have very mild weather from May to November, although July and August can be rainy – these two months usually see around half of Tibet's annual rainfall.

October and November often bring some dazzlingly clear weather, and daytime temperatures can be quite comfortable at the lower altitudes of Tibet. However, trekkers will need suitably warm clothing through these two months.

The coldest months are from December to February. It is not impossible to visit Tibet in the winter, but high-altitude trekking becomes almost impossible. High passes sometimes become snowbound, which can make travel difficult. The low-altitude valleys (around Lhasa, Shigatse and Tsetang) see very little snow.

Spring does not really get under way until April, although March can have warm sunny days and is not necessarily a bad month to be in Tibet. Again, though, sudden cold snaps can dump snow on passes at this time of the year.

ECOLOGY & ENVIRONMENT

The Tibetan plateau is of global ecological importance, not only as the earth's highest ecosystem and one of its last remaining great wildernesses but also as the source of Asia's greatest rivers: the Ganges, Yarlung

Tsangpo (Brahmaputra), Indus, Karnali, Sutlej, Yangzi, Yellow, Mekong, Salween and Irrawady. Over 47% of the world's population (over 85% of Asia) gets its water from these rivers. Furthermore, it is thought that the high plateau affects global jet streams and even influences the Indian monsoon. The Dalai Lama would like to see Tibet turned into a 'zone of peace' and perhaps even the world's largest national park.

The Buddhist view of the environment stresses the intricate and interconnected relationship between the natural world and human beings, a viewpoint closely linked to the concept of death and rebirth. As early as 1642 the fifth Dalai Lama issued an edict protecting animals and the environment. Buddhist practice in general stands for moderation and against overconsumption, and forbids hunting, fishing and the taking of animal life. Nomads, in particular, live in a fine balance with their harsh environment.

Modern communist experiments, such as collectivisation and the switching of century-old farming patterns (for example, from barley to wheat and rice), upset this fragile balance and resulted in a series of great disasters and famines in the 1960s (as indeed they did in the rest of China). By the mid-1970s, the failure of collectivisation was widely recognised, and Tibetans have since been allowed to return to traditional methods of working the land.

Other resources are less easily renewed. When the Tibetan government-in-exile sent three investigative delegations to Tibet in the early 1980s, among the shocking news they returned with was that Tibet had been denuded of its wildlife. Stories of Chinese troops machine gunning herds of wild gazelles circulated with convincing frequency, and it has sadly become necessary to travel to extremely remote locations to see the wildlife that once roamed freely on the plains of Tibet. Commercial trophy hunting, often by foreigners paying tens of thousands of US dollars, has had an effect on the numbers of antelope and argali sheep, in particular.

Rapid modernisation threatens to bring industrial pollution, a hitherto almost un-known concept, onto the high plateau. Several cement factories on the edge of Lhasa create huge clouds of noxious smoke, which regularly blankets parts of western Lhasa.

Tibet has enormous potential for hydro-electricity, although current projects at Yamdrok-tso and elsewhere have come in for criticism both from local Tibetans and from foreign environmental groups. For more information see the boxed text 'Down the Drain' in the Tsang chapter.

The region also has abundant supplies of geothermal energy thanks to its turbulent geological history. The Yangpachen Geothermal Plant already supplies Lhasa with much of its electricity. Portable solar panelling has also enjoyed some success; the plateau enjoys some of the longest and strongest sunlight outside the Saharan region. Experimental wind-power stations have been set up in northern Tibet.

In late 2001, Chinese scientists announced the discovery of almost five billion tons of oil and gas in the Changtang region of remote north-west Tibet.

Deforestation is a pressing problem, particularly in eastern Tibet as Chinese logging teams continue their relentless advance from Sichuan province. It has been estimated that US$54 billion worth of timber has been felled from the Tibetan region since 1959. Locals have described logging trucks in Kham as so regular that '15 fully laden trucks pass by in the time it takes to drink a cup of tea'. The potential effect on sediment and run-off levels for rivers downstream, especially in flood-prone China, is considerable; over half the world's population lives downstream of Tibet.

If you want to find out more about environmental issues in Tibet, visit the useful Web site of Tibet Environmental Watch at W www.tew.org.

FLORA

The vast differences in altitude in Tibet give rise to a spread of ecosystems from alpine to subtropical. The high-altitude plains of the Changtang, for example, support little in the way of vegetation beside grasses such as spear grass.

Juniper trees and willows are common in the valleys of central Tibet and it is possible to come across wildflowers such as the pansy and the oleander, as well as unique indigenous flowers such as the *tsi-tog* (a light pink, high-altitude bloom).

To the south, along the lower-altitude borders with Nepal, are forests of pines, firs and spruces. The east of Tibet, which sees higher rainfall than the rest of Tibet, has an amazing range of flora, from coniferous forests to deciduous forests with oaks, elms and birches, to subtropical plants and flowers including rhododendrons, azaleas and magnolias.

FAUNA

If you are not trekking in Tibet and your travels are restricted to sights off the Friendship Hwy, you are unlikely to see anything much in the way of wildlife. On the road out to Mt Kailash, however, it is not unusual to see herds of Tibetan gazelles *(owa)* and wild asses *(kyang)*.

Marmots *(chiwa* or *piya)* are very common, and can often be seen perched up on their hind legs sniffing the air curiously outside their burrows – they make a strange birdlike sound when distressed. The pika *(chipi)*, or Himalayan mouse-hare, a relative of the rabbit, is also very common. Pikas that live on Mt Everest have been observed at 5250m, thus earning the distinction of having the highest habitat of any mammal.

A surprising number of migratory birds make their way up to the lakes of the Tibetan plateau through spring and summer. Tibet has over 30 endemic birds; 480 species have been recorded on the plateau. Birds include the black-necked crane, the bar-headed goose and the lammergeier, as well as grebes, pheasants, snow cocks and partridges. Two of the best places to go

Yakety-Yak

Fifty years ago, an estimated one million wild yaks roamed the Tibetan plateau. Now it is a rare treat to catch a glimpse of this impressive black bovine, which weighs up to a tonne, whose shoulder height reaches over 1.8m and whose sharp, slender horns span 1m. Wild yaks have diminished in number to 15,000 as a result of the increased demand for yak meat and a rise in hunting. Although eating yak meat is not sacrilegious in Tibetan culture, hunting wild yaks is illegal.

Few, if any, of the yaks that travellers see are *drong* (wild yaks). In fact most are not even yaks at all but rather dzo, a cross between a yak and a bull. A domestic yak rarely exceeds 1.5m in height. Unlike its wild relative, it varies in shade from black to grey and, primarily around Kokonor in Qinghai, white. Seeing only one yak of a certain colour in a herd is considered a bad omen, while seeing two or more yaks is considered a sign of luck.

Despite their massive size, yaks are surprisingly sure-footed and graceful on steep, narrow trails, while burdened by loads of up to 70kg. Yaks panic easily and will struggle to stay close together. This gregarious instinct allows herders to drive packs of animals through snow-blocked passes, and thus to create a natural snowplough.

Most impressive is the yak's ability to thrive in high altitudes. In fact, a descent below 3000m may impair the reproductive cycle and even expose the yak to parasites and disease. Cloaked in layers of shaggy, coarse hair and blanketed by a soft undercoat, the yak uses its square tongue and broad bird-watching in summer are the lakes Yamdrok-tso and Nam-tso; a section of the latter has been designated a bird preserve, at least on paper. Flocks of huge vultures can often be seen circling monasteries looking for a sky burial.

Endangered Species

About 80 species of animal that are threatened with extinction have been listed as protected by the Chinese government. These include the snow leopard *(gang-zig)*, ibex *(capra)*, white-lipped deer *(shawa chukar)*, musk deer *(lawa)*, Tibetan antelope *(chiru)*, Tibetan wild ass *(khyang)*, bharal or blue sheep *(nawa na)*, black-necked crane and wild yak. Omitted from the list is the very rare Tibetan brown bear *(dom gyamuk)*, which stands up to 2m tall and can only be found in the forests of southern Tibet and the remote Changtang plateau.

The Tibetan red deer was recently 'discovered' only 75km from Lhasa after a 50-year hiatus, as was a hitherto unknown breed of ancient wild horse in the Riwoche region of eastern Tibet. The horses bear a striking resemblance to those shown in Stone-Age paintings.

The chiru, a rare breed of antelope, was recently placed on the Red List, a list of threatened species maintained by the World Conservation Union. Numbers in Tibet have dropped from over a million half a century ago to as few as 65,000 today. Poachers kill the animal for its *shatoosh* wool (wool from the animal's undercoat).

The illegal trade in antelope cashmere, musk, bear's paw and gall bladder, deer antlers and other body parts and bones remains a problem. You can often see Tibetan traders huddled on street corners in major Chinese cities selling these and other medicinal cures.

Yakety-Yak

muzzle to forage close to the soil in temperatures that frequently drop to minus 40°C. With three times more red blood cells than the average cow, the yak thrives in the oxygen-depleted high altitudes. Its curious lung formation, surrounded by 14 or 15 pairs of ribs rather than the 13 typical of cattle, allows a large capacity of inhaling and expelling air; thus the Latin name *Bos grunniens*, which translates literally as 'grunting ox'.

For centuries the Tibetan nomads have valued the yak. Legends suggest that Guru Rinpoche first domesticated the yak. Tibetans rely on yak milk for cheese, as well as for butter for the ubiquitous butter tea and offerings to butter lamps in monasteries. The outer hair of the yak is woven into tent fabric and rope, and the soft inner wool is spun into *chara* (a type of felt) and is used to make bags, blankets and tents. Tails are used in both Buddhist and Hindu religious practices. (Yak tail hair was the main material used to produce Father Christmas beards in 1950s America!) Yak hide is used for the soles of boots and the yak's heart is used in Tibetan medicine. Rare hornless yaks are in demand for riding. In the nomadic tradition, no part of the animal is wasted and even yak dung is required as a fundamental fuel, left to dry in little cakes on the walls of most Tibetan houses. Yaks are generically referred to as *nor*, meaning 'wealth', therefore a man's worth is measured by the size of his herd. So important are yaks to the Tibetans that yaks are individually named, like children.

Herders take great care to ensure the health and safety of their animals. Relocation three to eight times a year provides adequate grazing. Every spring the yaks' thick coats are carefully trimmed. Nomads rely on unique veterinarian skills, which they use to lance abscess, set broken bones and sear cuts. For some wounds the herders use a technique of wrapping the affected area in felt and keeping it moist with human urine.

Of the 14 million domesticated yaks worldwide, five million reside on the Qinghai-Tibetan plateau. The yak, with its extraordinary composition and might, has been perhaps the sole enabler of the harsh life of Tibet's *drokpas*, or nomads, and the two coexist in admirable harmony.

NATIONAL PRESERVES

Nature preserves officially protect over 20% of the TAR, although many exist on paper only. The reserve with the highest profile is the Qomolangma Nature Preserve, a 34,000-sq-km protected area straddling the 'third pole' of the Everest region. The park promotes the involvement of the local population, which is essential as some 67,000 people live within the park. For more information on the park see the boxed text 'Qomolangma Nature Preserve' in the Trekking chapter.

Tibet's newest preserve is the Changtang Nature Preserve, set up in 1993 with the assistance of famous animal behaviourist George Schaller. At 247,120 sq km (larger than Arizona in the USA), this is the largest nature reserve in the world after Greenland National Park. Endangered species in the park include bharal, argali sheep, wolves, lynxes, gazelles, snow leopards, wild yaks, antelopes, brown bears and wild asses.

Other reserves include the Medog (Metok) Nature Reserve to the south of Namche Barwa, the Dzalyul (Zayu) Reserve along the far south-east border with Assam, and the Kyirong and Nyalam reserves near the Nepali border. Unfortunately these reserves enjoy little protection or policing.

GOVERNMENT & POLITICS

Unfortunately it is necessary to make a distinction between how Tibet is run today by the Chinese and how it might govern itself should it ever have the chance to administer its own affairs.

The Communist State

Since 1965 Tibet has been administered as the Tibetan Autonomous Region. Not that there is anything particularly autonomous about its government. The Chinese make much of the fact that many high-ranking government positions are filled by Tibetans. One thing is certain: Any Tibetan officials are out the minute they stop toeing the Chinese line.

The TAR is made up of the municipality of Lhasa and six prefectures – Ali, Shigatse, Nagchu, Shannan, Nyingtri and Chamdo – divided into 70 counties. The whole affair is presided over by the Communist Party of the TAR, which calls all the shots. There are numerous other working committees and consultative bodies beneath the Communist Party right down to a local village level.

China is engaged in several border disputes with India, in particular over the 20% of Kashmir known as Aksai Chin, currently

Tibet in Exile

Modern political boundaries and history have led to the fracture of the Tibetan nation. Large areas of historical and ethnic Tibet are now incorporated into the Chinese provinces of Qinghai and Gansu (traditionally known as Amdo), and Sichuan and Yunnan (traditionally known as Kham).

Then figure on the 120,000 Tibetans in exile. Refugees continue to brave high passes and rapacious border guards to get to Kathmandu, paying as much as Y800 for a guide to help them across. The trek can take up to 25 days with no supplies other than all the dried yak meat and *tsampa* (roasted-barley flour) they can carry, and no equipment to help them get over the 6000m passes except canvas shoes. Refugees who make it to Mustang, Namche Bazaar or Kathmandu are interviewed by the United Nations High Commission for Refugees (UNHCR) and then transferred to India. Dharamsala and McLeod Ganj in India's Himachal Pradesh have become de facto Tibetan towns, although the Dalai Lama, after personally meeting each refugee, actively encourages many of them to return to Tibet.

The great monasteries of Tibet have also relocated, many to the South Indian state of Karnataka. Here in the tropical heat not far from the Indian city of Mysore you can find replicas of Sera, Ganden and Drepung Monasteries. There are also large communities of Tibetans in mountainous Switzerland and the USA; you can even find prayer flags gracing the Scottish glens of Samye Ling Monastery in Dumfrieshire.

held by China, and the regions of Sikkim and Arunachal Pradesh.

Hu Jintao, the Chinese head of the TAR during the bloody Tibetan demonstrations of 1988, is tipped to become Chinese president when current president Jiang Zemin steps down in 2002, which would make him arguably the most powerful man in China.

Tibetan Government-in-Exile

The immediate result of the 1959 Lhasa uprising was the flight of the Dalai Lama and eventually 80,000 Tibetan refugees to India, Nepal and Bhutan. It is estimated that there are now some 120,000 Tibetan refugees in 45 settlements on the subcontinent, and they look to the Dalai Lama's administration in Dharamsala as their government.

The government-in-exile initially consisted of the Dalai Lama's cabinet, the Kashag, but elections were called in 1960 for the establishment of a new body known as the Commission of People's Deputies. In 1963, a constitution of Tibet was promulgated. This constitution, which combines the qualities of Buddhism with the needs of modern government, is still in draft form, awaiting the final approval of the people of Tibet, should they ever have the opportunity to vote for their own constitution. The government is supported by voluntary taxes from the exiled Tibetan community and by business interests.

ECONOMY

While perhaps not quite matching the juggernaut pace of economic reform elsewhere in China, the economy of Tibet is seeing rapid changes. The Chinese government claims that economic growth in Tibet stands at 9%. Communications are constantly being improved and local officials have been encouraging foreign investment. The successes of such reforms are inevitably exaggerated, but changes are obvious to anyone who returns to Tibet after being away for a couple of years.

When the Chinese took over Tibet, the local economy had developed little in hundreds of years. It was largely agricultural and self-sufficient in its basic needs. Im-

ports of things such as tea, porcelain, copper and iron from China were compensated by exports of wool and skins. Trading was usually carried out in combination with pilgrimage or by nomads. This movement provided a flow of goods to isolated farming communities that generally harvested barley for *tsampa* (roasted-barley flour), the Tibetan staple. Animal husbandry was and still is extremely important in Tibet, and there are around 21 million head of livestock in the region.

Mining

The Chinese have since looked to other methods of developing the high plateau. One of these has been mining, which was traditionally inimical to the Tibetans, who thought it disturbed the sacred essence of the soil.

However, extensive surveys of Tibet's mining potential have brought to light rich deposits of gold, zinc, chromium, lithium, copper, silver, boron, uranium and other metals. A single mine in northern Tibet is said to hold over half the world's total deposits of lithium. Eastern Tibet is rich in both copper and gold. Reports indicate that over 120 new mining sites have been opened up in recent years to exploit these resources and that mining now accounts for one-third of Tibet's industrial output. The Chinese name for Tibet, Xizang, or the Western Treasure House, now has a ring of prophetic irony.

Chinese Investment & Migration

Tibet, like other outlying regions of China with rich resources and cheap labour, is attracting considerable investment from the booming east-coast regions of China. China's major drive to develop its western hinterland has had a considerable impact on investment in Tibet. In 2000 alone the Chinese government pledged over US$3.8 billion to complete over 100 construction projects. Expenditure on road building alone, for example, will treble between 2001 and 2005. There are even plans to make Lhasa a Special Economic Zone.

Outside investment has also brought with it a surge in Han immigration to Tibet.

Although no figures are available, it is obvious that many Chinese people, attracted by preferential loans and tax rates, a less strictly enforced one-child policy, stipends for a hardship posting and easy business opportunities, are setting up shop in urban centres all over Tibet. The government-in-exile estimates that of Lhasa's 13,000 shop-keepers only 300 or so are Tibetan. Not all Chinese are here to earn money though. Wealthy urban Chinese tourists are starting to flock to Tibet in droves, and tourism, both domestic and foreign, is becoming an increasingly important source of revenue.

Meanwhile, standards of living in the countryside remain relatively static; the average annual income is less than Y800 (less than US$100). There is an increasing economic and social divide in Tibet.

Many Tibetans maintain that Chinese immigrants are the real winners in the race to get rich in Tibet, while China protests that it is simply developing and integrating one of its most backward provinces, at a large financial loss.

POPULATION & PEOPLE

China's 1996 population survey put the population of the TAR at 2.44 million, with a natural growth rate of 16.2%, the highest in China. Figures are likely to be higher than this if Han immigrants and PLA troops stationed in Tibet (perhaps up to 200,000) are included, but the Chinese government is very coy about releasing figures that would make it clear just how many Chinese there are in Tibet.

Official statistics claim 95% of the TAR's population is Tibetan, a figure that is hotly contested by almost everyone except the government. Chinese figures for the population of Lhasa, for example, indicate it is just over 87% Tibetan and just under 12% Han Chinese, a ratio that stretches the credulity of anyone who has visited the city in recent years. It is more likely that somewhere in the vicinity of 50% of Lhasa's population is Han Chinese. The recent flood of Chinese immigrants into Tibet has been termed China's 'second invasion', and ethnic dilution has been pinpointed by the

Dalai Lama as probably the gravest threat to the survival of Tibetan culture.

A census conducted in 1990 indicated that there are another 2.5 million ethnic Tibetans in Qinghai, Sichuan and Gansu provinces. There are also thought to be around 120,000 more Tibetans in exile, mainly in India but also in the USA, Canada and Europe (especially Switzerland).

Population Control

Population control is a cornerstone of Chinese government policy but regulations are generally less strictly enforced in Tibet. 'Minority nationalities', as the Tibetans are classified, are allowed two children before they lose certain stipends and housing allowances; a stricter one-child policy applies in the rest of China.

In contrast to world demographic trends, there were 12 million Tibetans a millennium ago, four million by the 18th century and barely a million by 1949. The reason for the dramatic decline is neither plague nor invasion, but rather the tendency of families to send at least one son into the monkhood. Ironically, the most effective form of birth control in modern Tibet still seems to be to join a monastery.

Ethnic Groups

Like the Han Chinese (and almost all the other ethnic minorities of China), the Tibetans are classified as belonging to the Mongoloid family of peoples. They are probably descended from a variety of nomadic tribes who migrated from the north and settled to sedentary cultivation of Tibet's river valleys. About a quarter of Tibetans, however, are still nomadic. There are considerable variations between regional groups of Tibetans. The most recognisable of these are the Khampas of eastern Tibet, who are generally larger and a bit more rough-and-ready than other Tibetans and who wear red or black tassels in their long hair. Women from Amdo are especially conspicuous because of their elaborate braided hairstyles and jewellery.

There are pockets of other minority groups, such as the Lhopa (Lhoba) and

Monpa, in the south-east of Tibet, although these make up less than 1% of the total population. A more visible ethnic group are the Hui Muslims. Tibet's original Muslim inhabitants were largely traders or butchers (a profession that most Buddhists abhor), although most of the recent migrants are traders and restaurant owners from southern Gansu province. The Tibetans' closest ethnic cousins are the Qiang, who now live mostly in northern Sichuan province. Tibetans are also closely related to the Sherpas of Nepal and the Ladakhis of India.

EDUCATION

Education was once the exclusive domain of the monasteries, and the introduction of a secular education system has been a major goal of the Communist government. The number of schools has increased many times over, although literacy rates still hover around 60%. Just over 50% of Tibetan children under 12 attend primary school. Much primary teaching is carried out in Tibetan, although almost all higher education is carried out in Chinese. A knowledge of Chinese is essential for advancement in Tibet, particularly in government jobs.

ARTS

Almost all Tibetan art, with perhaps the exception of some folk crafts, is inspired by Buddhism. Wall hangings, paintings, architecture, literature, even dance, all in some way or another attest to the influence of the Indian religion that found its most secure resting place in Tibet.

At the same time, the arts of Tibet represent the synthesis of many influences. The Buddhist art and architecture of the Pala and Newari kingdoms of India and Nepal were an important early influence, as were the Buddhist cultures of Khotan and Kashmir. Newari influence is clearly visible in the early woodcarvings of the Jokhang, and Kashmiri influence is particularly strong in the murals of Tsaparang in western Tibet. As China came to play an increasingly major role in Tibetan affairs, Chinese influences too were assimilated, as is clear at Shalu Monastery near Shigatse and in the Karma Gadri style prevalent in eastern Kham. A later, clearly Tibetan style known as Menri was perfected in the monasteries of Drepung, Ganden and Sera.

Tibetan art is deeply conservative and conventional. Personal expression and innovation are not valued and indeed individual interpretation can actually become an obstacle to art's main purpose, which is to represent the path to enlightenment. Artists generally remain anonymous in Tibet. Colour is decided purely by convention and rigid symbolism.

Much of Tibet's artistic heritage fell victim to the Cultural Revolution. What was not destroyed was in many cases ferreted away to China or onto the Hong Kong art market. In recent years over 13,500 images have been returned to Tibet, a fraction of the number stolen. Worse still, many of Tibet's traditional artisans were persecuted or fled Tibet. It is only in recent years that remaining artists have again been able to return to their work and start to train young Tibetans in skills that faced the threat of extinction.

Dance & Drama

Anyone who is lucky enough to attend a Tibetan festival should have the opportunity to see performances of *cham*, a ritual dance performed over several days by monks and lamas. Although every movement and gesture of cham has significance, it is no doubt the spectacle of the colourful masked dancers that awes the average pilgrim.

Cham is about the suppression of malevolent spirits and is a throwback to the pre-Buddhist Bön faith. It is a solemn masked dance accompanied by long trumpets, drums and cymbals. The chief officiant is an unmasked Black Hat lama who is surrounded by a mandalic grouping of masked monks who represent manifestations of various protective deities. The act of exorcism – it might be considered as such – is focused on a human effigy made of dough or perhaps wax or paper in which the evil spirits are thought to reside.

The proceedings of cham can be interpreted on a number of levels. The Black Hat lama is sometimes identified with the monk who slew Langdharma, the anti-Buddhist king of the Yarlung era, and the dance is seen as echoing the suppression of malevolent forces inimical to the establishment of Buddhism in Tibet. Some anthropologists, on the other hand, have seen in cham a metaphor for the gradual conquering of the ego, which is the aim of Buddhism. The ultimate destruction of the effigy that ends the dance might represent the destruction of the ego itself. Whatever the case, cham is a splendid, dramatic performance and it well worth going out of your way to see it.

Performances of cham are most of the time accompanied by other, less significant performances that seem to have evolved as entertainment in festivals. *Lhamo*, not to be confused with cham, is Tibetan opera. A largely secular art form, it portrays the heroics of kings and the villainy of demons, and recounts events in the lives of historical figures. Lhamo was invented in the 14th century by Tangtong Gyelpo, known as 'Tibet's Leonardo da Vinci' because he was also an engineer, a major bridge-builder and physician. Traditional performances still include a statue of Tangtong on the otherwise bare stage. Performances were traditionally performed by travelling troupes and would last the entire day. After the stage has been purified, the narrator gives a plot summary in verse and the performers enter, each with his or her distinct step and dressed in the bright and colourful silks of the aristocracy.

Other festival dances might depict the slaying of Langdharma or the arrival of the Indian teachers in Tibet at the time of the second diffusion of Buddhism. Light relief is provided by masked clowns or children.

Music

Music is one aspect of Tibetan cultural life in which there is a strong secular tradition. In urban centres, songs were an important vent for social criticism, news and official lampooning. In Tibetan social life, both work and play are occasions for singing. Even today it is not uncommon to see monastery reconstruction squads pounding on the roofs of buildings and singing in unison. Where there are groups of men and women, the singing alternates between the two groups in the form of rhythmic refrains. Festivals and picnics are also occasions for singing.

Tibet also has a secular tradition of wandering minstrels. It's still possible to see minstrels in Lhasa and Shigatse, where they play on the streets and occasionally (when they are not chased out by the owners) in restaurants.

Generally, groups of two or three singers perform heroic epics and short songs to the accompaniment of a Tibetan four-stringed guitar and a nifty little shuffle. In times past, groups of such performers travelled around Tibet, providing entertainment for villagers who enjoyed few distractions from the constant round of daily chores. These performers were sometimes accompanied by dancers and acrobats.

While the secular music of Tibet has an instant appeal for foreign listeners, the liturgical chants of Buddhist monks and the music that accompanies cham dances is a lot less accessible. Buddhist chanting creates an eerie haunting effect but soon becomes very monotonous. The music of cham is a discordant cacophony of trumpet blasts and boom-crash drums – atmospheric as an accompaniment to the dancing but not exactly the kind of thing you would want to slip into the CD player.

Tibetan religious rituals use cymbals (*rolmo* and *silnyen*), suspended drums (*nga*), hand drums (*damaru*) and bells (*drilbu*), as well as long trumpets known as *dungchen*, conical oboes (formerly made from human thigh-bones) known as *kangling*, and conch shells (*dungkar*). Secular instruments include a six-stringed lute known as a *dranyen*, a two-stringed fiddle known as a *piwang* and a Chinese-style zither known as a *gyumang*.

Most recordings of traditional Tibetan music have been made in Dharamsala or Dalhousie in India. Tibet's biggest musical export (or rather exile) is Yungchen Lhamo, who sings traditional Tibetans songs, normally a cappella. She also appeared on Natalie Merchant's *Ophelia*. Another Tibetan singer based in the West is Dadon Dawa

Dolma. If you fancy a listen, try the following recordings available in the West:

Anthology of World Music: Music of Tibetan Buddhism
Chö Choying Drolma & Steve Tibbets (Hannibal Music Label) A stunning introduction to Tibetan religious music; highly recommended
Coming Home Yungchen Lhamo (Real World, 1998)
Dhama Suna Tibetan Institute of Performing Arts (Detour)
Freedom Chants from the Roof of the World The Gyuto Monks (Rykodisc)
Rain of Blessings: Vajra Chants Lama Gyurme & Jean-Philippe Rykiel (Real World)
Tibet Incantations: The Meditative Sound of Buddhist Chants (Nascente)
Tibet Tibet Yungchen Lhamo (Real World, 1996)
Tibetan Tantric Choir The Gyuto Monks (Windham Hill)

Literature

The development of a Tibetan written script is credited to a monk by the name of Tonmi Sambhota and corresponded with the early introduction of Buddhism during the reign of King Songtsen Gampo. Accordingly, pre-Buddhist traditions were passed down as oral histories that told of the exploits of early kings and the origins of the Tibetan people. Some of these oral traditions were later recorded using the Tibetan script.

But for the most part literature in Tibet was dominated by Buddhism; first as a means of translating Buddhist scriptures from Sanskrit into Tibetan; and second, as time went by, in association with the development of Tibetan Buddhist thought. There is nothing in the nature of a secular literary tradition – least of all novels – such as can be found in China or Japan.

One of the great achievements of Tibetan culture was the development of a literary language that could, with remarkable faithfulness, reproduce the concepts of Sanskrit Buddhist texts. The compilation of Tibetan-Sanskrit dictionaries in the early 9th century ensured consistency in all subsequent translations.

Alongside Buddhist scriptures exists an ancient tradition of storytelling, usually concerning the taming of Tibet's malevolent spirits to allow the introduction of Buddhism. Many of these stories were passed from generation to generation orally, but some were recorded. Examples include the Gesar epic and the story of Guru Rinpoche, who is said to have been born in a lotus in the ancient kingdom of Swat before coming to Tibet and performing countless miracles to prepare the land for the diffusion of Buddhism.

Through the 12th and 13th centuries, Tibetan literary endeavour was almost entirely consumed by the monumental task of translating the complete Buddhist canon into Tibetan. The result was the 108 volumes of canonical texts (Kangyur), which record the words of the Historical Buddha, Sakyamuni (Sakya Thukpa), and 208 volumes of commentary (Tengyur) on the Kangyur by Indian masters that make up the basic Buddhist scriptures shared by all Tibetan religious orders. What time was left from this was used in the compilation of biographies and the collection of songs of revered lamas. Perhaps most famous among these is the *Hundred Thousand Songs of Milarepa*; Milarepa was an ascetic to whom many songs and poems concerning the quest for buddhahood are attributed.

Wood-block printing has been in use in Tibet for centuries and is still the most common form of printing in monasteries. Blocks are carved in mirror image; printers then work in pairs putting strips of paper over the inky block and shuttling an ink roll over it. The pages of the text are kept loose, wrapped in cloth and stored along the walls of monasteries. Tibet's most famous printing presses were in Derge in modern-day Sichuan, at Nartang Monastery and at the Potala.

Very little of the Tibetan literary tradition has been translated into English. Translations that may be of interest include *The Tibetan Book of the Dead*, a mysterious but fascinating account of the stages and visions that occur between death and rebirth; *The Jewel Ornament of Liberation*, which describes the path to enlightenment as seen by the chief disciple of Milarepa and founder of the Kagyupa order; and *The Life of Milarepa*, the autobiography of Tibet's most famous ascetic.

Architecture

Most early Tibetan religious architecture – the Jokhang in Lhasa for example – owed much to Pala (Indian) and especially Newari (Nepali) influences. Still, a distinctively Tibetan style of architectural design soon emerged, and found its greatest expression in the Kumbum of Gyantse, the monasteries of Samye and Tashilhunpo, and the Potala. The great American architect Frank Lloyd Wright is said to have had a picture of the Potala on the wall of his office.

Chörtens

Probably the most prominent Tibetan architectural motif is the stupa, or *chörten* as it is known in Tibet. Chörtens were originally built to house the cremated relics of the Historical Buddha, Sakyamuni (Sakya Thukpa), and as such have become a powerful symbol of the Buddha and his teachings. Later, chörtens also served as reliquaries for lamas and holy men. Larger monumental versions would often encase whole mummified bodies, as is the case with the tombs of the Dalai Lamas in the Potala. And the tradition is very much alive: A stunning gold reliquary chörten was constructed in 1989 at Tashilhunpo Monastery to hold the body of the 10th Panchen Lama.

In the early stages of Buddhism, images of the Buddha did not exist and chörtens became the major symbol of the new faith. Over the next two millennia chörtens took many different forms across the Buddhist world, from the sensuous stupas of Burma to the pagodas of China and Japan. Most elaborate of all are the *kumbums*, or 100,000 Buddha images, of which the best remaining example in Tibet is at Gyantse. Many chörtens were built to hold ancient relics and sacred texts and so have been plundered over the years by treasure seekers and vandals.

Monastery Layout

Tibetan monasteries are based on a conservative design and share a remarkable continuity of layout. Many are built in spectacular high locations above villages. Most were originally surrounded by an outer wall, built to defend the treasures of the monastery from bands of brigands, Mongolian hordes or even rival monasteries. Most monasteries have a *kora*, or pilgrimage path, around the complex, replete with holy rocks and meditation retreats high on the hillside behind.

Inside the gates there is usually a central courtyard used for special ceremonies and festivals and a flag pole known as a *darchen*. Surrounding buildings usually include a main assembly or prayer hall (*dukhang*) with side protector chapels (*gönkhang* or *sumkhang*) and subsidiary chapels (*lhakhang*), as well as monks' quarters, a library and, in the case of larger monasteries, colleges (*tratsang*), halls of residence (*kangtsang*), kitchens and a printing press (*barkhang*).

The main prayer hall consists of rows of low seats and tables often strewn with cloaks, hats, ritual instruments, drums and huge telescopic horns. There is a small altar with seven bowls of water, butter lamps, and offerings of mandalas made from seeds. The main altar houses the main statues, often Sakyamuni (Sakya Thukpa), Jampa (Maitreya) or a trinity of the Past, Present and Future Buddhas and perhaps the founder of the monastery or past lamas. There may be an inner room behind the main hall, whose entrance is flanked by protector gods, one often blue, Chana Dorje (Vajrapani), the other red, Tamdrin (Hayagriva). There may well be an inner kora of prayer wheels. At the entrance to most buildings are murals of the Four Guardian Kings and perhaps a Wheel of Life or a mandala mural. Side stairs lead up from here to higher floors.

Protector chapels are dark and spooky halls that hold wrathful manifestations of deities, often covered with a cloth because of their terrible appearance. Murals are often traced against a black background and walls are decorated with Tantric deities or skeletons. Pillars are decorated with festival masks, weapons and sometimes stuffed animals such as snakes and wolves.

The monastery roof usually has excellent views as well as vases of immortality, victory banners, dragons, and copper symbols of the Wheel of Law flanked by two deer.

Chörtens are highly symbolic. The five levels represent the four elements and eternal space: The square base symbolises earth, the dome is water, the spire is fire, and the top moon and sun are air and space. The 13 discs of the ceremonial umbrella can represent the branches of the tree of life or the 10 powers and three mindfulnesses of the Buddha. The top seed-shaped pinnacle symbolises enlightenment, and in fact the chörten as a whole can be seen as a representation of the path to enlightenment. The construction can also physically represent the Buddha, with the base as his seat and the dome as his body.

Secular Architecture Typical features of Tibetan secular architecture, which are also used to a certain extent in religious architecture, are buildings with inward-sloping walls made of large tightly fitting stones or sun-baked bricks. Below the roof is a layer of twigs, squashed tight by the roof and painted to give Tibetan houses their characteristic brown band. Roofs are flat, as there is little rain or snow, made from pounded earth and edged with walls. You may well see singing bands of Tibetan men and women pounding a new roof with sticks weighted with large stones. In larger structures, the roof is supported inside by wooden pillars. The exteriors are generally whitewashed brick, although in some areas, such as Sakya in Tsang, other colours may be used. In rural Tibet, homes are often surrounded by walled compounds, and in some areas entrances are protected by painted scorpions and swastikas.

Nomads, who take their homes with them, live in *bar* (yak-hair tents) which are normally roomy and can accommodate a whole family. An opening at the top of the tent lets out smoke from the fire.

Painting
Tibetan painting is almost exclusively devotional in nature. As with other types of Tibetan art, it is also very symbolic and can be seen on many different levels.

Styles The strongest influence on Tibetan art came from India. Paintings usually followed stereotyped forms with a central Buddhist deity surrounded by smaller, lesser deities. Poised above the central figure was often a supreme buddha figure of which the one below it was an emanation. Later came depictions of revered Tibetan lamas or Indian spiritual teachers, often surrounded by incidents from the lama's life or lineage lines.

Chinese influence began to manifest itself more frequently in Tibetan painting from around the 15th century. The freer approach of Chinese landscape painting allowed some Tibetan artists to break free from some of the more formalised aspects of Tibetan religious art and employ landscape as a decorative motif in the context of a painting that celebrated a particular religious figure. This is not to say that Chinese art initiated a new movement in Tibetan art. The new, Chinese-influenced forms coexisted with older forms, largely because painting in Tibet was passed on from artisan to apprentice in much the same way that monastic communities maintained lineages of teaching.

Thangkas Religious paintings mounted on brocade and rolled up between two sticks are called *thangkas*. Their eminent portability was essential in a land of nomads, and they were often used by mendicant preachers and doctors as a visual learning aid. Not so portable are the huge thangkas, the size of large buildings, that are unfurled every year during festivals. Traditionally, thangkas were never bought or sold.

The production of a thangka is an act of devotion and the process is carefully formalised. Linen (or now more commonly cotton) is stretched on a wooden frame, stiffened with glue and coated with a mix of chalk and lime called gesso. Iconography is bound by strict mathematical measurements. A grid is drawn onto the thangka before outlines are sketched in charcoal, starting with the main central deity and moving outwards.

Colours are added one at a time, starting with the background and ending with shading. Pigments were traditionally natural: blue from lapis, red from cinnabar and yellow from sulphur. Most thangkas are burnished with at least a little gold. The last part of the thangka to be painted is the eyes, which are filled in during a special 'opening the eyes' celebration. Finally a brocade backing of three colours and a 'curtain' are added, the latter to protect the thangka.

Statuary & Sculpture

Tibetan statuary, like Tibetan painting, is religious in nature. Ranging from several centimetres to several metres in height, statues usually depict deities and revered lamas. Most of the smaller statues are hollow and are stuffed with paper prayers and relics when consecrated.

Metal statues are traditionally sculpted in wax and then covered in clay. When the clay is dry it is heated. The wax melts and is removed, leaving a mould that can be filled with molten metal. Statues are then often gilded and painted.

Sculptures are most commonly made from bronze or stucco mixed with straw but can even be made out of butter and tsampa. Butter sculptures are normally made on wooden frames and symbolise the impermanence of all things.

Handicrafts

Tibet has a 1000-year history of carpet making; the carpets are mostly used as seat covers, bed covers and saddle blankets. Knots are double tied (the best carpets have 100 knots per square inch) which results in a particularly thick pile. Tibet's secret carpet ingredient is its particularly high-quality sheep wool, which is hand spun and coloured with natural dyes such as indigo, walnut, madder and rhubarb. Gyantse and Shigatse were the traditional centres of carpet production, although the modern industry is based almost exclusively in Tibetan exile communities in Nepal.

Inlaid handicrafts are common, particularly in the form of prayer wheels, daggers, temple horns, butter lamps and bowls, although most of what you see these days in Lhasa is made by Tibetan communities in Nepal. Nomads in particular wear stunning silver jewellery; you may also see silver

flints, amulets known as *gau*, and ornate chopstick and knife sets.

Tibetan singing bowls, made from a secret mix of seven different metals, are a meditation device that originated from pre-Buddhist Bön practices. The bowls produce a 'disassociated' mystic hum when a playing stick is rotated around the outer edge of the bowl.

Woodcarving is another valued handicraft, used in the production of brightly coloured Tibetan furniture and window panels, not to mention wood blocks.

SOCIETY & CONDUCT

The Tibetans are such a deeply religious people that at least a basic understanding of Buddhism is essential in making any sense of their world. Buddhism permeates most facets of Tibetan daily life and shapes the aspirations of Tibetans in ways that are often quite alien to the Western frame of mind. The idea of accumulating merit, of sending sons to be monks, of undertaking pilgrimages, of devotion to the sanctity and power of natural places are all elements of the unique fusion between Buddhism and the older shamanistic Bön faith.

Traditional Culture

Traditionally there have been at least three distinct segments of Tibetan society: the nomads *(drokpa)*; the farmers of the Tibetan valleys *(rongpa)*; and the community of monks and nuns *(sangha)*. Members of these groupings each led very different lives, although all shared a deep faith in Buddhism. For more information on Tibet's nomads, see the boxed text 'Nomads' in the Ü chapter. For more information on monastic communities, see the boxed text 'The World of a Monk' later in this chapter.

Besides Buddhism, one thing these communities have shared over the centuries is a remarkable resistance to change. While religious orders rose and fell from power and the Mongolians and Chinese jostled for control of the high plateau, the fundamentals of the Tibetan lifestyle remained unchanged and technological innovation of any kind was unheard of. Until the early

20th century, Tibet was a land in which virtually the only use for the wheel was as a device for activating mantras.

Traditional Tibet has changed more in the past 50 years than it did in the 500 before that, although many traditional social structures have endured Chinese attempts at iconoclasm.

Farming communities in Tibet usually comprise a cluster of homes surrounded by agricultural lands once owned by the nearest large monastery. Most strategic agricultural valleys are protected by the ruins of a *dzong*, or fort, perched on a high outcrop. The farming itself is carried out with the assistance of a dzo, a cross between a bull and a female yak; or, if no cattle are available, by hand. Some wealthier farmers own a small 'walking tractor'. Harvested grain is carried by donkeys to a threshing ground where it is trampled by cattle or threshed with poles. The grain is then cast into the air from a basket and the task of winnowing carried out by the breeze.

Until recently such communities were effectively self-sufficient in their needs, and although theirs was a hard life it could not be described as grinding poverty. Village families pulled together in times of need, and plots of land were usually graded in terms of their quality and then distributed so that the land of any one family included both good-quality and poorer-quality land. This is changing rapidly as many regions become economically more developed and immersed in a cash economy. Most villages have at least one entrepreneur who has set up a shop and begun to ship in Chinese goods from the nearest urban centre.

Individual households normally have a shrine in the house or in a small building in the family compound. There might also be several religious texts, held in a place of honour, which are traditionally reserved for occasions when a monk or holy man visits the village. There are also ceremonies for blessing yaks and other livestock to ensure a productive year. At the same time, one of the highlights of the year for rural Tibetans is visiting nearby monasteries at festival times or making a pilgrimage to a holy site.

The World of a Monk

The Western term 'monk' is slightly misleading when it is used in the context of Tibetan Buddhism. The Tibetan equivalent would probably be *trapa*, which means literally 'scholar' or 'student', and is an inclusive term that covers the three main categories of monastic inmates. Monks in these categories should also be distinguished from lamas, who as spiritual luminaries have a privileged position in the monastic hierarchy, may have considerable wealth and, outside the Gelugpa order, are not necessarily celibate.

The first step for a monk, usually after completing some prior study, is to take one of two lesser vows, the *genyen* or *getsul* ordination – a renunciation of secular life that includes a vow of celibacy. This marks the beginning of a long course of study that is expected to lead to the full *gelong* vows of ordination. While most major monasteries have a number of gelong monks, not all monks achieve gelong status.

These three categories do not encompass all the monks in a monastery. There are usually specific monastic posts associated with administrative duties, with ritual and with teaching. Gelong vows are also supplemented by higher courses of study, which are rewarded in the Gelugpa order by the title *geshe*. In premodern Tibet, the larger monasteries also had divisions of so-called 'fighting monks', or monastic militias. To a large extent they served as a kind of police force within a particular monastery, but there were also times when their services were used to hammer home a doctrinal dispute with a rival monastery.

Before the Chinese invasion, entertainment traditionally included the occasional arrival of *lhamo* (Tibetan opera) troupes or wandering bands of musicians. As traditional life reasserts itself, many of these traditions are slowly making a comeback.

Tibetans still use the lunar calendar for traditional events. Years are calculated in a 60-year cycle and divided into five elements and 12 zodiac animals. Thus 2002 is the year of the water horse.

Marriage Traditionally, marriage has been arranged by the families involved, in consultation with a lama or shaman. In the fairly recent past, many Tibetan farming villages practised polyandry. When a woman married the eldest son of a family she also married his younger brothers (providing they did not become monks). The children of such marriages referred to all the brothers as their father. The practice was aimed at easing the inheritance of family property (mainly the farming land) and avoiding the break-up of small plots.

Death Although the early kings of Tibet were buried with complex funerary rites, ordinary Tibetans have not traditionally buried their dead. The very poor were usually dumped in a river when they died and the very holy were cremated and their ashes enshrined in a chörten. But in a land where soil is at a premium and wood for cremation is scarcer still, most people were, and still are, disposed of by sky burial.

After death, the body is kept for 24 hours in a sitting position while a lama recites prayers from *The Tibetan Book of the Dead* to help the soul on its journey through the 49 levels of Bardo, the state between death and rebirth. Three days after death the body is blessed and early-morning prayers and offerings are made to the monastery. The body is folded up and carried on the back of a close friend to the *dürtro* or burial site. Here, special body-breakers known as *rogyapas* cut off the deceased's hair, chop up the body and pound the bones together with tsampa for vultures to eat, although as often as not the job of eating the body might be done by wild dogs.

There is little overt sadness at a sky burial as the soul is considered to have already departed – the burial itself is considered to be mere disposal. Sky burial is, however, very much a time to reflect on the impermanence of life. Death is seen as a powerful agent of transformation and spiritual progress. Tibetans are encouraged to witness the disposal of the body and to confront death openly and without fear. This is one of the reasons why Tantric ritual objects such as trumpets and bowls are made from human bone.

Sky Burial

Naturally, Tibetans are often very unhappy about camera-toting foreigners heading up to sky-burial sites. The Chinese authorities do not like it either and may fine foreigners who attend a burial. You should never pay to see a sky burial and you should *never* take photos. Even if Tibetans offer to take you up to a sky-burial site, it is unlikely that other Tibetans present will be very happy about it. Sky burials are funeral services. Nobody invited you. Don't go.

Dress

Many Tibetans in Lhasa are beginning to wear Western (or rather Chinese) clothes, but in the countryside traditional dress is still the norm. The Tibetan national dress is a *chuba* or long-sleeved sheepskin cloak, tied around the waist with a sash and often worn off the shoulder with great bravado by nomads and Khampas (those from the region of Kham). Chubas from eastern Tibet in particular have super-long sleeves, which are tied around the waist. An inner pouch is often used to store money belts, amulets and even lunch. Most women wear a long dress with a colourful striped apron over the front. Traditional boots are made of leather strips and have turned-up toes, so as, it is said, to kill fewer bugs when walking.

Women generally set great store in jewellery, and their personal wealth and dowry are often invested in it. Coral is particularly valued (as it is so far from the sea), as are amber, turquoise and silver. The Tibetan *zee*, a unique elongated agate stone with black and white markings, is also highly prized. Earrings are common in both men and women and they are normally tied on with a piece of cord. You can see all these goodies for sale around the Barkhor in Lhasa.

Tibetan women, especially those from Amdo (north-eastern Tibet and Qinghai), traditionally wear their hair in 108 braids. Khampa men plait their hair with red or black tassels and wind the lot around their head. Cowboy hats are popular in summer and fur hats are common in winter. Most pilgrims carry a gau, or amulet, with a picture of the owner's personal deity or the Dalai Lama inside.

Dos & Don'ts

The Tibetans are among the easiest people in Asia to get along with. Their smiles are infectious and it is rare for major cultural differences to get in the way of communication. Problems do occur, however, and it is worth remembering that there is a lot of anger and long-harboured resentment under the surface in Tibet. Moreover, many Tibetans in business and administration operate within the Chinese scheme of things, and some have picked up habits that are encountered all too often by travellers elsewhere in China: for example, rudeness, overcharging and obstructionism.

In general negotiations it is a good idea to ensure that the person you are dealing with does not lose face, does not appear to be wrong and is not forced to back down in front of others. A negotiated settlement is always preferable and outright confrontation is a last resort. It is best to try to sort out problems with smiling persistence – when one tack fails, try another.

The giving of gifts is a useful way to establish a relationship where there was not one before. If you are a smoker, walking up to someone with a smile and handing them a cigarette is a very effective way of getting business off to a good start. Tibetans show respect to an honoured guest or a lama by placing a *kathak* (prayer scarf) around their neck. When reciprocating, hold the scarf out in both hands with palms turned upwards.

Be aware that Tibetans often gesture with their lips to indicate a particular direction, so if a member of the opposite sex pouts at you they are just showing you where to go. Older country folk may stick out their tongue when they meet you, a very traditional form of respect that greeted the very first travellers to Tibet centuries ago. Some sources say that this was traditionally done to prove that the person was not a devil, because devils have green tongues even when they take human form.

The most common hitching gesture is to stick out one or two fingers towards the ground and wave them up or down.

See the boxed text 'Visiting Monasteries and Temples' in the Lhasa chapter for more tips on etiquette.

RELIGION
Buddhism

A basic understanding of Buddhism is essential to getting beneath the skin of things in Tibet. Buddhism's values and goals permeate almost everything Tibetan. Exploring the monasteries and temples of Tibet and mixing with its people, yet knowing nothing of Buddhism, is like visiting Rome and knowing nothing of Christianity. To be sure, it might still seem an awe-inspiring experience, but much will remain hidden and indecipherable.

For those who already do know something of Buddhism, who have read something of Zen, for example, Tibet can be baffling on another level. The grandeur of the temples, the worship of images and the fierce protective deities that stand in doorways all seem to belie the basic tenets of an ascetic faith that is basically about renouncing the self and following a path of moderation.

On a purely superficial level, Buddhism has historically encompassed the moral precepts and devotional practices of lay followers, the scholastic tradition of the Indian Buddhist universities and a body of mystic Tantric teachings that had a particular appeal to followers of the shamanistic Bön faith.

Tibetan Buddhism's reaction with existing Bön spirit worship and the Hindu pantheon created a huge range of deities, both wrathful and benign (although these are all merely aspects of the human ego). Apart from a whole range of different buddha aspects there are also general protector gods called *dharmapalas* and personal meditational deities called *yidams* (either male *herukas* or female *dakinis*), which Tantric students adopt early in their spiritual training. Yet for all its confusing iconography the basic tenets of Buddhism are very much rooted in daily experience. Even high lamas and monks come across as surprisingly down-to-earth.

Sacred Items & Symbols

Swastika
The swastika is an ancient symbol of Buddhism and is often found painted on houses to bring good luck. Swastikas that point clockwise are Buddhist; those that point anticlockwise are Bön.

Sun & Moon
Another popular protective motif that is painted on houses, the sun and moon symbolise complementary opposites, in the form of wisdom and compassion.

Prayer Flags
Strips of coloured cloth printed with Buddhist sutras are strung up at the top of passes, near streams and on houses to purify the air and pacify the gods. When the flags flutter, prayers are thought to be released to the heavens. The colours are highly symbolic – red, green, yellow, blue and white represent the elements of fire, wood, earth, water and iron.

Prayer Wheels
Prayer wheels, which range from the hand-held variety to huge water-powered versions, are filled with up to a mile of prayers; the prayers are 'recited' with each revolution of the wheel. A wheel can be the size of a fist or a small building and can be powered by hand, water, wind or even hot air (in the case of cylinders made from paper and suspended over a hot flame).

Koras (pilgrimage paths) are lined with prayer wheels; circumambulating pilgrims spin the wheels to gain merit and to concentrate the mind on the mantras and prayers they are reciting.

Wind Horse
The wind horse, or *longda*, is the main symbol found on prayer flags. The horse carries the Three Jewels of Buddhism (the Buddha, dharma and sangha) on his back and carries prayers to the heavens.

Mani Stones
Mani stones are carved with sutras as an act of merit and placed in long walls, often hundreds of metres long, at holy sites.

'Om Mani Padme Hum'
The mantra *'om mani padme hum'* is the mantra most commonly carved on mani stones. The six syllables mean 'hail to the jewel in the lotus' and form the mantra of Chenresig (Avalokiteshvara), the Bodhisattva of Compassion. Other mantras include those of Guru Rinpoche (*'om ah hum vajra guru padma siddhi hung'*) and Jampelyang (*'om ahra paza nu dhi dhi'*).

Skull Drum
A skull drum is a small double-sided hand drum traditionally made from two halves of a skull covered in leather or even human skin.

Buddhism is perhaps the most tolerant of the world's religions. Wherever it has gone it has adapted to local conditions, like a dividing cell, creating countless new schools of thought. Its basic tenets have remained very much the same and all schools are bound together in their faith in the value of the original teachings of Sakyamuni (Sakya Thukpa), the Historical Buddha.

Closely linked to Bön and Buddhism is the folk religion of Tibet, known in Tibetan as *mi chös*, or 'the dharma of man', which is primarily concerned with spirits. These spirits include *nyen*, which reside in rocks and trees; snake-bodied spirits known as *lu* or *naga*,

which live at the bottom of lakes, rivers and wells; *sadok*, lords of the earth, which are connected with agriculture; *tsen*, air spirits which shoot arrows of illness and death at humans; and *dud*, demons linked to the Buddhist demon Mara. The religious beliefs of the average Tibetan are a fascinating melange of Buddhism, Bön and this folk religion.

History Buddhism originated in the northeast of India around the 5th century BC, at a time when the local religion was Brahmanism. Some Brahmin, in preparation for presiding over offerings to their gods, partook of an asceticism that took them to

Sacred Items & Symbols

Thunderbolt & Bell

The thunderbolt *(dorje)* and bell *(drilbu)* are ritual objects symbolising male and female aspects used in Tantric rites. They are held in the right and left hands respectively. The indestructible thunderbolt cuts through ignorance.

Ritual Dagger

The ritual dagger, or phurbu, is used in Tantric rituals to drive the invocation on its way. Its three sides pierce the heart of passion, aggression and ignorance. The design is based on the peg that Guru Rinpoche used to nail down evil spirits.

Seven Bowls of Water

Found on all altars and replenished twice a day, the seven bowls of water refer to the Seven Examined Men – the first seven monks in Tibet.

Tsatsa

Tsatsa are small icons fashioned from the clay collected from sacred sites.

Rosary Beads

Dried seeds (traditionally 108) are strung together as beads. Prayers are marked off by each bead; a second string is used to mark off higher multiples. Spies working for the British used adapted rosaries to keep records of distances as they secretly mapped large areas of Tibet during the 19th century.

Torma

Torma are small offerings made of yak butter and *tsampa* (roasted-barley flour) adorned with medallions of butter, which are often coloured. Most are made during the Shötun festival and remain on display throughout the year.

Kalachakra Seal

This seal is closely associated with the Kalachakra meditation deity and mandala, and also with the Dalai Lama.

Four Harmonious Brothers

This Buddhist parable is painted on walls at the entrance to many monasteries. The image is of a bird atop a hare, atop a monkey, atop an elephant. On its most basic level the image symbolises cooperation and harmony with the environment.

Spirit Trap

A spirit trap is a series of interlocking threads, often placed on a tree, which are supposed to ensnare evil spirits and which are burnt after their job is done.

Butter Lamp

Butter lamps, or *chömay*, are kept lit continuously in all monasteries and many private homes, and are topped up continuously by visiting pilgrims equipped with a tub of butter and a spoon.

remote places where they fasted, meditated and practiced yogic techniques.

The teachings of some of these ascetic Brahmin have their base in the underlying principle of the cosmos known as the brahman. This principle had its equivalent in the human mind, and was referred to as atman, the universal self. The yogic practitioner who achieved identity with atman achieved liberation from the cycle of death and rebirth and merged into brahman.

Thus, many of the fundamental concepts of Buddhism find their origin in the Brahmin society of this time. The Buddha himself was one of many wandering ascetics whose teachings led to the establishment of rival religious schools. Jainism, a religion that found a basic life principle in all objects and aimed to attain identity with that principle through ascetic practices and even self-mutilation, was one of these schools. Buddhism was another.

Life of the Buddha The historical dates for the life of the Buddha are much debated, and recent scholarship has put previously long-held beliefs into question. A commonly accepted compromise is something like 480–400 BC, give or take half a century.

The Buddha was born Siddhartha Gautama in the small kingdom of Sakka on the

Basic Buddhist Concepts

Rebirth

Life is a cycle of rebirths. The common assumption is that there are many rebirths, but in Buddhist thought they are innumerable. The word 'samsara' (Tibetan: *khorwa*), literally 'wandering on', is used to describe this cycle, and life is seen as wandering on limitlessly through time, and through the birth, extinction and rebirth of galaxies and worlds. There are six levels of rebirth, or realms of existence. It is important to accumulate enough merit to avoid the three lower realms, although in the long cycle of rebirth all beings pass through them at some point. The three lower realms comprise hells of torment, ghost worlds and the world of animals. The three higher realms are those of human beings, demigods and gods. These six levels are depicted on the Wheel of Life. All beings are fated to tread this wheel continuously until they make a commitment to enlightenment.

Karma

All beings pass through the same cycle of rebirths. Their enemy may once have been their mother, and like all beings they have lived as an insect and as a god, and suffered in one of the hell realms. Movement within this cycle, though, is not haphazard. It is governed by karma.

Karma is a slippery concept. It is sometimes translated simply as 'action', but it also implies the consequences of action. Karma might be thought of as an overarching condition of life. Every action in life leaves a psychic trace that carries over into the next rebirth. It should not be thought of as a reward or punishment, but simply as a result. In Buddhist thought karma is frequently likened to a seed that ripens into a fruit: Thus a human reborn as an insect is harvesting the fruits of a previous immoral existence.

Merit

Given that karma is a kind of accumulated psychic baggage that we must lug through countless rebirths, it is the aim of all practising Buddhists to try to accumulate as much 'good karma', or merit, as possible. Merit is best achieved through the act of rejoicing in giving, although merit can even be achieved through giving that is purely motivated by a desire for merit. The giving of alms to the needy and to monks, the relinquishing of a son to monkhood, acts of compassion and understanding are all meritorious and have a positive karmic outcome.

The Four Noble Truths

If belief in rebirth, karma and merit are the basis of lay-followers' faith in Buddhism, the Four Noble Truths might be thought of as the deep structure of the faith, or its philosophical underpinning. The

---

border of contemporary Nepal. The name Sakyamuni (Sakya Thukpa), given to him in the Mahayana tradition, has its origin in the kingdom of Gautama's birth; Sakyamuni (Sakya Thukpa) means 'sage of Sakya'.

Little is known about the life of Sakyamuni. It was probably not until some 200 years after his death that biographies were compiled, and by that time many of the circumstances of his life had merged with legend. It is known that he was born of a noble family and that he married and had a son before renouncing a life of comfort on a quest

to make sense of the suffering in the world. Traditional Buddhist biographies, however, do not start with the birth of Sakyamuni, but with his early lives '100,000 aeons ago'. Thus in his striving for buddhahood he passed through countless rebirths before he attained perfection.

At 29, Sakyamuni left his home, his wife and his newly born son. This action is explained as having been for the benefit of all sentient beings and having set a precedent for the renunciation of domestic life by the members of later monastic communities.

Basic Buddhist Concepts

Buddha systematised the truths in the manner of the medical practice of his time: (1) diagnose the illness, (2) identify its cause, (3) establish a cure, and (4) map a course for the cure. Their equivalents in Buddhism's diagnosis of the human condition are: (1) suffering (dukkha), caused by (2) desire *(tanha)*, which may be cured by (3) cessation of desire (*nibbana*, or nirvana), which can be achieved by means of (4) the Noble Eightfold Path, or the Middle Way.

The first of the Four Noble Truths, then, is that life is suffering. This suffering extends through all the countless rebirths of beings, and finds its origin in the imperfection of life. Every rebirth brings with it the pain of birth, the pain of ageing, the pain of death, the pain of association with unpleasant things, the loss of things we are attached to, and the failure to achieve the things we desire.

The reason for this suffering is the second Noble Truth, and lies in our dissatisfaction with imperfection, in our desire for things to be other than they are. What is more, this dissatisfaction leads to actions and karmic consequences that prolong the cycle of rebirths and may lead to even more suffering, much like a mouse running endlessly in a wheel.

The third Noble Truth was indicated by the Buddha as nibbana (Tibetan: *namtrol*), which is known in English as nirvana. It is the cessation of all desire, an end to attachment. With the cessation of desire comes an end to suffering, the achievement of complete nonattachment and an end to the cycle of rebirth – nirvana, the ultimate goal of Buddhism. Nit-pickers might point out that the will to achieve nirvana is a desire in itself. Buddhists answer that this desire is tolerated as a useful means to an end, but it is only when this desire too is extinguished that nirvana is truly achieved.

The Noble Eightfold Path

The Noble Eightfold Path is the fourth of the Noble Truths. It prescribes a course that for the lay practitioner will lead to the accumulation of merit and for the serious devotee may lead to nirvana. The components of this path are (1) right understanding, (2) right thought, (3) right speech, (4) right action, (5) right livelihood, (6) right effort, (7) right mindfulness and (8) right concentration. Needless to say, each of these has a 'wrong' corollary.

The Ten Meritorious Deeds

The ten deeds are: do not kill, do not steal, and refrain from inappropriate sexual activity, lying, gossiping, cursing, sowing discord, envy, malice and opinionatedness.

He studied with many of the great teachers of the day, passing up opportunities to become a teacher himself. Later he embarked on a course of intense asceticism, before he concluded that such a path was too extreme.

At this point, rather than give up his quest, Sakyamuni recalled an earlier meditative state he had once achieved, a state of great bliss and great peace. In the place that is now known as Bodhgaya, he sat beneath a bo tree and meditated. Over the course of three moonlit nights he achieved knowledge of the final obstacles to his enlightenment, and at the break of dawn at the end of the third night he became a buddha (awakened one).

After achieving enlightenment, Sakyamuni sat for another three or four weeks contemplating his achievement. During this time Brahma Sahampata, the god of compassion, asked Sakyamuni to share his perfect knowledge with those who were ready to hear his teachings. Sakyamuni's compliance with this request is seen as evidence of

[Continued on page 53]

IMPORTANT FIGURES OF TIBETAN BUDDHISM

This is a brief iconographical guide to some of the gods and goddesses of the vast Tibetan Buddhist pantheon, as well as to important historical figures. It is neither exhaustive nor scholarly, but it may help you to recognise a few of the statues you encounter during your trip. Tibetan names are given first, with Sanskrit names provided in parentheses. (The exception is Sakya Thukpa, who is often known in Tibet by his Sanskrit name, Sakyamuni.)

Buddhas

Sakyamuni (Sakya Thukpa) The Historical Buddha, or the Buddha of the Present Age, was born in Lumbini in southern Nepal in the 5th century BC with the name Gautama. He attained enlightenment under a bo tree and his teachings set in motion the Buddhist faith. In Tibetan-style representations he is always pictured sitting cross-legged on a lotus-flower throne. His hair is dark blue and there is a halo of enlightenment around his head. The Buddha is recognised by 32 marks on his body, including a dot between his eyes, a bump on the top of his head and the Wheel of Law on the soles of his feet. In his left hand he holds a begging bowl; his right hand touches the earth in the 'witness' mudra. He is often flanked by two disciples or bodhisattvas.

Marmedze (Dipamkara) The Past Buddha, Marmedze came immediately before Sakyamuni (Sakya Thukpa) and spent 100,000 years on earth. His hands are shown in the 'protection' mudra and he is often depicted in a trinity with the Present and Future Buddhas.

Öpagme (Amitabha) The Buddha of Infinite Light resides in the 'pure land of the west'. The Panchen Lama is considered a reincarnation of this buddha. He is red, his hands are held together in his lap in a 'meditation' mudra and he holds a begging bowl.

Tsepame (Amitayus) The Buddha of Longevity, like Öpagme (Amitabha), is red and holds his hands in a meditation gesture, but he holds a vase containing the nectar of immortality.

Medicine Buddhas (Menlha) A medicine buddha holds a medicine bowl in his left hand and herbs in his right. He is often depicted in a group of eight buddhas.

Dhyani Buddhas (Gyawa Ri Gna) Each of the five Dhyani buddhas is a different colour, and each of them has different mudras, symbols and attributes. Öpagme (Amitabha) is one of the Dhyani buddhas.

Inset: Fifth Dalai Lama

Sakyamuni (Sakya Thukpa)

Tsepame (Amitayus)

Jampa (Maitreya)

Chenresig (Avalokiteshvara)

Jampelyang (Manjushri)

Drölma (Green Tara)

Drölkar (White Tara)

Nagpo Chenpo (Mahakala)

Tamdrin (Hayagriva)

Chana Dorje (Vajrapani)

Palden Lhamo (Shri Devi)

Guru Rinpoche

Tsongkhapa

Fifth Dalai Lama

King Songtsen Gampo

Milarepa

Jampa (Maitreya) Jampa, the Future Buddha, is passing the life of a bodhisattva until it is time to return to earth in human form 4000 years after the disappearance of Sakyamuni (Sakya Thukpa). He is normally seated, with a scarf around his waist, his legs hanging down and his hands by his chest in the mudra of turning the Wheel of Law.

Bodhisattvas

These are beings who have reached the state of enlightenment but vow to save everyone else in the world before they themselves enter nirvana. Unlike buddhas, they are often shown decorated with crowns and jewels.

Chenresig (Avalokiteshvara) The glorious gentle one, Chenresig is the Bodhisattva of Compassion; his name means 'he who gazes upon the world with suffering in his eyes'. The Dalai Lama is considered a reincarnation of Chenresig (as is King Songtsen Gampo), and pictures of the Dalai Lama and Chenresig are interchangeable, depending on the political climate. The current Dalai Lama is the 14th manifestation of Chenresig.

In the four-armed version pictured in this book (known more specifically in Tibetan as Tonje Chenpo), his body is white and he sits on a lotus blossom. He holds crystal rosary beads and a lotus and clutches to his heart a jewel that fulfils all wishes. A deer skin is draped over his left shoulder.

There is also a powerful 11-headed, 1000-armed version. The head of this version is said to have exploded when confronted with a myriad of problems to solve. One of his heads is that of wrathful Chana Dorje (Vajrapani), and another (the top one) is that of Öpagme (Amitabha), who is said to have reassembled Chenresig's body after it exploded. Each of the 1000 arms has an eye in the palm. His eight main arms hold a bow and arrow, lotus, rosary, vase, wheel and staff.

Jampelyang (Manjushri) The Bodhisattva of Wisdom, Jampelyang is regarded as the first divine teacher of Buddhist doctrine. School children often offer prayers to him. His right hand holds the flaming sword of awareness, which cuts through ignorance. His left arm cradles a scripture on a half-opened lotus blossom and his left hand is in the 'teaching' mudra. He is often yellow and may have blue hair or an elaborate crown.

Drölma (Tara) A female bodhisattva with 21 different manifestations or aspects, Drölma is also known as the saviouress. She was born from a tear of compassion that fell from the eyes of Chenresig (Avalokiteshvara) and is thus considered the female version of Chenresig and a protectress of the Tibetan people. She also symbolises purity and fertility and is believed to be able to fulfil wishes. Images usually represent Green Tara, who is associated with night, or Drölkar (White Tara), who is associated with day. The green version sits in a half-lotus position with her right leg down, resting on a lotus flower. The white version sits in the full lotus position and has seven eyes, including ones in her forehead, both palms and both soles of her feet. She is often seen as part of a longevity triad, along with red Tsepame (Amitayus) and three-faced, eight-armed female Namgyelma (Vijaya).

Protector Deities

Chökyong (Lokpalas) The Chökyong, or Four Guardian Kings, are normally seen at the entrance hallway of monasteries and are possibly of Mongol origin. They are the protectors of the four cardinal directions: The eastern chief is white with a lute; the southern is blue and holds a sword; the western is red and holds a thunderbolt. Namtöse (Vaishravana), the protector of the north, doubles as the god of wealth and can be seen with a yellow body, riding a snow lion, and holding a banner of victory and a jewel-spitting mongoose.

Dorje Jigje (Yamantaka) Dorje Jigje is a favourite protector of the Gelugpa order. A wrathful form of Jampelyang (Manjushri), he is also known as the destroyer of Yama, or the Lord of Death. He is blue with eight heads, the main one of which is the head of a bull. He wears a garland of skulls around his neck and a belt of skulls around his waist, and holds a skull cup and a flaying knife in his 34 arms. He tramples on eight Hindu gods, eight mammals and eight birds with his 16 feet.

Nagpo Chenpo (Mahakala) A wrathful Tantric deity and manifestation of Chenresig (Avalokiteshvara), Nagpo Chenpo, or the Great Black One, has connections to the Hindu god Shiva. There are many varieties with anything from two to six arms. He is blue with fanged teeth and a tiara of skulls, and carries a trident and a skull cup. In a form known as Gompo, he is believed by nomads to be the guardian of the tent.

Tamdrin (Hayagriva) Another wrathful manifestation of Chenresig (Avalokiteshvara), Tamdrin has a red body. His right face is white, his left face is green, and he has a horse's head in his hair. He wears a tiara of skulls, a garland of 52 severed heads and a tiger skin around his waist. His six hands hold a skull cup, a lotus, a sword, a snare, an axe and a club, and his four legs stand on a sun disc trampling corpses. On his back are the outspread wings of Garuda and the skins of a human and an elephant. He is shown in this book embracing a blue consort. He has close connections to the Hindu god Vishnu.

Chana Dorje (Vajrapani) The name of the wrathful Bodhisattva of Energy means 'thunderbolt in hand'. In his right hand he holds a thunderbolt (*dorje* or *vajra*), which represents power and is a fundamental symbol of Tantric faith. He is blue with a tiger skin around his waist and a snake around his neck. He also has a peaceful, standing aspect.

Palden Lhamo (Shri Devi) The special protector of Lhasa, the Dalai Lama and the Gelugpa order, Palden Lhamo is a female counterpart of Nagpo Chenpo (Mahakala). Her origins probably lie in the Hindu goddess Kali. She is blue, wears clothes of tiger skin and human skin, and has earrings made of a snake and a lion. She carries a club in her right hand and a skull cup full of blood in the left. She holds the moon in her hair, the sun in her belly and a corpse in her mouth, and rides a mule with an eye in its rump.

Demchok (Chakrasamvara) This meditational deity has a blue body with 12 arms, four faces, and a crescent moon in his top knot. His main hands hold a dorje and bell, and others hold an elephant skin, an axe, a hooked knife, a trident, a skull, a hand drum, a skull cup, a lasso and the head of Brahma. He also wears a garland of 52 heads and clothes made from tiger skin.

Historical Figures

Guru Rinpoche The 'lotus-born' 8th-century master from modern-day Swat in Pakistan, Guru Rinpoche subdued Tibet's evil spirits and helped to establish Buddhism in Tibet. Known in Sanskrit as Padmasambhava, he is regarded by followers of Nyingmapa Buddhism as the second Buddha and wears a red Nyingmapa-style hat. His domain is the copper-coloured mountain called Zangdok Pelri. He has a curly moustache, and holds a thunderbolt in his right hand, a skull cup in his left hand, and a staff topped with three heads – one shrunken, one severed and one skull – in the crook of his left arm. He has a *phurbu* (ritual dagger) in his belt. Guru Rinpoche has eight manifestations, known collectively as the Guru Tsengye.

Tsongkhapa Founder of the Gelugpa order and a manifestation of Jampelyang (Manjushri), Tsongkhapa (1357–1419) wears the yellow hat of the Gelugpas. He is normally portrayed in a triad with his two main disciples, Kedrub Je and Gyatsab Je. His hands are in the 'teaching' mudra and he holds two lotuses. He was the founder and first abbot of Ganden Monastery and many images of him are found there.

Fifth Dalai Lama The greatest of all the Dalai Lamas, the fifth (Ngawang Lobsang Gyatso; 1617–82) unified Tibet and built the bulk of the Potala. He was born at Chongye (in the Yarlung Valley) and was the first Dalai Lama to exercise temporal power. He wears the Gelugpa yellow hat and holds a thunderbolt in his right hand and a bell *(drilbu)* in his left. He may also be depicted holding the Wheel of Law (symbolising the beginning of political control of the Dalai Lamas) and a lotus flower or other sacred objects.

King Songtsen Gampo Tibet was unified under Songtsen Gampo, who introduced Buddhism to the country early in the 7th century. He has a moustache and wears a white turban with a tiny red Öpagme (Amitabha) poking out of the top. He is flanked by Princess Wencheng, his Chinese wife, on the left, and Princess Bhrikuti, his Nepali wife, on his right.

King Trisong Detsen The founder of Samye Monastery reigned from 755 to 797. He is normally seen in a trio of kings with Songtsen Gampo and King Ralpachen (r. 817–36). He is regarded as a manifestation of Jampelyang (Manjushri) and so holds a scripture on a lotus in the crook of his left arm and a sword of wisdom in his right. Images show him with features similar to Songsten Gampo's but without the buddha in his turban.

Milarepa A great 11th-century Tibetan magician and poet, Milarepa is believed to have attained the supreme enlightenment of buddha-hood in the course of one lifetime. He became an alchemist in order to poison an uncle who had stolen his family's lands and then spent six years meditating in a cave in repentance. During this time he wore nothing but a cotton robe and so became known as Milarepa (Cotton-Clad Repa). Most images of Milarepa depict him smiling, holding his hand to his ear as he sings. He may also be depicted as green because he lived for many years on a diet of nettles.

[Continued from page 47]

his compassion, compassion being the ideal complement of perfected wisdom.

Early Teachings Buddhism's early teachings are based on the insights of Sakyamuni (Sakya Thukpa) and form the basis of all further Buddhist thought. The later Mahayana school (to which Tibetan Buddhism belongs) diverged from these early teachings in some respects, but not in its fundamentals.

The Buddha began his teachings by explaining that there was a Middle Way that steered a course between sensual indulgence and ascetic self-torment – a way of moderation not renunciation. This Middle Way could be followed by taking the Noble Eightfold Path. The philosophical underpinnings of this path were the Four Noble Truths, which addressed the problems of karma and rebirth. These basic concepts are the kernel of early Buddhist thought.

Schools of Buddhism Not long after Sakyamuni's (Sakya Thukpa's) death, disagreements began to arise among his followers (as they tend to in all religious movements) over whose interpretations best captured the true spirit of his teachings. The result was the development of numerous schools of thought and eventually a schism that saw the emergence of two principal schools: Hinayana and Mahayana.

Hinayana, also known as Theravada, might be seen as the more conservative of the two, a school that encouraged scholasticism and close attention to what were considered the original teachings of Sakyamuni (Sakya Thukpa). Mahayana, on the other hand, with its elevation of compassion as an all-important idea, took Buddhism in a new direction. It was the Mahayana school that made its way up to the high plateau and took root there, at the same time travelling to China, Korea and Japan. Hinayana retreated into southern India and took root in Sri Lanka and Thailand.

Mahayana The claims that Mahayanists made for their faith were many, but the central issue was a change in orientation from individual pursuit of enlightenment to bodhisattvahood. The bodhisattva, rather than striving for complete nonattachment, aims, through compassion and self-sacrifice, to achieve enlightenment for the sake of all beings.

In another development, Sakyamuni (Sakya Thukpa) began to take on another form altogether. Mahayanists maintained that Sakyamuni had already attained buddhahood many aeons ago and that he was a manifestation of a long-enlightened transcendent being who sent such manifestations to many worlds to assist all beings on the road to enlightenment. There were many such transcendent beings, the Mahayanists argued, living in heavens or 'pure lands', and all were able to project themselves into the innumerable worlds of the cosmos for the sake of sentient life there.

The philosophical reasoning behind the Mahayana transformation of Buddhism is extremely complex, but it had the effect of allowing Mahayanists to produce newly revealed texts that recorded the words of Sakyamuni (Sakya Thukpa) as they appeared in dreams and visions. It also had the effect of producing a pantheon of bodhisattvas, a feature that made Mahayana more palatable to cultures that already had gods of their own. In Tibet, China, Korea and Japan, the Mahayana pantheon came to be identified with local gods. In Tibet, in particular, many stories of the taming of local gods by their Mahayana equivalents came into being.

Tantrism (Vajrayana) A further Mahayana development that is particularly relevant to Tibet is Tantrism, or Vajrayana. The words of Sakyamuni (Sakya Thukpa) were recorded in sutras and studied by students of both Hinayana and Mahayana, but according to followers of Tantrism, a school that emerged from around AD 600, Sakyamuni (Sakya Thukpa) left a corpus of esoteric instructions to a select few of his disciples. These were known as Tantra (Gyü).

Tantric adepts claimed that through the use of unconventional techniques they could jolt themselves towards enlightenment, and shorten the long road to bodhisattvahood. The process involved identification with a tutelary deity invoked through deep meditation and recitation of the deity's mantra. The most famous of these mantras is the 'om mani padme hum' mantra of Chenresig (Avalokiteshvara). Tantric practice employs Indian yogic techniques to channel energy towards the transformation to enlightenment. Such yogic techniques might even include sexual practices. Tantric techniques are rarely written down, but rather are passed down verbally from tutor to student.

Most of the ritual objects and images of deities in Tibetan monasteries and temples are Tantric in nature. Together they show the many facets of enlightenment – at times kindly, at times wrathful. Sometimes these deities are pictured at the centre of a mandala, which is a representation of the world they inhabit. The Tantric adept who identifies with a particular deity will visualise the mandala as a three-dimensional world, a feat of meditational concentration that takes many years of training to achieve.

Buddhism in Tibet The story of the introduction of Buddhism to Tibet is attended by legends of the taming of local gods and spirits and their conversion to Buddhism as protective deities. This panoply of buddhas, bodhisattvas and sages occupies a mythical world in the Tibetan imagination. Chenresig (Avalokiteshvara) is perhaps chief among them, manifesting himself in early Tibetan kings and later in the Dalai Lamas. Guru Rinpoche, the Indian sage who bound the native spirits and gods of Tibet into the service of Buddhism, is another. And there are countless others worshipped in images throughout the land: Drölma (Tara), Jampelyang (Manjushri), Milarepa, Marpa and Tsongkhapa, among others. While the clerical side of Buddhism concerns itself largely with textual study and analysis, the Tantric shamanistic-based side seeks revelation through identification with these deified beings and through their *terma* ('revealed' words or writings).

It is useful to consider the various schools of Tibetan Buddhism as revealing something of a struggle between these two orientations: shamanism and clericalism. Each school finds its own resolution to the problem. In the case of the last major school to arise, the Gelugpa order, there was a search for a return to the doctrinal purity of clerical Buddhism. But even here, the Tantric forms were not completely discarded; it was merely felt that many years of scholarly work and preparation should precede the more esoteric Tantric practices.

The clerical and shamanistic orientations can also be explained as the difference between state-sponsored and popular Buddhism respectively. There was always a tendency for the state to emphasise monastic Buddhism, with its communities of rule-abiding monks. Popular Buddhism, on the other hand, with its long-haired, wild-eyed ascetic recluses capable of performing great feats of magic, had a great appeal to the ordinary people of Tibet, for whom ghosts and demons and sorcerers were a daily reality.

Nyingmapa Order The Nyingmapa order is the Old School, and traces its origins back to the teachings and practices of Guru Rinpoche, who came to Tibet from India and lived in the country in the 8th and 9th centuries. As Buddhism fell into decline until the second diffusion of the faith in the 11th century, the Nyingmapa failed to develop as a powerful, centralised school, and for the most part prospered in villages throughout rural Tibet, where it was administered by local shamanlike figures.

With the second diffusion of Buddhism in Tibet and the emergence of rival schools, the Nyingmapa order experienced something of a revival through the 'discovery' of hidden texts in the 'power places' of Tibet visited by Guru Rinpoche. In many cases these terma, or 'revealed' texts, were discovered through yogic-inspired visions by spiritually advanced Nyingmapa practitioners, rather than found under a pile of rocks or in a cave. Whatever their origins, these terma gave the Nyingmapa a new lease of life.

The terma gave rise to the Dzogchen teachings, or Great Perfection teachings. Much maligned by other Tibetan schools,

Religious Symbols in Tibetan Buddhism

The Eight Auspicious Symbols (Tibetan: Tashi Targyel) are associated with gifts made to Sakyamuni (Sakya Thukpa) upon his enlightenment, and appear as protective motifs throughout Tibet.

Precious Parasol
Usually placed over buddha images to protect them from evil influences, the precious parasol is a common Buddhist motif also seen in Thailand and Japan.

Banner of Victory
This heralds the triumph of Buddhist wisdom over ignorance.

White Conch Shell
Blown in celebration of the enlightenment of Sakyamuni (Sakya Thukpa) and the potential of all beings to be awakened by the sound of dharma, the shell is often used to signal prayer time.

Knot of Eternity
Representing the entwined, never-ending passage of time, harmony and love and the unity of all things, the knot of eternity is commonly seen on embroidery and tents.

Golden Fishes
Shown leaping from the waters of captivity, they represent liberation from the Wheel of Life. (Once the symbol of Lhasa Beer!)

Vase of Great Treasure
The vase is a sacred repository of the jewels of enlightenment or the water of eternity.

Lotus Flower
The lotus flower, or *padma*, stands for the purity and compassion of Sakyamuni (Sakya Thukpa). The pure lotus rises from the muddy waters of earthly existence.

Wheel of Law
Representing the Noble Eightfold Path to salvation, the wheel is also referred to as the Wheel of Dharma. The wheel turns twelve times, three times for each of the Four Noble Truths.

Dzogchen postulates a primordial state of purity that pre-existed the duality of enlightenment and samsara, and offered a Tantric short cut to nirvana. Such ideas were to influence other orders of Buddhism in the 19th century.

The Nyingmapa never had the centralised power of other major Tibetan schools of Buddhism, and can be considered to represent an extreme of the shamanistic orientation.

Its fortunes improved somewhat with the accession of the fifth Dalai Lama, who was born into a Nyingmapa family. He personally saw to the expansion of Mindroling and Dorje Drak Monasteries, which became the head Nyingmapa monasteries of Ü and all Tibet.

Kagyupa Order The Kagyupa (Whispered Transmission) order traces its lineage back to early Indian teachers, but the impetus behind its establishment was Marpa (1012–93), a married Tibetan yogi renowned for his translations and Tantric powers. He took on a disciple, Milarepa (1040–1123), who in turn became a renowned yogi, meditating in high mountain caves and composing songs. Milarepa is a perfect example of the non-monastic ascetic for whom textual study is less important than Tantric experience, and legends accumulated around him: In particular, he is supposed to have overcome and taught mountain goddesses with the use of Tantric sexual techniques.

The influence of one of Milarepa's disciples, Gampopa (1079–1153), led to the establishment of numerous monasteries that became major teaching centres, eventually overshadowing the ascetic-yogi origins of the Kagyupa. The yogi tradition did not die out completely, however, and Kagyupa monasteries also became important centres for synthesising the clerical and shamanistic orientations of Tibetan Buddhism.

Several suborders of the Kagyupa sprung up with time, the most prominent of which was the Karma Kagyupa, also known as the Karmapa. The practice of renowned lamas reincarnating after death probably originated with this suborder, when the abbot of Tsurphu Monastery, Dusum Khyenpa (1110–93),

announced that he would be reincarnated as his own successor. The 16th Karmapa died in 1981, and his disputed successor fled to India in 2000. Other Kagyupa schools, the Drigungpa and Taglungpa, are based at Drigung Til and Talung Monasteries in Ü.

Sakyapa Order With the second diffusion of Buddhism in the 11th and 12th centuries, many Tibetan monasteries became centres for the textual study and translation of Indian Buddhist texts. One of the earliest major figures in this movement was Kunga Gyaltsen (1182–1251), known as Sakya Pandita (literally 'scholar from Sakya').

Sakya Pandita's renown as a scholar led to him, and subsequent abbots of Sakya, being recognised as a manifestation of Jampelyang (Manjushri), the Bodhisattva of Insight. Sakya Pandita travelled to the Mongolian court in China, with the result that his heir became the spiritual tutor of Khublai Khan. In the 13th and 14th centuries, the Sakyapa order became embroiled in politics and implicated in the Mongol overlordship of Tibet. Nevertheless, at the same time Sakya emerged as a major centre for the scholastic study of Buddhism, and attracted students such as Tsongkhapa, who initiated the Gelugpa order.

Many Sakyapa monasteries contain images of the Sakyapa protector deity Gompo Gur and photographs of the school's four head lamas: the Sakya Trizin, Ngawang Kunga (head of the Sakyapa order), Chogye Trichen Rinpoche (head of the Tsarpa subschool), and Ludhing Khenpo Rinpoche (head of the Ngorpa subschool).

Gelugpa Order It may not have been his intention, but Tsongkhapa (1357–1419), a monk who left his home in Kokonor at the age of 17 to study in central Tibet, is regarded as the founder of the Gelugpa (Virtuous School) order, which came to dominate political and religious affairs in Tibet.

Tsongkhapa studied with all the major schools of his day, but was particularly influenced by the Sakyapa and the Kadampa orders. The Kadampa order had its head monastery at Netang, near Lhasa, and it was here that the 11th-century Bengali sage Atisha (Jowo-je) spent the last of his days. The Kadampa had sustained the teachings of Atisha, which are a sophisticated synthesis of conventional Mahayana doctrine with the more arcane practices of Tantric Buddhism, and emerged as a major school, emphasising scholastic study. It may never have matched the eminence of the Kagyupa and Sakyapa orders, but in the hands of Tsongkhapa the teachings of the Kadampa order established a renewal in Tibetan Buddhism.

After having a vision of Atisha (Jowo-je), Tsongkhapa elaborated on the Bengali sage's clerical-Tantric synthesis in a doctrine known as *lamrim*, or 'the graduated path'. Tsongkhapa basically advocated a return to doctrinal purity and monastic discipline as prerequisites to advanced Tantric studies. He did not, as is sometimes maintained, advocate a purely clerical approach to Buddhism, but he did reassert the monastic body as the basis of the Buddhist community, and he maintained that Tantric practices should be reserved for advanced students.

Tsongkhapa established a monastery at Ganden, which was to become the head of the Gelugpa order. Other monasteries were also established at Drepung, Sera and Shigatse. Although the abbot of Drepung was the titular head of the order (and is to this day), it was the Dalai Lamas who came to be increasingly identified with the order's growing political and spiritual prestige.

Bön

In Tibet the establishment of Buddhism was marked by its interaction with the native religion Bön. This shamanistic faith, which encompassed gods and spirits, exorcism, talismans and the cult of dead kings among other things, almost certainly had a major influence on the direction Buddhism took in Tibet.

Many popular Buddhist symbols and practices, such as prayer flags, sky burial, the rubbing of holy rocks, the tying of bits of cloth to trees and the construction of spirit traps, all have their roots deep in Bön tradition. The traditional blessing of dipping a finger in water or milk and flicking it to the sky derives from Bön and can still be seen today in the shamanistic folk practices of Mongolia.

But it was Bön that was transformed and tamed to the ends of Buddhism and not vice

Red Hats versus Yellow Hats

The terms 'Red Hat' and 'Yellow Hat' have been avoided in this book, although they are widely used elsewhere. The main reason is that they represent a simplification that gives rise to confusion. The old adage 'Don't judge a Buddhist by his bowler' is a good one to follow in Tibet.

The distinction between the two is actually Chinese. The Chinese differentiated between the yellow-hatted Gelugpa order and the red-hatted Kagyupa order – disputants for religious and political ascendancy until the 17th-century Mongol intervention – through their headgear. By extension, the distinction identified the Gelugpa as the Yellow Hats and all other Tibetan schools of Buddhism as Red Hats.

It is a distinction that makes little sense of the complexity of Tibet's religious orders. Confusion also arises from the fact that the Karmapa, head of the Karma Kagyupa suborder, is often referred to as the Black-Hat lama. It makes a lot more sense to see the major orders of Tibetan Buddhism not in terms of their dress sense, but in terms of their respective historical rise to power.

The Nyingmapa order, then, is the oldest of the Tibetan schools of Buddhism, and traces its origins back to the early establishment of Buddhism in the reign of King Songtsen Gampo. Tibetans sometimes refer to this school as the Old School. The middle period of the second diffusion of Buddhism in the 11th century saw the rise of the New-School Kagyupa and Sakyapa orders. The 15th-century search for doctrinal purity gave rise to the Gelugpa order, which by the 17th century had become dominant in Tibet.

versa. The Bön order, as it survives today, is to all intents and purposes a school of Buddhism. You may see Bönpo pilgrims circumambulating monuments and mountains anticlockwise and reciting the Bön mantra *'om matri muye sale du'*. Mt Kailash and Bönri are Bön's holiest mountains. Major Bön monasteries include Menri and Yungdrungling in central Tibet, and Tengchen in eastern Tibet. Other pockets of Bön exist in the Changtang region of northern Tibet and the Aba region of northern Sichuan. The main centre of Bön in exile is at Dolanji, near Solan, in India's Himachal Pradesh.

For more on this faith see the boxed text 'Bön' in the Kham (Eastern Tibet) chapter.

LANGUAGE

Tibetan and (Mandarin) Chinese are the two main languages of Tibet. Tibetan is spoken by over seven million people throughout the Himalayan region, although there are considerable local variations. Lhasa-ke is the standard honorific dialect, although this is barely understood by speakers of Kham-ke and Amdo-ke in the east and north-east of the country respectively. Very few Tibetans outside Lhasa speak English, although most Tibetans in China now speak at least basic Chinese. For more information on Tibetan and Chinese, and some handy phrases in both, see the Language chapter near the back of this book.

Facts for the Visitor

HIGHLIGHTS

The highlights of Tibet will depend largely on your interests. For trekkers, for example, Tibet offers the opportunity to tread pilgrim paths in some of the world's highest places. Others will appreciate the rich religious life of the country, while a few will be satisfied with the wildness of a remote land. For an overview of some of the main highlights of Tibet see the boxed text 'Highlights'.

It's also worth trying to make it to a couple of sites that are off the beaten track. Tibet is full of small monasteries and these can be some of the most enjoyable places to visit. The monks are often very happy to have a foreign visitor and will sit down to share some tea with you and show you around.

The other highlights of a visit to Tibet are harder to define. The joy of hitching on an open-air truck, hiking out to a secluded monastery, or following a *kora* (ritual circumcambulation path) with a happy band of pilgrims all rate highly. But perhaps the memories that remain the longest are those of the Tibetan people: drinking *chang* (Tibetan barley beer) by the side of the road with complete strangers, or seeing the veneration and dedication of pilgrims at any religious site. Then there is the rare sense of calm and space that emanates from what is one of the most beautiful and unique places on earth. Few people come away unaffected or unimpressed by Tibet.

SUGGESTED ITINERARIES

The chief goal of travellers to Tibet is of course Lhasa itself. Lhasa must rank as one of the most enigmatic cities in the world, and it is the focal point and spiritual heart of the nation. There is enough to see in and around the city to keep you busy for at least a week, perhaps 10 days. The monastic institutions of Drepung and Sera are close by, and Ganden and Tsurphu Monasteries are easy day trips away.

There are plenty of other excursions to be made from Lhasa. A three-day return trip can

take you to the stunning lake Nam-tso. Another three-day option is to head up to Drigung Til Monastery and Tidrum Nunnery, both to the east of Lhasa.

Highlights

Monasteries & Temples

Drepung & Sera Once the largest and second-largest monasteries, respectively, in the world, Drepung and Sera are still recovering from the Chinese onslaught, but both are a highlight of a trip to Lhasa.

Ganden This monastery, in a stunning location 40km east of Lhasa, is the scene of frantic rebuilding. Take the early-morning pilgrim bus from Lhasa for a great day trip.

Jokhang A hushed silence pervades Lhasa's holiest collection of shrines. The Jokhang is the spiritual heart of Tibet and is always full of a murmuring, shuffling crowd of pilgrims.

Riwoche This dramatic, towering and remote temple in eastern Tibet, founded in 1276, dwarfs those who make pilgrimages to it.

Sakya This eerie, fortress-like monastery with the most spectacular assembly hall in Tibet is an easy 25km detour off the Friendship Hwy and worth an overnight stop.

Samye Tibet's first monastery has a relaxing location beside the Yarlung Tsangpo. There's good accommodation, and the monastery can be used as a base for walks to meditation retreats in surrounding parts of Ü.

Tashilhunpo The traditional seat of the Panchen Lama, Tashilhunpo Monastery in Tsang is possibly Tibet's best-preserved and most spectacular monastery.

Other Buildings

Gyantse Kumbum The pinnacle of Tibetan architecture, this multifaceted stupa is well worth visiting en route from Lhasa to Shigatse.

Potala Palace The focus of travellers for centuries, the impressive palace of the Dalai Lama remains eerily empty.

Yumbulagang Reputed to be the first building in Tibet, this structure is stunningly located in the birthplace of the Tibetan nation.

Natural Beauty

Draksum-tso This alpine lake in eastern Tibet features a lovely monastery sited on a very photogengic island.

Lake Manasarovar & Mt Kailash It's a rugged two-week trip to get to Tibet's holiest and most compelling mountain and its most venerated lake, but the high-altitude scenery along the way is stunning.

Mt Everest Quite literally the high point of Tibet. The views of the mountain from Rongphu Monastery are unsurpassed.

Nam-tso A stunning turquoise lake set below a range of 7000m peaks, Nam-tso is a great place to glimpse nomadic life and experience Tibet's awesome sense of space.

Rawok-tso Beyond the sandy beaches and turquoise waters of Rawok-tso lie snowcapped peaks; the views in the area are magical.

Yamdrok-tso This holy lake in Tsang is shaped like a scorpion. The best views of the coiling body of water come from the high pass of Kampa-la.

Pilgrim Circuits

Barkhor Lhasa's pilgrim circuit around the Jokhang is infinitely interesting – this is one place worth coming back to again and again.

Ganden The main seat of the Gelugpa order features both a high and a low kora circuit, and attracts bands of pilgrims.

Lingkhor Lhasa's 8km pilgrim path has some fascinating spots to see en route and is a good way to see the city's hidden sights.

From Lhasa, fewer travellers head east towards the Yarlung Valley but a visit to Samye Monastery and Yumbulagang are easily fitted into an eight-day Land Cruiser trip to the border. Samye Monastery could conceivably be visited as an overnight trip from Lhasa, although it's better to spend a couple of nights there.

The road between Lhasa and Kathmandu in Nepal is the main travellers' route through Tibet. This route, which basically follows the Friendship Hwy from Lhasa to Kathmandu, allows a number of detours to the highlights of Tsang province. These include Yamdrok-tso, the *kumbum* (literally '100,000 images') at Gyantse, and Shigatse's Tashilhunpo Monastery. Both Gyantse and Shigatse are worth a stop for a day or two to see the sights and to get a glimpse of urban life outside of Lhasa. A popular destination en route is Sakya, a small monastery town just 25km off the Friendship Hwy.

Closer to the border, and emerging as the most popular trekking destination in Tibet, is the Everest region. Many people drive right up to Everest Base Camp and leave the next day, but it's much better to fit in an extra day to enjoy the extraordinary views. If you are trekking or hitching, allow a week to get to Rongphu and back from the Friendship Hwy, although you could do it in less time if you're lucky with lifts.

Much talked about, but little visited, is Mt Kailash out in western Tibet. Those travelling out there are looking at a return journey of around 15 to 20 days by Land Cruiser and up to a month if hitching. If heading to Nepal from here you can cut down south on the way back to join the Friendship Hwy at Nyalam.

Equally remote are the stunningly scenic routes through eastern Tibet. Road conditions make the trip unreliable from May to September but at other times of the year this is an excellent route into or out of Tibet. It's also possible to do a five- to seven-day loop trip to Kongpo from Lhasa, which takes in Draksum-tso and Lamaling temple and returns via Tsetang.

Remember that further is not necessarily better; there are endless remote monasteries, pilgrimage places and lakes that remain off the beaten track just a few kilometres from the main sites. The biggest constraint on where you go will be either the time on your visa or the permit situation.

Two Weeks

In two weeks you could see most of the sites of Lhasa and then head down on a seven- or eight-day Land Cruiser trip to Kathmandu, taking in the sights of Yamdrok-tso, Gyantse, Shigatse, Sakya and possibly Everest Base Camp. If you are not heading for Nepal, you could spend the second week travelling on public transport to Shigatse and Gyantse. If you have the money to travel by Land Cruiser, you could probably squeeze in an overnight stay at Samye.

One Month

With one month you have more time to add on some excursions, perhaps to Nam-tso or Drigung Til Monastery. You could also extend your trip to the border to take in Samye Monastery. If travelling by public transport you will need this extra time to cover the basic two-week itinerary. You could make it out to western or eastern Tibet and back in a month but you wouldn't have enough time to see much more of the country.

Two Months

This is a nice amount of time to be able to enjoy Tibet slowly. In two months you can make a trip to Mt Kailash and back and still have time to see the main highlights of the country. If you are not heading out west you can see most of the main sites in central Tibet in around two months and leave Tibet via the east.

PLANNING
When to Go

Climate is not such a major consideration when visiting Tibet as many people might imagine. Winter is very cold and snowfalls can sometimes make travel difficult, but some travellers swear by the winter months. There are few travellers about at this time and Lhasa, for example, is crowded with nomads and at its most colourful.

Spring, early summer and late autumn are probably the best times to be in Tibet. March is a politically sensitive month in Tibet (see Public Holidays later in this chapter) and there is occasional tightening of restrictions on travellers heading into Tibet at this time. April brings reliable weather in eastern Tibet. Prices for accommodation and Land Cruiser rental in Lhasa are generally discounted in April and May and the weather is good. Everest is particularly clear during this time. From mid-July through to the end of September, the monsoon starts to affect parts of Tibet. Travel to western Tibet becomes more difficult, the roads to the east are washed out and the Friendship Hwy sometimes becomes impassable on the Nepal side or on the border itself. Trips to Mt Kailash can be undertaken from April to October, although September and October are considered the best months. This is also the best time to make a trip out to the east. Lhasa and its environs don't get *really* cold until the end of November.

It's worth trying make your trip coincide with one of Tibet's main festivals. New Year (Losar) is an excellent (although cold) time to be in Lhasa. Saga Dawa (April or May) is also a good time to be in Lhasa or Mt Kailash.

Maps

It shouldn't come as a surprise that good mapping for Tibet is not easy to come by. Stock up on maps before you leave.

Maps of Tibet In Lhasa three maps are available: two in Chinese (and possibly also Tibetan) and one in English. The 166-page *Xizang Zizhiqu Dituceng* (Tibet Autonomous Province Atlas) is very detailed; it shows major roads and towns and has a scale of up to 1:300,000. A fold-out version is available with a scale of 1:2,200,000. Both are of very limited use, however, if you do not read Chinese. Even if you do, most of the place names are known locally in Tibetan only, not Chinese.

The English-language map *China Tibet Tour Map*, by the Mapping Bureau of the Tibet Autonomous Region, is the best local

alternative if you are just travelling around Tibet by road.

Road maps to look out for in Kathmandu include *Tibet – South-Central* by Nepa Maps; *Latest Map of Kathmandu to Tibet* by Mandala Maps; the *Namaste Trekking Map*; and *Lhasa to Kathmandu*, a mountain-biking map by Himalayan Map House. They are marginally better than the Chinese-produced maps but still aren't up to scratch.

Back at home, look out for the Nelles Verlag *Himalaya* map, which has excellent detail of central Tibet. Geocenter's *Tibet, Nepal, Bhutan* is also good. Bartholomew's *Tibet & the Mountains of Central Asia* is a good geographic overview but shows little detail. A good map if you are doing a lot of travelling is the *Tibet Road Map* by Berndtson & Berndtson. It has a detailed insert of central Tibet and is laminated, so it won't rip like all the others.

A specialist map, fascinating but of little practical use, is the *Terrain Map of Qinghai-Xizang Plateau*, coproduced by the Chinese Academy of Science & Woodlands Mountain Institute. It provides fascinating geographical information in the form of a satellite photo of the Tibetan plateau. You can find it in the gift shops of top-end hotels in Lhasa, but it's pricey at around US$15 to US$20.

Some of the most detailed maps of China and Tibet available in the West are the aerial survey Operational Navigation Charts (Series ONC). These are prepared and published by the Defense Mapping Agency Aerospace Center, St Louis Air Force Station, MO 63118, USA. Cyclists, trekkers and mountaineers rate these maps highly for their extraordinary detail.

The best maps available for Tibet, published by the US Department of Defense, are the Joint Operations Graphic (JOG) Series 1501 at a scale of 1:250,000. These maps are difficult to obtain and are semiclassified, but remarkably they have been reprinted in Victor Chan's *Tibet Handbook – A Pilgrimage Guide*, with key additions of religious sites and trekking routes added. For anyone really serious about mapping, this alone should make the book worth buying.

For detailed online maps of Tibet, try the Tibet Map Institute Web site at **W** http://perso.wanadoo.fr/tibetmap/.

Maps of Lhasa If you intend to explore Lhasa in detail, look out for *Lhasa City* (1:12,500) published by the Amnye Machen Institute in Dharamsala (**W** www.amnyemachen.org). The detail of the maps is awesome and includes many unorthodox sites. It is available from Stanfords (see Map Suppliers following) for UK£10.95.

On This Spot – Lhasa, published by the International Campaign for Tibet (ICT), is a unique political map of the Lhasa region, pinpointing the location of prisons, demonstrations, human-rights abuses and more. It's a really fascinating read, but it's too politically subversive to take into Tibet. It costs US$5.95 and can be ordered from ICT (for contact details, see Useful Organisations later in this chapter).

A less practical but equally fascinating map is *Tibetan Old Buildings and Urban Development in Lhasa 1948–1985–1998* by the Tibet Heritage Fund. It shows the development, or rather destruction, of the Tibetan quarter over recent years. The 1948 map of Lhasa is based on the original surveys of Peter Aufschnaiter, Heinrich Harrer's erstwhile companion. The map can be hard to find; you could contact the cartographers at **e** thf@chinaonline.com.cn.net. See the Web site **W** www.asianart.com/lhasa_restoration for more information.

Map Suppliers Several map suppliers have Web sites where you can view catalogues or even the actual maps. Mail-order suppliers include:

Australia
Mapland (☎ 03-9670 4383) 372 Little Bourke St, Melbourne, Vic 3000
The Travel Bookshop (☎ 02-9241 3554) 20 Bridge St, Sydney, NSW 2000

Germany
GeoCenter ILH (☎ 0711-788 93 40, fax 788 93 54, **e** geocenterilh@t-online.de) Schockenriedstrasse 44, D-70565 Stuttgart

UK
Maps Worldwide (☎ 01225-707 004, **W** www.mapsworldwide.co.uk) Datum House, Lancaster Rd, Melksham SN12 6TL
Stanfords (☎ 020-7836 1321, fax 7836 0189, **W** www.stanfords.co.uk) 12–14 Long Acre, Covent Garden, London WC2E 9LP
Upton Map Shop (☎ 01684-593 146, fax 594 559, **W** www.themapshop.co.uk) 15 High St, Upton-upon-Severn, Worcestershire WR8 0HJ

USA
Chessler Books (☎ 800-654 8502, 303-670 0093, fax 303-670 9727, **W** www.chesslerbooks.com) PO Box 4359, Evergreen, CO 80437
Map Link (☎ 805-692 6777, fax 692 6787, **W** www.maplink.com) 30 S La Patera Lane, Unit 5, Santa Barbara, CA 93117

What to Bring

Bring as little as possible to Tibet. It is much better to buy things as you need them than to throw things away because you have too much to carry. 'Lightweight' and 'compact' are two words that should be etched in your mind.

Carrying Bags A day-pack is good for hiking and for carrying extra food, books etc on long bus rides. You can even dump your main luggage in a hotel's storage and travel light for a couple of days with a medium-sized day-pack. A belt-pack is OK for maps, extra film and other miscellanea, but do not use it for valuables such as travellers cheques, plane tickets and your passport – it is an easy target for pickpockets.

Clothes In Tibet, no matter what time of year you are travelling, you should come prepared with some warm clothing. In the summer months, a couple of T-shirts and a good sweater or fleece will do the trick unless you are planning to be trekking at high altitudes or heading out to western Tibet. At other times of the year, ideally you should have thermal underwear, a down jacket, gloves and even a balaclava to protect your ears. A waterproof jacket can be surprisingly useful in summer, particularly if you are heading out to eastern Tibet.

Some clothing can be bought in Lhasa or Shigatse, but the selection is limited. It is much better to come prepared. Good walking boots and heavy socks are essential. Items such as a wide-brimmed hat to keep off the sun can be bought in Lhasa very cheaply. Baseball caps are widely available but won't protect your ears against the strong Tibetan sunshine.

Shorts are not a very suitable option in Tibet. The days can get pretty hot but wearing shorts in Tibet is akin to walking around with 'TOURIST!' tattooed on your forehead.

Sleeping Bag The question of whether you need a sleeping bag or not depends entirely on where you plan to go and how you plan to travel. Those who aim to spend time in Lhasa and then head down to Nepal via the sights of Tsang could do without one, although they are always a nice comfort, especially in budget hotels. Anyone planning on trekking or heading out to remoter areas such as Nam-tso, Everest or western Tibet should definitely bring one along. A silk lining for your sleeping bag will keep it clean and add extra warmth. If you are passing through Chengdu you can buy silk in the Chengdu Department Store for about Y20 per metre (get four metres) and get a tailor to make you a liner for less than US$1. A roll-up mat, although not essential, can also be useful.

Necessities & Accessories A good pair of sunglasses is absolutely essential to block out the UV light and protect your eyes. Also essential is high-factor sunscreen lotion. There are one or two places in Lhasa that sell sunscreen, but to be sure you should bring your own. A compact umbrella is a versatile shelter from rain, sleet, snow and sun.

Shaving cream, decent razor blades, mosquito repellent, deodorant, dental floss, tampons and contact-lens cleaning solution are hard to find. Bring a supply of lip salve: Most travellers' lips start to crack within a few days of arriving in Tibet, and if untreated this can become *very* painful. Cold medicines and throat pastilles are useful, as many travellers develop a cold and cough symptoms as a result of altitude. Shampoo

is available throughout Tibet in convenient one-use sachets, as is laundry soap and travel packs of tissues. A supply of zip-lock bags is useful. Take particular care when re-opening things such as tubes of sunscreen and shampoo after a flight to or from Lhasa, as the change in pressure can cause messy explosions of volcanic proportions.

Instant hot drinks such as coffee and soup are useful, as boiling water is available everywhere. A packet of mixed spices can really enliven the dreaded instant noodles. Water bottles are essential; try to get one that you can use to cool boiled water (thus doubling as a hot-water bottle!).

An alarm clock is essential for getting up on time to catch flights and buses. A strong torch (flashlight) is necessary for viewing the inside of most monasteries; Chinese versions are of poor quality. Following is a checklist of essential and nonessential items to consider packing:

Passport, photocopy of passport, visa, documents (vaccination certificate, student ID card), small emergency stash of cash in US currency, money-belt or vest, separate list of travellers cheque numbers, air ticket, copy of address book, reading matter, pens, notepad, name cards, visa photos, Swiss army knife, camera and accessories, extra camera battery, radio, padlock, cable lock (to secure luggage on trains), sunglasses, alarm clock, leak-proof water bottle, torch (flashlight) with batteries and bulbs, comb, compass, day-pack, long pants, long-sleeved shirt, T-shirt, nylon jacket, sweater or fleece, razor and razor blades, sewing kit, spoon, sun hat, sunscreen (UV) lotion, compact umbrella, toilet paper, tampons, toothbrush, toothpaste, dental floss, deodorant, shampoo, cord for a laundry line, flip-flops, tweezers, vitamins, laxative, diarrhoea medicine, condoms, contraceptives, any special medications you use, and medical kit (see Health later in this chapter).

Gifts It is nice to be able to cement friendships or reward favours with a gift. Pictures of you and your family are good for breaking the ice when no-one speaks English.

The obvious gift is a photograph of the Dalai Lama, although be aware that these are currently illegal in Tibet and you are committing a crime by bringing them into the country. Moreover you may be placing the recipient in danger of a fine or jail sentence from the Chinese authorities. Pictures of the Dalai Lama with the Tibetan national flag are even 'more' illegal.

RESPONSIBLE TOURISM

Tourism has already affected many areas in Tibet. Most children will automatically stick their hand out for a sweet, a pen or anything. Tibetans in some regions, eg, around Mt Everest, have become frustrated at seeing a stream of rich tourist groups but few tangible economic results. Please try to bear the following in mind as you travel through Tibet:

- Revenues created by organised group tourism go largely into the pockets of the Chinese authorities, so try to patronise as many small local Tibetan businesses, restaurants and guesthouses as possible.
- Support ecofriendly tourist initiatives wherever you see them.
- Don't hand out sweets or pens to children – you'll turn them into beggars. Similarly, doling out medicines can encourage people not to seek proper medical advice. If you wish to contribute something constructive, it's better to give pens directly to schools and medicines to rural clinics, or make a donation to an established charity.
- Monastery admission fees go largely to local authorities, so if you want to donate to the monastery leave your offering on the altar.
- Don't buy skins or hats made from endangered animals.
- Don't pay to take a photograph of someone and don't photograph someone if they don't want you to. If you agree to send a photograph of someone please follow through on this.
- If you have any pro-Tibetan sympathies be very careful with whom you discuss them. Don't put Tibetans in a difficult or even potentially dangerous situation. This includes handing out pictures of the Dalai Lama and politically sensitive materials.
- Always offer to pay for accommodation if it is offered. At monasteries, leave a donation even if no payment is required.
- Never disturb a collection of prayer flags or rock carvings. Similarly never buy artwork or relics belonging to a monastery or chapel, even if offered by a monk.
- Act respectfully when visiting temples and monasteries. Always circle a monastery building, statue or *chörten* (stupa) in a clockwise direction (unless it is a Bön monastery).

For more on the etiquette of visiting monasteries see the boxed text 'Visiting Monasteries & Temples' in the Lhasa chapter. For information on responsible trekking see the Trekking chapter.

TOURIST OFFICES

Tibet is officially a province of China and does not have tourist offices as such. There are a number of Chinese state-sponsored travel agencies that provide information on tours to Tibet, but they will all deny that it's possible to get to Tibet as an independent traveller. They can sometimes book domestic train and plane tickets to Chengdu and Golmud. See Organised Tours in the Getting There & Away chapter for details.

Similarly, the Tibetan government-in-exile does not provide information specifically relateing to travel in Tibet. Several of the Tibet-related information services offer travel advice; see Useful Organisations later in this chapter.

Tibet Tourism Bureau

The main function of the state-sponsored Tibet Tourism Bureau (TTB) is to direct travellers into group tours in Tibet. It issues the permits necessary to enter Tibet (see Travel Permits under Visas and Documents later in this chapter), although very few travellers deal with it directly.

The main TTB office outside Tibet is in Shanghai (☎ 021-6321 1729, fax 6323 1016, W www.tibet-tour.com) at 6/F Laojiefu Bldg, 233 Nanjing Donglu, Shanghai 200002.

There are also TTB offices in Beijing (☎ 010-6410 5822); Chengdu (☎ 028-333 3988); Kathmandu (☎ 977-01-119787) at 10 Renmin Beilu; and Hong Kong.

VISAS & DOCUMENTS
Passport

Chinese embassies will not issue a visa if your passport has less than six months of validity remaining. Be sure that your passport has at least a few blank pages for visas and entry and exit stamps.

Losing your passport is very bad news indeed. Getting a new one takes time and money, particularly if you are in Tibet. If you do lose your passport, you will probably need to travel to Beijing to apply for a new one, although we have had reports that some travellers have been able to get a certificate in English from the Public Security Bureau (PSB; China's police force) enabling them to travel to Nepal and apply for a new passport there. You will definitely need some photo identification.

Hong Kong residents have reported problems entering Nepal on a British National Overseas (BNO) passport after exiting China on their brown Huixiangzhen (used for travelling in China), as the BNO passport then lacks a Chinese exit stamp. If you are travelling this way, try to get an exit stamp put in your BNO passport.

Visas

Visas for individual travel in China are easy to get from most Chinese embassies. China will even issue visas to individuals from countries that do not have diplomatic relations with the People's Republic of China (PRC). The Chinese government has been known to stop issuing individual visas during summer or the run-up to sensitive political events, in an attempt to control the number of tourists.

Most Chinese embassies and consulates will issue a standard 30-day, single-entry tourist ('L' category) visa in three to five working days. 'L' stands for *lüxing* or 'travel'. Fees vary according to how much your country charges Chinese citizens for a visa. At the time of writing, a standard 30-day visa cost A$30 in Australia, €30.50 in France, UK£25 in the UK and US$30 in the USA. Fees must be paid in cash at the time of application and you'll need two passport-sized photos. It's best to get an application form in person at the embassy or consulate, although it is possible to obtain one online at embassy Web sites. Most Chinese embassies in Western countries offer a postal service for a fee but this takes around three weeks. Express services cost double the normal fee. Your application must be written in English, and you are advised to have one entire blank page in your passport for the visa.

Visas for Hong Kong & Macau

At the time of writing, nationals of most Western countries did not require visas to visit Hong Kong or Macau (British nationals can stay for up to six months without a visa). However, now that Hong Kong has been reunified with China, be aware that new visa regulations could be issued at any time. Note that if you cross from China into Hong Kong or Macau your passport will be stamped and you will need another Chinese visa or a double-entry visa to re-enter China.

The visa application form asks you a lot of questions (your entry and exit points, travel itinerary, means of transport etc), but once in China you can deviate from this as much as you like. Regulations state that you should have a ticket out of the country but this is rarely enforced. Whatever you do, however, *do not* let on that you plan to visit Tibet when you fill in this section. When listing your itinerary, pick the obvious contenders: Beijing, Shanghai and so on. Don't list your occupation as journalist and don't mention bicycles (otherwise you may be told erroneously that you have to take a tour to travel by bike – see the Getting Around chapter).

Visas valid for more than 30 days can be difficult to obtain anywhere other than Hong Kong, although some embassies abroad (in the UK, for example) may give you 60 days out of high season if you ask nicely. This saves you the considerable hassle of getting a visa extension in Tibet. Most agencies in Hong Kong should be able to arrange a 90-day visa.

A standard single-entry visa is activated on the date you enter China, and must be used within three months from the date of issue. There is some confusion over the validity of Chinese visas. Most Chinese officials look at the 'valid until' date, but on most 30-day visas this is actually the date by which you must have *entered* the country, not the visa's expiry date. Longer-stay visas are often activated on the day of issue, not the day you enter the country, so there's no point in getting one too far in advance of your planned entry date. Check with the embassy if you are unsure.

If you want more flexibility to enter and leave China several times, most Chinese embassies will issue a double-entry visa. Note that only travellers with tourist visas are currently allowed into Tibet. It is very difficult to get a TTB permit for Tibet if you have a business, resident or student visa (most multiple entry visas are business visas).

Hong Kong In Hong Kong, the cheapest 30-day visas (HK$100 for next-day service, HK$250 for same-day service) can be obtained from the visa office (☎ 2827 1881) at the Ministry of Foreign Affairs of the PRC, 5th floor, Low Block, China Resources Bldg, 26 Harbour Rd, Wanchai. US citizens (unless of Chinese descent) face an additional surcharge of HK$160. You'll have to queue – do not expect so much as a smile – but you'll save a few dollars. It is open 9am to 12.30pm and 2pm to 5pm Monday to Friday, and 9am to 12.30pm on Saturday. From Tsimshatsui on the Kowloon side, the cheapest and easiest way to get there is to take the Star Ferry to Wanchai Pier (not to Central!), one block away from the China Resources Building.

China Travel Service (☎ 2315 7188), on the 1st floor, Alpha House, 27–33 Nathan Rd, Tsimshatsui (enter from Peking Rd), is a convenient and popular place to get a visa. Tourist visas of up to 90 days cost HK$380 for same-day service (hand your passport in before noon, pick up at 6.30pm), HK$250 for next-day service and HK$180 for two-day service. Passport photos are available here for HK$30.

Two other reliable agencies are Phoenix Services (☎ 2722 7378), 6th floor, Milton Mansion, 96 Nathan Rd, Tsimshatsui, Kowloon; and Shoestring Travel (☎ 2723 2306), 4th floor, Block A, Alpha House, 27 Peking Rd, Tsimshatsui, Kowloon.

Kathmandu Try to obtain a Chinese visa before you get to Kathmandu, either at home, or in Delhi or Bangkok; it will save you a whole series of headaches once you get to Tibet. Note that the Chinese embassy changes regulations frequently. At the time of writing the embassy *was* issuing 30-day tourist visas to individual travellers, but these regulations change like the wind. The visa section is only open from 9.30am to 11am on Monday, Wednesday and Friday, and is closed on all Chinese and Nepali holidays.

If the embassy has stopped issuing visas to individual travellers you will have to get the travel agency that is arranging your tour to Tibet in Kathmandu (see Kathmandu under Gateway Cities in the Getting There & Away chapter for details) to arrange the visa as well. You will probably be put on a group visa, which is actually a separate sheet of paper with all the names and passport numbers of the group members. Come the end of your tour in Lhasa you will either have to return with the group or split from this group visa. This can only officially be done by the Chinese partner of the Nepali travel agency that arranged your travel into Tibet and the process is both awkward and pricey. Agencies in Lhasa will need your passport and a couple of days to deal with the bureaucratic procedures.

When restrictions are tight the Chinese embassy may cancel your individual visa and put you on a group visa anyway, but it's still worth turning up in Kathmandu with an individual Chinese visa. It gives you more freedom and saves you the potential hassle of having to split from a group visa and then extending your visa inside Lhasa.

Visa Extensions The foreign affairs section of the local PSB handles visa extensions. Extensions of up to a week are often available in Lhasa within seven days of the visa's expiration if you can produce proof that you are leaving Tibet (a plane ticket to Chengdu will do). It is far easier to extend your visa in Chengdu, Xining or Xi'an, where a month's extension is commonplace. It may be possible to get a visa extension in Ali or Chamdo if you are on a legitimate tour. Fees vary according to your nationality but generally cost between Y100 and Y200.

For extensions of longer than a week it's worth going direct to a travel agency (see Information in the Lhasa chapter) rather than revealing your plans to the PSB.

Travel agencies should be able arrange a visa extension for as long as you are on one of their tours.

The penalty for overstaying your visa is Y500 per day. Lonely Planet does not recommend that you overstay your visa under any circumstances. However, you should be aware that the PSB has the power to lower fines. Many travellers have said they are students or claimed ignorance, sickness or road closures, and have paid lower fines.

Travel Permits

Tibet Tourism Bureau Permit The official Tibetan government line is that a TTB permit is required to visit Tibet full stop. This is partly true. However, even if you fork out whatever local authorities are charging for the 'permit', you will probably never see anything that looks remotely like a travel permit (especially if you take the bus from Golmud). You are basically paying a 'fee' that will allow you to travel to Tibet independently. If you fly from Chengdu you *will* need to show this permit when you check in and one member of your group will probably carry the group TTB permit on the plane and hand it over to the guide at Lhasa.

See the Getting There & Away chapter for more information on buying air and bus tickets into Tibet from Kathmandu, Golmud or Chengdu. The amount of time you can stay in Tibet is normally determined by the length of time on your visa, not the TTB permit.

TTB permits are also needed by groups travelling by Land Cruiser but this will be arranged by the travel agency organising the trip.

The Latest Word

Permit and visa regulations for Tibet change every year, sometimes every month, and are notoriously hard to keep track of. For the latest information and travellers' reports check out the Postcards and Thorn Tree sections of the Lonely Planet Web site (**w** www.lonelyplanet .com), as well as our latest online Tibet upgrade, published every six months or so.

Alien Travel Permit Once you have a visa and have managed to wangle a TTB permit, you'd think you were home dry. Think again. You'll probably need to arrange a travel permit for much of your travel around Tibet.

Tibet is slightly more complicated when it comes to travel permits than elsewhere in China. An Alien Travel Permit (usually just called a 'travel permit') is granted by the PSB for travel (independent or group) to an area that is officially closed.

At the time of research, travel permits were *not* needed for the towns of Lhasa, Shigatse and Tsetang, or for places in the Lhasa region (not just Lhasa town), or for nonstop travel on the Friendship Hwy. The Lhasa region includes such places as Ganden, Tsurphu, Nam-tso, Drigung Til and Reting, giving you quite a lot of scope.

Gyantse, Sakya, Samye, the Yarlung Valley, the Everest region and western Tibet all require permits. At the time of research, however, the only places that were actively checking permits were Samye, the Yarlung Valley and the road to Mt Kailash, although in theory you could be checked anywhere outside these places.

Lhasa PSB will not issue travel permits to individuals and will direct you to a travel agency. Agencies can arrange a travel permit to almost anywhere but only if you book a Land Cruiser, driver and a guide.

The only glimmer of light in this situation is Shigatse PSB (God bless them). For some reason that nobody can quite work out, Shigatse PSB will issue permits to individuals for most places in Shigatse prefecture (Sakya, Everest Base Camp, Nangartse, Shalu, Gyantse and anywhere on the Friendship Hwy). Permits are issued on the spot for Y50. You may have to pay a fully refundable Y200 deposit for a permit to Gyantse. You are then free to catch a bus or hitch to these places without having to book an expensive tour. Shigatse PSB has had to cut down on the number of permits it hands out in recent years and may well soon stop the practice completely.

Travel permits for Samye and Tsetang are almost impossible to come by without booking a tour. At the time of research there were only sporadic checks at Samye. Permits for the Yarlung Valley were only available from Tsetang PSB and were only issued when you booked transport and a guide with Tsetang's China International Travel Service (CITS).

Permits cost Y50, are valid for the duration of your visa and can list any number of destinations. They are well worth getting if you can. If you get caught by the PSB without a permit (most likely when you check into a hotel) you face a fine of between Y200 and Y500, which is probably still cheaper than booking a tour. Get a receipt to ensure you don't get fined a second time during your return to Lhasa.

Beware that the permit situation is subject to rapid and unpredictable change by the Chinese government so it's worth checking the current situation with other travellers in Lhasa. Don't trust the travel agencies on this one, as they have a vested interest in booking you on one of their tours.

You should give your agency an absolute minimum of four working days to arrange your permits, longer if military or other permits are required (see below). If you are arranging a Land Cruiser trip from abroad the travel agency may ask for up to one month to arrange permits.

Other Permits Sensitive border areas such as Mt Kailash and eastern Tibet also require a military permit and a foreign-affairs permit.

For Thöling and Tsaparang in western Tibet you will also need a permit from the local Cultural Antiquities Department. All these will be arranged by the tour agency if you book a tour.

For remote places such as the Yarlung Tsangpo gorges or the Bönri kora in eastern Tibet, or for any border area, you may not be able to get permits even if you book a tour through an ordinary travel agency. For this you will need an agency that has connections with the military authorities.

Travel Insurance

A travel insurance policy to cover theft, loss and medical problems is a good idea. The policies handled by STA Travel and other student travel organisations are usually good value. There is a wide variety of policies available so check the small print. Some policies specifically exclude 'dangerous activities', which normally includes trekking. Check that the policy covers ambulances or an emergency flight home. Paying for your air ticket with a credit card often provides limited travel accident insurance – ask your credit card company what it covers.

You may prefer a policy that pays doctors or hospitals directly rather than you having to pay on the spot and claim later. If you have to claim later, make sure you keep all documentation. Some policies ask you to call (reverse charges) a centre in your home country where an immediate assessment of your problem is made.

Some policies offer a cheaper plan that covers only medical cover and not baggage loss. This can be worthwhile if you're not carrying any pricey valuables in your grotty backpack. Most policies require you to pay the first US$100 or so anyway and only cover valuables up to a set limit. In case of loss of baggage or valuables, you will almost certainly need a police report to show the insurance company.

Insurance policies can normally be extended while you are on the road by a simple phone call to the insurance company or agency you bought it from. Make sure you do this *before* it expires or you may have to buy a new policy, often at a higher premium.

Student & Youth Cards

International student or youth cards such as ISIC or GO 25 cards may get you cheaper fares to China or Nepal, but are of little use inside Tibet. The only times you'll use one is for a 50% discount at some monasteries, but these don't worry too much about selling you a ticket anyway. Chinese student cards, bona fide or otherwise, are more useful.

Other Documents

Given the Chinese preoccupation with impressive bits of paper, it is worth carrying a few business cards, student cards and anything else that is printed and laminated in plastic. These additional IDs are useful for leaving with bicycle hirers, who often want a deposit or some form of ID as security. Some hotels also require you to hand over your passport as security, even if you've paid in advance – an old expired passport is useful in these situations.

If you are travelling with your spouse, a photocopy of your marriage certificate just might come in handy if one of you is Chinese. Useful, although not essential, is an International Health Certificate that records your vaccinations.

Youth hostel cards, driving licences, senior citizen's cards and the like are all of little use in Tibet.

Copies

All important documents (passport data page, Chinese visa, credit cards, travel insurance policy, air ticket etc) should be photocopied before you leave home. Leave one copy with someone at home and keep another with you, separate from the originals. It's also a good idea to keep a list of your travellers cheque numbers separate from the cheques themselves.

You can store details of your vital travel documents in Lonely Planet's free online Travel Vault in case you lose the photocopies or can't be bothered with them. Your password-protected Travel Vault is accessible online anywhere in the world – create it at **W** www.ekno.lonelyplanet.com.

EMBASSIES & CONSULATES
Chinese Embassies

In major cities abroad, Chinese embassies include those in:

Australia (☎ 02-6273 4780, 6273 4781, **W** www.chinaembassy.org.au) 15 Coronation Dr, Yarralumla, ACT 2600

Canada (☎ 613-789 3509, **W** www.chinaembassy canada.org) 515 St Patrick St, Ottawa, ON KIN 5H3

Denmark (☎ 039-625806, 625484) 25 Oregards Alle, 2900 Hellerup, Copenhagen

France (☎ 01 47 36 02 58, fax 01 36 34 46, **W** www.amb-chine.fr) 9 Ave Victor Cresson, 921130 Issy Les Mounlineaux, Paris

Germany (☎ 0228-361095, **W** www.china botschaft.de) Kurfürstenallee 125–300 Bonn 2 (Bad Godesberg)

India (☎ 011-611 6682, fax 688 5486) 50-D Shantipath, Chanakyapuri, New Delhi 110021

Italy (☎ 06-3630 8534, 3630 3856) Via Della Camilluccia 613, Roma 00135

Japan (☎ 03-3403 3380, 3403 3065) 3–4–33 Moto-Azabu, Minato-ku, Tokyo 106

Nepal (☎ 01-411740, fax 414045) Baluwatar, Kathmandu

Netherlands (☎ 070-355 1515) Adriaan Goekooplaan 7, 2517 JX, The Hague

New Zealand (☎ 04-587 0407, **W** www.china embassy.org.nz) 104A Korokoro Rd, Pentone, Wellington

UK (☎ 020-7636 8845, 24-hour premium-rate visa information 0891-880808, fax 020-7436 9178, **W** www.chinese-embassy.org.uk) 31 Portland Place, London WIN 5AG

USA (☎ 202-328 2500, 338 6688, fax 558 9760, faxback 265 9809, **W** www.chinaembassy.org) Room 110, 2201 Wisconsin Ave NW, Washington DC 20007

For embassies not listed here see the Chinese Foreign Ministry Web site at **W** www.fmprc.gov.cn/eng/.

Consulates in Tibet

The only diplomatic representation in Tibet is the Nepali consulate in Lhasa (☎ 682 2881, fax 683 6890, **e** rncglx@public.ls.x.cn), which is on a side street just south of the Lhasa Hotel and north of the Norbulingka. Visa application hours are 10am to 12.30pm Monday to Friday. Visas are issued within 24 hours. Visa fees change regularly, but at the time of research they were Y255 for a 30-day visa (Y425 if you have visited Nepal in the same calendar year). A double-entry visa costs between Y425 and Y765, depending on whether you have visited Nepal before. All visas are valid for six months from the date of issue. Remember to bring one visa photo.

It is also possible to obtain visas for the same costs as above at Kodari, the Nepali border town, although it would be sensible to check first that this has not changed.

Embassies in Beijing

If you need to contact your embassy while in Tibet you will need to ring or fax Beijing, where all of China's foreign embassies are located. It is not a good idea to send your passport by post to any of the addresses listed in order to obtain a visa for the next stop on your travels.

There are also consulates for Laos, Myanmar (Burma) and Thailand in Kunming, and consulates for Australia, France, Germany, Japan, Thailand and Vietnam in Guangzhou (Canton).

In a real emergency the nearest Western diplomatic representation is the US consulate (☎ 028-558 3992, after hours ☎ 1370-800 1422, fax 558 3520) at 4 Lingshiguan Lu, Section 4, Renmin Nanlu, Chengdu.

In Beijing (☎ code 010) there are two embassy compounds – Jianguomenwai and Sanlitun. The following embassies are in Jianguomenwai, Beijing:

India (☎ 6532 1908, fax 6532 4684) 1 Ritan Donglu
Ireland (☎ 6532 2691, fax 6532 2168) 3 Ritan Donglu
Japan (☎ 6532 2361, fax 6532 4625) 7 Ritan Lu
New Zealand (☎ 6532 2731, fax 6532 4317) 1 Ritan Dong Er Jie
Thailand (☎ 6532 1903, fax 6532 1748) 40 Guanghua Lu
UK (☎ 6532 1961, fax 6532 1937) 11 Guanghua Lu
USA (☎ 6532 3831, fax 6532 6057) 3 Xiushui Beijie
Vietnam (☎ 6532 5414, fax 6532 5720) 32 Guanghua Lu

The Sanlitun compound in Beijing is home to the following embassies:

Australia (☎ 6532 2331, fax 6532 6957) 21 Dongzhimenwai Dajie
Canada (☎ 6532 3536, fax 6532 4072) 19 Dongzhimenwai Dajie
Denmark (☎ 6532 2431, fax 6532 2439) 1 Sanlitun Dong Wu Jie
France (☎ 6532 1331, fax 6532 4841, W www .ambafrance-cn.org) Dongsan Jie 3, Chaoyang
Germany (☎ 6532 2161, fax 6532 5336) 17 Dongzhimenwai Dajie
Myanmar (Burma; ☎ 6532 1584, fax 6532 1344) 6 Dongzhimenwai Dajie
Nepal (☎ 6532 1795, fax 6532 3251) 1 Sanlitun Xi Liu Jie
Netherlands (☎ 6532 1131, fax 6532 4689, W www.nlembassypek.org) 4 Liangmahe Nanlu
Pakistan (☎ 6532 2504) 1 Dongzhimenwai Dajie

CUSTOMS

Chinese border crossings have gone from being severely traumatic to exceedingly easy for travellers. There are clearly marked 'green channels' and 'red channels'; take the latter only if you have something to declare.

You are allowed to import 400 cigarettes (or the equivalent in tobacco products), 2L of alcoholic drink and one pint of perfume. You are allowed to import a maximum of 72 rolls of film. Importation of fresh fruit is prohibited. It's also officially forbidden to bring more than 20 pieces of underwear into the PRC (we kid you not).

You can legally bring in or take out only Y6000 in Chinese currency. There are no such restrictions on foreign currency except that you should declare any cash amount exceeding US$5000 (or its equivalent in other currencies).

It is illegal to import any printed material, film, tapes etc 'detrimental to China's politics, economy, culture and ethics'. This is a particularly sensitive subject in Tibet, but even here it is highly unusual to have Chinese customs officials grilling travellers about their reading matter. Maps and political books printed in Dharamsala, India, could cause a problem. It is currently illegal to bring into China pictures, books, videos or speeches of or by the Dalai Lama. Be very circumspect if you are asked to take any packages, letters or photos out of Tibet for anyone else, including monks.

Some travellers have reported being asked whether they have a Tibet guidebook with them when crossing the border from Nepal to Tibet. This is the exception rather than the rule, however, and the appropriate answer is 'no'.

Anything made in China before 1949 is regarded as a cultural treasure and cannot be taken out of the country.

MONEY
Currency

The Chinese currency is known as Renminbi (RMB) or 'people's money'. The basic unit of this currency is the yuan, designated in this book by a 'Y'. In spoken Chinese, the word 'kuai' is almost always substituted for the word 'yuan'. Ten jiao (in spoken Chinese, pronounced 'mao') make up one yuan. Ten fen make up one jiao, but fen are becoming rare because they are worth so little – some people will not accept them.

RMB comes in paper notes issued in denominations of one, two, five, 10, 20, 50 and 100 yuan; one, two and five jiao; and one, two and five fen. Coins are in denominations of one yuan; five jiao; and one, two and five fen. A new red Y100 bill was introduced in 1999. Older bills feature the communist pantheon of Mao Zedong, Zhou Enlai, Zhu De and Liu Shaoqi. Both are legal tender.

Exchange Rates

At the time of writing, exchange rates were as follows:

country	unit		yuan
Australia	A$1	=	Y4.19
Canada	C$1	=	Y5.37
Euro zone	€1	=	Y7.55
Hong Kong	HK$1	=	Y1.06
Japan	¥100	=	Y6.58
Nepal	Rs 100	=	Y11.34
New Zealand	NZ$1	=	Y3.42
UK	UK£1	=	Y11.56
USA	US$1	=	Y8.26

Exchanging Money

In Tibet, the only place to change foreign currency and travellers cheques is the Bank of China. The top-end hotels in Lhasa have exchange services but they are only available to guests. The sensible thing to do is to change as much money in Lhasa as you think you'll need. The only other places to change money are in Shigatse, Zhangmu, Purang and Ali (cash only at the last two), and at the airport on arrival. If you are travelling upcountry, try and get your cash in small denominations: Y100 and Y50 bills are sometimes difficult to get rid of in rural Tibet.

The currencies of Australia, Canada, the US, the UK, Hong Kong, Japan, the Euro zone and most of the rest of Western Europe are acceptable at the Bank of China. For cash transactions outside the bank, you will need to have US dollars. The official rate is given at all banks and most hotels so there is little need to shop around for the best deal. The standard commission is 0.75%.

Since the floating of the RMB, there is no problem taking the currency out of the country. However, it would be sensible to change it back into a more useful currency. There are plenty of moneychangers at Zhangmu who will change yuan into Nepali rupees and vice versa. Yuan can also easily be reconverted in Hong Kong. Keep your exchange receipts as you'll need these to change your yuan back to dollars at the Bank of China.

Cash If you don't like the idea of turning up at the border with no Chinese currency, you can buy cash RMB from banks in Hong Kong and the Bank of China in large cities such as London and New York.

Travellers Cheques Besides the advantage of safety, travellers cheques are useful to carry in Tibet because the exchange rate is higher (by about 3%) than it is for cash. Cheques from most of the world's leading banks and issuing agencies are now accepted at the Bank of China – stick to the major companies such as Thomas Cook, Citibank, American Express and Bank of America and you'll be OK.

Credit Cards You'll get very few opportunities to splurge on the plastic in Tibet unless you spend a few nights in a top-end hotel. Flights out of Lhasa can not be paid using a credit card, although this may change in the future. The Lhasa central branch of the Bank of China is the only place in Tibet that provides credit card advances. A 3% commission is usually deducted and the minimum advance is normally Y1200.

International Transfers Getting money sent to you in Lhasa is possible but it can be a drag. One option is through the Bank of China's central office in Lhasa. Staff claim that it takes seven days for money to arrive but you should budget more time than that. Money should be wired to the Bank of China, Lhasa branch, bank account No 148340001.

You should double-check wiring instructions with the bank beforehand.

The second option is via Western Union, which can wire money via Express Mail Service (EMS; see Post & Communications later in this chapter) at the main post office (☎ 682 6314) on Dekyi Shar Lam in Lhasa. See the Web site W www.westernunion.com for details.

Black Market There is not really much of a black market in Tibet any more. Money-changers still work the streets of Lhasa, but as they offer almost the same rates as the bank and there is a *big* problem with counterfeit notes in China, you would be foolish to use their services unless you get caught without cash after hours.

Counterfeit Notes Chinese authorities have recently been confronted with a deluge of counterfeit notes. Very few Tibetans or Chinese will accept a Y100 or Y50 note without first subjecting it to intense scrutiny, and many will not accept old, tattered notes. Check the watermark when receiving any Y100 note.

Security

A moneybelt or pockets sewn inside your clothes is the safest way to carry money.

Keeping all your eggs in one basket is not advised – you should keep an emergency cash stash of small-denomination notes in US dollars separate from your main moneybelt, along with a record of your travellers cheque serial numbers, emergency contact numbers and your passport number.

Costs

How much it costs to travel in Tibet depends on how much you want to see and how quickly you want to see it. Accommodation is still very economical in Tibet, while food is a little more expensive than elsewhere in China, but the major expense – unless you have plenty of time and enjoy rough travelling – is getting around. There is little in the way of public transport in Tibet and hitching can be time-consuming, so if you really

want to see a lot in a short space of time you will probably have to consider hiring a vehicle (plus driver) at rates of approximately US$0.50 per kilometre.

Of course travel costs can be reduced by sharing transport with other travellers, but even so you will probably spend more money getting around than you would in other parts of China. The per-person cost for a group of six travelling with stops from Lhasa to the Nepali border, for example, is around US$120. Getting into Tibet is also relatively expensive. Even the bus fare from Golmud has risen to around US$200, while the cheapest package by air costs around US$350. Most hired transport tends to work out at around US$20 to US$30 per person per day.

If you don't hire transport (and it is still perfectly possible to see many of the places covered in this guide if you don't) costs are very reasonable. If you are staying in Lhasa and visiting the surrounding sights you can do it comfortably on US$15 per day – US$3 for dormitory accommodation, US$5 for food and the rest for transport and admission fees. Outside the main cities of Lhasa, Shigatse and Tsetang, daily costs can drop drastically, especially if you're hitching or hiking out to remote monasteries and living on instant noodles.

One Country, Two Prices For years in China foreigners have been charged more for most things, and Tibet is no exception. In the last couple of years, dual pricing for things such as hotel accommodation, train and plane tickets and admission prices has been phased out. Interestingly, in Tibet, Chinese tourists are feeling the other end of the boot – while Tibetans pay only Y1 to get into the Potala, Chinese tourists have to pay Y40 like everyone else.

Still, after years of official encouragement to charge foreigners more, many Chinese (and unfortunately Tibetans, too) view upping the price for foreigners as their patriotic duty. A student card sometimes serves to waive these surcharges, and in some situations determined haggling can bring prices down.

Tipping & Bargaining

Tibet is one of those wonderful places where tipping is not done and almost no-one asks for a tip. If you go on a long organised trip out to eastern or western Tibet, your guide and driver will probably expect a tip at the end of the trip, assuming all went well. Figure on around Y50 to Y100 per person.

Basic bargaining skills are essential for travel in Tibet. You can bargain in shops, hotels, street stalls and travel agencies, and with pedicab drivers and most people – but not everywhere. In small shops and street stalls, bargaining is expected, but there is one important rule to follow: Be polite.

Tibetans are no less adept at driving a hard deal than the Chinese and, like the Chinese, aggressive bargaining will usually only serve to firm their conviction that the original asking price is the one they want. Try to keep smiling and firmly whittle away at the price. If this does not work, try walking away. They might call you back, and if they don't there is always somewhere else.

Taxes

Although big hotels and top-end restaurants may add a tax or 'service charge' of 10% to 15%, all other consumer taxes are included in the price tag. For information on departure tax see the Getting There & Away chapter.

POST & COMMUNICATIONS

Tibet is increasingly well connected to the rest of the world. Even in small towns it is possible to make international calls. Email connections are possible in towns such as Lhasa, Shigatse, Tsetang and Chamdo. Lhasa is the only place in Tibet from where it is possible to send international parcels.

Postal Rates

An airmail letter of up to 20g costs Y6.40 to any country. Postcards cost Y4.20 and aerograms cost Y5.20.

There are cheaper rates for printed matter and small packets, but pricing regulations rapidly become complicated. It will cost you around Y50 to send a small 500g packet by airmail.

Rates for parcels vary depending on the country of destination and seem quite random. As a rough guide, a 1kg airmail package costs around Y175 at the letter rate, Y135.50 at the printed-matter rate and Y147 at the small-packet rate. A 5kg packet to the UK costs Y523 by airmail, Y368 by surface mail and Y201 by sea mail. Surface and sea mail takes around two months. The maximum weight you can send or receive is 30kg.

Post offices are very picky about how you pack things; do not finalise your packing until the parcel has its last customs clearance. If you have a receipt for the goods, then put it in the box when you are mailing it, since it may be opened again by customs further down the line.

Express Mail Service (EMS), a worldwide priority mail service, can courier documents to most foreign countries within a couple of days. Packages up to 500g cost Y170 to Australia, Y230 to Western Europe and Y190 to the US, with each additional 500g costing from Y55 (Australia) to Y75 (US and Europe). There are charges of Y2.30 for recorded delivery and Y6.50 for registered mail.

Sending Mail

The international postal service seems efficient, and airmail letters and postcards will probably take around seven to 10 days to reach their destinations. If possible, write the country of destination in Chinese, as this should speed up the delivery.

Receiving Mail

There is a reliable poste restante service at the main post office in Lhasa, but it would be foolhardy to risk sending poste restante letters anywhere else in Tibet. Things are arranged almost alphabetically – check for your first name, surname and even 'M' for Mr, Miss, Ms or Mrs. Bring your passport. There is a charge of Y1.50 for each item of mail you receive.

Telephone

China's phone system has been rapidly modernised and domestic direct dialling is available almost everywhere. Major post offices and telecom offices can place long-distance and international calls, although it is easiest in Lhasa, Tsetang or Shigatse. Most hotels in Lhasa have direct-dial international telephones but levy a hefty 30% surcharge on calls.

Domestic long-distance rates from Lhasa vary according to distance, but are cheap. International rates have fallen dramatically in recent years. Rates for station-to-station calls to most countries in the world recently fell from Y15 to Y8.2 per minute. Cardphones cost half this. Hong Kong is Y2.2 per minute. There is normally a minimum charge of one minute although it's best to check this before you dial.

Calls are placed by paying a deposit of Y200 and then calling direct from a phone booth. Time the call yourself if you want to limit your call to a certain duration. After you make the call, the cost is deducted from your deposit and the balance returned to you. The time is computer controlled and you are not going to be cheated. If you get through to a recorded message or fax you will be charged the minimum one-minute charge. Lines are amazingly clear considering where you are. In fact, the biggest problem will probably be the guy yelling in the booth next door on a call to Shigatse.

It is still impossible to make collect calls (reverse-charge calls) or to use foreign telephone debit cards. The best you can do is give someone your number and get them to call you back.

Local area codes are given at the start of each town's entry within this guidebook.

Phonecards There's a wide range of local and international phonecards.

Lonely Planet's eKno Communication Card is aimed specifically at independent travellers and provides budget international calls, a range of messaging services, free email and travel information. For local calls you are usually better off with a local card. You can join online at W www.ekno.lonely planet.com, or by phone from China by dialling ☎ 10800-180-0073. Once you have joined, dial ☎ 10800-180-0072 to use eKno from China. Check the eKno Web site for

joining and access numbers from other countries and updates on super budget local access numbers and new features.

The introduction of the Internet phone (IP) system has slashed the cost of international calls. In March 2001 rates were reduced to Y2.40 per minute to the US and Canada and Y3.60 to Western Europe, Australia, Japan, Singapore, Malaysia and Thailand. 'Domestic' calls cost Y1.50 per minute to Hong Kong, Macau and Taiwan and Y0.30 elsewhere in China. The service is only available in Lhasa.

To take advantage of these rates you have to buy an IP card. These are available from telecom offices in increments of Y30 (most common), Y50 and Y100. You dial in a local access number, then punch in your card number (followed by #), a password number (followed by #) and finally the number you wish to call (followed by a final #). English-language instructions are available. You can make IP-card calls on most public and private phones but not on cardphones. You may have to search around for a phone that will accept the number you are trying to ring. Public phones charge a service fee of around Y0.3 per minute or a flat fee of Y1 to use their phones. You cannot currently use a card purchased in Lhasa (called a '17908 card') in other areas of Tibet or other provinces of China, although the service will probably spread to Shigatse before long.

Regular cardphones (which take cards known as IC cards) are also found in most telecom offices and major hotels. Most IC cards cost Y50. Calls made on cardphones cost the standard rate of about Y8 per minute and are charged by the minute so you may be left with up to US$1 (less than Y8) of unusable credits on a card.

Direct Dialling To dial into China from elsewhere, dial ☎ 86 (the country code for China), followed by the Chinese local area code (minus the 0) and the local number.

To dial out of China, dial the international access code ☎ 00, followed by your country code, the local area code (minus the first 0) and then the number.

Fax

Telecom offices in major towns and business centres in the top-end hotels offer reliable fax services, although prices are generally high. Most places charge the basic cost of the call, plus a service charge of Y8 to Y10 per page, bringing the total for a one-page fax to around Y24. Problems arise if you are sending a fax to a combined fax and phone and someone at the other end picks up the phone. Make sure you get a print-out confirming that the fax actually went through. Be aware that some hotels charge up to US$10 *just to receive a fax*.

Email & Internet Access

It is possible to send and receive emails in Lhasa, Shigatse, Tsetang, Ali and Chamdo, either in private Internet bars (which double as video arcades) or in the 'business centres' of telecom offices. Most places charge around Y5 for an hour's Internet access. Some Web sites, such as the BBC's, have been blacklisted by the Chinese government and are unavailable.

DIGITAL RESOURCES

The World Wide Web is a rich resource for travellers. You can research your trip, book hotels, check on weather conditions or chat with locals and other travellers about the best places to visit (or avoid!).

The Lonely Planet Web site (W www.lonelyplanet.com) has succinct summaries on travelling to most places on earth, postcards from other travellers and the Thorn Tree bulletin board, where you can ask questions before you go or dispense advice when you get back. You can also find travel news and upgrades to many of our most popular guidebooks, and the subWWWay section links you to the most useful travel resources elsewhere on the Web.

The Tibet-L list is an email circular for those with a deep interest in all things Tibet, from politics to art exhibitions. To subscribe, send an email to e listserv@listserv.indiana.edu with 'SUBSCRIBE TIBET-L' and your name in the body of the message.

For details of Web sites of Tibetan organisations see Useful Organisations later in this chapter. The pick of general Web sites on Tibet is listed here:

Asian Arts (W www.asianart.com) An online journal with articles and online galleries of Tibetan art

Australia Tibet Council (W www.atc.org.au/travel) Includes excellent information on travel to Tibet, including the latest travel restrictions

Canada Tibet Committee (W www.tibet.ca) A useful, free news-gathering service on issues relating to Tibet

China Tibet Information (W www.tibetinfor.com/en) News, background and tourism information from the Chinese perspective

Himalayan Art (W www.himalayanart.org) Hundreds of online examples of Tibetan art from dozens of collections

Office of the Dalai Lama in London (W www.tibet.com) Provides lots of background information on Tibet

Tibet Information Network (W www.tibetinfo.net) Another news-gathering service with a good rundown of tourist regulations in Tibet

Tibet Map Institute (W www.tibetmap.com) Highly detailed downloadable maps of almost every region of Tibet, with an overview of other commercial map sources

Tibet Online (W www.tibet.org) Operated by the Tibet Support Group; articles on Tibet and good links to other Tibet-related sites

Tibet Tourism Bureau, Shanghai Branch (W www.tibet-tour.com) Contains mostly information about pricey tours but has some useful information such as flight timetables for Lhasa

Tibetan Government-in-Exile (W www.tibet.net) General information on Tibet from Dharamsala, India

Tibetan Studies WWW Virtual Library (W www.ciolek.com/wwwvl-tibetanstudies.html) Excellent list of Tibetan Web sites and general information on Tibet

BOOKS

Literature on Tibet is abundant. Quite a bit of it is of the woolly 'how to find enlightenment in the mysterious Land of Snows' variety, but there is still a lot of very good stuff about.

Bring your own reading material because the only way you will find anything worthwhile to read in Tibet is to swap with other travellers.

If you are coming in from either Kathmandu or Hong Kong, you'll find that both are excellent places to stock up on reading material. Kathmandu, which has dozens of cheap bookshops simply brimming with novels and books about India, Nepal and Tibet, is the best place to stock up. Its shops not only have cheap second-hand books and anything new and current, they also have many expensive and rare books, including Indian reprints of very rare editions.

Publishers specialising in books on Tibet and Tibetan Buddhism include Shambhala Publications (Ⓦ www.shambhala.com), Snowlion Publications (Ⓦ www.snowlion pub.com) and Wisdom Publications (Ⓦ www .wisdom pubs.org).

Lonely Planet

If you are heading for the Tibetan countryside then you'll find Lonely Planet's *Tibetan phrasebook* a lifesaver. Guides to neighbouring regions include *China, South-West China, Nepal, Trekking in the Nepal Himalaya, Bhutan* and *North India*.

Buddhist Stupas in Asia: The Shape of Perfection by Joe Cummings & Bill Wasseman is an accessible and lavishly illustrated exploration of the spread of Buddhism and stupa building across India and Asia, and it has a chapter devoted to Tibet.

Guidebooks

The market has been flooded with guides to Tibet in recent years. Interestingly, however, general guides aimed at the first-time visitor to Tibet are sparse on the ground.

The Odyssey Illustrated Guide to Tibet is an exception to this rule, and provides good background reading on Tibet and its attractions in an appealing format. Unlike some of the other books around it is also fairly portable, although very few independent travellers take it to Tibet.

Books that assume a reasonably deep interest in Tibet and possibly some prior study of the culture include Stephen Batchelor's classic *The Tibet Guide*, the pick of the pack for serious travellers to central Tibet. Consider getting a copy if you have a strong interest in identifying the myriad images found in Tibetan monasteries. Unfortunately there's very little practical information along the lines of useful maps or places to stay.

There are a couple of encyclopedic guides to Tibet. Victor Chan's *Tibet Handbook – A Pilgrimage Guide* is without a doubt the most comprehensive guide (1099 pages) ever written on Tibet and any serious student of Tibetan culture should get hold of a copy. Unfortunately, for the average traveller the book is simply too bulky, too baffling in its organisation and too comprehensive to be a useful guide. The book is a remarkable, fascinating achievement but probably better off on the bookshelf than in your backpack.

A less bulky companion for the serious traveller is the *Tibet Handbook* by Gyurme Dorje. If you have been to Tibet before, have a specialist interest and are interested in *really* getting off the beaten track, this is currently the pick of the pack. It covers both Tibet and the Tibetan areas of Sichuan, Qinghai and Gansu provinces.

Mapping the Tibetan World, published by Khotan, is strong on maps, as you would expect, but the text is limited. Only one-third of the guide is concerned with the Tibetan Autonomous Region (TAR).

Tibet Overland: A Route and Planning Guide for Mountain Bikers and Other Overlanders by Kym McConnell is strong on the Lhasa-Kathmandu route.

Finally, the best companion to the book you are holding in your hands is *Trekking in Tibet – A Traveler's Guide* by Gary McCue. This well-researched guide has detailed information on treks around Lhasa, Ü, Tsang and western Tibet, and is indispensable for anyone whose primary interest in Tibet is in exploring the country on foot.

Travel

There are a number of books around documenting the exploits of visitors to Tibet. A classic is Heinrich Harrer's *Seven Years in Tibet* translated from the German in 1952 and made into a film in 1997. It is an engaging account of Harrer's sojourn in Tibet in the final years before the Chinese takeover. He wrote a somewhat less engaging sequel in *Return to Tibet*.

For starry-eyed dreamers *Magic & Mystery in Tibet* by Alexandra David-Neel has the lot – flying nuns, enchanted daggers, ghosts and demons, and also some interesting background information on the mystic side of Tibet. Another David-Neel title to look out for is *My Journey to Lhasa*. See the boxed text 'Alexandra David-Neel' later in this chapter for information about the author and her travels in Tibet.

Anyone heading out to western Tibet simply has to get hold of a copy of *A Mountain in Tibet* by Charles Allen. This superbly crafted book takes a look at the holy Mt Kailash and the attempts of early European explorers to reach it and to determine its geographical significance. Allen builds on this work with the recent *Search for Shangri-La* in which he returns to western Tibet to examine the region's pre-Buddhist history and mythology, focusing on Bön. For other books on Mt Kailash, see the boxed text 'Kailash & Manasarovar Books' in the Ngari (Western Tibet) chapter.

Peter Hopkirk's *Trespassers on the Roof of the World – The Race for Lhasa* is another book that is primarily concerned with the European assault on Tibet, and it makes superb reading.

An interesting, little-known book worth looking out for is *Captured in Tibet* by Robert Ford. This is the account of a radio operator employed by the Tibetan government in Chamdo who was incarcerated for four years by the Chinese after their takeover for the alleged murder of a pro-Chinese lama. Ford is not blind to the inefficiencies that characterised the former lamaist government but at the same time has a great sympathy for the Tibetan people.

A Stranger in Tibet by Scott Berry tells the fascinating story of Kawaguchi Ekai, a young Japanese monk who was one of the first foreigners to reach Lhasa in 1900 and who managed to stay over a year in the capital before his identity was discovered and he was forced to flee the country.

There are a couple of early travel books around that make for good reads. One of the classics is Robert Byron's *First Russia, Then Tibet*. Peter Fleming's *Bayonets to Lhasa* is an exciting blow-by-blow account of the British invasion of Tibet in 1904 led by Francis Younghusband.

Running a Hotel on the Roof of the World by Alec Le Seur is a comic recollection of the day-to-day (mis)adventures of the former Lhasa Holiday Inn in the 1980s and 1990s by a manager who worked there for five years. It takes time to kick into gear but really hits its stride describing the hotel's surreal culture clashes, eccentric characters and various doomed PR schemes.

Below Another Sky: A Mountain Adventure in Search of a Lost Father by Rick Ridgeway ruminates on a journey made through Tibet to Minyak Gonkar in western Sichuan with the daughter of a friend of Ridgeway's whose father died on the mountain during an earlier 1980 expedition. More than just a mountaineering book, Ridgeway reflects (often movingly) on the interconnected meanings of life, death and mountains.

Frank Kingdon Ward's Riddle of the Tsangpo Gorges, edited by Kenneth Cox, is a large-format book that presents Ward's original 1924–25 text alongside details of recent expeditions into the remote areas around Namche Barwa.

Finally, Walt Unsworth has written a 700-page book simply called *Everest*. This is the perfect companion for a trip to Base Camp and further, even if it is a bit hefty to lug around with you. It has fascinating accounts of all the early attempts to reach the peak and some of the key successful later attempts.

History & Politics

It is difficult to find a general history of Tibet that is worth recommending. The standard text is *Tibet and Its History* by Hugh Richardson, a book that is weak on the early history of Tibet and concentrates mainly on the years from the Gelugpa ascendancy to the Chinese takeover.

A Cultural History of Tibet by David Snellgrove & Hugh Richardson is perhaps a better introduction to the history and culture of Tibet, but is marred for the general reader by the use of a scholarly and at times indecipherable transliteration system of Tibetan;

Samye Monastery, for example, is rendered 'bSam-yas'.

The most accessible history of modern Tibet is *Tears of Blood – A Cry for Tibet* by Mary Craig. This riveting and distressing account of the Tibetan experience since the Chinese takeover should be read by every visitor to Tibet.

An excellent scholarly account of modern Tibet is Melvyn Goldstein's *A History of Modern Tibet 1913–1959 – The Demise of the Lamaist State*. It gives a blow-by-blow account of the critical years that saw Tibet lose what independence it had to its powerful eastern neighbour. Interestingly, it pulls no punches in showing the intrigues, superstitions and governmental ineptitude that led to the demise of the Lhasa government.

The Snow Lion and the Dragon, also by Melvyn Goldstein, is worth wading through if you want a dispassionate and unsentimental analysis of the historically complex issue of China's claims to Tibet, and the Dalai Lama's options in dealing with the current Chinese leadership.

Another detailed (but weighty) look at modern Tibetan history, this time since 1947, is *The Dragon in the Land of Snows* by Tsering Shakya. This is the definitive account for anyone with a serious interest in modern Tibetan history.

The Search for the Panchen Lama by Isabel Hilton is a look at the political intricacies of Tibet, with an emphasis on the controversial Panchen Lama and China's abduction of his current reincarnation.

Biography

Another illuminating glimpse of the Tibetan experience is provided by *Freedom in Exile: The Autobiography of the Dalai Lama*. With great humility the Dalai Lama outlines his personal philosophy, his hope to be reunited with his homeland and the story of his life. *Kundun* by Mary Craig is a biography of the family of the Dalai Lama.

Fire Under Snow: Testimony of a Tibetan Prisoner by Palden Gyatso is a moving autobiography that recounts Gyatso's life as a Buddhist monk imprisoned for 33 years for refusing to denounce the Dalai Lama.

Sorrow Mountain: The Journey of a Tibetan Warrior Nun by Ani Pachen & Adelaide Donnelly offers a slightly different perspective, this time from that of a nun who became a resistance leader and was imprisoned by the Chinese for 21 years before escaping to India.

People & Society

Probably the best wide-ranging introduction to Tibet can be found in *Tibet: Its History, Religion and People* by Thubten Jigme Norbu & Colin Turnbull. It is an account from within Tibet (the principal author is the Dalai Lama's brother) and is perhaps not as objective as it might have been. The book does, however, offer a great deal of insight into how Tibetans perceive and organise their world. Written in 1972, it can be a bit hard to find.

Also highly recommended is John Avedon's *In Exile from the Land of Snows*. This is largely an account of the Tibetan community in Dharamsala, but is an excellent and informative read.

Kate Karko's *Namma: A Tibetan Love Story* is the unusual story of a young woman from London who married a Tibetan and lived with his extended family of nomads on the plains of north-eastern Tibet for six months. The book offers an interesting, insightful and humorous close-up look at traditional Tibetan life and at the differences between Western and Tibetan cultures.

Those with a more academic bent should look out for *Civilised Shamans – Buddhism in Tibetan Societies* by Geoffrey Samuel, a fascinating anthropological investigation into the nature of Tibetan Buddhism and its relationship with the indigenous Bön faith – heavy but rewarding reading.

The authoritative work on Bön is *The Bon Religion of Tibet* by Per Kvaerne.

Art

The Art of Tibet by Robert Fisher is a portable colour guide to all the arts of Tibet, from the iconography of *thangkas* (Tibetan religious paintings usually framed by silk brocade) to statuary.

If you are interested in actually creating, not just understanding, Tibetan art, look for the master work on the subject, *Tibetan Thangka Painting: Methods & Materials* by David P Jackson & Janice A Jackson.

Buddhism

A good, lucid exposition of Tibetan Buddhism? Well, they are not that easy to come by. A lot of books seem to assume that you want to practise Buddhism rather than just know about it, which of course is a tricky theoretical distinction.

A good primer for Buddhism in general is *A Short History of Buddhism* by Edward Conze.

The classic introduction to Tibetan Buddhism – although many of its conclusions and observations are disputed by contemporary Tibetologists – is Charles Bell's *The Religion of Tibet*. For a more modern overview, try *Introduction to Tibetan Buddhism* by John Powers.

Keith Dowman's *Sacred Life of Tibet* builds on his earlier *Power Places of Central Tibet* to provide an excellent insight into how Tibetans see the spiritual landscape of their land. It also offers a pilgrim's perspective on travelling in Tibet.

The Dalai Lama is a one-man publishing empire – it's amazing he gets the time! Many of the books attributed to the Dalai Lama are actually transcripts of public lectures. The best place to start is with the most popular titles: *The Art of Happiness*, *Ethics for the New Millennium*, *The Meaning of Life* and *The Power of Compassion*.

The Tibetan Book of Living and Dying by Sogyal Rinpoche is an excellent background commentary on *The Tibetan Book of the Dead* and the Dzogchen tradition. Sogyal has a long tradition of contact with Western students, and several travellers have recommended the book for both beginners and advanced practitioners.

There are many other modern guides to practising Tibetan Buddhism – a quick search for Western authors such as Lama Surya Das and Pema Chodron will yield a good selection of books dealing with Tibetan Buddhist concepts in a modern context.

Fiction

The enduring myth of Shangri-la owes much to James Hilton's 1937 classic novel *Lost Horizon*, which tells the story of a group of Westerners who crash land into an earthly paradise somewhere in remote Tibet. The Chinese recently claimed to have proof that Hilton based his Shangri-la on Tibetan communities in north-west Yunnan.

Sherlock Holmes – The Missing Years by Jamyang Norbu chronicles Holmes' two years in Tibet. (Holmes was killed off by Arthur Conan Doyle, only to be resurrected two years later by public demand.) Fans of Conan Doyle or Kipling's *Kim* will love this pastiche. The first half set in India is classic Conan Doyle; the New Agey climax is harder to swallow.

The Third Eye by Lobsang Rampa was a fabulously popular first-hand account of Tibetan mysticism in the 1950s, selling millions of copies until it came out that the author Lobsang Rampa was actually one Cyril Hoskins, a plumber from Cornwall.

The Rose of Tibet by Lionel Davidson, also from the Lobsang Rangpa school of Tibetan history, is very readable and surprisingly informative. The novel's Yamdring Monastery is closely based on the Samding Monastery with its female incarnate lama.

Children's Books

The Mountains of Tibet by Mordicai Gerstein is a pictorial book for young children which a few readers have recommended. In Kathmandu there are several bookshops that sell Tibetan thangka and mandala colouring books.

Finally, kids (and most adults) will love Hergé's timeless *Tintin in Tibet*.

FILMS

In 1997 Tibet was Hollywood's flavour of the month (see the boxed text 'Tibet Chic'), with two big-box-office releases focused on Tibet.

Seven Years in Tibet was the crowd puller. The US$70-million film tells the story of the daring escape of Heinrich Harrer (as portrayed by Brad Pitt) and Peter Aufschnaiter (David Thewlis) from a prisoner-of-war

Tibet Chic

Hollywood's flirtation with Tibet started way back in 1937 with the film version of James Hilton's classic *Lost Horizon* featuring Ronald Coleman, John Howard and Jane Wyatt. The pseudo-Tibet theme continued with such films as *The Golden Child* (1986), apparently inspired by the young Karmapa of Tsurphu Monastery, and Bernardo Bertolucci's *Little Buddha* (1993). But it was the release of *Seven Years in Tibet* and *Kundun* in 1997, two films detailing the Chinese invasion of Tibet, that really made Tibet chic.

Richard Gere remains the most outspoken advocate of Tibetan independence in Tinseltown, using the Academy Awards ceremony in 1992 as a platform to publicise the cause. But the Hollywood connection doesn't end here. Robert Thurman, the father of actress Uma Thurman, is the Tsongkhapa Professor of Indo-Tibetan Studies at Columbia University. Other stars with an active interest in Tibetan Buddhism include Harrison Ford, Goldie Hawn, Oliver Stone and Phil Jackson, the coach of the Chicago Bulls. Harrison Ford's wife Melissa Matheson wrote the screenplay for *Kundun* and Ford apparently spent several days reading the script out to the Dalai Lama to gauge his Holiness's reaction. Perhaps most surprising of all was the announcement that Steven Seagal, the pony-tailed kick-boxing movie star, has been discovered to be a reincarnated *trulku* (incarnate lama) of the Nyingmapa order of Tibetan Buddhism.

None of this is good PR for China. The Chinese government tried to get *Kundun* scrapped by holding hostage its business deals with Disney (the film's backers), but Disney admirably held firm. *Seven Years in Tibet* was all set to be filmed in northern India until the Indian authorities buckled under Chinese diplomatic pressure. Brad Pitt soon joined Richard Gere on the list of counter-revolutionary actors banned from entering China.

Tibet chic has spread to the music industry. Adam Yauch of the Beastie Boys, a confirmed Tibetan Buddhist, is the organiser of the now annual Tibet Freedom Concert, which has featured artists such as U2, Björk, Alanis Morissette, Radiohead, Blur, the Foo Fighters and Patti Smith. Other Buddhist musicians include Natalie Merchant and composer Phillip Glass, who composed the soundtrack for *Kundun*. Annie Lennox and Peter Gabriel have also voiced public support for the Tibetan cause.

Whether all this media fuss has actually helped the Tibetan cause is up for debate. Some argue that the hype merely helps to perpetuate a media myth of Tibet: that somehow Tibet is a remote fantasy and that the suffering of the Tibetan people isn't real and doesn't require any hard action. Back in Hollywood they grin knowingly: 'There's no such thing as bad press'.

---

camp in northern India, their epic trek across Tibet and their seven-year sojourn in Lhasa as aides to the young Dalai Lama.

A better film is Martin Scorsese's *Kundun* (*kundun* means 'presence' and is one of the names used to refer to the Dalai Lama). The film features an all-Tibetan and -Chinese cast, many of them descendants of the figures they portray (the Dalai Lama's mother, for example, is played by the Dalai Lama's niece). The cinematography in particular is gorgeous.

The Cup (Phörpa) is a Bhutanese comedy chronicling the increasingly desperate attempts of two Tibetan refugees in India to watch the World Cup final on TV. The film

(the first Tibetan-language feature film) features an all-monk cast and is well worth digging up. The first-time director Kyentse Norbu is himself an important Buddhist reincarnation.

Himalaya, by director Eric Valli, tells the epic story of Tibetan herders on the salt caravan from Nepal to Tibet. The cinematography is particularly gorgeous (it was filmed largely in Dolpo in Nepal) and, again, the cast is all Tibetan. The film was also released under the name *Caravan*.

Windhorse, by director Paul Wagner, is a drama set in Lhasa. It follows a Tibetan singer (played by singer Dadon Dawa Dolma) popular with the Chinese who faces a crisis of conscience when her cousin, a nun, is imprisoned and tortured for her religious beliefs. Some parts of the film were shot illegally in Tibet.

A Chinese film worth watching out for is acclaimed director Tian Zhuangzhuang's *The Horse Thief*, a documentary-style look at the nomads of eastern Tibet.

Possibly one to miss is the epic Chinese production *Red River Valley*, which depicts the Younghusband invasion from a very Chinese perspective (and features one of the authors of an earlier edition of this book as an extra!).

NEWSPAPERS & MAGAZINES

Unless you are fluent in Chinese or Tibetan, you can forget about browsing through newspapers while you are in Tibet. The Beijing English-language publication the *China Daily* occasionally turns up a couple of weeks late, but it is a boring read anyway. No foreign newspapers or magazines are available in Lhasa, even at the Lhasa Hotel. The lobby of the Pentoc Hotel keeps a print-out of world news downloaded from the Internet which is worth a browse if you're feeling cut off from the world.

A handful of Tibetan Buddhist 'lifestyle' magazines are published in the US:

Mandala This quarterly magazine is published by the Foundation for the Preservation of the Mahayana Tradition (FPMT).

Shambhala Sun (W www.shambhalasun.com) A bi-monthly US publication, Shambhala Sun has articles on various aspects of Buddhism and information on meditation centres, books, tour companies, music and retreats.

Tricycle (W www.tricycle.com) An American quarterly devoted to Buddhism, this magazine features frequent articles on Tibet.

RADIO & TV

There is unlikely to be anything that you would want to watch or listen to on the television or the radio while you are in Tibet. Tibet has its own TV channel (although most of it is in Chinese) and there are even local stations such as Shigatse TV! Broadcasts are made in both Mandarin and Tibetan.

If you have a short-wave radio you can pick up the BBC World Service and Voice of America. Frequencies vary according to the time of day. Both also broadcast a Tibetan-language service.

VIDEO SYSTEMS

China subscribes to the PAL video standard, the same as Australia, New Zealand, the UK and most of Europe.

PHOTOGRAPHY & VIDEO
Film & Equipment

Tibet is one of the most photogenic countries in the world and you should bring twice as much film as you think you'll need. It is fairly easy to pick up print film in Lhasa and Shigatse – Fuji and Konika film are available, almost always in 100ASA. It is more difficult to find slide film, but you can buy Sensia or Ektachrome film in Lhasa for around Y45 for 36 exposures. You won't find any slide film outside of Lhasa.

For video cameras, make sure you keep the batteries charged and have the necessary charger, plugs and transformer (see Electricity later in this chapter). It is possible to obtain video cartridges in Lhasa but make sure you buy the correct format. It is usually worth buying at least a few cartridges duty-free to start off your trip.

Believe it or not, it is actually possible to process print film in Lhasa, and with fairly good results. Down in the Potala area are a number of shops with the latest Japanese photo-processing machines. Photos can be processed in a few hours for around Y25.

Don't even think about processing slide film in Tibet, even if someone in Lhasa claims it is possible. Save your processing for home, Bangkok or Hong Kong. Even in Kathmandu, with the exception of a couple of professional outfits, it is a very risky proposition.

Technical Tips

Bear in mind, when taking photographs in Tibet, that special conditions prevail. For one, the dust gets into everything – make a point of carefully cleaning your lenses as often as possible. The high altitudes in

Tibet also mean that you are dealing with unusual light conditions. The best time to take photographs is when the sun is low in the sky: early in the morning and late in the afternoon. This does not mean that you should not take photographs at other times, but simply that getting a good exposure becomes more difficult – you are likely to end up with a shot full of dark shadows and bright points of light.

One useful accessory to cope with Tibet's harsh light conditions is a polarising filter. When using it, turn the filter until the contrast improves; if there are any clouds in the sky, they will become whiter as the sky itself becomes a deeper shade of blue.

Properly used, a video camera can give a fascinating record of your holiday. As well as videoing the obvious things – sunsets and spectacular views – remember to record some of the ordinary everyday details of life in the country. Often the most interesting things occur when you're actually intent on filming something else. Remember, too, that unlike still photography, video 'flows' – so, for example, you can shoot scenes of countryside rolling past the bus window, to give an overall impression that isn't possible with ordinary photos.

One good rule for beginners to follow is to try to film in long takes, and don't move the camera around too much. Otherwise, your video could well make your viewers seasick! If your camera has a stabiliser, you can use it to obtain good footage while travelling on various means of transport, even on bumpy roads.

Restrictions

Photography from planes and photographs of airports and military installations are prohibited; bridges may even be a touchy subject, but this is unlikely. Don't take any photos or especially video footage of civil unrest or public demonstrations. The Chinese are paranoid about foreign TV crews filming unauthorised documentaries on Tibet.

Restrictions on photography are also imposed at most monasteries, museums and archaeological sites. This has absolutely nothing to do with religious sensitivity and

everything to do with China protecting its inept postcard industry; in the case of flash photography, such restrictions do protect wall murals from damage. Inside the larger monasteries, a fee is often imposed in each room or building for taking a photograph. Generally this is Y50 per shot but you can often negotiate with the monks. Video fees can be up to Y800 (US$100!) in some monasteries. You are free, however, to take photographs of the exteriors of monasteries.

Be aware that these rules are generally enforced. If you want to snap a few photos where you shouldn't, then start with a new roll of film. This way, if it is ripped out of your camera, you won't lose 20 photos from some other part of Tibet as well.

Photographing People

Tibet is a great place for portraits. Generally, Tibetans do not mind their photograph being taken. Naturally, it is best to ask first. Tibetans, like other Asian people, do not like having their photograph taken while they are working (eg, monastery restoration crews) and cannot understand why anyone would want to take such a photograph anyway. Be discreet in taking such photographs and try not to upset anyone. The same rules apply for video – having a video camera shoved in their face is probably even more annoying and offensive for locals than a still camera. Always ask permission first.

It's not uncommon for Tibetans to ask you to take their photograph. Usually this is because they assume you have a Polaroid camera and can hand them the results immediately. You should try and explain, with sign language if necessary, that you can't give them a photograph on the spot before shooting. If you agree to send them a copy of the photo, please follow through on this.

TIME

Time throughout China – including Tibet – is set to Beijing time, which is eight hours ahead of GMT/UTC. When it is noon in Beijing it is also noon in far-off Lhasa, even if the sun only indicates around 9am or 10am.

ELECTRICITY

Electricity is 220V, 50 cycles AC. Plugs come in at least four designs – three-pronged angled pins (like in Australia), three-pronged round pins (like in Hong Kong), two flat pins (US style but without the ground wire) or two narrow round pins (European style), and three rectangular pins (British style). Conversion plugs are easily purchased in Hong Kong but are damn near impossible to find in China. Interestingly, Chinese extension lines often end in a unit that accommodates all the different styles of plug in regular use.

Considering the remoteness of Tibet, it is surprising just how many towns and villages are supplied with electricity. Nevertheless, most monasteries are very poorly lit and in western Tibet there is very little in the way of electricity. Bring a small but good-quality torch (flashlight) from abroad. Chinese torches are awful – 50% of the time they do not work and the bulbs seldom last as long as the batteries.

WEIGHTS & MEASURES

The metric system is widely used in China. However, traditional Chinese measures are often used for domestic transactions and you may come across them. Chinese traders measure fruit and vegetables by the *jin* (500g). Smaller measurements (eg, for dumplings) are measured in *liang* (50g). The following conversions may help:

metric	Chinese	imperial
1m	3 *chi*	3.28 feet
1km	2 *li*	0.62 miles
1 hectare	15 *mu*	2.47 acres
1L	1 *gongsheng*	0.22 gallons
1kg	2 *jin*	2.2 pounds

LAUNDRY

The Kirey and Banak Shol hotels in Lhasa offer free laundry services, while others such as the Pentoc charge around Y15 for a bagful. Top-end hotels charge considerably more. The Tenzin Hotel in Shigatse also washes clothes.

Otherwise you are pretty much on your own. All but the crummiest hotel rooms provide a bowl for washing, even if the water supply is less than reliable. Small packets of soap powder (eg, Tide) can be bought almost anywhere.

TOILETS

Chinese toilets might be fairly dismal, but Tibetan toilets make them look like little bowers of heaven. The standard model is a deep hole in the ground that bubbles and gives off noxious vapours. Many people (including women with long skirts) urinate and defecate in the street. On the plus side there are some fabulous 'toilets with a view' in Tibet. Honours go to the Samye Monastery Guesthouse, the Sakya Guesthouse, the public toilets in the Potala, and the small village of Pasum on the way to Everest Base Camp.

With the exception of the odd hotel here and there, toilets in Tibet are of the squat variety – as the cliches go, good for the digestion and character building too. Stock up on toilet paper in Lhasa and Shigatse. Be warned that toilets are not secure – keep an eye on valuables. And finally, a tip for the boys: If there's nobody about, the women's toilets are always cleaner than the men's.

HEALTH

Tibet poses particular risks to your health, although for the large part these are associated with the high average altitude of the plateau. There is no need to be overly worried: Very few travellers are adversely affected by the altitude for very long, and greater risks are present in the form of road accidents and dog bites. Insect-borne and infectious diseases are quite rare because of the altitude.

Sensible travellers will rely on their own medical knowledge and supplies when travelling to Tibet. It is a very isolated place, and outside Lhasa there is very little in the way of expert medical care available. Read the following section carefully for information on how to make your trip a safer one.

Predeparture Planning

Immunisations China does not officially require any immunisations for entry into the country, but the further off the beaten track

A Fall from Grace (or Full of Shit?)

In Lhasa I wanted to use a typical public toilet, so I went to the ones across from the Holiday Inn (now the Lhasa Hotel). I have never had problems with toilets in China before, and although I read in the Lonely Planet guide that the toilets in Lhasa were particularly disgusting, I didn't think it would be a problem. It was bad luck (or perhaps stupidity) that led me to the wrong entrance to the toilet, the entrance from whence the shit is collected. It was like a swimming pool. It was quite dark inside, but I could see it was very dirty and I knew I had to be careful not to fall down. To me it looked like a real floor, I thought the shit was only on the surface. It wasn't.

I took one step, and fell in. I went under (it was really deep – I am 1.8m tall!), swallowed a mouthful, and then I managed to get out. All I could do when I got out was laugh – I could not believe something like that could really happen! There was a Canadian guy waiting for me in the main street and when he saw me I had to laugh again. The only thing I could say was that I was full of shit!

We went to the Holiday Inn, but the staff wouldn't allow me inside. A group of Italians outside the hotel tried to hose me down on the lawn next door. The water was extremely cold. I took my clothes off piece by piece. Fortunately a very nice man from the management of the Holiday Inn sent somebody to take me inside the hotel. I felt quite embarrassed as I walked through the lobby, freezing, almost naked and still very dirty. Everyone was staring at me!

I took a long hot shower. The hotel staff gave me some salt water to make me vomit, and the Canadian guy bought me some underwear and nice Chinese clothes. I went to the doctor because I was concerned that swallowing shit may not be good for your health. The doctor gave me some medicine for worms and to cleanse my insides.

I had to throw away my little backpack and its contents (including Lonely Planet's *China* and *Tibet*, both new). Also my money went a funny colour and was very wet and stinky for a few days, so I had some trouble spending it. Neither my passport nor student card looked very nice, and I had to get new ones.

I read in the Lonely Planet that, thank God, no-one has ever fallen into a Tibetan toilet! In your new edition you may have to correct that.

Kerstin Knopf

you go the more necessary it is to take precautions. The World Health Organization (WHO) requires travellers who have come from an area infected with yellow fever to be vaccinated before entering the country. Record all vaccinations on an International Health Certificate, available from a doctor or government health department.

Plan ahead for getting your vaccinations: Some of them require more than one injection, while some vaccinations should not be given together. Note that some vaccinations should not be given during pregnancy or to people with allergies.

It is recommended that you seek medical advice at least six weeks before travelling. Be aware that there is a greater risk of all kinds of disease with children and during pregnancy.

Discuss your requirements with your doctor, but vaccinations you should consider for this trip include the following (for more details about the diseases themselves, see the individual disease entries later in this section).

Diphtheria & Tetanus Vaccinations for these two diseases are usually combined and are recommended for everyone. After an initial course of three injections (usually given in childhood), boosters are necessary every 10 years.

Hepatitis A The vaccine for Hepatitis A (eg, Avaxim, Havrix 1440 or VAQTA) provides long-term immunity (possibly more than 10 years) after an initial injection and a booster at six to 12 months. Alternatively, an injection of gamma globulin can provide short-term protection against hepatitis A – two to six months, depending on the dose given. It is not a vaccine, but is ready-made antibody collected from

Medical Kit Check List

Following is a list of items you should consider including in your medical kit – consult your pharmacist for brands available in your country.

☐ **Aspirin or paracetamol (acetaminophen in the USA)** – for pain or fever

☐ **Antihistamine** – for allergies, eg, hay fever; to ease the itch from insect bites or stings; and to prevent motion sickness

☐ **Cold and flu tablets, throat lozenges and nasal decongestant**

☐ **Multivitamins** – consider for long trips, when dietary vitamin intake may be inadequate

☐ **Antibiotics** – consider including these if you're travelling well off the beaten track; see your doctor, as they must be prescribed, and carry the prescription with you

☐ **Loperamide or diphenoxylate** – 'blockers' for diarrhoea

☐ **Prochlorperazine or metaclopramide** – for nausea and vomiting

☐ **Rehydration mixture** – to prevent dehydration, which may occur, for example, during bouts of diarrhoea; particularly important when travelling with children

☐ **Insect repellent, sunscreen, lip balm and eye drops**

☐ **Calamine lotion, sting relief spray or aloe vera** – to ease irritation from sunburn and insect bites or stings

☐ **Antifungal cream or powder** – for fungal skin infections and thrush

☐ **Antiseptic (such as povidone-iodine)** – for cuts and grazes

☐ **Bandages, Band-Aids (plasters) and other wound dressings**

☐ **Water purification tablets or iodine**

☐ **Scissors, tweezers and a thermometer** – note that mercury thermometers are prohibited by airlines

☐ **Sterile kit** – in case you need injections in a country with medical hygiene problems; discuss with your doctor

☐ **Homeopathic medicines** – useful homeopathic medicines include gentiana for altitude sickness, echinacea, and tea-tree oil for cuts and scrapes

blood donations. It is reasonably effective and, unlike the vaccine, it is protective immediately, but because it is a blood product, there are concerns about its long-term safety. Hepatitis A vaccine is also available in a combined form, Twinrix, with hepatitis B vaccine. Three injections over a six-month period are required, the first two providing substantial protection against hepatitis A.

Hepatitis B China (although not so much Tibet) is one of the world's great reservoirs of hepatitis B infection. This disease is spread by contact with blood or by sexual activity. Vaccination involves three injections, the quickest course being over three weeks with a booster at 12 months.

Polio This serious, easily transmitted disease is still prevalent in many developing countries, including China. Everyone should keep up to date with this vaccination, which is normally given in childhood. A booster every 10 years maintains immunity.

Rabies Officially there is no rabies in Tibet. All the same, there are an awful lot of rabid-looking dogs about. Recent surveys by the Chinese indicate that instances of rabies may have occurred in Qinghai, which borders Tibet. Vaccination should be considered if you are spending a month or longer in Tibet, especially if you are cycling, handling animals, caving or travelling to remote areas, and for children (who may not report a bite). Pretravel rabies vaccination involves having three injections over 21 to 28 days. The vaccine will not give you 100% immunity, but will greatly extend the time you have for seeking treatment. If someone who has been vaccinated is bitten or scratched by an animal they will require two booster injections of vaccine, while those not vaccinated will require more.

Tuberculosis The risk of tuberculosis (TB) to travellers is usually very low, unless you will be living with or closely associated with local people in high-risk areas. As most healthy adults do not develop symptoms, a skin test before and after travel to determine whether exposure has occurred may be considered. A vaccination (BCG) is recommended for children and young adults living in these areas for three months or more.

Typhoid This is an important vaccination to have in Tibet where hygiene standards are low. Available either as an injection or oral capsules. A combined hepatitis A–typhoid vaccine was launched recently but its availability is still limited – check with your doctor to find out its status in your country.

Yellow Fever This disease is not endemic in China and a vaccine for yellow fever is required only if you are coming from an infected area.

Health Insurance Make sure you have adequate health insurance. Keep in mind that Tibet is a very isolated place, and if you become seriously injured or very sick here, you may need to be evacuated by air. Under these circumstances, you don't want to find yourself without health insurance. For more information, see Travel Insurance under Visas & Documents earlier in this chapter.

Travel Health Guides Lonely Planet's *Healthy Travel Asia & India* is a handy pocket size and is packed with useful information including pretrip planning, emergency first aid, immunisation and disease information, and what to do if you get sick on the road. *Travel with Children* from Lonely Planet also includes advice on travel health for younger children.

Other detailed health guides include:

CDC's Complete Guide to Healthy Travel Recommendations for international travel from the US Centers for Disease Control & Prevention.
Staying Healthy in Asia, Africa & Latin America by Dirk Schroeder. A detailed and well-organised guide.
Travellers' Health by Dr Richard Dawood. This is comprehensive, easy to read, authoritative and highly recommended, although it's rather large to lug around.
Where There Is No Doctor by David Werner. A very detailed guide intended for people going to work in a developing country.

There are also a number of excellent travel health sites on the Internet. From the Lonely Planet Web site (W www.lonelyplanet.com) there are links to the WHO and the US Centers for Disease Control & Prevention.

Other Preparations Make sure you're healthy before you start travelling. If you are going on a long trip make sure your teeth are OK. If you wear glasses, take a spare pair and your prescription.

If you require a particular medication take a good supply, as it may not be available in Tibet. Take part of the packaging showing the generic name rather than the brand, which will make getting replacements easier. To avoid problems, it's a good idea to have a legible prescription or letter from your doctor to show that you legally use the medication.

Basic Rules

Food There is an old colonial adage that says 'If you can cook it, boil it or peel it you can eat it…otherwise forget it'. Vegetables and fruit should be washed with purified or bottled water or peeled where possible. Beware of ice cream that is sold in the street or anywhere it might have been melted and refrozen; if there's any doubt (eg, a power cut in the last day or two) steer well clear. Undercooked meat should be avoided.

If a place looks clean and well run and the vendor also looks clean and healthy, then the food is probably safe. In general, places that are packed with travellers or locals will be fine, while empty restaurants are questionable. Chinese food in particular is cooked over a high heat, which kills most germs.

Water The number-one rule is *be careful of the water* and especially ice. If you don't know for certain that the water is safe assume the worst. In urban centres Tibetans, like the Chinese, boil their drinking water making it safe to drink hot or cooled. In the country you should boil your own water or treat it with water-purification tablets. Milk should be treated with suspicion as it will

Everyday Health

Normal body temperature is up to 37°C (98.6°F); more than 2°C (4°F) higher indicates a high fever. The normal adult pulse rate is 60 to 100 per minute (children 80 to 100, babies 100 to 140). As a general rule the pulse increases about 20 beats per minute for each 1°C (2°F) rise in fever.

Respiration (breathing) rate is also an indicator of illness. Count the number of breaths per minute: Between 12 and 20 is normal for adults and older children (up to 30 for younger children, 40 for babies). People with a high fever or serious respiratory illness breathe more quickly than normal. More than 40 shallow breaths a minute may indicate pneumonia.

be unpasteurised in the countryside, although boiled milk is fine if it is kept hygienically. Soft drinks and beer are always available wherever there is a shop, and these are always safe to drink, as is tea. Locally brewed beer, *chang*, is another matter. It is often made with contaminated well water and there is always some risk in drinking it.

Water Purification The simplest way to purify water is to boil it thoroughly. At Tibet's high altitude water boils at a lower temperature and germs are less likely to be killed, so make sure you boil water for at least 10 minutes.

Consider purchasing a water filter for a long trip. There are two main kinds of filters. Total filters take out all parasites, bacteria and viruses, and make water safe to drink. They are often expensive, but they can be more cost effective than buying bottled water. Simple filters (which can even be a nylon mesh bag) take out dirt and larger foreign bodies from the water so that chemical solutions work much more effectively; if water is dirty, chemical solutions may not work at all. It's very important when buying a filter to read the specifications, so that you know exactly what it removes from the water and what it doesn't. Simple filtering will not remove all dangerous organisms, so if you cannot boil water it should be treated chemically.

Chlorine tablets (eg, Puritabs or Steritabs) will kill many pathogens, but not giardia and amoebic cysts. Iodine is more effective for purifying water and is available in tablet form (eg, Potable Aqua). Follow the directions carefully and remember that too much iodine can be harmful.

Medical Problems & Treatment

Self-diagnosis and treatment can be risky, so you should always seek medical help. Although we do give drug dosages in this section, they are for emergency use only. Correct diagnosis is vital.

In Tibet the top-end hotels can usually recommend a good place to go for advice. In most places in Tibet standards of medical attention are so low that for some ailments the best advice is to go straight to Lhasa and in extreme cases get on a plane to Chengdu or Kathmandu.

Global Doctor (☎ 028-678 6746, fax 678 6746), in the Holiday Inn Crowne Plaza, 31 Zongfu Lu, Chengdu, offers pre-Tibet medical examinations and a Tibet Travellers Assist Package that can be useful if you are worried about an existing medical condition. See the Web site ⓦ www.eglobaldoctor .com for details.

Antibiotics should ideally be administered only under medical supervision. Take only the recommended dose at the prescribed intervals and use the whole course, even if the illness seems to be cured earlier. Stop immediately if there are any serious reactions and don't use the antibiotic at all if you are unsure that you have the correct one. Some people are allergic to commonly prescribed antibiotics such as penicillin; carry this information (eg, on a bracelet) when travelling.

Environmental Hazards

Acute Mountain Sickness Lack of oxygen at high altitudes (over 2500m) affects most people to some extent. The effect may be mild or severe and it occurs because less oxygen reaches the muscles and the brain at high altitude, requiring the heart and lungs to compensate by working harder. Acute mountain sickness (AMS), or altitude sickness, is common at high altitudes; relevant factors are the rate of ascent and individual susceptibility. The major risk factor in AMS is the speed with which you make your ascent. Any traveller who flies or buses into Lhasa, whose elevation is just over 3600m, is likely to experience some symptoms of AMS. You should take care to acclimatise slowly and take things easy for the first couple of days. On average, one tourist a year dies in Tibet from altitude sickness – make sure it is not you.

AMS is a notoriously fickle affliction and can affect even trekkers and walkers accustomed to walking at high altitudes. AMS has been fatal at 3000m, although 3500m to 4500m is the usual range.

Acclimatisation AMS is linked to low atmospheric pressure. Those who travel up to Everest Base Camp, for instance, reach an altitude where atmospheric pressure is about half of that at sea level.

With an increase in altitude the human body needs time to develop physiological mechanisms to cope with the decreased oxygen. This process of acclimatisation is still not fully understood, but is known to involve modifications in breathing patterns and heart rate induced by the autonomic nervous system, and an increase in the blood's oxygen-carrying capabilities. These compensatory mechanisms usually take about one to three days to develop at a particular altitude. Once you are acclimatised to a given height you are unlikely to get AMS at that height, but you can still get ill when you travel higher. If the ascent is too high and too fast, these compensatory reactions may not kick into gear fast enough.

Symptoms Mild symptoms of AMS are very common in travellers visiting high altitudes, and usually develop during the first 24 hours at altitude. Most visitors to Tibet will suffer from some symptoms; these will generally disappear through acclimatisation in several hours to several days.

Symptoms tend to be worse at night and include headache, dizziness, lethargy, loss of appetite, nausea, breathlessness and irritability. Difficulty sleeping is another common symptom, and many travellers have trouble sleeping for the first few days after arriving in Lhasa.

AMS may become more serious without warning and can be fatal. Symptoms are caused by the accumulation of fluid in the lungs and brain, and include breathlessness at rest, a dry irritative cough (which may progress to the production of pink, frothy sputum), severe headache, lack of coordination (typically leading to a 'drunken walk'), confusion, irrational behaviour, vomiting and eventually unconsciousness.

The symptoms of AMS, however mild, are a warning – be sure to take them seriously! Trekkers should keep an eye on each other as those experiencing symptoms, especially severe symptoms, may not be in a position to recognise them. One thing to note is that while the symptoms of mild AMS often precede those of severe AMS, this is not always the case. Severe AMS can strike with little or no warning.

Prevention The best way to prevent AMS is to avoid rapid ascents to high altitudes. If you fly or bus into Lhasa, take it easy for at least three days – for most travellers this is enough to get over any initial ill-effects. At this point you might step up your program by visiting a few sights around town. Within a week you should be ready for something a bit more adventurous, but do not push yourself to do anything that you are not comfortable with. If you are driving up from Kathmandu you will experience rapid altitude gain. An itinerary that takes you straight up to Everest Base Camp is unwise; plan to see it on your way back if possible.

To prevent acute mountain sickness:

- Ascend slowly. Have frequent rest days, spending two to three nights at each rise of 1000m. If you reach a high altitude by trekking, acclimatisation takes place gradually and you are less likely to be affected than if you fly directly to high altitude.
- Trekkers should bear in mind the climber's adage 'Climb high, sleep low'. It is always wise to sleep at a lower altitude than the greatest height reached during the day. High day climbs followed by a descent back to lower altitudes for the night are good preparation for high-altitude trekking. Also, once above 3000m, care should be taken not to increase the sleeping altitude by more than 400m per day. If the terrain won't allow for less than 400m of elevation gain, be ready to take an extra day off before tackling the climb.
- Drink extra fluids. The mountain air is dry and cold, and moisture is lost as you breathe. Evaporation of sweat may occur unnoticed and result in dehydration.
- Eat light, high-carbohydrate meals for more energy.
- Avoid alcohol as it may increase the risk of dehydration, and don't smoke.
- Avoid sedatives.
- When trekking, take a day off to rest and acclimatise if feeling over-tired. If you or anyone else in your party is having a tough time make allowances for unscheduled stops.

• Don't push yourself when climbing up to passes; rather, take plenty of breaks. You can usually get over the pass as easily tomorrow as you can today. Try to plan your itinerary so that long ascents can be divided into two or more days. Given the complexity and unknown variables involved with AMS and acclimatisation, trekkers should always err on the side of caution and ascend mountains slowly.

Treatment Treat mild symptoms by resting at the same altitude until recovery, usually a day or two. Take paracetamol or aspirin for headaches. If symptoms persist or become worse, however, *immediate descent* is necessary – even 500m can help.

The most effective treatment for severe AMS is to get down to a lower altitude as quickly as possible. In less severe cases the victim will be able to stagger down with some support; in other cases they may need to be carried down. Whatever the case, do not delay, as any delay could be fatal.

AMS victims may need to be flown out of Tibet as quickly as possible – make sure you have adequate travel insurance.

The drugs acetazolamide (Diamox) and dexamethasone are recommended by some doctors for the prevention of AMS. However, you should be aware that their use is controversial. They can reduce the symptoms, but they may also mask warning signs; severe and fatal AMS has occurred in people taking these drugs. Drug treatments should never be used to avoid descent or to enable further ascent.

Several hotels in Lhasa sell a Tibetan herbal medicine recommended by locals for easing the symptoms of mild altitude sickness. The medicine is known as *solomano* in Tibetan and *hongjingtian* in Chinese. A box of vials costs around Y25.

Heat Exhaustion Dehydration and salt deficiency can cause heat exhaustion. Take time to acclimatise to high temperatures, drink sufficient liquids and do not do anything too physically demanding.

Salt deficiency is characterised by fatigue, lethargy, headaches, giddiness and muscle cramps; salt tablets may help, but adding extra salt to your food is better.

Hypothermia Winter in Tibet is not to be taken lightly. Even in mid-summer, passes and high areas around northern Tibet and the Changtang can be hit without warning by sudden snow storms. You should always be prepared for cold, wet or windy conditions, especially if you're out walking, hitching or trekking at high altitudes or even taking a long bus trip over mountains (particularly at night).

Hypothermia occurs when the body loses heat faster than it can produce it and the core temperature of the body falls. It is surprisingly easy to progress from very cold to dangerously cold through a combination of wind, wet clothing, fatigue and hunger, even if the air temperature is above freezing.

It is best to dress in layers; silk, wool and some of the new artificial fibres are all good insulating materials. A hat is important, as a lot of heat is lost through the head. A strong, waterproof outer layer and a 'space' blanket for emergencies are essential. Carry basic supplies, including food that contains simple sugars to generate heat quickly, and fluid to drink.

Symptoms of hypothermia are exhaustion, numb skin (particularly toes and fingers), shivering, slurred speech, irrational or violent behaviour, lethargy, stumbling, dizzy spells, muscle cramps and violent bursts of energy. Irrationality may take the form of sufferers claiming they are warm and trying to take off their clothes.

To treat mild hypothermia, first get the person out of the wind and rain, remove their clothing if it's wet and replace it with dry, warm clothing. Give them hot liquids (not alcohol) and some high-energy, easily digestible food. Do not rub victims; instead, allow them to slowly warm themselves. This should be enough to treat the early stages of hypothermia. The early recognition and treatment of mild hypothermia is the only way to prevent severe hypothermia, which is a critical condition.

Frostbite This is the freezing of extremities, including fingers, toes and nose. Signs and symptoms of frostbite include a whitish or waxy cast to the skin, or even crystals on the surface, plus itching, numbness and pain. Warm the affected areas by immersing them in warm (not hot) water or with blankets or clothes, only until the skin becomes flushed. Frostbitten parts should not be rubbed. Pain and swelling are inevitable. Blisters should not be broken. Get medical attention right away.

Motion Sickness Eating lightly before and during a trip will reduce the chances of motion sickness. If you are prone to motion sickness try to find a place that minimises movement – near the wing on aircraft, near the centre on buses. Fresh air usually helps; reading and cigarette smoke don't. Commercial preparations for motion-sickness, which can cause drowsiness, have to be taken before the trip commences. Ginger (available in capsule form) and peppermint (including mint-flavoured sweets) are natural preventatives.

Sunburn It is very easy to get sunburnt in Tibet's high altitudes. Sunburn is more than just uncomfortable. Among the undesirable effects are premature skin ageing and possible skin cancer in later years. Sunscreen with a high sun protection factor (SPF), sunglasses and a wide-brimmed hat are good means of protection. Calamine lotion is good for treating mild sunburn.

Those with fair complexions should bring reflective sunscreen (containing zinc oxide or titanium oxide) with them. Apply the sunscreen to your nose and lips (and especially the tops of your ears if you are not wearing a hat).

Infectious Diseases
Respiratory Infections Upper respiratory tract infections (eg, the common cold) are a common ailment all over China, including Tibet. Why are they such a serious problem in China? Respiratory infections are aggravated by the high altitude, cold weather, air pollution, chain-smoking and overcrowded conditions which increase the opportunity for infection. But the main reason is that Chinese people spit a lot, thereby spreading the disease. It is a vicious circle: They are sick because they spit and they spit because they are sick.

Symptoms of influenza include fever, weakness and sore throat. Any upper respiratory tract infection, including influenza, can lead to complications such as bronchitis and pneumonia which may need to be treated with antibiotics. Seek medical help in this situation.

The Chinese treat bronchitis, which can be a complication of flu, with a powder made from the gall bladder of snakes – a treatment of questionable value, but there is no harm in trying it.

No vaccine offers complete protection, but there are vaccines against influenza and pneumococcal pneumonia which might help. The influenza vaccine is good for no more than a year.

Diarrhoea Simple things such as a change of water, food or climate can all cause a mild bout of diarrhoea (*la duzi* or 'spicy stomach' in Chinese), but a few rushed toilet trips with no other symptoms are not indicative of a major problem. Even Marco Polo got the runs.

Dehydration is the main danger with any diarrhoea, particularly in children or the elderly as it can occur quite quickly. Under all circumstances *fluid replacement* (at least equal to the volume being lost) is the most important thing to remember. Weak black tea with a little sugar, soda water, or soft drinks allowed to go flat and diluted 50% with clean water are all good. With severe diarrhoea a rehydrating solution is preferable to replace lost minerals and salts. Commercially available oral rehydration salts (ORS) are very useful; add them to boiled or bottled water. In an emergency you can make up a solution of six teaspoons of sugar and half a teaspoon of salt to a litre of boiled or bottled water. You need to drink at least the same volume of fluid that you are losing in bowel movements and vomiting. Urine is the best guide to the adequacy of replacement – if you have small amounts of concentrated urine, you need to drink more. Keep drinking small amounts often. Stick to a bland diet as you recover.

Loperamide or diphenoxylate can be used to bring relief from the symptoms, although they do not actually cure the problem. However, neither is available in China. A good Chinese equivalent is berberine hydrochloride *(huang lian su)*. Only use these drugs if you do not have access to toilets, eg, if you *must* travel. For children under 12 years these drugs are not recommended. Do not use these drugs if you have a high fever or are severely dehydrated.

In certain situations antibiotics may be required: diarrhoea with blood or mucus (dysentery), any diarrhoea with fever, profuse watery diarrhoea, persistent diarrhoea not improving after 48 hours and severe diarrhoea. These suggest a more serious cause of diarrhoea, in which case gut-paralysing drugs should be avoided.

In these situations, a stool test may be necessary to diagnose what bug is causing your diarrhoea, so you should seek medical help urgently. Where this is not possible the recommended drugs for bacterial diarrhoea (the most likely cause of severe diarrhoea in travellers) are norfloxacin 400mg twice daily for three days or ciprofloxacin 500mg twice daily for five days. These are not recommended for children or pregnant women. The drug of choice for children would be co-trimoxazole (Bactrim, Septrin or Resprim) with dosage dependent on weight. A five-day course is given. Ampicillin or amoxycillin may be given in pregnancy, but medical care is necessary.

Two other causes of persistent diarrhoea in travellers are giardiasis and amoebic dysentery.

Giardiasis (commonly known as giardia) is caused by a common parasite, *Giardia lamblia*. It is a type of diarrhoea that is relatively common in Tibet. Mountaineers often suffer from this problem. The parasite causing this intestinal disorder is present in contaminated water. Many kinds of mammals harbour this parasite, so you can get it easily from drinking 'pure mountain water' unless the area is devoid of animals. Just brushing your teeth using contaminated water is sufficient to get giardiasis, or any other gut bug. Symptoms include stomach cramps, nausea, a bloated stomach, watery, foul-smelling diarrhoea and frequent gas. Giardiasis can appear several weeks after you have been exposed to the parasite. The symptoms may disappear for a few days and then return; this can go on for several weeks.

Amoebic dysentery, caused by the protozoan *Entamoeba histolytica*, is characterised by a gradual onset of low-grade diarrhoea, often with blood and mucus. Cramping abdominal pain and vomiting are less likely than in other types of diarrhoea, and fever may not be present. It will persist until treated and can recur and cause other health problems.

You should seek medical advice if you think you have giardiasis or amoebic dysentery, but where this is not possible, tindazole or metronidazole are the recommended drugs. Treatment is a 2g single dose of tindazole or 250mg of metronidazole three times daily for five to 10 days.

Metronidazole is not easily obtained in Tibet, although equivalent drugs are available in Lhasa. If you are going to be travelling in high mountain areas, it might be a good idea to keep your own stock of metronidazole with you.

Hepatitis This is a general term for inflammation of the liver. Hepatitis is a common disease worldwide. There are several different viruses that cause hepatitis, and they differ in the way that they are transmitted. The symptoms are similar in all forms of the illness, and include fever, chills, headache, fatigue, feelings of weakness and aches and pains, followed by loss of appetite, nausea, vomiting, abdominal pain, dark urine, light-coloured faeces, jaundiced (yellow) skin and yellowing of the whites of the eyes. People who have had hepatitis should avoid alcohol for some time after the illness, as the liver needs time to recover.

Hepatitis A is transmitted by contaminated food and drinking water. You should seek medical advice, but there is not much you can do apart from resting, drinking lots of fluids, eating lightly and avoiding fatty foods.

Hepatitis A is most often spread in China and Tibet as a result of the custom of sharing food from a single dish rather than using separate plates and a serving spoon. It is wise to use the disposable chopsticks now freely available in most restaurants in Tibet, or else buy your own chopsticks and spoon. Hepatitis E is transmitted in the same way as hepatitis A; it can be particularly serious in pregnant women.

There are almost 300 million chronic carriers of hepatitis B in the world, and China has more cases than any other country – almost 20% of the population are believed to be carriers. It is spread through contact with infected blood, blood products or body fluids, for example through sexual contact, unsterilised needles and blood transfusions, or contact with blood via small breaks in the skin. Other risk situations include having a shave, tattoo or body piercing with contaminated equipment. The symptoms of hepatitis B may be more severe than those for type A and the disease can lead to long-term problems such as chronic liver damage, liver cancer or a long-term carrier state. Hepatitis C and D are spread in the same way as hepatitis B and can also lead to long-term complications.

There are vaccines against hepatitis A and B, but there are currently no vaccines against the other types of hepatitis. Following the basic rules about food and water (hepatitis A and E) and avoiding risk situations (hepatitis B, C and D) are important preventative measures.

HIV & AIDS Infection with the human immunodeficiency virus (HIV) may lead to acquired immune deficiency syndrome (AIDS), which is a fatal disease. Any exposure to blood, blood products or body fluids may put the individual at risk. The disease is often transmitted through sexual contact or dirty needles – vaccinations, acupuncture, tattooing and body piercing can be potentially as dangerous as intravenous drug use. HIV/AIDS can also be spread through infected blood transfusions; some developing countries cannot afford to screen blood used for transfusions.

HIV is not thought to be a major problem in Tibet, although anyone who intends to work or study in Tibet for longer than 12 months is required by the Chinese authorities to undergo an AIDS test.

If you do need an injection, ask to see the syringe unwrapped in front of you, or take a needle and syringe pack with you. Fear of HIV infection should never preclude treatment for serious medical conditions.

Sexually Transmitted Infections HIV/AIDS and hepatitis B can be transmitted through sexual contact – see the relevant sections earlier for details. Other sexually transmitted infections (STIs) include gonorrhoea, herpes and syphilis. Sores, blisters or rashes around the genitals and discharges or pain when urinating are common symptoms. In some STIs, such as wart virus or chlamydia, symptoms may be less marked or not observed at all, especially in women. Syphilis symptoms eventually disappear completely but the disease continues and can cause severe problems in later years. While abstinence from sexual contact is the only 100% effective prevention, using condoms is also effective. Gonorrhoea and syphilis are treated with antibiotics. The different STIs each require specific antibiotics. There is no cure for herpes or AIDS.

Condoms are available in China – the word is *baotao*, which translates literally as 'insurance glove'.

Cuts, Bites & Stings
See Less Common Diseases later for information on rabies, which is passed through animal bites.

Cuts & Scratches Wash any cut well and treat it with an antiseptic such as povidone-iodine. Where possible avoid bandages and Band-Aids, which can keep wounds wet.

Bedbugs & Lice Bedbugs live in various places, but particularly in dirty mattresses and bedding, evidenced by spots of blood on bedclothes or on the wall. Bedbugs leave itchy bites in neat rows. Calamine lotion or a sting-relief spray may help.

All lice cause itching and discomfort. They make themselves at home in your hair (head lice), your clothing (body lice) or in your pubic hair (crabs). You catch lice through direct contact with infected people or by sharing combs, clothing and the like. Powder or shampoo treatment will kill the lice. Infected clothing should then be washed in very hot, soapy water and left in the sun to dry.

Bites & Stings Bee and wasp stings are usually painful rather than dangerous. However, people who are allergic to them may have severe breathing difficulties and require urgent medical care. Calamine lotion or a sting-relief spray will give relief and ice packs will reduce the pain and swelling.

Leeches In the damp low-lying areas of eastern Tibet, leeches may be present; they attach themselves to your skin to suck your blood. Trekkers often get them on their legs or in their boots. Salt or a lighted cigarette end will make them fall off. Do not pull them off, as the bite is then more likely to become infected. Clean and apply pressure if the point of attachment is bleeding. An insect repellent may help keep them away.

Women's Health
Gynaecological Problems Antibiotic use, synthetic underwear, sweating and contraceptive pills can lead to fungal vaginal infections, especially when travelling in hot climates. Fungal infections are characterised by a rash, itch and discharge. Nystatin, miconazole or clotrimazole pessaries or vaginal cream are the usual treatment, but some people use a more traditional remedy involving vinegar or lemon-juice douches, or yogurt. Maintaining good personal hygiene and wearing loose-fitting clothes and cotton underwear may help prevent these infections.

Sexually transmitted infections are a major cause of vaginal problems. Symptoms include a smelly discharge, painful intercourse and sometimes a burning sensation when urinating. Medical attention should be sought and sexual partners must also be treated. For more information, see Sexually Transmitted Infections earlier. Besides abstinence, the best thing is to practise safe sex using condoms.

Pregnancy It is not advisable to travel to some places while pregnant as some vaccinations normally used to prevent serious diseases are not advisable during pregnancy (eg, yellow fever). In addition, some diseases are much more serious for the mother (and may increase the risk of a stillborn child) in pregnancy.

Most miscarriages occur during the first three months of pregnancy. Miscarriage is not uncommon and can occasionally lead to severe bleeding. The last three months should also be spent within reasonable distance of good medical care. A baby born as early as 24 weeks stands a chance of survival, but only in a good modern hospital. Pregnant women should avoid all unnecessary medication, although vaccinations should still be taken where needed. Additional care should be taken to prevent illness and particular attention should be paid to diet and nutrition. Alcohol and nicotine, for example, should be avoided.

Less Common Diseases
The following diseases pose a small risk to travellers, and so are only mentioned in passing. Seek medical advice if you think you may have any of these diseases.

Cholera This is the worst of the watery diarrhoeas and medical help should be sought. Outbreaks of cholera are generally widely reported, so you can avoid such problem areas. *Fluid replacement is the most vital treatment* – the risk of dehydration is severe as you may lose up to 20L a day. If there is a delay in getting to hospital, then begin taking tetracycline. The adult dose is 250mg four times daily. It is not recommended for children under nine years nor for pregnant women. Tetracycline may help shorten the illness, but adequate fluids are required to save lives.

Rabies This fatal viral infection is found in many countries. Although officially there is no rabies in Tibet, it would be foolish not to get treatment if you are bitten. Many animals can be infected (such as dogs, cats, bats and monkeys) and it is their saliva that is infectious. Any bite, scratch or even lick from an animal should be cleaned immediately and thoroughly. Scrub with soap and running water, and then apply alcohol or iodine solution. Medical help should be sought promptly to receive a course of injections to prevent the onset of symptoms and death.

At the time of writing, treatment for rabies was not available anywhere in Tibet and it was necessary to fly to Kathmandu or Chengdu. If you think you've been infected, get to Lhasa as quickly as you can and seek medical advice.

WOMEN TRAVELLERS

Sexual harassment is extremely rare in Tibet and foreign women seem to be able to travel here with few problems. Naturally, it is worth noticing what local women are wearing and how they are behaving, and making a bit of an effort to fit in, as you would in any other foreign country. Probably because of the harsh climate, Tibetan women dress in bulky layers of clothing that mask their femininity. It would be wise to follow their example and dress modestly, especially when visiting a monastery. Several women have written of the favourable reactions they have received from Tibetan women when wearing Tibetan dress.

Women may be forbidden to enter the *gönkhang* (protector chapel) of some monasteries.

GAY & LESBIAN TRAVELLERS

Homosexuality has historical precedents in Tibet, especially in Tibetan monasteries, where male lovers were known as *trap'i kedmen*, or 'monk's wife'. The Dalai Lama has sent mixed signals about homosexuality, describing gay sex as 'sexual misconduct', 'improper' and 'inappropriate', but also saying 'There are no acts of love between adults that one can or should condemn'.

The official attitude to gays and lesbians in China is also ambiguous, with responses ranging from Draconian penalties to tacit acceptance. Travellers are advised to act with discretion. Chinese men routinely hold hands and drape their arms around each other without anyone inferring any sexual overtones.

The Gay Buddhist Open Forum is an email group discussing Buddhist teachings and practise for gay men. To subscribe send a blank email to **e** gbof-subscribe@yahoo groups.com or visit the Web site **w** http://groups.yahoo.com/group/gbof.

Alexandra David-Neel

If you have doubts about going to Tibet as a solo woman then take Alexandra David-Neel as your inspiration. Traveller, operetta singer and one-time director of the Tunis Casino, David-Neel lived a fascinating and uncompromising life, making several trips to Tibet and neighbouring Tibetan areas. In 1912 she became the first Western woman to have an audience with a Dalai Lama, in this case the 13th Dalai Lama in Sikkim, who deemed her to be an emanation of Dorje Phagmo, Tibet's only female incarnation. At various times David-Neel spent 18 months in retreat in a cave in Sikkim, lived for two years at Kumbum Monastery in Amdo, lived for a while at Tashilhunpo Monastery on the invitation of the Panchen Lama and in 1924 became the first Western woman ever to enter Tibet (in disguise), travelling with a Sikkimese monk who became her adopted son. Caught in China during the outbreak of war, she spent most of WWII in Kangding in eastern Tibet.

Surprisingly, for such a nomadic soul, David-Neel had married in 1904 in Tunis and settled down for seven years before dreams of Tibet finally pulled her away again. Her husband tolerated and even encouraged her wanderlust (eventually becoming her manuscript editor) and the two corresponded regularly, even after their separation. It was a fascinating relationship that endured over 40 years. Alexandra David-Neel died in 1968, just before her 101st birthday.

DISABLED TRAVELLERS

Tibet can be a hard place for disabled travellers. The high altitudes, rough roads and lack of access make travel difficult. Monasteries in particular often involve a hike up a hillside or steep, very narrow steps. Few hotels offer any facilities for the disabled.

The Nepal-based company Navyo Nepal (☎ 01-280056, fax 227070, W www.navyo nepal.com) has some experience in running tours for the disabled to Tibet and Nepal. Its postal address is GPO Box 8974, PCN 329, Kathmandu, Nepal.

SENIOR TRAVELLERS

The main risks to senior travellers in Tibet are the altitude and the prevalence of China Syndrome or chronic bronchitis. See Respiratory Infections under Health for more details. When planning a trip try not to pack too much into a short time.

Eldertreks (☎ 800-741 7956, 416-588 5000, fax 416-588 9839, W www.eldertreks .com), 597 Markham St, Toronto, ON M6G 2LZ, Canada, offers organised trips to Tibet for over 50s.

If you wish to travel more independently but still require some health care, contact Travel Aides International (☎ 530-873 2977, W http://members.tripod.com/~Travel_us), which provides travel companions qualified in health care.

TRAVEL WITH CHILDREN

Once again altitude is the major problem in Tibet. Be especially careful with children as they won't be on the lookout for the signs of altitude sickness. Children don't get on with Tibetan food or toilets any better than grown ups. They also tire more easily from an endless round of visiting monasteries. Bring along *Tintin in Tibet* for when morale flags.

On the upside children can be a great icebreaker and generally generate a lot of interest. Many hotels have family rooms, which normally have three or four beds arranged in two connected rooms.

Tibet is probably not a great place to bring a very small child. You should bring all supplies (including nappies and medicines) with you. Small spoons can be useful

as most places have only chopsticks. There's plenty of boiling water to sterilise bottles etc. It's possible to make a cot from the copious numbers of duvets supplied with most hotel rooms.

USEFUL ORGANISATIONS

There are numerous Tibet-related information services scattered around the world. For some travellers these may be worth contacting for a wide range of information, from background information on Tibet to upcoming events, dharma talks, language courses, Tibet-related products, news items and charitable donations. Most advocate some form of independence for Tibet. Some of these offices are as follows:

Australia
Australian Tibetan Society (☎ 02-9489 0353, fax 9489 8563) PO Box 347, Killara, NSW 2071
Australia Tibet Council (☎ 02-9283 3466, fax 9283 3846, W www.atc.org.au) PO Box 1236, Potts Point, NSW 2011; contact Tony Williams, ATC Travel Officer at ☎ 03-9850 3200 or e travel@atc.org.au
Tibet Information Office (☎ 02-6285 4046, fax 6282 4301) 3 Weld St, Yarralumla, ACT 2600

Canada
Canada Tibet Committee (☎ 514-487 0665, fax 487 7825, W www.tibet.ca) 4675 Coolbrook Avenue, Montreal, QC H3X 247; plus branches throughout Canada

UK
Free Tibet Campaign (☎ 0870-770 0328, 020-7833 9958, W www.freetibet.org) 1 Rosoman Place, London EC1R 0JY
Tibet Foundation (☎ 020-7930 6001, fax 7930 6002, W www.tibet-foundation.org) 1 St James Market, London SWC1 Y4SB. The foundation runs language courses, provides information about upcoming events, produces a newsletter, sells Tibetan music and runs a shop.
Tibet House (☎ 020-7722 5378, fax 7722 0326, e tibetlondon@gn.apc.org) 1 Culworth St, London NW8 7AF
Tibet Information Network (TIN; ☎ 020-7814 9011, fax 7814 9015, W www.tibetinfo.net) 188–196 Old St, London EC1 9FR UK
Tibet Society (☎ 020-7272 1414, fax 7272 1410, W www.tibet-society.org.uk) Tower House, 139 Fonthill Rd, Finsbury Park, London N4 3HF

USA
Conservancy for Tibetan Art & Culture (☎ 703-755 1533, fax 847 8805, W www.tibetan culture.org) PO Box 6598, McLean, VA 22106-6598. The conservancy aims to preserve and promote Tibetan culture through teachings, exhibitions, symposia and cultural research.
International Campaign for Tibet (☎ 202-785 1515, W www.savetibet.org) 1825 K St NW, Suite 520, Washington DC 20006
Tibetan Cultural Center (☎ 812-855 8222) 3655 South Snoddy Rd, Bloomington, IN 47402
Tibet House Cultural Centre (☎ 212-807 0563, fax 807 0565, W www.tibethouse.org) 22 West 15th St, New York, NY 10011
Students for a Free Tibet (☎ 212-358 0071, W www.tibet.org/sft/) 735 E 9th St, #1FW, New York, NY 10009. This organisation has chapters at many university campuses.

DANGERS & ANNOYANCES
Theft
Tibet is very poor and it is to be expected that there will be a risk of theft when travelling here. Trekkers in the Everest region have reported problems with petty theft, and pickpockets work parts of Lhasa. That said, Tibet is safer than most other provinces of China and indeed safer than most countries in the region.

Pickpocketing is the most common form of theft. The best protection is attentiveness to your surroundings and avoiding situations where you are caught up in crowds. The big cities of China are far more dangerous in this respect than Lhasa and the rest of Tibet.

Do not leave anything valuable in hotel rooms, particularly dormitories. There are at least a few people who subsidise their journey by ripping off their fellow travellers. Other items of little or no apparent value to the thief, eg, film, should also be safeguarded, since to lose them would be a real heartbreak to you.

Small padlocks are useful for backpacks and some dodgy hotel rooms. Bicycle chain locks come in handy not only for hired bikes but for attaching backpacks to railings or luggage racks.

If something of yours is stolen, you should report it immediately to the nearest foreign affairs branch of the PSB. They will ask you to fill in a loss report before investigating the case and they sometimes even recover the stolen goods.

If you have travel insurance (which is recommended), it is essential to obtain a loss report so you can claim compensation.

Staring Squads
It is very unusual to be surrounded by staring Tibetans and Chinese in Lhasa, unlike other remote parts of China, but visiting up-country is another matter. Trekkers will soon discover that it is not a good idea to camp beside Tibetan villages. The spectacle of a few foreigners putting up tents is probably the closest some villagers will ever come to TV. It is not unusual to get up in the morning and find half the village still sitting and watching.

Beggars
Being a devout Buddhist region, Tibet has a long tradition of begging for alms. It is unusual to sit down in a restaurant in Tibet without being pestered by women with babies in their arms, wizened old men, urchins dressed in rags, boy monks and even itinerant musicians. Generally, they will approach you with thumbs up and mumble 'guchi guchi' – 'please, please' (not a request for Italian designer clothes). Only the monks are occasionally pushy. Often it is food that is being sought and restaurant owners seem to tolerate this – the instant you push your plate to one side (or get up to leave) anything remaining on it is likely to disappear instantly.

Tibetans with money are generally very generous with beggars and usually hand out a couple of mao to anyone who requests it.

If you do give (and the choice is entirely yours), give the same amount Tibetans do; do not encourage beggars to make foreigners a special target by handing out large denominations. In this case it's worth keeping all your small change in one pocket – there's nothing worse than pulling out a Y100 note! Banks will swap a Y10 note for a wad of one-mao notes and these will go a long way.

Bookjacking

Tibetans are a very curious and devout people and so the slightest glimpse of a photo of a monastery or a Dalai Lama picture will result in the temporary confiscation of your Lonely Planet guide. For many Tibetans this is their only chance to see other parts of their country so try to be patient, even after the 10th request in five minutes. A good deed like this can often open hitherto locked doors (literally) in the place you are visiting.

Dogs

Lhasa used to be infested with packs of mangy, rabid-looking dogs that made catching a predawn bus a frightening, even life-threatening experience. However, a series of clean-up campaigns by the Chinese in Lhasa and Shigatse has largely done away with these. Dogs can still be a problem in other towns though, and you should be especially vigilant when exploring back streets or seeking out an obscure monastery. Hurling a few rocks in their direction will let them know you are not in the mood for company, while a hefty stick is good for action at close quarters. The most dangerous dogs belong to remote homesteads or nomad encampments and should be given an extremely wide berth. See Health earlier in this chapter for information on what to do if you are bitten.

LEGAL MATTERS

Only the most serious cases are tried in front of a judge (never a jury). Most lesser crimes are handled administratively by the PSB, which acts as police, judge and executioner.

China takes a particularly dim view of opium and all its derivatives. It's difficult to say what attitude the Chinese police will take towards foreigners caught using marijuana – they often don't care what foreigners do if it's not political and if Chinese aren't involved. Then again the Chinese are fond of making examples of wrong-doings and you don't want to be the example.

Public Security Bureau

The Public Security Bureau (PSB) is the name given to China's police, both uniformed and plain clothed. The foreign affairs branch of the PSB deals with foreigners. This branch (also known as the 'entry-exit branch') is responsible for issuing visa extensions and Alien Travel Permits.

The PSB is responsible for introducing and enforcing regulations that concern foreigners. So, for example, they bear responsibility for the exclusion of foreigners from certain hotels. If this means you get stuck for a place to stay, they can offer advice. Do not pester them with trivia or try to 'use' them to bully a point with a local street vendor. Do turn to them for mediation in serious disputes with hotels, restaurants, taxi drivers and so on. This often works since the PSB wields god-like power – especially in remote areas.

In Tibet it is fairly unusual for foreigners to have problems with the PSB. It does of course depend on what you get up to when you are there. Making an obvious display of pro-Tibetan political sympathies is guaranteed to lead to problems. Photographing Tibetan protests or military sites will lead to the confiscation of your film and possibly a brief detention. Attempting to travel into or out of Tibet on any of the closed routes (mainly to Sichuan or Yunnan) is likely to end in an unpleasant encounter somewhere en route. If you are caught in a closed area without a permit you face a fine of Y200 to Y500, which can often be bargained down. Some officers have been known to offer a 'student discount' on fines!

If you do have a serious run-in with the PSB, you may have to write a confession of your guilt and pay a fine. In the most serious cases, you can be expelled from China (at your own expense). But in general, if you are not doing anything particularly nasty (such as smuggling suitcases of dope through customs), the PSB will probably not throw you in prison.

BUSINESS HOURS

Banks, offices, government departments and the PSB are open Monday to Friday, with perhaps a half-day on Saturday. As a rough guide only, they open from around 8am to 9am, close for two hours in the middle of the day (often one hour in winter or three hours during a heat wave in summer), then reopen until 5pm or 6pm. Saturday and Sunday are public holidays.

Many of Lhasa's main tourist attractions are open only in the morning. Most smaller monasteries have no set opening hours and will open up chapels for you once you've tracked someone down. Others, such as Samye, are notorious for only opening certain rooms at certain times. In general it's best to try to tag along with pilgrims or a tour group.

PUBLIC HOLIDAYS

The PRC has nine national holidays during the year. These are mainly Chinese holidays and mean little to many Tibetans, but they are still a good opportunity to catch a Tibetan opera or join families picnicking in a local park.

New Year's Day 1 January
Chinese New Year Usually February
International Working Women's Day 8 March
International Labour Day 1 May
Youth Day 4 May
Children's Day 1 June
Anniversary of the founding of the Communist Party of China 1 July
Anniversary of the founding of the People's Liberation Army 1 August
National Day 1 October

The Chinese New Year, otherwise known as the Spring Festival, starts on the first day of the old lunar calendar. Although officially it lasts only three days, many people take a week off from work. Be warned: This is China's only three-day holiday and this is definitely not the time to cross borders (especially the Hong Kong one) or to run out of money. In general, however, Spring Festival has a minor effect in Tibet compared to the chaos engendered in the rest of China.

Be aware that 10 March is a politically sensitive date, as it is the anniversary of the 1959 Tibetan uprising and flight of the Dalai Lama. Also, 23 May marks the signing of the *Agreement on Measures for the Peaceful Liberation of Tibet*, while 1 September

marks the anniversary of the founding of the Tibetan Autonomous Region (TAR). Other politically sensitive dates marking political protests are 5 March, 27 September, 10 December and 1 October. It may be impossible for travellers to fly into Tibet for a few days before these dates.

SPECIAL EVENTS

Tibetan cultural heritage took such a hammering during the Cultural Revolution that traditional festivals, once important highlights of the Tibetan year, are only now starting to revive.

Tibetan festivals are held according to the Tibetan lunar calendar, which usually lags at least a month behind our Gregorian calendar. We have included forthcoming dates for some of the festivals listed below, but you will need to ask around for the exact dates of many festivals because these are often only fixed by monasteries a few months in advance. To check Tibetan lunar dates against Western Gregorian dates, try the Web site W www.ntic.qc.ca/~rloise/astro tibet/calendrier/calactuel.html.

The following are some of the more important festivals; you might try to plan your trip to coincide with these:

January
Shigatse New Year Festival Held in the first week of the 12th lunar month.

February–March
Year End Festival Dancing monks can be seen on the 29th of the 12th lunar month in this festival which is held to dispel the evil of the old year and auspiciously usher in the new one.

New Year Festival (Losar) Taking place in the first week of the first lunar month, Losar is a colourful week of activities; Lhasa is probably the best place to be. There are performances of Tibetan drama and pilgrims making incense offerings, and the streets are thronged with Tibetans dressed in their finest. Forthcoming dates: 3 March 2003, 21 February 2004, 9 February 2005.

Lantern Festival This is held on the 15th of the first lunar month; huge yak-butter sculptures are placed around Lhasa's Barkhor circuit. Forthcoming dates: 18 March 2003, 6 March 2004, 23 February 2005.

Mönlam (Great Prayer Festival) Held midway through the first lunar month (officially culminating on the 25th). Monks from Lhasa's three main monasteries assemble in the Jokhang and an image of Jampa (Maitreya) from Lhasa's Jokhang is borne around the Barkhor circuit, attracting enthusiastic crowds of locals and pilgrims. The festival was first instituted by Tsongkhapa in 1409 at Ganden Monastery.

May–June

Birth of Sakyamuni (Sakya Thukpa) This is not exactly a festival, but rather the seventh day of the fourth lunar month is an important pilgrimage date and sees large numbers of pilgrims in the Holy City of Lhasa and other sacred areas in Tibet. Festivals are held at this time at Tsurphu (detailed following), Ganden, Reting and Samye Monasteries.

Tsurphu Festival *Cham* dancing (ritual dancing carried out by monks) and chang drinking are the order of the day at this festival on the 10th day of the fourth lunar month. The highlight used to be the dance of the Karmapa (the spiritual leader of the Karma Kagyupa suborder, now in India) so it remains to be seen how the festival continues.

Saga Dawa (Sakyamuni's Enlightenment) The 15th day of the fourth lunar month (full moon) marks the date of Sakyamuni's (Sakya Thukpa's) conception, moment of enlightenment and entry into nirvana. It is an occasion for outdoor operas and also sees large numbers of pilgrims at Lhasa's Jokhang and on the Barkhor circuit. Many pilgrims climb Gephel Ri, the peak behind Drepung Monastery, to burn juniper incense. Saga Dawa is also a particularly good time to be at Mt Kailash. Any kora is bursting with extra pilgrims. Forthcoming dates: 26 May 2002, 14 June 2003, 3 June 2004, 23 May 2005.

June–July

World Incense Day A day of incense burning and picnicking.

Gyantse Horse-Racing Festival A traditional festival whose date authorities are trying to fix to the middle of June to boost the number of tourists. The fun and games include dances, picnics, archery and equestrian events.

Worship of the Buddha During the second week of the fifth lunar month, the parks of Lhasa, in particular the Norbulingka, are crowded with picnickers.

Tashilhunpo Festival During the second week of the fifth lunar month, Shigatse's Tashilhunpo Monastery becomes the scene of a three-day festival, and a huge thangka is hung.

Samye Festival Held from the 15th day of the fifth lunar month (full moon) for two days. Special ceremonies and cham dancing in front of the Ütse are the main attractions. The monastery guesthouse is normally booked out at this time so bring a tent.

August–September

Chökor Duchen Festival Held in Lhasa on the fourth day of the sixth lunar month, this festival celebrates Buddha's first sermon at Sarnath near Varanasi in India.

Guru Rinpoche's Birthday Held on the 10th day of the sixth lunar month, this festival is particularly popular in Nyingmapa monasteries.

Ganden Festival On the 15th day of the 6th lunar month, the Ganden Monastery displays its 25 holiest relics, which are normally locked away. A large offering ceremony accompanies the unveiling.

Drepung Festival The 30th day of the sixth lunar month is celebrated with the hanging of a huge thangka at Drepung Monastery. Lamas and monks do masked dances.

Shötun (Yogurt Festival) Held in the first week of the seventh lunar month, this festival starts at Drepung and moves down to the Norbulingka. Operas and masked dances are held, and locals take the occasion as another excuse for more picnics. Forthcoming dates: 8–15 August 2002, 27 August–3 September 2003, 15–22 August 2004, 3–10 September 2005.

September–October

Bathing Festival The end of the seventh and beginning of the eighth lunar months sees locals washing away the grime of the previous year in an act of purification that coincides with the week-long appearance of the planet Venus in the night sky.

Horse-Racing Festival Held in the first week of the eighth lunar month, this festival featuring horse racing, archery and other traditional nomad sports is held in Damxung and Nam-tso. A similar and even larger event is held in Nagchu a few weeks earlier, from 10–16 August.

Onkor In the first week of the eighth lunar month Tibetans in central Tibet get together and party in celebration of this traditional harvest festival.

November–December

Lhabab Düchen Commemorating Buddha's descent from heaven, the 22nd day of the ninth lunar month sees large numbers of pilgrims in Lhasa.

Palden Lhamo (Shri Devi) Held on the 15th day of the 10th lunar month, this festival features a procession in Lhasa around the Barkhor bearing

Palden Lhamo (Shri Devi), protective deity of the Jokhang.

Tsongkhapa Festival Respect is shown to Tsongkhapa, the founder of Gelugpa order, on the anniversary of his death on the 25th of the 10th lunar month; monasteries light fires and carry images of Tsongkhapa in procession. Check for cham dances at the monasteries at Ganden, Sera and Drepung.

ACTIVITIES

Tibet offers the type of topography to delight mountaineers, white-water rafters, hang-gliding enthusiasts, and others. The problem, as always, is those faceless, sombre figures known collectively as 'the authorities'. High-ranking cadres, the PSB, the military, CITS and others in China with the power to extort money know a good business opportunity when they see it. In many cases, it is doubtful that the law really requires a permit but many local governments simply make up the law as they go along.

In general, when foreigners do something that is deemed unusual – and hang-gliding, bungee jumping, kayaking and so on are unusual in China – a permit will be required and a fee will be charged. The more unusual the activity, the higher the fee demanded.

Trekking

One of the remarkable things about Tibet, considering the difficulties placed in the way of those heading up there by Chinese authorities, is that once you are up on the high plateau there is considerable freedom to strike off on foot and explore the Tibetan valleys and ranges. Of course no-one at CITS or any other Chinese organisation will tell you this, but nevertheless it is the case. Experienced and hardy trekkers have the opportunity to visit places that are almost impossible to reach any other way, and are unlikely to find any official obstacles. For information on trekking routes see the Trekking chapter.

Mountaineering

There are some huge peaks in Tibet, including the 8000m-plus giants of Cho Oyu, Shisha Pangma and, of course, Everest, which are enough to send a quiver of excite-

ment through vertically inclined explorers. Unfortunately, the Chinese government charges exorbitant fees for mountaineering permits, which puts mountaineering in Tibet out of the range of most individuals or groups devoid of commercial sponsorship.

For more information on mountaineering in Tibet, contact Tibet International Sports Travel (☎ 633 1421, fax 633 4855, e tist@ public.ls.xn.cn), Himalaya Hotel, Lhasa, or the Chinese Mountaineering Association, 9 Tiyuguan Lu, Beijing 100763. Foreign travel companies such as High Asia and OTT Expeditions arrange mountaineering trips to Tibet – see Organised Tours in the Getting There & Away chapter for details.

Cycling

Tibet offers some of the most extreme and exhilarating mountain biking in the world. If you are fit and well-equipped it's possible to visit most places in this book by bike, although the most popular route follows the Friendship Hwy from Shigatse down to Kathmandu. For more information on cycling see Bicycle in the Getting Around chapter.

COURSES

It is possible to enrol in a Tibetan language course at Tibet University. Tuition costs US$1000 per semester; semesters run from March to July and September to January. There are two hours of classes a day and around 70 foreign students currently attend, although many are undercover missionaries. For a an application form contact the Foreign Affairs Office (☎ 0891-634 3254, e fsd@utibet.edu.cn), Tibet University, Lhasa 850000, Tibetan Autonomous Region. Once you are accepted the university will help arrange a student ('X') visa and, after three months, residency status in Lhasa. Students have to stay in campus accommodation, which costs Y40 per day for a private room with toilet, but no hot-water shower or heating in winter.

It should also be possible to hire a private tutor from the university for around Y20 per hour.

Many people find it more convenient to study at Dharamsala in India or Kathmandu, although students say that the mix of dialects and high levels of English make it a less effective place to study. Courses offered there include Tibetan Buddhist philosophy, Tibetan language and Tibetan performing arts.

The various Tibetan organisations around the world offer courses and meditation retreats. Contact them for details (see Useful Organisations earlier in this chapter). The Tibet Foundation (☎ 020-7404 2889) in London, for example, offers a 10-week Tibetan language course for UK£130.

WORK

It might be possible to get work as an English teacher at Lhasa University, although it's a long shot, especially as most teachers seem to double as Christian missionaries. For a time US citizens were banned from teaching English in Tibet.

ACCOMMODATION

Outside Lhasa, Shigatse and Tsetang, travellers in Tibet are not overwhelmed with accommodation options. The standard hotel in rural Tibet is a dirt-floor truck stop with a row of rooms each containing four or five beds. Hot water is provided in thermoses and a basin is usually provided for washing. Electricity and running water are luxuries that cannot be expected. At least such places are cheap – from around Y8 to Y15 on average – and bedding is provided.

In urban centres such as Lhasa, Shigatse, Gyantse, Tsetang and Zhangmu, there is more choice and conditions are better. As a result of demand, hot showers are becoming more common in such hotels. Accommodation along the Friendship Hwy is also becoming increasingly developed.

In the towns, the Chinese government keeps a pretty tight lid on which places can and cannot accept foreigners. Most tourists will only come up against this problem in Tsetang, where the bottom-end hotels are not permitted to accept foreigners.

Camping

A large proportion of the Tibetan population is nomadic, and there is a strong tradition of making your home wherever you can ham-

mer in a tent peg. You probably run the risk of an unpleasant run-in with the PSB if you attempt to set up a tent in Lhasa, but get 20km or so out of town and the nearest patch of turf is yours for the picking.

Truck Stops

Travellers making their way out to Mt Kailash will probably get to sample quite a few truck stops. They are basically just places to crash after a long day of travelling. The bedding is usually filthy so it's a good idea to have a sleeping bag (and even a ground sheet!). If you value your privacy it is also a good idea to pay for a whole room (usually four or five beds), because drivers turn up at all times of the night. Some truck stops will have an attached restaurant, but this is less likely to be the case in remote parts of western Tibet.

Army Camps

An increased number of privately run guesthouses and truck stops in Tibet means that travellers rarely have to stay in army camps any more – a frequent occurrence, even on the road between Lhasa and the border with Nepal, back in the early days of individual travel.

Cyclists, however, might have to make use of road-maintenance camps (*daoban* in Chinese), recognisable by the steering wheel symbol. In free-market China these camps are normally open to foreigners and go under such glamorous names as the '22nd Team Road Maintenance Division Guesthouse'. Rates are usually around Y15 per bed and food there is usually available.

Homestays

It is sometimes possible for trekkers to stay with Tibetan families. Some families living on popular trekking routes have a room that they hire out to foreign trekkers. Food is sometimes available, but if not they can usually offer you hot water. Sometimes a charge of Y1 is asked for hot water – which is not a lot of money considering the effort involved in producing the stuff. Be careful not to force any hospitality, as it is technically illegal for foreigners to stay in a Tibetan home without the host first registering with the PSB and your host could be open to a fine if found out.

Guesthouses & Hotels

Most of the accommodation used by foreigners in Tibet could be classed as guesthouse accommodation. In Lhasa there are several clean, well-run Tibetan-style guesthouses. Similar set-ups can be found in Shigatse, Sakya and Tingri. Some monasteries, such as Samye, Ganden, Drigung Til, Dorje Drak, Mindroling, Tidrum and Reting also have guesthouses that charge a standard Y15. Remoter monasteries often have a spare room, or even a chapel, which they may be willing to let out. If no fee is asked, leave a Y15 donation in the prayer hall.

Tibetan-style guesthouses tend to be much more friendly and homy than Chinese guesthouses; prices are also lower. In Lhasa, Tibetan guesthouses have dorms for around Y25 per person. Accommodation elsewhere in Tibet is cheaper – around Y15 – but standards are not as high as those in Lhasa. Outside Lhasa and Shigatse, you cannot expect to find budget guesthouses with running water, although all guesthouses will provide hot water for drinking; if there is enough, you can use it for a quick wash. The only place conspicuously lacking in budget accommodation is Tsetang, where the cheapest rooms currently cost around Y100.

There is comfortable hotel-style accommodation in Lhasa, Shigatse, Gyantse, Tsetang and Zhangmu. Choice and range has increased dramatically in the last couple of years, especially in Lhasa where there are now dozens of two-star and above hotels. Most of these are Chinese style and Chinese managed. They are all pretty much anonymous but share several traits: The plumbing is often very dodgy, the carpets are dotted with a mosaic of cigarette burns, and all offer a ratty pair of flip-flops so you don't have to touch the bathroom floor. Hotel rates range from Y60 to Y400 for a double room. Few of the top-end hotels have single room rates.

Some hotels price their accommodation per bed (generally the cheaper ones) rather than per room. (For example, one person might pay Y60 to stay in a double room, whereas two people would pay Y120.) Paying by the bed rather than by the room works well for solo travellers. To guarantee that you have the room to yourself you would theoretically have to pay for all beds (and few hotel owners will try to force you to do so), but normally that's not necessary. If you are alone in a double room or are a couple in a triple room, staff will not normally put others in the room, although they have the right to. They may possibly put other foreigners in the room, but it is rare for a hotel to mix foreigners and Chinese or Tibetans in one room. This depends largely on your negotiations.

In some areas of Tibet, notably in Lhasa, accommodation prices vary seasonally. Throughout this book, the prices provided apply in the high season (from June to September). Rates can be a little lower in April, May and October, and lower still in winter.

All hotels and guesthouses offer plentiful thermoses of boiled water for making your own tea or coffee.

FOOD

The food situation in Tibet has improved vastly over the last five or six years. Fresh vegetables are more widely available than they once were, and there are now a lot more (mainly Chinese) restaurants around.

Tibetan

Tellingly, the basic Tibetan meal is *tsampa*, a kind of dough made with roasted-barley flour and yak butter (if available) mixed with water, tea or beer – something wet. Tibetans skilfully knead and mix the paste by hand into dough-like balls – not as easy as it looks! Tsampa with milk powder and sugar makes a pretty good porridge and is a fine trekking staple, but only a Tibetan can eat it every day and still look forward to the next meal.

Tibetan cuisine is not going to win any prizes. In Lhasa there are a few restaurants that have elevated a subsistence diet into the beginnings of a cuisine. But outside Lhasa, Tibetan food is limited mainly to greasy *momos* and *thugpa*.

Momos are small dumplings filled with meat or vegetables or both. They are normally steamed but can be fried and are actually pretty good.

More common is thugpa, a noodle soup with meat or vegetables or both. Variations on the theme include *hipdu* (squares of noodles and yak meat in a soup) and *thanthuk* (more noodles). More ambitious and harder to find are *shemdre* (potatoes and yak meat on a bed of rice) and *shya vale* (pancake-style pasties, fried, with a yak-meat filling).

Also popular among nomads is dried yak (*yaksha*) or lamb meat. It is normally cut into strips and left to dry on tent lines and is pretty chewy stuff. Sometimes you will see bowls of little white lumps drying in the sun that even the flies leave alone – it is dried yak cheese and it's eaten as a sweet. For the first half-hour it is like having a small rock in your mouth, but eventually it starts to soften up and taste like old, dried yak cheese.

Chinese

Han immigration into Tibet may be a tragic threat to the very essence of Tibetan culture…but it's done wonders for the restaurant scene (!). Even most Tibetans have to admit that Chinese food is better than tsampa, momos and thugpa. All of the Tibetan urban centres have Chinese restaurants these days, and they can also be found on major roads, even on the road out to Mt Kailash. Chinese restaurants in Tibet are generally around 50% more expensive than Chinese restaurants in the rest of China.

Chinese food in Tibet is almost exclusively Sichuanese. This is the hottest of the Chinese regional cuisines, but in Tibet it is rarely made with as many spices as it is in Sichuan. You may find that some dishes include *huajiao* (flower pepper), a curious mouth-numbing spice that tastes a little bit like washing detergent. Another interesting sauce is *yuxiang*, a spicy, piquant sauce that is supposed to resemble the taste of fish (probably the closest thing you'll get to fish in Tibet). Sichuanese dishes are usually stir-fried quickly over a high flame and so tend to be more hygienic than their Tibetan counterparts.

Very few Chinese restaurants have menus in English. Usually the dishes on offer are written on a board, and if you do not read Chinese the only thing you'll gather from it is the range of prices. This is rarely a problem, as in most restaurants you can wander out into the kitchen and point to the vegetables and meats that you want fried up. The main snag with this method is that you'll miss out on many of the most interesting sauces and styles and be stuck with the same dishes over and over.

Chinese snacks are excellent and worth trying. The most common are ravioli-style dumplings called *shuijiao*, ordered by the bowl or weight (half a jin is enough for one person) and steamed dumplings called *baozi*, similar to momos and normally ordered by the steamer. You can usually get a bowl of noodles anywhere for around Y5; *shaguo mixian* is a particularly tasty form of rice noodles cooked in a clay pot. Fried noodles (*chaomian*) are not as popular as in the West but you can get them in many Chinese and backpacker restaurants. Likewise, the backpacker staple of egg fried rice (*dan chao fan*) is rarely eaten by the Chinese but most cooks will rustle it up for around Y5 a bowl.

For a list of the most common dishes see the Language chapter.

Muslim

The Muslim restaurants found in almost all urban centres in Tibet are an interesting alternative to Chinese or Tibetan food. These are normally recognisable by a green flag hanging outside or Arabic script on the restaurant sign. Most chefs come from the Linxia area of Gansu. The food is based on noodles, and of course there's no pork.

Dishes worth trying include *ganbanmian*, a kind of stir-fried spaghetti bolognaise made with beef (or yak) and sometimes green peppers, and *chaomianpian*, fried noodle squares with meat and vegetables. Muslim restaurants also offer good breads and excellent Eight Treasure Tea (*baba-ocha*), which is made with dried raisins, plums and rock sugar and only releases its true flavour after several cups. Most restaurants will sell you take-away packets of the tea if you really like it. You can often go into the kitchen and see your noodles being hand made.

Breakfasts

You can get decent breakfasts of yogurt, muesli and toast at backpacker hotels in Lhasa and Shigatse, but elsewhere you are more likely to be confronted by Chinese-style dumplings, fried bread sticks and rice porridge. One good breakfast-type food that is widely available is scrambled eggs and tomato (*fanqie chaojidan* in Chinese).

Self-Catering

There will be a time when you'll need to be self-sufficient, whether you're staying overnight at a monastery, arriving at a town late at night, or heading off on a trip to Mt Kailash or Nam-tso. Unless you have a stove, your main saviour will be instant noodles. After a long trip to Mt Kailash and back you will know the relative tastes of every kind of packet noodle sold in Tibet. Your body will also likely be deeply addicted to MSG. Even the faintest smell of noodles will leave you gagging.

Fortunately the range of foods available in most towns has improved greatly in the last couple of years. Instant options now include fruit (dried, fresh and in jars), vegetables, cans of tuna, soup mixes, sweets (White Rabbit is the best brand), sausages, biscuits and many others. Imports such as Western chocolate, instant coffee and even Pringles are available in Chinese supermarkets.

Vegetables such as onions, carrots, and bok choy can save even the cheapest pack of noodles from culinary oblivion. You can also find a type of red-fruit roll in Lhasa which travels well. Even Tashi restaurant's take-away fried apple momos travel quite well.

DRINKS
Nonalcoholic Drinks

The local beverage that every traveller ends up trying at least once is yak-butter tea (see the boxed text).

The more palatable alternative to yak-butter tea is sweet, milky tea, or *cha ngamo*. It is similar to the tea drunk in neighbouring

Pakistan. Chinese green tea is also widely available. Tibetans do not drink coffee and you will not find any outside Lhasa and Shigatse. Soft drinks and mineral water are widely available throughout Tibet. The most popular Chinese soft drink is Jianlibao, a honey-and-orange drink (sometimes translated on restaurant menus as 'Jellybowl'!).

In many remote areas, even if there is nothing else available to drink, there will at least be beer and Pepsi on sale.

Yak-Butter Tea

Bŏ cha, literally Tibetan tea, is unlikely to be a highlight of your trip to Tibet. Made from yak butter mixed with salt, milk, soda, tea leaves and hot water all churned up in a wooden tube, the soupy mixture has more the consistency of bouillon than of tea (one traveller described it as 'a cross between brewed old socks and sump oil'!). When mixed with *tsampa* (roasted-barley flour) and yak butter it becomes the staple meal of most Tibetans and you may well be offered it at monasteries, people's houses and even while waiting for a bus by the side of the road. Most Tibetans mix it in a small wooden bowl and knead the mixture into small balls, which they pop into their mouths – not as easy as it looks!

At most restaurants you mercifully have the option of drinking *cha ngamo* (sweet, milky tea) but there will be times when you just have to be polite and down a cupful of bŏ cha (without gagging). Most nomads think nothing of drinking up to 40 cups of the stuff a day. At least it stops your lips from cracking.

Most distressing for those not sold on the delights of yak-butter tea is the fact that your cup will constantly be refilled every time you take even the smallest sip, as a mark of the host's respect. There's a pragmatic reason for this as well; there's only one thing worse than hot yak-butter tea – cold yak-butter tea.

JENNY BOWMAN

Alcoholic Drinks

The Tibetan brew is known as *chang*, a fermented barley beer. It has a rich, fruity taste, and ranges from disgusting to pretty good. Connoisseurs serve it out of a jerry can. Those trekking in the Everest region should try the local variety, which is served in a big pot. Hot water is poured into the fermenting barley and the liquid is drunk through a wooden straw – it is very good.

On our research trips we have never suffered any adverse effects from drinking chang. However, you should be aware that it is often made with contaminated water, and there is always some risk in drinking it. The dirtiness of the jerry cans that chang is sometimes carried in also poses a risk. Still, sharing chang is a great way to get to know local people, if drunk in small quantities. Trekkers might prefer to be extra cautious and avoid it – no-one wants stomach problems (or a hangover) on a trek.

The main brands of beer available in Tibet are Wuquan, Huanghe (Yellow River) and Green Leaf. Lhasa Beer is brewed in Lhasa, originally under German supervision. Pabst Blue Ribbon (*landai* in Chinese) is a US beer brewed in Sichuan under franchise; no-one admits to drinking Pabst in the US, but out in Tibet it tastes pretty good. Domestic beer costs around Y4 in a shop, Y7 in most restaurants and Y12 in swanky bars.

Supermarkets in Lhasa stock several types of Chinese red wine, including Shangri-La, produced in the Tibetan areas of north-east Yunnan using methods handed down by French missionaries at the beginning of the 19th century. A bottle costs around Y50.

ENTERTAINMENT

Hopefully entertainment in Tibet is not high on your list of priorities. If it is, go somewhere else. The Tibetan idea of fun is having a picnic and getting sloshed on chang. In general, foreigners make their own entertainment in Tibet, and evenings in the hotels of Lhasa and Shigatse often see groups of travellers knocking back a couple of beers and swapping tall stories while someone strums 'Tears from Heaven' or 'Knocking on Heaven's Door' (not *again*!) in the background.

Lhasa has a burgeoning nightlife scene, but very little in the way of cultural entertainment. As with the rest of China, karaoke bars have taken off in a big way in urban centres. Lhasa is the karaoke capital of Tibet, but you will also find bars in Shigatse, Gyantse, Tsetang and even far away Ali. It is worth dropping into one of them once, but you would have to be weird to make a habit of it.

A karaoke bar will have drinks available at slightly inflated prices (from Y10 to Y15 or more for a beer) and customers have to pay to sing a song – the price depends on the bar. Some bars in Lhasa alternate between karaoke sessions and dancing, and can be innocent, good fun. Be aware, however, that some karaoke bars are a front for prostitution.

The PSB does not look too kindly on foreigners seeking out night-time entertainment in venues frequented by locals. Some travellers have been warned off from dancing and chatting with locals. Proceed with caution.

Those seeking out cultural entertainment will probably have to wait for a festival. Festivals often include performances of cham dancing and Tibetan opera, but unfortunately such times represent your only opportunity to see them.

Tibetans are not big on sports. The horse-racing festivals such as those in Gyantse and Nagchu (see Special Events earlier in this chapter) are probably your only chance to see any sporting action.

SHOPPING

Tibet is not a bad place for souvenir hunting, although much of the stuff you see in markets, particularly the bronzes, has been humped over the high passes from Nepal and can probably be bought cheaper in Kathmandu, where you will have a better selection of quality goods.

Some travellers buy a Tibetan carpet and send it home. There are carpet factories in Lhasa and Shigatse producing new carpets of average quality. Good-quality traditional carpets, on the other hand, are harder to come by. A small contingent of frequent travellers to Tibet have made carpets their business and if you fall in with some of them they may give you some tips on finding one for yourself.

For an overview of possible purchases in Tibet, the best place to look is the Barkhor in Lhasa. The entire Barkhor circuit is lined with stalls selling all kinds of oddities. Prayer flags, shawls, prayer wheels and daggers are all popular buys. Itinerant pilgrims may also come up to you with things to sell – the proceeds will often finance their trip home.

Most of the stalls on the Barkhor circuit seem be selling jewellery and most (some would say all) of it is fake. If you are travelling via Kathmandu you will find better quality jewellery at cheaper prices there, but with a little knowledge and some hard bargaining you can still pick up some nice trinkets in Lhasa. The vast majority of the jewellery on offer is turquoise and coral; Tibetans believe that turquoise is good for the liver and coral for the heart. Locals will tell you that the turquoise comes from the mountains and the coral from the lakes of Tibet – more likely sources are Taiwan and China (if it doesn't come from a factory, that is).

It is easy to tell fake turquoise (or 'new turquoise' as the stall holders call it) from the real thing ('old turquoise'). The fake stuff is bluer and is flawless; beware of a string of identically shaped and rounded beads – nature did not intend them to be this

way. The final test is to scratch the surface with a sharp metal object, the fake turquoise will leave a white line, the real stuff won't show a thing. When you've established what you're buying have a closer look at the stone to make sure it's all in one piece. Unscrupulous stall holders glue together tiny bits of turquoise with black glue to make larger pieces of stone.

The same rules apply to coral – if you see a perfectly formed set of red beads the chances are they aren't real. Look for bubbles and imperfections. But if you're happy with what you're buying and the price you're paying, that's all that matters.

You will also see Buddha eye beads, known as *zee* – black or brown oblong beads with white eye symbols. These are replicas of fossils found in rocks in the mountains containing auspicious eye symbols thought to represent the eyes of the Buddha. The real thing is priceless; copies are more affordable. The more eyes the higher the price.

Be prepared to bargain hard for any purchase, especially in the Barkhor. You can probably reckon on at least halving the price, but there are no hard-and-fast rules. Shop around for a while and get a feel for prices.

Other possible buys are Tibetan ceiling drapes and thangkas. Some of the ceiling drapes and door curtains are very tasteful and can be bought in Lhasa and Shigatse. Most of the thangkas for sale are gaudy – good ones do not come cheap. There are a couple of workshops in Lhasa where you can see thangkas being painted.

Getting There & Away

Warning

The information in this chapter is particularly vulnerable to change: Prices for international travel are volatile, routes are introduced and cancelled, schedules change, special deals come and go, and rules and visa requirements are amended. Airlines and governments seem to take a perverse pleasure in making price structures and regulations as complicated as possible. You should check directly with the airline or a travel agency to make sure you understand how a fare (and ticket you may buy) works. In addition, the travel industry is highly competitive and there are many lurks and perks.

The upshot of this is that you should get opinions, quotes and advice from as many airlines and travel agencies as possible before you part with your hard-earned cash. The details given in this chapter should be regarded as pointers and are not a substitute for your own careful, up-to-date research.

Tibet is not the most accessible of destinations, but then getting there is half the fun. For most international travellers, getting to Tibet will involve at least two legs; the first to the gateways of Kathmandu (Nepal) or Chengdu (China) and the second from these cities into Tibet. The first section of this chapter details long-haul options to China and Nepal, while the second section details the practicalities of actually getting into Tibet. The Gateway Cities section offers basic information for travellers transiting through Kathmandu or Chengdu.

Once you are in the region, direct air access to Lhasa is basically limited to flights from either Kathmandu or Chengdu. There are also connections from Chongqing, Xining and Xi'an, but these tend to involve considerably more bureaucratic hassle.

Overland routes into Tibet involve days of gruelling travel from either Nepal or China. The only officially sanctioned overland routes into Tibet are via the Qinghai-Tibet Hwy, which runs between Lhasa and Golmud, or the Friendship Hwy, which runs from Kathmandu to Lhasa.

At the time of writing, bureaucratic obstacles to entering Tibet (a potentially more insurmountable barrier than the Himalaya) had loosened enough to make entry relatively easy, although there is a cost involved. Travellers heading from Nepal or flying from China still have to join a nominal tour in order to get into Lhasa but after that you can break off on your own.

Political events, both domestic and international, heavily affect regulations for entry into Tibet. Travel restrictions tightened in 2001 during the 50th anniversary 'celebrations' of the founding of the Tibetan Autonomous Region (TAR). The previous year, Americans faced temporary difficulties getting permits after the spy plane collision incident. It would be wise to check on the latest developments in Tibet before setting out. For some contacts to use as starting points, see Useful Organisations in the Facts for the Visitor chapter.

AIR

Air travel is complicated because there are no direct long-haul flights to Tibet. You will probably have to stop over in Kathmandu, Beijing or Hong Kong if you are making a beeline for Lhasa.

Generally, flights to Kathmandu are not all that cheap as there are a limited number of carriers operating out of the Nepali capital. Depending on where you are coming from, it may be cheaper to fly to Delhi and make your way overland from there.

To China, you generally have the choice of flying first to Beijing or Hong Kong, although there are a small number of flights direct to Chengdu or Kunming from South-East Asia. Hong Kong has traditionally enjoyed the cheapest flights but these days this is not always the case. If there's little difference in the fares, then it's just a choice of which city you would prefer to visit. It costs more to fly to Chengdu from Hong Kong than from Beijing, but fares even up if you fly from Shenzhen, just over the Guangdong border from Hong Kong. Hong Kong is the easiest place to get a 60- or 90-day Chinese visa.

If you are heading straight to Chengdu you could fly to Bangkok and then take a direct flight from there to Chengdu.

Buying Tickets

Buying a plane ticket is a major outlay so it's well worth spending time looking into the various routings and the airlines that fly into China or Nepal and their comparative costs.

Although you will not find a round-the-world (RTW) fare that includes Lhasa, it should not be so difficult to find one that includes Hong Kong or Kathmandu. The drawback is that you will probably have to return to your point of origin after visiting Tibet to pick up your onward flight, unless you can arrange an overland sector in the ticket.

If you want to get to Tibet as quickly as possible (perhaps to get the maximum use from your visa) consider buying a domestic Air China ticket to Chengdu as part of your international ticket to, say, Beijing. Some Air China offices will give you a discount of up to 50% on the domestic leg if you buy the long-haul leg through them.

Another ticket worth looking into is an open-jaw ticket. This might involve, for example, flying into Hong Kong and then flying out of Kathmandu, allowing you to travel overland across Tibet. If there are no open-jaw tickets available then consider buying two one-way tickets. Travel agencies may have trouble booking a one-way inbound ticket but can normally manage something if you book the outbound ticket at the same time.

Start early: Some of the cheapest tickets have to be bought months in advance, and some popular flights sell out early. Find out the fare, the route and the duration of the flight (and the stopover if there is one), and check for restrictions on the ticket.

In the UK and the USA many of the cheapest fares are those offered by small 'bucket shops', which should be approached with caution. Avoid agencies that demand that you pay the full price in advance. Always demand a receipt and ring the airline to confirm that you really are booked on the flight.

An alternative to these risks is to pay a little more up front and use a reputable, well-established agency.

Once you have bought your ticket, copy out the ticket and flight numbers and keep this information separate from the ticket. If the ticket is lost or stolen, this information will help you to get a replacement.

Try to buy travel insurance as early as possible. If you buy it the week before you fly you may find, for example, that you are not covered for delays in your flight due to industrial action.

Travellers with Special Needs

With advance notice, most international airlines can cater for special needs, eg, travellers with disabilities, people with young children or those with dietary preferences. Contact the airline directly.

Airlines usually carry babies up to two years of age at 10% of the adult fare, although a few carry them free of charge. For children between the ages of two and 12, international fares are usually 50% of the standard fare and 67% of a discounted fare.

Departure Tax

The international departure tax from China is Y90, payable at check-in. The domestic departure tax is Y50.

The UK

There are some very good deals available in London's bucket shops for flights to Beijing, Hong Kong and major Indian cities, mainly Delhi. Check the travel sections of newspapers, and magazines like *Time Out*.

Most British travel agencies are registered with the Association of British Travel Agencies (ABTA). If you have paid for your flight with an ABTA-registered agency that then goes out of business, the ABTA will

Air Travel Glossary

Baggage Allowance This will be written on your ticket and usually includes one 20kg item to go in the hold, plus one item of hand luggage.

Cancellation Penalties If you have to cancel or change an Apex or other discounted ticket, there are often heavy penalties involved and you may well lose the entire value of the ticket.

Check-In Airlines ask you to check in a certain time ahead of the flight departure (usually one to two hours on international flights). If you fail to check in on time and the flight is overbooked, the airline can cancel your booking and give your seat to somebody else.

Lost Tickets If you lose your airline ticket an airline will usually treat it like a travellers cheque and, after inquiries, issue you with another one. Legally, however, an airline is entitled to treat it like cash and if you lose it then it's gone forever.

Onward Tickets Some (although few) Chinese embassies ask for proof that you have a ticket out of the country. If you're unsure of your next move, the easiest solution is to buy the cheapest onward ticket to a neighbouring country or a ticket from a reliable airline that can be refunded if you do not use it.

Overbooking Airlines hate to fly empty seats and since every flight has some passengers who fail to show up, airlines often book more passengers than they have seats. Usually any excess passengers can fly because of the no-shows, but occasionally somebody gets bumped. Guess who it is most likely to be? The passengers who check in late.

Reconfirmation At least 72 hours prior to departure of an onward or return flight, you may have to contact the airline and 'reconfirm' that you intend to be on the flight. Check with your airline.

Restrictions Discounted tickets often have various restrictions on them, such as needing to be paid for in advance and incurring a penalty to be altered. Others are restrictions on the minimum and maximum period you must be away, such as a minimum of 14 days or a maximum of one year.

Round-the-World Tickets RTW tickets give you a limited period (usually a year) in which to circumnavigate the globe. You can go anywhere the carrying airlines go, as long as you always travel in the same direction (either west or east). The number of stopovers or total number of separate flights is decided before you set off and these tickets usually cost a bit more than a basic return flight.

Transferred Tickets Airline tickets cannot be transferred from one person to another. Travellers sometimes try to sell the return half of their ticket, but officials can ask you to prove that you are the person named on the ticket. This is less likely to happen on domestic flights, but on an international flight, tickets may be compared with passports.

then provide you with either a refund or an alternative.

London's best-known agencies for bargain tickets include:

Bridge the World (☎ 020-7911 0900) 47 Chalk Farm Rd, Camden Town, London NW1 8AH
Council Travel (☎ 020-7478 2000, fax 7734 7322, e infouk@councilexchanges.org.uk) 52 Poland St, London W1V 4JQ
Flight Bookers (☎ 020-7757 2444, w www .flightbookers.co.uk)
STA (☎ 020-7361 6262, w www.statravel.co .uk) Priory House, 6 Wrights Lane, London W8 6TA

Trailfinders (☎ 020-7938 3366, fax 7937 9294, w www.trailfinders.com) 42–50 Earl's Court Rd, Kensington, London W8 6EJ; (☎ 020-7938 3939) 194 Kensington High St, London W8 7RG

Those looking at travelling via the Indian subcontinent and shaving costs wherever possible will find it cheapest to fly to Delhi and then travel overland to Nepal. Fares to India generally start from around UK£220 one way or from UK£325 to UK£440 return. The cheapest high-season return fares to Kathmandu are around UK£650 with

Royal Nepal Air. The cheapest one-way fares from Kathmandu to London cost around US$400 with Gulf Air.

There are sometimes great offers to Beijing on Air China (☎ 020-7630 7678) or British Airways (☎ 0345-222 111). Several specialist agencies in London can book both international and Chinese domestic tickets. China Travel Service and Information Centre (☎ 020-7388 8838, W www.china travel.co.uk), 124 Euston Rd, London NW1 2AL, offers some of the lowest fares to China and offers a 30% discount on any domestic Air China ticket booked in conjunction with an international Air China ticket.

Summer peak-season fares to Beijing cost around UK£300 one way and UK£500 return, although low-season return flights can be as little as UK£340. Virgin Atlantic offers excellent fares to Shanghai for around UK£400 return, from where it's relatively easy to get to Chengdu. Cheap flights (often with Middle Eastern Airlines) to Hong Kong cost around the same price.

Continental Europe

From Europe you have the option of flying to Beijing with Air China and bypassing Hong Kong, which is useful for those wanting to get to Tibet as quickly as possible. Numerous other airlines fly to Hong Kong, which should cost around the same as flying to Beijing.

In France, make inquiries at STA Travel (☎ 01 43 59 23 69), 49 rue Pierre Charron, or Council Travel (☎ 01 44 41 74 74), 1 place de l'Odéon, F-75006 Paris. In the Netherlands, NBBS Travels (☎ 20-620 7051), Leidestraat 53, 1017 NV, Amsterdam is a reliable agency. In Germany, try STA Travel (☎ 49-69 430 1910), Bergerstrasse 118, Frankfurt-am-Main, or Council Travel (☎ 030-2884 8590), Oranienburger Strasse 13–14, 10178 Berlin.

Air fares to the Indian subcontinent are much cheaper in the UK than they are in the rest of Europe.

The USA & Canada

It is far cheaper to fly to Hong Kong or Beijing from the USA or Canada than it is to fly to India. This might work out quite well if your ultimate destination is India. Overland travel from Hong Kong to Nepal and India via Tibet is reasonably time-consuming – but what a trip!

The cheapest tickets to Hong Kong are offered by bucket shops run by ethnic Chinese in San Francisco, Los Angeles and New York. Good deals are also available at more reliable long-running agencies; these include Council Travel (☎ 800-226 8624, W www.counciltravel.com), STA Travel (☎ 800-777 0112, W www.sta.com), Overseas Tours (☎ 800-323 8777, 650-692 4892, W www.overseastours.com) in Milbrae, California, and Gateway Travel (☎ 800-441 1183, 214-960 2000).

A good Web site with information on international and domestic air fares in China is W www.flychina.com.

From the west coast, the cheapest one-way/return fares to Hong Kong start at around US$385/750. To Beijing return fares begin at US$860. From New York to Hong Kong, one-way/return fares start at around US$410/900. Fares are likely to be higher at the peak of summer.

Tickets from the west coast cost around US$1350 return to Delhi or Mumbai (Bombay), and US$1500 return to Kathmandu. From the east coast you are looking at around US$1000 return to Delhi. From Kathmandu, a one-way ticket with Northwest or Thai International to the west coast costs US$673.

Canadian prices are similar to those in the USA. Try Travel Cuts (☎ 800-667 2887, W www.travelcuts.com) for excellent deals on tickets to Asia. Canadian Airlines and Korean Air have the cheapest flights to Hong Kong.

Australia & New Zealand

Check major newspapers such as the *Age*, the *Sydney Morning Herald* and the *Australian* for information on long-haul travel agencies. Both STA Travel (☎ Australia-wide 131 776, W www.statravel.com.au) and Flight Centre (☎ Australia-wide 131 600, W www.flightcentre.com.au) are represented in most Australian and New Zealand cities.

Air Routes

All of the following flights operate in both directions. Fares given are one way.

from	to	flights per week	fare (yuan)
Lhasa	Beijing	2	2040[1]
Lhasa	Chamdo	1	720
Lhasa	Chengdu	21	1270
Lhasa	Chongqing	1	1400
Lhasa	Guangzhou	1	2100[2]
Lhasa	Kathmandu	3	2290
Lhasa	Shanghai	2	2310[3]
Lhasa	Xi'an	4	1420
Lhasa	Xining	4	1390
Lhasa	Zhongdian	1	1250
Chamdo	Chengdu	3	750
Zhongdian	Kunming	7	560
Kunming	Lijiang	7	520
Xining	Chengdu	7	900
Xining	Golmud	7	540

[1] via Chengdu
[2] via Chongqing
[3] via Xining

The cheapest flights from Australia to China generally go via one of the South-East Asian capitals, such as Kuala Lumpur, Bangkok or Manila. The cheapest one-way (low-season) tickets from Australia to Hong Kong cost around A$840; return tickets will cost at least A$1100. Flights from New Zealand cost around NZ$990/1345 for a one-way/return fare.

Return fares to Kathmandu from the east coast of Australia range from around A$1300 to A$1500, depending on the season. A one-way ticket costs A$1046 with Singapore Airlines and A$1091 with Thai Airways. Return flights from New Zealand cost from around NZ$1820 to NZ$2170.

Hong Kong

Hong Kong is the main entry point for China and is now formally part of the People's Republic of China. (For visa-related information on Hong Kong and Macau, see Visas &

Documents in the Facts for the Visitor chapter.) Most travellers make their way from Hong Kong into China by train or ferry, but there are also daily direct flights from Hong Kong to Chengdu with Dragonair and China Southwest Airlines for around HK$2330/3710 one way/return.

It is considerably cheaper to fly from Shenzhen (HK$1250 bought in Hong Kong, as low as Y900 bought in Chengdu) or Guangzhou (HK$1170) to Chengdu than from Hong Kong. The Shenzhen airport is just a Turbojet hydrofoil ride (HK$189) from Hong Kong's Tsim Sha Tsui district. As a comparison, the 40-hour train ride from Guangzhou to Chengdu costs around Y500/800 for a hard/soft sleeper. China International Travel Service (CITS; see Chinese State Travel Agents Abroad later in this chapter) can book all these tickets and also offers a discount deal on hydrofoil tickets booked in conjunction with a flight out of Shenzhen.

A flight from Hong Kong to Kathmandu costs around US$320 one way.

South-East Asia

There are direct flights from Bangkok and Singapore to Chengdu and from Bangkok, Chiang Mai, Yangon (Rangoon), Vientiane and Singapore to Kunming.

Bangkok is a popular place to pick up air tickets, and prices are generally very competitive. The best place to shop around is the Bangkok backpacker ghetto of Khao San Rd. Flights with China Southwest Airlines from Bangkok to Chengdu/Kunming cost around US$255/180 one way. It's also possible to fly direct three times a week from Chiang Mai to Kunming for around US$100 (Y1450 in Kunming). Flights to Kathmandu can be picked up for around US$300. Don't forget to organise your visa for China in Bangkok.

STA Travel has branches in Singapore, Bangkok and Kuala Lumpur.

LAND

There are countless ways to cross overland into China. There's the Torugart Pass from Kyrgyzstan, the Karakoram Hwy from Pakistan, the Eurasian rail link from Kazakhstan, the Trans-Siberian railway from Russia and Mongolia, and the subtropical crossings from Vietnam, Laos and even, if you are lucky, Myanmar (Burma).

For more information on these crossings see Lonely Planet's *Karakoram Highway*, *China*, *South-West China* or *Trans-Siberian Railway* guides, or other publications such as *The Trans-Siberian Rail Guide* by Robert Strauss and the *Trans-Siberian Handbook* by Bryn Thomas.

The Karakoram Hwy, in particular, provides travellers with the opportunity to do a subcontinental circuit through Tibet, Nepal, India and Pakistan and back into China (in any order you like).

ORGANISED TOURS

The following companies all offer group tours to Tibet. They can be a useful way to see a lot in a short time, although most are pretty draining on the wallet. Most lead standard tours along the Friendship Hwy, but some offer adventurous exploratory trips into the back of beyond. Short tour descriptions are given for most of the companies listed here, although they generally change their programs every couple of years.

Australia

Adventure World (☎ 02-8913 0755, fax 9956 7707, @ info@adventureworld.com.au, W www .adventureworld.com.au) 3rd floor, 73 Walker St, North Sydney, NSW 2060. Adventure World is an agent for Explore Worldwide (see the UK listing) and others.

Intrepid Adventure Travel (☎ 1300-360 667, W www.intrepidtravel.com.au) 13 Spring St, Fitzroy, Vic 3065. Includes 'Roam' trips for 18- to 35-year-olds, billed as the cheapest adventure holidays in the world.

Peregrine Adventures (☎ 03-9663 8611, fax 9663 8618, @ websales@peregrine.net.au, W www.peregrine.net.au) 258 Lonsdale St, Melbourne, Vic 3000. Allied with Exodus (see UK listing).

Thor Adventure Travel (☎ 1800-801 119, 08-8232 3155, fax 08-8232 3541, @ tashi@olis .net.au) 228 Rundle St, Adelaide, SA 5000

World Expeditions (☎ 02-9264 3366, fax 9261 1974, @ enquiries@worldexpeditions.com.au, W www.worldexpeditions.com.au) 3rd floor, 441 Kent St, Sydney, NSW 2000

France

Allibert Voyages (☎ 08 25 09 01 90, W www .allibert-voyages.com) route de Grenoble, 38530 Chapareillan

Terres D'Adventure Services (☎ 01 53 73 77 53, fax 01 40 46 95 22) 16 rue St Victor, 75005 Paris

New Zealand

Adventure World (☎ 0800-652 954, 09-524 5118, fax 09-520 6629, @ discover@adven tureworld.co.nz, W www.adventureworld.co .nz) 101 Great South Rd, Remeura, Auckland. Australasian agent for Explore Worldwide (see UK listing) and others.

UK

China International Travel Service (CITS; ☎ 020-7836 9911) 7 Upper St Martin's Lane, London WC2H 9DL. Pricey tours of four days to one week from Chengdu or Kathmandu.

Exodus (☎ 020-8675 5550, fax 8673 0779, W www.exodus.co.uk) 9 Weir Rd, London SW12 0LT. Interesting tours through eastern Tibet, plus treks and overland trips.

Explore Worldwide (☎ 01252-760001, 319448, fax 343170, @ info@explore.co.uk, W www .explore.co.uk) 1 Frederick St, Aldershot, Hants GU11 1LQ. Offers a standard 15-day tour that covers all the main highlights.

Haiwei Trails (W www.haiweitrails.com) New British company that operates out of Lijiang in Yunnan province and runs jeep trips and charters into central and eastern Tibet.

Himalayan Kingdoms (☎ 01453-844400, fax 844422, W www.himalayankingdoms.com) Old Crown House, 18 Market St, Wotton-under-Edge, Gloucestershire GL12 7AE. Trekking and mountaineering.

Imaginative Traveller (020-8742 3049, fax 8742 3045, @ info@imaginative-traveller.com, W www .imaginative-traveller.com) 14 Barley Mow Passage, Chiswick, London W4 4PH. Small-group tours to Yunnan and Sichuan.

KE Adventure Travel (☎ 017687-73966, 72267, fax 74693, W www.keadventure.com) 32 Lake Rd, Keswick, Cumbria CA12 5DQ. Tours, treks to Mt Kailash, mountaineering on Mt Shisha Pangma and mountain-biking trips from Lhasa to Kathmandu.

OTT Expeditions (☎ 0114-258 8508, fax 255 1603, @ andy@ottexpd.demon.co.uk, W www .ottexpeditions.co.uk) Unit 5B, Southwest Centre, Troutbeck Rd, Sheffield S7 2QA. Hardcore mountaineering, including an ascent of 8201m Cho Oyu.

Regent Holidays (☎ 0117-921 1711) 15 John St, Bristol BS1 2HR. Tours and do-it-yourself pre-booked trips.

Sherpa Expeditions (☎ 020-8577 2717, fax 8572 9788, W www.sherpa-walking-holidays .co.uk) 131A, Hounslow, Middlesex TW5 0RD

Steppes East (☎ 01285-810267, fax 810693, e sales@steppeseast.co.uk, W www.steppes east.co.uk) Castle Eaton, Cricklade, Swindon, Wiltshire SN6 6JU. Standard tour of Tibet with a well-respected company.

Trans-Himalaya (☎ 1373-455518, fax 455594, e gd@trans-himalaya.demon.co.uk, W www .trans-himalaya.ndirect.co.uk) 4 Foxcote Gardens, Frome, Somerset BA11 2DS. Specialist in exploratory trips throughout the Tibetan region.

Travelbag Adventures (☎ 01420-541007, fax 541002, e info@travelbag-adventures.co.uk, W www.travelbag-adventures.co.uk) 15 Turk St, Alton, Hampshire GU34 1AG. Small-group adventure tours.

World Expeditions (☎ 01753-581808, fax 581809) 101C Slough Rd, Datchet, Berkshire SL3 9AQ. Trekking and mountain-biking tours.

USA

Adventure Center (☎ 800-228 8747, 510-654 1879, fax 654 4200, W www.adventurecenter .com) 1311 63rd St, Suite 200, Emeryville, CA 94608. An information and booking agent for Explore Worldwide, Intrepid (see UK listing) and others.

Asian Pacific Adventures (☎ 818-886 5190, fax 818-935 2691, W www.asianpacificadven tures.com) 9010 Reseda Blvd, Suite 227, Northridge, CA 91324

Boojum Expeditions (☎ 800-287 0125, 406-587 0125, fax 585 3474, W www.boojum.com) 14543 Kelly Canyon Rd, Bozeman, MT 59715. Offers horse treks in Chinese parts of eastern Tibet.

Geographic Expeditions (☎ 800-777 8183, 415-922 0448, e info@geoex.com, W www .geoex .com) 2627 Lombard St, San Francisco CA 94123. Specialises in itineraries it has pioneered.

High Asia (☎/fax 800-809 0034, W www.high asia.com) PO Box 2438, Basalt, CO 81621. Ground-breaking and eco-aware touring, trekking and mountaineering trips to eastern Tibet, the Changtang, Bonri, the Tsangpo gorges, Tsari and Lapchi.

Himalayan High Treks (☎ 800-455 8735, 415-861 2391, fax 415-861 2391) 241 Dolores St, San Francisco, CA 94103. Offers a Humla-Kailash trek.

Latitudes, Expeditions East (☎ 800-580 4883, fax 415-680 1522, e info@weblatitudes.com) 870 Market St, Suite 482, San Francisco, CA

94102. Standard tours of Tibet with a trek to Kharta.

Mountain Travel-Sobek (☎ 888-MTSOBEK, 510-527 8100, fax 525 7710, e info@mtsobek .com, W www.mtsobek.com) 6420 Fairmount Ave, El Cerrito, CA 94530. Trekking activities.

Snow Lion Expeditions (☎ 1800-525 8735, fax 801-355 6566, W www.snowlion.com) Oquirrh Place, 350 South 400 East, Suite G2, Salt Lake City, UT 84111. Mountain biking, trekking and overland trips.

Wilderness Travels (☎ 800-368 2794, 415-548 0420, fax 548 0347) 801 Allston Way, Berkeley, CA 94710. Trekking activities.

Chinese State Travel Agents Abroad

China International Travel Service (CITS) and China Travel Service (CTS), the main Chinese state travel bureaus, predominantly organise travel arrangements for group tours. As an individual traveller in Tibet, you are even less likely to have much contact with this organisation than you are in China. However, offices abroad can book hotels, domestic flights, train tickets and travel arrangements from Hong Kong to China, which can save you time and hassle in China if you have a tight itinerary.

China International Travel Service

CITS has offices worldwide and a general Web site at W www.cits.net.

Australia
(☎ 03-9621 2198, fax 9621 2919) 99 King St, Melbourne, Vic 3000

Canada
(☎ 604-267 0033, fax 267 0032) 5635 Cambie St, Vancouver, BC V5Z 3A3

Denmark
(☎ 039-3391 0400, 3312 3688) Ved Vester-port 4, DK-1612, Copenhagen V

France
(☎ 01 42 86 88 66, fax 01 42 86 88 61) 30 rue de Gramont, 75002 Paris

Hong Kong
(☎ 852-2732 5888, fax 2721 7154, e market ing@cits.com.hk) New Mandarin Plaza, Tower A, 12th floor, 14 Science Museum Rd, Tsim Sha Tsui East

Japan
Osaka: (☎ 06-6910 6635, fax 6910 6640, e cits-osk@magical.egg.or.jp) 2–16 YK Building, 9th floor, Hinomachibashi, Chuo-Ku, Osaka

Tokyo: (☎ 03-3499 1245, fax 3499 1243) 24–2 Shu Building, 6th floor, Shibuya 1-Chome, Shibuya-Ku, Tokyo 150
Fukuoko: (☎ 92-441 8180, fax 441 8160, e cits-fuk@magical3.egg.or.jp) SS Building 3–21–15, 7th floor , Hakada, Fukuoko

Sweden
(☎ 08-702 2280, fax 702 2330, e tinaxz@swipnet.sc) Gotgatan, 41, 1tr, 11621 Stockholm

USA
New York: (☎ 718-261 7329, fax 261 7569, e citsusa@aol.com) 71–01 Austin St, Suite 204, Forest Hills, NY 11375
Pasadena: (☎ 626-568 8993, fax 568 9207, e citslaz@aol.com) 975 East Green St, Suite 101, Pasadena, CA 91106

China Travel Service Outside China, CTS is represented in countries including these:

Australia
(☎ 02-9211 2633, fax 9281 3595) 757–759 George St, Sydney, NSW 2000

Canada
Vancouver: (☎ 1800-663 1126, 604-872 8787, fax 604-873 2823) 556 West Broadway, Vancouver, BC V5Z 1E9
Toronto: (☎ 1800-387 6622, 416-979 8993, fax 416-979 8220) Suite 306, 438 University Ave, Box 28, Toronto, ON M5G 2K8

France
(☎ 01 44 51 55 66, fax 01 44 51 55 60) 32 rue Vignon, 75009 Paris

Germany
Frankfurt: (☎ 69-223 8522) Düsseldorfer Strasse 14, D-60329, Frankfurt-am-Main
Berlin: (☎ 30-393 4068, fax 391 8085) Beusselstrasse 5, D-10553, Berlin

Hong Kong
Central: (☎ 852-2853 3888, fax 2541 9777, e ctsdmd@ctshk.com, w www.ctshk.com) 4th floor, CTS House, 78–83 Connaught Rd, Central
Tsim Sha Tsui: (☎ 852-2315 7188, fax 2721 7757) 1st floor, Alpha House, 27–33 Nathan Rd, Tsim Sha Tsui

UK
(☎ 020-7836 9911, 7836 3121, e cts@ctsuk .com) 7 Upper St Martin's Lane, London WC2H 9DL

USA
San Francisco: (☎ 1800-899 8618, 415-398 6627, e info@chinatravelservice.com, w www.chinatravelservice.com) 575 Sutter St, San Francisco, CA 94102
Los Angeles: (☎ 1800-890 8818, fax 626-457 8955, e usctsla@aol.com) 119 S Atlantic Blvd, Suite 303, Monterey Park, CA 91754

Gateway Cities

KATHMANDU
☎ 01 • pop 500,000 • elevation 1300m

Kathmandu has long been a popular destination for travellers, but there are a couple of drawbacks to entering Tibet from here, namely the uncertainty of getting a Chinese visa and the potential hassles involved in arranging a group tour. For detailed information, see Visas & Documents in the Facts for the Visitor chapter, and Air later in this chapter.

The Thamel district of Kathmandu is a travellers' mecca and the place to get a yak steak, repair a sleeping bag, buy a backpack or a 'Free Tibet' T-shirt (don't take it into China!), shop for souvenirs or purchase hard-to-find books on Tibet. Pilgrim's Bookstore (w www.pilgrimsbooks.com) has the best selection.

During the June to August monsoon (when most people travel to or from Tibet) it is hot, humid and rainy in Kathmandu. The huge *chörten* (stupa; containing the cremated remains of important lamas) at Bodnath, 6km east of Kathmandu, serves as a focus for the Tibetan community. See Lonely Planet's *Nepal* for more details.

Money
Check exchange and commission rates at both banks and licensed moneychangers as they vary. One of the most popular places to change money in Thamel is Nepal Grindlays Bank. Citibank has an office at the Yak & Yeti Hotel, east of Thamel in Hattisar district. The US dollar is worth around Rs 75 (75 rupees).

Airlines
China Southwest Airlines (☎ 411302) is a 10-minute walk east of Thamel, but it won't sell you a ticket to Lhasa without a Tibet Tourism Bureau (TTB) permit.

International airlines include:

Aeroflot (☎ 227399) Kamaladi
Air India (☎ 415637) Hattisar
British Airways (☎ 222266) Durbar Marg
Gulf Air (☎ 430456) Hattisar
Indian Airlines (☎ 410906) Hattisar

Japan Airlines (☎ 224854) Durbar Marg
Lufthansa (☎ 223052) Durbar Marg
Pakistan International Airlines (PIA;
  ☎ 439234) Hattisar
Qatar Airlines (☎ 256579) Kantipath
Royal Nepal Airlines (☎ 220757) Kantipath
Singapore Airlines (☎ 220759) Durbar Marg
Thai International (☎ 223565) Durbar Marg

There are three important rules concerning flights out of Kathmandu: reconfirm, reconfirm and reconfirm! This applies particularly to Royal Nepal Airlines. Make sure you get to the airport very early as people at the end of the queue can be left behind.

Organised Tours
Many agencies in Thamel offer budget tours to Tibet and these are currently the only way to get into Tibet. The following agencies are the most reliable, although none is particularly recommended:

Dharma Adventures (☎ 430499, fax 421053,
  ⒠ info@shivatours.com) PO 5385, Gairidhara
Explore Nepal Richa Tours & Travels
  (☎ 423064, 420710, fax 421573, ⒠ explore@
  ecomail.com.np, ⒲ www.explorenepalricha
  .com) PO Box 167, Thamel
Green Hill Tours, Treks & Expeditions
  (☎ 424968, fax 414803, ⒠ ghill@wlink.com
  .np, ⒲ www.greenhilltours.com) PO Box
  5072, Thamel

Places to Stay
There are dozens of places to stay in the tourist ghetto of Thamel. Listed here are a few to get you started.

Kathmandu Guest House (☎ 413632, ⒠ *kgh@wlink.com.np)* Singles without/with washbasin US$2/10, doubles without/with washbasin US$3/12, singles with private bathroom US$17-20, doubles with private bathroom US$20-30, singles/doubles with air-con US$50/60. This was the first hotel to open in the area and is still one of the most popular. It's often booked out weeks in advance during the high season. There's a 12% tax on top of all prices at this place.

Hotel Potala (☎ 419159, fax 416680) Rooms with shared bathroom Rs 200-250. Close to the heart of Thamel, almost opposite the popular KC's Restaurant, this small and friendly Tibetan-run place is cheap and cheerful.

Hotel Horizon (☎ 220904, ⒠ *horizon@ hons.com.np)* Rooms with private bathroom Rs 200-750. This is a good choice off the main street, down near the bank of tapestry shops, and has a range of rooms at quite reasonable prices.

Siddhartha Garden Guest House (☎ 227 119) Doubles with shared bathroom US$5, singles/doubles with private bathroom US$8/12. This French-run hotel not far from Hotel Utse has stylish rooms, Tibetan staff and a pleasant fruit garden that doubles as a restaurant.

Hotel Utse (☎ 226946, ⒠ *utse@wlink .com.np)* Singles/doubles US$15/22, deluxe rooms US$17/24. The Utse is a well-run Tibetan hotel in Jyatha, with spotlessly clean and very comfortable rooms. It has a good rooftop area, and it is often full in the high season.

Hotel Manang (☎ 410993, ⒠ *htlmnang@ vishnu.ccsl.com.np)* Singles/doubles US$55/ 65, deluxe rooms US$80/90. This modern three-star hotel in Paknajol has everything you could need. Many rooms have magnificent views and all have TV, air-con, phone and minibar. Rooms are often discounted to US$40/55. Next door, the *Hotel Marshyangdi (☎ 414105,* ⒠ *htlgold@mos.com.np)* is of a similar standard. A 10% tax is added on to all rooms at this place.

Kantipur Temple House (☎ 250131, ⒠ *kan tipur@tmplhouse.wlink.com.np)* Singles/ doubles US$50/60. Along a short alley at the southern end of Jyatha, this interesting new hotel has been built in the style of an old Newari temple, has tastefully decorated rooms and is eco-friendly. Rooms incur a 12% task on top of the room rate.

Getting Around
Taxis are fairly reasonably priced and most drivers will use the meter for short trips around town, which rarely come to more than Rs 50. In the evening you may have to negotiate a fare.

Three-wheeled autorickshaws are common and cost as little as half the taxi fare. Cycle rickshaws cost Rs 30 to 50 for most rides around town. Always agree on a price before you get in.

To/From the Airport Kathmandu's Tribhuvan International Airport is about 2km east of town. You will find an organised taxi service in the ground-floor foyer area immediately after you leave the baggage collection and customs section. The taxis have a fixed fare of Rs 250 to Thamel or Rs 200 to Durbar Marg.

Hotel touts outside the international terminal will offer you a free lift to their hotel, but you are less likely to get a discounted room rate this way as touts receive a hefty commission.

You should be able to get a taxi from Thamel to the airport for Rs 100.

CHENGDU
☎ 028 ● pop 11.3 million ● elevation 126m
It normally takes a day or two to arrange a ticket and permit to Lhasa so to fill in the time you could take a taxi or cycle out to the Panda Research Centre, 12km north-east of the city, or visit the teahouses in Renmin Park and the Wenshu Monastery.

It's best to change money at a Bank of China branch; there's one in the lobby of the Traffic Hotel.

In an emergency, Chengdu has a US consulate (☎ 558 3992) at 4 Lingshiguan Lu, in the south of town. See Lonely Planet's *South-West China* for more details.

Airlines
China Southwest Airlines, opposite the Jinjiang Hotel, will not sell air tickets to Lhasa (see also Organised Tours below).

Dragonair (☎ 675 5555 ext 6105, fax 675 5170) has an office at the Sichuan Hotel, Zongfu Lu.

Organised Tours
You can only buy an air ticket to Lhasa in conjunction with a tour. For this most travellers use the budget travel agencies at the Traffic Hotel, such as Tibet Budget Tour (☎ 554 1376), Traffic Travel Service (☎ 553 1285) and George of the Jungle. All offer the same prices and services.

Depending on how tight restrictions are, the Highfly Cafe (☎ 550 1572) and Sam's Backpacker Guesthouse (☎ 777 2593) can sometimes also arrange air tickets.

Places to Stay
Traffic Hotel (Jiaotong Fandian; ☎ *555 1017, fax 558 2777, 77 Linjiang Lu)* Dorm beds with air-con Y40, doubles/triples with private bathroom Y200/300. Conveniently located next to the Xinnanmen Bus Station, this is the main backpacker option and it's pretty good. All the rates include a terrible breakfast.

Sam's Guesthouse (☎ *609 9022,* e *sam tour@yahoo.com, 130 Shanxi Jie)* Dorm beds Y25, doubles with private bathroom without/with air con Y100/150. Sam's is inside the Rongcheng Hotel; enter through the gate on the hotel's left, head into the building straight ahead and you'll find reception down the first hall on the left. Facilities include left luggage, cafe, email, travel service, laundry, bike rental and book exchange.

Jindi Fandian (☎ *691 5339)* Singles/doubles with private bathroom Y160/230. This two-star hotel in the north-west of town has bright, clean, air-conditioned rooms.

Chengdu Hotel (Chengdu Dajiudian; ☎ *317 3888)* Doubles with bathroom Y300-400. Rooms are large, clean and comfortable; you may find that they are discounted to between Y120 and 240.

Minshan Hotel (Minshan Fandian; ☎ *558 3333,* e *mhotel@swww.com.cn, Renmin Nanlu)* Four-star standard rooms from Y800. This hotel has several bars, restaurants and a coffee shop and is popular with tour groups.

Jinjiang Hotel (Jinjiang Binguan; ☎ *558 2222, fax 558 23448, 80 Renmin Nanlu)* New-wing doubles Y1180, old-block singles/doubles Y788/960. This five-star giant has nonsmoking rooms.

Tibet Hotel (Xizang Fandian; ☎ *318 3388, fax 318 5678, 10 Renmin Beilu Yiduan)* Doubles Y400-600. This three-star hotel in the north of town has an ersatz Tibetan feel.

The next three hotels listed offer five-star luxury for about US$140 a night for doubles: *Holiday Inn Crowne Plaza (Zongfu Huangguan Ri Jiudian;* ☎ *678 6666, fax 678 6599,*

31 Zongfu Jie); **Yinhe Dynasty Hotel** *(Yinhe Wangshao Dafandian;* ☎ *661 8888,* e *dy nasty@mail.sc.cninfo.net, 99 Xiaxishuncheng Jie)*; and **Sheraton Chengdu Lido Hotel** *(Tianhu Lido Duxilaideng Fandian;* ☎ *676 8999, 15 Section 1, Renmin Zhonglu).*

Places to Eat

Paul's Oasis This funky backpacker-oriented place is on the north river bank, across from the Traffic Hotel. There are plenty of Western and Chinese snacks on offer and it's very popular for a beer in the evening. There are many small Chinese restaurants next door.

Weizhiyu Restaurant (30 Hongxing Zhonglu Si Duan) If you fancy something a bit more authentic, try this excellent local restaurant five-minutes' walk north of the Traffic Hotel.

Getting Around

The most useful bus is No 16, which runs from Chengdu's north train station to the south train station along Renmin Nanlu. Regular buses cost Y1, while the double-deckers cost Y2. Taxis have a flag fall of Y5 (Y6 at night), plus Y1.4 per kilometre. Both Sam's Guesthouse and the Traffic Hotel rent bikes for about Y10 per day, with a Y200 deposit.

To/From the Airport Shuangliu Airport is 18km west of the city. The Civil Aviation Authority of China (CAAC) runs a bus every half-hour between the ticket office on Renmin Nanlu and the airport (Y8). Taxis will take you to the airport for Y10 per person (minimum two people) from outside the ticket office. On the meter the ride is about Y40, plus an expressway toll.

Tibet

This section details how to get into Tibet from Nepal or China.

AIR

The only airline that flies into Tibet is China Southwest Airlines, which is based in Chengdu.

Flights to and from Lhasa are frequently cancelled or delayed in the winter months, so if you are flying at this time give yourself a couple of days' leeway in Chengdu if you have a connecting flight.

To/From Nepal

Flights between Kathmandu and Lhasa operate twice weekly in the low season (departing Tuesday and Saturday) and three times a week in the high season.

Individual travellers cannot buy air tickets from the China Southwest Airlines office without a TTB permit. Your only option is to buy a three- to eight-day package tour through a travel agency.

At the time of research, the cheapest package was a three-day tour for around US$360. This included the flight ticket (US$273), airport transfer to Kathmandu and Lhasa, TTB permits and dormitory accommodation for three nights in Lhasa.

The Chinese embassy in Kathmandu is not in the habit of giving Chinese visas to individual travellers so it is important that you arrive in Kathmandu with a Chinese visa in your passport. See the Visas & Documents in the Facts for the Visitor chapter for more on visas in Kathmandu.

Flights between Kathmandu and Lhasa may be cancelled at the slightest whiff of trouble in Lhasa and may also be shut down during the winter months.

To/From Chengdu

Flights between Chengdu and Lhasa cost Y1270, but you'll be very lucky if this is all you end up paying for the flight. Both in Chengdu and other cities, China Southwest Airlines will not normally sell you a ticket to Lhasa unless you already have a TTB permit.

To get around this, many travel agencies, especially those near the Traffic Hotel in Chengdu, will sell you a 'tour' that allows them to arrange a ticket for you. What the tour consists of depends largely upon the political climate in Lhasa. Out of the high tourist season (July to September) you can normally get away with booking only a ticket and airport transfers. However, at the height of summer, agencies may have to book your transport from Gongkar airport to Lhasa, three nights' dormitory accommodation and a tour in Lhasa, plus require either a cash deposit of Y200 to Y400 (which can be used towards onward travel) or a return ticket.

In May 2001 a standard Tibet package, consisting of two transfers, a one-way flight and three nights' dormitory accommodation and tour swung between Y2000 and Y2700. Packages are generally cheaper in March and April and start rising by May, reaching a peak in August. Travellers must travel in groups of five, although the agencies can normally rustle up enough individual travellers to form a small group. Everyone goes their own way once in Lhasa. Agencies normally need 24 hours to process the mythical TTB permit. This is still the most cost-effective way to enter Tibet.

Whether you actually see your TTB permit is unlikely, although your travel agency will wave it at check-in and airport security to allow you through. One group member will probably have to carry the permit and hand it to the guide at Gongkar airport.

With some advance planning it is sometimes possible to buy a Chengdu-Lhasa ticket from Air China offices abroad. The price for this is normally higher than Y1200 but you won't have to pay for any permits. The main problem arises when you try to board the plane in Chengdu without a TTB permit. You might be able to bluff your way through, but this is unlikely and not worth the gamble.

On a clear day the views from the plane are stupendous so try to get a window seat. In general the best views are from the left side of the plane from Chengdu to Lhasa and on the right side from Lhasa to Chengdu.

To/From Zhongdian & Kunming

In 2001 China Southwest Airlines introduced a weekly flight from Kunming to Lhasa via Zhongdian in north-west Yunnan. The flight alone costs Y1720 from Kunming and Y1250 from Zhongdian, but as with other flights to Lhasa, foreigners need to sign up on a tour to get their hands on a ticket.

The cheapest tour package means you start in Zhongdian; the package costs around Y2250 (including the air ticket, TTB permit, airport transfers and three nights' worth of dormitory accommodation in Lhasa), which is cheaper than flying from Chengdu. You must arrange the TTB permit and pick it up in Kunming, although the flight ticket can be picked up in either Zhongdian or Kunming.

Mr Chen is a travel agent located in Kunming in room 3116, building three, at the Camellia Hotel (Chahua Binguan; ☎ 0871-318 8114, mobile 0871-138 882 87389). He operates in affiliation with the TTB and offers packages for air travel on weekly Kunming-Zhongdian-Lhasa flights as follows: Prices are Y2550 from Kunming and Y2400 from Zhongdian; it may be possible to negotiate down from the latter figure. The packages include a one-way flight, a TTB permit, airport transfers and a three-day guided tour.

To/From Other Chinese Cities

From elsewhere in China there are direct flights to Lhasa weekly from Chongqing (Y1400) and four times weekly from Xining (Y1390). There is also a weekly flight from Chengdu to Chamdo in eastern Tibet (Y720).

Flight connections operate to/from Beijing (Y2040) twice a week via Chengdu, to/from Shanghai (Y2310) twice a week via Xining, to/from Xi'an (Y1420) four times a week via Xining and to/from Guangzhou (Y2100) once a week via Chongqing. All connections require you to change planes.

Buying tickets for these connections from Lhasa is no problem. However, 99% of travellers flying from China into Lhasa go from Chengdu or Zhongdian, because arranging a permit is so much easier from there.

LAND

Many individual travellers make their way to Tibet as part of a grand overland trip through China, Nepal, India and onwards. In many ways, land travel to Tibet is the best way to go, not only for the scenery en route but also because it can help spread the altitude gain over a few days.

In theory there are a number of land routes into Tibet. In practice, however, most travellers only use one of two officially sanctioned routes: Kathmandu to Lhasa via the Friendship Hwy or Golmud to Lhasa via the Qinghai-Tibet Hwy. Other possible routes (for now officially closed) are the Sichuan-Tibet Hwy, the Yunnan-Tibet Hwy and the Xinjiang-Tibet Hwy. Of these the Yunnan-Tibet Hwy is the 'most closed' (ie, very few travellers are getting through to Tibet this way); the 'least closed' is the Xinjiang-Tibet Hwy.

By 2010 there should be a rail link between Golmud and Lhasa. See the boxed text 'Mission Impossible' later for details.

Friendship Highway (Nepal to Tibet)

The 920km stretch of road between Kathmandu and Lhasa is known as the Friendship Hwy. The journey is without a doubt one of the most spectacular in the world.

From Kathmandu (elevation 1300m) the road travels gently up to Kodari (1873m), before leaving Nepal to make a steep switchback ascent to Zhangmu (2300m), the Tibetan border town. From here the road climbs and climbs, past Nyalam (3750m) to the top of the Tong-la (5120m), where travellers from Kathmandu are likely to feel decidedly weak and wobbly as a result of the altitude. Tingri (4390m) provides fabulous views of Mt Everest and the Himalaya and is where many travellers spend the night.

It is essential to watch out for the effects of altitude sickness during the early stages of this trip (see Health in the Facts for the Visitor chapter). Try to slip in a rest day at Tingri or Nyalam if you are heading up to Everest Base Camp at 5200m. See the Tsang chapter for details of sights and landmarks en route.

This highway is very well travelled nowadays and is a pleasant journey, except for one major problem – the Chinese authorities will not let individual travellers enter Tibet without a TTB permit and tour.

Because of this, several of Kathmandu's travel agencies offer 'budget' tours of Tibet to get you into Lhasa. At the time of research the cheapest of these tours cost US$220 per person for a basic three-day Land Cruiser trip to Lhasa, stopping in Zhangmu, Lhatse and Lhasa. An eight-day trip via Everest Base Camp, Sakya Monastery, Shigatse and other places costs US$450 per person. Prices include transport, permits, basic accommodation, guide and admission fees (group size is a minimum of five people). Agencies might pool their clients so you may find yourself travelling in a larger group than expected and perhaps a bus instead of the promised Land Cruiser. Other potential inconsistencies may include having to share a room when you were told you would be given a single.

It's best to obtain an individual Chinese visa before arriving in Kathmandu and ensure that you are not put on a group visa. For more information on potential visa snags see Visas & Documents in the Facts for the Visitor chapter.

China is 2¼ hours ahead of Nepali time.

Qinghai-Tibet Highway

The 1115km journey between Golmud and Lhasa is the subject of an ancient Chinese curse: 'May you travel by Chinese bus from Golmud to Lhasa'. Actually, I made that one up – but it deserves to be.

Golmud (3200m), the drab little Chinese town where the long journey begins, is approached by rail (13 to 18¼ hours), bus or even plane from Xining (capital of Qinghai province). If Golmud were not one of the most utterly depressing places in China, it would probably serve as a good place to hang out for a few days and acclimatise to the altitude. But it *is* one of the most utterly depressing places in China and consequently most people jump on a Lhasa-bound bus quicker than a CITS official can say 'give us your cash'.

If Golmud did not exist, CITS would have to invent it. It is a perfect bottleneck to capture Lhasa-bound individual travellers and screw them for every yuan possible. CITS officials make it their job to form welcoming parties for all incoming buses and trains.

CITS-approved buses for Lhasa leave from the Tibet bus station on Jinfen Lu at around 5pm. Foreigners are usually picked up at the Golmud Hotel and taken by CITS to the station. Foreigners are required to buy their tickets from CITS (☎/fax 413 003) on the 1st floor of the Golmud Hotel, at a massive mark-up.

Current regulations require that foreigners have not only a TTB permit (see Travel Permits in Facts for the Visitor), insurance and a minimum three-day tour, but also a return ticket to either Kathmandu, Chengdu or Golmud, and they must travel in a groups with a minimum of five people. The cheapest and most popular package currently costs Y1660, which includes the return bus fare to Golmud. If you want to stay in Tibet for more than three days, in theory you have to pay an extra Y100 per day. However, once in Lhasa you should be able to extend the date of departure at either the bus station or CAAC office. Otherwise cancel the ticket – either way you'll lose about 10% of the ticket price. When you purchase your ticket, make sure that CITS provides you with the ticket, not just a receipt.

Most people either pay up and then throw their return ticket away when they arrive in Lhasa, or they try one of the numerous touts offering lifts from Golmud.

You won't have to go looking for the guys offering seats on a bus to Tibet, they will find you. They generally ask for between Y600 and Y1000 to Lhasa. It's assumed that this price includes a bribe to the PSB along the way. There is no way to guarantee that you will get to Lhasa or that you won't be fined and sent back. Some travellers have made it to Lhasa hassle-free.

The main check post lies 25km south of Golmud and your ticket will be checked here. If you decide to try to hitch, bear in mind that some travellers have been sent back from Nagchu, about three-quarters of the way to Lhasa!

In contrast, travellers making their way from Lhasa to Golmud by sleeper bus can just buy a ticket from Lhasa bus station (Y210).

Tibetan Tasters

If you are heading to Golmud overland there are several worthwhile detours you can make to give you an idea of what you are in for. Labrang Monastery, around 100km south of Lanzhou in Gansu, is one of the six major monasteries of the Gelugpa Buddhist order and is well worth a visit. Another of the six is Ta'ersi (Kumbum) Monastery, 26km southeast of Xining. Both are easily visited on the way from Xi'an to Golmud.

The Qinghai-Tibet Hwy is cold, bleak and almost devoid of interesting sights. Before setting off you should stock up on munchies and drinks and, if you have not already done so, buy some warm clothing – toasty-warm People's Liberation Army (PLA) overcoats are available for around Y65. Golmud has several markets and numerous shops where you can buy supplies.

The trip itself takes anywhere between 30 and 50 hours, longer if there is a serious breakdown. Even in summer it can get bitterly cold, especially up on the high passes, the highest of which is Tangu-la (5180m). It is one of those once-in-a-lifetime trips.

Sichuan-Tibet Highway

The road between Chengdu and Lhasa is around 2400km or 2100km, depending on whether you take the northern or southern route.

While the occasional intrepid traveller still manages to make it through on this road, if your destination is Lhasa, this is not the most sensible of routes to take. The Sichuan section of the Sichuan-Tibet Hwy is now open to foreigners as far as the Tibetan border. Beyond this, the road is closed to individual travellers, although the occasional tour group and renegade explorer passes along it. Be prepared for a difficult trip that might end with a fine and an abrupt return.

There is very little in the way of public transport. Truck drivers face fines of up to Y2000 and the loss of their licence for carrying foreigners in their trucks, and it is a dangerous trip – numerous accidents have occurred on it. Perhaps your best chance is to hook up with a truck that is itself slightly illegal and therefore inclined to drive through the check posts at night. Apart from the check posts the likeliest place to be caught is at a hotel.

Food and accommodation is of a better standard and more widely available than on the Qinghai-Tibet Hwy (where there is basically nothing) or in western Tibet. For details of the Tibetan areas of Sichuan and Yunnan see Lonely Planet's *South-West China* guide. There are public buses as far as Derge on the northern branch and Batang on the southern branch.

The northern route involves a detour off the southern road just west of Kangding, travelling via Derge and Chamdo and rejoining the southern route around Pomda. A less-trafficked route heads due west from Chamdo to Nagchu.

On the southern route, onward travel from Batang, over the Dri-chu (Jinsha Jiang, or Yangzi River) and the Tibetan border to Markham, a further 275km west of Litang, is likely to be more difficult. Markham is where the Yunnan-Tibet Hwy joins the Sichuan-Tibet Hwy and so the local PSB is particularly scrupulous about making sure that no travellers continue on to Lhasa.

The 780km stretch of road between Markham and Bayi is likely to be the biggest hurdle for travellers making their way to Lhasa. There are PSB offices in most towns, particularly Pomi, Lunang and Nyingtri. If you make it as far as Bayi, you will have to deal with the Bayi PSB. Many travellers have had problems with this PSB, and the best advice is to tell them you have come from Lhasa and let them have the pleasure of sending you back. Be patient and try not to be belligerent.

For details on the routes through eastern Tibet and an overview of routes through western Sichuan see the Kham (Eastern Tibet) chapter.

Yunnan-Tibet Highway

The Yunnan-Tibet Hwy would be a wonderful way to approach Tibet if it were ever to open. From Lijiang a road heads up to the Tibetan towns and monasteries of Zhongdian (Gyeltang) and Deqin (Jol), from where there are public buses north across the Tibetan border (and check post) 112km to Yanjing. From here it's 111km to Markham on the Sichuan southern route. For details on the Tibetan areas of north-west Yunnan see Lonely Planet's *South-West China*. For an outline of the Tibetan section of this trip, see the Kham (Eastern Tibet) chapter.

Unfortunately, the Yunnan route is closed to individual travellers, who are normally stopped, fined and turned back at Yanjing or Markham. A few travel companies are starting to organise tours along this route. CITS (☎ 0887-822 2238) in Zhongdian was offering a 12-day Land Cruiser trip for Y15,000, which works out at around US$500 per person travelling in a group of four. Other companies that might be able to arrange this kind of trip are Haiwei Trails (see Organised Tours earlier) and Gyaltang Travel (☎ 887-822 3646, fax 822 3620, ⓔ uttara@chengdu.net) in Zhongdian.

Xinjiang-Tibet Highway

The Xinjiang-Tibet Hwy is officially off limits, but interestingly, at the time of research, quite a large number of travellers were managing to get through, even on bicycles. Approximately 1350km of road separates Kashgar from Ali in western Tibet and for the adventurous this can form an extension to a trip along the Karakoram Hwy. For information on travelling between Ali and Lhasa or Zhangmu see the Getting There & Away section of the Ngari (Western Tibet) chapter.

With at least two passes over 5400m, the Xinjiang-Tibet Hwy is the highest road in the world. It can be bitterly cold and closes down for the winter months from December to February. The whole trip takes around four days of travel, depending on how lucky you are with lifts.

From Kashgar there are buses every halfhour to Yecheng (Karghilik; Y23, five hours). There is no reliable onward public transport from Yecheng to Ali but some

Mission Impossible

Chinese engineers and bureaucrats love to prove the dominance of Chinese technology and mass mobilisation over Mother Nature – just look at the Three Gorges Dam or even the Great Wall of China. But there's one project that still stumps China's finest technocrats: how to build a railway line to China's most 'backward' province, the only one today without a rail connection.

Since 1958 there have been repeated investigations into building a railway line from Golmud to Lhasa, a project that would involve drilling dozens of ice tunnels through the Nyenchen Tanglha (Tangula) mountains. Finally, in 1979, it was declared impossible.

Then in 1998 they tried again, this time investigating a potential 1654km routing from Dali in Yunnan province to Lhasa, linking Lhasa to Bangkok. It was calculated that almost half of the line, some 710km, would have to consist of tunnels or bridges at an estimated cost of US$8 billion.

In February 2001 the Chinese government announced it had approved construction of a 1118km railway line from Golmud to Lhasa, to be the world's highest railway line, as part of its campaign to boost economic development in its western hinterland. Tibetan support groups fear the line will prove disastrous for local Tibetans, opening the demographic and economic floodgates to Han Chinese immigrants and troops (much like the recent line to Kashgar in troubled Xinjiang province), and leading to increased exploitation of Tibet's mineral resources. The Dalai Lama has condemned the plan and called for international corporations to boycott the venture. The railway is slated to be finished by 2010 at a cost of US$2.5 billion, but may well be operational before then.

travellers have successfully hitched lifts with trucks for a few hundred yuan. For details of the route, see Xinjiang to Ali in the Ngari (Western Tibet) chapter.

Other Routes into Tibet

Since 1994 another route into Tibet has been open, to tour groups only, passing through Purang (Nepali: Taklakot). Special visas are required for this trip. Trekkers start by travelling by road or flying from Kathmandu to Nepalganj, then flying from there to Simikot in the far west of Nepal. From Simikot it's a five- or six-day walk to the Tibetan border, crossing the Humla Karnali. You can then drive the 28km to Purang and 107km on to the Mt Kailash area via Manasarovar. For details on the route from the Nepali border to Mt Kailash see the Ngari (Western Tibet) chapter.

The border between Nepal and China is sometimes closed to foreigners, especially when tensions are high between the authorities and the Maoist rebels based in western Nepal. At the time of writing the rebels were charging some trekkers a US$60 'fee' to walk through the territory they held. See Lonely Planet's *Trekking in Nepal* for more information.

Indian travellers are now reportedly allowed to cross into Tibet in specially arranged groups from Sikkim via the Natula and the Jelep-la, along the former trading routes between Lhasa and Kalimpong. Other foreign travellers are not yet allowed on this route.

Getting Around

Tibet's transport infrastructure is poorly developed and, with the exception of the Friendship Hwy and the Qinghai-Tibet Hwy, most of the roads are in very poor condition. Some work is being undertaken to improve this situation – a vital aspect of Chinese plans to develop Tibet – but it is unlikely that travel in Tibet will become comfortable or easy in the near future.

The main problem for travellers short on time is the scarcity of public transport. There are no flights (except those in or out of Tibet), no rail system, and only a handful of buses and minibuses plying the roads between Lhasa and other major Tibetan towns such as Shigatse and Tsetang. So-called public 'pilgrim buses' to monastery attractions have become more widespread in recent years, but are generally restricted to the major monastic sites in the Lhasa region.

For those who would like to tour Tibet by car or motorcycle, the news is bleak: Basically it's impossible to drive unless you have a Chinese driving licence. This leaves many travellers in the position of having to band together to hire 4WDs and drivers to get around Tibet. The availability of such vehicles has increased recently, but in the peak summer months of August and September there can still be a squeeze and prices can rise. Travellers should bear in mind that, if they have limited time and want to see as much of Tibet as possible, they are probably going to end up spending quite a bit of money renting vehicles.

The other main option is to hitch. If you can get the necessary travel permits (see Travel Permits in the Facts for the Visitor chapter) and you have time this isn't a bad idea. You will still have to pay, but only a fraction of the amount for a Land Cruiser. You'll need to be much more self-sufficient, and be prepared to wait for hours, if not days, for a truck driver willing to take you. Hitching in Tibet can be very frustrating.

Those with more time can, of course, trek or cycle their way around the high plateau.

BUS

Bus travel in Tibet is slow and gruelling. Most bus services originate in Lhasa and connect the capital with Shigatse, Tsetang and local sites such as Ganden Monastery. There are also buses from Shigatse to Gyantse and Sakya. Many routes go to places off limits to foreigners, such as Yatung or Bayi, and you'd be lucky to be allowed to board.

If travelling by bus, try to avoid sitting in the back of the bus. The combination of bad suspension and shocking roads makes for very bumpy journeys, and the back of the bus is the worst place to be. You will almost certainly be required to stow your baggage on the roof if you have a bulky backpack. If possible, check that it is tied down properly (bus drivers normally do a good job of checking such details) and lock your pack as a precaution against theft. Try to see what everyone else is paying before you hand over your cash.

MINIBUS

Private entrepreneurs are taking to the roads in increasing numbers, and minibus services are now available to many areas that are not served by buses. Unfortunately, local authorities occasionally fine minibus services between Lhasa and Shigatse (and sometimes other destinations) because they don't have government permission (and insurance) to take foreigners. Consequently, some minibus drivers are cautious of taking foreigners.

Minibuses operate out of Lhasa to monastic sites such as Drepung, Tsurphu, Ganden and Samye, and to Tsetang and Shigatse. From Shigatse, minibuses run to Gyantse and Lhatse. Ticket prices are cheap but you can expect to spend a lot of time sitting around waiting for the minibus to fill up.

It is often possible to get a ride from Lhasa to the Nepali border (with an overnight stop in Shigatse) on minibuses heading down to pick up groups arriving from Kathmandu. Ask at travel agencies or look for advertisements on hotel notice boards. You'll pay between Y250 and Y350 for a seat. Be warned that if the group doesn't run, neither does the minibus, and the agency won't bother to tell you. There are no discounts if you are only going to Tingri or Lhatse.

CAR & MOTORCYCLE

Renting a vehicle has become the most popular way of getting around in Tibet. Tourists are not yet permitted to drive rental vehicles in China; however, on Tibet's roads you're not likely to mind.

There is currently only one agency in Lhasa authorised to deal with vehicle rental, although this may change in the future (see Travel Agencies in the Lhasa chapter). Prices depend largely on the kilometres driven (roughly Y3.50 per kilometre) not the time taken, meaning that you can often add

Dealing with an Agency

When dealing with an agency to rent a vehicle, you need to establish a few ground rules. First, work out an itinerary for your trip. This will allow the agency to give you a firm quote based on distance covered and number of days on the road. The agency may even suggest changes to your proposal based on the current road conditions, travel times, accommodation en route and so on.

You'll need to fix the rate for any extra days that may need to be tacked onto an itinerary. For delays caused by bad weather, blocked passes, swollen river crossings and so on, there should be no extra charge for jeep hire. At the very least the cost for extra days should be split 50% between your group and the agency. For delays caused by vehicle breakdowns, driver illness etc then the agency should cover 100% of the costs and provide a backup vehicle if necessary.

Second, ask the agency about its policy on refunds for an uncompleted trip. Some agencies refuse any kind of refund, others are more open to negotiation.

Third, make sure that the price you agree on covers all permit costs, and establish which costs are not covered in the price (for example, the Y400 vehicle fee to drive to Everest Base Camp).

Finally, be aware that the vehicle you receive has probably been subcontracted from outside the agency. You should ensure that the vehicle and driver have the necessary permits and insurance required to carry foreigners. Also, and more importantly, you should verify that the agency will take responsibility in the event of a vehicle breakdown. Some reputable agencies will calmly refuse to take any role in disputes between you and the owner of the vehicle. Find out where you stand in advance.

Once you are sorted with the agency it's a good idea to organise a meeting between your group and the driver(s) and guide a day or two before departure. Make sure the drivers are aware of your itinerary (it may be the first time they have seen it!). Ensure that the guide speaks fluent Tibetan, good Chinese and useable English. Strong personality clashes would suggest a change of personnel.

Unless you are qualified mechanic, inspecting the soundness of the vehicle may prove to be difficult, but you should carry out the following basic checks. First make sure that the 4WD can at least be engaged (not just that the stick moves!) and that the 'diff lock' can be locked and unlocked (this is usually done via tabs on the front wheel hubs). For longer trips, make sure that at least one shovel and a long steel tow cable (rope cables are useless) is supplied. Snow chains are apparently available for trucks but not for Land Cruisers. Tyres and spares on both vehicles should be in reasonable condition (by Tibetan standards). Check that fuel cans don't leak and that there's rope to tie baggage to the roof rack.

The only other predeparture issues to consider for long trips are warm clothing, a good sleeping bag, plenty of food and perhaps a small stove. A tent is an excellent backup. A few plastic barrels or sacks (available in most markets) are useful to protect your gear from the dust and general thrashing it will get in the back of the truck. Jerry cans to carry water (and even *chang*, or Tibetan barley beer!) are a good idea.

Andre Ticheler

an extra day to your itinerary for the same cost. If you are not returning with your vehicle (from Lhasa to the Nepali border, for example) you can expect to pay an extra 50% of the one-way hire rate for the vehicle to return empty. Prices are higher on trips where a permit and both guide and driver are needed. Guide fees are normally calculated at Y150 per day.

Toyota Land Cruisers are the most widely seen rented vehicles plying the high plateau loaded with backpackers. They have room for six people and their luggage, although five is more comfortable. Three can go in the back, two in the front and there is often a fold-down seat in the boot. For longer trips where a guide is required it's worth limiting the number of passengers in a Land Cruiser to four (plus the guide) as any more than that is a real grind.

Beijing jeeps are cheaper but can only hold around four people with their luggage, which ends up making them more expensive per person. Pajero jeeps are the choice of high-ranking party cadres and so are hard to find. Renting a minibus with 20 or more seats really spreads the costs around – but who can be bothered looking for 19 other travel companions?

The best place to hire vehicles is Lhasa. Before organising a vehicle, check the notice boards at the main budget hotels. There are usually dozens of notices advertising seats on trips to all quarters of Tibet. The most popular destinations are the Nepali border, Nam-tso, Drigung Til and Mt Kailash, and there will probably be a few notices about more-obscure destinations.

Actually hiring a vehicle is subject to all kinds of pitfalls (see the boxed text 'Dealing with an Agency' for some guidelines). If possible, it is a good idea to reach an agreement that payment be delivered in two instalments: one before setting off and one on successful completion of the trip. This gives you more leverage in negotiating a refund if your trip was unsuccessful (one reason why agencies are loathe to do this).

Drawing up a contract in English and Tibetan or Chinese is a good idea, but carries much less weight in Tibet than it would

elsewhere in the world. Keep contracts short and to the point. List your exact itinerary, the price and method of payment. Clauses that prevent the driver from picking up 'friends' and 'relatives' en route are useful if you do not want to be squeezed by freeloaders. Above all, get together with the driver before the trip and go through the main points of the contract verbally. You are likely to have far fewer problems if you can reach friendly terms with your driver by treating him with respect – giving him some cigarettes or some kind of small gift – rather than waving a contract in his face.

BICYCLE

Long-distance cyclists are once again appearing on the roads of Tibet. Most pack their bikes onto their tour to Lhasa and then cycle back along the Friendship Hwy. Others buy mountain bikes in China and bring them up to Lhasa; some even buy their bikes in Lhasa. Any of these options is currently feasible, and local authorities appear to be turning a blind eye to the phenomenon.

Bringing a Bicycle into Tibet

There don't seem to be any regulations on bringing a bike into Tibet from Kathmandu or elsewhere. If you enter from Nepal, however, you will not be allowed to ride on from Zhangmu. Instead, you will have to put your bike on the roof of a Land Cruiser, drive all the way to Lhasa and then cycle back!

Rental

The only place in Tibet where you can easily rent bicycles is Lhasa. Rates of Y2 to Y3 per hour or Y20 to Y30 per day prevail, and the bikes are usually clunky Chinese Flying Pigeons, useless on anything other than (downhill) tarmac. Test the brakes and tyres before taking the bike out onto the streets. An extra padlock might be a good idea, as there is a problem with bicycle theft in the capital.

Purchase

Nowadays it is possible to buy a Chinese-made or (better) Taiwanese-made mountain bike in Lhasa for about Y500. Shop around in the area near the Potala on Dekyi Nub Lam. Standards aren't all that bad, although you should check the gears in particular. Do not expect the quality of such bikes to be equal to those you might buy at home – bring plenty of spare parts. Bikes have a relatively high resale value in Kathmandu and you might even make a profit if the bike is in good shape (which is unlikely after a trip across Tibet!).

Touring

Most Public Security Bureau (PSB) officials have no idea whether foreigners are allowed to cycle around Tibet, which means that most will leave you alone as long as you have a valid Chinese visa and a travel permit.

Despite the official ambivalence, Tibet still poses unique challenges to the individual cyclist. The roads are generally very bad. Even though there's not much traffic, wind squalls and dust storms can make your work particularly arduous, the warm summer months can bring flash flooding, and then there is the question of your fitness. Tibet's high-altitude mountainous terrain is sure to test the determination of all cyclists who set out on its roads.

You will need to be prepared to do your own repairs. A full bicycle-repair kit, several spare inner tubes, and a spare tyre and chain are essential. Preferably bring an extra rim and some spare spokes. Extra brake wire and brake pads are useful (you'll be descending 3000m from Lhasa to Kathmandu!). Other useful equipment includes reflective clothing, a helmet, a dust mask, goggles, gloves and padded trousers.

You will also need to be prepared with supplies: food, water-purifying tablets and camping equipment, just as if you were trekking. Most long-distance cyclists will probably find formal accommodation and restaurants only available at two- or three-day intervals. It may be possible to stay with army and road repair camps in remote places. See the boxed text 'Kilometre Markers along the Friendship Highway' in the Tsang chapter and 'Kilometre Markers along the Yarlung Tsangpo: Chushul to Tsetang' in the Ü chapter.

Obviously you need to be in good physical condition to undertake road touring in Tibet. Experienced cyclists recommend a program of distance training before heading off. Spend some time acclimatising to the altitude and taking leisurely rides around Lhasa (for example) before setting off on a long trip.

On the plus side, while Tibet has some of the highest-altitude roads in the world, gradients are usually quite manageable. Tibetan roads are designed for low-powered Chinese trucks, and tackle the many high passes of the region with low-gradient switchback roads. Most cyclists report there are few occasions when it is necessary to get off their bikes and push.

Touring Routes The most popular touring route at present is Lhasa-Kathmandu, along the Friendship Hwy. It is an ideal route in that it takes in most of Tibet's main sights, offers you superb scenery and (for those travelling from Lhasa) features a spectacular roller-coaster ride down from high La Lung-la into the Kathmandu valley. The trip takes a minimum of two weeks, although to do it justice and include stopovers at Gyantse, Shigatse and Sakya, this will expand to 20 days. The entire trip is just over 940km, although most people start from Shigatse. Watch for the kilometre markers, as these can be a very useful way of knowing exactly how far you have gone and how far you still have to go. For detailed information on this route, see the Tsang chapter.

It is also possible to cycle to Everest Base Camp, although very few travellers have attempted this tour. Keen cyclists with good mountain bikes might want to consider this option as a side trip on the Lhasa-Kathmandu route. The trip would have to be tackled from the Shegar turn-off, and it would take around two days to Rongphu Monastery.

Other possibilities are endless. Tsurphu and Ganden Monasteries are relatively easy (although uphill) trips. Drigung Til also makes a good destination. Cycling in the Yarlung Valley region would be a wonderful option if it were not for the permit problems. Some cyclists even tackle the trip to

Nam-tso, although the nomads' dogs can be a real problem here.

Hazards Cycling in Tibet is not to be taken lightly. Traffic on Tibetan roads is relatively light, but cyclists do have to be prepared for some very erratic driving. Some cyclists have also complained of deliberate offensive driving by Chinese troop convoys, for whom forcing a couple of foreign cyclists off the road is a brief escape from the tedium of soldiering up on the high plateau. It would be wise to pull off the road and wait for such convoys to pass.

Dirt roads prevail in Tibet, and these present particular problems. Cyclists who pick up too much speed on downhill stretches run the grave risk of slipping on gravel. Numerous cycling trips have been brought to an abrupt halt by such a misadventure. Be sensible. Wear a cycling helmet and lightweight leather gloves and, weather permitting, try to keep as much of your body covered with protective clothing as possible. A denim jacket, jeans, gloves and a helmet will protect you from the worst of gravel rash and head injuries if you take a tumble. It goes without saying that cyclists should also be prepared with a comprehensive medical kit. See the boxed text 'Medical Kit Check List' under Health in the Facts for the Visitor chapter for details.

Dogs are a major problem for cyclists in Tibet, especially in more remote areas. You may have to pedal like mad to outpace them. Children have been known to throw stones at cyclists.

HITCHING

Hitching is never entirely safe in any country in the world, and we don't recommend it. Travellers who decide to hitch should understand that they are taking a small but potentially serious risk. However, in Tibet, hitching is often the only alternative to hiring an expensive Land Cruiser and so has become a fairly established practice. The advice that follows should help to make journeys as fast and safe as possible.

With the exception of travellers hitching out to western Tibet and the very small number making their way illegally from Chengdu to Lhasa, few foreigners travel long distances by truck these days. The main reason is that the authorities impose heavy fines on truck drivers caught transporting foreign travellers and may even confiscate their licence. This is particularly the case on the Lhasa-Chengdu route, where fines of Y2000 prevail, plus whatever local officials demand in bribes. There seems to be little stopping truck drivers from picking up travellers off the main highways, however, especially if there are no check posts en route. Sometimes you can get a lift on a pilgrim truck or an organised passenger truck.

The most frequently seen truck in Tibet is the Dongfeng (East Wind), a sturdy and basic Chinese-made vehicle with a carrying capacity of around 10 tonnes. It comes in a variety of models. The occasional Japanese-made truck also turns up.

If you hitch by truck in Tibet, be prepared to share the hardships of a trucker's life. You will probably end up helping to drag the vehicle out of rivers and sand drifts, and assisting in repairs. Particularly in western Tibet, the roads are atrocious and accidents, breakdowns and delays are par for the course. If you are headed out to fairly remote destinations you should be equipped to camp out for the night if you don't get a ride. One guy we heard of waited so long for a lift to Mt Kailash that he built a *chörten* (stupa) from stones out of boredom. By the time he got a ride it was over 1m tall!

Trucks aren't the only transport on the roads. There are also plenty of half-empty Land Cruisers heading down the Friendship Hwy to pick up a group, or returning after having dropped one off. It's a wonderful feeling to finally get a lift in an empty Land Cruiser after being rejected all day by a stream of dilapidated trucks travelling at 30km/h!

Bear in mind that nowadays it is very unusual to hear of people getting free lifts in Tibet. It does occur occasionally, but more often than not you will be expected to pay for your lift. The amount is entirely negotiable, but in areas where traffic is minimal, drivers will often demand quite large sums.

One point to keep in mind when scouring a town for a lift is that a truck's number plate tells you where it is registered, and therefore where it is likely to be heading to. The following letters indicate places of registration:

letter	place of registration
A	Lhasa
B	Chamdo
C	Shannan (for Tsetang)
D	Shigatse
E	Nagchu
F	Ali
G	Nyingtri
J	Golmud

It's worth investing in a face mask (readily available in Lhasa) as the roads in Tibet are very dusty.

Back in the early days of travelling in Tibet, truck depots were good places to organise lifts with trucks. Nowadays you will be drawing unwanted attention to yourself by popping into depots in Tibet's urban centres. It is far better to find a lift out on the road. Those planning on hitching along the Friendship Hwy, from Lhasa for example, should at least get as far as Shigatse, and preferably Lhatse, before 'extending a thumb'. See the boxed text 'Travelling to Ngari' in the Ngari (Western Tibet) chapter for information on hitching out to Mt Kailash.

It's a good idea to start hitching a few kilometres out of town because then you know that traffic is going in your direction and is not about to turn off after 400m. This is especially important if there is a check post nearby. It's best to walk through the check post yourself and wait for a lift a couple of kilometres on the other side.

LOCAL TRANSPORT

Local transport is only available in Lhasa and Shigatse. In some parts of Tibet it is possible to get short lifts with tractors, an extremely uncomfortable way to travel.

Bus

Minibuses ply the streets of Lhasa and Shigatse these days, and it is possible to travel quickly from one end of town to the other for just Y2.

Pedicab

Pedicabs (pedal-operated tricycles that take passengers) are available in Lhasa, Gyantse, Shigatse and Bayi. They are a slow and expensive way to get around. For example, in Lhasa it costs a minimum of Y10 to go from one end of town to the other and it is a much more time-consuming process than travelling by minibus. Some serious haggling is required for hiring pedicabs.

Autorickshaw

A couple of towns in eastern Tibet, such as Pomi and Bayi, have motorised three-wheeler rickshaws that take passengers around town or to destinations (eg, monasteries) just outside of town. Negotiate the fare before you set off.

Tractor

In Shigatse, tractors serve as the town's public transport system and rides cost around Y2 or Y3. Elsewhere in Tibet the tractor can be a good option for short trips, especially in the Yarlung Valley. For a few yuan, drivers are normally quite happy to have some passengers in the back. Rides of anything over 10 minutes quickly become excruciatingly painful.

Taxi

One result of China's economic infusion into Tibet is the large number of taxis now available in most towns, even Ali in western Tibet. Taxis in Lhasa, Shigatse and Ali charge a standard Y10 anywhere in the city; for longer trips negotiate a fare. Fixed-route passenger taxis also run between Lhasa, Gongkar airport and Tsetang and you only need to pay for your seat.

ORGANISED TOURS

Nominally, organised tours must be arranged before you enter Tibet (see Organised Tours in the Getting There & Away chapter for a list of companies that offer tours from outside Tibet). Moreover, to get into Tibet from Chengdu or Kathmandu you have to book a so-called 'tour' of three days which includes transport, accommodation, transfers and a guide (although most travellers skip the 'tour' section once they've arrived in Lhasa).

However, if you hire a Land Cruiser, along with a driver and often a guide, you have effectively arranged a kind of do-it-yourself tour within Tibet. For detailed information on such 'do-it-yourself' tours, see Car & Motorcycle earlier in this chapter; see also Rental Vehicles in the Lhasa chapter.

Travellers who arrive independently in Lhasa, but who want to undertake a tour organised by someone else, are limited to arranging travel through the Family (or Foreign) and Independent Traveller (FIT) offices run by the Tibet Tourism Bureau (TTB). For more information, see Travel Agencies in the Lhasa chapter.

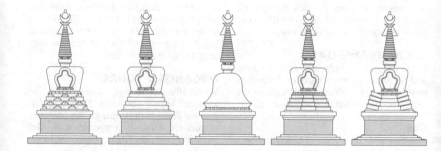

Lhasa

☎ 0891 • pop 200,000 • elevation 3595m

Lhasa, the heart and soul of Tibet, for centuries the abode of the Dalai Lamas, and object of devout pilgrimage is still a city of wonders, despite the large-scale encroachments of Chinese influence.

As you enter the Kyi-chu Valley, either on the long haul from Golmud or from Gongkar airport, your first hint that Lhasa is close at hand is the sight of the Potala, a vast white and ochre fortress soaring over this, one of the world's highest cities. It is a sight that has heralded the marvels of the Holy City to travellers for close to four centuries.

While the Potala dominates the Lhasa skyline and, as the residence of the Dalai Lamas, serves as a symbolic focus for Tibetan hopes of self-government, it is the Jokhang, some 2km to the east of the Potala, that is the spiritual heart of the city. A curious mix of sombre darkness, wafting incense and prostrating pilgrims, the Jokhang is the most sacred and active of Tibet's temples. Encircling it is the Barkhor, the holiest of Lhasa's devotional circumambulation circuits. It is here that most visitors first fall in love with Tibet. The medieval push and shove of crowds from another time and place, the street performers, the stalls hawking everything from prayer flags to jewel-encrusted yak skulls, and the devout tapping their foreheads to the ground at every step is an exotic brew that few newcomers can resist.

However, the Potala and the Jokhang, though prominent, are just two of the sights that Lhasa has to offer. Close to the Jokhang are a number of smaller active temples that are little visited by foreign travellers. The alleys running off the Barkhor circuit are cluttered with pool tables, market stalls and milling crowds from all over Tibet. The Norbulingka, summer palace of the Dalai Lamas, is a short distance away in the western part of town; and in Lhasa's low-lying surrounding hills are the important Gelugpa monasteries of Sera and Drepung.

Highlights

- Letting yourself be swept around the Barkhor, Lhasa's fascinating medieval pilgrim circuit, brimming with religious artefacts and prostrating pilgrims
- Joining the shuffling, murmuring pilgrims around the network of shrines of the Jokhang, the spiritual heart of Tibet
- Winding your way through the Potala, the deserted but impressive home of the Dalai Lamas
- Exploring Sera and Drepung, two of the largest and most intact of Tibet's great monasteries
- Making an easy day trip from Lhasa to Ganden Monastery, with its fine pilgrim circuit
- Walking Lhasa's pilgrim circuits, while rubbing shoulders with pilgrims
- Visiting one of Lhasa's small off-the-beaten-track temples

And just a word of warning: It's not uncommon to feel breathless, suffer from headaches and sleep poorly if you fly straight into Lhasa. Take things easy for the first few days and try to drink lots of fluids. For detailed information on acute mountain sickness (AMS; also known as altitude sickness), its symptoms and its treatment, see Health in the Facts for the Visitor chapter.

HISTORY

Lhasa rose to prominence as an important centre of administrative power in the 7th century AD, when Songtsen Gampo (c. 618–49), a local ruler in the Yarlung Valley, continued the task initiated by his father of unifying Tibet in concert with other local chieftains. Songtsen Gampo moved his capital to Lhasa and built a palace on the site that is now occupied by the Potala. At this time the temples of Ramoche and the

Jokhang were established to house Buddha images brought as the dowries of Songtsen Gampo's Chinese and Nepali wives.

The rule of the Yarlung kings from their new capital, Lhasa, lasted some 250 years. There is little to draw on in imagining the kind of capital Lhasa might have been during this time. Chinese records from Dunhuang state that the capital of Lhasa was a walled city with flat-roofed houses and refer to the 'king and his nobles' as living 'in felt tents'. The same records refer to an aversion to washing, the eating of *tsampa* (roasted-barley flour) and the plaited hair of Tibetan women – customs that persist to the present day.

With the break-up of the Yarlung empire, Buddhism enjoyed a gradual resurgence at monastic centres outside Lhasa. It was at Sakya that the next large-scale Tibetan regime emerged with Mongol support in the 13th century. Subsequent Tibetan governments were located in Nedong (Ü) and Shigatse (Tsang). No longer the capital, Lhasa languished in the backwaters of Tibetan history until the fifth Dalai Lama (1617–82) defeated the Shigatse Tsang kings with Mongol support.

The fifth Dalai Lama moved his capital to Lhasa. He built his palace, the Potala, on the site of Songtsen Gampo's 7th-century palace. Lhasa has remained Tibet's capital since 1642, and most of the city's historical sights date from this second stage of the city's development. Very little remains of Lhasa's 7th-century origins.

Modern Lhasa in many ways provides the visitor with both the best and the worst of contemporary Tibet. After all, despite the city's rich historical associations and colourful Tibetan population, it is here that Chinese control is at its most trigger-happy, and much of the city's charm has fallen prey to Chinese 'modernisation'.

Photographs of the city taken before October 1950 reveal a small town nestled at the foot of the Potala and linked by an avenue to another cluster of residences in the area of the Jokhang. The population of the city before the Chinese takeover is thought to have been between 20,000 and 30,000.

Today the city has a population of over 150,000, and Chinese residents outnumber Tibetans.

Shöl, the village at the foot of the Potala, has all but disappeared, and the old West Gate, through which most people entered the Holy City, was torn down during the Cultural Revolution to be replaced by a smaller, modern version in 1995. The area in front of the Potala has been made into a Tiananmen-style public square, and what used to be known as Gumolingka Island, once a traditional picnic spot for Tibetans, has been replaced by a Chinese-style shopping and karaoke complex. At the time of research, there were even plans to erect a 35m-tall monument in front of the Potala to 'celebrate' the 50th anniversary of Tibet's 'liberation'.

The Tibetan quarter is now an isolated enclave in the eastern end of town, comprising only around 4% of the total area of contemporary Lhasa. Even these lingering enclaves of tradition are under threat despite official protection. Lhasa has probably changed more in the last twenty years than in the thousand years before.

ORIENTATION

While Lhasa has emerged as a surprisingly sprawling city in recent years, orientation is still a relatively simple affair. The city divides clearly into a western (Chinese) section and an eastern (Tibetan) section. The Chinese section holds most of Lhasa's upmarket accommodation options, along with Chinese restaurants, bars and the Nepali consulate. The Tibetan eastern end of town is more colourful and has all the lower-end accommodation popular with individual travellers.

The principal thoroughfare for orientation is Dekyi Nub Lam, which becomes Dekyi Shar Lam in the east of town (in Tibetan, *nub* means west, *shar* means east). This road, known in Chinese as Beijing Zhonglu and Beijing Donglu, runs from west to east past the Tibet Hotel, the Lhasa Hotel (formerly the Holiday Inn), the yak statues, the Potala and the main post office, and into the Tibetan part of town, passing the Yak and

Banak Shol hotels, two of the most popular budget accommodation options.

The Barkhor circuit and the Jokhang, at the centre of the Tibetan quarter, are about five minutes' walk south-east of the Yak Hotel. There's a small Muslim quarter with a few mosques south-east of the Barkhor.

The Jokhang and Barkhor Square are between Dekyi Shar Lam and Chingdröl Shar Lam (Jiangsu Lu) and are connected to these two main roads by a web of winding alleyways lined with the white-washed facades of traditional Tibetan homes. This Tibetan area is not particularly extensive. Rather than worry about orientation it is more fun to simply slip away from the Barkhor circuit at some point and aimlessly wander the alleys. You won't stay lost for long.

Lhasa's Pilgrim Circuits

For Tibetan pilgrims, who approach the Holy City with priorities somewhat different from those of the average Western visitor, the principal points of orientation are Lhasa's three *koras* (pilgrimage circuits): the Nangkhor, the Barkhor and the Lingkhor. For the visitor, all the koras are well worth following, especially during festivals such as Saga Dawa, when the distance between tourists and pilgrim can become very fine. Remember always to proceed clockwise.

The Nangkhor
This kora encircles the inner precincts of the Jokhang.

The Barkhor
This traces the outskirts of the Jokhang in a circuit of approximately 800m. It is the most famous of Lhasa's pilgrimage circuits and probably the best introduction to the old town for newcomers. For more details, see Barkhor Area later in this chapter.

The Lingkhor
This is the devotional route that traditionally encompassed the entirety of the old city. Nowadays the Lingkhor includes a great deal of scenery that is of a decidedly secular and modern nature, but it is still used by pilgrims. The route is marked on the Lhasa and Barkhor Area maps. You can join the circuit anywhere. One option is to walk south of Barkhor Square onto Chingdröl Shar Lam and head west. After about 2km, a small alley turns north (look out for the stone carvers) and then west to the excellent rock carvings of Chagpo Ri. From here the trail continues west and then north up to the Kunde Ling. Where the trail hits the main road there are some holy 'rubbing stones' which pilgrims rub their backs and legs against. Head east along Dekyi Nub Lam, past the Gesar Ling, and turn left at the golden yak statue up to the chörtens near the Lukhang. From here follow the main road east along Lingkhor Chang Lam (Linkuo Beilu) and then south down Lingkhor Shar Lam. Turn right towards the main city mosque and head west past the Ani Sangkhung Nunnery and a second smaller mosque until you reach the Lho Rigsum Lhakhang on your right. From here the Lingkhor turns south onto Chingdröl Shar Lam, taking you back to where you started. The whole kora is around 8km long and takes most of the morning, longer if you make many stops en route.

The Potala Kora
Another popular kora encircles the holy Potala palace and follows an almost continuous circuit of prayer wheels. The route leads past teahouses, chörtens, stone carvers, rock paintings and often buskers, and is worth a visit, especially if you wish to visit the Lukhang.

Other Koras
There are koras at Drepung, Ganden and Sera Monasteries (see Around Lhasa later in this chapter).

Maps

The *Lhasa Tour Map* is a relatively useful English-language map of the city produced by the Mapping Bureau of Tibet Autonomous Region. This and other local maps are available at the Xinhua bookstores, the post office bookstore, and the gift shops of the top-end hotels.

For details of other maps of Lhasa available abroad, see Maps in the Facts for the Visitor chapter.

INFORMATION

Useful information is scarce in Lhasa. Most travellers find out more about what is going on and how things work by sitting around chatting among themselves in the courtyard of the Yak Hotel or at Tashi I or II restaurants than they do by calling in to travel agencies. The information boards at the Pentoc Guesthouse and the Yak, Banak Shol, Snowlands and Kirey hotels can be very useful if you are looking for travel partners, a ride on a Land Cruiser, or even a second-hand Lonely Planet guidebook. If you post up a question, chances are that someone will scribble up an answer before too long.

Nepali Consulate

The Nepali consulate (☎ 682 2881, fax 683 6890, ⓔ rncglx@public.ls.x.cn) is on a side street just south of the Lhasa Hotel (formerly the Holiday Inn) and north of the Norbulingka. For information on obtaining visas here, see Embassies & Consulates in the Facts for the Visitor chapter.

Money

The Bank of China branch on Dekyi Shar Lam, between the Banak Shol and Kirey hotels, changes cash and travellers cheques without fuss and is the most conveniently located option (though it can't give cash advances on a credit card). Opening hours are 8.30am to 1.30pm and 3.30pm to 5.30pm Monday to Friday.

For credit-card advances and foreign exchange during the weekend, you'll need to go to the main Bank of China office, just north of Dekyi Nub Lam, west of the Potala. Visa, MasterCard, Diners Club and American Express cards are accepted; there's a 3% commission and the minimum withdrawal is Y1200. This is also the place to arrange a bank transfer (see Money in the Facts for the Visitor chapter). Opening hours are 9am to 6.30pm Monday to Friday and 10am to 3pm Saturday and Sunday (opening and closing half an hour later in winter).

The top-end hotels all have an exchange service, but this is normally available only to hotel guests.

Post

The main post office is on Dekyi Shar Lam, about 15 minutes' walk west of the Yak

---

Visiting Monasteries & Temples

Most monasteries and temples extend a warm welcome to foreign guests and in remote areas will often offer a place to stay for the night. Please maintain this good faith by observing the following courtesies:

- Always circumambulate Buddhist monasteries and other religious objects clockwise, thus keeping shrines and *chörtens* (stupas) to your right.
- Don't touch or remove anything on an altar.
- Don't take prayer flags or *mani* (prayer) stones.
- Don't take photos during a prayer meeting. At other times always ask permission to take photos, especially when using a flash. The larger monasteries charge photography fees, though some monks will allow you to take a quick picture for free. If they won't there's no point getting angry; you don't know what pressures they may be under.
- Don't wear shorts or short skirts in a monastery.
- Take your hat off when you go into a chapel.
- Don't smoke in a monastery.
- If you have a guide, try to ensure that he or she is a Tibetan, as Chinese guides invariably know little about Tibetan Buddhism or monastery history.

Hotel. It is open from 9am to 8pm Monday to Saturday and 10am to 6pm Sunday. The counter in the far left corner as you walk through the main doors sells stamps.

All poste restante is kept at a counter in the same area; a collection charge of Y1.50 is required for each letter. Bring along your passport for identification.

Stamps and packaging for parcels are available at the same counter. It is a good idea to leave the parcel unsealed until you get to the post office as the staff will want to check the contents for customs clearance.

There's another post office five minutes' walk north-east of the Banak Shol hotel, open from 9am to 7pm daily.

Telephone & Fax

The most convenient telecom office is in the main post office building, open 8.30am to 10pm daily. There is a smaller telecom building at the northern end of Lingkhor Shar Lam in the east of town, open 8am to midnight daily. The main telecom building is on Dekyi Nub Lam, east of the Grand Hotel, and keeps similar hours.

International calls require a deposit of Y200. Change is provided after the cost of the call is deducted. The deposit is refunded in total if you don't get through. Prepaid international call (IC) cards and Internet phone (IP) cards are also available (for information on phonecards see Telephone under Post & Communications in the Facts for the Visitor chapter). IC cards can be used at any card machine inside or outside the building, whereas IP cards have to be used at public phones. IC cardphones are also available 24 hours a day in the foyer of the Lhasa Hotel.

The business centre at the Pentoc Guesthouse (Panduo Lüguan; ☎ 632 6686, fax 633 0700, e pentoc@public.east.cn.net), 5 Mentsikhang Lam, is conveniently located for making calls and sending faxes but levies a Y10 service charge on top of standard China Telecom rates. Receiving a fax costs Y10. It is only open 9am to 6pm Monday to Friday. You can also make international calls from the lobby of the Banak Shol hotel.

Email & Internet Access

There are dozens of places in Lhasa offering Internet access for around Y5 per hour. Popular ones include the Khangli Internet Bar opposite the Banak Shol hotel (open 9am to midnight), the Internet bars scattered around the nearby junction of Dekyi Shar Lam and Lingkhor Shar Lam, and the telecom office on Dekyi Shar Lam.

Travel Agencies

At the time of research, independent travel agencies had been outlawed by the Tibetan government and all independent travellers had to arrange travel with one of two Family (or Foreign) and Independent Traveller (FIT) offices run by the Tibet Tourism Bureau (TTB). These offices are located in the Snowlands hotel (☎ 634 9239, fax 634 3854) and the Banak Shol hotel (☎ 634 4397, fax 681 5615). Despite the enforced monopoly, service levels don't seem to have dropped significantly, though prices have risen. In our experience the Banak Shol branch is far more professional, reliable and easy to deal with.

Policies change like the wind in Tibet so you may find that private agencies have reappeared. In fact, one or two agencies, such as Tibet Yekyl Tour Shop (☎ 634 1391) near the Snowlands hotel, are already starting to make ad hoc travel arrangements, albeit illegally. They offer cheaper prices but have problems obtaining travel permits so are probably best used for trips around Lhasa and along the Friendship Hwy.

More-reliable (and more-expensive) agencies are located in the western part of town. At the time of research, they could not make arrangements for independent travellers, but again this may change:

China Tibet Travel & Tours (CTTT; ☎ 682 4305) Room 1688, Lhasa Hotel
Tibet Holiday International Travel Service (☎ 682 4305, fax 683 4957, e thits@public .ls.xz.cn) Ground floor, Lhasa Hotel
Tibet Holyland International Travel Service (☎ 681 4304, fax 683 4472) 215 Dekyi Nub Lam
Tibet Wind-Horse Adventure (☎ 683 3009, fax 683 6793) Room 1120, Lhasa Hotel

Public Security Bureau

The Lhasa Public Security Bureau is at 4 Dekyi Shar Lam; it is open 9am to noon and 3.30pm to 6pm Monday to Saturday. It is not a good place for visa extensions, but then no PSB offices in Tibet are. Extensions of up to a week are normally given if you can conjure up some evidence of planned departure, such as an air ticket out of Tibet. If you're looking for a longer extension then it's wiser to inquire at one of the private travel agencies before revealing your plans to the PSB.

Travel permits are rarely given to individual travellers in Lhasa and you're better off trying in Shigatse (for more information, see Shigatse in the Tsang chapter).

Bookshops

There is very little in the way of decent mapping or non-Chinese reading material available in Lhasa. The Xinhua Bookstore on Yuthok Lam (Yutuo Lu), about 10 minutes' walk west of Barkhor Square, has some maps, postcards and photo books, but there's a better selection at the branch on Dekyi Nub Lam, east of the Tibet Hotel.

The gift shops at the Lhasa Hotel, the Himalaya Hotel, the Potala and the Norbu-

---

LHASA

PLACES TO STAY
11 Himalaya Hotel
24 Airway Hotel
45 Grand Hotel
49 Lhasa Hotel; Tibet Holiday International Travel Service; Tibet Wind-Horse Adventure; China Tibet Travel & Tours
57 Tibet Hotel

PLACES TO EAT
25 Teahouses
31 Guingi Chakhang (Teahouse)
52 Yeti Café
54 Snow Dragon Restaurant

OTHER
1 Tibetan Antelope Travel and Transportation Co Ltd

2 Gymnasium
3 Drapchi Prison
4 Public Security Bureau
5 Mountaineers Statue
6 Telecom Office; Post Office
7 City People's Hospital
8 Lhasa Public Security Bureau
9 Eastern Suburbs Bus Station
10 Tibet University
12 Carpet Factory
13 Ramoche Temple; Tsepak Lhakhang
14 Tibetan Autonomous Region People's Hospital
15 Minibus No 3 to Drepung Monastery
16 Yuthok Bridge
17 Xinhua Bookstore (Main Branch)
18 Lhasa Department Store

19 Photographic Shops
20 New Century Supermarket
21 Minibus No 5 to Sera Monastery
22 China Southwest Airlines; Civil Aviation Authority of China
23 Main Post Office; Telecom Office
26 North Col Outdoor Equipment Shop
27 The Potala
28 Three Chörtens
29 The Lukhang
30 Chörten (Former West Gate)
32 Drubthub Nunnery
33 Palha Lupuk
34 Bank of China (Main Office)
35 Golden Yak Statues
36 Gesar Ling
37 Kunde Ling

38 Tibet Tourism Bureau
39 Rock Carvings
40 Main Bus Station (Long-Distance Buses)
41 Cultural Department Office
42 Tibet Museum
43 Main Telecom Building
44 Lhasa Foreign Trade Building Supermarket
46 Gleckes Fresh Beer
47 Tibetan Dance & Drama Theatre
48 Nepali Consulate
50 Last Bus (Bar)
51 China International Travel Service
53 Music Kitchen
55 Tibet Holyland International Travel Service
56 Xinhua Bookstore

To Nechung (1.25km) & Drepung Monastery (2.5km)

Dekyi Nub Lam (Beijing Zhonglu)

Minzu Beilu

Se'erku Lu

Deji Linka Lu

The Norbulingka

See The Norbulingka Map p155

Mirig Lam (Minzu Nanlu)

Norbulingka Lam (Luobulinka Lu)

Chingdröl Kyil Lam (Jinzhu Xilu)

Parma Ri

To Gongkar Airport (92km)

Lhasa River (Kyi-chu)

0   0.5   1km
0   0.25   0.5mi
Minor Roads not Depicted

········· Lingkhor Kora (Pilgrimage Circuit)
------- Potala Kora (Pilgrimage Circuit)

lingka are good places to track down glossy coffee-table books, though the books here are inevitably more expensive than those at Xinhua.

The Makye Amye restaurant on the Barkhor circuit has a small library of books on Tibet which you can borrow after leaving a small deposit.

Laundry
The Banak Shol and Kirey hotels offer a free laundry service to guests. Snowlands hotel's laundry charges Y2 per piece. The Pentoc charges Y15 to Y20 for a bagful.

Medical Services
In the case of an emergency you will probably be taken or directed to the City People's Hospital on Lingkhor Shar Lam. Hygiene standards are minimal, but the staff are competent.

Several hotels around town sell Tibetan herbal medicine recommended by locals for easing the symptoms of altitude sickness (also known as AMS, which stands for acute mountain sickness). The medicine is known as *solomano* in Tibetan and *hongjingtian* in Chinese. A box of vials costs around Y25.

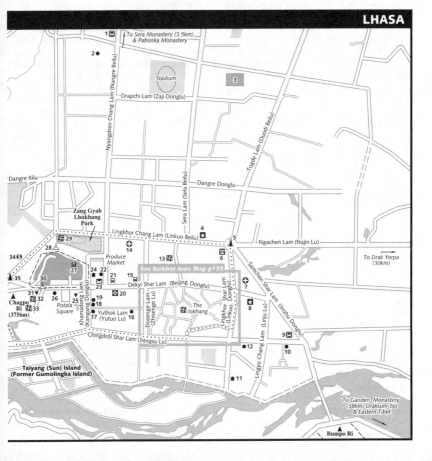

BARKHOR AREA

The first stop for most newcomers to Lhasa is the Jokhang in the heart of the old Tibetan part of town. But before you even venture into the Jokhang it is worth taking a stroll around the Barkhor, Lhasa's most interesting *kora* (pilgrimage circuit), a quadrangle of streets that surrounds the Jokhang and some of the old buildings adjoining it. It is an area unrivalled in Tibet for its fascinating combination of deep religiosity and push-and-shove market economics. This is both the spiritual heart of the Holy City and the main commercial district for Tibetans.

As you follow the crowds into the Barkhor circuit, there is a curious sensation of having slipped backwards through time into a medieval carnival. This is one part of Lhasa that has resisted any invasion of the modern world. Pilgrims from Kham, Amdo and further afield step blithely around a prostrating monk and stop briefly to finger a jewel-encrusted dagger at a street stall; children dressed like bit players in a stage production of Oliver Twist tug at the legs of a foreign visitor and beg for Dalai Lama pictures; a line of monks sit cross-legged on the paving stones before their alms bowls muttering mantras.

The whole circuit is lined with stalls selling everything a Tibetan or visiting tourist could possibly need. Some of the stalls sport a wide variety of souvenir items of dubious quality (be prepared to bargain very hard), others specialise: some in cowboy-style hats or *chubas* (long-sleeved sheepskin cloaks), others in carpets, some in prayer scarves and prayer flags, others in turquoise or clothes – great browsing even if you are not in the mood for a purchase. One curiosity worth noting is that many of the stall keepers and customers these days are Chinese. How times change. From razing monasteries to the ground and stripping monks of their vestments, the Chinese have moved to cashing in on the booming market for Tibetan religious items.

Barkhor Square

For your first visit to the Barkhor area, enter from Barkhor Square (at the eastern end of Yuthok Lam), a large plaza that was cleared in 1985 and renovated in 2000. No doubt the clearing of a plaza in the centre of Lhasa makes it easier for the Chinese to keep an eye on the activities of locals (watch out for video cameras on the roofs above the square), but the square has still become a focus for protest and has been the scene of pitched battles between Chinese and Tibetans on several occasions, most noticeably in 1998 when several Tibetans were killed and a Dutch tourist was shot in the shoulder. At least the Chinese resisted the temptation to plunk a Mao statue in the middle of it all.

Close to the entrance to the Jokhang is a constant stream of Tibetans following the Barkhor circumambulation route in a clockwise direction. Look for the two pot-bellied, stone *sangkang* (incense burners) in front of the Jokhang. There are four altogether, comprising the four extremities of the Barkhor circuit; the other two are positioned at the rear of the Jokhang. Behind the first two sangkang are two enclosures. The northern stele is inscribed with the terms of the Sino-Tibetan treaty of 822. The inscription guarantees mutual respect of the borders of the two nations – an irony seemingly lost on the Chinese authorities. The southern one harbours the stump of an ancient willow tree, known as the hair of the Jowo, allegedly planted by Songtsen Gampo's Chinese wife, Princess Wencheng, and a stele erected in 1793 commemorating smallpox victims.

For your first few visits to the Barkhor circuit, it's best to let yourself be dragged along by the centrifugal force of the pilgrims, but there are also several small, often fascinating temples to pop into en route.

Walking Tour

As you follow the flow of pilgrims past sellers of religious photos, fake antiques and horse tackle, you will see a couple of narrow alleys leading off to the north that are worth exploring. The alley that heads up to Dekyi Shar Lam and emerges just east of the Yak Hotel is notable for its outdoor pool tables where Khampas from the east of Tibet huddle over weathered felts and rarely

BARKHOR AREA

PLACES TO STAY
4 Hotel Kyichu; Kyichu Art Gallery
9 Yak Hotel
11 Dhood Gu Hotel
15 Kirey Hotel; Tashi II Restaurant
22 Banak Shol; Kailash Restaurant; Family & Independent Traveller Office
26 Pata Hotel
35 Mandala Hotel
39 Snowlands; Snowlands Laundry; Tashi Gallery; Family & Independent Traveller Office
41 Tashi Targyel Hotel; Tashi Targyel Restaurant; Teahouse
42 Pentoc Guesthouse
44 Shangbala Hotel
56 Tibet Xiongbala Hotel
61 Flora Hotel

PLACES TO EAT
6 Tashi I
7 French Restaurant
10 Dunya
13 Turquoise Dragon Teahouse
20 Muslim Restaurant
24 Yuyi Restaurant
28 Makye Amye Restaurant
38 Snowlands Restaurant
45 Tibet Lhasa Kitchen
46 Gangki Restaurant
51 Native Tibetan Restaurant

OTHER
1 Tsome Ling
2 Tsome Ling Tent Workshop
3 Shide Tratsang
5 Mount Green Trekking
8 Dorje Antique Shop
12 Minibuses to Shigatse, Samye & Nagchu
14 Wholesale Food Shops
16 Gyüme (Lower Tantric College)
17 Meru Sarpa Monastery
18 Outlook Outdoor Equipment
19 Bank of China
21 Cinema
23 Khangli Internet Bar
25 Internet Bars
27 Karmashar Temple
29 Meru Nyingba Monastery
30 Mani Lhakhang
31 Jampa Lhakhang
32 Gongkar Chöde Chapel; Jambhala Lhakhang
33 Thangka Workshops
34 Ticket Office for Bus to Ganden Monastery
36 Minibuses to Tsurphu Monastery; Buses to Ganden Monastery, Samye & Tsetang
37 Snow Leopard Carpet Industries
40 Tibet Yekyl Tour Shop
43 Tengye Ling
47 Minibuses to Drepung Monastery
48 Tibetan Traditional Hospital (Mentsikhang)
49 Minibus No 3 to the Norbulingka
50 Nepali Shops
52 Lugu Bus Station
53 Minibuses to Dagtse
54 Lho Rigsum Lhakhang
55 Mosque
57 Rabtse Temple
58 Thangka Workshop
59 Ani Sangkhung Nunnery
60 Main City Mosque
62 Nuoling Tsongkhang Nepali Shop

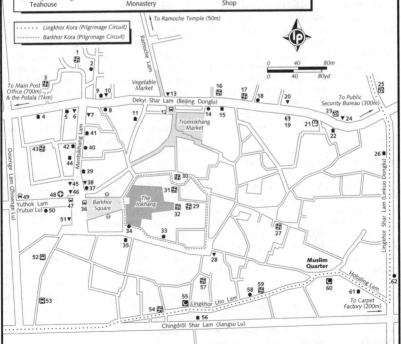

Lingkhor Kora (Pilgrimage Circuit)
Barkhor Kora (Pilgrimage Circuit)

To Ramoche Temple (50m)

To Main Post Office (700m) & the Potala (1km)

Ramoche Lam

Vegetable Market

Dekyi Shar Lam (Beijing Donglu)

To Public Security Bureau (300m)

Tromsikhang Market

Mentsikhang Lam

Dosenge Lam (Zhisenge Lu)

The Jokhang

Barkhor Square

Yuthok Lam (Yutuo Lu)

Lingkhor Shar Lam (Linkuo Donglu)

Muslim Quarter

Hobaling Lam

To Carpet Factory (200m)

Linkhor Lho Lam

Chingdröl Shar Lam (Jiangsu Lu)

0 40 80m
0 40 80yd

pot a ball. Alleys also head north-east to the bustling market area of the **Tromsikhang**. One busy alley heads south from here back down to the Barkhor.

Continuing around the Barkhor clockwise you'll soon see a small building on the right, set off from the main path but very much part of the pilgrim circuit. This is the **Mani Lhakhang**, a small chapel that houses a huge prayer wheel set almost continuously in motion. To the right of the building is the grandiose entrance of the former city jail and dungeons, known as the Nangtse Shar.

If you head south from here, after about 10m you will see the entrance to the **Jampa Lhakhang** (or Jamkhang) on the right. The ground floor of this small temple has a two-storey statue of Miwang Jampa, the Future Buddha, flanked by rows of various protector gods. Pilgrims ascend to the upper floor to be blessed with a sprinkling of holy water (the temple is also known as the Water Blessing Temple) and the touch of a holy *dorje* (thunderbolt).

Continue down the alley following the prayer wheels, then pass through a doorway into the old **Meru Nyingba Monastery**. This small but active monastery (Tibetan: *gompa*) is a delight. The main attraction is less the chapel than the courtyard area, which is invariably crowded with Tibetans thumbing prayer beads or lazily swinging prayer wheels and chanting under their breath. The chapel itself is administered by Nechung Monastery and so has several images of the Nechung oracle inside. The building, like the adjoining Jokhang, dates back to the 7th century but most of what you see today is of very recent construction.

On the west side of the courtyard up some narrow stairs is the small **Gongkar Chöde** chapel. Below is the **Jambhala Lhakhang**, with a central image of Marmedze (Dipamkara), the Past Buddha, and a small inner kora path.

From here you can return north or head east to join up with the Barkhor circuit. The eastern side of the circuit has more shops and even a couple of small department stores on the right side specialising in turquoise. In the south-east corner is a *darchen* (prayer pole) marking the spot where Tsongkhapa planted his walking stick in 1409. The southern stretch has several *thangka* (religious painting) workshops, where you can watch the artists at work. The empty southern square of the Jokhang used to host annual teachings by the Dalai Lama during the Mönlam festival. The circuit finally swings north by a police station back to Barkhor Square.

THE POTALA

The Potala *(admission Y40; open 8.30am-3.30pm Mon, Wed & Fri, 9.30am-3.30pm Tues, Thur, Sat & Sun; interior chapels close 4.30pm)* is Lhasa's cardinal landmark and one of the wonders of Eastern architecture. It looks best from a distance and it can be viewed and photographed from various places around town – notably from the top of Chagpo Ri.

The Potala is a structure of massive proportions, an awe-inspiring place to explore, but still many visitors come away slightly disappointed. Unlike the Jokhang, which hums with activity, the Potala lies dormant like a huge museum, and the lifelessness of the highly symbolic building constantly reminds visitors that the Dalai Lama has been forced to take his government elsewhere. That said, your first sight of the Potala will be a magical moment that you will remember for a long time. It's hard to take your eyes off the place.

It's a modern irony that the Potala now hums with large numbers of Chinese tourists staring with wonder at the building the generation before them tried so hard to destroy.

Pilgrims get free access to the Potala on Monday, Wednesday and Friday so crowds for many of the chapels are bigger then, though the presence of pilgrims adds interest to a visit. It's worth getting there early as there's a lot to see and rooms tend to close briefly around 1pm for lunch. There are extra charges for access to the roof and the exhibition room, both Y10. Guides in English are available for Y50.

[Continued on page 148]

THE JOKHANG

The Jokhang, also known in Tibetan as the Tsug-lhakhang, is the most revered religious structure in Tibet. Although little remains of its 7th-century origins and most of the sculptures that adorn its interior postdate the Cultural Revolution, the Jokhang, bustling with worshippers and redolent with mystery, is an unrivalled Tibetan experience.

Entry is free, except for tour groups and for visitors with guides, who pay Y25 per person. The inner chapels are open daily from around 8am to midday and sometimes from 3pm to 5.30pm, though the outer halls and the roof are effectively open daily from sunrise to sundown if you enter by the side door to the right of the main entrance.

After you've explored the interior of the Jokhang, the best part is arguably spending some time on the roof, with its stunning views. Monks often debate up here in the late afternoon. There is also a small teahouse. The orange building on the north side holds the private quarters of the Dalai Lama.

It's worth finishing off a visit with a walk around the Nangkhor *kora* (pilgrimage circuit), which encircles the Jokhang's inner sanctum. If you're not utterly exhausted you could have a brief look at the **Drölma Chapel**, featuring Drölma (Tara) flanked by her green and white manifestations and others of her 21 manifestations. Pilgrims sometimes pop into the **Guru Rinpoche Chapel**, a series of three interconnected shrines stuffed with images of Guru Rinpoche.

History

Estimated dates for the Jokhang's founding range from 639 to 647. Construction was initiated by King Songtsen Gampo to house an image of Mikyöba (Akshobhya) brought to Tibet as part of the dowry of his Nepali wife Princess Bhrikuti. The Ramoche Temple was constructed at the same time to house another Buddha image, Jowo Sakyamuni (Sakya Thukpa), brought to Tibet by his Chinese wife Princess Wencheng. It is thought that after the death of Songtsen Gampo, Jowo Sakyamuni was moved from Ramoche for its protection and hidden in the Jokhang by Princess Wencheng. The image has remained in the Jokhang ever since (Jokhang, or Jowokhang, means 'chapel of the Jowo'), and is the most revered Buddha image in all of Tibet.

It is said that Princess Wencheng chose the site of the Jokhang, and that just to be difficult she chose Lake Wothang. The lake had to be filled in, but it is said that a well in the precincts of the Jokhang still draws its waters from those of the old lake. Over the years, many legends have emerged around the task of filling in Lake Wothang. The most prominent of these is the story of how the lake was filled by a sacred goat (the Tibetan word for goat, *ra*, is etymologically connected with the original name for Lhasa – Rasa). A small carving of the goat can be seen in the Chapel of Jampa on the south wall of the Jokhang's ground-floor inner sanctum.

Inset: Wheel of Law (Illustration by Jenny Bowman)

Demoness-Subduing Temples

Buddhism's interaction with Bön – a shamanistic folk religion of ghosts and demons – combined with the inhospitable high places of the Tibetan plateau has led to many fables about Buddhism's taming and domestication of Tibet. The story of the early introduction of Buddhism to Tibet is attended by the story of a vast, supine demoness whose body straddled all the high plateau.

It was Princess Wencheng, the Chinese wife of King Songtsen Gampo, who divined the presence of this demoness. Through Chinese geomantic calculations she established that the heart of the demoness lay beneath a lake in the centre of Lhasa, while her torso and limbs lay far away in the outer dominions of the high plateau. As in all such fables, the demoness can be seen as symbolic of the inhospitableness of Tibet and its need to be tamed before Buddhism could take root there. It was decided that the demoness would have to be pinned down.

The first task was to drain the lake in Lhasa of its water (read life-blood of the demoness) and build a central temple that would replace the heart of the demoness with a Buddhist heart. The temple built there was the Jokhang. A stake through the heart was not enough to put a demoness of this size out of action, however, and a series of lesser temples, in three concentric rings, were conceived to pin the extremities of the demoness.

There were four temples in each of these rings. The first are known as the *runo* temples and form a protective circle around Lhasa, pinning down the demoness' hips and shoulders. Two of these are Trandruk Monastery in the Yarlung Valley and Katsel Monastery on the way to Drigung. The second group, known as the *tandrul* temples, pin the knees and elbows of the demoness. Buchu Monastery near Bayi in eastern Tibet is one of these. And the final group, known as *yandrul* temples, pin the hands and feet. These last temples are found as far away as Bhutan and Sichuan, though the location of two of them is unknown.

Over the centuries, the Jokhang has undergone many renovations, but the basic layout is ancient and differs from that of many other Tibetan religious structures. One crucial difference is the building's east-west orientation; it is said to face towards Nepal to honour Princess Bhrikuti. Alterations were undoubtedly undertaken during the centuries when Lhasa played second fiddle to other centres of power, but the most drastic renovations took place during the reign of the fifth Dalai Lama in the 17th century. Lhasa returned to the centre stage of Tibetan affairs at this time and the Jokhang was enlarged accordingly. Only a few carved pillars and entrance arches remain from the original 7th-century work of Newari artisans from Nepal's Kathmandu Valley.

In the early days of the Cultural Revolution, much of the interior of the Jokhang was desecrated by Red Guards and many objects are thought to have been removed. At one stage the monks' quarters were renamed Guesthouse No 5 and it is claimed that part of the Jokhang

THE JOKHANG

1 Sino-Tibetan Treaty Stele
2 Smallpox Stele and Ancient Willow Tree

GROUND FLOOR
3 Guardian Kings
4 Ticket Office
5 Main Assembly Hall
6 Naga Chapel
7 Nojin Chapel
8 Jampa Statue
9 Jampa Statue
10 Jampa Statue
11 Guru Rinpoche Statue
12 Chenresig Statue
13 Guru Rinpoche Statue
14 Chapel of Tsongkhapa & His Disciples

15 Chapel of the Buddha of Infinite Light
16 Chörten
17 Chapel of the Eight Medicine Buddhas
18 Chapel of Chenresig
19 Chapel of Jampa
20 Chapel of Tsongkhapa
21 Chapel of the Buddha of Infinite Light
22 Chapel of Jowo Sakyamuni
23 Chapel of Jampa
24 Chapel of Chenresig (Riding a Lion)
25 Guru Rinpoche Shrine; Rock Painting

26 Chapel of Tsepame
27 Chapel of Jampa
28 Chapel of the Hidden Jowo
29 Chapel of the Seven Buddhas
30 Chapel of the Nine Buddhas of Longevity
31 Chapel of the Kings
49 Drölma Chapel
50 Guru Rinpoche Chapel

FIRST FLOOR
32 Chapel of Lhobdak Namka Gyaltsen
33 Chapel of Sakyamuni
34 Chapel of Eight Medicine Buddhas

35 Chapel of Sakyamuni
36 Chapel of Five Protectors
37 Anteroom
38 Chapel of the Three Kings
39 Chapel of Songtsen Gompo
40 Chapel of Chenresig
41 Chapel of Sakyamuni
42 Prayer Wheel
43 Chapel of Guru Rinpoche & Sakyamuni
44 Chapel of Songtsen Gampo
45 Zhelre Lhakhang (Inacessible)
46 Chapel of Guru Rinpoche
47 Chapel of Samvara
48 Palden Lhamo Statues

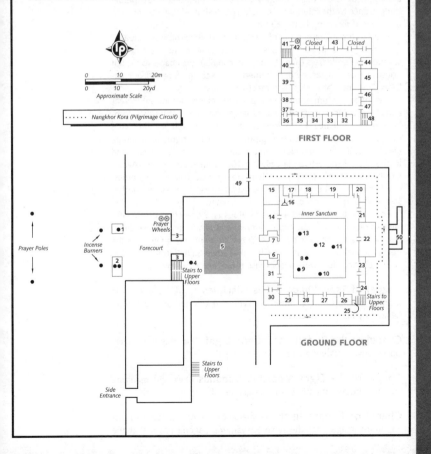

was utilised as a pigsty. Since 1980 the Jokhang has been restored, and without the aid of an expert eye, you will see few signs of the misfortunes that have befallen the temple in recent years.

Ground Floor

In front of the entrance to the Jokhang is a forecourt generally crowded with prostrating pilgrims. Take a look at the paving stones worn smooth by centuries of devotion and enter around two huge prayer wheels.

Just inside the entrance to the Jokhang are the **Four Guardian Kings** (Tibetan: Chökyong), two on either side. Beyond this point is the **main assembly hall** or *dukhang*, a paved courtyard that is open to the sky. During festivals the hall is often the focus of ceremonies. Just before the entrance to the interior of the Jokhang itself is a long altar marked by a row of flickering butter lamps.

Entry to the Jokhang proper is via a short, dark corridor punctuated midway by a chapel on either side. The chapel to the right houses several *naga* goddesses (naga being water spirits); the chapel to the left houses fierce, red-faced *nojin*, benign subterranean dragon-like creatures. Together they serve as protective deities.

The inner sanctum of the Jokhang houses its most important images and chapels. Most prominent are six larger-than-life statues that dominate the central area. In the foreground and to the left is a 6m statue of Guru Rinpoche. The statue opposite it, to the right, is of Jampa (Maitreya), the Future Buddha. At the centre of the hall, between and to the rear of these two statues, is a 1000-armed Chenresig (Avalokiteshvara). At the far right are two more Jampa (Maitreya) statues, one behind the other, and to the far rear, behind Chenresig, is another statue of Guru Rinpoche, encased in a cabinet.

Encircling this enclosed area of statues is a collection of chapels. Tibetan pilgrims circle the central area of statuary in a clockwise direction, visiting the chapels en route. There are generally queues for the holiest chapels, particularly the Chapel of Jowo Sakyamuni.

The chapels, following a clockwise route, are as follows:

Chapel of Tsongkhapa & His Disciples Tsongkhapa was the founder of the Gelugpa order, and you can see him seated centre, flanked by his eight disciples.

Chapel of the Buddha of Infinite Light This chapel is usually closed. Just outside is a large *chörten* (stupa).

Chapel of the Eight Medicine Buddhas The eight medicine buddhas are recent and not of special interest.

Chapel of Chenresig This chapel contains the Jokhang's most important image after the Jowo Sakyamuni. Legend has it that the

Roof detail: The spokes of the Wheel of Law represent the eight parts of the Noble Eightfold Path.

GREG CAIRE

Buddhism meets business: A woman sells her wares outside the Jokhang.

CRAIG PERSHOUSE

CRAIG PERSHOUSE

BERNARD NAPFTHINE

NICK TAPSELL

HANNAH LEVY

A hushed silence pervades the Jokhang. Butter lamps light the darkness; prayer wheels concentrate the mind.

statue of Chenresig (Avalokiteshvara) sprang spontaneously into being and combines aspects of King Songtsen Gampo, his wives and two wrathful protective deities. The doors of the chapel are among of the few remnants of the Jokhang's 7th-century origins and were fashioned by Nepali artisans.

Chapel of Jampa Inside are statues of Jampa (Maitreya) and four smaller bodhisattvas: Jampelyang (Manjushri), Chenresig (Avalokiteshvara), Chana Dorje (Vajarapani) and Drölma (Tara). Öpagme (Amitabha) and Tsongkhapa are also present, as are two chörtens, one of which is of the original sculptor.

Chapel of Tsongkhapa This chapel's image of Tsongkhapa, founder of the Gelugpa order, was commissioned by the subject himself and is said to be a precise resemblance. It is the central image to the left of the raised chapel.

Chapel of the Buddha of Infinite Light This is the second of the chapels consecrated to Öpagme (Amitabha), the Buddha of Infinite Light. The outer entrance is protected by two fierce deities, red Tamdrin (Hayagriva) and blue Chana Dorje (Vajrapani). There are also statues of the eight bodhisattvas. Pilgrims generally pray here for the elimination of impediments to viewing the most sacred image of the Jokhang, that of Jowo Sakyamuni, which waits in the next chapel.

Outside the chapel are statues of King Songtsen Gampo with his two queens and also Guru Rinpoche (with a big nose).

Chapel of Jowo Sakyamuni The most important shrine in Tibet, this chapel houses an image of Sakyamuni (Sakya Thukpa) at the age of 12 years. You enter via an anteroom containing the Four Guardian Kings and two protector statues: Miyowa (Achala) and Chana Dorje (Vajrapani). There are several bells on the anteroom's roof. The 1.5m statue of Sakyamuni is covered in silks and jewellery and flanked by silver pillars with dragon motifs. Pilgrims touch their forehead to the statue's left leg before being tapped on the back by a monk bouncer when it's time to move on.

To the rear of Sakyamuni are statues of the seventh and 13th Dalai Lamas, Tsongkhapa and 12 standing bodhisattvas.

Chapel of Jampa The Jampa (Maitreya) enshrined here is a replica of a statue that came to Tibet as part of the dowry of Princess Bhrikuti, King Songtsen Gampo's Nepali wife. Surrounding the statue are eight images of Drölma (Tara), a goddess who is seen as an embodiment of the enlightened mind of Buddhahood and who offers protection against the eight fears – hence the eight statues.

Chapel of Chenresig (Riding a Lion) The statue of Chenresig (Avalokiteshvara) on the back of a lion is second from the left (it's not the largest of the icons within). The other eight statues of the chapel are all aspects of Chenresig (Avalokiteshvara).

Some pilgrims exit this chapel and then follow a flight of stairs to the next floor, while others complete the circuit on the ground floor. If you're chapelled out (you've seen the important ones already), continue on upstairs, but look out first for a small hole in the wall to the right of the chapel, against which pilgrims place their ear to hear the beating wings of a mythical bird that lives under the Jokhang.

Guru Rinpoche Shrine Two statues of Guru Rinpoche and one of King Trisong Detsen can be found next to the stairs. Next to the shrine is a painting of the Medicine Buddha protected by an iron grill.

Chapel of Tsepame Inside are nine statues of Tsepame (Amitayus), the red Buddha of Longevity, in *yabyum* (sexual and spiritual union) pose.

Chapel of Jampa This, another Jampa (Maitreya) chapel, houses the Jampa statue that is borne around the Barkhor on the 25th day of the first lunar month for the Mönlam festival. Jampa's yearly excursion is designed to hasten the arrival of the Future Buddha.

Jampelyang (Manjushri) and Chenresig (Avalokiteshvara) flank the Buddha. Look out also for the tiny carving of the sacred goat mentioned under History earlier in this section; it's in the far left corner.

Chapel of the Hidden Jowo This is the chapel where Princess Wencheng is said to have hidden Jowo Sakyamuni for safekeeping after the death of her husband. Inside is a statue of Öpagme (Amitabha) and the eight medicine buddhas.

Other Chapels From this point there are several chapels of limited interest to non-Tibetologists. The **Chapel of the Seven Buddhas** is followed by the **Chapel of the Nine Buddhas of Longevity**. The last of the ground-floor chapels is the **Chapel of the Kings**, which contains some original statues of Tibet's earliest kings. The central figure is Songtsen Gampo, and he is flanked by images of King Trisong Detsen (left) and King Ralpachen (right). Pilgrims touch their head to the central pillar. On the wall outside the chapel is an interesting mural depicting the original construction of the Jokhang and the Potala, with musicians, dancers, wrestlers and horse races.

First Floor

At this point you should return clockwise to the rear of the ground floor (if you did not do so earlier) and climb the flight of stairs to the upper floor of the Jokhang. The upper floor of the Jokhang's inner sanctum is also ringed with chapels, though some of them are closed. Notice the doorframes of the **Chapel of Samvara** (showing Samvara with consort) and the **Chapel of Guru Rinpoche**, which date back to the 7th century.

As you begin the circuit, you will pass several new rooms featuring **Sakyamuni** flanked by his two main disciples, and one featuring the **eight medicine buddhas**. The chapel near the south-east corner features Pabonka Rinpoche, Sakyamuni (Sakya Thukpa), Tsongkhapa and Atisha (Jowo-je); the chapel in the south-west corner is the **Chapel of Five Protectors** and has some fearsome statues of Tamdrin (Hayagriva), Palden Lhamo (Shri Devi) and other protector deities. Next is the **Chapel of the Three Kings**, dedicated to Songtsen Gampo, Trisong Detsen and Ralpachen. Also featured in the room are Songtsen Gampo's two wives, various ministers, and symbols of royalty such as an elephant and a horse.

Also worth a look is the **Chapel of Songtsen Gampo**, the principal Songtsen Gampo chapel in the Jokhang. It is positioned in the centre of the west wall (directly above the entrance to the ground-floor inner sanctum). The bejewelled king, with a tiny buddha protruding from his head, is flanked by his two consorts, his Nepali wife to the left and his Chinese wife to the right. His animal-headed container for *chang* (barley beer) is placed opposite him behind a grill.

Most of the other rooms have been closed for years, the main exception being the meditation cell or Chapel of Songtsen Gampo near the floor's north-eastern corner, which has an incredible carved doorway smeared with decades' worth of yak butter. Before you leave the 1st floor by the stairs in the south-east corner, ascend half a floor up to two statues of the protectress Palden Lhamo (Shri Devi), one wrathful, the other benign. You can sometimes gain access to a Tantric chapel up on the 2nd floor.

[Continued from page 140]

Entrance to the Potala is via Shöl village, nestled at the southern foot of Marpo Ri. This was once Lhasa's red-light district as well as housing a prison, a printing press and some ancillary government buildings. Today it is an undistinguished cluster of Tibetan-style buildings and gift shops. Two steep access ramps snake up the southern side of the hill from Shöl and will almost certainly leave you puffing. Visitors who arrive by car or bus (taxis are not allowed) can drive up the back road to the top of the Potala via the west gate and then ascend floor by floor. (We describe the attractions from top to bottom, assuming you arrived on foot.)

The eastern entrance to the Potala takes you into **Deyang Shar**, the external courtyard of the White Palace, where there is a small gift shop. From here a triple flight of steps leads up into the White Palace and the former living quarters of the Dalai Lamas. (At the top of the triple stairs look out for the golden handprints of the 13th Dalai Lama on the wall to the left.) From there, you continue up to the roof of the Red Palace and then make a gradual journey downwards into the labyrinthine bowels of the Potala, before exiting from the northern side.

Photography of the interior of the Potala is forbidden and all rooms are wired with motion sensors and video cameras.

A morning visit to the Potala can easily be combined with an afternoon excursion to some of the sights nearby, such as Drubthub Nunnery, Palha Lupuk, Chagpo Ri, Parma Ri, Lukhang Temple, or a circuit of the Potala kora.

History

Marpo Ri, the 130m-high 'Red Hill' that commands a view of all Lhasa, was the site of King Songtsen Gampo's palace in the mid-7th century, long before the construction of the present-day Potala. There is little to indicate what this palace looked like, but it is clear that royal precedent was a major factor in the fifth Dalai Lama's choice of this site when he decided to move

the seat of his Gelugpa government here from Drepung Monastery.

Work began first on the White Palace, or Karpo Potrang, in 1645. The nine-storey structure was completed three years later, and in 1649 the fifth Dalai Lama moved from Drepung Monastery to his new residence. However, the circumstances surrounding the construction of the larger Red Palace, or Marpo Potrang, are subject to some dispute. It is agreed that the fifth Dalai Lama died in 1682 and that his death was concealed until the completion of the Red Palace 12 years later. In some accounts, the work was initiated by the regent who governed Tibet from 1679 to 1703 and foundations were laid in 1690 (after the fifth Dalai Lama's death). In other accounts, the Red Palace was conceived by the fifth Dalai Lama as a funerary chörten and work was well under way at the time of his death. In any event, the death of the fifth Dalai Lama was not announced until he was put to rest in the newly completed Red Palace.

There is also some scholarly debate concerning the Potala's name. The most probable explanation is that it derives from the Tibetan name for Chenresig's (Avalokiteshvara's) 'pure land', or paradise, also known as Potala. Given that Songtsen Gampo and the Dalai Lamas are believed to be reincarnations of Chenresig (Avalokiteshvara), this connection is compelling.

Since its construction, the Potala has been the home of each of the successive Dalai Lamas, although since construction of the Norbulingka summer palace in the late 18th century, it has served only as a winter residence. It has also been the seat of the Tibetan government, and with chapels, cells, schools for religious training and even tombs for the Dalai Lamas, it was virtually a self-contained world.

The 13th Dalai Lama undertook some renovation work in the early 20th century, demolishing sections of the White Palace to expand some chapels. The Potala was also shelled briefly during the 1959 popular uprising against the Chinese. Fortunately, and miraculously, the damage was not extensive. The Potala was spared again during the

Cultural Revolution, reportedly at the insistence of Zhou Enlai, the Chinese premier, who is said to have deployed his own troops to protect it. The Potala was reopened to the public in 1980 and final touches to the US$4-million renovations were completed in 1995.

Roof of the White Palace

As you arrive on the roof turn right into the private quarters of the 13th and 14th Dalai Lamas. The first room you come to is the **throne room**, where the Dalai Lamas would receive official guests. The large picture on the left is of the 13th Dalai Lama – the matching photo of the present Dalai Lama has been removed. The trail continues clockwise to the **reception hall**, which has a fine collection of bronze statues and fine views from the balcony. Next comes the **meditation room**, which still displays the ritual implements of the present Dalai Lama on a small table to the side of the room. Protector gods here include Nagpo Chenpo (Mahakala), the Nechung oracle and Palden Lhamo (Shri Devi). The final room, the **bedroom of the Dalai Lama**, has some personal effects of the Dalai Lama on show, such as his bedside clock. The mural above the bed is of Tsongkhapa, the founder of the Gelugpa order of which the Dalai Lama is the head. The locked door leads into the Dalai Lama's private bathroom.

From the roof you can catch some great views of Lhasa before heading across the courtyard and up into the Red Palace. See the floor plans for orientation.

Red Palace

Third Floor The main attractions on this floor are the Chapel of Jampa and the tomb of the 13th Dalai Lama. The **Chapel of Jampa** contains an exquisite image of Jampa (Maitreya) commissioned by the eighth Dalai Lama; it stands opposite the throne of the successive Dalai Lamas. To the right of the throne is a wooden Kalachakra mandala. The walls are stacked with the collected works of the fifth Dalai Lama. The chapel was unfortunately damaged in a fire in 1984 (caused by an electrical fault) and many valuable thangkas were lost. From here you can ascend onto the roof of the Red Palace for an extra Y10 before continuing onto the other halls.

The **Chapel of Three-Dimensional Mandalas** houses spectacular jewel-encrusted mandalas of the three principal Tantric deities of the Gelugpa order. There are some fine blackened murals near the throne of the seventh Dalai Lama. The **Chapel of the Victory over the Three Worlds** houses a library and displays examples of Manchu texts. The main statue is a golden Chenresig (Avalokiteshvara), while the thangka by the exit is of the Manchu Chinese emperor Qianlong in Mongol dress. The **Chapel of Immortal Happiness** was once the residence of the sixth Dalai Lama, whose throne remains; it is now dedicated to Tsepame (Amitayus), the Buddha of Longevity, who is opposite the throne. Next to him is the Dzogchen deity Ekajati (Tsechigma), with a black hat and a single fang.

From here a long corridor leads off the main circuit to a gallery that overlooks the **tomb of the 13th Dalai Lama**. You can normally look down on the chörten from above and then descend to look at it at ground level, but the room was closed at time of research.

The north-west corner houses the **Lhama Lhakhang** and the **tomb of the Seventh Dalai Lama**, constructed in 1805. From here steps lead up into the small but important **Chapel of Arya Lokeshvara**. Allegedly this is one of the few corners of the Potala that dates from the time of Songtsen Gampo's 7th-century palace. It is the most sacred of the Potala's chapels, and the image of Arya Lokeshvara inside is the most revered image housed in the Potala. The statue is flanked to the left by the seventh Dalai Lama and Tsongkhapa, and to the right by the fifth, eighth and ninth Dalai Lamas and Chana Dorje (Vajrapani). The left cabinet holds the stone footprints of Guru Rinpoche and Tsongkhapa. The prominent painting is of Tibet's three famous kings – Songtsen Gampo, Trisong Detsen and Ralpachen.

The last two rooms on this floor are the jewel-encrusted **tombs of the Eighth and Ninth Dalai Lamas**.

RED PALACE OF THE POTALA

THIRD FLOOR

SECOND FLOOR

GROUND FLOOR

THIRD FLOOR
1 Chapel of Jampa
2 Chapel of Three-Dimensional Mandalas
3 Chapel of the Victory over the Three Worlds
4 Chapel of Immortal Happiness
5 Tomb of the 13th Dalai Lama
6 Lhama Lhakhang
7 Tomb of the Seventh Dalai Lama
8 Chapel of Arya Lokeshvara
9 Tomb of the Eigth Dalai Lama
10 Tomb of the Ninth Dalai Lama

SECOND FLOOR
11 Chapel of Kalachakra
12 Chapel of Sakyamuni
13 Chapel of the Nine Buddhas of Longevity
14 Treasures of the Potala Exhibition
15 Chapel of Sakyamuni
16 King Songsten Gampo's Meditation Chamber
17 Lima Lhakhang
18 Lima Lhakhang
19 Lima Lhakhang
20 Rest Area

GROUND FLOOR
21 Assembly Hall
22 Throne
23 Chapel of Lamrim
24 Rigsum Lhakhang
25 Chapel of the Dalai Lamas' Tombs
26 Chapel of the Holy Born

Approximate Scale

0   25   50m
0   25   50yd

· · · · · · Suggested Route

Second Floor If you're exhausted already (still two floors to go!) you can rest your legs at a reception area in the middle of the floor. Otherwise the first of the chapels you come to on the 2nd floor is the **Chapel of Kalachakra**. It is noted for its stunning three-dimensional mandala, which is over 6m in diameter and finely detailed with over 170 statues. A statue of the Tantric deity Dukhor (Kalachakra) stands in the far right corner. Other statues include a variant of Jampelyang (Manjushri) riding a snow lion, and Guru Rinpoche in the corner. The next two halls hold the **Chapel of Sakyamuni** and the **Chapel of the Nine Buddhas of Longevity**. In the latter hall look for the murals by the window – the left side depicts Tangtong Gyelpo and his celebrated bridge (now destroyed) over the Yarlong Tsangpo near Chushul.

The last room on the south side houses a **Treasures of the Potala exhibition**. The collection is small but of a very high quality and includes such famous items as a three-dimensional mandala made of over 200,000 pearls, a crystal Sakyamuni (Sakya Thukpa) Buddha, and a bronze statue of a lotus whose leaves open out to reveal miniature statues inside. Other items include antique armour, festival costumes and thangkas. Entry to this room costs an additional Y10. The **Chapel of Sakyamuni** is next door.

Continue clockwise to the north-western corner where you'll find a small corridor that leads to **King Songtsen Gampo's meditation chamber**, which, along with the Chapel of Arya Lokeshvara on the 3rd floor, is one of the oldest rooms in the Potala. The most important statue is of Songtsen Gampo himself, to the left. To his left is his minister Tonmi Sambhota and to the right are his Chinese and Nepali wives. The king's Tibetan wife (the only one to bear a son) is in a cabinet by the door. The fifth Dalai Lama lurks behind (and also on) the central pillar.

The next three rooms are all linked and are chock-a-block full of Chinese statuary.

First Floor This floor was closed to visitors at the time of research and was unlikely to reopen soon.

Ground Floor The lower floor is reached via a number of steep, dark staircases and holds the beautiful **assembly hall**, which is the largest hall in the Potala and is its physical centre. Note the fine carved pillar heads. The large throne that dominates one end of the hall was the throne of the sixth Dalai Lama. Four important chapels adjoin the hall.

The first chapel you come to is the **Chapel of Lamrim**. *Lamrim* means literally 'the graduated path', and refers to the graduated stages that mark the path to enlightenment. The central figure in the chapel is Tsongkhapa, the founder of the Gelugpa order, with whom lamrim texts are usually associated.

The next chapel, the long **Rigsum Lhakhang**, is consecrated to eight Indian teachers who brought various Tantric practices and rituals to Tibet. The central figure is a silver statue of Guru Rinpoche (one of the eight), who is flanked by his consorts, as well as statues of the eight teachers on his left and a further eight statues of himself in different manifestations on the right.

In the west wing of the assembly hall is one of the highlights of the Potala, the awe-inspiring **Chapel of the Dalai Lamas' Tombs**. The hall is dominated by the huge 14m-high chörten of the fifth Dalai Lama, gilded with some 3700kg of gold. Flanking it are two smaller chörtens containing the 10th (right) and 12th (left) Dalai Lamas, who both died as children. Eight other chörtens represent the eight major events in the life of the Buddha. Before proceeding to the next chapel take a look at the murals of the assembly hall.

The final chapel visited is the **Chapel of the Holy Born**. First is the statue and chörten of the 11th Dalai Lama, who died at the age of 17. Then come statues of the eight medicine buddhas, the fifth Dalai Lama and Sakyamuni (Sakya Thukpa), followed by the first four Dalai Lamas and several Guru Rinpoches.

At this point, you exit the Potala by a path that winds down to the prayer wheels of the Potala kora and Dekyi Nub Lam. A path takes you back down on to Dekyi Nub

Lam at the site of Lhasa's former West Gate. Several chörtens have been rebuilt and you can get some good shots of the Potala from here. If energies are flagging you can stop for a cup of sweet tea at the Tibetan-style Guingi Chakhang.

DRUBTHUB NUNNERY & PALHA LUPUK

On the south side of Dekyi Nub Lam, a road leads around the eastern side of Chagpo Ri, the hill that faces Marpo Ri, site of the Potala. Take this road past piles of mani stones and prayer flags to the Drubthub Nunnery on the right (west). The nunnery is dedicated to Tangtong Gyelpo, the 15th-century bridge maker, medic and inventor of Tibetan opera, whose white-haired statue graces the nunnery's main hall.

After the nunnery, look for a flight of stairs 100m on the right. The stairs lead up to Palha Lupuk (admission Y15), a cave temple said to have been the 7th-century meditational retreat of King Songtsen Gampo.

The main attraction of the cave is its relief rock carvings. Some of them are thought to be more than 1000 years old. Altogether there are over 70 carvings of bodhisattvas in the cave and on the cave's central column. Work on the carvings was probably undertaken during three different historical periods, but the oldest are generally the ones lowest on the cave walls. Many of the carvings were damaged in the Cultural Revolution and have since been repaired.

The yellow building above Palha Lupuk is a chapel that gives access to the less interesting meditation cave of King Songtsen Gampo's Chinese wife, Princess Wencheng.

CHAGPO RI

Apart from Palha Lupuk, there are a couple of other points of interest on Chagpo Ri (Iron Mountain), although the steel telecom mast that graces the mountain's summit is probably not one of them. The hill was once the site of Lhasa's principal Tibetan medical college. Founded in 1413 by the fifth Dalai Lama, the college was destroyed in the 1959 popular uprising.

Today, the hill's main point of interest is a series of rock carvings on cliff walls at three different places. Altogether there are over 5000 carvings, some of them dating back to the 7th century. The first carvings are thought to have been commissioned by King Songtsen Gampo and executed by Nepali artists. The tradition of carving images on the cliffs of Chagpo Ri continued for another 1000 years.

The best place to see the carvings is on the south-west end of the hill, where there is a large painting of a blue Tsepame (Amit-ayus), among others. It costs Y5 to take photos in this area. Get here by following the Lingkhor kora (see the boxed text 'Lhasa's Pilgrim Circuits' earlier in this chapter) or by taking a track that leads southward from Dekyi Nub Lam. There are more rock carvings on the north-east end of the hill.

Finally, for stunning views of the Potala, take the trail that begins opposite the exit from the Potala and walk 20 minutes to the summit of Chagpo Ri.

PARMA RI

Several hundred metres to the west of Chagpo Ri, Parma Ri is another hill with a couple of interesting sights. At the foot of the hill, close to Dekyi Nub Lam, is one of Lhasa's four former royal temples, Kunde Ling. The ling (royal) temples were appointed by the fifth Dalai Lama, and it was from one of them that regents of Tibet were generally appointed. There are only a couple of restored chapels open, but it is worth a quick look all the same.

At the top of the hill is the Gesar Ling (admission Y7), a Chinese construction that dates back to 1793. It is the only Chinese-style temple in Lhasa and is a quiet place for an afternoon walk. The main temple has a statue of Gesar (linked to Guanyu, the Chinese God of War), flanked by Guru Rinpoche on the left and Ekajati, the Dzogchen deity, on the right. A separate yellow chapel on the kora behind has statues of an orange Jampelyang (Manjushri) flanked by Sakyamuni (Sakya Thukpa), Chana Dorje (Vajrapani) and Chenresig (Avalokiteshvara).

LHASA

LUKHANG

Lukhang (*admission Y10; open around 9am-5pm daily*) is a little-visited temple on a small island on a lake behind the Potala. The lake is in the Zang Gyab Lhukang Park (*admission Y2; open 9am-8pm daily*), formerly known as Chingdröl Chiling (Liberation) Park, which is entered from north of the Civil Aviation Authority of China (CAAC) building or from directly behind the Potala. Bike parking here costs Y1.

The Lake of the Naga King in the park was created during the construction of the Potala. Earth used for mortar was excavated from here, leaving a depression that was later filled with water. *Naga* (also known as *lu*) are subterranean dragon-like spirits that were thought to inhabit the area, and the Lukhang, or Chapel of the Dragon King, was built by the sixth Dalai Lama to propitiate them. You can see Luyi Gyalpo, the naga king, at the rear of the ground floor of the Lukhang. He is riding an elephant and protective snakes rise from behind his head. The naga spirits were finally imprisoned in the Palha Lupuk.

The Lukhang is celebrated for its 2nd- and 3rd-floor murals, which date from the 18th century. Bring a torch. The 2nd-floor murals tell a story made famous by a Tibetan opera, while the murals on the 3rd floor depict different themes on each of the walls – Indian yogis demonstrating yogic positions (west), 84 *mahisaddhas* or masters of Buddhism (east), and the life cycle as perceived by Tibetan Buddhists (north), with the gods of Bardo, the Tibetan underworld, occupying its centre. Look for the wonderful attention to detail, down to the hairy legs of the sadhus and the patterns on the clothes. The 3rd floor also contains a statue of an 11-headed Chenresig (Avalokiteshvara) as well as a meditation room used by the Dalai Lamas. It is reached by a flight of stairs around the back.

RAMOCHE TEMPLE

Ramoche (*Ramoche Lam; admission Y20; open 9am-5pm daily*) is the sister temple to the Jokhang. It was originally built to house the Jowo Sakyamuni image that is now in the Jokhang. The principal image in Ramoche is Mikyöba (Akshobhya), brought to Tibet in the 7th century as part of the dowry of King Songtsen Gampo's Nepali wife, Princess Bhrikuti. The image represents Sakyamuni (Sakya Thukpa) at the age of eight years. It is said to have been badly damaged by Red Guards during the Cultural Revolution.

Ramoche was built at the same time as the Jokhang, but it is thought that unlike the Jokhang, it was originally built in Chinese style. By the mid-15th century it had become Lhasa's Upper Tantric College, Gyutö (see Gyüme, following, for information about Lhasa's Lower Tantric College). Today Ramoche is a little tired and down at heel.

The Mikyöba (Akshobhya) image can be seen in the **Tsangkhang**, a small chapel at the far rear of the temple. There is a circumambulation circuit lined with prayer wheels around the perimeter of the temple. Many people consider that the temple's Y20 entry fee isn't worth it.

TSEPAK LHAKHANG

As you exit Ramoche look for an entrance just to the right. Pass a row of prayer wheels to reach a delightful chapel, Tsepak Lhakhang, with three large statues. The central image is Tsepame (Amitayus), the buddha associated with longevity, flanked by Jampa (Maitreya) and Sakyamuni (Sakya Thukpa). There are smaller statues of Dorje Chang (Vajradhara) and Marmedze (Dipamkara). The young monks tending this place are very friendly and the chapel is popular with pilgrims.

GYÜME

Gyüme (*15 Dekyi Shar Lam*), or the Lower Tantric College, is just down the road from the Yak Hotel, across from the Kirey Hotel. It is easy to miss – look for an imposing entrance set back from the road. This place gets very few foreign visitors, and its opening hours are irregular.

Gyüme was founded in the mid-15th century and in its time was one of Tibet's foremost Tantric training colleges. In Lhasa, its importance was second only to the monasteries of Sera and Drepung. More than 500 monks were once in residence, and students of the college underwent a physically and intellectually gruelling course of study. The college was thoroughly desecrated during the Cultural Revolution, but a growing number of monks are now in residence.

On the left as you enter the courtyard is a small chapel filled with butter lamps. The main *dukhang* (assembly hall) has statues of Tsongkhapa, the 13th Dalai Lama and Sakyamuni (Sakya Thukpa). Look for the monks' alms bowls encased in crafted leather, hanging from the rafters. Behind are statues of Tsongkhapa and his two main disciples and next door is a fearsome statue of Dorje Jigje (Yamantaka). The 2nd- and 3rd-floor chapels are often shut.

MERU SARPA MONASTERY

This small but active monastery *(Dekyi Shar Lam; admission free)* is opposite the Kirey Hotel. The building in the middle of the central compound houses a traditional wood-block printing press. In the north-west corner is an atmospheric chapel with a central statue of 1000-armed Chenresig (Avalokiteshvara). The main chapel behind the printers is usually closed.

KARMASHAR TEMPLE

Situated about 150m south-east of Barkhor Square, this quiet but interesting temple was once the home of the Karmashar, Lhasa's main oracle. Look for the spooky icon painted on a pigskin bag and for the Karmashar statue on the far right. There are also some nice original murals of Atisha (Jowo-je), Tsongkhapa and Tsepame (Amitayus) on the upper walls. Enter from the south side.

ANI SANGKHUNG NUNNERY

This small, active nunnery *(Lingkhor Lho Lam; admission Y10)* is the only one within the precincts of the old Tibetan quarter. The nuns (*ani* in Tibetan) are friendly and seem genuinely pleased to have a foreign guest.

The site of the nunnery probably dates back to the 7th century, but it housed a monastery until at least the 15th century. The main hall is up a flight of stairs, on the 2nd floor. The principal image is a 1000-armed

Chenresig (Avalokiteshvara). A small alley to the side of the main chapel leads down to the former meditation chamber of Songtsen Gampo, the 7th-century king of Tibet.

The nunnery is a little difficult to find. It is on a narrow street south-east of the Bark-hor Square. Look for the only yellow building on the street or ask for the *ani gompa*. Just next to the entrance is an excellent and very friendly thangka workshop.

LHO RIGSUM LHAKHANG

This small but popular chapel is on the Lingkhor and is one of four chapels surrounding the Jokhang at cardinal points. The chapel, which is almost completely ignored by tourists, houses a central statue of Tsepame (Amitayus), flanked by the four main bodhisattvas, and has its own inner kora. The chapel is looked after by monks from Ganden Monastery.

OTHER TEMPLES

Down the alleys off Dekyi Shar Lam are three obscure temples which can be visited if you've seen everything else.

Tsome Ling is the most interesting of the three. One of the four *ling* (royal) temples of Lhasa (along with Kunde Ling and Tengye Ling), this small site consists of two temples. To the east is the Karpo Potrang (White Palace), built in 1777, and to the west is the Marpo Potrang (Red Palace), built at the beginning of the 19th century. Both buildings have fine murals. The Karpo Potrang has statues of Öpagme (Amitabha), Jampa (Maitreya) and a famous tutor of the Dalai Lama. The Marpo Potrang has statues of Tsongkhapa, Atisha (Jowo-je) and the eighth Dalai Lama. There are two smaller chapels behind the central hall.

The obscure and rarely visited **Tengye Ling** chapel is a Nyingmapa sect temple dedicated to the deity Tseumar (whose statue is next to those of Guru Rinpoche), Pehar (a protector connected to Samye) and Tamdrin (Hayagriva). The chapel is hidden in the backstreets west of the Snowlands hotel and hard to find. To access the temple look for the red walls, enter the adjacent apartment block and proceed to the roof.

The badly ruined temple of **Shide Trat-sang** is connected to Reting Monastery and was once one of the six principal temples encircling the Jokhang. It is down a back alley near Tashi I restaurant but little remains.

MUSLIM QUARTER

There are a couple of mosques in the area south-east of the Barkhor circuit, serving Lhasa's 2000-strong Muslim population. It is dubious whether it is worth the effort of seeking them out (non-Muslims are denied entry to the prayer halls), but the Muslim quarter is worth a stroll, especially at lunch time on Friday when weekly prayers are held and the quarter is full of men with wispy beards and skullcaps. The main city mosque is in a small market square south-east of the Barkhor and a newer mosque is west of the Ani Sangkhung Nunnery.

The Muslim quarter, Lho Rigsum Lha-khang and Ani Sangkhung Nunnery are all best visited as part of a walk around the Lingkhor circuit (see the boxed text 'Lhasa's Pilgrim Circuits' earlier in this chapter).

THE NORBULINGKA

The Norbulingka *(Mirig Lam; foreigners/ Tibetans Y25/1; open 9am-1pm & 2.30pm-6pm daily)*, the summer palace of the Dalai Lamas, is about 10 minutes' walk south of the Lhasa Hotel in the western part of town. It ranks well behind the other points of interest in and around Lhasa, such as the Jokhang and the Potala. The gardens are poorly tended and the palaces themselves are something of an anticlimax, especially as most rooms are closed to the public. Avoid the zoo at all costs – it is thoroughly depressing.

This said, the Norbulingka is still worth a visit, and the park is a great place to be at festival times and public holidays. During the seventh lunar month of every year the Norbulingka is crowded with picnickers for the Shötun festival. Traditional Tibetan opera performances are also held at this time.

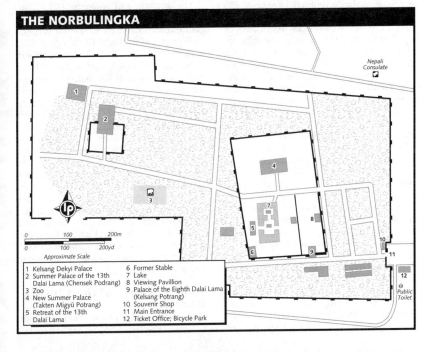

THE NORBULINGKA

1 Kelsang Dekyi Palace
2 Summer Palace of the 13th Dalai Lama (Chensek Podrang)
3 Zoo
4 New Summer Palace (Takten Migyü Potrang)
5 Retreat of the 13th Dalai Lama
6 Former Stable
7 Lake
8 Viewing Pavillion
9 Palace of the Eighth Dalai Lama (Kelsang Potrang)
10 Souvenir Shop
11 Main Entrance
12 Ticket Office; Bicycle Park

History

The first summer palace to be constructed in the Norbulingka (whose name literally means 'jewel park') was founded by the seventh Dalai Lama in 1755. Rather than use the palace as a retreat, he decided to use the wooded environs as a summer base from which to administer the country, a practice that was to be followed by each of the succeeding Dalai Lamas. The grand procession of the Dalai Lama's entourage relocating from the Potala to the Norbulingka became one of the highlights of the Lhasa year.

The eighth Dalai Lama (1758–1804) initiated further work on the Norbulingka, expanding the gardens and digging a lake which can be found south of the New Summer Palace. The 13th Dalai Lama (1876–1933) was responsible for the three palaces in the north-west corner of the park, and the 14th Dalai Lama built the New Summer Palace in 1956.

In 1959 the 14th Dalai Lama made his escape from the Norbulingka disguised as a Tibetan soldier. Unfortunately all the palaces of the Norbulingka were damaged by Chinese artillery fire in the popular uprising that followed the Dalai Lama's flight. At the time the compound was surrounded by some 30,000 Tibetans determined to defend the life of their spiritual leader. Repairs have been undertaken but have failed to restore the palaces to their full former glory.

Palace of the Eighth Dalai Lama

This palace (also known as Kelsang Potrang) is the first you come to from the entrance to the Norbulingka. It was first used as a summer palace by the eighth Dalai Lama and was used by every Dalai Lama up to the 13th. It is of limited interest to visitors today. Only the main audience hall is open; it features 65 hanging thangkas and a throne backed by statues of the eight medicine buddhas.

New Summer Palace

The New Summer Palace (or Takten Migyü Potrang) in the centre of the park was built by the present (14th) Dalai Lama between 1954 and 1956 and is without a doubt the most interesting of the Norbulingka palaces.

The first of the rooms you visit is the **Dalai Lama's audience chamber**. Note the murals on the chamber's walls. They depict the history of Tibet in 301 scenes. As you stand with your back to the window the murals start on the left wall with Sakyamuni (Sakya Thukpa) and show the mythical beginnings of the Tibetan people and the first agricultural field in Tibet. The wall in front of you depicts the building of the circular monastery of Samye, as well as Ganden, Drepung and other monasteries. The right wall contains the histories of the Dalai Lamas, concluding with the reincarnation of the current Dalai Lama and the building of the Norbulingka.

Next come the **Dalai Lama's private quarters**, which consist of a meditation chamber and a bedroom. The rooms have been maintained almost exactly as the Dalai Lama left them, and apart from the usual Buddhist images they contain the occasional surprise: a Soviet radio and a stylish European bed, among other things.

The **assembly hall**, where the Dalai Lama would address heads of state, is home to a gold throne backed by wonderful cartoon-style murals of the Dalai Lama's court (left, at the back) and all 14 Dalai Lamas (right). Look out for British representative Hugh Richardson in a trilby hat, and several Mongolian ambassadors. The first five of the Dalai Lamas on the right wall lack the Wheel of Law; this symbolises their lack of governmental authority. There are also murals depicting the lives of Sakyamuni or Sakya Thukpa (at the top) and Tsongkhapa (below). The final room to be visited is the meeting room of the Dalai Lama's mother.

South of the New Summer Palace is the artificial lake commissioned by the eighth Dalai Lama. The only pavilion open here during the time of research was the personal retreat of the 13th Dalai Lama in the south-western corner, featuring a library, a 1000-armed Chenresig (Avalokiteshvara) statue, and a stuffed tiger in the corner!

Summer Palace of the 13th Dalai Lama

The summer palace of the 13th Dalai Lama (Chensek Potrang) is in the western section of the Norbulingka, north-west of the zoo (the shrieks of deranged monkeys are warning enough to give the zoo a wide berth).

There is not a lot to see in the two-storey palace, but it is worth a quick visit. The ground-floor assembly hall holds the throne of the 13th Dalai Lama and is stuffed full of various buggies, palanquins and bicycles. The 2nd-floor living quarters are closed.

Nearby is a smaller building, the **Kelsang Dekyi Palace**, also built by the 13th Dalai Lama, but this is also closed.

TIBETAN TRADITIONAL HOSPITAL

Lhasa's original Tibetan Traditional Hospital sat atop Chagpo Ri opposite the Potala, but was destroyed by artillery fire in the 1959 uprising. The current one, on the north side of Yuthok Lam, was set up by the 13th Dalai Lama in 1916 and Tibetan doctors still train here. Known in Tibetan as the Mentsikhang, the hospital has a dispensary on the north side of the Barkhor Square.

Tours are available but only for groups with a special interest and a prior booking *(Y10; open 9.30am-12.30pm & 3.30pm-6pm Mon-Sat)*. The new building has a room with modern thangkas and statues of three famous medics: Yutok Yonten Gonpo, the founder of Tibetan medicine; Desi Sangye Gyatso, the founder of Chakpo Ri; and Khyenrab Norbu, the physician of the 13th Dalai Lama. There are plans to build a museum in the old block to hold the hospital's old medical thangkas.

Tibetan Medicine

The basic teachings of Tibetan medicine share much with those of other Asian medical traditions, which according to some scholars made their way to the East via India from ancient Greece. While the Western medical tradition treats symptoms that indicate a known medical condition (measles or mumps, say), the Eastern medical tradition looks at symptoms as indications of an imbalance in the body and seeks to restore that balance.

It is wrong to assume, however, that Tibetan medicine was practised by trained doctors in clinics scattered across the land. The Tibetan medical tradition is largely textual, derives from Indian sources and was studied in some monasteries in much the same way that Buddhist scriptures were studied. When Tibetans needed medical help they usually went to a local 'apothecary' who sold concoctions of herbs; equally, help was sought in prayers and good-luck charms.

The theory of Tibetan medicine is based on an extremely complex system of checks and balances between what can be broadly described as three 'humours' (related to state of mind), seven 'bodily sustainers' (related to the digestive tract) and three 'eliminators' (related to the elimination of bodily wastes). And if the relationship between bodily functions and the three humours of desire, egoism and ignorance were not complex enough, there is the influence of harmful spirits to consider. There are 360 harmful female influences, 360 harmful male influences, 360 malevolent *naga* influences (naga being water spirits) and finally 360 influences stemming from past karma. All these combine to produce 404 basic disorders and 84,000 illnesses!

How does a Tibetan doctor go about assessing the condition of a patient? The most important skill is pulse diagnosis. A Tibetan doctor is attuned to 360 'subtle channels' of energy that run through the body's skin and muscle, internal organs, and bone and marrow. The condition of these channels can be ascertained through six of the doctor's fingers (the first three fingers of each hand). Tibetan medicine also relies on urine analysis as an important diagnostic tool.

If Tibetan diagnostic theory is mainly Indian in influence, treatment owes as much to Chinese medicine as to Indian. Herbal concoctions, moxibustion and acupuncture are all used to restore balance to the body. Surgery was practised in the early days of Tibetan medicine, but was outlawed in the 9th century when a king's mother died during an operation.

For more on Tibetan medicine see the Web site W www.tibetan-medicine.org.

TIBET MUSEUM

This grand-looking new museum (☎ 681 2210; adults/students Y25/5; open 9am-1pm & 2pm-6pm daily) out in the west of town just opposite the Norbulingka isn't too bad as long as you can see through the offensive propaganda. The adult ticket includes a useful audio tour (student ticket holders pay an extra Y10 for this) but the commentary suffers from terrible Americanised pronunciation (Da-**lai** La-**maaarr**!).

The halls start logically with prehistory, highlighting Neolithic sites around Chamdo in eastern Tibet. The 'History of Integration' hall is full of boring seals and misleading Chinese political spin. The more interesting third hall covers Tibetan script, masks, musical instruments, medical thangkas and statuary. The next hall concentrates on thangkas, many of which are new or have been shipped in from China. The final hall has a good display of folk handicrafts, ranging from coracle boats to nomad tents and leather ware. At the time of research a history section was due to open soon on the upper floors, though you can expect the propaganda to be thick as yak butter here. There are toilets and a shop.

SPECIAL EVENTS

If it is at all possible, try to time your visit to Lhasa with one of the city's festivals. Winter and the New Year festivals see thousands of pilgrims flood into town, and the city's pilgrim circuits take on a colourful, party atmosphere. The day of the Saga Dawa festival sees huge numbers of pilgrims making pilgrim circuits around Lhasa late into the night. Many Lhasa residents trek up to the summit of Gephel Ri, the peak behind Drepung Monastery.

For a list of festivals in Lhasa see Special Events in the Facts for the Visitor chapter.

PLACES TO STAY

Accommodation in Lhasa can be divided into inexpensive Tibetan-style accommodation in the central Barkhor area and less conveniently located upmarket digs on the outskirts of town. Almost all independent travellers head straight for the Barkhor area, where five Tibetan-style hotels (the first five reviewed here) dominate the market. This is simply because the Barkhor area is the most interesting part of town, the service in these hotels is friendly (if basic) and the five are the best places to meet other travellers and get the current lowdown on travel in Tibet.

The past couple of years have seen a rise in the number of mid-range options. Most of these are in shiny faceless Chinese hotels, but the old backpacker hotels offer excellent mid-range rooms with private bathroom, carpet, TV and so on, and remain the best places to stay.

Prices given here (and throughout this book) apply in the high season. Rates can be a little lower in April, May and October and lower still in winter.

PLACES TO STAY – BUDGET & MID-RANGE

Yak Hotel (Ya Binguan; ☎ 632 3496, 100 Dekyi Shar Lam) Dorm beds Y20, doubles with shared bathroom Y50-60, triples with shared bathroom Y125, doubles with private bathroom Y260. Possibly the most popular place with individual travellers, the hotel has two courtyards: one at the front and one at the rear. The rooms that front onto the rear courtyard are quietest but can be dark. The doubles in the new block above reception are much brighter. The excellent pricier doubles with Tibetan-style decor are often booked out by tour groups so try to book ahead. The dorms can be somewhat gloomy but the toilets are clean. Hot showers, in the far corner of the rear courtyard, are available morning and evening. Internet access is available for Y10 per hour and there is a bicycle hire.

Banak Shol (Balangxue; ☎ 632 3829, 143 Dekyi Shar Lam) Dorm beds Y25, singles Y35, doubles Y60-150. Once *the* place to stay back in the early days of independent travel, this is the second most popular hotel among individual travellers. It is not as clean or as efficiently run as the Yak, but it does have a charm that the larger Yak doesn't. Guests can titillate themselves with the thought they have checked into a medieval monastic retreat (well, almost) as they enjoy the cosy Tibetan-style rooms fronted by verandas that face the inner courtyard. The main downside is that the walls are paper thin and most look onto the noisy main road. The doubles in the new block come with carpet, water boiler and an immaculate bathroom with 24-hour hot water. In the off-season they can be discounted to Y120 or even Y100, making them the best-value rooms in Lhasa. The cheaper doubles in the block below the Kailash Restaurant are shabby and poorer value, although the restaurant itself has taken off as one of Lhasa's most popular places to eat and socialise. Laundry is free, though you won't get your crusty socks washed after a week's trekking.

Snowlands *(Xueyu Binguan;* ☎ *632 3687, 4 Mentsikhang Lam)* Dorm beds Y25, doubles Y60-360. Snowlands is another one of Lhasa's long-stayers. It was a favourite with backpackers back in the 1980s, but the mood has changed a bit since then and the place seems to have been hijacked by officials based at the FIT office here. You'll probably get to stay here for the first night or two as part of your tour package. Most people quickly move to one of the other guesthouses. Snowlands is quieter than the Yak or the Banak Shol, though you pay for your solitude with lower service standards. The shower block in the corner of the courtyard has unreliable water and there's a frustrating lack of wash basins elsewhere. The rooms in the plush block at the back of the central quadrangle are clean and spacious, but not quite such good value as those at the Yak or the Banak Shol. There's a small shop selling basic items, and Internet access is available.

Kirey Hotel *(Jiri Binguan;* ☎ *632 3462, 105 Dekyi Shar Lam)* Dorm beds Y20, doubles Y50-120. The fourth and least popular of the Barkhor area's Tibetan-run hotels, the Kirey deserves more custom than it gets. It is super friendly and clean, and has reliable hot water from 9am to 9pm in the shower block around the back. The doubles with private bathroom are at the back of the main courtyard and are looking a bit tired these days. Tashi II restaurant is

on the premises and there's a sitting area on the roof above reception. Laundry service is free – put your washing in the bags provided and hand it in to reception before 9am. The only grumble we have is the dodgy plumbing in the toilets.

Lhasa Signs – Chinese

Throughout this chapter you'll find transliterations from (Mandarin) Chinese of many hotel names, street names and so on. In the Places to Stay and Places to Eat listings, these appear in parentheses after the Tibetan name of each hotel/restaurant, but before the address. On maps, they appear in parentheses following Tibetan street names. They are intended only as a guide to pronunciation, so we haven't included the tonal marks. If your taxi driver doesn't understand your attempts to communicate, you could, if he's Chinese, show him the relevant script below. And if you're really keen to practise your spoken Chinese, tones and all, turn to the Language chapter near the back of this book.

Jokhang
  Dazhao Si 大昭寺
Barkhor
  Bakuo 八廓
Potala
  Budala Gong 布达拉宫
Norbulingka
  Luobulinka 罗布林卡
Sera Monastery
  Sela Si 色拉寺
Drepung Monastery
  Zhebang Si 哲蚌寺
Civil Aviation Authority of China (CAAC) office
  Zhongguo Minhang 中国民航
Bank of China
  Zhongguo Yinhang 中国银行
Banak Shol Hotel
  Balangxue lüguan 八郎学旅馆
Yak Hotel
  Ya Binguan 亚宾馆
Lhasa Hotel
  Lasa Fandian 拉萨饭店
Bus Station
  Keyun Zhan 客运站

Pentoc Guesthouse *(Panduo Lüguan; ☎ 632 6686, fax 633 0700,* e *pentoc@pub lic.east.cn.net, 5 Mentsikhang Lam)* Dorm beds Y25, singles/doubles Y40/65. The Pentoc is in a great location near the Snow-lands, 50m north of Barkhor Square. It's a stylish place with nice touches such as free videos every night at 8pm, print-outs of news reports and festival dates, and indi-vidual bed lights in the three-bed dormito-ries. There are plans for a coffee shop. Rooms overlooking the street can be noisy during the day. Credit cards are accepted for bills over Y400, with a 4.5% bank charge.

Pata Hotel *(☎ 633 8419, Lingkhor Shar Lam)* Dorm beds Y15, triples Y30-40 per bed, doubles with private bathroom Y180. This new place is a bit out of the way and attracts far fewer tourists than the other budget options, but it's therefore quieter and not a bad choice if you want to be out of the action. Rooms are arranged around a large courtyard and there's plenty of com-mon seating. The corner rooms come with a tiled Western bathroom and hot water.

Tashi Targyel Hotel *(Zaxi Dajie Bin-guan; 8 Mentsikhang Lam)* Doubles/triples Y25 per bed, doubles with private bathroom Y100. Further up from the Pentoc and Snowlands, the Tashi Targyel offers fairly grim rooms and is only worth checking out if everything else is full. The doubles with private bathroom are tiny.

Hotel Kyichu *(Lasa Jiqu Fandian; ☎ 633 8824, fax 632 0234, 18 Dekyi Shar Lam)* Singles/doubles Y180/260, deluxe doubles Y320. The Kyichu is a friendly and well-run choice west of Tashi I restaurant, and a welcome exception to the usual Chinese-style hotels that are either bursting with tour groups or deserted and languishing in life-less apathy. All rooms have a basic private bathroom. A 20% winter discount is given from November to April inclusive.

Mandala Hotel *(Manzhai Jiudian; ☎ 633 8940, fax 632 4787, 31 South Barkhor)* Singles/doubles/triples with private bathroom Y180/260/300. This new hotel has a great lo-cation just off the Barkhor. The rooms are clean and comfortable and there's a rooftop teahouse and Nepali-style restaurant.

Flora Hotel *(☎ 632 4491, fax 632 4901,* e *flora@public.ls.xz.cn, Hobaling Lam)* Dorms Y35, doubles/triples with private bathroom Y250/350. The Flora is a well-run hotel in the interesting Muslim quarter (it's run by a Nepali Muslim). There are nice touches such as a minibar at local-shop prices, a stock of foreign magazines and a laundry service. Decent three-bed dorms out the back (with shared toilets and hot shower) offer a quiet alternative to Lhasa's backpacker hotels. There's also a fine Nepali restaurant here.

Himalaya Hotel *(Ximalaya Fandian; ☎ 632 1111, fax 623 2675, 6 Lingkhor Shar Lam)* Standard doubles/triples Y373/439, superior singles/doubles Y456/648, deluxe doubles Y747. This old stand-by was re-cently given a face-lift and now the choice is between the tatty and way overpriced old block, and the clean and quiet but still over-priced new block. Rates include breakfast and discounts of 20% are normally avail-able. There is a travel agency *(☎ 633 4082)* on the 4th floor. Credit cards are accepted.

Airway Hotel *(☎ 683 4444, 12 Khama-dong Lam)* Doubles Y320. Just east of the Potala, the Airway has excellent views of the Potala from the west-facing rooms. Rooms are pretty good, though the hotel lacks charm. Ask for the discounted rate of Y260. The place is run by the CAAC.

Tibet Xiongbala Hotel *(Xizang Xiong-bala Dajiudian; ☎ 633 8888, fax 633 1777, 28 Chingdröl Shar Lam)* Standard/deluxe doubles with private bathroom Y368/518. This is a new and well-run three-star Chi-nese hotel. Facilities include coffee bar, business centre and several restaurants; the upper floors have views of the Potala. The bathrooms are particularly nice. Discounts of 20% are likely to be available if you ask.

Shangbala Hotel *(Mentsikhang Lam)* Doubles Y400. Next to the Pentoc (and not to be confused with the Xiongbala Hotel listed earlier), this new Chinese blockhouse is totally out of place in its Tibetan sur-roundings. Rooms are standard, there's a decent restaurant and it has a useful loca-tion. It's popular with American groups. Rooms are sometimes discounted to Y320.

Dhood Gu Hotel (*Dungu Binguan;* ☎ *632 2555, fax 632 3555,* e *dhoodgu@public .ls.xz.cn, Near the Tromsikhang market*) Singles/doubles Y320/480. This stylish Nepali-run hotel has excellent Tibetan-style decoration if you are looking for a dash of style. Rooms come with modern bathrooms and kettles, though some are cramped. Breakfast is included in the price; the dinner buffet is Y40.

PLACES TO STAY – TOP END

All the following hotels offer a minimum 20% discount in the winter months (November to March inclusive). Prices quoted are for the high season.

Lhasa Hotel (*Lasa Fandian;* ☎ *683 2221, fax 683 5796,* e *sales@public.ls .xz.cn, 1 Mirig Lam*) Standard/superior doubles Y1020/1328, economy triples Y980, Tibetan suites Y1555. Until recently there was only one place in town that even approached international standards. However, in 1997, the Holiday Inn group pulled out of Tibet under increasing pressure from pro-Tibetan groups. The hotel was returned to the government and it reverted to its original name, the Lhasa Hotel. Standards have certainly slid (the staff can be particularly clueless) but there is still a decent selection of restaurants and bars, international direct-dial phones, nonsmoking rooms, satellite TV, in-house movies, a clinic with both Western and Tibetan doctors, a dirty pool and a small fitness centre. The restaurant apparently opens at 4.30am for travellers taking morning flights. The hotel has its own travel agency, China Tibet Travel & Tours (CTTT).

Tibet Hotel (☎ *683 9999, fax 683 6787, 64 Dekyi Nub Lam*) Doubles/triples Y880/980. A couple of hundred metres up the road from the Lhasa Hotel is the Tibet Hotel. In keeping with its name, it strives to create a Tibetan ambience, but the results are somewhat surreal. Service tends to dodder somewhere between apathy and incompetence and the rooms are overpriced. This said, the plush rooms come with nice touches such as a hair dryer and shaving mirror. Like the Lhasa Hotel, the Tibet

Hotel has international direct-dial phones, satellite TV and foreign exchange. A new four-star block was due to open soon after we visited.

Grand Hotel (☎ *682 6096, fax 683 2195, 196 Dekyi Nub Lam*) Economy/standard Y120, suites Y460. This hotel used to serve as the government guesthouse but now operates as a three-star option. It's not quite as plush as it looks and the cheaper rooms in particular are quite run-down.

PLACES TO EAT
Restaurants & Cafes

The restaurant scene in Lhasa has improved immensely over the past few years, though sadly this is for the most part a result of Han Chinese immigration.

Tibetan Quarter Most individual travellers stick to the Tibetan quarter around the Barkhor Square area when it comes to meals. Tibetan cooking may not be one of the world's most exciting cuisines, but there are a few Tibetan restaurants in this area that serve up some very tasty dishes.

Tashi I (*Cnr Mentsikhang Lam & Dekyi Shar Lam*) Dishes Y8-15. This place deserves a special mention because it has been running for a while now, and despite increased competition continues to be a favourite. The service is friendly (though the waitresses can get a bit sarcastic), the prices are cheap and everything on the menu is good. Special praise is reserved for the *bobis* (chapatti-like unleavened bread), which most people order with seasoned cream cheese and fried vegetables or meat. The Western dishes such as the pizza (Y10) are less authentic and portions can be small. Tashi's cheesecakes (with chocolate and pineapple) are still to die for.

Tashi II (☎ *632 3462, Dekyi Shar Lam*) Located in the Kirey Hotel, Tashi II offers the same menu as Tashi I but is a little quieter and has charming staff.

Kailash Restaurant (*Banak Shol hotel*) This is definitely one of the best hotel restaurants. Prices are a little higher than at the Tashi restaurants but dishes on offer include vegetarian lasagne and yak burgers (as good as those at the Lhasa Hotel and much cheaper). The chicken sizzler (Y20) could well be the best meal in Lhasa. The roof is a great place for a beer in summer. The restaurant's breakfasts (muesli brought in from Kathmandu, among other things) have also achieved a devoted following.

Snowlands Restaurant (☎ 632 3687, *Mentsikhang Lam*) Dishes Y25-35. Attached to the Snowlands hotel, this is a slightly more upmarket place that serves a mix of Tibetan and Nepali food in civilised surroundings.

French Restaurant (*Fashi Canting*) Originally set up by a French woman, the French Cafe, or Tcheu Tang, is an unexpected oasis of tasty treats you won't get elsewhere in Lhasa. Specialities include proper coffee (Y7), crepes (Y12 to Y16), homemade bread, quiche (Y14), freshly baked croissants (Y3), Italian cheese (Y10) and to-die-for chocolate mousse (Y14).

Dunya (*Dekyi Shar Lam*) Dishes Y30-40. With sophisticated decor, excellent and wide-ranging food and interesting specials, this foreign-run place has a very Western feel. It's pricier than most other places in town but it's very popular with groups and travellers who aren't on a shoestring.

Makye Amye (☎ 632 3829, *Barkhor Circuit*) Mains Y18-25. The prize for the best location in town must go to this restaurant on the 1st floor of a building overlooking the south-east corner of the Barkhor circuit. The food is a decent mix of Italian, Nepali and Tibetan cuisine but the desserts in particular have suffered since the foreign managers left a few years back. Still, it has a pretty good vibe, and, voyeurism aside, it's a great place to kick back with a beer or a pot of tea and watch the Barkhor below.

Gangki Restaurant Dishes Y10-20. Down in the Barkhor Square area, this place has a rooftop dining area with great views of the Jokhang and Barkhor Square.

Native Tibetan Restaurant Dishes Y10-25. This is a better place with a fine view over the Barkhor, either from inside or from the rooftop. The inside features some lovely Tibetan murals. Food is a good mixture of Tibetan, Chinese and Nepali.

There are also many other local restaurants in the Tibetan quarter. The **Yuyi Restaurant** across from the Banak Shol hotel offers good and cheap Chinese dishes with an English menu of sorts. Along Dekyi Shar Lam between the Kirey and Banak Shol hotels are a number of Muslim restaurants. One such restaurant with an English menu can be found on Dekyi Shar Lam opposite the Bank of China. The best Muslim restaurants are in the Muslim district. There are some excellent and cheap noodle dishes on offer, including *chao mianpian* (fried noodle squares) and *ganban mian*, a kind of stir-fried spaghetti bolognaise.

With the arrival of half a dozen Nepali restaurants, Lhasa now rivals Kathmandu in the Nepali food stakes (though prices are a little higher). All offer a mix of Indian, pseudo-Chinese and Western dishes such as pizza for around Y25, though Indian veggie dishes are cheaper at Y10-12. If you are hankering for enchiladas, chocolate pudding, peach lassis and other Thamel favourites, these are the places to come.

Tashi Targyel Restaurant (*Mentsikhang Lam*) Dishes Y12-25. This restaurant is probably the pick of the bunch. Prices are lowest, service is impeccable and the food is good. The Nepali dishes (try the thali for Y20) and Chinese dishes are the best bets.

Tibet Lhasa Kitchen (*Mentsikhang Lam*) Dishes Y15-30. Along similar lines to the Snowlands Restaurant, and just across the road, this upstairs restaurant is popular for its cosy atmosphere, good Nepali food and occasional cultural show.

The best places for breakfast are probably the Makye Amye, Dunya and Kailash restaurants.

Western Lhasa The best Chinese food in town is found in the west of town, which is predominantly Han Chinese. This area is such a long hike from the Tibetan quarter that few travellers make the effort. In the vicinity of the Lhasa Hotel are some upmarket dining options, both Tibetan and Chinese, but the best upmarket restaurants are actually in the hotel itself: The **Zampu** serves Chinese food, the **Everest** has an international buffet, and the *Himalaya* serves Tibetan. The Y170 buffet price tag (Y130 for breakfast) will put these out of reach for most travellers, but for those with some extra cash to spend on a splash-out meal this is some of the best food available in Lhasa.

One Minzu Lane Snacks Y20-40. If you can't afford the hotel restaurants this snack bar, just off the foyer, has affordable coffee, sandwiches and ice cream sundaes.

Hard Yak Café Meals Y60-90. Still inside the Lhasa Hotel and next door to One Minzu Lane, the Hard Yak serves good meals including the famous yak burger with French fries (Y68). The 'seafood in a basket' beggars belief.

Yeti Café (Xueren Jiudian; ☎ *681 5755, 206-210 Dekyi Nub Lam)* Dishes Y15-40. This cafe is a more modest restaurant opposite the Lhasa Hotel where you can get some unusual Tibetan dishes in very pleasant surroundings. There's not much for vegetarians here.

Snow Dragon Restaurant (Xuelong Canting; ☎ *683 4699, 28 Dekyi Nub Lam)* Dinner Y40. A clone of the nearby Yeti Café, with exactly the same menu, this Tibetan-style restaurant is aimed more at groups. Every night at 6.30pm it features a Tibetan show with dinner.

Teahouses

There are several Tibetan teahouses around town where you can grab a cheap cup of *cha ngamo* (sweet tea). Most are grungy Tibetan-only places, blasted by high-decibel kungfu videos, but there are a few exceptions. The best places are the *Turquoise Dragon Teahouse*, a Tibetan-style place with a fine balcony overlooking Dekyi Shar Lam, the *teahouse* underneath the Tashi Targyel Hotel and the pleasant *teahouses* around the ponds to the east of Potala Square.

Self-Catering & Trekking Supplies

Lhasa is the best place to stock up on food supplies for trips to Mt Kailash and the Nepali border. The town has many supermarkets, mostly Chinese-run, which sell everything from sachets of shampoo to bottles of red wine. One of the largest is on the ground floor of the Lhasa Foreign Trade Building on Dekyi Nub Lam, though cheaper supermarkets can be found across the road.

In the Tibetan quarter, the *wholesale shops* near and behind the Kirey Hotel offer the best prices for basic food supplies and are the places to stock up for a long trip.

The *Tromsikhang Market* area just south of here has a small selection of fresh vegetables, puffed rice and yogurt as well as Tibet's best selection of dried fruits and nuts. Roasted peanuts are good trekking food and are available for about Y5 per *jin* (500g) from the various Chinese mobile stalls that sell duck and dubious cuts of roast meat.

The old town has a couple of Tibetan-run Nepali supermarkets selling everything from muesli and chocolate spread to Indian spices, though at prices far higher than in Nepal. Try the *Nuoling Tsongkhang* shop, 300m south of the junction of Dekyi Shar Lam and Lingkhor Shar Lam.

Ramoche Lam, the street leading to the Ramoche Temple, has a small *vegetable market*, but the best *produce market* lies in a covered lane just east of the Potala.

For trekking supplies and imported luxury items such as Pringles and Cornflakes, check out the *Pentoc Guesthouse shop*. Items past their use-by date are sold at 30% discount.

ENTERTAINMENT

There is not a great deal in the way of entertainment options in Lhasa. In the evening most travellers head to one of the restaurants in the Tibetan quarter and then retire to the Yak or Banak Shol hotels, which sometimes become the scene of an impromptu party.

Makye Amye (☎ *632 3829, Barkhor Circuit)* Makye Amye is a good place for a beer or hard-to-find drinks such as Kahlúa (mixers cost Y40), and sometimes stays open until the early hours if there are enough people around.

Dunya (Dekyi Shar Lam) The upstairs bar is popular with local expats and tour groups. A beer costs Y12; happy hour means a Y2 discount between 7pm and 9.30pm on Friday.

Gleckes Fresh Beer (☎ 682 6552, Dekyi Nub Lam) Open 10am-midnight daily. In the west of town near the Grand Hotel, Gleckes brews its own dark and lager-style beer and it's pretty good. A glass of light/dark beer costs Y10/12; pitchers are Y23/28. Food is served but it's nothing special.

Last Bus (Mu Ban Che; ☎ 688 4990) Funky design makes this bar popular with Lhasa's trendies, mostly Chinese and male. Bottled beer costs Y12. It's easy to find – look for the bus stuck into the wall across from the Lhasa Hotel!

Music Kitchen, part of a string of bars and restaurants near the Lhasa Hotel, boasts the best Western music in Lhasa.

Karaoke bars and *discos* are a recent addition to the nightlife scene. Generally not many travellers venture into these places and some of those who have claim to have been harassed by plain-clothed PSB officers. Of more interest are the *Tibetan dance halls* around town, which offer a mix of disco music and traditional Tibetan dance, with a bit of karaoke thrown in for good measure. Locations change regularly so try to go with a Tibetan friend.

Lhasa's *cinemas* and *video halls* mostly blast out Hindi musicals and Hong Kong kung fu flicks, though the cinemas show the occasional Hollywood blockbuster dubbed into Chinese. The *Pentoc Guesthouse* shows free videos most nights at 8pm in its lobby.

Unfortunately there is almost nothing in the way of cultural entertainment in Lhasa. Restaurants like the *Tibet Lhasa Kitchen* and *Crazy Yak* in the courtyard of the Kirey Hotel have song-and-dance performances for diners. For authentic performances of Tibetan opera and dancing you will probably have to wait for one of Lhasa's festivals (see Special Events earlier in this chapter).

Tibetan Dance & Drama Theatre (Cnr Mirig Lam & Dekyi Nub Lam) Opposite the Lhasa Hotel, the theatre is mostly a lost cause, although it might be worth inquiring at the Lhasa Hotel whether there will be any performances that coincide with your visit – it is unlikely.

SHOPPING

Lhasa is no longer the backwater it once was, and it is now a good place to stock up on basic supplies. Items such as medical supplies, books, water-purifying tablets and deodorant are still not easy to find.

Lhasa Department Store (Lasa Baihuo Dalou) is a good one-stop shop for most supplies, especially clothes, though it's a little more expensive than elsewhere.

Photography

It is still a good idea to come with your own film supplies, but slide film is now relatively easy to find in Lhasa (though slide processing is impossible). A profusion of *photographic shops* are clustered around the entrance to the Workers' Cultural Palace, east of the Potala Square. Prices for 100ASA Sensia can normally be haggled down to about Y45 for 36 exposures, less if you buy in bulk; Elitechrome is a little cheaper. Print film is available everywhere for between Y20 and Y25 (36 exposures). Advantix film costs around Y65. Camera batteries (2CRS) cost around Y60.

Chinese black-and-white film is cheap to buy but expensive to process in Lhasa so you won't save much over colour film.

The Pentoc Guesthouse develops film the same day for Y6.5, plus Y0.9 to Y1.8 per print, if you hand in your film before 11am.

Travel & Trekking Equipment

For basic items such as thermoses and water canisters, the best places to shop are the lanes that run from the Tromsikhang Market down to the Barkhor circuit. Cheap pots and pans (ideal for instant noodles) are available at the stalls on the east side of the Potala, near the Airway Hotel. For details of places to buy food supplies for trekking, see Self-Catering & Trekking Supplies under Places to Eat earlier in this chapter.

Mount Green Trekking (Dekyi Shar Lam) Basic trekking gear is available here for rent: sleeping bags (Y15 per day), mats (Y5), petrol stoves (Y10) and tents (Y25 per day, including two mats). It also sells Nepali-made fleeces, jackets, hats and gloves. You can get hard-to-find items such as sunscreen, deodorant and lip cream here; otherwise dig around in the Nepali-stocked shops around the Barkhor.

***Outlook Outdoor Equipment** (☎/fax 634 5589, 11 Dekyi Shar Lam,* W *www.ontheway.com.cn)* This great trekking shop is across from the Kirey Hotel. Apart from Western-quality sleeping bags, Gore-Tex jackets and tents, it's also full of hard-to-find travel knick-knacks such as altimeters, trekking socks, food supplies and gloves. Prices are almost as high as in the West but quality is high. If you buy one of the trekking gas canisters (Y60 to Y70) you can rent the burner for free. Also available for rent are Primus multifuel stoves (Y40 per day), mats (Y10 to Y20), sleeping bags (Y15 to Y25) and tents (Y35 to Y70). Prices and deposits for equipment rental are negotiable here and at some other outdoor shops.

***North Col Outdoor Equipment Shop** (☎ 681 6379)* At North Col you'll find a good collection of mid-range Chinese-made Western outdoor clothes (Gore-Tex jackets start at US$40). You can rent sleeping bags (Y15 to Y25 per day), tents (Y25 to Y35) and rucksacks (Y20 to Y30), and buy mountaineering equipment and gadgets such as ski poles and altimeters. Gas canisters cost Y60.

Canned oxygen is available at the Pentoc Guesthouse.

Souvenirs

Most travellers do their souvenir shopping on the Barkhor circuit. Expect to be asked outrageous prices for anything you are interested in and then settle down for some serious and persistent haggling. There is an awful lot of junk for sale in this part of town, but even some of the junky items have a certain charm. Popular purchases include prayer wheels, rings, daggers and prayer flags, all of which are fairly portable. Tibetan clothing such as chubas, Tibetan dresses, cowboy hats, Chinese silk jackets, Tibetan brocade and fur hats are good buys.

The majority of shops in the Barkhor sell jewellery, most of it turquoise and coral and almost all of it fake. If you are thinking of investing money in this stuff, first read the pointers under Shopping in the Facts for the Visitor chapter.

There are **carpet stalls** at a couple of different points on the Barkhor circuit. If you have a particular interest in buying carpet you might want to check out the **carpet factory** *(24 Chingdröl Shar Lam)*, in the south-eastern part of town near the Tibet University, although it doesn't sport a particularly exciting selection.

***Snow Leopard Carpet Industries** (☎ 632 1481, fax 633 3249, 2 Mentsikhang Lu)*, next to the Snowlands Restaurant, sells a collection of high-quality carpets and interesting souvenirs and can arrange delivery abroad.

There are a couple of **thangka workshops** on the south side of the Barkhor circuit and several others in the surrounding back streets.

The ***Tsomeling Tent Workshop*** in the backstreets north of the Yak Hotel sells ready-made tents and door hangings (Y40) and will make anything you ask for in a day or so. Stalls sell similar goods around the Barkhor.

For better-quality souvenir items at marked-up prices, look out for the antique shops tucked away behind the stalls on the Barkhor circuit. Shops like ***Tashi Gallery*** near the Snowlands hotel, ***Dorje Antique Shop*** opposite the Yak Hotel and the ***Kyichu Art Gallery*** in the Hotel Kyichu offer excellent-quality items at high prices.

Pentoc Guesthouse shop has some interesting items such as yak tails, knucklebone games, hand-made Tibetan paper, and fabulous kitsch such as *'om mani padme hum'* ('hail to the jewel in the lotus') fridge magnets! It has the best postcards in town, as well as Tibetan calendars.

Most tourist sites and top-end hotels have some souvenir shops. Those around the Potala and the Norbulingka offer a selection of oil paintings by local artists, thangkas, antiques, souvenir books and the best selection of T-shirts in town, although prices have been pushed up by the tour groups.

Most shops of this kind are run by Han Chinese from other provinces. Tibetans sell

LHASA

trinkets from blankets outside the Potala and the Lhasa Hotel.

If you need to get customs clearance for an antique you will need to go the Cultural Department office (Wenhua Ju), just south of the Tibet Museum.

GETTING THERE & AWAY

While there are theoretically a number of ways to get to Lhasa, the main routes are by air from Chengdu (in Sichuan), by bus from Golmud (in Qinghai), and overland or by air from Kathmandu. For information on these and other services into Tibet, see the Getting There & Away chapter; the table 'Air Routes' shows flights and fares between Lhasa and regional destinations.

Air

Flying *out* of Lhasa is considerably easier and cheaper than flying in. No permits are necessary – just turn up to the office of the CAAC and China Southwest Airlines (☎ 633 3446) at 88 Nyangdren Chang Lam (Nangre Beilu) and buy a ticket, preferably several days in advance. To book a ticket you need to fill out a form, get a reservation and then pay (in cash only) at the cashier. The office is open from 9am to 8pm daily. Fares discounted by up to 25% are sometimes available on flights between Kathmandu and Lhasa. You can buy onward tickets from Chengdu here, but not at discounted prices.

If you cancel a ticket the penalty depends on how far in advance you cancel. More than 24 hours before departure the penalty is 5% of the ticket cost (ie, you get a 95% refund); two to 24 hours before is 10%; less than two hours before is 20%; and after the flight has departed the penalty is 50%.

There is no TTB permit check on arrival or departure, though you should hold on to your luggage stub as officials check these zealously. Departure tax is Y50 for domestic flights, Y90 for flights to Kathmandu, paid at check-in.

Bus & Minibus

To/From Golmud The only bus service between Lhasa and the outside world is to Golmud in Qinghai province.

Tickets for sleeper buses from Lhasa to Golmud (Y210, 30 to 50 hours) can be bought at the main bus station south of the Lhasa Hotel. Buses depart at 8.30am. There are also sleeper buses that continue on all the way to Xining, the capital of Qinghai province (Y334, 2½ days) and even Chengdu (3287km, three days and four nights, via Golmud). For more information on the Lhasa-Golmud route, see Qinghai-Tibet Highway in the Getting There & Away chapter.

To/From Nepal There are no longer direct buses to the Nepali border (at Zhangmu), though there are occasional advertisements in the Tibetan quarter for seats in minibuses or Land Cruisers to Zhangmu. These are vehicles that are travelling to pick up groups, so beware that if a tour is cancelled so is the vehicle (and your booking). Seats cost around Y350 for the two-day trip, normally with an overnight stop at Shigatse.

Around Tibet Other services operating from the main bus station include those to Shigatse (Y38, 9am), Tsetang (Y27 to Y30, 9am, 10am and 11am) and Nagchu (Y63, eight hours, 8.30am). Buses to Bayi (Y80, 8.30am) and Chamdo (Y230, daily, non-sleeper) are currently off-limits to foreign travellers. You can buy tickets up to three days in advance at the ticket office. Bring your passport. If you cancel your ticket 24 hours or more before departure you get 90% of the ticket price back. Private buses depart from the front of the main bus station for Samye, Tsetang and Shigatse.

Private buses also depart for Shigatse (Y38) from the junction of Ramoche Lam and Dekyi Shar Lam at around 7.30am. Some travellers have been thrown off private buses to Shigatse as they don't have permits to carry foreign travellers. The government bus to Shigatse also waits here to pick up passengers at around 7.30am but beware as it only drives to the bus station and waits until 9am. Buses normally also depart for Samye and Nagchu (Naqu) from here or in front of the Kirey Hotel at the same time.

A minibus direct to Gyantse leaves the main bus station at around 6.30am on alternate days (Y63, eight hours). You may find other services departing later in the day. Otherwise take a bus to Shigatse and change there.

Lhasa's Lugu Bus Station is located south-west of the Barkhor Square and has several departures daily to both Medro Gungkar (Mozhu Gongka), for visits to Drigung Til Monastery, and Lhundrub (Linzhou), for the road to Reting Monastery. There are also buses to Chushul and Nyemo. Minibus No 9 departs frequently from here for Dagtse (Y3).

The Eastern Suburbs Bus Station (Dongjiao Qike Keyunzhan) has buses to Lhundrub (Y12, 7.30am) and Meldro Gongkar (Y12, 10am, 2pm and 4pm) and lots of buses to Bayi (Y80 to Y100), which at the time of research was off-limits to foreigners. There are also buses to Yangpachen (Y15), Ritok (Y25, 10am), Nyima Jangre (for Drigung) and Zashu (9am, for Drigung), and every three days to Pangduo. Buses from Lugu station to Tsetang, Samye and the airport also pick up passengers here. There are lots of buses to Bayi from here, but foreigners are not allowed on these.

Buses to popular pilgrim destinations leave early in the morning from the west side of Barkhor Square. Buses leave around 6.30am for Ganden Monastery (2½ hours), 7am to 7.30am for the Samye ferry crossing (Y25, 3½ hours), 7.30am for Tsurphu Monastery (Y15, 2½ hours), 8am for Tsetang (advertised as Shannan, the Chinese name of the county; Y30) and between 8am and 9am for Dranang. Buses depart when full.

An exciting development is the inauguration of a bus service between Lhasa and Ali in western Tibet. Buses run every week, leave at 9pm and take anywhere from 50 to 60 hours nonstop. Berths cost Y600, Y700 or Y800, depending on the location in the bus (the cheaper berths are at the back and in the upper tier) and there are a couple of seats for Y550. The company claims that passengers don't need travel permits for Ali but that foreigners have to 'get off at Lhatse and walk around one checkpoint'! For details and bookings contact the Tibetan Antelope Travel and Transportation Co Ltd (Zanglingyang Lüyun Youxian Gongsi; ☎ 681 1588) at 37 Nyangdren Chang Lam. The office is four doors to the right of the Ali Prefectural Office (Ali Banshi Chu), which most taxi drivers know. Minibus No 5 goes past here en route to Sera Monastery.

Rental Vehicles

Rental vehicles have emerged as the most popular way to get away from Lhasa in recent years, even though you can still travel along most of the main routes by public transport. The most popular route is a leisurely and slightly circuitous journey down to Zhangmu on the Tibet-Nepal border, taking in Yamdrok-tso, Gyantse, Shigatse, Sakya, Everest Base Camp and Tingri along the way (see the Tsang chapter for more information). Mt Kailash and Nam-tso are also popular destinations.

At the time of research, all Land Cruiser trips were supposed to be organised through FIT (see Travel Agencies under Information earlier in this chapter), though for trips around the Lhasa region (which require no permits) there is nothing to stop you talking directly to a driver or other travel agency. If you are organising a long trip then read the advice given in the boxed text 'Dealing with an Agency' in the Getting Around chapter.

Prices for Land Cruiser hire (with driver) fluctuate throughout the year depending upon the season, the number of available vehicles and the number of tourists. August and September tend to be the most expensive months in which to hire a vehicle.

A seven-day trip to the Nepali border via Yamdrok-tso, Gyantse, Shigatse, Sakya and Everest Base Camp will cost between Y4500 and Y6000. The price includes permits and guide and should also include the fee of Y400 to enter the Qomolangma Nature Preserve by Land Cruiser (though it generally does not cover the Y65 individual entry fee). A trip that returns to Lhasa from Everest Base Camp should be a little cheaper.

If you are headed to the Yarlung Valley then a three- or four-day trip to Samye,

Mindroling Monastery, Tsetang and back costs Y2500 to Y2800, including a guide and permits.

For the cost of trips to western Tibet see that chapter. See specific destinations for other approximate Land Cruiser costs.

If independent travel agencies return to the scene you'll have to talk to other travellers and get the latest on which are most reliable. Remember it's often worth spending a few hundred yuan extra (it's not much spread between six people) to hire a vehicle from a bigger and more reliable agency.

GETTING AROUND

For those travellers based in the Tibetan quarter of Lhasa, most of the major inner-Lhasa sights are within fairly easy walking distance. Sights such as the Norbulingka over in the west of town, however, mean a long trudge and it's better to take a minibus or hire a bicycle.

To/From Gongkar Airport

Gongkar airport is an inconvenient 95km from Lhasa. Airport buses leave at 6am for the morning flights to Kathmandu and Chengdu, and at 10am and 3pm, from the courtyard in front of the CAAC building. Buses wait for flights outside the terminal building. The price is Y25, except for the early bus from Lhasa, which costs Y35. It is possible to stay the night at Gongkar if you can't face the early start (see the Ü chapter). There are also buses from Gongkar airport to Shigatse (Y50).

Signs on the notice boards at the Yak, Snowlands and Banak Shol hotels and at the Pentoc Guesthouse regularly advertise seats on Land Cruisers hired for the trip to the airport. Hiring a vehicle for this trip should cost around Y400, which is fairly reasonable if you can get six or seven people together. Taxis are cheaper at around Y200 but can only fit three comfortably. The road has been asphalted for its entire length and it is a relatively smooth drive.

Shared taxis sometimes run to and from Gongkar airport for Y25 per person. This price assumes that there are four paying passengers in the car. These airport taxis can be tricky to track down in Lhasa, but you could try around the office of the CAAC and China Southwest Airlines, 88 Nyangdren Chang Lam.

Minibus

Privately run minibuses are frequent on Dekyi Shar Lam and if you need to get up to the area around the Lhasa Hotel or the bus station this is the quickest and cheapest way to do it. There is a flat Y2 charge.

The main minibus routes are:

No 2 From a block west of Barkhor Square, eastward past the Potala to the Norbulingka and main bus station and back
No 3 From a block west of Tashi I restaurant along Dekyi Shar Lam past the Potala and the Lhasa Hotel and out to Drepung Monastery; returns east along the same route except that it detours behind the Potala and the Lukhang
No 5 From Nyangdren Chang Lam (and sometimes Dekyi Shar Lam) north to the Sera Monastery

Taxi

Taxis are plentiful and charge a standard fare of Y10 to anywhere within the city. Few Chinese drivers know the Tibetan names for even the major sites, so you may have to refer (or point) to the boxed text 'Lhasa Signs – Chinese' earlier in this chapter, for a list of Chinese names and characters.

Pedicab

There is no shortage of pedicabs plying the streets of Lhasa, but as they are slow and relatively expensive there is little incentive to use them. A trip between the Yak Hotel and the Lhasa Hotel, for example, costs at least Y10 (after much haggling) and takes around 25 minutes. If you are heading to the Potala, bear in mind that pedicabs are not allowed to proceed further west than Nyangdren Chang Lam so you'll have to walk half the distance anyway. You'd be better off hiring a bicycle and peddling yourself around.

Bicycle

Bicycle is without a doubt the best way to get around once you have acclimatised to the altitude. You can hire bicycles at the Banak Shol/Snowlands hotel for Y2/3 per hour or Y20 per day. No deposit is required if you are a guest of the hotel, otherwise you'll have to hand over Y200 to Y400.

Bicycle theft is a problem in Lhasa, so always park your bike in the designated areas patrolled by matronly bicycle attendants (the standard charge is Y0.30). A lock and chain is a good idea.

It is possible to buy mountain bikes in Lhasa nowadays. Check the area in the vicinity of the Potala on Dekyi Nub Lam for bike shops. Prices fluctuate around Y500. Don't expect the quality to be up to international standards, but plenty of travellers manage to do long trips without having the bikes fall apart. Be sure to check the gears.

Around Lhasa

Within easy cycling distance of central Lhasa are the major Gelugpa monasteries of Sera and Drepung. Both are well worth visiting, even if you have only a brief stay in Lhasa.

DREPUNG MONASTERY
About 8km west of central Lhasa, Drepung *(adults/students Y35/25, open 9am-4.30pm daily)* was once the world's largest monastery, with a population of up to 10,000 monks. The word Drepung literally translates as 'rice heap', a reference to the huge numbers of white monastic buildings that once piled up on the hillside. It suffered through the ages with assaults by the kings of Tsang and the Mongols, but was left relatively unscathed during the Cultural Revolution and there is still much of interest intact. Rebuilding and resettlement continue at a pace unmatched elsewhere in Tibet and the site once again resembles a small village. There is a far greater sense of community here than at Lhasa's other great monasteries.

Interior photography costs Y20 per chapel. A *restaurant* near the bus stop serves reviving tea for three mao a glass and *momos* (dumplings) for two mao each.

History
Drepung was founded in 1416 by a charismatic monk and disciple of Tsongkhapa called Jamyang Chöje. He was able to raise funds for the project quickly and within a year of completion the monastery already hosted a population of some 2000 monks.

In 1530 the second Dalai Lama established the Ganden Palace, the palace that was home to the Dalai Lamas until the fifth built the Potala. It was from here that the early Dalai Lamas exercised their control over central Tibet, and the second, third and fourth Dalai Lamas are all entombed here. By the time of the fifth Dalai Lama in the early 17th century, the number of resident monks was somewhere between 7000 and 10,000. Today there are around 600 monks in residence.

Ganden Palace
From the car park follow the kora circuit clockwise around the outside of the monastery until you reach the steps up to the Ganden Palace. Prior to the construction of the Potala, this was the residence of the Dalai Lamas and headquarters of the Tibetan government. You can see the former residence of the Dalai Lamas at the top right of the main building.

The first hall on the left is the Sanga Tratsang, a recently renovated chapel housing statues of the protectors Namse (Vairocana), Nagpo Chenpo (Mahakala), Dorje Jigje (Yamantaka), Chögyel (Dharmaraja), Palden Lhamo (Shri Devi; on a horse) and the Nechung oracle, all arranged around a central statue of the fifth Dalai Lama.

Head up across the main courtyard, where performances of *cham* (a ritual dance) are still held during the Shötun festival and where several woodcarvers and printers sell their craft. There is a single chapel on the first floor of the main building and above here are three chapels making up the apartments of the early Dalai Lamas. The second of the three chapels has wonderfully detailed murals and the throne of the fifth Dalai Lama next to a 1000-armed statue of Chenresig (Avalokiteshvara). The third is a bare meditation room.

LHASA

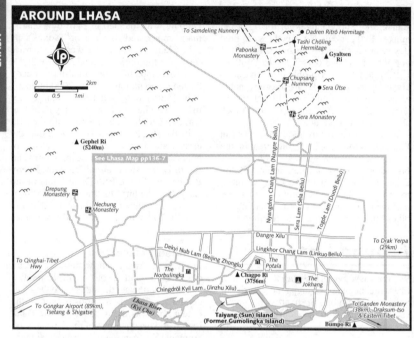

AROUND LHASA

From here, descend and cross over to a final chapel whose entrance is defaced by a rare Cultural Revolution–era Chairman Mao painting complete with political slogans. Signs lead past a teahouse to the exit to the north.

Main Assembly Hall

The main assembly hall, or *tsogchen*, is the principal structure in the Drepung complex. The hall is reached through an entrance on the west side.

The huge interior is very atmospheric, draped with thangkas and supported by over 180 supporting columns, some of which are adorned with ancient armour used for festival dances. Sculptures of interest include a two-storey Jampelyang (Manjushri), flanked by the 13th Dalai Lama; Sakyamuni (Sakya Thukpa) Buddha; Tsongkhapa; Jamyang Chöje, Drepung's founder, in a cabinet to the right; and Sakyamuni (Sakya Thukpa) Buddha, flanked by five of the Dalai Lamas.

At either end of the altar is a group of eight *arhats* (literally 'worthy ones').

The back-room chapel is flanked by the protector deities Chana Dorje (Vajrapani, blue) and Tamdrin (Hayagriva, red) and features statues of Sakyamuni (Sakya Thukpa) Buddha with his two disciples, the Buddhas of the Three Ages, and nine chörtens above. The walls and pillars are lined with statues of the eight bodhisattvas. To the east is Tsongkhapa. To the left there is also a statue of Lamdrin Rinpoche (a former abbot of Drepung whose photo is one of the most commonly seen in Tibet); next to it is his chörten.

Back by the main entrance, steps lead up to the 1st and 2nd floors. At the top of the stairs to the right is the Hall of the Kings of Tibet, featuring the fifth Dalai Lama, and to the left is a chapel containing the head of a two-storey Jampa (Maitreya) statue. Pilgrims prostrate themselves here and drink from a sacred conch shell.

Continue clockwise through the Sakyamuni Chapel, stuffed with chörtens, and then descend to the **Chapel of Jampa**. This chapel contains the assembly hall's most revered image, a massive statue of Jampa (Maitreya), the Future Buddha, at the age of 12. The statue rises through three floors of the building from a ground-floor chapel that is usually closed, and is flanked by Tsongkhapa and Jamyang Chöje. The chörtens behind contain the remains of the second Dalai Lama (at the back) and Jamyang Chöje (at the front). At the front right are statues of seven of the Dalai Lamas.

To the right of this chapel is a Drölma chapel. Drölma (Tara) is a protective deity, and in this case the three Drölma (Tara) images in the chapel (to the immediate right) are responsible for protecting Drepung's drinking water, wealth and authority respectively. There are also some lovely examples of Tibetan Kangyur scriptures here. The central statue is a form of Sakyamuni (Sakya Thukpa) whose amulet is said to contain one of Tsongkhapa's teeth.

Exit the building from the western side of the second floor.

Ngagpa College

Ngagpa is one of Drepung's four colleges, and was devoted to Tantric study. The chapel is dedicated to Dorje Jigje (Yamantaka), a Tantric meditational deity who serves as an opponent to the forces of impermanence. The cartoon-style Dorje Jigje (Yamantaka) image is said to have been fashioned by Tsongkhapa himself. Working clockwise, other statues include Palden Lhamo (Shri Devi; second clockwise), Nagpo Chenpo (Mahakala; fourth), Drölma (White Tara; fifth), Tsongkhapa (sixth), the fifth Dalai Lama (eighth), the Nechung oracle in the corner and, by the door, a small Dorje Drakden (see Nechung Monastery later in this chapter). Look for Chögyel (Dharmaraja) to the right with his hand thrusting out of the glass cabinet.

As you follow the pilgrim path (clockwise) around the back of the assembly hall you will pass the small Jampelyang Temple where pilgrims peer in to see a holy rock painting and get hit on the back with a holy iron rod.

Loseling College

Loseling is the largest of Drepung's colleges, and studies here were devoted to logic. The main hall houses a throne used by the Dalai Lamas, an extensive library and a long altar decorated with statues of various Dalai Lamas, Tsongkhapa and former Drepung abbots. The chörten of Loseling's first abbot is covered with financial offerings. There are three chapels to the rear of the hall. The one to the left houses 16 arhats which pilgrims walk under in a circuit. The central chapel has a large image of Jampa and interesting photos of the new and old Nechung oracle; the chapel to the right has a small statue of Sakyamuni (Sakya Thukpa).

On the 2nd floor you'll come to a small chapel full of angry deities and then you pass under the body of a stuffed goat draped with one-mao notes before entering the *gönkhang* (protector chapel). There are more protective deities here, including Nagpo Chenpo (Mahakala), Dorje Drakden and Dorje Jigje (Yamantaka).

Gomang College

Gomang is the second largest of Drepung's colleges and follows the same layout as Loseling. The main hall has a whole row of images, including Jampa, red Tsepame (Amitayus), and the seventh Dalai Lama. Again there are three chapels to the rear: The one to the left houses three deities of longevity, but more important is the central chapel, chock-a-block with images. As at Loseling, there is a single protector chapel on the upper floor. Women are sometimes not allowed into this chapel.

Deyang College

The smallest of Drepung's colleges, this one can safely be missed if you have had enough. The principal image in the main hall is Jampa (Maitreya), flanked by Jampelyang (Manjushri), Drölma (Tara), the fifth Dalai Lama and others.

East of here are a cluster of friendly colleges, including the **Jurche Mitze**, once

LHASA

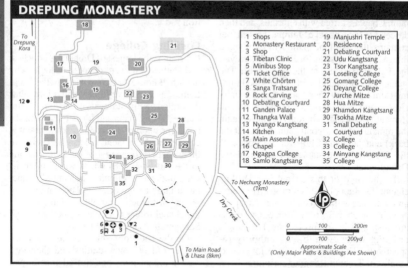

DREPUNG MONASTERY

1 Shops	19 Manjushri Temple
2 Monastery Restaurant	20 Residence
3 Shop	21 Debating Courtyard
4 Tibetan Clinic	22 Udu Kangtsang
5 Minibus Stop	23 Tsor Kangtsang
6 Ticket Office	24 Loseling College
7 White Chörten	25 Gomang College
8 Sanga Tratsang	26 Deyang College
9 Rock Carving	27 Jurche Mitze
10 Debating Courtyard	28 Hua Mitze
11 Ganden Palace	29 Khamdon Kangtsang
12 Thangka Wall	30 Tsokha Mitze
13 Nyango Kangtsang	31 Small Debating
14 Kitchen	Courtyard
15 Main Assembly Hall	32 College
16 Chapel	33 College
17 Ngagpa College	34 Minyang Kangtsang
18 Samlo Kangtsang	35 College

To Nechung Monastery (1km)

To Main Road & Lhasa (8km)

Dry Creek

0   100   200m
0   100   200yd
Approximate Scale
(Only Major Paths & Buildings Are Shown)

home to students from Inner Mongolia, and the **Khamdon Kangtsang**, which is defaced with many faded Mao slogans and images. More buildings sport English signs saying that visitors are welcome.

Drepung Kora

The lovely Drepung kora climbs up to around 3900m and probably should not be attempted until you have had four or five days acclimatising in Lhasa. The walk takes about 1½ hours at a leisurely pace (it is possible to do it more quickly at hiking speed). Look for the path that continues uphill from the turn-off to the Ganden Palace. The path passes several rock paintings, climbs up past a high wall used to hang a giant thangka during the Shötun festival, peaks at a valley of prayer flags and then descends to the east via an encased Drölma (Tara) statue and several more rock carvings. There are excellent views to be had along the way.

Hard-core acclimatised trekkers might want to consider the three-hour climb up to a white **retreat** perched high behind the monastery on the steep rock face of Gephel Ri, which offers spectacular views.

Getting There & Away

It takes around 45 minutes to cycle from the Barkhor area to the base of the hill on which Drepung is situated (look for Drepung above you and to the right). A dirt road leaves the main road up to Drepung; unless you have a mountain bike, it's best to leave your bike at the base of the hill or put it on a tractor. There should be someone to look after your bike just after the turn-off. The walk up to Drepung takes around 30 minutes.

The easy way to get out to Drepung is by minibus. Buses run all day from the minibus area in front of Barkhor Square (though there aren't many between 11am and 3pm) and cost Y3 to the base of the hill or, if you're lucky, up to the parking area in front of Drepung. The No 3 minibus also goes there from a block west of Tashi 1 restaurant.

NECHUNG MONASTERY

Nechung (*admission free; open 9am-4pm daily*) is only 10 minutes' walk downhill from Drepung. Until 1959, it was the seat of the State Oracle. The oracle at Nechung was the medium of Dorje Drakden, an aspect of Pehar, the Gelugpa protector of the Buddhist state, and the Dalai Lamas would make

The Nechung Oracle

Every New Year in Lhasa until 1959, the Dalai Lama would consult the Nechung oracle on important matters of state. In preparation for the ordeal the oracle would strap on bracelets in the shape of a human eye and an elaborate headdress of feathers, so heavy that it had to be lifted onto his head by two men.

The oracle would whip himself into a trance in an attempt to dislodge the spirit from his body. Eyewitness accounts describe how his eyeballs would swell and roll up into his sockets, and how his mouth would open wide, his tongue curl upward and his face redden. As he began to discern the future in a steel mirror the oracle answered questions in an anguished, tortured, hissing voice, which would then be translated for the court by a clerk. After the trance the oracle would faint and have to be carried away.

no important decision without first consulting him. In 1959 the State Oracle fled with the Dalai Lama to India, and Nechung is now cared for by a small number of monks.

Nechung Monastery is an eerie place associated with possession, exorcism and other pre-Buddhist rites. Note the blood-red doors at the entrance painted with flayed human skins and the scenes of torture along the top of the outer courtyard. For images of Dorje Drakden, the protective spirit manifested in the State Oracle, see the backroom chapel to the left of the main hall. The statue on the left shows Dorje Drakden in his wrathful aspect; the one on the right has him in a more conciliatory frame of mind. In between the two is a sacred tree.

On the 1st floor is an audience chamber with a throne used by the Dalai Lamas when they consulted with the State Oracle. The 2nd floor features a huge new statue of a wrathful Guru Rinpoche.

Nechung is easily visited as a day trip along with Drepung. Bring some lunch.

SERA MONASTERY

Sera Monastery (admission Y35; open 9am-5pm daily), around 5km north of central Lhasa, was along with Drepung one of Lhasa's two great Gelugpa monasteries. Its once huge monastic population of around 5000 monks has now been reduced to several hundred, and building repairs are still continuing. Nevertheless the monastery is worth a visit, particularly from around 3.30pm onwards when debating is usually held in the monastery's debating courtyard. Once you're inside the monastery walls there are no ticket checks. Interior photography costs Y30 per chapel; video fees are an outrageous Y850. Near the monastery entrance there is a basic *restaurant*.

History

Sera was founded in 1419 by Sakya Yeshe, a disciple of Tsongkhapa also known by the honorific title Jamchen Chöje. In its heyday, Sera hosted a huge monastic population and five colleges of instruction, but at the time of the Chinese invasion in 1959 the colleges numbered three. Like those of Drepung, the colleges of Sera specialised: Sera Me in the fundamental precepts of Buddhism; Sera Je in the instruction of itinerant monks from outside central Tibet; and Sera Ngagpa in Tantric studies.

Sera survived the ravages of the Cultural Revolution with light damage, although many of the colleges were destroyed.

Sera Me College

Follow the pilgrims clockwise, past the Shampa Kangtsang residential hall and several minor buildings, to the Sera Me College. This college dates back to the original founding of the monastery.

The central image of the **main hall** is a copper Sakyamuni (Sakya Thukpa), flanked by Jampa (Maitreya) and Jampelyang (Manjushri). To the rear of the hall are four chapels. To the far left is a dark chapel dedicated to Ta-og, dharma protector of the east, and Dorje Jigje (Yamantaka). Look out for the masks on the ceiling. Women may be refused entry to this chapel.

Continue to the central chapel, which contains statues of the Present, Future and Past Buddhas (Sakyamuni or Sakya Thukpa, Jampa or Maitreya, and Marmedze or

LHASA

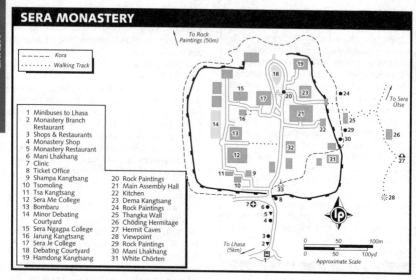

SERA MONASTERY

- – – – Kora
- · · · · · · Walking Track

1 Minibuses to Lhasa
2 Monastery Branch Restaurant
3 Shops & Restaurants
4 Monastery Shop
5 Monastery Restaurant
6 Mani Lhakhang
7 Clinic
8 Ticket Office
9 Shampa Kangtsang
10 Tsomoling
11 Tsa Kangtsang
12 Sera Me College
13 Bombaru
14 Minor Debating Courtyard
15 Sera Ngagpa College
16 Jarung Kangtsang
17 Sera Je College
18 Debating Courtyard
19 Hamdong Kangtsang
20 Rock Paintings
21 Main Assembly Hall
22 Kitchen
23 Dema Kangtsang
24 Rock Paintings
25 Thangka Wall
26 Chöding Hermitage
27 Hermit Caves
28 Viewpoint
29 Rock Paintings
30 Mani Lhakhang
31 White Chörten

To Rock Paintings (50m)

To Sera Ütse

To Lhasa (5km)

Approximate Scale

Dipamkara), as well as 16 arhats depicted in their mountain grottos.

The next chapel is home to Miwang Jowo, a Sakyamuni (Sakya Thukpa) statue that dates from the 15th century and is the most sacred of the college's statues. At the back are Tsepame (Amitayus) and eight bodhisattvas. The entrance to the chapel is flanked by the protectors Tamdrin (Hayagriva; red) and Achala (blue). The last chapel is dedicated to Tsongkhapa and there are also images of several Dalai Lamas as well as of Sakya Yeshe, Sera's founder and first abbot.

There are also two chapels on the upper floor. The first, after you mount the stairs, is dedicated to Sakyamuni (Sakya Thukpa). The second, approached over a walkway, is a Drölma (Tara) chapel and has 1000 statues of this protective deity. The third has 1000 statues of Chenresig (Avalokiteshvara).

Sera Ngagpa College

A Tantric college, Ngagpa is also the oldest structure at Sera. The **main hall** is dominated by a statue of Sakya Yeshe (wearing a black hat), surrounded by other famous Sera lamas. There are two chapels to the

rear of the hall, one with 16 arhats and a large Sakyamuni (Sakya Thukpa) statue and one with a statue of the protective deity Dorje Jigje (Yamantaka), as well as Namtöse (Vaishravana), the guardian of the north, to the right, who rides a snow lion and holds a mongoose that vomits jewels. There are also a couple of rooms upstairs featuring Tsepame (Amitayus) and the eight medicine buddhas (Menlha).

Jarung Kangtsang

Most pilgrims pay a quick visit to this residential college.

Sera Je College

This is the largest of Sera's colleges. It has a breathtaking **main hall**, hung with thangkas and lit by shafts of light from high windows. Several chörtens hold the remains of Sera's most famous lamas.

To the left of the hall is a passage that leads, via a chapel dedicated to the Present, Future and Past Buddhas, to the most sacred of Sera Monastery's chapels, the **Chapel of Tamdrin**. Tamdrin (Hayagriva) is a wrathful meditational deity whose name means 'horse headed'. He is the chief protective deity of Sera, and there is often a line of pilgrims waiting to touch their forehead to his feet in respect. Take a look at the weapons hanging from the ceiling. There is a second chapel for him on the upper floor, but here he is in another aspect with nine heads. The chapels to the rear of the hall are of less interest. There are three altogether: One is devoted to Jampa (Maitreya) and the 16 arhats, who are depicted in lovely sandalwood statues; another is devoted to Tsongkhapa, flanked by Sakyamuni (Sakya Thukpa) and Öpagme (Amitabha); and another to Jampelyang (Manjushri), who is depicted in the mudra (hand position) of turning the Wheel of Law, flanked by Jampa (Maitreya) and another Jampelyang (Manjushri).

To the north-east of Sera Je is Sera's **debating courtyard**. There is usually debating practice here in the afternoons from around 3.30pm to 4pm. You will hear it (with much clapping of hands to emphasise points) as you approach Sera Je. It is well worth your time and provides a welcome relief from peering at Buddhist iconography.

Hamdong Kangtsang
Hamdong served as a residence for monks studying at Sera Je College. The back left chapel contains a bearded image of a Sera lama who died in 1962; in a case to the right is an image of Drölma (Tara), who is said to protect Sera's water supply.

As you walk downhill, note the wonderful **rock paintings** of Jampelyang (Manjushri), Chenresig (Avalokiteshvara), Chana Dorje (Vajrapani) and Green Tara.

Main Assembly Hall
The main assembly hall is the largest of Sera's buildings and dates back to 1710. The main hall is particularly impressive and is noted for its wall-length thangkas. A statue of Jampa (Maitreya) is the centrepiece. He is flanked by other figures including Dalai Lamas on your right, while to the left is the large throne of the 13th Dalai Lama. Behind the throne is a figure of Sakyamuni (Sakya Thukpa) flanked by the 13th Dalai Lama and Sakya Yeshe, the founder of Sera.

Of the three chapels to the rear of the hall, the central is the most important, with its 6m-high Jampa (Maitreya) statue. The statue rises up to the upper floor, where it can also be viewed from the central chapel. Also on the upper floor (to the far left of the central chapel) is a highly revered statue of a 1000-armed Chenresig (Avalokiteshvara). Pilgrims put their forehead to a pole that connects them directly to the heart of the Bodhisattva of Compassion. The pilgrim path enters the building from the back so this may be the first chapel you come across.

Sera Kora
The Sera kora takes less than an hour and is well worth the time. It starts outside the entrance and heads west, following an arc around the monastery walls. On the eastern descent, look out for several brightly coloured rock paintings. The largest ones on the eastern side of the monastery are of Dorje Jigje (Yamantaka), Tsongkhapa and others. You can cut through to here by heading east from the Hamdong Kangtsang. Next to the rock paintings is a support wall used to hang a giant thangka during festivals.

A path leads up the side steps of this wall to the **Chöding hermitage**, a short uphill climb. The hermitage was a retreat of Tsongkhapa, and predates Sera. There is not a great deal to see, but it is a short walk and the views from the hermitage are worthwhile. A path continues south around the hillside past a holy spring to a viewpoint that has fine views of Sera and Lhasa beyond.

The kora continues into the monastery complex past two large chörtens.

Sera Ütse
Sera Ütse was another retreat used by Tsongkhapa. It is of more interest than Chöding, but it is also more of a climb. From Sera the walk takes around 1½ hours. To get there, take the path towards Chöding hermitage and branch off to the left before you get there, climbing the ridge via a switchback path until you reach the yellow building. This walk should not really be attempted until you have had at least a few days in Lhasa acclimatising to the altitude.

LHASA

Monasteries in Tibet

The great Gelugpa monasteries of Drepung, Sera and Ganden were once like self-contained worlds. Drepung, the largest of these monasteries, was home to around 10,000 monks at the time of the Chinese takeover in 1951. Like the other major Gelugpa institutions, Drepung operated less as a single unit than as an assembly of colleges, each with its own interests, resources and administration.

The colleges, known as *dratsang*, were in turn made up of residences, or *kangtsang*. A monk joining a monastic college was assigned to a kangtsang according to the region he was born in. For example, it is thought that 60% of monks at Drepung's Loseling College were from Kham, while Gomang college was dominated by monks from Amdo and Mongolia. In total, Loseling had 23 kangtsang, but the three most powerful kangtsang were all Kham controlled. This gave the monastic colleges a distinctive regional flavour, and meant that loyalties were generally grounded much deeper in the colleges than in the monastery itself.

At the head of a college was the abbot or *khenpo*, a position that was filled by contenders who had completed the highest degrees of monastic studies. The successful applicant was chosen by the Dalai Lama. Beneath the abbot was a group of religious heads who supervised prayer meetings and festivals and a group of economic managers who controlled the various kangtsang estates and funds. There was also a squad of huge monks known as *dob-dobs*, who were in charge of discipline and administering punishments.

In the case of the larger colleges, estates and funds were often extensive. Loseling College had over 180 estates and 20,000 serfs who worked the land and paid taxes to the monastery. Monasteries were involved in most forms of trade. For the most part, these holdings were not used to support monks – who were often forced to do private business to sustain themselves – but to maintain an endless cycle of prayer meetings and festivals that were deemed necessary for the spiritual good of the nation.

The white granite rock faces of the hills around Sera give off a lot of glare and can make for hot walking, particularly in the summer months, so get an early start and take lots of water.

Getting There & Away

Sera is only a half-hour bicycle ride from the Barkhor area of Lhasa. Leave your bicycle next to the monastery restaurant.

Alternatively, head down to the intersection of Nyangdren Chang Lam and Dekyi Shar Lam (the last turn before the main post office as you head west) and look for the No 5 minibuses and jeeps that wait on the corner. They head up to Sera every 10 minutes or so (whenever they are full) and cost Y2.

PABONKA MONASTERY

Pabonka Monastery (*admission free; open dawn-dusk*) is one of the most ancient Buddhist sites in the Lhasa region. It is little visited, but is only a one-hour walk from the

Sera Monastery turn-off and is well worth the effort.

Built on a flat-topped granite boulder, Pabonka may even predate the Jokhang and Ramoche. It was built in the 7th century by King Songtsen Gampo. The Tibetan king Trisong Detsen, Guru Rinpoche and Tibet's first seven monks all meditated here. A monk named Thonmi Sambhota reputedly invented the Tibetan alphabet here. It was destroyed in 841 by the anti-Buddhist King Langdharma and rebuilt in the 11th century. It was restored again by the fifth Dalai Lama, who added an extra floor to the two-storey building. It suffered more damage in the Cultural Revolution and has undergone repairs in recent years.

The first building you come across is the **Rigsum Gonpo Temple**, whose most famous relic is the carved mantra 'om mani padme hum' to the left of the entrance. Inside is a fine statue and mural of an 11-headed Chenresig (Avalokiteshvara). The

The Potala, the traditional but deserted residence of the Dalai Lamas, is a reminder of Tibetan hopes for self-government.

Be transported in Lhasa, the heart and soul of Tibet. Walking the city's *koras* (pilgrimage paths) is a sure way to lose yourself – or find yourself.

inner chapel contains 'self-arising' carvings depicting the trinity of Chenresig (Avalo-kiteshvara), Jampelyang (Manjushri) and Chana Dorje (Vajrapani), after which the chapel is named.

Continue uphill past a row of chörtens, walking clockwise around the Pabonka rock (said to represent a female tortoise) to the **Palden Lhamo Cave** on the west side, where King Songtsen Gampo once meditated. Images inside are of Songtsen Gampo, Guru Rinpoche, Trisong Detsen and the protector Palden Lhamo (Shri Devi).

The **Pabonka Potrang** is placed on top of the ancient rock. There is nothing to see on the ground floor, but the upper floor has an assembly hall with a 'self-arising' Sakya-muni (Sakya Thukpa) statue on a pillar to the right. The inner room is a protector chapel. The four-pillared Kashima Lha-khang is lined with various lamas and kings. The rooftop quarters of the Dalai Lama have a fine statue of the meditational deity Demchok (Chakrasamvara) and offers fine views.

Further above the Pabonka Potrang are the remains of 108 chörtens and the yellow temple of Princess Wencheng, which has a ground-floor room dedicated to various manifestations of Tsongkhapa and an upper-floor chapel with a small statue of Wen-cheng herself (in the far right). There is a sky-burial site to the east.

Walks Around the Monastery

A few intrepid (and fit) travellers use Pabonka as a base for walks further afield. The half-day kora around Pabonka, Tashi Chöling hermitage and Chupsang Nunnery makes a nice addition to a visit to Sera Monastery. Midday can be hot here so bring enough water.

For those who aren't so fit, an easy, short walk from Pabonka leads 20 minutes up to **Tashi Chöling hermitage**. There is not a lot left to see at the hermitage, but again it affords good views. From the back of the Pabonka kora follow the path diagonally up the hillside following the electricity poles.

From Tashi Chöling, the trail drops down into a ravine and follows this down for 30

minutes to **Chupsang Nunnery**. There are some 80 nuns resident at Chupsang and it's a very friendly place. You could also get to the nunnery from the road between Sera and Pabonka and then follow paths west around the base of the hill to Pabonka itself. It's about 40 minutes' walk from the nunnery to the main road into Lhasa.

An alternative route from Tashi Chöling is to hike 40 minutes north-east up the ravine to the cliffside hermitage of **Daden Ritrö**. You can see the hermitage from the trail.

Samdeling Nunnery is a tough four-hour hike from Tashi Chöling (allow around two hours for the descent). This is a serious day hike and should not be attempted until you are well adjusted to the altitude. Take water with you, though you will probably receive some butter tea from the nuns if you make it to the top. The trail heads to the north-west from Tashi Chöling and follows a steep ridge. The nunnery, home to more than 80 nuns, is at an altitude of over 4200m.

Getting There & Away

To get to Pabonka, take a minibus or jeep to the Sera Monastery turn-off (see Sera Monastery earlier in this chapter). Rather than take the turn to Sera, look for a left turn a little up the road before the military base. The walk from here is fairly straightforward. You need to make a right turn at a T-junction, but you will see Pabonka up ahead to the left perched on its granite boulder. The 'monastery' to the right is actually Chupsang Nunnery.

GANDEN MONASTERY
elevation 4500m

Ganden *(admission Y25; open dawn-dusk)*, just 40km north-east of Lhasa, was the first Gelugpa monastery and has remained the main seat of this major Buddhist order ever since. If you only have time for one monastery excursion outside Lhasa, Ganden would probably be the best choice. With its stupendous views of the surrounding Kyi-chu Valley and fascinating kora, Ganden is an experience unlike the other major Gelugpa monasteries in the Lhasa area.

LHASA

The monastery was founded in 1409 by Tsongkhapa, the revered reformer of the Gelugpa order, after the very first Mönlam festival was performed here. Images of Tsongkhapa and his first two disciples, Gyatsab Je and Kedrub Je, are found throughout the monastery. When Tsongkhapa died in 1411, the abbotship of the monastery passed on to these disciples. The post came to be known as the Ganden Tripa and was earned through scholarly merit, not reincarnation. It is the Ganden Tripa, not, as one might expect, the Dalai Lama, who is the head of the Gelugpa order.

Ganden means 'joyous' in Tibetan and is the name of the Western Paradise (also known as Tushita) that is home to Jampa (Maitreya), the Future Buddha. There is a certain irony in this, as of all the great monasteries of Tibet, it was Ganden that suffered most at the hands of the Red Guards, possibly because of its political influence. In 1959 there were 2000 monks at Ganden.

Today it is the scene of extensive rebuilding, but this does not disguise the ruin that surrounds the new. The destruction was caused by artillery fire and bombing in 1959 and 1966. New chapels and residences are being opened all the time, so even pilgrims are often unsure in which order to visit the chapels.

Ganden was temporarily closed to tourists in 1996 after violent demonstrations against the government's banning of Dalai Lama photos. The number of monks in Ganden seems to have dropped in recent years and those who remain aren't very knowledgeable or too interested in foreigners. Interior photography fees are Y20 per chapel; video fees are an amazing Y1500.

For details on trekking from Ganden to Samye, see the Trekking chapter.

Ngam Chö Khang

The first chapel you reach from the parking area is Ngam Chö Khang. It is built on the site of Tsongkhapa's original assembly hall, or dukhang, and has a small shrine with images of Tsongkhapa. On the left is a protector chapel, or gönkhang, that houses four protective deities. The largest image is of Dorje Jigje (Yamantaka).

Debating Courtyard

South-east of the Gomde Khang residence is the debating courtyard. You should be able to hear the clapping of hands as you pass if there is a debate in progress.

Tomb of Tsongkhapa

The red fortress-like structure of Tsongkhapa's mausoleum, also known as the Serkhang, is probably the most impressive of the reconstructed buildings at Ganden. Look for its inclining walls and the four

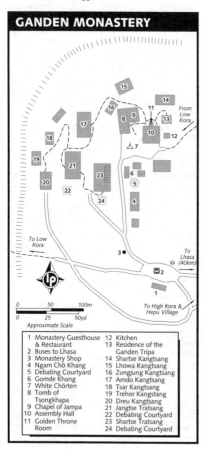

GANDEN MONASTERY

From Low Kora

To Low Kora

To Lhasa (40km)

To High Kora & Hepu Village

0   50   100m
0   25   50yd
Approximate Scale

1 Monastery Guesthouse & Restaurant	12 Kitchen
2 Buses to Lhasa	13 Residence of the Ganden Tripa
3 Monastery Shop	14 Shartse Kangtsang
4 Ngam Chö Khang	15 Lhowa Kangtsang
5 Debating Courtyard	16 Zungjung Kangtsang
6 Gomde Khang	17 Amdo Kangtsang
7 White Chörten	18 Tsar Kangtsang
8 Tomb of Tsongkhapa	19 Trehor Kangtsang
9 Chapel of Jampa	20 Dreu Kangtsang
10 Assembly Hall	21 Jangtse Tratsang
11 Golden Throne Room	22 Debating Courtyard
	23 Shartse Tratsang
	24 Debating Courtyard

high windows above a prominent white chörten.

The main entrance leads to an ad hoc printing press selling wood blocks. A small chapel is dedicated to Sakyamuni (Sakya Thukpa). The protector chapel ahead and to the right is the domain of the protective deity Chögyel (Dharmaraja). Women are not allowed into this chapel.

Exit this building, turn to the left and take the stairs leading to the upper floors. Here you'll find the throne of the Dalai Lamas.

Next to the hall is the Yangchen Khang chapel, which houses Tsongkhapa's tomb. The chapel is named after the stone in the back left, which is said to have flown from India. Both the original tomb and the preserved body of Tsongkhapa inside it were destroyed by Red Guards. The new silver and gold chörten was built to house salvaged fragments of Tsongkhapa's skull. The images seated in front of the chörten are of Tsongkhapa flanked by his two principal disciples. The room also holds several holy relics attributed to Tsongkhapa. Monks here write votive inscriptions in gold ink for pilgrims. Look out for the huge butter lamps.

Chapel of Jampa
This small chapel (Jampa Lhakhang) just across from the exit of the Tomb of Tsongkhapa holds two large images of the Future Buddha.

Assembly Hall
The recently renovated assembly hall has statues of the 16 arhats and two huge statues of Tsongkhapa. Stairs lead up to the inner sanctum, the Golden Throne Room (Ser Trikhang), which houses the throne of Tsongkhapa, where pilgrims get thumped on the back by the yellow hat of the Dalai Lama.

There are two entrances on the north side of the building. The west one gives access to a second-floor view of the Tsongkhapa statue and the east one houses a library.

Residence of the Ganden Tripa
East of the Golden Throne Room, this residence (also known as Zimchung Tridok Khang) contains another, lesser throne, this time used by the Ganden Tripa. Other rooms include a protector chapel, with statues of Demchok (Chakrasamvara) and Nagpo Chenpo (Mahakala; in the form of Gompo), and a Tsongkhapa chapel. The room where Tsongkhapa died is currently closed. The upper-floor chapel has a round platform used for creating sand mandalas.

Amdo Kangtsang
The 'Amdo' of Amdo Kangtsang's name refers to the Tibetan province that is now Qinghai. Tsongkhapa himself was from Amdo, and many monks came from the province to study here. There are some interesting chapels to the rear of the building. To the left of the main chapel you'll find paintings of the 35 confession buddhas.

Ganden Kora
The Ganden kora is a simply stunning walk and should not be missed. There are superb views of the Kyi-chu Valley along the way and there are usually large numbers of pilgrims and monks offering prayers, rubbing holy rocks and prostrating themselves along the path.

There are actually two parts to the walk: the high kora and the low kora. The high kora climbs Angkor (Wanbo) Ri south of Ganden and then drops down the ridge to join up with the lower kora.

To walk the **high kora** follow the path south-east of the car park, away from the monastery. After a while the track splits – the left path leads to Hepu village on the Ganden-Samye trek, the right path heads pretty much straight up the ridge to a collection of prayer flags. Try to follow other pilgrims up. It's a tough 40-minute climb up to the top of the ridge, so don't try this one unless you're well acclimatised. Here pilgrims burn juniper incense and give offerings of tsampa before heading west down the ridge in the direction of the monastery, stopping at several other shrines en route.

The **low kora** is an easier walk of around 45 minutes. From the car park bear left for the trail that heads west up and then around the back of the ridge behind the monastery.

LHASA

The trail winds past several isolated shrines and rocks that are rubbed for their healing properties or squeezed through to test the amount of sin a pilgrim has amassed. At one point pilgrims all peer at a rock through a clenched fist in order to see visions. There are also several rock carvings and a **sky-burial site** along the route. The sky-burial site is reached shortly after the path begins to descend. Some pilgrims undertake a ritual simulated death and rebirth at this point, rolling around on the ground.

Towards the end of the kora, on the eastern side of the ridge, is **Tsongkhapa's hermitage**, a small building with relief images of Atisha (Jowo-je), Sakyamuni (Sakya Thukpa), Tsepame (Amitayus) and Palden Lhamo (Shri Devi). These images are believed to have the power of speech. Above the hermitage is a brilliantly coloured rock painting that is reached by a narrow, precipitous path. From the hermitage the kora drops down to join the main buildings of the monastery.

Places to Stay & Eat
Basic accommodation is available at the *Monastery Guesthouse* to the south of the car park for Y15 per room. The *restaurant* underneath the guesthouse has low-grade *thugpa* (Tibetan noodles) and occasional fried rice. Just up the road from the car park is a well-stocked *shop* with everything from sweets and candles to instant noodles and beer, but you're better off bringing some of your own food.

Getting There & Away
Ganden is one of the few sights in Ü that is connected to Lhasa by public transport. At least one bus, sometimes more (including a speedier minibus service), leaves from in front of the Barkhor Square sometime between 6.30am and 7am. The bus takes around 2½ hours to get out to Ganden and leaves the monastery for the return journey at around 2pm. Tickets cost Y18 return. Pilgrims usually buy their tickets the day before from a tin shack near the south-east corner of Barkhor Square, but foreigners can buy tickets on the bus.

On the way back to Lhasa the public bus normally stops at the Gensukhang Temple and picnic spot near the turn-off to Ganden, and also at **Sanga Monastery**, set at the foot of the ruined **Dagtse Dzong** (or Dechen Dzong; *dzong* means 'fort'). The monastery has some excellent murals but you'll need to bring a torch to see them.

If you can get a group of people together, Ganden is worth visiting in a rented vehicle. This way you can stop for photos on the long, panoramic haul up to the monastery itself, and have control over when you leave. A Land Cruiser for the day trip should cost around Y400; guides are not required.

DRÖLMA LHAKHANG
This small but significant monastery (*admission free; open dawn-dusk*) is full of relics and hidden treasures. It's only 30 minutes by bus south-west of Lhasa and is worth a stop for those interested in Tibetan Buddhism.

As you take the Lhasa-Tsetang road out of Lhasa, you will pass a blue **rock carving** of the Medicine Buddha at the base of a cliff about 11km south-west of town. Netang village and the monastery are about 6km further on.

Drölma Lhakhang is associated with the Bengali scholar Atisha (982–1054). Atisha (Jowo-je) came to Tibet at the age of 53 at the invitation of the king of the Guge kingdom in western Tibet and subsequently travelled extensively in Tibet. His teachings were instrumental in the so-called second diffusion of Buddhism in the 11th century. Drölma Lhakhang was established at this time by one of Atisha's foremost disciples, Drömtonpa, who also founded the Kadampa order, to which the monastery belongs. Atisha died at Netang aged 72.

The monastery was spared desecration by the Red Guards during the Cultural Revolution after a direct request from Bangladesh (which now encompasses Atisha's homeland) that the monastery be left untouched. Apparently, Chinese premier Zhou Enlai intervened on its behalf.

The entrance and exit of the monastery are both protected by two ancient guardian deities, which may even date back to the 11th-century founding of the monastery.

From the entrance, you pass into the first chapel, the Namgyel Lhakhang, which contains a number of chörtens. The Kadampa-style chörten to the right reputedly holds the staff of Atisha and the skull of Naropa, Atisha's teacher. Statuary includes Atisha and the eight medicine buddhas.

The middle chapel houses a number of relics purported to be associated with Atisha. The statues at the top include an 11th-century statue of Sakyamuni (Sakya Thukpa) and statues of the 13th Dalai Lama and Serlingpa, another teacher of Atisha. A 13th-century statue of Chenresig (Avalokiteshvara) was reputedly stolen from here recently by art thieves. The central statue behind the grill is an image of Jampa (Maitreya) that was reputedly saved from Mongol destruction when it shouted 'Ouch!'. There are also 21 statues of Drölma (Tara), after whom the monastery and the chapel are named.

The final Tsepame Chapel has original statues of Tsepame (Amitayus), made with the ashes of Atisha, flanked by Marmedze (Dipamkara), the Past Buddha, Jampa (Maitreya), the Future Buddha, and the eight bodhisattvas. The small central statue of Atisha is backed by his original throne. As you leave the chapel look out for two sunken white chörtens, which hold Atisha's robes.

Upstairs is the throne room of the Dalai Lama (look for the fine old quivers and arrows on the pillars) as well as a living room featuring a fine tree-of-life thangka depicting the Gelugpa lineages.

Really keen gompa stompers can plod out a further hour west from Drölma Lhakhang to **Ratö Monastery**. This Gelugpa institution is renowned for its fine wall murals. It is reached via a track that heads south from the main road just after Drölma Lhakhang.

Any bus heading south from Lhasa (ie, to Shigatse, Samye Monastery, Tsetang) will take you past the entrance to Drölma Lhakhang. You could also take a minibus from the Lugu Bus Station to Chushul (Y10) or Gongkar. It's probably easier to visit on the way back from Shigatse or the Yarlung Valley, since getting back to Lhasa you can flag down anything that comes by.

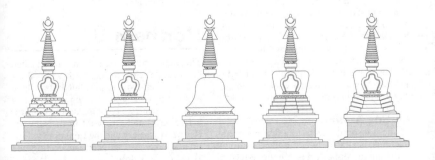

Ü

The traditional province known in Tibetan as Ü is the more easterly of the two central provinces (the other being Tsang) that have long been at the centre stage of Tibetan politics and history. In modern Chinese terms Ü consists mainly of Lhasa and Shannan prefecture.

The province of Ü is effectively the heartland of all Tibet. It was from here, in the Yarlung Valley, that the earliest Tibetan kings launched their 6th-century conquest and unification of the Tibetan plateau and ruled from Lhasa for three centuries. Political power later shifted to Sakya and Shigatse in Tsang, but returned to Ü when the fifth Dalai Lama reunited the country with Mongol support in 1642, and again made Lhasa the capital.

For most independent travellers, Ü's main attractions are Ganden, Tsurphu and Samye Monasteries and the turquoise lake called Nam-tso. Ganden and Tsurphu can be visited as day trips from the capital, whereas it's best to take around three days for a visit to either Samye Monastery or Nam-tso.

Travel in the Lhasa region (not just Lhasa town) does not require a permit, but once you leave the region you need a permit from the Public Security Bureau (PSB).

The ancient province is also host to a large number of other sights that are little visited by foreign travellers. The wide valley of the Yarlung Tsangpo has numerous side valleys sheltering a wealth of monasteries and settlements that are rarely visited by foreigners. In particular, the Yarlung Valley, site of Yumbulagang and the nearby tombs of the Tibetan kings at Chongye, is well worth a visit. Around 100km north-east of Lhasa, Drigung Til Monastery and nearby Tidrum Nunnery offer an excellent three-day trip deep into the Tibetan countryside.

Getting Around

Public transport, except to a few major attractions, is a rarity in Ü. Ganden, Tsurphu and Samye Monasteries are linked with

---

Lhasa by public bus and minibus, as is Tsetang, the nearest major town south-east of Lhasa and a good base for visits to the Yarlung Valley. Several sights have public transport part of the way – eg, to Medro Gungkar for Drigung Til, Lhundrub for Reting – from where you can hike or hitch. Otherwise, rented vehicles, hiking and hitching are the only ways to get around.

Ü offers many hiking possibilities. Day hikes around Lhundrub, Samye Monastery and the Yarlung Valley are covered in this chapter. The Ganden to Samye and Tsurphu to Yangpachen treks are described in the Trekking chapter.

Northern Ü

The sights in this section are often visited on separate trips: to the north-west (Tsurphu and Nam-tso), north (Lhundrub, Talung and Reting) and east (Tidrum and Drigung Til). You can also combine destinations for a five-day Land Cruiser trip to Nam-tso, Reting Monastery and the Lhundrub valley, or a six-day trip to Nam-tso, Reting and Drigung Til/Tidrum.

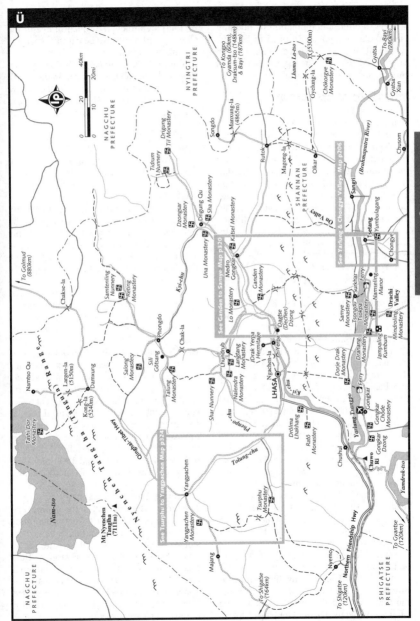

It's possible to get to all the sights in this section through a combination of hitching and hiking, though you'll need to be self-sufficient in food and have some time up your sleeve. None of the sights described in this section requires a permit.

TSURPHU MONASTERY
elevation 4480m

Tsurphu Monastery *(admission Y10)*, around 70km west of Lhasa, is the seat of the Karmapa branch of the Kagyupa order of Tibetan Buddhism. The Karmapa are also known as the Black Hats, a title that dates back to 1256, when the second Karmapa was invited to China by the emperor of the Yuan dynasty, Kublai Khan, and presented with a black hat embellished with gold. This hat, said to be made from the hair of holy women, is now kept at Rumtek Monastery in Sikkim, India.

It was the first Karmapa, Dusum Khyenpa (1110–93), who instigated the tradition of *trulku* (whereby a lama could choose his next reincarnation), and the Karmapa lineage has been maintained until this day. Before his death, Dusum Khyenpa indicated to followers certain signs that would enable them to find his reincarnation. This practice was widely adopted by other orders, notably the Gelugpa in the form of the Dalai Lama and Panchen Lama lineages. For more information, see the boxed text 'Reincarnation Lineages' in the Facts about Tibet chapter.

The 16th Karmapa fled to Sikkim in 1959 after the popular uprising in Lhasa and founded a monastery in Rumtek. He died in 1981. His reincarnation, an eight-year-old Tibetan boy from Kham, Ugen Thinley Dorje, was announced amid great controversy by the Dalai Lama and other religious leaders in June 1992. In December 1999, the 17th Karmapa made a dramatic escape from Tibet into India (see the boxed text 'The Karmapa Connection').

With his departure, things are pretty quiet at Tsurphu, and only a handful of pilgrims visit each day. The few travellers who venture out here are usually planning to make the three- or four-day trek to Yangpachen Monastery (detailed in the Trekking chapter).

Because of the political attention given to it, Tsurphu attracts the watchful eye of the Chinese authorities, so be careful what you say and to whom.

Tsurphu has an annual festival around the time of the Saga Dawa festival in the fourth lunar month of the Tibetan calendar. There is plenty of free-flowing *chang* (Tibetan barley beer), as well as ritual *cham* dancing by monks and lamas.

Officially you don't need a permit to visit Tsurphu, but some travellers have reported being turned away by authorities when they've tried to stay overnight.

History

Tsurphu was founded in the 1180s by Dusum Khyenpa, some 40 years after he founded the Karmapa order in Kham, his birthplace. It was the third Karmapa monastery to be built, and after the death of the first Karmapa it became the head monastery for the order.

The Karmapa order traditionally enjoyed strong ties with the kings and monasteries of Tsang, a legacy that proved a liability when conflict broke out between the kings of Tsang and the Gelugpa order. When the fifth Dalai Lama invited the Mongolian army of Gushri Khan to do away with his opponents in Tsang, Tsurphu was sacked (in 1642) and the Karmapa's political clout effectively came to an end. Shorn of its political influence, Tsurphu nevertheless bounced back as an important spiritual centre and is one of the few Kagyupa institutions still functioning in the Ü region. When Chinese forces invaded in 1950, there were around 1000 monks in residence. There are now about 400 monks.

Viewing the Monastery

The large **assembly hall** in the main courtyard houses a *chörten* (stupa) containing the relics of the 16th Karmapa, as well as statues of Öpagme (Amitabha) and Sakyamuni (Sakya Thukpa), the Historical Buddha. You can visit the former audience chamber of the present Karmapa on the upper floor, although there's little to see. The monks will offer you a blessing from the Karmapa's empty throne.

Walking west (clockwise) around the monastery complex you come to the **protector chapel** *(gönkhang)* of the main hall. There are five main rooms here, all stuffed to the brim with wrathful deities.

The first room is dedicated to Tsurphu's protector deity, an aspect of blue Nagpo Chenpo (Mahakala) called Bernakchen. There are also statues of Palden Lhamo (Shri Devi) and Tamdrin (Hayagriva).

The Karmapa Connection

Anyone who thinks of the Tibetans as a lofty, spiritually absorbed people should think again. Tibetan history has been dogged by factional intrigue, continuing into the 21st century.

In 1981 the 16th Karmapa died in Chicago. Administration of the Karmapa sect in Sikkim was passed down to four regents, two of whom, Situ Rinpoche and Shamar Rinpoche, have become embroiled in a dispute that has caused a painful rift in the exiled Tibetan community.

At the centre of the dispute is Ugen Thinley Dorje, the young man who until recently resided at Tsurphu Monastery – the 17th Karmapa. In early 1992 the four regents announced the discovery of a letter written by the 16th Karmapa that provided critical clues as to the whereabouts of his reincarnation. Curiously, just a month later, one of the regents was killed in a car crash in Sikkim. The local press declared 'suspicious circumstances', but these allegations were never investigated, apparently at the request of figures close to the regent.

Two weeks after the accident, Shamar Rinpoche announced that the mystery letter was a fraud, but it was too late. By early June clues from the letter had been deciphered, Ugen Thinley Dorje had been found in eastern Tibet and the Dalai Lama had made a formal announcement supporting the boy's candidature.

Shamar Rinpoche opposed the Dalai Lama's decision and began a letter-writing campaign. Meanwhile, the Chinese authorities formally enthroned the 17th Karmapa at Tsurphu, using the occasion to announce that they had a 'historical and legal right to appoint religious leaders in Tibet'. In March 1994, Shamar Rinpoche announced that he had discovered the rightful reincarnation, a boy named Tenzin Chentse (also known as Thaye Dorje) who had been spirited out of China to Delhi. In December 1999, the then 14-year-old 17th Karmapa dramatically fled Tibet into India. In a letter left behind at Tsurphu he told the Chinese he was going to collect the black hat of the Karmapa (taken to India by the 16th Karmapa when he fled Tibet in 1959), as well as several relics, including a human skull encased in silver.

The stakes are high. The Karmapa sect has assets estimated to be worth US$1.2 billion and up to one million followers, including many in the USA. Both Karmapas have received death threats. Sikkim's Rumtek Monastery (now the head Karmapa monastery) was briefly occupied in 1993 by Indian troops to break up brawling by monks divided over the issue.

The flight of the Karmapa was a particular blow for the Chinese. The Karmapa ranks as the third-most important lama in Tibet after the Panchen Lama and the Dalai Lama. Moreover, with the recognition of the Chinese-backed Reting Rinpoche disputed by Dharamsala, the Karmapa is the only high-level reincarnation recognised by both the Chinese and Tibetan authorities. With the Dalai Lama now in his late 60s, many Tibetans are increasingly looking to the Karmapa as head of a new generation of spiritual leaders.

For the moment, at least, there is a stalemate. The Karmapa has been granted refugee status and residence at the Gyuto Monastery in Dharamsala, but the Indian authorities, in an attempt to avoid a political dispute with China, have not allowed him to travel to Rumtek (China does not recognise India's claim to Sikkim).

For more on the starkly differing viewpoints, see the pro-Karmapa Web site at ⓦ www.kagyu.org and the pro–Shamar Rinpoche sites at ⓦ www.karmapa.org and ⓦ www.karmapa-issue.org.

The third room features a wrathful form of Guru Rinpoche and the fourth room features the Kagyu protector Dorje Phurba holding a ritual dagger. The fifth room contains a statue of Tseringma, a protectress associated with Mt Everest, on a snow lion.

The large building behind the gönkhang is the **Serdung Chanpo**, which served as the residence of the Karmapa. It is usually possible to visit the cavernous ground-floor assembly hall, which features a large statue of Sakyamuni flanked by Guru Rinpoche and the 16th Karmapa, who wears the characteristic black hat. It is sometimes possible to go into the upper chapels featuring new statues of all 16 previous Karmapas. A room at the rear of the courtyard, beside the assembly hall, houses three chörtens.

The **Lhakhang Chenmo** to the right of the Serdung Chanpo houses a new and remarkably ugly 20m-high statue of Sakyamuni (Sakya Thukpa); this replaced a celebrated 13th-century image destroyed during the Cultural Revolution.

Behind the Serdung Chanpo and the Lhakhang Chenmo is the sprawling **Chökang Gang Monastery**, the residence of the regent of Tsurphu, where a room on the 2nd floor and another downstairs have been restored. There is also an assembly hall accessed from a side entrance just by the main western entrance, which has statues of Sakyamuni, flanked by Jampa (Maitreya) and Guru Rinpoche and protected by blue Nagpo Chenpo (Mahakala) and red Tamdrin (Hayagriva).

Tsurphu Kora

The Tsurphu *kora* (ritual circumambulation circuit), a walk of two or three hours, is quite taxing if you are not acclimatised to the altitude. It winds up some 150m, providing splendid views of Tsurphu below. Above the monastery are some meditation retreats and traces of rock paintings. You may not have time for the kora if you have to return to Lhasa on the public minibus.

To follow this kora take the road west of Tsurphu and bear left. Ahead is a turn-off that snakes uphill, eventually to the top of the ridge overlooking the monastery. From here the trail is fairly obvious, descending eastward down the ridge into a gully before returning to the entrance of Tsurphu.

Places to Stay & Eat

Monastery Guesthouse Dorm beds Y25. This new guesthouse, opposite the main assembly hall, has pleasant dorm rooms overlooking the river.

There are a couple of very basic *restaurants* and some small *shops* selling soft drinks, instant noodles and biscuits.

Getting There & Away

A minibus goes to Tsurphu from Barkhor Square in Lhasa sometime between 7.30am and 8am, leaving when full (Y15/25 one way/return). The timing is not ideal as the minibus takes at least 2½ hours to get to Tsurphu and returns at around 1.30pm, allowing only a couple of hours to look around. You'll have to stay overnight if you want a better look or want to do the kora.

You could hire a Land Cruiser for Y400 to Y600 return, or even tag a visit here onto a trip to Nam-tso. You should organise this in advance with your travel agency. Some will let you detour to Tsurphu for free, others will add up to Y150 to the price of the tour.

NAM-TSO
elevation 4718m

Nam-tso, approximately 190km north-west of Lhasa, is the second-largest saltwater lake in China, the first being Koko Nor (Qinghai Lake) in Qinghai province. It is over 70km long and reaches a width of 30km. The Nyenchen Tanglha (Tangula) range, with peaks of more than 7000m, towers over the lake to the south – it was these mountains that Heinrich Harrer and Peter Aufschnaiter crossed on their incredible journey to Lhasa. Nam-tso is a tidal lake and the ring marks of earlier lake levels are clearly visible by the shoreline.

Visits to Nam-tso have become increasingly popular with independent travellers over the past few years. In clear weather the water is a miraculous shade of turquoise and there are magnificent views of the nearby mountains. The wide open spaces, dotted with the tents of local *drokpas* (nomads), are intoxicating.

Whatever you do, however, do not sign up for a lift out here until you have been in Lhasa for at least a week. It is not unusual for visitors to get altitude sickness on an overnight stay out at the lake. The sudden altitude gain of 1100m is not to be treated lightly.

Before you cross the mountain passes into the Nam-tso basin you will have to pay an entry fee of Y35 per person. There is a second, highly dubious Y5 'entrance fee' to the Tashi Dor area, which is fenced off with a couple of bits of wire.

Those seeking detailed information on Nam-tso should refer to *Divine Dyads: Ancient Civilization in Tibet* by John Vincent Bellezza.

Tashi Dor Monastery

Most travellers head for Tashi Dor, situated on a hammerhead of land that juts into the south-eastern corner of the lake. Here at the foot of two wedge-shaped hills are a couple of small chapels, with views back across the clear turquoise waters to the huge snowy Nyenchen Tanglha massif (7111m).

The 'monastery' is really just a small chapel to the east of the accommodation area. Inside is an image of the local deity, Nyenchen Tanglha, which has its roots in Bön belief and resides in the nearby mountain of the same name. (It is also the protector of Marpo Ri, the hill on which the Potala is built.) There are several other chapels and retreats honeycombed into the rock face.

There are some fine walks in this area. The short **kora path** takes less than an hour. It leads off west from the accommodation area to a chapel hidden behind a large splinter of rock. The trail continues round to a rocky promontory of cairns and prayer flags, where pilgrims undertake a ritual washing, and then continues past several caves and a *chaktsal gang* (prostration point). The twin rock towers here look like two hands in the *namaste* greeting and are connected to the male and female attributes of the meditational deity Demchok (Chakra-

samvara). Pilgrims squeeze into the deep slices of the nearby cliff face as a means of sin detection. They also drink water dripping from cave roofs, and some even ingest 'holy dirt'.

From here, the path curves around the shoreline and passes a group of ancient rock paintings, where pilgrims test their merit by attempting to place a finger in a small hole with their eyes closed. Nearby is a footprint of Guru Rinpoche. At the north-eastern corner of the hill is the Mani Ringmo, a large *mani* (prayer) wall at whose end is a crumbling chörten with a *chakje* (handprint) of the third Karmapa. From here you can hike up to the top of the hill for good views.

If you have enough time it's well worth walking around the larger of the two hills. There are superb views to the north-east of the Nyenchen Tanglha (Tangula) range, which marks the modern border between Tibet and Amdo.

Another main attraction of a trip to Nam-tso is the opportunity to get a peek at the otherwise inaccessible nomadic life of the Changtang, Tibet's vast northern plateau. You may get the opportunity to stop at the brown or black spider-like tents of nomads. Make sure you are not forcing anyone's hospitality, and watch out for vicious dogs.

Trekking to Nam-tso

The easiest trek to Nam-tso is by way of the Largen-la (5150m), following the road up from Damxung. It takes about two days to reach the southern shore of the lake at Tashi Dor. There are many good camping places here but the only water comes from the lake, which is slightly brackish.

You can also reach Nam-tso from Damxung via the Kong-la (5240m). An excellent circuit of about one week takes in both the Kong-la and Largen-la. This is a demanding and remote route and is best done with a guide.

Keep in mind that trekking on the vast northern plains of the Changtang demands special preparation, as this is the coldest, most windswept and most unpredictable part of Tibet. Blizzards can hit even in the middle of summer.

Nomads

The *drokpas* (nomads) of Tibet travel in groups of up to 20 or more families. They live in four-sided yak-hair tents, which are usually shared by one family, though a smaller subsidiary tent may be used when a son marries and has children of his own. The various families of a group pitch their tents at quite a distance from each other, usually because the poor quality of grazing land means that yaks have to cover a large area to feed. The decision to move from one area to another is made jointly by all the families in a particular group.

The interior of a nomad tent holds all the family's possessions. There will be a stove for cooking and boiling water. The principal diet of nomad people is *tsampa* (roasted-barley flour) and yak butter (mixed together with tea), dried yak cheese and sometimes yak meat. The tent will also house a family altar dedicated to Buddhist deities and various local protectors, including those of the livestock, tent pole and hearth. Next to the altar is a box that contains the family's jewellery and other valuables. In the warm summer months it is not unusual for nomad people to sleep outside their tent on a sheepskin, covering themselves with rough yak-hair blankets.

Tending the herds of yaks and sheep is carried out by the men during the day. Women and children stay together in the camp, where they are guarded by one of the men and the ferocious Tibetan mastiffs that are the constant companions of Tibet's nomads. The women and children usually spend the day weaving blankets and tanning sheep skins. Women are normally in charge of making dairy products such as butter and cheese.

Nomads graze their herds through the summer months and into late autumn. By this time the herds should be strong and healthy, and with the onset of winter it is time to go to the markets of an urban centre. The farmers of Tibet do the same, and trade between nomads and farmers provides the former with tsampa and the latter with meat and butter. Most nomads these days have a winter home base and only make established moves to distant pastures during the rest of the year.

The nomads of Tibet have also traditionally traded in salt, which is collected from the Changtang (northern plateau) and transported south in bricks, often to the border with Nepal, where it is traded for grain. These annual caravans are fast dying out. Traditional life suffered its greatest setback in 1968 when nomads were collectivised and forcibly settled by the government. In 1981 the communes were dissolved and the collectivised livestock divided equally, with everyone getting five yaks, 25 sheep and seven goats. Nomads today generally rank among the poorest people in Tibet.

Nomads' marriage customs differ from those of farming communities in many ways. When a child reaches a marriageable age, inquiries are made, and when a suitable match is found the two people meet and exchange gifts. If they like each other, these informal meetings and ritual exchanges of gifts may go on for some time. The date for a marriage is decided by an astrologer, and when the date arrives the family of the son rides to the camp of the prospective daughter-in-law to collect her. On arrival there is a custom of feigned mutual abuse that appears to verge on giving way to violence at any moment. This may continue for several days before the son's family finally carry off the daughter to their camp and she enters a new life.

Places to Stay & Eat

The good news is that there are now at least two places to stay at Tashi Dor. The bad news is that development has brought generators, motorbikes and rising levels of rubbish, all of which are beginning to take their toll. Please remember to carry out your own rubbish and as much of other people's rubbish as possible, before the site turns into a huge rubbish dump. There is still no toilet at Tashi Dor, so bury faecal waste and burn your toilet paper. Bedding is provided at all places but nights can get very cold, so it's a good idea to bring a sleeping bag and warm clothes.

The main *guesthouse* is a white U-shaped building. Beds cost Y25 or Y35 depending on the thickness of the mattress.

There's no toilet but you get thermoses of hot water and electricity in the evenings.

A second *guesthouse*, next door, offers traditional mattress-style beds for Y20 each in a four-bed room.

A *canteen* to the left of the two guesthouses offers food at slightly inflated prices; eg, Y10 for *thugpa* (a traditional noodle dish) and Y15 for a vegie dish. It also offers *accommodation* in a tent for Y20 per person.

There is good *camping* 100m west of the monastery at the foot of the cliffs. You can get boiled lake water (there's no taste of salt) at the canteen for Y2 a flask.

There are two decent hotels in Damxung, the nearest town to Nam-tso that is linked to Lhasa by public transport.

Tianhu Hotel (☎ *0891-611 2098*) Dorm beds Y20, doubles/triples Y50/40 per bed. By the turn-off from the main highway to Nam-tso, this place is a pretty good option; it's popular with foreigners.

Damxung Nyenchen Tanglha Hotel (☎ *0891-611 2086*) Doubles with private bathroom Y40-60 per bed, triples/quads Y45/40 per bed. This place is five minutes' walk north of the turn-off to Nam-tso. The bathrooms are clean and there's a shower house downstairs (Y5).

There are several *restaurants* in Damxung, the best of which are the Muslim noodle joints. The only shops are at Namtso Qu, the local government centre 25km east of Tashi Dor, where there is also a basic *guesthouse* with cheap rooms.

Getting There & Away

There is no public transport to Nam-tso. Most travellers get a group together and hire a Land Cruiser for the six- or seven-hour drive from Lhasa. The price for a three-day return trip is around Y1500 (Y300 to Y400 per person). Many groups also stop off at the concrete hot-spring pools at Yangpachen (entry Y20) or Tsurphu Monastery or both, often for no extra charge. It's possible to return to Lhasa via Reting Monastery and either Drigung Til or the Lhundrub valley, making for an interesting and adventurous loop, for around Y2800.

The nearest town to Nam-tso that is linked to Lhasa by public transport is Damxung (Dangxiong) on the Qinghai-Tibet Hwy. One option is to take a Nagchu-bound bus as far as Damxung (Y30 to Y35); the other is to take a minibus from in front of the Kirey Hotel in Lhasa (Y35), departing at 7am.

From Damxung, you have the option of hitching or trekking out to the village of Namtso Qu or to Tashi Dor Monastery, 66km away. By road it's 11km to the check post where you pay the entry fee, a further 17km to the Largen-la and then a circuitous 38km to Tashi Dor. Some travellers have been lucky and hitched lifts with trucks or even jeeps, but it seems that most end up walking at least half the way since most traffic heads for Namtso Qu, not Tashi Dor. The road to the lake is being upgraded but until it's finished rain and snow can quickly turn the tracks into a quagmire.

Some intrepid travellers have made it out to Nam-tso on a mountain bike, though the shiny wheels seem to drive most nomads' dogs even more berserk than normal. Wolves have been spotted around the Largen-la and the Kong-la.

See Trekking to Nam-tso earlier for information on the demanding walk to the lake.

DRAK YERPA

For those with a particular interest in Tibetan Buddhism, Drak Yerpa hermitage, about 30km north-east of Lhasa, is one of the holiest cave retreats in Ü. Among the many ascetics who have sojourned here and contributed to the area's great sanctity are Guru Rinpoche and Atisha (Jowo-je), the Bengali Buddhist who spent 12 years proselytising in Tibet. King Songtsen Gampo also meditated in a cave here, after his Tibetan wife established the first of Yerpa's chapels. The site is deeply peaceful and has stunning views.

At one time the hill at the base of the cave-dotted cliffs was home to Yerpa Drubde Monastery, the summer residence of Lhasa's Gyutö College at the Ramoche Temple. The monastery was destroyed in 1959, and more destruction occurred during the Cultural Revolution.

Monks have begun to return to Yerpa (there are currently 14 monks) but numbers are strictly controlled by the government, which tore down several 'unauthorised' chapels as recently as 1998.

The Caves

The first building most people come to is the kitchen. Next door is the **Lhalung-puk**, the cave where the monk Lhalung meditated after assassinating the anti-Buddhist king Langdharma. The chapel is being rebuilt.

Above and to the right is the **Dawa-puk** (Moon Cave), where Guru Rinpoche (the main statue) is said to have spent seven years. Look for the painting of Ekajati (Tschigma) to the left and the footprints of Guru Rinpoche and Lhalung to the right.

Heading west, climb to the **Chögyal-puk**, the Cave of Songtsen Gampo. The interior chapel has a central 1000-armed Chenresig (Avalokiteshvara) statue known as Chaktong Chentong. As you start to walk around the central pillar look for the eyes of a 'self-arising' lion face. A small cave and statue of Songtsen Gampo are in the right-hand corner.

The yellow **Jampa Lhakhang** has a two-storey statue of Jampa flanked by Chana Dorje (Vajrapani) to the left and Namse (Vairocana) and Tamdrin (Hayagriva) to the right. Other statues are of Atisha (Jowo-je) flanked by the fifth Dalai Lama and Tsongkhapa.

The upper cave is the **Drubthub-puk**, recognisable by its black overhang. Continue to the **Atisha Zim-puk**, the cave where Atisha meditated. Around here are several caves dedicated to Chana Dorje (Vajrapani), which were the first in the complex to be rebuilt.

Below the main caves and to the east is the **Neten Lhakhang**, where the practice of worshipping the 16 *arhats* (literally 'worthy ones') was first introduced. Below here is where Atisha is said to have taught. Further east is the holy mountain of Yerpa Lhari, topped by prayer flags and encircled by a kora path.

There are several caves and retreats higher up the cliff face if you have time to explore.

Places to Stay

It is often possible to stay in one of the *caves* (normally the Dawa-puk), but don't count on it. You can sleep on the cushions provided, but you'll need a sleeping bag and preferably a mat. The caretaker is very kind and can provide boiling water and tea. If you are allowed to stay make an offering of Y10 to Y15 per person. Bring your own food and drinks and some extra supplies to offer to the monks. Water comes from a spring below the caves.

Getting There & Away

It is possible to hike from Lhasa to Yerpa in about seven to eight hours, but you should be able to hitch the first 16km to Yerpa village. In Lhasa, head east along Ngachen Lam, near the intersection of Lingkhor Chang Lam and Lingkhor Shar Lam in the north-east of town. Hike, hitch or take the No 7 minibus to its terminus several kilometres out of town. The road follows the northern bank of Kyi-chu east, passing a hydroelectric power station en route. Shortly after this the road bears left up a mountain-side to the low Ngachen-la. Yerpa village is visible on the other side of the pass. A small shop by the roadside sells water and biscuits and other basics.

From Yerpa village it's a three-hour hike up the side valley to Drak Yerpa. The trail passes two ruined *dzongs* (forts) and a disused dam, before leaving the road and ascending the hillside behind a village to the back of a white chörten. From here trails lead up to the caves. The walk back to the road takes about two hours.

An alternative onward route from Yerpa is to walk three hours east to Dagste bridge, over the Kyi-chu. From the northern shore you could hitch to Lhundrub and Reting Monastery. From the southern shore you can take a minibus back to Lhasa from Dagtse or continue on to Ganden Monastery or Drigung Til.

LHUNDRUB VALLEY
☎ 0894 • elevation 3800m

This lovely valley, also known in Tibetan as the Phenpo valley, is linked to Lhasa by public transport and dotted with interesting monasteries, so it offers plenty of scope for adventurous do-it-yourself exploration. It would also be a great destination for mountain bikes. Few travellers get here. Two of the easiest monasteries to visit in the valley are Nalendra and Langtang Monasteries.

Lhundrub

The main town in the valley is Lhundrub (Chinese: Linzhou), which serves as a useful base. The north-western section of town has the main shops, the centre has the Ganden Chökhorling Monastery, and the southeast has a couple of *Muslim restaurants* and the bus station.

Bus Station Hotel Doubles Y20 per bed, quads Y10 per bed. There are no luxuries here but it is a passable place to stay in the south-east of town. The outside toilets are in the bus yard below.

Buses to Lhundrub run from Lhasa's Lugu and Eastern Suburbs Bus Stations. The last bus back to Lhasa returns in the early afternoon but you might still find a ride after that.

Nalendra Monastery

Nalendra Monastery was founded in 1435 by Rongtongpa, a contemporary of Tsongkhapa, the 14th-century founder of the Gelugpa order and Ganden Monastery. It was largely destroyed in 1959, and ruins still dwarf the rebuilding work.

To get an idea of the original layout, look closely at the mural on the immediate left as you enter the **main assembly hall**. A chapel on the left houses 21 manifestations of Drölma (Tara), with Guru Rinpoche and Sakyamuni (Sakya Thukpa). The nearby gönkhang has a central Gompo Kur (a form of Nagpo Chenpo (Mahakala) and protector of the Sakyapa school), as well as statues of Pehar and Namse (Vairocana; in the left corner on a snow lion), plus Palden Lhamo (Shri Devi) and Dorje Rabden to the right. Look for the huge wild yak's head. The main hall has a statue of Rongtongpa in a glass case. The inner sanctum features Rongtongpa, flanked by two Sakyapa lamas, and an inner kora.

Below the assembly hall is the Tsar Kangtsang, the monastic residential quarters, which have lovely new murals. Other buildings include the Jarung Kangtsang, the Chuchikhang, which houses Rongtongpa's throne and two statues of Tangtong Gyelpo, a Jampa chapel and a debating courtyard. The friendly monks are usually happy to show visitors around.

It may be possible to spend the night at the monastery if you have a sleeping bag and supplies. A kora path leads up to more ruins above the monastery and offers fine views down into the valley.

Nalendra and Langtang Monasteries make an excellent half-day trip by tractor (Y50 to Y100) or motorbike (Y100 per bike), both available for hire if you ask around Lhundrub. You'll need to haggle.

Alternatively, you can walk to Nalendra from Lhundrub in a day, stopping at Langtang en route. From Lhundrub bus station head south over the bridge and follow the tracks as they swing west parallel to the mountain ridge, or head due west out of town from the Bus Station Hotel. You can see the former road to Lhasa snaking up the mountainside to the south.

Langtang Monastery

On the way back from Nalendra it's worth stopping off at Langtang Monastery, visible from afar because of its huge Kadampa-style chörten and the ring of trees encircling the lovely village. The monastery was founded in 1093 and once had 200 monks. Today only two chapels and the ruins of the main assembly hall remain, served by 26 monks. Like Nalendra, Langtang was built as a Kadampa monastery but was subsumed into the Sakyapa school. The main hall has a central statue of Kunga Gyaltsen (Sakya Pandita; 1182–1251), plus, to the right, a small statue of Drölma (Tara) that is said to have the power of speech. The building to the left is a protector chapel which has a central image of Langtangpa, the 11th-century founder of the monastery. To the far right are some lovely old texts in gold leaf, recovered from the nearby chörtens when they were dynamited by the Chinese.

For information on reaching Langtang Monastery, see Nalendra Monastery earlier.

Other Monasteries

From Nalendra it's also possible to hike half a day to **Shar Nunnery** on the northwestern side of the valley, sleep the night there and return the next day to Lhundrub via Nakar Monastery. You will need a sleeping bag and all food. A tent would be a sensible backup.

Other monasteries worth exploring at the northern end of the valley include Lhundrub Dzong and Nisu Monastery, the latter visible from the main road and recognisable by its row of eight chörtens. At the head of the valley the road switchbacks up to the Chakla and then drops down towards Talung Monastery.

TALUNG MONASTERY
elevation 4150m

The sprawling monastic complex of Talung (or Taglung), around 65km north of Lhasa, was dynamited by Red Guards and now lies in ruins in the green fields of the Pak-chu valley. Rebuilding is being undertaken, but not on the scale of other more important monasteries in the area.

Talung was founded in 1228 as the seat of the Talung school of the Kagyupa order. At one time it may have housed some 7000 monks (it currently has 45 monks), but it was eventually eclipsed in importance and grandeur by the Riwoche Monastery in eastern Tibet. Talung is worth a visit if you have your own transport but it lacks the charm of nearby Reting.

The site's most important structure was its **Tsuglhakhang** (literally 'grand temple'), also known as the Red Palace of Talung. The building is reduced to rubble but its thick stone walls remain. To the south in the main monastery building are the Jagi Lhakhang and the Choning Lhakhang, which has some fine cham masks and a statue of a bearded Tashipel, one of the monastery's founders. The other main building is the recently rebuilt Targye Lhakhang. Look out for the destroyed set of three chörtens, one of which was the funeral chörten of Drom-

tonpa, the founder of Reting Monastery. A pleasant kora path climbs the hill behind the main monastery.

Down in the centre of the village is the recently renovated Tashikang Tsar, the residence of the local rinpoche.

A 30-minute walk north of the turn-off to Talung brings you to **Sili Götsang**, an amazing eagle's-nest hermitage perched high above the valley. At the base of the cliff face are several long mani walls and drokpa tents.

There's no accommodation at Talung. The monastery is a pleasant 2km walk west of the main road to Phongdo. Public transport in this part of Ü is almost nonexistent. For information on reaching the monastery, see Reting Monastery, following.

RETING MONASTERY
elevation 4100

Pre-1950 photographs show Reting Monastery *(admission Y10)* sprawling gracefully across the flank of a juniper-clad hill in the Rong-chu valley. Like Ganden Monastery, it was devastated by Red Guards and its present remains hammer home the tragic waste caused by the ideological zeal of the Cultural Revolution. Still, the site is one of the most beautiful in the region. The Dalai Lama has stated that should he ever return to Tibet it is at Reting, not Lhasa, that he would like to reside.

The monastery dates back to 1056. It was initially associated with Atisha (Jowo-je) but in its later years had an important connection with the Gelugpa order and the Dalai Lamas. Two regents – the de facto rulers of Tibet for the interregnum between the death of a Dalai Lama and the majority of his next reincarnation – were chosen from Reting abbots. The fifth Reting Rinpoche was regent from 1933 to 1947. He played a key role in the search for the current Dalai Lama and served as his senior tutor. He was later accused of collusion with the Chinese and died in a Tibetan prison.

The sixth Reting Rinpoche died in 1997. In January 2001 the Chinese announced that a young boy named Sonam Phuntsog had been identified out of 700 candidates as the seventh Reting Rinpoche. Significantly, the announcement came just two days after the Karmapa set off on his flight from Tibet to India (see the boxed text 'The Karmapa Connection' earlier in this chapter). The Dalai Lama refuses to recognise the choice, and denounces it as part of a long-term strategy by the Chinese government to control religious leadership in Tibet.

The young rinpoche currently resides under PSB protection at his official residence, 2km below the monastery by the riverside. For this reason all foreign tour groups are expected to register there with the PSB.

Viewing the Monastery

Monks have begun the slow and arduous process of rebuilding Reting. The current main assembly hall, or Tsogchen, occupies only one side of the original hall. Enter the hall to the right to get to the main inner shrine, the Ütse. The central statue of Jampai Dorje is an unusual amalgam of the gods Jampelyang (Manjushri), Chana Dorje (Vajrapani) and Chenresig (Avalokiteshvara). To the left is a Drölma (Tara) statue credited with the power of speech; to the right are Tsongkhapa and, on the wall, four ancient *thangkas* (religious paintings).

To the left of the Ütse entrance is a rare mural of the 14th (current) Dalai Lama; to the right of the entrance is a picture of the current Reting Rinpoche and a footprint and photo of the fifth Reting Rinpoche. At the back of the kora path around the Ütse is a small chapel containing drums and masks used during cham dances held on the 15th day of the first and fourth lunar months.

As you leave the chapel look for a second hall to your right. The hall contains a gold chörten with the remains of the sixth Reting Rinpoche, Tenzin Jigne. To the right is a silver box that holds a huge festival thangka. Lining the back wall are statues of the six previous Reting Rinpoches.

The monastery is still graced by surrounding juniper forest, said to have sprouted from the hairs of its founder. A 40-minute **kora** leads around the monastery, passing several stone carvings, a series of eight chörtens and an active *dürtro* (sky-

burial site). Further up the hillside is the retreat where Tsongkhapa composed the Lamrim Chenmo, or Graduated Path, a key Gelugpa text. The large escarpment to the right is the Sengye Drak, or Lion's Rock, where there are several more retreats.

A pleasant hour-long walk north-east of Reting leads to **Samtenling Nunnery**, home to over 170 nuns. The main chapel houses the meditation cave of Tsongkhapa. The trail leads off from the sky-burial site to the north-east of the monastery.

Getting There & Away

Talung and Reting Monasteries are probably best visited together in a rented vehicle. It might be a little difficult to find companions to share costs with, but there is usually a reasonable number of travellers in Lhasa with an interest in Tibetan Buddhism and a will to escape the madding crowd.

The cost of a two-day Land Cruiser trip should be Y1000 to Y1300. A guide and permits are not necessary. You could tack on Drigung Til Monastery and make a nice loop for a few hundred yuan more.

On public transport you could get as far as Lhundrub, if not a little further, on a daily bus from Lhasa's Eastern Suburbs or Lugu Bus Stations. After this you'd have to rely on hitching, though if you have food and enough time you shouldn't have any major problems. Reting is 28km from Phongdo village, which has a ruined dzong.

ROAD TO DRIGUNG TIL MONASTERY

Drigung Til and Tidrum Monasteries, around 120km north-east of Lhasa, are becoming increasingly popular destinations for independent travellers. They can only be reached by rented transport or by hitching. There are few sights here, but the valleys have an untouched and timeless quality that makes them seem much further from Lhasa than they actually are. Most people who make it out here agree that it is well worth the effort.

Medro Gungkar and Drigung Qu don't have many attractions in their own right, but can be useful as places to break the journey.

Medro Gungkar

The road to Drigung leaves the main highway at the small town of Medro Gungkar. If you have time it's worth stopping at **Katsel Monastery**, just across the Kyi-chu from the town. There's not much to see, but the temple is significant as one of the original demoness-subduing temples (see the boxed text 'Demoness-Subduing Temples' in the special section 'The Jokhang').

In case you get stuck without transport there are a couple of places to stay in Medro Gungkar.

Plateau Hotel (Gaoyuan Luguan) Triples with shared bathroom Y20 per bed. This is probably the best choice; it's on the northern side of the road.

Trade Hotel (Maoyi Lüshe) Y12 per bed. This is cheaper but a more basic option, with outside toilets, on the southern side of the road above the vegetable market.

There are several *restaurants* and shops offering basic supplies.

Drigung Qu

As you continue up the valley from Katsel Monastery you pass two enormous ruined chörtens on the right. Halfway up the valley you come to Drigung Qu village (also known as Nyima Jiangre), set at the auspicious confluence of three rivers.

A 20-minute walk north-west of town is the Drigungpa-school **Dzongsar Monastery**. Apart from the usual statues of Guru Rinpoche and Sakyamuni (Sakya Thukpa) inside the main chapel, there are also icons of Abchi, the white female protector of the region, and a two-armed standing Chenresig (Avalokiteshvara), as well as the founder of the Drigung school, Jikten Gonpo (and his golden footprints). Behind the monastery two chörtens stand sentinel over the beautiful upper Kyi-chu valley.

Also nearby is **Sha Monastery**, 2km south-east of Drigung Qu and dedicated to the Dzogchen suborder. As you go in past two inscribed pillars, look up at the stuffed snow leopard. To the right is a side protector chapel with the Dzogchen trinity Dorje Lekpa, Rahulla and Ekajati. Continue on through an unusual courtyard encircling a huge chörten, to the upstairs chapel above the entrance.

Up a side valley from Sha Monastery is the Nyingmapa-sect Shalung Nunnery. Across the river valley from Dzongsar Monastery is **Una Monastery**. There is also a **ruined dzong** 3km south of town.

The only *accommodation* is at the end of the only street in town, above a shop with a pool table in front. Beds in the clean upstairs dormitory cost Y15. *Congratulations Restaurant* has *momos* (dumplings), thugpa, beer, tea and basic fried dishes.

From Drigung Qu it is about 35km to Drigung Til.

DRIGUNG TIL MONASTERY

Drigung Til Monastery *(admission Y15)* is the head monastery of the Drigungpa school of the Kagyupa order. Although it suffered some damage in the Cultural Revolution, the monastery is in better shape than most of the other monastic centres in this part of Ü. It was first established in 1167. By 1250 it was already vying with Sakya for political power – as it happened, not a particularly good move. The Sakya forces joined with the Mongol army to sack Drigung Til in 1290. Thus chastened, the monastery subsequently devoted itself to the instruction of contemplative meditation. There are 210 monks at Drigung Til.

Drigung Til sprouts from a high, steep ridge overlooking the Drigung valley. A steep thread of a path makes its way up into the monastic complex, although there is also vehicle access from the eastern end of the valley. The 180-degree views from the main courtyard are impressive and a serene stillness pervades the site.

The **main assembly hall** is probably the most impressive of the buildings. The central figure inside is Jigten Sumgon, the founder of the monastery. Guru Rinpoche and Sakyamuni (Sakya Thukpa) are to the left. Upstairs on the 1st floor you can see statues of Jigten Sumgon and his two successors, all wearing red hats. Jigten's footprint is set in a slab of rock at the foot of the statue. From the 1st floor you can go upstairs to a balcony and a circuit of prayer wheels. Steps lead up from here to the chörtens of two previous abbots.

The monastery **kora** then heads up the hill to the main dürtro. This is the holiest sky-burial site in the Lhasa region – people travel hundreds of kilometres to bring their deceased relatives here. It is sometimes possible to observe a sky burial but it is absolutely essential that you gain permission from both the family of the deceased and the senior lama who conducts the ceremony. The lama requests that you do not take photos. Please do not abuse his and the deceased family's hospitality by sneaking any shots. If they do not want you to attend then just let it go. It's not worth coming all the way to Drigung Til just on the off-chance that there will be a burial. (For more information on sky burials, and on issues to consider in requesting permission to attend one, see the boxed text 'Sky Burial' in the Facts about Tibet chapter.)

As you follow the kora along the ridge and down to the monastery, ask the monks for the path to the gönkhang. This **protector chapel** is dedicated to Abchi, the protectress of Drigung, who can be seen to the left of the main statue of Jigten Sumgon. To the right of the chapel there is another statue of Abchi riding a horse, which is next to Tseringma, the goddess of Mt Everest, riding a snow lion. Also look out for the pair of yak horns on the left wall of the chapel, after which Drigung is said to be named (a *dri* is a female yak and *gung* means 'camp'), and the stuffed snow leopard on the right.

It is possible to stay in the *Monastery Guesthouse* in the main courtyard for Y15 per night. There's a small monastery shop here but no food, so bring supplies with you. Boiled water is available.

For information on reaching Drigung Til see Getting There & Away under Tidrum Nunnery, following.

TIDRUM NUNNERY
elevation 4325m
About three hours' walk from the main valley, north-west of Drigung Til and 16km up a side valley, is Tidrum Nunnery with its **medicinal hot springs** (*admission Y5*).

Tidrum has a great location in a narrow gorge at the confluence of two streams. The small nunnery has strong connections to Yeshe Tsogyel, the wife of King Trisong Detsen. The Kandro-la, the resident spiritual leader of the nunnery, is considered a reincarnation of Yeshe Tsogyel.

The hot springs are delightful and are in a mercifully concrete-free zone. There are separate men's and women's bathrooms. Bring a towel and flip-flops.

If you have a day to spare you could do a tough day hike circumambulating the caves of Yeshe Tsogyel. Take a guide from the nunnery as the trail can be hard to find.

For a short walk, head north up the gorge behind the nunnery for about 1½ hours until you get to Dranang Monastery, where the valley divides.

Places to Stay & Eat
There are two guesthouses next to the springs. Both offer beds for Y15 to Y30, but the *Nunnery Guesthouse* is much nicer than the *government blocks*. There is a *shop* selling biscuits and beer – bring all your food with you.

Getting There & Away
The best way to get to Drigung Til and Tidrum is by rented vehicle. The trip takes around four hours from Lhasa. It's worth spending at least one night in Tidrum or Drigung, more if you want to do any hikes. A two- or three-day trip will cost around Y1500. It is also possible to visit Drigung as part of a loop taking in Reting (around Y1500), or as a longer five-day trip taking in Nam-tso and Reting (around Y2500).

Alternatively, public transport runs to Drigung Qu, from where you'll have to hitch the 35km to Drigung Til and then to Tidrum. There's very little traffic on this last section so you may need to wait a day for a lift to arrive.

If you are hitching, there are buses from Lhasa's Eastern Suburbs Bus Station at 10am, 2pm and 4pm to Medro Gungkar (Y12), from where it's relatively easy to get a ride to Drigung Qu. There is also a daily bus from Lhasa's Eastern Suburbs Bus

Station to Zashu at 9am, which will drop you in Drigung Qu at around 2pm. A monastery bus shuttles between Lhasa and Drigung Til Monastery every three days but it's easier to track down in Drigung Til.

From Drigung Qu it's theoretically possible to head directly up to Reting on the daily 11am bus from Lhasa, but both the bus service and the road are unreliable.

Yarlung Tsangpo Valley

Although it's only a couple of hours by bus or taxi from Lhasa, the Yarlung Tsangpo valley offers plenty of opportunities to get off the beaten track without launching a major expedition. The ease of transport means you can jump on and off public transport to visit any combination of sights near the roadside, while with more time you could spend days exploring the various side valleys on foot or by mountain bike.

Permits are theoretically needed for all places in this section. In reality, only the Yarlung Valley, and possibly Samye, require permits. See those entries later for details.

GONGKAR
☎ 0891

Gongkar's main claim to fame is its airport. A further 3km towards Lhasa are the ruins of **Gongkar Dzong** and neighbouring Sundruling Monastery. Nearby, by the roadside, you can normally see small coracle boats, which ferry passengers across the Yarlung Tsangpo to Sinpo Ri.

Gongkar Chöde Monastery
Around 10km back along the road to Lhasa is this surprisingly large Sakyapa monastery (*admission Y10, if collected*), founded in 1464 and famed for its 16th-century Kyenri-style murals. It lies 400m south of the highway; the turn-off is marked by a blue sign and a brown shrine.

The assembly hall has statues of founder Dorje Denpa (1432–96), Guru Rinpoche and Sakya Pandita, and a mandala sculptured

Kilometre Markers along the Yarlung Tsangpo	
Chusul to Tsetang	
marker	feature
72	Chuwo Ri, one of Ü's four holy mountains
73	Monastery on side of Chuwo Ri
80–81	Ruins of Gongkar Dzong & Shedruling Monastery
84	Gongkar Chöde Monastery
93–94	Gongkar airport
102/3	Gongkar Xian town
112	Ferry to Dorje Drak Monastery
117	Dongphu Chukhor Monastery
140	Ferry to Drak Valley
142	Turn-off to Dranang Monastery (signposted as 'Zhatong')
147	Road to Mindroling Monastery
148–49	Tsongdu Tsokpa Monastery
155	Samye ferry
161	Namseling Manor turn-off
190	Tsetang town

from *tsampa* (roasted-barley flour). To the left is the gönkhang, whose outer rooms have black murals depicting sky burial. The inner hall has a statue of the Sakyapa protector Gonpo Gur and some amazing spirit traps (to the right). The inner sanctum has fine Kyenri-style murals of the Sakyapa founders by the entrance, and a kora path. There are more Kyenri murals in the Chinese landscape style in a small chapel to the right.

The upper floor has lovely old murals, including some showing the original monastery layout, and an adjacent gönkhang. On either side of the roof is the Kyedhor Lhakhang, which has fine protector murals in *yabyum* (Tantric sexual union) pose, and the Kangyur Lhakhang. The top floor has three new chapels to the left, as well as the Lama Lhakhang, and the Neten Lhakhang, dedicated to the 16 arhats.

The original monastery once had two additional colleges on either side and a thangka wall at the rear where a gigantic thangka was unfurled on the 15th day of the first lunar month.

Die-hards can hike a further 5km up the side valley to visit the Dechen Chokhor Monastery on the hillside.

Places to Stay & Eat

There are a couple of decent places to stay near the airport if you can't face an early bus trip or you want to use Gongkar as a base from which to explore the valley.

Airport Hotel (☎ 618 2171) Doubles Y50-100, triples Y30 per bed. The recently renovated main block has comfortable standard rooms but unreliable hot water. The old block has the cheaper and better-value rooms, which also come with a bathroom. Breakfast costs Y10. The hotel is right by the terminal building.

Wujin Hotel (☎ 618 2240) Doubles with private bathroom Y50-60 per bed, doubles/triples without bathroom Y40/30 per bed. This privately run place, next to the Airport Hotel, has box-like doubles and better triples. The pricier rooms suffer from grim toilets. Hot showers cost Y6 extra. All in all, the Airport Hotel is a better bet.

Zhuhangkong Binguan (2nd floor, Cnr main & airport roads) Doubles with private bathroom Y30 per person. The rooms are pretty good and there's a public hot shower in the basement (Y6), making this the best budget bet.

Gongkar has lots of Chinese *restaurants*, all overpriced but with decent food.

Getting There & Away

Airport buses run daily from the office of the Civil Aviation Authority of China (CAAC) in Lhasa to Gongkar at 6.30am (Y35), 10am (Y25) and 3pm (Y25). Return buses to Lhasa (and less-frequent buses to Shigatse and Bayi) are timed to coincide with the arrival of flights. There are plenty of minibuses and shared taxis running from Tsetang to Gongkar, particularly in the afternoon.

Taxis take passengers to Lhasa for Y25 per person (Y100 per taxi), though you may get the entire taxi for less if it's returning anyway. Otherwise, you should not have to wait too long to find a bus returning to Lhasa from Samye or Tsetang.

DORJE DRAK MONASTERY

Dorje Drak, along with Mindroling, is one of the two most important Nyingmapa monasteries in Ü. It is less accessible than Mindroling, and not as well restored, and consequently gets few Western visitors.

Dorje Drak was forcibly relocated to its present site in 1632 by the kings in Tsang and then sacked by the Dzungar Mongols in 1717. The monastery is headed by a line of incarnate lamas known as the Rigdzin, named after the first Rigdzin Godemachen, who are thought to be reincarnations of Guru Rinpoche. The 10th Rigdzin Lama currently resides in Lhasa.

A demanding **kora path** leads around the back of the rock behind the monastery to a ruined retreat atop the rock. The path passes a pleasant wooded sandy bay. You have to slog through sand dunes to get up to the retreat but the views are stunning.

Tibetan-style beds are available at the *Monastery Guesthouse* for Y10. Bring a sleeping bag and food.

The monastery, on the northern bank of the Yarlung Tsangpo, can be reached via a ferry from kilometre marker 112 on the Lhasa-Tsetang road. Boats run in the morning and late afternoon (Y3, 30 minutes) or you can charter a boat for Y35. Some trekkers approach Dorje Drak from Lhasa, which means a hike of around four days.

DRANANG MONASTERY & VALLEY

A further 48km from Gongkar airport is the turn-off to Dranang (Dratang) Monastery *(admission Y15)*, 3km south of the highway. This small Sakyapa monastery of only 15 monks is of interest mainly to art specialists for its rare murals, which combine Indian and central Asian styles. Bring a torch for the murals.

The assembly hall has central statues of Dorje Chang (Vajradhara) and the monastery's founder, Drapa Ngonshe. Look out for the interesting oracle costume and mirror, in which the oracle would discern his visions. The inner sanctum holds all that remains of the murals, the best of which are on the back (western) wall.

A side protector chapel is accessed by steps outside and to the left of the main entrance. The chapel (whose central image is that of a yak's head) has a secret passage at the back that leads to a rooftop chapel and kora path.

To get to the monastery, walk 2km south from the highway, through the modern town of Dranang (and quickly past the PSB office on the right-hand side) into the old town, until the road curves to the right. Dranang has several shops and restaurants but no hotel. There are also restaurants by the turn-off.

Also worth visiting if you have a particular interest are the ruins of the **Jampaling Kumbum**, a 30-minute walk south-east of Dranang. The 13-storey chörten, built in 1472, was one of the largest in Tibet, with an attendant monastery of 200 monks, before it was dynamited by the Chinese in 1963. It's worth climbing up the hillside above the ruins to get an overview of the scale of the site, which includes a ruined assembly hall east of the chörten.

The only reconsecrated chapel is the Jampa Lhakhang, rebuilt in 1985, which features a large Jampa (Maitreya), flanked by Atisha (Jowo-je) and Tsongkhapa. Look out for a lonely brass toe, the only surviving part of the original statue. An old photo shows the magnificent original chörten.

To get to the Jampaling, walk south out of Dranang Monastery and after a couple of minutes turn left, following a path to the base of the ruins visible on the hillside above.

Explorers with a tent and supplies could easily spend a couple of days in the Dranang valley, hiking up the valley past the village and monastery of **Gyeling Tsokpa**, 8km from Dranang, to **Dingboche Monastery**, 14km from Dranang.

MINDROLING MONASTERY

Mindroling Monastery is a worthwhile detour from the Lhasa-Tsetang road between the Dranang turn-off and the Samye ferry crossing. It is the largest and, along with Dorje Drak, one of the most important Nyingmapa monasteries in Ü. Parts of it were dynamited during the Cultural Revolution, but most of it has been beautifully restored.

Although a small monastery was founded at the present site of Mindroling as early as the 10th century, the date usually given for the founding of Mindroling is the mid-1670s. The founding lama, Terdak Lingpa (1646–1714), was highly esteemed as a scholar and counted among his students the fifth Dalai Lama. Subsequent heads of the monastery were given the title Minling Trichen. The monastery was razed in the Mongol invasion of 1718 and later restored.

Mindroling has cham dancing on the 10th day of the fifth Tibetan lunar month and the fourth day of the fourth lunar month. The latter festival features the creation of a sand mandala.

There are two entrances to the monastery. If you come by foot you will probably enter from the east; cars enter from the south. The central **Tsuglhakhang** is an elegant brown stone structure on the west side of the courtyard. Note in particular the impressive masonry – the fit between the many different-sized stones used in the building is nearly perfect.

As you walk clockwise the first chapel is the **Zhelre Lhakhang**, with statues of Guru Rinpoche and Terdak Lingpa. The main hall itself has another statue of Terdak Lingpa, along with Dorje Chang (Vajradhara) and a row of Kadam-style chörtens. The inner chapel has a large Sakyamuni (Sakya Thukpa) statue surrounded by eight ornaments. Only the statue's head is original; the body was smashed by the Chinese for its relics.

Upstairs, the Tresor Lhakhang houses a famed old thangka with the gold footprints and handprints of Terdak Lingpa, which was given to the fifth Dalai Lama. Also here is the Pema Wangyal Chapel, featuring Guru Rinpoche, Terdak Lingpa, King Trisong Detsen and the Indian translator Shantarakshita.

The top floor holds the Lama Lhakhang, with some fine ancient murals of the Dzogchen lineages, plus a central statue of Gundu Sangba (Samanthabadri). The Dalai Lama's quarters remain empty.

The other main building, to the right, is the **Sangok Potrang**, used for Tantric practices. As you enter the hall to the right look for a famous mural of Guru Rinpoche. Several photos are on display in the hall: those of Namcai Norbu, the famous Nyingmapa teacher based in Italy; the current Minling Trichen (in exile); and the current abbot of Mindroling. The inner chapel has a large statue of Guru Rinpoche flanked by Shantarakshita and King Trisong Detsen, plus the eight manifestations of Guru Rinpoche.

A new white **chörten** has recently been built with Taiwanese funds just outside the monastery to replace an original 13-storey chörten destroyed in the Cultural Revolution. It's possible to climb past the ground-floor statue of Jampa to upper floors and sometimes the roof.

Nice walks lead off from the kora path around the Tsuglhakhang, west up the valley through the village to the ruins of what used to be a nunnery.

On the main road 1.5km towards Tsetang is the small **Tsongdu Tsokpa Monastery**. The original monastery across the road has been converted into a housing block.

Places to Stay & Eat

It's possible to stay the night at the *Monastery Guesthouse* for Y15. A small *shop* outside the south gate sells noodles, Pepsi and the like.

Getting There & Away

There is no direct public transport to Mindroling. One possibility is to take the Lhasa-Tsetang bus and get off at kilometre marker 147 by the English sign to the monastery. The monastery is around 8km south of the road, up the Drachi valley, and the last section involves a climb (it's not too punishing). You won't see the monastery until you round a ridge and are below it. You should be able to hitch a lift pretty easily from the highway turn-off, where there is a shop.

Mindroling is easily slotted into a Yarlung Valley excursion if you have a rented vehicle. It should add very little to the cost of your trip, as it is a detour of only 16km all up.

SAMYE MONASTERY

Samye is deservedly the most popular destination for travellers in the Ü region. The monastery, in the middle of the sandy Samye valley and approached via a beautiful river crossing, has a magic about it that causes many travellers to stay longer than they had intended. No journey in Ü is complete without a visit to Samye. (For details of the trek from here to Ganden, see the Trekking chapter.)

History

Samye was Tibet's very first monastery and has a history that spans over 1200 years. It was founded in the reign of King Trisong Detsen (who was born nearby), though the exact date is subject to some debate – probably between 765 and 780. Whatever the case, Samye represents the Tibetan state's first efforts to allow the Buddhist faith to set down roots in the country. The Bön majority at court, whose religion prevailed in Tibet prior to Buddhism, were not at all pleased with this development.

The victory of Buddhism over the Bön-dominated establishment was symbolised by Guru Rinpoche's victory over the massed demons of Tibet at Hepo Ri, just to the east of Samye. It was this act that paved the way for the introduction of Buddhism to Tibet.

Shortly after the founding of the monastery, Tibet's first seven monks (the 'seven examined men') were ordained here by the monastery's Indian abbot, Shantarakshita, and Indian and Chinese scholars were invited to assist in the translation of Buddhist texts into Tibetan.

Before long, disputes broke out between followers of Indian and Chinese scholarship. The disputes culminated in the Great Debate of Samye, an event that is regarded by Tibetan historians as a crucial juncture in the course of Tibetan Buddhism. The debate, which probably took place in the early 790s, was essentially an argument between the quietist Indian approach to bodhisattva-hood via textual study and scholarship, and the more immediate Chan- (Zen-) influenced approach of the Chinese masters, who decried scholarly study in favour of

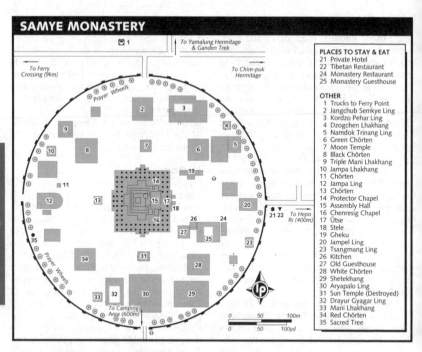

SAMYE MONASTERY

To Yamalung Hermitage
& Ganden Trek

To Ferry
Crossing (9km)

To Chim-puk
Hermitage

Prayer Wheels

To Hepo
Ri (400m)

Prayer Wheels

To Camping
Area (600m)

PLACES TO STAY & EAT
21 Private Hotel
22 Tibetan Restaurant
24 Monastery Restaurant
25 Monastery Guesthouse

OTHER
1   Trucks to Ferry Point
2   Jangchub Semkye Ling
3   Kordzo Pehar Ling
4   Dzogchen Lhakhang
5   Namdok Trinang Ling
6   Green Chörten
7   Moon Temple
8   Black Chörten
9   Triple Mani Lhakhang
10 Jampa Lhakhang
11 Chörten
12 Jampa Ling
13 Chörten
14 Protector Chapel
15 Assembly Hall
16 Chenresig Chapel
17 Ütse
18 Stele
19 Gheku
20 Jampel Ling
23 Tsangmang Ling
26 Kitchen
27 Old Guesthouse
28 White Chörten
29 Shetekhang
30 Aryapalo Ling
31 Sun Temple (Destroyed)
32 Drayur Gyagar Ling
33 Mani Lhakhang
34 Red Chörten
35 Sacred Tree

contemplation on the absolute nature of Buddhahood. The debates came out on the side of the Indian scholars.

Samye has never been truly the preserve of any one of Tibetan Buddhism's different orders. However, the influence of Guru Rinpoche in establishing the monastery has meant that the Nyingmapa order has been most closely associated with Samye. Images of the Guru dominate here. When the Sakyapa order came to power in the 15th century it took control of Samye, and Nyingmapa influence declined, though not completely.

Samye has been damaged and restored many times throughout its long history. Inevitably, the most recent assault on its antiquity was by the Chinese during the Cultural Revolution. Many of the monastery's structures, including the all-important, gold-topped Ütse, were badly damaged, and vast numbers of relics and images were stolen or destroyed. Nevertheless, Samye did not fare

as badly as some of the other temples in Ü. Extensive renovation work has been going on since the mid-1980s and there are now 130 monks at Samye.

Permits

A travel permit is theoretically needed to visit Samye and it's difficult to get one without organising a tour and guide. At the time of research there were only occasional permit checks, at the ferry point on the Tsetang side and at Samye itself. No-one is checked for weeks and then suddenly a bunch of travellers are fined. You'll have to ask other travellers or just give it a try. Don't rely on travel agencies in Lhasa to tell you about the current situation.

If you are stopped without a permit you may be subject to a fine of up to Y500, though you can normally plead stupidity and negotiate down to Y100 or less. Trekkers coming from Ganden Monastery have been a particular target for fines in the past.

Viewing the Monastery

Samye Monastery is designed to represent the Buddhist universe, and many of the buildings in the courtyard are cosmological symbols. The square in front of the monastery guesthouse has some interesting bits and pieces. The stubby isolated building to the north constitutes the remains of a nine-storey tower used to display festival thangkas.

The Ütse The central building of Samye, the Ütse, comprises a synthesis of architectural styles. The ground and 1st floors were originally Tibetan in style; the 2nd floor was Chinese and the 3rd floor Indian.

Just to the left of the entrance is a **stele** dating from 779. The elegant Tibetan script carved on its surface proclaims Buddhism as the state religion of Tibet by order of King Trisong Detsen.

From here the entrance leads into the first of the ground-floor chambers: the **assembly hall**. As you enter the hall a row of figures greet you straight ahead: Namse (Vairocana); Shantarakshita, Samye's first abbot; Guru Rinpoche (a copy of a famous statue whose photo lies to the left); Trisong Detsen; and Songtsen Gampo (with an extra head in his turban). On the right are two groups of three statues: the first group is associated with the Kadampa order; the second group is multidenominational, and includes lamas from the Nyingmapa, Sakyapa and Gelugpa orders.

To the rear of the assembly hall are steps leading into Samye's most revered chapel, the **Jowo Khang**. You enter the inner chapel via three doors – an unusual feature. They symbolise the Three Doors of Liberation: those of emptiness, signlessness and wishlessness. A circumambulation route around the inner chapel follows at this point.

The centrepiece of the inner chapel is a 4m statue of Sakyamuni (Sakya Thukpa). Ten bodhisattvas and two protective deities line the side walls of the chapel, and the walls themselves are decorated with ancient murals. Look also for the panelled ceiling – each of the panels is adorned with a Tantric mandala.

The Samye Mandala

Samye's overall design was based on that of the Odantapuri Temple of Bihar, in India, and is a mandalic representation of the universe. The central temple represents Mt Meru (or Sumeru), and the temples around it in two concentric circles represent the oceans, the continents and the subcontinents that ring the mountain in Buddhist cosmology.

At the centre of the monastery grounds is the Ütse, the most impressive of the monastery buildings, and at the centre of this is a pole that represents the core of the universe. Directly to the north is a Moon Temple and to the south a Sun Temple (now destroyed). Ringing the Ütse are four large *chörtens* (stupas), which are named after their colours: red, black, green and white. These were destroyed in the Cultural Revolution but were rebuilt recently – they look decidedly concrete and slightly out of place. Surrounding the chörtens are 12 *ling* chapels (lesser, outlying chapels), four major and eight minor ones. The four major ling chapels represent the four continents; the minor ling chapels are subcontinents. The complex originally had 108 buildings (an auspicious number to Tibetans) and there were 1008 chörtens on the circular wall that rings the monastery.

To the right of the hall is a gönkhang with statues of deities so terrible that they must be masked. Watch out for the stuffed snake over the exit.

Before ascending to the 1st floor, take a look at the **Chapel of Chenresig**, outside and to the left of the main assembly hall, which features a dramatic 1000-armed statue of Chenresig (Avalokiteshvara) and some ancient bas-relief plates.

The main feature of the **2nd floor** is an upper extension of the inner chapel. This houses an image of Guru Rinpoche in a semiwrathful aspect, plus Shantarakshita, Trisong Detsen and Sakyamuni. There is an inner kora path around the hall.

Some of the murals outside this hall are very impressive; those on the southern wall depict Guru Rinpoche, while those to the left of the main door show the fifth Dalai Lama with the Mongol Khan Gushri and various ambassadors showing obeisance. Also on this floor are the Dalai Lama's quarters (left) and another protector chapel and Tsepame (Amitayus) chapel (right).

The **3rd floor** is a recent addition to the Ütse. It holds a mandala base as well as four statues of Namse (Vairocana). Walk around the back to a ladder leading up to the **4th floor**. This is a sacred chapel of great significance. The main image is of Dukhor (Kalachakra), a Tantric deity. The pillars around the central core symbolise the Four Guardian Kings, the 16 arhats and the 21 manifestations of Drölma (Tara).

Back on the ground floor you can follow the prayer wheel circuit around the Ütse, and look at the interesting murals showing the founding of the monastery. It is also possible to climb up to the monks' quarters on the outer 1st floor and then up onto the roof.

Ling Chapels & Chörtens As renovation work continues at Samye, the original *ling* chapels (lesser, outlying chapels) and the coloured chörtens are gradually being restored. Wander around and see which are open. Following is a clockwise tour of those open at the time of research.

The **Tsangmang Ling**, once the monastery printing press, is now open; look for the sacred stone in the centre. The **Shetekhang** is a residential college for monks. The restored **Aryapalo Ling** was Samye's first building and is now looked after by a couple of charming monks. The **Drayur Gyagar Ling** was originally the centre for the translation of texts, as depicted on the wall murals. The main statue on the upper floor is of Sakyamuni (Sakya Thukpa), flanked by his Indian and Chinese translators.

The **Jampa Ling** on the west is where Samye's Great Debate was held. On the right as you go in, look out for the mural depicting the original design of Samye with zigzagging walls. There is an unusual semicircular inner pilgrimage path here that is decorated with images of Jampa. Just north of here is a chörten that pilgrims circumambulate; south is a sacred tree to which pilgrims tie stones. The triple **Mani Lhakhang** to the north has some lovely murals.

The green-roofed **Jangchub Semkye Ling** houses a host of bodhisattvas around a 3-D wooden mandala. East of here is the **Kordzo Pehar Ling**, the home of the oracle Pehar until he moved to Nechung Monastery outside Lhasa. There are several protector chapels here, including an upper-floor chapel with unusual gods including Dorje Phurbu, whose lower half is a dagger, sitting astride fantastic beasts such as a nine-headed boar.

It is also possible to enter the four reconstructed concrete chörtens, though there is little of interest inside.

Hepo Ri

Hepo Ri is the hill east of Samye where Guru Rinpoche vanquished the demons of Tibet. King Trisong Detsen later established a palace here. Paths lead up the side of the hill from the road leading from Samye's east gate. A 30-minute climb up the side ridge takes you to an incense burner, festooned with prayer flags and offering great views of Samye below. Early morning is the best time for photography.

Chim-puk Hermitage

Chim-puk hermitage is a warren of caves that was once a retreat for Guru Rinpoche. It is a popular day hike for travellers spending a few days at Samye. The walk takes around four or five hours up and three hours down. Take some water with you. If you are lucky you might find a pilgrim truck headed up there, or you could hire a tractor in Samye (Y50). Ask at reception at the Monastery Guesthouse.

Chim-puk is north-east of Samye. If you head out of the monastery in this direction you should be able to find a path leading east through some fields. Keep following this track, bearing left. The path crosses through desert-like territory for a couple of hours before ascending into the surprisingly lush area in which the caves are found.

There is a small monastery built around Guru Rinpoche's original **meditation cave** halfway up the hill. Follow the pilgrims around the various other shrines. It might be possible to stay the night here if you have a sleeping bag and food. There are splendid views of the Samye valley from up here.

If you are feeling fit and acclimatised it is possible to climb to the top of the peak above Chim-puk. You'll probably only have enough time to do this if you get a lift to Chim-puk or stay the night there. To make this climb from the Guru Rinpoche cave follow the left-hand valley behind the caves and slog it uphill for 1½ hours to the top of the ridge, where there are several clumps of prayer flags. From here you can drag yourself up along a path for another 90 minutes to the top of the conical peak, where there are a couple of meditation retreats and fine views of the Yarlung Tsangpo valley. On clear days you can see several massive Himalayan peaks to the south-east.

If you managed to get a lift up to Chim-puk it is possible to take another route back to Samye in around three to four hours. From the peak descend back down to the ridge line above Chim-puk, but instead of heading straight down the way you came up, cut down the other (western) side of the ridge that divides Chim-puk from the Samye valley. Follow paths along the western side of this ridge, slowly descending in the direction of Samye. After two hours you reach the valley floor, from where it is an easy one-hour walk to Samye.

Other Attractions

It is possible to head up the valley directly behind Samye to **Yamalung hermitage**, around 20km from Samye. It's really too far to hike there and back in a day but you could probably hire a tractor to take you there for around Y50 return. For details of this valley see the final stages of the Ganden to Samye trek and the relevant map in the Trekking chapter.

Places to Stay & Eat

Monastery Guesthouse Rooms Y10-25. This is really the only place to stay. It's just in front of the Ütse compound. It lacks the intimacy of the old guesthouse next door

(now used by monks) but it's still pretty good. Top-floor rooms include the much-sought-after corner room, with its great views of the Ütse. The *shops* either side of the guesthouse are well stocked with snacks, soft drinks, beer (essential for any monastic sojourn) and religious knick-knacks.

There is fine *camping* in an orchard 10 minutes' walk south of the Ütse. Take your own water.

Monastery Restaurant Dishes Y5. This place, just east of the guesthouse, offers basic food such as thugpa and fried noodles. Prices are cheap, the food is average and there's an English menu.

Tibetan Restaurant Chinese dishes Y8-18. This private teahouse outside the eastern gate of the monastery is the only other place to eat. Decent Chinese dishes are available, as well as standbys like thugpa and mugs of milk tea (Y1).

Getting There & Away

All buses from Lhasa to Tsetang pass by the Samye ferry departure point, which makes getting to Samye fairly easy.

A bus service also runs from just west of Barkhor Square in Lhasa to the Samye ferry. It leaves at around 8am (get there 30 minutes earlier) and costs Y30. There is also a bus to Tsetang (referred to as the bus to Shannan, the name of the prefecture) that leaves an hour or so later. A minibus to Samye leaves from opposite the Kirey Hotel in Lhasa at roughly the same time. Buses to Tsetang also leave from Lhasa's main bus station at 9am, 10am and 11am (Y27 to Y30).

All buses drop Samye passengers at the ferry crossing compound, where there is a basic restaurant and guesthouse if you arrive late (and have a permit). River crossings are irregular, operating whenever there are enough people, in flat-bottomed boats powered with a small motor. Locals pay Y3 for the crossing, but foreigners (especially those with a guide) are sometimes charged Y10.

The river crossing, one of the few in Tibet, is a fantastic ride, though it can be hot and there's no shelter. It takes a little over an hour, with much careful navigation around the sandbanks.

It is 9km from the ferry drop to Samye and almost everyone – Tibetans included – jumps on a truck or tractor for the ride (30 minutes, Y3). There are views of five chörtens to the left and lovely desert views to the right.

Trucks (and occasionally monastery minibuses) leave Samye for the ferry terminal at around 8am and 2pm, though it's worth checking these times with the guesthouse manager. Buses to Tsetang and Lhasa wait for passengers on the other side of the river, as does the PSB. There are occasional trucks direct to Tsetang via the northern shore of the Yarlung Tsangpo and the bridge over to Tsetang, but it's a longer, hot and dusty drive.

NAMSELING MANOR

This ruined multistorey family mansion is a minor site but you might find it worth a visit if you have your own transport. It is perhaps the only building of its type still standing in Tibet. There are a few murals left but the ruins are unstable in places so you should take care when exploring. The building is 3km south of the main highway near kilometre marker 161.

TSETANG

☎ 0893 • elevation 3500m

Tsetang, 183km south-east of Lhasa, is the second-largest town in the Ü region and the third-largest in Tibet. It is the capital of Shannan prefecture and an important Chinese administrative centre and army base. For travellers Tsetang is of interest mainly as a jumping board for exploration of the Yarlung Valley. The major obstacles are a lack of budget accommodation, permit hassles (see Yarlung Valley later in this chapter) and a concerted effort on the part of the Chinese to charge foreigners double for everything.

Tsetang is divided into a new Chinese town and an old Tibetan quarter. The Tibetan quarter is in the east of town, clustered around Gangpo Ri, one of Ü's four sacred mountains. The former dzong and village of Nedong has been subsumed into Tsetang's southern suburbs.

Information

The telecom office is the place to make international calls. Tsetang Hotel is the only place in town that changes money, for hotel guests only. There several Internet bars near the post office (Y6 per hour). The Tsetang PSB is the most unfriendly in Tibet. If you don't have a permit, keep a low profile.

The China International Travel Service (CITS; ☎ 782 5555 ext 1109, fax 782 1855) has an office in the Tsetang Hotel. Really it is only interested in large groups but will organise overpriced independent day trips (with guide and permits) to the sights of the Yarlung Valley for around Y400 per person.

Monastery Kora

There are a couple of small monasteries in the Tibetan quarter that are worth a brief visit. Most pilgrims visit them in a clockwise circuit.

From the market head east to a small square and continue down the street to the right of the bank. After 200m you'll come to **Tsetang Monastery** (also known as Ganden Chökhorling). This 14th-century monastery was originally a Kagyupa institution but by the 18th century the Gelugpas had taken it over. The Chinese smashed the place up but the three storeys have been well restored.

From here head north and then east to **Ngachö Monastery**, a somewhat livelier place. On the top floor are the bed and throne of the Dalai Lama. A side chapel is devoted to medicine, with images of the eight medicine buddhas.

A pilgrim path leads down from the monastery, follows the base of Gangpo Ri to a small shrine and then heads up to a bundle of prayer flags. From here one path ascends the hill to hermitage caves, the other descends to **Sang-ngag Zimche Nunnery**. The principal image here is of a 1000-armed Chenresig (Avalokiteshvara), dating back to the time of King Songtsen Gampo. According to some accounts, the statue was fashioned by the king himself.

Places to Stay & Eat

Finding good budget accommodation is a real problem in Tsetang. There are cheap

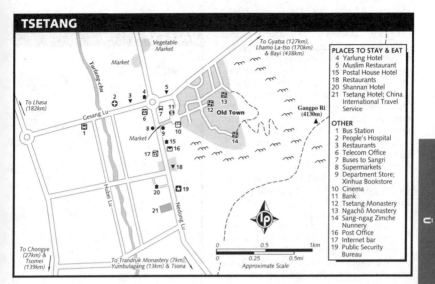

TSETANG

Vegetable Market

Market

To Lhasa (182km)

Yarlung-chu

Gesang Lu

To Gyatsa (127km), Lhamo La-tso (170km) & Bayi (438km)

Old Town

Gangpo Ri (4130m)

Market

Hubei Lu

Nedong Lu

To Chongye (27km) & Tsomei (139km)

To Trandruk Monastery (7km), Yumbulagang (13km) & Tsona

0   0.5   1km
0   0.25   0.5mi
Approximate Scale

PLACES TO STAY & EAT
4   Yarlung Hotel
5   Muslim Restaurant
15 Postal House Hotel
18 Restaurants
20 Shannan Hotel
21 Tsetang Hotel; China
    International Travel
    Service

OTHER
1   Bus Station
2   People's Hospital
3   Restaurants
6   Telecom Office
7   Buses to Sangri
8   Supermarkets
9   Department Store;
    Xinhua Bookstore
10 Cinema
11 Bank
12 Tsetang Monastery
13 Ngachö Monastery
14 Sang-ngag Zimche
    Nunnery
16 Post Office
17 Internet bar
19 Public Security
    Bureau

hotels, like the *Yarlung Hotel* (beds Y15 to Y30) on the main roundabout, but they are prevented from accepting foreigners by Tsetang's strong PSB presence.

Shannan Hotel (☎ 782 6168) Doubles Y280-380. This mid-range hotel isn't bad but the less expensive doubles are small, stained and overpriced. There are cheaper doubles for Y60 but foreigners aren't allowed to stay in these. Hot water flows from 9.30pm to midnight. All prices include breakfast.

Tsetang Hotel (Zedang Fandian; ☎ 782 5666, fax 782 1855, 21 Nedong Lu) Doubles Y888. This is Tsetang's premier lodging, with 24-hour hot water, money exchange and a decent restaurant, but it's still terribly overpriced.

Postal House Hotel (Youdian Gongyu; ☎ 782 1888, Nedong Lu) 4-bed dorms Y60, doubles with shared bathroom Y150, rooms with private bathroom Y280-300. This is the cheapest option in town but the dingy rooms are still grossly overpriced, as foreigners pay a 50% surcharge.

The main north-south drag is the best place to seek out restaurants; north of the Tsetang Hotel all the way to the traffic circle

the road is lined with *Chinese restaurants*. A couple of good (if noisy) *Muslim restaurants* east of the circle serve up tasty noodles.

There are several well-stocked *supermarkets* on the main road that are good for hiking supplies.

Getting There & Away

Buses for Tsetang leave Lhasa early in the morning from the long-distance bus station and Lhasa's Barkhor Square, though most travellers make their way first to Samye, spend a day or so at the monastery, and then travel on to Tsetang.

Buses and minibuses heading back to Lhasa (via the Samye ferry) depart from the bus station every hour between 7am and 10am, and at 3.30pm (Y27 to Y40). Afternoon minibuses to Gongkar run until about 5.30pm. There are also three or four buses a week south to Tsomei (via Chongye) and Tsona (via Yumbulagang) but you'll be lucky to get on them since both destinations are off limits to foreigners. There is supposed to be a bus every Friday at 8am to Nangartse on the shores of Yamdrok-tso.

Minibuses to Sangri leave when full from a depot just east of the main intersection.

GANGPO RI

Gangpo Ri (4130m) is a mountain of special significance for Tibetans as it is the legendary birthplace of the Tibetan people (see the boxed text 'Mythology of the Yarlung Valley' later in this chapter). The **Gangpo Ri Monkey Cave**, where the monkey meditated, can be visited near the summit of the mountain. The walk there and back will take close to a full day. Do it in the spirit of a day walk in the hills, rather than as a trip specifically to see the Monkey Cave, as the cave itself is rather disappointing.

The most direct trail leads up from the Sang-ngag Zimche Nunnery, climbing about 550m to the cave. If in doubt, head for the collection of prayer flags.

There is a pilgrimage circuit around Gangpo Ri, but the 10-hour walk would probably require two days. The walk starts a few kilometres east of town, along the road to Bayi, and heads south up a dry valley to the Gangpo-la and the Monkey Cave. You could probably sleep here if you had a sleeping bag, some food and a sense of adventure, before descending the next day to the main road south of Tsetang.

YARLUNG VALLEY

Yarlung is considered the cradle of Tibetan civilisation and it was from Yarlung that the early Tibetan kings unified Tibet in the 7th century. The massive burial mounds of these kings can be seen in Chongye. Yumbulagang, another major attraction of the area, is perched on a crag like a medieval European castle and is considered Tibet's oldest building.

The major attractions of the Yarlung Valley can just about be seen in a day, but this is a beautiful part of Tibet for extended hiking and day walks. The main problem is the permit situation (see Permits later). Yarlung sees far fewer foreign travellers than the other major destinations of Ü.

Some travellers band together in Lhasa for a three- or four-day trip out to the Yarlung Valley by way of Tsetang. This way it is possible to visit Samye Monastery, drive on to Tsetang and spend the night there, visit the Yarlung Valley sights and

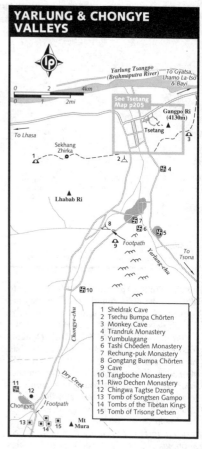

YARLUNG & CHONGYE VALLEYS

1 Sheldrak Cave
2 Tsechu Bumpa Chörten
3 Monkey Cave
4 Trandruk Monastery
5 Yumbulagang
6 Tashi Chöeden Monastery
7 Rechung-puk Monastery
8 Gongtang Bumpa Chörten
9 Cave
10 Tangboche Monastery
11 Riwo Dechen Monastery
12 Chingwa Tagtse Dzong
13 Tomb of Songtsen Gampo
14 Tombs of the Tibetan Kings
15 Tomb of Trisong Detsen

head back to Lhasa via Mindroling Monastery and possibly Gongkar. The total cost (including permits and guide) for a Land Cruiser on a trip of this sort is around Y2800. It's more cost-effective to add a Yarlung extension onto a trip to the Nepali border if you are heading that way.

Permits

Permits are needed to visit anywhere outside Tsetang town, though there weren't any formal permit checks in the valley during our research visit. If you head off on foot before dawn to Yumbulagang or Rechung-puk there is little chance of being caught, but the likelihood rises rapidly in Chongye, especially if you stay the night.

If you are on a Land Cruiser tour your driver or guide will arrange a permit from Tsetang PSB. The only other way to get a permit is to hire a Land Cruiser from Tsetang CITS, which will cost an arm and a leg.

Sheldrak Cave

Sheldrak Cave is the preserve of hardy hikers and Tibetan pilgrims. It is a tough six-hour climb to the west of Tsetang with an altitude gain of around 1000m.

For Tibetans, Sheldrak is one of Tibet's holiest pilgrimage destinations. It is the site of Guru Rinpoche's first meditation cave. King Trisong Detsen invited Guru Rinpoche to Tibet to exorcise the land of demons and the influence of Tibet's indigenous Bön faith. According to legend, it was here in the Crystal Cave that he got the job done. Unless you have a keen interest in Tibetan pilgrimage sites, it would be best to treat this as a strenuous hike rather than as a serious attraction.

The cave is reached from the road that heads out to Chongye from Tsetang. About 4km from the centre of Tsetang there is a large chörten known as the Tsechu Bumpa. It's worth trying to hitch a ride on a tractor along this section. From the chörten a trail heads west from the Chongye road up the Sheldrak valley to Sekhang Zhirka village, a sky-burial site and then a small monastery. From here it is a tough climb of less than an hour to Sheldrak. The cave has a small chapel and provides great views of the surrounding countryside.

Trandruk Monastery

Around 7km south of the Tsetang Hotel, Trandruk is one of the earliest Buddhist monasteries in Tibet, having been founded at the same time as the Jokhang and Ramoche in Lhasa. Dating back to the 7th-century reign of Songtsen Gampo, it is one of the demoness-subduing temples of Tibet (see the boxed text in the special section 'The Jokhang'). Trandruk's location corresponds to the demoness's left shoulder.

Trandruk was significantly enlarged in the 14th century and again under the auspices of the fifth and seventh Dalai Lamas. The monastery was badly desecrated by Red Guards during the Cultural Revolution, and extensive restoration work has been carried out since 1988.

The entrance of the monastery opens into a courtyard area ringed by cloisters. The building to the rear of the courtyard has a ground plan similar to that of the Jokhang, and indeed shares the same Tibetan name: Tsuglhakhang. The open room in the centre is the main assembly hall, and surrounding it is a walkway with chapels off to the sides.

Most of Trandruk's valuable images and murals were damaged during the Cultural Revolution and have been replaced with new ones. The principal chapel, to the rear centre, holds a statue of Tara known as Drölma Sheshema (under a parasol), next to the five Dhyani buddhas. The Chogyel Lhakhang to the left houses a statue of Songtsen Gampo. The Tuje Lhakhang to the right has Chenresig (Avalokiteshvara), Jampelyang (Manjushri) and Chana Dorje (Vajrapani), who form the Tibetan trinity known as the Rigsum Gonpo. Note the stove to the right, said to have belonged to Princess Wencheng, the Chinese consort of Songtsen Gampo. There are plenty of other chapels to explore, and fine murals depicting Dzogchen deities and the life of Sakyamuni.

Upstairs and to the rear is a central chapel containing a famous thangka of Drölma (Tara) made of 29,000 pearls, and an ancient applique thangka showing Sakyamuni.

Trandruk has an atmospheric, medieval feel and is a significant stop for Tibetan pilgrims, making it well worth a visit en route to Yumbulagang. Theoretically, there is an entry charge, but the monks do not seem particularly concerned about collecting it.

Trandruk is in a small Tibetan village around 7km south of the Tsetang Hotel. It is possible to walk here in 1½ hours, but there is also a steady stream of tractors plying the road between Trandruk and Tsetang. Try to head out around dawn if you don't have a travel permit (see Permits earlier), though the monastery may not open until 7am.

Mythology of the Yarlung Valley

The Yarlung Valley is considered the cradle of the Tibetan people. The story goes that Chenresig (Avalokiteshvara), the Bodhisattva of Compassion, descended from the heavens to the Land of Snows long ago in the form of a monkey. He meditated in a cave on the slopes of Gangpo Ri, before being drawn from his solitude by Sinmo, a white demoness (and manifestation of the goddess Drölma, or Tara). It seems she got his attention by sitting outside his cave and weeping – the oldest trick in the book, but one that is especially effective with a Bodhisattva of Compassion. One thing led to another and before too long they had six children – the beginnings of the Tibetan race. A strip of land nearby (at one time known less than romantically as 'Commune No 9') is the site of the legendary 'first field in Tibet'.

The contours of the valley shelter a wealth of other such legends. The mountain of Lhabab Ri is said to be the site where the first of the Tibetan kings, Nyentri Tsenpo, descended from heaven on a sky cord. Subsequent Tibetan kings all ascended back to heaven using the handy sky cord until Drigum Tsenpo (whose name means 'slain by pollution') accidentally cut the cord in a show of marksmanship. From this time the remains of Tibetan kings remained earthbound and were buried in the funerary mounds of nearby Chongye.

In the same valley in 1943, three Americans fell from the sky. They had lost their bearings and run out of fuel while flying supplies from India to Kunming over 'The Hump', China's only supply line during WWII. They managed to bail out of their B-24 bomber and touched down on mountain slopes above Tsetang. They finally made it to Lhasa and then safely back home to Idaho, but only after they narrowly escaped a mob of Tibetans furious that foreigners had been high enough to look down on the Dalai Lama.

Yumbulagang

Yumbulagang, a fine, tapering finger of a structure that sprouts from a craggy ridge overlooking the patchwork fields of the Yarlung Valley, is reputed to be the oldest building in Tibet. At least that is the claim for the original structure. Most of what can be seen today dates from 1982. It is still a remarkably impressive sight, with a lovely setting, and should not be missed.

The founding of Yumbulagang stretches back to a time of legend, and myths converge on the structure in bewildering profusion. The standard line is that it was built to accommodate King Nyentri Tsenpo, a historical figure who has been swallowed up in the mythology of Tibet. Legend has him descending from the heavens and being received by the people of the Yarlung Valley as a king. More than 400 Buddhist holy texts (known collectively as the 'Awesome Secret') are said to have fallen from the heavens at Yumbulagang in the 5th century. Murals at Yumbulagang depict the magical arrival of the texts.

There has been no conclusive dating of the original Yumbulagang, though some accounts indicate that the foundations may have been laid more than 2000 years ago. It is more likely that it dates back to the 7th century, when Tibet first came under the rule of Songtsen Gampo.

The design of Yumbulagang indicates that it was originally a fortress and probably much larger than the present structure. Today it serves as a chapel and is inhabited by a couple of monks. Its most impressive feature is its **tower**, and the prominence of Yumbulagang on the Yarlung skyline belies the fact that this tower is only some 11m tall.

The ground-floor **chapel** is consecrated to the ancient kings of Tibet. A central buddha image is flanked by Nyentri Tsenpo on the left and Songtsen Gampo on the right. Other kings and ministers line the side walls. There is another chapel on the upper floor with an image of Chenresig (Avalokiteshvara) similar to the one found in the Potala. There are some excellent murals by the door which depict, among other things,

Nyentri Tsenpo descending from heaven on a sky cord, Trandruk Monastery, and Guru Rinpoche arriving at Sheldrak. As you exit look to the left for the mural of the local mountain deity Yarlha Shampo.

It does not take all that long to explore Yumbulagang. Perhaps the best part of a visit is the walk up along the ridge above the building. There are fabulous views of Yumbulagang and the Yarlung Valley from a promontory topped with prayer flags. It is an easy five-minute climb.

Unless you have hired transport, you will have to walk or hitch the 6km from Trandruk Monastery to Yumbulagang along a dusty new road. From Tsetang it takes around three hours.

Rechung-puk Monastery

The remains of Rechung-puk Monastery are really only an attraction for serious pilgrim types or those with time to hike around the Yarlung Valley region. The monastery is easily accessible on foot from Trandruk Monastery or from Tsetang, but little is left of its former grandeur. As ever, it's most interesting to visit with a bunch of pilgrims.

Rechung-puk is associated with the illustrious Milarepa (1040–1123), founder of the Kagyupa order and revered by many as Tibet's greatest songwriter and poet. It was his foremost disciple, Rechungpa (1083–1161), who founded Rechung-puk as a cave retreat. Later a monastery was founded at the site; it eventually housed up to 1000 monks. For pilgrims, the draw of the monastery is the cave of Black Heruka, where they are hit on the back with holy relics. There are statues of Milarepa and Guru Rinpoche.

To get to Rechung-puk, follow the road between Yumbulagang and Trandruk and take the road to the west (left) at kilometre marker 132, about halfway between the two. You can see the ruins of the monastery up on the ridge that divides the two channels of the Yarlung Valley. The road enters a small village and then bends to the south (left), finally crossing a river next to a small school. A couple of kilometres from the main road is a second village, Khurmey,

from where it is a steep 20-minute walk up to the monastery, passing a white chörten.

An alternative from Yumbulagang is to walk west and then north through village paths to the small Tashi Chöeden Monastery and then north to Rechung-puk.

A path leads over the ridge from the Heruka cave, past some ruined chapels and down to the minor road. From here, you can head west along a dirt track towards the large Gongtang Bumpa chörten and then join the main road from Tsetang to Chongye.

Alternatively you can walk down the eastern side of the Chongye valley to a holy cave; a couple of hours after that you'll reach Tangboche Monastery.

Tangboche Monastery

Around 15km south-west of Tsetang on the road to Chongye, Tangboche is a minor site. The monastery is thought to date back to 1017 and was instrumental in the revival of Buddhism in central Tibet. Atisha (Jowo-je), the renowned Bengali scholar, stayed here in a meditation retreat. The murals, which for most visitors with an interest in things Tibetan are the main attraction of the monastery, were commissioned by the 13th Dalai Lama in 1913. They can be seen in the monastery's main hall – one of the few monastic structures in this region that was not destroyed by Red Guards.

Tangboche is easily visited if you are travelling by rented transport between Tsetang and Chongye. You should be able to see the building on the left once you're about 15km out of Tsetang. You have to look carefully, as it is partially obscured by a village. There is a short trail from the road to the village and monastery. It is a dusty 12km walk from Trandruk Monastery to Tangboche.

CHONGYE VALLEY

Most visitors to Chongye go there as a day trip from Tsetang, and combine the visit with the attractions in the Yarlung Valley. It is possible to stay in the town of Chongye but you leave yourself open to permit hassles this way. If you want to visit the surrounding sites and don't have a permit, it's worth detouring around the central PSB office and generally keeping a low profile. A road on the eastern side of the valley bypasses the centre of town and leads to the Chongye tombs.

There's probably not enough of interest to the average traveller to warrant a stay of more than a day or two. The huge burial mounds of the ancient kings of Ü are pretty much just mounds, not particularly exciting for anyone without a degree in archaeology.

Chongye is a beautiful valley enclosed by rugged peaks. The views from some of the burial mounds are superb. It is also well worth climbing up to Riwo Dechen Monastery and the ruins of the old dzong behind it for more views of the mounds.

Chongye Town

Chongye town is a dusty street lined with the occasional shop and restaurant, and culminates in a T-junction. To the far right of the junction as you come from Tsetang there is a basic *government guesthouse* (next to the PSB compound) with beds for around Y20. It is not a town in which you'll want to linger, but it makes a good base for hikes in the Chongye valley area. Chongye is around 27km south of Tsetang and hitching here is not that easy, though by no means impossible.

From Chongye town, most of the important sights are easily accessible on foot.

Chongye Burial Mounds

The Tombs of the Kings at Chongye represent one of the few historical sites in the country that gives evidence of a pre-Buddhist culture in Tibet. Most of the kings interred here are now firmly associated with the rise of Buddhism on the high plateau, but the methods of their interment point to the Bön faith. It is thought that the burials were probably officiated at by Bön priests and accompanied by sacrificial offerings. Archaeological evidence seems to suggest that earth burial, not sky burial, might have been quite widespread in the time of the Yarlung kings, and may not have been limited to royalty.

Accounts of the location and number of the mounds differ. Erosion of the mounds

has also made some of them difficult to identify positively. It is agreed, however, that there is a group of 10 burial mounds just south of the Chongye-chu.

The most revered of the mounds, and the closest to the main road, is the **Tomb of Songtsen Gampo**. It is the largest of the mounds and has a small Nyingmapa temple atop its 13m-high summit.

The southernmost of the group of mounds, high up on the slopes of Mt Mura, is the **Tomb of Trisong Detsen**. It is about a one-hour climb, but there are superb views of the Chongye valley from up here.

Chingwa Tagtse Dzong

The dzong, or fort, can be seen clearly from Chongye town and from the burial mounds, its crumbling ramparts straddling a ridge of Mt Chingwa. It was once one of the most powerful forts in central Tibet and dates back to the time of the early Yarlung kings. The dzong is also celebrated as the birthplace of the fifth Dalai Lama. There is nothing to see in the fort itself, but again you are rewarded with some great views if you take the hour or so walk up from Chongye town. Paths lead up from the centre of town, from the nearby ruins of the red chapel and from the gully behind Riwo Dechen Monastery.

Riwo Dechen Monastery

The large and active Gelugpa-sect Riwo Dechen Monastery sprawls across the lower slopes of Mt Chingwa below the fort. There are some nice walks up to the ridge to the north of the monastery and then down to the fort.

Riwo Dechen Monastery can be reached by a half-hour walk from Chongye's excellent old Tibetan quarter. Turn west at the town's T-junction and ask for the 'gompa'. Halfway up is a grand, new chörten. It is sometimes possible to stay the night at the monastery – a magical experience.

LHAMO LA-TSO

Around 115km north-east of Tsetang, Lhamo La-tso is one of Ü's most important pilgrimage destinations. The *la* of La-tso is a Tibetan word that means 'soul' or 'life spirit'. La resides in both animate and inanimate forms, including lakes, mountains and trees. The two may sometimes be connected, as in the Tibetan custom of planting a tree at the birth of a child – such a tree is known as a *la-shing*. In the case of Lhamo La-tso, 'la' is identified with the spirit of Tibet itself.

The Dalai Lamas have traditionally made pilgrimages to Lhamo La-tso to seek visions that appear on the surface of the oracle lake. The Tibetan regent journeyed to the lake in 1933 after the death of the 13th Dalai Lama and had a vision of a monastery in Amdo that led to the discovery of the present Dalai Lama. The lake is also considered the home of Palden Lhamo.

Places to Stay & Eat
Lhamo La-tso is difficult to reach and receives few foreign visitors. You should come prepared with a tent and enough food for a week. Be prepared for cold weather: the lake is at an altitude of over 5000m.

The nearest accommodation to Lhamo La-tso is at *Chökorgye Monastery*, from where it's a hard four-hour walk to the view of the lake from a high pass at around 5300m. You

have to be fit, acclimatised and well equipped to attempt it. There is no charge for staying at the monastery, but it is appropriate to make a donation when you leave. Do your best to keep the monks well disposed towards the occasional foreign visitor.

Getting There & Away
Most travellers approach Lhamo La-tso by rented vehicle via Gyatsa Xian, where a bridge spans the Yarlung Tsangpo. On the other side a truck is sometimes available to ferry pilgrims and travellers up to Chökorgye Monastery. From Tsetang, it may be possible to hitch a lift to Gyatsa Xian, from where it is a two-day walk up to Chökorgye Monastery. You will have to keep a low profile in Gyatsa Xian if you have no permit.

The most interesting way to reach the lake is to trek from Rutok (six days, via Dzingchi and the Magong-la) or from Sangri, both routes via the Gyelung-la. For detailed information on this trek see Gary McCue's *Trekking in Tibet – A Traveler's Guide*. We met one cyclist who had made it along this route on a mountain bike but ended up dragging his bike half the way and losing his shoes in a river crossing!

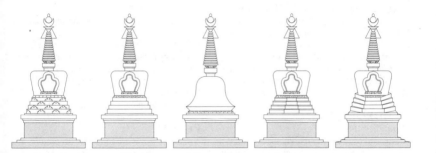

Tsang

The traditional Tibetan province of Tsang lies to the west of Ü, the province with which Tsang has long shared political dominance over the Tibetan plateau. With the decline of the Lhasa kings in the 10th century, the epicentre of power moved to Sakya, under Mongol patronage from around the mid-13th to the mid-14th centuries.

After the fall of the Sakya government, power shifted back to Ü and then again back to Tsang. However, until the rise of the Gelugpa order and the Dalai Lamas in the 17th century, neither Tsang nor Ü effectively governed the whole of central Tibet, and the two provinces were usually rivals for power. Some commentators see the rivalry between the Panchen Lama and Dalai Lama as a latter-day extension of this provincial wrestling for political dominance.

The two major urban centres of Tsang are Shigatse and Gyantse. Both contain important historical sights and have emerged as popular destinations for travellers.

A large number of travellers make their way through Tsang travelling from Lhasa to Kathmandu – usually in rented vehicles – via Yamdrok-tso, Gyantse, Shigatse, Sakya, Everest Base Camp, Tingri and Zhangmu. It is a convenient route along the 725km Friendship Hwy that takes in Tsang's most important attractions. By public transport it is possible to get as far as Lhatse but after that you must rely on your thumb.

Most of Tsang's sights involve detours from the highway. Sakya is 21km from the highway, close to Lhatse, while Everest Base Camp is 71km from Shegar by road or a three-day trek from Tingri.

The entries in this chapter follow a south-westerly route through Tsang from Lhasa to the border with Nepal, taking in the main attractions of the area on the way.

YAMDROK-TSO
elevation 4488m
On the old road between Gyantse and Lhasa, dazzling Yamdrok-tso can be seen from the

Highlights

- Gazing at the turquoise waters of Yamdrok-tso, the coiling scorpion-shaped lake
- Visiting Tashilhunpo Monastery and the spectacular tombs of the Panchen Lamas
- Climbing through the levels of Gyantse Kumbum, the most stunning architectural wonder in Tibet
- Touring the breathtaking assembly hall of Sakya Monastery, one of Tibet's greatest treasures
- Taking in the magnificent views of Mt Everest's north face

summit of the Kamba-la (4794m). The lake lies several hundred metres below the road, and in clear weather is a fabulous shade of deep turquoise. Far in the distance is the huge massif of Mt Nojin Kangtsang (7191m).

Yamdrok-tso is a coiling, many-armed body of water shaped like a scorpion. It doubles back on itself on the western side, effectively creating a large island within its reaches. For Tibetans, it is one of the four holy lakes of Tibet (the others are Lhamo La-tso, Nam-tso and Manasarovar), and the home of wrathful deities. The Chinese, on the other hand, have a more pragmatic interest in the lake: It is the site of a power station that generates hydroelectricity (see the boxed text 'Down the Drain').

Devout Tibetan pilgrims and the occasional Western trekker circumambulate the lake, a walk of around seven days. Most Western travellers, however, are content with a glimpse of the lake from Kamba-la and views from the town of Nangartse, where you can stay the night. If you're interested in a day walk on the lakeshore, see Samding Monastery later in this chapter.

Permits
Yamdrok-tso is in Shannan prefecture and officially you need a permit from Tsetang

212

Public Security Bureau (PSB) to visit independently, but it's unlikely you'll be checked. If you hire a vehicle the agency will arrange your permit for you.

Nangartse
☎ 0893 • elevation 4500m

Nangartse is the largest town on the lakeside and a popular stop for the night. It's not a particularly attractive place but there is a small monastery in the south of town, an old Tibetan quarter and a small *dzong* (fort) to the north (famed as the birthplace of the mother of the fifth Dalai Lama). There are also plenty of opportunities for walks nearby (see Samding Monastery, following). You can't actually walk to the lakeshore as you will soon find yourself up to your knees in bog, but the views are still good and birdwatchers in particular will have a field day in Nangartse during the summer months.

There is a telephone in town, but don't expect to find any showers.

Grain Guesthouse Dorm beds Y20. The best place to stay is the Tibetan-style Grain Guesthouse located above the Sichuan Restaurant on the south side of the street. Look for a green sign that says 'Guesthouse'. The pit toilets will make your eyes water but it's a friendly and comfortable place.

Hotel for Foreigners Beds Y20. The rooms here are comfortable and there are nice views from the veranda, but the place lacks the charm of the Grain Guesthouse across the street.

The People's Guesthouse Doubles Y45 per person. The rooms here have a TV and you might want to pay extra for the reasonably clean tiled toilets. To get to the guesthouse, continue on as the main road turns left and you'll see its red roof on the right.

Lhasa Restaurant Soup Y10. Even if the owners try to usher you upstairs, grab a seat downstairs among the friendly locals knitting and playing cards. There's an English menu.

There are also several relatively expensive Chinese restaurants in town, including the *Sichuan Restaurant* on the ground floor of the Grain Guesthouse.

Samding Monastery

Samding *(admission Y10)* sits on the shores of Yamdrok-tso, around 10km east of Nangartse. Sited on a ridge that separates the

Down the Drain

Yamdrok-tso is one of Tibet's holiest lakes and an important centre for pilgrimage. Yet what one devout Tibetan Buddhist perceives as a sacred body of water, another pragmatic Chinese engineer views as a natural resource just waiting to be utilised for the development of the country.

Yamdrok-tso has an unusual location locked in a high bowl above the Yarlung Tsangpo (Brahmaputra River) and the Chinese government has long harboured a plan to utilise gravity to create a hydroelectric supply. By the mid-1980s the Chinese leadership had sanctioned a plan to build a 6km tunnel 10m below the surface of the lake that would send the waters of the lake dropping some 846m into the Yarlung Tsangpo. Work was temporarily halted after opposition by the Panchen Lama, but by 1997 the turbines had started to produce electricity for the Lhasa region. You can see the pumps from the Lhasa-Shigatse road, 15km west of Chushul.

The project is highly controversial, and not only because of the reverence Tibetans have for the lake. Yamdrok-tso is a dead lake with no outlet and no perennial source of water. Water drained from it can never be replenished naturally. Chinese scientists claim that excess power will pump river water back up into the lake. Environmentalists fear that the lake, an important breeding ground for the endangered black-necked crane, could be dry within 20 years.

Water levels do indeed seem to be dropping and the section of water around Nangartse is now cut off from the main body of the lake. Many Tibetans further claim that the energy produced by the lake's hydroelectric supply will be directed mainly at fuelling Chinese migration into Lhasa. The Chinese reaction is predictable: Other hydroelectric sites are in the pipeline.

TSANG

northern arm of the lake from Dumo-tso (a smaller lake between the northern and southern arms of Yamdrok-tso), the monastery provides excellent views of the Dumo plain and the mountains to the south. You can walk here from Nangartse in about two hours.

Samding is noted for the unusual fact that it is traditionally headed by a female incarnate lama named Dorje Phagmo (Diamond Sow). When Mongolian armies invaded Samding in 1716, Dorje Phagmo changed her nuns into pigs to help them escape the terrors. Her current incarnation works for the government in Lhasa.

The monastery is undergoing extensive renovations, but it's possible to visit the main *dukhang* (assembly hall), a chapel dominated by a statue of Sakyamuni (Sakya Thukpa) and an eerie protector chapel. There are 27 monks and 10 nuns in residence at the monastery who live in separate quarters but share the use of the main buildings.

To walk to Samding, take the dirt road leading from the north end of Nangartse across to a small village recognisable by its trees. Once you get here, take the path on the right and follow it all the way to the monastery. It's worth climbing up the ridge

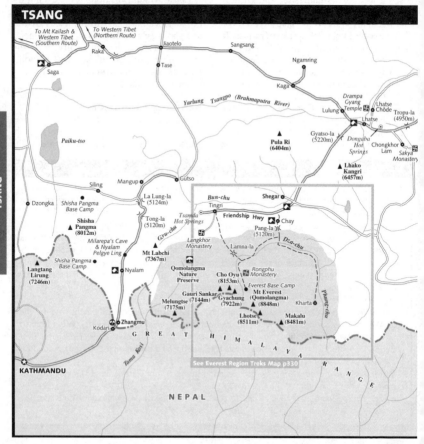

TSANG

See Everest Region Treks Map p330

behind the monastery for the fantastic views. It's also possible to drive here in a Land Cruiser, although the road turns to glue after it rains.

Talung & Ralung Monasteries

If you have your own transport and you want to get right off the beaten track you could make a detour to either Talung Monastery, 13km south of the Nangartse-Gyantse road, or Ralung Monastery, 5km south of the road after the Karo-la. Both monasteries are extremely remote and if you want to visit them you'll have to arrange this itinerary in advance with your travel agency.

Getting There & Away

A bus to Nangartse (Y40, six hours) departs Lhasa's main bus station at around 8.30am on alternate days. The bus returns at 8.30am the next day from the main street in Nangartse.

Many people travelling in rented vehicles include Yamdrok-tso in their trip to the border en route from Lhasa to Gyantse. It's also possible to hire a vehicle for a four-day loop from Lhasa visiting the lake, Gyantse and Shigatse.

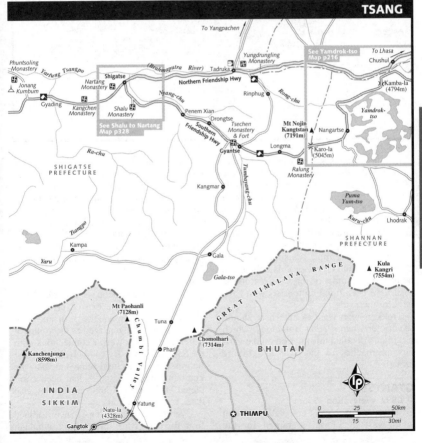

TSANG

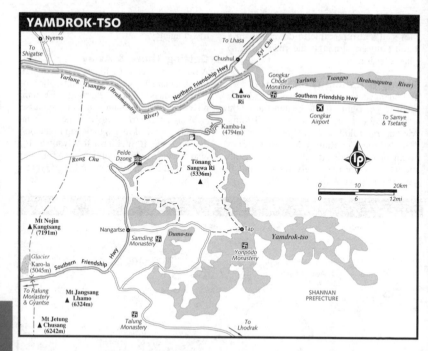

Leaving Yamdrok-tso is as spectacular as arriving, since you have to cross the 5045m Karo-la, with its awesome roadside views of the Nojin-Kangtsang Glacier. It was here that Colonel Younghusband's British troops clashed with Tibetan forces en route to Lhasa (see the boxed text 'Bayonets to Gyantse' later in this chapter).

There is no public transport between Yamdrok-tso and Gyantse, and hitching can be difficult as most of the vehicles on the road have been hired by tourists who have paid for their ride.

Trekkers who want to hike here should see Victor Chan's *Tibet Handbook*, which has highly detailed information on the various approaches to the lake and hiking around it.

GYANTSE
☎ 0892 • elevation 3950m
Gyantse, in the Nyang-chu valley 254km south-west of Lhasa, is famed for the Gyantse Kumbum, the largest *chörten* (stupa) in Tibet. The chörten is a magnificent tiered structure that has only one ruined and remote contemporary in the Buddhist world at Jonang, 60km north-east of Lhatse (see Phuntsoling Monastery & Jonang Kumbum later in this chapter). It's worthwhile spending a couple of days exploring Gyantse and you can also visit the Pelkor Chöde Monastery and the Gyantse Dzong.

There are no conclusive records that a settlement at Gyantse existed prior to the 14th century. Between the 14th and 15th centuries the town emerged as the centre of a fiefdom with powerful connections with the Sakyapa order. By 1440 Gyantse's most impressive architectural achievements – the kumbum and the dzong – had been completed. The Pelkor Chöde Monastery also dates from this period.

Gyantse's historical importance declined from the end of the 15th century, although the town continued to be a major centre for the trade of wood and wool between India and Tibet – Gyantse carpets were considered the finest in Tibet. Its position at the crossroads of trade routes leading south to Bhutan, west to Shigatse and north-east to Lhasa turned Gyantse into the third-largest town in Tibet by the time of the Chinese takeover. In 1904 it became the site of a major battle during Colonel Younghusband's advance on Lhasa, and British troops spent a month in the Gyantse Dzong before continuing to Lhasa (see the boxed text 'Bayonets to Gyantse' later in this chapter).

Gyantse has a horse racing and archery festival in the summer. It is traditionally held in the middle of the fourth lunar month (June or July).

Most people travelling in hired vehicles heading to the Nepali border pass through Gyantse. It's also possible to visit the town independently. Three-day permits are available from Shigatse PSB (Y50 with a Y200 deposit), but many travellers take the risk without one.

Orientation

Finding your way around Gyantse is a fairly straightforward affair. Buses stop at the town's only major intersection. To the north is the old Tibetan part of town. It is concentrated around the main road leading to Pelkor Chöde Monastery past the dzong, which looms over the town on a high ridge. To the south is an incipient Chinese quarter, with government buildings, shops, restaurants and a couple of hotels.

Pelkor Chöde Monastery

The monastery compound in the far north of town houses both Pelkor Chöde Monastery (☎ 817 2680, Pelkor Rd; admission Y30; open around 8.30am-1pm & 3pm-7.30pm daily) and the Gyantse Kumbum. Founded in 1418, Pelkor Chöde was once a complex of 15 monasteries. They were a particularly interesting collection of monasteries in that they brought together three different orders of Tibetan Buddhism in the one compound: a rare instance of multidenominational tolerance. Nine of the monasteries were Gelugpa,

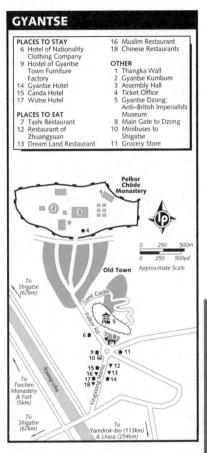

GYANTSE

PLACES TO STAY		16	Muslim Restaurant
6	Hotel of Nationality Clothing Company	18	Chinese Restaurants
9	Hostel of Gyantse Town Furniture Factory		**OTHER**
		1	Thangka Wall
14	Gyantse Hotel	2	Gyantse Kumbum
15	Canda Hotel	3	Assembly Hall
17	Wutse Hotel	4	Ticket Office
		5	Gyantse Dzong; Anti–British Imperialists Museum
PLACES TO EAT			
7	Tashi Restaurant	8	Main Gate to Dzong
12	Restaurant of Zhuangyuan	10	Minibuses to Shigatse
13	Dream Land Restaurant	11	Grocery Store

three were Sakyapa and three belonged to the obscure Büton suborder whose head monastery was Shalu near Shigatse (see Shalu Monastery later in this chapter).

Today much of the sprawling courtyard, enclosed by walls that cling to the hills backing onto the monastery, is bare; the remaining structures are attended by Gelugpa monks. The best way to get an idea of the original extent of Pelkor Chöde is to view it from the Gyantse Dzong.

The ticket office is just inside the main gates. The admission price for the monastery includes entry into the Gyantse Dzong.

The Chinese government has produced a slick souvenir CD-ROM that you may be forced to buy for an extra Y10, but it's of little interest if you can't speak or read Chinese and the monks would clearly prefer you didn't purchase it.

The **assembly hall** is a gloomy place and if you want a good look at the various murals and *thangkas* (Tibetan religious paintings) it is a good idea to bring a torch. The entrance is flanked by statues of the Four Guardian Kings instead of the usual paintings. Keep an eye out for the jewel-vomiting mongoose. Just by the entrance on the left is a particularly spooky protector chapel.

The main chapel is to the rear of the assembly hall. There is an inner route around the chapel, which is lined with murals. Inside, the central image is of Sakyamuni (Sakya Thukpa), who is flanked by the Past and Future Buddhas. Images of bodhisattvas line the walls.

To the left of the main chapel is another chapel that is worth taking a look inside. It is crowded with images, some of which are particularly noteworthy for their fine artistic accomplishment.

There are also a number of interesting chapels on the upper floors. Some of the statuary may be of Indian origin, but whatever the case, there are many beautiful images here with startlingly vivid and lifelike facial expressions. The first chapel to the left after you mount the stairs is noted in particular for a three-dimensional mandala that dominates the room, the paintings of the 84 *mahasiddhas* (highly accomplished Tantric practitioners) that adorn the walls, and clay images of key figures in the Sakyapa lineage. Take a look at the 84 mahasiddhas, each of whom is unique and shown contorted in a yogic posture. Other chapels are dedicated to Jampa (Maitreya), Tsongkhapa and the 16 *arhats* (literally 'worthy ones').

Gyantse Kumbum

Commissioned by one of the early Gyantse princes in 1427, the mystical Gyantse Kumbum (admission to which is included in the entry to Pelkor Chöde) is rated by many as the town's foremost attraction. The chörten is packed with exquisite Tibetan sculpture and painting and rises 35m over four main symmetrical floors surmounted by a gold dome. The dome rises like a crown over four sets of eyes that gaze serenely out in the directions of the cardinal points. As you climb upwards through the chapels of the kumbum you are drawn through progressively higher levels on the Tantric path.

A clockwise route leads murmuring pilgrims up through the six floors, taking in the 77 chapels that line the walls. There are two sets of four central chapels that extend to the floor above from the 1st and 3rd floors, and each of these is surrounded by smaller chapels in diminishing numbers and size as the floors ascend.

Much of the statuary in the chapels was damaged in the Cultural Revolution but has now been restored. The murals, however, have weathered very well. They are of 14th-century provenance and if they were not created by Newari (Nepali) artisans they are obviously influenced by Newari forms. Experts also see evidence of Chinese influence and, in the fusion of these Newari and Chinese forms with Tibetan sensibilities, the emergence of a syncretic but distinctly Tibetan style of painting.

Whatever the case, there are an awful lot of murals to look at (*kumbum* means '100,000 images'!) and unless you have a particular interest in the evolution of Tibetan Buddhist art it is difficult not to hurry through the last two floors. Lingering in a few of the chapels and having a close look at the wall frescoes is enough to give you an idea of what is on offer in other chapels. For a superb view of the whole chörten, climb the hills behind the monastery.

Depending on the position of the sun, certain chapels are sometimes illuminated with a warm, soft light that allows flashless photographs. There is a photography charge of Y10.

First Floor This floor has four main chapels, oriented according to the cardinal points. These are dedicated to Sakyamuni (along with two disciples, medicine buddhas and Guru Rinpoche) in the south; Sukhavati, the 'pure land of the west' and home of red Öpagme (Amitabha) in the west; Marmedze (Dipamkara, the Past Buddha) in the north; and Tushita (another 'pure land' and the home of Jampa) in the east. In between are some excellent murals depicting minor Tantric and protector deities. Murals of the Four Guardian Kings in the east lead the way to the upper floors.

Second Floor The first four chapels in order clockwise from the stairs are dedicated to Jampelyang (Manjushri), Chenresig (Avalokiteshvara), Tsepame (Amitayus) and Drölma (Green Tara). Most of the other chapels are devoted to wrathful protector deities, while others include Drölma (White Tara; 12th chapel from the stairs), Chana Dorje (Vajrapani; 14th chapel) and Mikyöba (Akshobhya; 15th chapel), a blue buddha who holds a *dorje* (thunderbolt).

Third Floor This floor is dominated by a second series of two-storey chapels at the cardinal points portraying the four Dhyani Buddhas – red Öpagme (Amitabha) in the south, yellow Rinchen Jungne (Ratnasambhava) in the west, green Donyo Drupa (Amoghasiddhi) in the north and blue Mikyöba (Akshobhya) in the east. There are several other chapels devoted to the fifth Dhyani Buddha, white Namse (Vairocana). Again most of the other chapels are filled with wrathful deities.

Fourth Floor The 11 chapels on this floor consist largely of teachers, interpreters and translators of obscure orders of Tibetan Buddhism. Exceptions include the Three Kings of Tibet (8th chapel clockwise from the steps) and Guru Rinpoche (10th chapel). You circumambulate this floor in a clockwise direction and find the passageway to the upper floors hidden behind the fourth statue in the eastern chapel – it's easy to miss in the gloom.

Upper Floors The 5th floor, also known as the Bumpa, has four chapels and gives access to the roof. A pathway at the back of the floor leads up to the 6th floor and takes you out onto the veranda at the level of the eyes painted on the wall. From here there are great views of the town and monastery. There is also a series of murals painted around a central cube. The top floor portrays a Tantric manifestation of Sakyamuni (Sakya Thukpa), but you may find it locked.

Gyantse Dzong

The 14th-century Gyantse Dzong (☎ 817 2116; admission Y25; open around 8.30am-8.30pm daily), or fort, is worth the stiff 20-minute climb to its upper limits. This is more for the amazing views of Gyantse, the monastery compound at the end of town and the surrounding Nyang-chu valley, than for what is left of the dzong itself, which is not much.

Some of the dzong's buildings can be entered and explored, sometimes to upper floors, by means of rickety wooden ladders. But generally there is very little to see. About midway up through the fort complex is an **Anti–British Imperialists Museum** featuring a fabulously warped version of the 1904 British invasion. The displays start off with the predictable 'Tibet is an inalienable part of the motherland…'. Some of the more spurious facts quoted include references to the '10,000 British troops' (the British claim 1000 troops and 10,000 servants), the death of reporter Edmund Chandler (he actually returned home to write a bestseller) and the claim that Tibetan troops were 'fighting to safeguard the (Chinese) motherland'.

Entry to the dzong is via the large gate on the roundabout. You can also enter through the back way from Pelkor Rd via the alley marked 'Lane Castle'.

Places to Stay

Accommodation in Gyantse has been in flux for the last couple of years. Rooms are expensive, a situation aggravated by the fact that officially only the Wutse, Canda and Gyantse Hotels are open to foreigners.

Places to Stay – Budget

Wutse Hotel (☎ 817 2909, fax 817 2880, Yingxiong Nanlu) Dorm beds Y40, singles/

TSANG

Bayonets to Gyantse

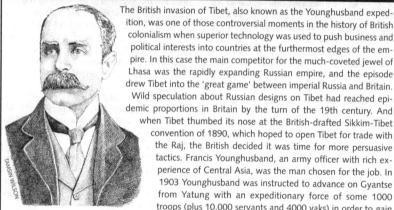

The British invasion of Tibet, also known as the Younghusband exped-ition, was one of those controversial moments in the history of British colonialism when superior technology was used to push business and political interests into countries at the furthermost edges of the em-pire. In this case the main competitor for the much-coveted jewel of Lhasa was the rapidly expanding Russian empire, and the episode drew Tibet into the 'great game' between imperial Russia and Britain. Wild speculation about Russian designs on Tibet had reached epi-demic proportions in Britain by the turn of the 19th century. And when Tibet thumbed its nose at the British-drafted Sikkim-Tibet convention of 1890, which hoped to open Tibet for trade with the Raj, the British decided it was time for more persuasive tactics. Francis Younghusband, an army officer with rich ex-perience of Central Asia, was the man chosen for the job. In 1903 Younghusband was instructed to advance on Gyantse from Yatung with an expeditionary force of some 1000 troops (plus 10,000 servants and 4000 yaks) in order to gain 'satisfaction' from the Tibetans.

Francis Younghusband

Despite previous brushes with British firepower, the Tibetans seemed to have had little idea about what they were up against. Not far from the village of Tuna (about halfway between Yatung and Gyantse), a Tibetan army of some 1500 troops armed with swords, matchlock rifles and a motley assortment of foreign firearms confronted a British force armed with light artillery, Maxim machine guns and modern rifles. The Tibetan trump card was a charm marked with the seal of the Dalai Lama himself, which each of the troops had been given with the assurance by the monks that it would protect them from British bullets. It didn't. Firing began after a false alarm and the British killed 700 Tibetans in four minutes.

The British buried the Tibetan dead (the Tibetans dug them up at night and carried them off for sky burial) and set up a field hospital, apparently dumbfounding the wounded Tibetans, who could not understand why the British would try to kill them one day and save them the next.

The British continued their advance on Gyantse. On arrival they found that the Gyantse Dzong had been deserted by its troops. Curiously, rather than occupy the dzong, the British camped on the outskirts of Gyantse, content to watch the Union Jack flutter on top of the fort. After a month in

---

doubles with private bathroom Y250/300. Most travellers stay in the comfy dorms of this new hotel. Rooms have TV; there are clean showers and a pleasant grassy court-yard complete with a shady Tibetan-style tent.

Hostel of Gyantse Town Furniture Fac-tory (☎ *817 2254, Pelkor Rd*) Beds Y40. This hostel on the main junction is decent, but forbidden to foreigners. The rooms here are fairly clean, and toilets and grubby showers are available.

Hotel of Nationality Clothing Company (*Pelkor Rd*) Dorm beds Y25. A five-minute walk north-west of the roundabout is the Hotel of Nationality Clothing Company (don't you love these snappy names?). This truck stop has been the mainstay of budget travellers for years but it's now very run-down and you have to check the bedding for bedbugs. Showers may be available. Again, you'll have to avoid the PSB if you decide to stay here.

Places to Stay – Mid-Range
Canda Hotel (*Yingxiong Nanlu*) Doubles with private bathroom Y150. The Canda is a decent mid-range hotel with spotless rooms.

Bayonets to Gyantse

Gyantse waiting for officials from Lhasa to arrive (they never came), a force of 800 Tibetan troops reoccupied the dzong under the cover of darkness. Meanwhile Younghusband sped off up to the Karo-la to take on 3000 Tibetans who had dug themselves in at over 5000m – the highest battle in British military history and a fine example of frozen stiff upper lip.

In early July, over six months after setting out from Yatung and after nearly two months in Gyantse waiting for Lhasa officials, the British troops received orders from Britain to retake the Gyantse Dzong and march on Lhasa. The assault on the Gyantse Dzong involved a diversionary attack on the north-east front while the real attack took place on the south-west. Shelling was used to make breaches in the walls, and when one of the shells destroyed the Tibetan gunpowder supply (and much of the dzong with it) the Tibetans were reduced to throwing rocks at their attackers. The dzong fell in one day, with over 300 Tibetan dead and just four British casualties.

The fall of the Gyantse Dzong was the last straw in Tibetan attempts to repel the British incursion. The British proceeded to the Yarlung Tsangpo (Brahmaputra River), which they finally crossed after five days of continual ferrying, and reached Lhasa without further incident.

Once in Lhasa there were some fine moments of imperial culture clash while Younghusband tried to ascertain where the bloody hell the Dalai Lama was (he had fled to Mongolia). British soldiers roamed the bazaars, quite miffed that the Tibetans largely ignored them. The troops discovered that British goods were already trickling in – one British soldier wrote proudly how he managed to find a sausage machine made in Birmingham and two bottles of Bulldog stout on a shopping trip to the Barkhor. Others tried in vain to persuade monks to sell them the statues from inside the Jokhang. Earlier that year in Tuna, the stalwart British officers had even managed to rustle up a Christmas dinner of turkey, Christmas pudding and (frozen) champagne.

After a month Younghusband managed to get the Tibetan regent to sign an agreement in the throne room of the Potala, allowing the British to set up trade missions at Gyantse and Gartok (near Mt Kailash), and the troops withdrew from their camp behind the Potala. A more profound agreement was signed in 1906 between the British and Chinese authorities, which assigned Tibet to China's sphere of influence, effectively ending both British and Russian influence.

But for Younghusband himself the most significant event of the campaign was yet to come. As he looked out over Lhasa on the evening before his departure he felt a great wave of emotion, insight and spiritual peace rush over him: an almost religious awakening that changed his life. He went on to found the World Congress of Faiths in 1936, citing that 'that single hour on leaving Lhasa was worth all the rest of a lifetime'.

Gyantse Hotel (☎ 817 2222, fax 817 2366, 8 Yingxiong Nanlu) Doubles/triples with private bathroom Y550/658 high season, Y445/556 low season. This Chinese-style place is the main group-tourist pad. It has all you would expect – obsequious staff, shiny lobby, awful coffee and clocks showing the wrong time in all the major capitals. You can get laundry done here or splurge on a massage (Y160 for 45 minutes).

Places to Eat

Most restaurants can be found in the stretch of road opposite the Wutse Hotel.

Tashi Restaurant (☎ 817 2793, Main roundabout) Mains Y15-20. Tashi Restaurant, upstairs on the main junction, is no relation to the one in Lhasa. This is the main travellers' hang-out in Gyantse. The food is fairly ordinary Tibetan, Chinese and Western fare, but the atmosphere is relaxed and it has an English menu.

Restaurant of Zhuangyuan (Yingxiong Nanlu) Dishes Y10-25. The owners of the Zhuangyuan are very keen to please and offer reasonable Chinese dishes.

Dream Land Restaurant (☎ 817 2450, Yingxiong Nanlu) Dishes Y18-25. This

TSANG

place hopes to lure travellers in with its oversized TV screening VCD gems such as *The Sound of Music*. It serves up Western, Chinese and Tibetan fare.

Muslim Restaurant (Yingxiong Nanlu) Mains Y5-10. If you're after something a bit cheaper, try this place on the other side of the road where you can get a good plate of *ganbian* (home-made noodles fried with yak meat). The *chao mianpian* (fried noodle squares) are also recommended.

You can breakfast on *baozi* (Chinese dumplings) and *xifan* (rice porridge) in many of the *Chinese restaurants* opposite the Gyantse Hotel. For those who want to self-cater, there's a grocery store by the junction.

Getting There & Away

You may be able to track down a little-known minibus service that runs direct from Lhasa to Gyantse from the main bus station at around 6.30am on alternate days (Y63, eight hours). It returns the next day from Gyantse's main intersection at around 7am.

It's easier, however, to get to Gyantse from Shigatse and if you take this route you can get a permit for the trip. Minibuses depart from in front of Shigatse's main bus station from around 10am to 6pm daily (Y25, two to three hours). If you're starting from Lhasa, minibuses arrive in Shigatse from the capital at around 3pm, so it's possible to get all the way to Gyantse in one day. Minibuses from Gyantse to Shigatse leave around 8am or 9am daily from the main intersection in Gyantse.

Hitching to Yamdrok-tso is not easy; you're best off walking a way along the road and trying from there. You'll probably get a lift as far as the hydroelectric engineering works, 30km east of Gyantse, where there is a minor checkpoint that only bothers during 'emergencies'. From here hitching is tricky and your best bet is to walk about 1km east and hope for a truck bound for Nangartse.

Getting Around

All of Gyantse's sights can be reached comfortably on foot, which is just as well because apart from a few stray pedicabs there

is not much else. You can hire bikes from the Gyantse Hotel for a pricey Y5 per hour.

TSECHEN MONASTERY & FORT

The traditional village of Tsechen is around 5km north-west of Gyantse and offers a nice half-day trip out of the town. There is a small monastery above the village but the main reason to hike out here is to climb up the ruined fortress, wander along the defensive walls and enjoy great views of the (often flooded) river valley below. It's a good idea to bring a picnic.

The fortress was believed to have been built as early as the 14th century and was used by the British during their 1904 invasion, although it was already partly ruined by then. It's possible to hike up to the right side of the fortress and then cross over to the highest ramparts on the left.

To get to Tsechen you can either walk or hitch along the southern Friendship Hwy to Shigatse. The village is just past the turn-off south to Yatung. On the way back it's possible to cut through fields to the river and follow this back to the Gyantse Bridge. You might get a lift back on a tractor for a couple of yuan, otherwise it's an hour-long walk.

YUNGDRUNGLING MONASTERY

The Bönpo Yungdrungling Monastery *(admission free)* makes an impressive sight across the river on the northern road between Lhasa and Shigatse. It was once the second most influential Bönpo monastic institution in Tibet (the first was at nearby Menri) and home to 700 monks. The number of monks occupying the monastery is now limited to 45 by the Chinese government.

The monastery was destroyed during the Cultural Revolution and is now filled with the smell of fresh paint as the monks slowly rebuild it with their meagre funds. To the average visitor, Yungdrungling looks much like a Buddhist monastery – but note the swastikas swirling anticlockwise and remember to make the rounds in an anticlockwise direction as well. Foreigners are only permitted to visit the large dukhang, which houses the impressive thrones of the monastery's two resident lamas. There are

1300 small iron statues of Shiromo (Sakya Thukpa) lining the walls.

The monastery is 170km west of Lhasa on the north bank of the Yarlung Tsangpo (Brahmaputra River), just east of the point where the Nangung-chu meets it. You can easily cross the Yarlung Tsangpo via the ferry at Tadruka, but note that the ferry only runs when a vehicle is crossing. Foreigners are charged Y1/30 per passenger/vehicle. Once on the northern bank, follow the road for 2km along the Nangung-chu until you reach a footbridge across it. From here it's about 1km up to the monastery.

However, it's more fun to hire a yak-skin boat for the trip at Tadruka (around Y15 per person return). The current is very strong but the local boatmen are experts at manoeuvring their boats across this stretch of the river.

SHIGATSE
☎ 0892 • elevation 3900m
Around 250km to the south-west of Lhasa (via the northern Friendship Hwy), Shigatse is the second-largest town in Tibet and the traditional capital of Tsang. Since the Mongol sponsorship of the Gelugpa order, Shigatse has been the seat of the Panchen Lama, who is traditionally based in Tashilhunpo Monastery. Tashilhunpo is one of the highlights of Tibet and is Shigatse's foremost attraction.

The town has long been an important trading and administrative centre. The Tsang kings exercised their power from the once imposing heights of the Shigatse Dzong – the present ruins only hint at its former glory – and the fort later became the residence of the governor of Tsang.

Far too many travellers speed through Shigatse on their way to the Nepali border, leaving just one afternoon to poke around Tashilhunpo and a night to rest up. This is a pity because, while it may not be brimming with sights, Shigatse is a good place to hang out, kick back, and enjoy a few beers on the roof of the Tenzin Hotel gazing across at the ruins of the fort. It's also one of the few places in Tsang with reliable and frequent public transport connections with Lhasa.

During the second week of the fifth lunar month (June/July), Tashilhunpo Monastery becomes the scene of a three-day festival and a huge thangka is hung.

Orientation
Shigatse is not a particularly big town, but orientation can initially be a bit confusing. Like most modern Tibetan towns, it is divided into a distinct Tibetan quarter and a newer Chinatown.

The old Tibetan part of town is for the most part clustered higgledy-piggledy between Tashilhunpo Monastery and the high ramparts of the Shigatse Dzong. Here you'll find the Tibetan market and the Tenzin Hotel. Tashilhunpo Monastery effectively marks the western extent of town – beyond it is a nomad encampment – while the Shigatse Dzong does the same thing to the north.

The rapidly expanding Chinese part of town comprises two wide boulevards lined with building-block concrete cubes of the style beloved by Chinese town planners. They run north-south parallel to each other: Shandong Lu holds the main post office, and Jiefang Zhonglu has the Shigatse Hotel and the Bank of China.

Information
Money The Bank of China is next door to the Shigatse Hotel on Jiefang Zhonglu and exchanges money from around 9.30am to 1pm and 3.30pm to 6.30pm Monday to Friday. It's also open on Saturday and Sunday from 10am to 3pm in summer and 10am to 5pm in winter. Travellers cheques and cash in most currencies can be changed with a minimum of fuss, but it is not possible to arrange credit-card advances – you will have to go to Lhasa to do this.

Post & Communications The main post office is open 9am to noon and 4pm to 7pm. It is possible to send international letters and postcards from here, but *not* international parcels. You can send faxes and make international phone calls at the telecom office, 200m west of the post office on Zhufeng Lu (open until 11pm).

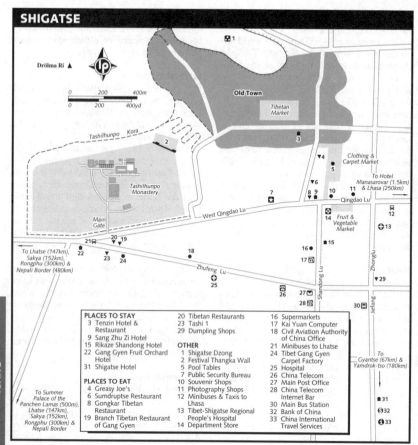

SHIGATSE

Drölma Ri ▲

0   200   400m
0   200   400yd

Old Town

Tibetan Market

Tashilhunpo   Kora

Clothing & Carpet Market

To Hotel Manasarovar (1.5km) & Lhasa (250km)

Tashilhunpo Monastery

Qingdao Lu

Main Gate

West Qingdao Lu

Fruit & Vegetable Market

To Lhatse (147km), Sakya (152km), Rongphu (300km) & Nepali Border (480km)

Zhufeng Lu

Shandong Lu

Zhonglu

Jiefang

To Gyantse (67km) & Yamdrok-tso (180km)

To Summer Palace of the Panchen Lamas (500m), Lhatse (147km), Sakya (152km), Rongphu (300km) & Nepali Border

PLACES TO STAY	20 Tibetan Restaurants	16 Supermarkets
3 Tenzin Hotel & Restaurant	23 Tashi 1	17 Kai Yuan Computer
9 Sang Zhu Zi Hotel	29 Dumpling Shops	18 Civil Aviation Authority of China Office
15 Rikaze Shandong Hotel		21 Minibuses to Lhatse
22 Gang Gyen Fruit Orchard Hotel	OTHER	24 Tibet Gang Gyen Carpet Factory
31 Shigatse Hotel	1 Shigatse Dzong	25 Hospital
	2 Festival Thangka Wall	26 China Telecom
PLACES TO EAT	6 Pool Tables	27 Main Post Office
4 Greasy Joe's	7 Public Security Bureau	28 China Telecom Internet Bar
6 Sumdruptse Restaurant	10 Souvenir Shops	30 Main Bus Station
8 Gongkar Tibetan Restaurant	11 Photography Shops	32 Bank of China
19 Branch Tibetan Restaurant of Gang Gyen	12 Minibuses & Taxis to Lhasa	33 China International Travel Services
	13 Tibet-Shigatse Regional People's Hospital	
	14 Department Store	

The China Telecom Internet Bar (☎ 882 1266) is just south of the post office on Shandong Lu and it has a good, fast connection for Y10 per hour. It's open 24 hours and is filled with cigarette smoke and teenagers toting virtual machine guns until the wee hours every night.

Alternatively there's the smaller Kai Yuan Computer (open 9am to 10pm daily) on Shandong Lu. It also charges Y10 per hour for Internet access.

Permits Shigatse is an open town and so a permit is not required. However, most other areas of Tsang are closed and you need to get a permit from the PSB in Shigatse to visit these or risk a fine of up to Y500. If you are on an official organised tour your agency will take care of all permits for you, but if you're travelling down to the Nepali border on the cheap your journey will be much easier if you can get a permit from the Shigatse PSB.

At the time of writing the PSB was issuing seven-day permits for all towns along the Friendship Hwy to the border (including Sakya, Rongphu and Everest Base Camp). Three-day permits for Gyantse and Shalu

Monastery were also available, but only with a Y200 deposit reclaimable upon return to Shigatse. The cost of any permit (no matter how many destinations it covers) is Y50 per person.

But be warned – it has not always been this easy. Recently many travellers have been refused permits for independent travel in Shigatse and the authorities could step up the restrictions again at any time. Your best bet is to ask other travellers, as the rules change like the wind. If you have trouble you could try asking for advice from Shigatse's China International Travel Service (CITS); for details, see Getting There & Away later in this section. CITS can book you a tour with all the necessary permits and they've even helped some travellers to get individual travel permits.

The PSB office is on Qingdao Xilu (signposted West Qingdao Lu) and is open 9am to 1pm and 4pm to 7pm Monday to Friday; if you're lucky you might catch it open on the weekend as well. This office does not have the power to extend your visa – you'll have to go to Lhasa to do this.

Tashilhunpo Monastery

Tashilhunpo Monastery (☎ 882 2114, West Qingdao Lu; admission Y45/55 without/with souvenir CD-ROM; open around 9am-noon & 4pm-6.30pm daily) is one of the six great Gelugpa institutions, along with Drepung, Sera and Ganden in Lhasa, and the Kumbum and Labrang in Amdo. It was founded in 1447 by a disciple of Tsongkhapa, Genden Drup. Genden Drup was retroactively named the first Dalai Lama and he is enshrined in Tashilhunpo. Despite its association with the first Dalai Lama, Tashilhunpo was initially isolated from the mainstream of Gelugpa affairs, which were centred in the Lhasa region. The monastery's standing rocketed, however, when the fifth Dalai Lama declared his teacher – then abbot of Tashilhunpo – to be a manifestation of Öpagme (Amitabha; a deification of the Buddha's faculty of perfected cognition and perception). Thus Tashilhunpo became the seat of an important lineage: the Panchen Lamas.

Panchen means 'great scholar' and the title was traditionally bestowed on abbots of Tashilhunpo. But with the establishment of the Panchen Lama lineage of spiritual and temporal leaders – second only to the Dalai Lamas themselves – the spectre of possible rivalry was introduced into the Gelugpa order. Naturally it did not take long to emerge. The next Panchen Lama was declared ruler of Tsang and western Tibet by the Qing dynasty in China, a move that has been seen by many as part of a continuing effort by the Chinese to manipulate a schism between the Panchen Lama and the Dalai Lama.

Of course it is arguable that such a schism did not require much prompting on the part of the Chinese. There have long been disputes between Lhasa and Shigatse over the autonomy of Tashilhunpo. In the early 1920s, a dispute between the ninth Panchen Lama and the 13th Dalai Lama over taxes (and ultimately Tashilhunpo's right to self-rule) led to the flight of the Panchen Lama to China. The ninth Panchen Lama never returned to Tibet. His successor, the 10th Panchen Lama, never escaped Chinese clutches and was largely kept in Beijing, only occasionally visiting Tashilhunpo. He died in 1989 (see the boxed text 'The Panchen Lamas' later in this chapter).

From the entrance to the monastery, visitors get a grand view. Above the white monastic quarters is a crowd of ochre buildings topped with gold – the tombs of the past Panchen Lamas. To the right, and higher still, is the great white wall that is hung with massive, colourful thangkas during festivals. The entire complex is surrounded by a high wall.

Information Tashilhunpo is one of the few monasteries in Tibet that weathered the stormy seas of the Cultural Revolution relatively unscathed. It is a real pleasure to explore the busy cobbled lanes twisting around the ancient buildings – the monastery is essentially a walled town in its own right. Go to Tashilhunpo several times if you can – there really is too much to see in a single visit.

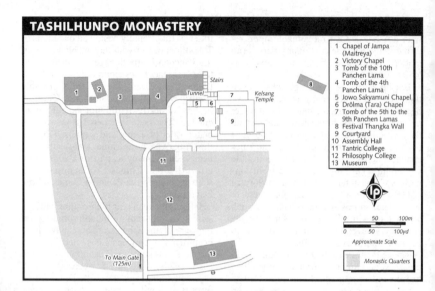

TASHILHUNPO MONASTERY

1 Chapel of Jampa (Maitreya)
2 Victory Chapel
3 Tomb of the 10th Panchen Lama
4 Tomb of the 4th Panchen Lama
5 Jowo Sakyamuni Chapel
6 Drölma (Tara) Chapel
7 Tomb of the 5th to the 9th Panchen Lamas
8 Festival Thangka Wall
9 Courtyard
10 Assembly Hall
11 Tantric College
12 Philosophy College
13 Museum

On the downside, the monastery has a very high profile as the largest functioning monastic institution in Tibet, a fact that does not escape the government. The monks here are sometimes unfriendly and there is conjecture that many of the English-speaking monks are in cohorts with the Chinese authorities. Be careful about voicing controversial opinions, and certainly don't hand out any Dalai Lama pictures.

Opening and closing hours at Tashilhunpo are fairly arbitrary. You may be told by monks at, say, 5pm (after you have already bought your ticket), that the monastery is closing in half an hour. If this happens they will usually let you in on the same ticket the next morning. It costs Y2 to park a Land Cruiser in front of the monastery.

There are severe restrictions on photography inside the monastic buildings. The going cost for a photograph varies, but be prepared for a pricey Y75 fee. This should cover a full roll of film.

Unfortunately, many of the smaller chapels that were once open to the public have been closed recently for renovation, including chapels inside the Kelsang Temple and the seven chapels in the Palace of the Panchen Lamas (although with luck they will reopen again soon). If you're very keen you could try asking one of the monks to find the keys. It's still possible to visit all the main buildings within the complex.

Chapel of Jampa Walk up through the monastery and bear left for the first and probably the most impressive of Tashilhunpo's sights – the Chapel of Jampa (Maitreya). An entire building is hollowed out to house the world's largest gilded statue – a 26m image of Jampa (Maitreya), the Future Buddha. It was made in 1914 under the auspices of the ninth Panchen Lama and took some 900 artisans and labourers four years to complete.

The impressive, finely crafted and serene-looking statue looms over the viewer. Each of Jampa's fingers is over 1m long, and more than 300kg of gold went into his coating, much of which is also studded with precious stones. On the walls surrounding the image are a thousand more gold paintings of Jampa against a red background.

Victory Chapel This chapel is a centre for philosophy and houses a large statue of

Tsongkhapa flanked by Jampa and Jampel-yang (Manjushri). If it's not open, ask one of the monks to let you in.

Tomb of the 10th Panchen Lama This impressive gold-plated funeral chörten holds the remains of the 10th Panchen Lama, who died in 1989 (see the boxed text 'The Panchen Lamas' later in this chapter). His image is displayed in front of the tomb, surrounded by kaleidoscopic rainbow swirls. The ceiling of the chapel is painted with a Kalachakra mandala and the walls are painted with real gold buddhas.

Tomb of the Fourth Panchen Lama The 11m silver-and-gold funerary chörten of the fourth Panchen Lama (1570–1662) was the only tomb chörten to escape destruction during the Cultural Revolution.

From here you pass through a dark walkway that leads out to the Kelsang Temple complex.

Kelsang Temple The centrepiece of this remarkable collection of buildings is a large **courtyard**, the focus of festival and monastic activities. This is a fascinating place to sit and watch the pilgrims and monks go about their business. Monks congregate here before their lunch-time service in the main assembly hall. A huge prayer pole rears up from the centre of the flagged courtyard, while the surrounding walls are painted with buddhas. There are splendid photo opportunities here.

The **assembly hall** is one of the oldest buildings in Tashilhunpo, dating back to the 15th-century founding of the monastery. The huge throne dominating the centre of the hall is the throne of the Panchen Lamas. The hall is an atmospheric place, with rows of mounted cushions for monks, and impressive thangkas depicting the various incarnations of the Panchen Lama suspended from the ceiling. The central inner chapel holds a wonderful statue of Sakyamuni, while the chapel to the right holds several images of Drölma (Tara). On the floor above the assembly hall is a tangle of small chapels currently closed to visitors.

You can also visit the huge new **Tomb of the Fifth to the Ninth Panchen Lamas**, built by the 10th Panchen to replace tombs destroyed in the Cultural Revolution. The Panchen Lama returned to Shigatse from Beijing to dedicate the tomb in 1989. He fulfilled his prediction that he would die on Tibetan soil just three days after the ceremony.

Other Buildings As you leave Tashilhunpo, it is also possible to visit the monastery's two remaining colleges. They are on the left-hand side as you walk down towards the main gate. The first is the **Tantric College** and the second is the brown **Philosophy College**. Neither is particularly interesting, but you might be lucky and find yourself in time for debating, which is held in the courtyard of the Philosophy College.

A new **museum** *(admission Y5)* has been opened a few hundred metres east of the main entrance to promote the friendly periods in the relationship between the 10th Panchen Lama and the Chinese government. There was not much of interest in the museum at the time of writing, but there are plans to open more rooms. Check out the scale model of Tashilhunpo and the photograph of the 10th Panchen Lama with former Australian prime minister Bob Hawke.

Tashilhunpo Kora The *kora* (pilgrimage path) around Tashilhunpo takes just an hour to walk around and provides photogenic views of the monastery.

From the main gate, follow the monastery walls in a clockwise direction and look out for an alley on the right. The alley follows the western wall for a while before opening out into a wider trail that leads into the hills above Tashilhunpo. The trail leads up past rock paintings of Guru Rinpoche and Chenresig (Avalokiteshvara) to the 13-storey white wall used to hang a giant thangka at festival time. The path then splits in two: down the hill to complete the circuit of the monastery, and (more interesting) along a ridge to the ruins of Shigatse Dzong, a walk of around 15 to 20 minutes.

For those staying at the Tenzin Hotel, the kora can also be approached by turning left

TSANG

out of the hotel and following the road past Tibetan homes before bearing left at the walls of the monastery. This alley leads down to the main road and to the entrance of the monastery, where you can continue along the kora, finishing back on the trail that leads back to the hotel. To avoid giving offence, try to follow the route clockwise.

Shigatse Dzong

Once the residence of the kings of Tsang and later the governor of Tsang, very little remains of the dzong. It was destroyed in the popular uprising of 1959. Pictures taken before the Chinese occupation, however, show an impressive structure that bears a remarkable resemblance to the Potala, albeit a smaller version.

The main attraction of the Shigatse Dzong today are the views it commands over Shigatse and the surrounding valleys. One approach is via the Tashilhunpo kora. The other is to turn left out of the Tenzin Hotel and after about 200m look for a paved alley

---

The Panchen Lamas

Traditional abbots of Tashilhunpo Monastery, frequent rivals to the central authority of Lhasa and often pawns in Chinese designs on the high plateau, the Panchen Lamas have been the focus of decidedly unspiritual squabbles. The ninth Panchen Lama (1883–1937) spent the last of his days in the clutches of a Chinese Nationalist warlord after attempting to use the Chinese as leverage to gain greater influence in Tibet during a disagreement with the 13th Dalai Lama. His reincarnation grew up in the control of the Chinese.

This Chinese connection hung over the 10th Panchen Lama like a grim cloud, and he was regarded with suspicion by his own people for much of his life. Even his authenticity was subject to doubt. There had been at least two other candidates for the position in Tibet itself, but the Chinese had forced Tibetan delegates in Beijing in 1951 to endorse the Chinese choice. It is said that in 1949, the 11-year-old Panchen Lama had written to Mao Zedong asking him to 'liberate' Tibet, although, to give him credit, it is unlikely he did it of his own volition. When the Panchen Lama became joint chairperson (with the Dalai Lama) of the Preparatory Committee for the Autonomous Region of Tibet (Pcart) and later vice-chairman of China's National People's Congress, it was commonly felt that he was a mere Chinese puppet.

The 10th Panchen Lama

By the time he died of a heart attack at Shigatse in 1989, however, the Panchen Lama was regarded throughout Tibet as a hero. From his triumphant arrival at Tashilhunpo Monastery as the Chinese trump card in 1951, the Panchen Lama had become by 1965 a 'big rock on the road to socialism' according to Chinese authorities. What happened?

It seems likely that the Panchen Lama had a major change of heart about his Chinese benefactors after the 1959 Lhasa uprising. In September 1961, the Panchen Lama presented Mao with a 70,000-character catalogue of the atrocities acted upon Tibet, and a plea for increased freedoms. The answer was a demand that he denounce the Dalai Lama as a reactionary and take the latter's place as spiritual head of Tibet. Not only did the Panchen Lama refuse but, in 1964, with tens of thousands of Tibetans gathered in Lhasa for the Mönlam festival, he announced to the crowds that he believed Tibet would one day regain its independence and the Dalai Lama would return in glory as its leader.

heading north (right). Watch out for dogs. The walk takes around 20 to 30 minutes.

Summer Palace of the Panchen Lamas

This building *(admission Y15)* is about 1km south of the Tashilhunpo Monastery, hidden in a walled compound. The straggly gardens form the Panchen Lamas' version of the Norbulingka, although there's a lot less to see.

The palace was built in 1844 by the Seventh Panchen Lama, Tenpei Nyima, and some of the rooms are open to visitors, including a number of **chapels** on the ground floor, the 10th Panchen Lama's lavishly adorned **sitting rooms** on the 1st floor, and his impressive **audience chamber** on the 2nd floor. On holidays the grounds are a popular picnic spot.

Places to Stay

Don't expect to get much sleep in Shigatse. By around 10pm packs of dogs begin to wake up with a few yelps and howls and by

The Panchen Lamas

It must have come as a shock to the Chinese to see their protege turn on them so ungratefully. They responded in time-honoured fashion by throwing the Panchen Lama into jail, where he remained for 14 years, suffering abuse and torture. His crimes, according to the Chinese, included participating in orgies, 'criticising China' and raising a private insurrectionary army. A 'smash the Panchen reactionary clique' campaign was mounted, and those close to the Panchen Lama were subject to 'struggle sessions' and in some cases were imprisoned.

After emerging from prison in early 1978, the Panchen Lama rarely spoke in outright defiance of the Chinese authorities, but continued to use what influence he had to press for the preservation of Tibetan cultural traditions. It is believed that shortly before his death he again fell out with the Chinese, arguing at a high-level meeting in Beijing that the Chinese occupation had brought nothing but misery and hardship to his people. Accordingly, many Tibetans believe that he died not of a heart attack but by poisoning. Others maintain that, exhausted and perhaps despairing, the Panchen Lama came home in 1989 to die as he always said he would on Tibetan soil.

Of course in Tibet the story doesn't just end here. In May 1995 the Dalai Lama identified Gedhun Choekyi Nyima, a six-year-old boy from Amdo, as the reincarnation of the Panchen Lama. Within a month the boy had been forcibly relocated to a government compound in Beijing and an irate Chinese government had ordered the senior lamas of Tashilhunpo to come up with a second, Chinese-approved choice. Chadrel Rinpoche, the abbot who lead the search that identified Gedhun, was later imprisoned for six years for 'splitting the country' and 'colluding with separatist forces abroad' (ie, consulting the Dalai Lama), and Tashilhunpo was closed to tourists for a few months.

Tashilhunpo's lamas eventually settled on Gyancain Norbu, the son of Communist Party members, who was formally approved in a carefully orchestrated ceremony. Beijing's interest is not only to control the education of Tibet's number-two spiritual leader, but also to influence the boy who could later himself be influential in identifying the reincarnation of the Dalai Lama.

Meanwhile the young 11th Panchen Lama remains under house arrest at an undisclosed location in China, causing him to be dubbed the 'world's youngest political prisoner'. For his ninth birthday the Canadian embassy presented Gedhun with 1000 birthday cards from well-wishers. His future remains uncertain though, as the Chinese don't appear to have softened their attitude towards him. In May 2001 Chadrel Rinpoche was due to be released from his six-year sentence. However, his prison sentence was reportedly extended until January 2002.

There are a number of groups campaigning to free the Panchen Lama. Check out the Web sites of the Tashilhunpo Monastery (**W** www.tashilhunpo.org/panchen.html), the Australia Tibet Council (**W** www.atc.org.au), and the Canada Tibet Committee, which has a page designed for kids (**W** www.tibet.ca/panchenlama).

midnight the night-time silence is torn to shreds by a cacophony of blood-curdling canine cries of attack and wild retreat.

Places to Stay – Budget

Tenzin Hotel (☎ 882 2018) Dorm beds from Y25, singles Y50, doubles Y60-80. The Tenzin, opposite the Tibetan market, is the most popular budget place in Shigatse, but be warned it's far from perfect: The hot showers trickle out before the end of their official hours (8pm to 10pm), you may find yourself sleeping on an itchy carpet and some of the walls are paper-thin. But apart from these small gripes (this is Tibet after all), the Tenzin is a delightful little inn. The upstairs veranda is a great place to lounge around in the late afternoons and evenings, and they even keep cold beer in the fridge. The modern double rooms have a view of the fort but can be noisy.

Gang Gyen Fruit Orchard Hotel (☎ 882 2282, 9 Zhufeng Lu) Dorm beds Y15, doubles/triples/quads Y40/30/25 per bed. The other hotel that sees a fair number of foreign guests is opposite the entrance to Tashilhunpo Monastery, and it comes from the concrete-box school of Chinese hotel design. The hot showers are unreliable, but at least it's pretty clean and the rooms have a TV. The hotel has a perfect location for visiting Tashilhunpo or for catching a morning minibus to Lhatse. The monastery owns the guesthouse, and 50% of its earnings go back there.

Places to Stay – Mid-Range & Top End

Hotel Manasarovar (☎ 883 2000, fax 882 8111, 20 Qingdao Lu) Dorm beds/doubles Y40/120. This new hotel is in the eastern end of town. It's a bit of a hike from the action but it's the best value for money in Shigatse. Rooms are spacious and spotless and have a TV, and the opulent shared bathrooms have 24-hour hot water. At the time of writing, a new wing was under construction; it will have rooms with private bathrooms. Prices sometimes drop to Y30 for dorm beds and Y80 for doubles when the hotel is not busy.

Sang Zhu Zi Hotel (☎ 882 2280, fax 882 1135, Qingdao Lu) Doubles with private bathroom Y182. Just down the road and around the corner from the Tenzin is this Chinese-style hotel, an uninspiring but comfortable-enough place to stay. It's often booked out by tour groups.

Rikaze Shandong Hotel (☎ 882 6138, fax 882 6124, 5 Shandong Lu) Singles/doubles with private bathroom Y558/588. This overpriced and soulless new hotel overlooks Shandong Lu from nine ugly storeys. It hopes to impress with its gargantuan chandelier, elevator and oxygen machines, but the hot water is unpredictable and the carpets are already stained; rooms have a TV. With a bit of bargaining you can knock Y50 to Y250 off the price depending on the season, but it's hardly worth the effort.

Shigatse Hotel (☎ 882 2525, fax 882 1900, 13 Jiefang Zhonglu) Singles & doubles Y400, triples Y450. The inconveniently located Shigatse Hotel is in the south of town next to the Bank of China. Prices here are reasonably negotiable, as occupancy rates are always likely to be low. The Chinese- and Tibetan-style rooms have private bathrooms with 24-hour hot water. High-flyers might like to inquire about the standard/Tibetan suites at Y980/1540. There's a 20% discount on all rooms from November to March.

Places to Eat

Shigatse is swarming with good restaurants, most of which are Chinese. Many travellers find the food here better than in Lhasa.

Sumdruptse Restaurant (☎ 882 4514) Meals Y10-20. This is the best restaurant of the collection near the Tenzin Hotel. It's a cavernous place with many rooms, including Chinese and Tibetan wings, and also has Western, Indian, Nepali and Japanese dishes on the menu. The food's great, the staff are friendly and what's more, they serve real coffee.

Greasy Joe's Breakfast Y3-5. Returned to this strip after being demolished in 1998, this is a good cheapie for breakfast. It serves up Chinese dishes in a flash for lunch or dinner as well. True to its name, Greasy

Joe's has a set of very greasy stairs to climb if there are no tables downstairs.

Tenzin Restaurant *(☎ 882 2018, Ground floor, Tenzin Hotel)* Meals Y8-25. This backpacker place is convenient if you're staying at the Tenzin Hotel. If there's no-one around to take your order, go through the back to the kitchen to rustle someone up.

Gongkar Tibetan Restaurant *(☎ 882 1139, Qingdao Lu)* Dishes Y10. Open late. West of the Sang Zhu Zi Hotel, this restaurant is Chinese-run but has an English menu.

The best area for Tibetan food is the west end of Zhufeng Lu, opposite the Gang Gyen Fruit Orchard.

Branch Tibetan Restaurant of Gang Gyen *(☎ 882 7788, Zhufeng Lu)* Dishes Y8-25. Owned by the monastery, this place is full of Tashilhunpo monks slurping on their *thugpa* (a traditional Tibetan noodle dish). Try the tasty vegie momo soup for Y6.

Tashi 1 *(☎ 882 2516, Zhufeng Lu)* Meals Y10-18. This friendly place sports the usual long menu of Chinese dishes. Be warned: The back room is armed with an elaborate karaoke VCD setup that may be loaded.

There are also some ***dumpling shops*** across the intersection from the main bus station – a good place to grab a snack while waiting for a bus.

If you're self-catering and you get up early you'll find a great range of fresh produce at the ***fruit and vegetable market*** *(Qingdao Lu)* from around 5.30am.

Shopping

Tibetan market In front of the Tenzin Hotel, this is probably the best place outside Lhasa to pick up souvenirs such as prayer wheels, rosaries and thangkas. Bargain hard.

Clothing and carpet market This market, near the old town, has a disintegrating collection of outdoor pool tables at the northern end – a good place to meet the locals.

Tibet Gang Gyen Carpet Factory *(☎ 882 2733, W www.tapis-du-tibet.com, 9 Zhufeng Lu)* Open 9am-1pm & 3pm-7pm daily. A five-minute walk from Tashilhunpo (follow the enormous signs), this slick French operation exports carpets to America and Europe. Women work on the carpets on the premises, singing as they weave, trim and spin, and you are free to take photographs. Expect to pay around US$200 plus shipping for a carpet measuring 185cm x 90cm.

Getting There & Away

From Lhasa to Shigatse, most travellers use the minibus service (Y38, about seven hours). Minibuses depart when full from 7.30am daily from the corner of Dekyi Shar Lam and Ramoche Lam (near the Kirey Hotel) in Lhasa. Some of the minibuses have been stopped and fined and the drivers told that they are not to take foreign passengers. If this happens you will be kicked off the bus, but most people get through without incident. Returning minibuses leave from around 8am to 9am from a crossroads on the eastern side of Shigatse. You can also catch the slower and less comfortable public bus service which runs from the main Lhasa bus station for the same price as the minibus.

Taxis do the trip from Lhasa to Shigatse for around Y70 per person (four hours), and wait for fares near the spot where the minibuses depart. You might even be able to find a seat in a Land Cruiser here for as little as Y50.

The Civil Aviation Authority of China (CAAC) runs a daily bus direct to the airport from its office on Zhufeng Lu for Y50. Book your ticket in advance.

Buses to Gyantse (Y25, two to three hours) depart about every two hours from the main bus station from 10am until 6pm daily.

Minibuses heading west leave from the junction outside Tashilhunpo Monastery. There are minibuses every other day at 8am for Sakya (Y27, six hours). These return to Shigatse the next day, so you get either an afternoon or 2½ days at Sakya – neither one is ideal. Minibuses for Lhatse depart daily at around 8am (Y30, five hours).

You can arrange to get on the Ali bus in Shigatse, but you must buy your ticket in Lhasa first. For details, see Ali in the Ngari (Western Tibet) chapter.

Those aiming for the Nepali border or Tingri really have very few options. One possibility is to inquire at the Shigatse or Tenzin Hotels about minibuses or Land

Cruisers heading out to the border to pick up tour groups. The cost for hooking up with one of these starts at Y400 but if demand is low you can negotiate down to Y250 or less. You will probably need to ask for three or four days in a row before you get lucky, and there is always the chance that you will not. Otherwise start hitching from Lhatse.

Renting vehicles in Shigatse is more difficult than in Lhasa. CITS (☎ 882 9688) is the only official agency in town. Its office next to the Shigatse Hotel is often closed, but you can track someone down through the Tashi 1 restaurant near Tashilhunpo Monastery (see Places to Eat earlier). CITS's prices are not cheap but it can arrange a permit for you if you can't get one directly from the PSB. Sample prices are Y3400 per vehicle for a three-day round-trip to Rongphu, or Y5000 to Rongphu and on to the border. Permits are extra (Y50 per person for the PSB permit and Y65 per person for entry to the Everest region), but unlike some of the tours offered in Lhasa, the price includes the Y405 charge for vehicle entry to the Everest region.

You could also try to hire a Land Cruiser unofficially by talking to the drivers who park outside the Tenzin Hotel. Expect to pay Y2500 to Y3000 for a vehicle to Rongphu and the Nepali border, but you'll have to arrange your own permits with the PSB and pay the entrance fees to Everest separately.

Getting Around

Shigatse is not that big and can be comfortably explored on foot. For trips out to the

---

Kilometre Markers along the Friendship Highway

The following towns, geographical features and points of interest along with their appropriate kilometre markers (signifying distance from Beijing) may be of help to travellers, hitchhikers and, in particular, mountain bikers. One point worth bearing in mind is that the kilometre-marker system changes at some points, and in certain regions the markers have disappeared – sometimes turning up as doorsteps in new buildings. There are enough of them left, however, for you to be able to keep a fairly accurate track of your progress and identify turn-offs to places of interest.

Lhasa to Shigatse

marker	feature
4646	Lhasa's eastern crossroads to Golmud or Shigatse
4656	Sakyamuni Buddha rock painting
4662	Netang village and Drölma Lhakhang
4673	Bridge on left to picnic grounds
4695–97	Chushul
4703	Bridge over the Yarlung Tsangpo to Nangartse; shops and restaurants
4712	Hydroelectric project on the far side of the river – the structure shaped like a golf ball atop the hill is a radar and meteorological centre
4718	Ruined fortress on left and village
4724	Village and ruined dzong
4732	Jagged peaks ahead and valley begins to narrow
4758	Bridge and road to Nyemo to north; restaurants
4768	Suspension footbridge to left
4780	Bridge over to south side
4801	Checkpoint, turn-off to Gyantse and shops
4821	Traduka – ferry to Yungdrungling Monastery and Yangpachen; restaurants
4857	Tree plantation
4876	Ferry to north bank
4900–05	Shigatse

Shigatse to Tingri

marker	feature
4900–05	Shigatse
4917	Nartang Monastery
4928	Gyeli village
4933	Very gentle mountain pass of Tso-la (4500m)
4936	Kangchen Monastery to right
4960–61	Gyading – checkpoint, ruined fort, restaurants and shops
4973	Dilong village

Shigatse Hotel, or just for fun, you might want to use the pedicabs or the tractors, which are abundant – there is usually a small crowd of them on every corner. Prices are negotiable, but should work out to around Y3 per head after a little haggling. A ride in a tractor from the centre of town to Tashilhunpo should cost Y3. A ride anywhere in town in one of the many taxis will cost Y10.

AROUND SHIGATSE

There are a number of sights around Shigatse, although few of them are visited by Western travellers, mainly because of access difficulties. En route to Lhatse you can visit **Nartang Monastery**, a Kadampa monastery famed for wood-block printing the Nartang

canon in the 18th century, and **Kangchen Monastery** – both are signposted in English just off the Friendship Hwy. For information on the trek from Shalu to Nartang see the Trekking chapter. It is even possible to visit Gyantse as a day trip from Shigatse.

If you're heading to Lhatse by Land Cruiser you can detour off the Friendship Hwy to check out Phuntsoling Monastery and the Jonang Kumbum (for details, see Around Lhatse later in this chapter).

Shalu Monastery

Shalu Monastery *(admission Y25)* is around 19km south of Shigatse, a few kilometres off the Shigatse-Gyantse road, and is easily spotted because of its Chinese-style, green-tiled roof. The monastery, which dates back

Kilometre Markers along the Friendship Highway

marker	feature	marker	feature
4977	Turn-off to Phuntsoling Monastery	5170	Village
4985–5005	Sealed road (in bad condition in places)	5193–94	Tingri
5000	Marker showing 5000km from Beijing, small monastery and dzong	**Tingri to Nyalam**	
5009	Village and start of climb to pass	**marker**	**feature**
5014	Tropu-la (4950m)	5193–94	Tingri
5028	Sakya bridge – turn-off to Sakya	5206	Tsamda Hot Springs
5036	Ruined dzong	5216	Two small Tibetan guesthouses
5041	Village and turn-off to Dongaba Hot Springs	5232	Gutso village; guesthouse and restaurant
5052–53	Lhatse	5237	Village on west side of the river
5058	Checkpoint and turn-off to western Tibet	5254	Small guesthouse and restaurant
5063	Start of climb to pass, with a height gain of around 1000m	5258	Ngakyoong monastery turn-off
		5276	La Lung-la (5124m)
5083	Gyatso-la (5220m)	5282	Bridge
5100	Terrible roads 5km either way	5289	Tong-la (5120m) and view of Cho Oyu and Mt Everest
5114	Views of Everest and the Himalaya	5292	Short cut down the hillside, used by Land Cruiser drivers
5124	Nunnery and fortress	5303	Roadworkers' hostel and village
5133–42	Good sealed road	5311	Village
5133	Shegar and turn-off to main town	5334	Gangka village and track to Milarepa's Cave
5139	Shegar checkpoint	5345	Nyalam
5145	Turn-off to Everest Base Camp	5376	Approximate check point
5155	Ruined dzong to left	5378	Zhangmu
5162	Village	5386	Nepali border

TSANG

to the 11th century, rose to prominence in the 14th century, when its abbot Büton Rinchen Drup emerged as the foremost interpreter and compiler of Sanskrit Buddhist texts of his day. A suborder, the Büton, formed around him. Shalu was also a centre for training in skills such as trance walking, made famous by the flying monks of Alexandra David-Neel's *Magic & Mystery in Tibet*.

Shalu is divided into a Tibetan-style monastery, founded in the 10th century, and the Chinese-influenced inner Serkhang, founded in the 15th century. The former was destroyed in the Cultural Revolution, but the Serkhang has survived reasonably well. The design of the monastery represents the paradise of Chenresig (Avalokiteshvara), a haven from all worldly suffering.

Shalu is noted for its 14th-century murals which fuse Chinese, Mongol and Nepali Newari styles, but it's hard for most non-specialists to discern this much. The best murals line the walls of a corridor that rings the central assembly hall – bring a torch to really appreciate these.

The inner Serkhang contains a statue of Büton on the left side, in front of three 14th-century mandalas. There are also statues of the monastery's founder and the Tantric deity Dukhor (Kalachakra). The west chapel has a black stone statue of Chenresig, the monastery's holiest relic.

From Shalu you can take an hour's walk up to the remote Ri-puk Monastery, a meditation centre with nice views of the Shalu valley. For a map of the valley and details of the trek from Shalu to Nartang, see the Trekking chapter.

The Shalu Monastery is one of the more accessible sights around Shigatse, as it is only 4km south off the main Shigatse-Gyantse road. If you take a Gyantse-bound minibus from Shigatse, get off at the village of Tsündu (also known as Shalu) and look out for the turn-off a couple of hundred metres past a hill covered with prayer flags. From here it's an hour's walk up to Shalu village, passing the small Gyanggong Monastery en route. A shop in Shalu village sells soft drinks, water and pot noodles. Bring a hat, sunscreen and water.

SAKYA
☎ 0892 • elevation 4280m

The monastic town of Sakya is one of Tsang's most significant attractions, and occupies an important place in Tibetan history. Of Sakya's two monasteries, on either side of the Trum-chu, the fortress-like southern monastery is the most interesting. Most of the original, northern monastery has been reduced to picturesque ruins, although restoration work is ongoing.

One characteristic feature of the Sakya region is the colouring of its buildings. Unlike the standard whitewashed effect that you see elsewhere in Tibet, in Sakya the buildings are ash grey with white and red vertical stripes. The colouring is thought to either symbolise the Rigsum Gonpo, who are the three most important bodhisattvas, or stand as a mark of Sakya authority, and at the end of the day it's probably a mixture of both. Sakya literally means 'pale earth'.

Don't expect too much of Sakya in terms of basic comforts – food is good but limited and accommodation is very basic. But if you are doing the grand tour of Tibet – Lhasa and environs, Gyantse, Shigatse, Everest and the border – Sakya offers the opportunity for an overnight stay or longer in a town that has suffered little from the encroachments of the modern Chinese world.

Permits

Officially you need a permit (Y50) from the PSB in Shigatse to visit Sakya, although if you turn up without one, no-one seems to care in the least. Those coming by rented vehicle from Lhasa will have one arranged by their travel agency.

Sakya Monastery

The immense, thick-walled southern monastery (☎ 824 2352; admission Y35/Y45 with/without souvenir CD-ROM) is Sakya's main attraction. Before the Cultural Revolution, Sakya Monastery was one of the largest monasteries in Tibet. It crouches grim and forbidding among the cluster of houses that make up Sakya township. It costs Y2 to park a Land Cruiser near the main entrance; taking photos costs Y5 each or Y20 for a roll.

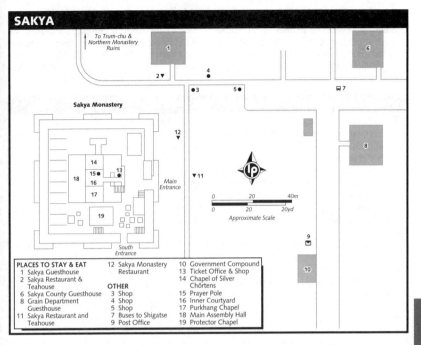

SAKYA

To Trum-chu &
Northern Monastery
Ruins

Sakya Monastery

Main Entrance

South Entrance

0   20   40m
0   20   20yd
Approximate Scale

PLACES TO STAY & EAT		10 Government Compound
1 Sakya Guesthouse	12 Sakya Monastery	13 Ticket Office & Shop
2 Sakya Restaurant &	Restaurant	14 Chapel of Silver
Teahouse		Chörtens
6 Sakya County Guesthouse	OTHER	15 Prayer Pole
8 Grain Department	3 Shop	16 Inner Courtyard
Guesthouse	4 Shop	17 Purkhang Chapel
11 Sakya Restaurant and	5 Shop	18 Main Assembly Hall
Teahouse	7 Buses to Shigatse	19 Protector Chapel
	9 Post Office	

The southern monastery was established in 1268 and is designed defensively, with watchtowers on each of the corners of its high walls. There may once have been further walls intervened by a moat, but no trace of them remains today. It is possible to walk around the top of these outer walls.

Directly ahead of the east-wall main entrance is the entrance to the central courtyard of the monastery, an impressive area with a towering prayer pole that is surrounded by chapels. Try to tag along with a group if possible as the monks will open up more rooms.

The chapel to the left (south) is the **Purkhang Chapel**. Central images are of Sakyamuni (Sakya Thukpa) and Jampelyang (Manjushri), while wall paintings behind depict Tsepame (Amitayus), Drölma (Tara) and Namgyelma (Vijaya), as well as a medicine buddha, two Sakyamunis and Jampa (Maitreya). Murals on the left wall depict Tantric deities central to the Sakya school.

The **main assembly hall** to the west of the courtyard is a huge structure with 3.5m-thick walls. It also tends to be very dark, although the morning sunshine lights the place up with a diffuse ambience. It is still a good idea to bring a good torch with you. The hall's ceiling is supported by massive sacred pillars. In the far corner of the hall is a huge drum.

The walls of the assembly hall are lined with larger-than-life buddhas, many of which also serve as reliquaries for former Sakya abbots. The buddha in the far left corner contains relics of Sakya Pandita; the one next to it houses those of the previous abbot of Sakya. The largest central buddha contains remains of the founder of the monastery. To the right of the central buddha are statues of Jamelyang and a seated Jampa. Sakya's famous **library** is accessed from this hall but it is rarely opened up to tourists.

To the north of the courtyard is a **chapel** containing 11 silver chörtens, again reliquaries for former Sakya abbots. Look to the left for the sand mandala. A door leads to another chapel with more amazing chörtens.

On either side of the east-wall entrance are stairs leading up to the smaller second-floor chapels, including a **Tsepame chapel** with 250 buddha images.

There are a couple of chapels open outside of this central complex, although the most interesting is the very spooky **protector chapel** of the Pakspa Lhakhang, where scary monsters, masks and stuffed wolves await you in the dark recesses.

Priests & Patrons: The Reign of the Sakyapas

It's hard to imagine today how the small town of Sakya would have looked during its glory days as the capital of Tibet from 1268 to 1354. It was here that the fascinating alliance between the Sakya lamas and Mongol Khans developed to rule Tibet. The alliance saved Tibet from the annihilation met by nearby countries trying to resist Mongol advances, and converted the entire Mongolian empire in east Asia to Tibetan Buddhism, led by the Sakya lama.

The Sakya Monastery was founded in 1073 by Kön Könchog Gyelpo (1034–1102), a member of the influential Kön family. The 11th century was a dynamic period in the history of Tibetan Buddhism, largely due to renewed contacts with Indian Buddhists. At this time, the Kagyupa order was founded by Marpa and his disciple Milarepa, and in Sakya, the Kön family established a school that came to be called the Sakyapa.

Unlike most other schools and monasteries that were headed by a succession of incarnate lamas, the abbotship of Sakya was hereditary and restricted to the sons of the Kön family. It is thought that in the early days of Sakya at least one Kön son would marry in order to continue the Kön line, but later the abbots of Sakya themselves married.

By the early 13th century, Sakya had emerged as an important centre of scholastic study. This was initially aided by the assistance of Indian translators such as Shakyashribhada, who came to Sakya in 1204. But before long Tibetan scholars began to make their own unique contributions to Buddhist scholarship. The most famous of these was a Sakya abbot, Kunga Gyaltsen (1182–1251), who came to be known as the Sakya Pandita, literally the 'scholar from Sakya'. Sakya Pandita wrote influential texts on perception and logic, and his learning gave rise to his being identified as a manifestation of Jampelyang (Manjushri), the Bodhisattva of Insight.

There is no doubt that it was Sakya Pandita's scholastic and spiritual eminence that led him to represent the Tibetan people to the Mongol prince Godan (the son of Ghengis Khan) when the Mongols threatened to invade Tibet in the mid-13th century. Sakya Pandita made a three-year journey to Mongolia, arriving in 1247, and after meeting with Godan offered him overlordship of Tibet. Sakya Pandita defended his actions by noting that resistance to the Mongols was pointless – they had already easily conquered Xixia, as well as other kingdoms that had resisted their advances.

After Sakya Pandita's death in 1251, one of his nephews became the abbot of Sakya and, therefore, with the Mongol support of Kublai Khan, also the ruler of all Tibet. This was the first religious government with a lama as head of state, and set an important precedent for Tibetan government.

The association between Tibetan lamas and their Mongol masters (which Tibetans characterised as like the relationship between religious teacher and patron) set yet another important precedent. The association was one that was open to various interpretations, would trouble the Tibetan state for centuries to come and help the Chinese justify claims over the high plateau.

As it was, Mongol overlordship and Sakya supremacy were relatively short-lived. Mongol corruption and rivalry between the Sakyapa and Kagyupa orders led to the fall of Sakya in 1354, when power fell into the hands of the Kagyupa and the seat of government moved to Nedong in Ü.

Sakya was to remain a powerful municipality, however, and like Shigatse enjoyed a high degree of autonomy from successive central governments. Even today, you can see homes across the plateau painted with the red, white and blue-black stripes associated with Sakya Monastery.

Finally, climb up onto the walls of the monastery for superb views of the surrounding valley and the interior buildings of Sakya Monastery.

Northern Monastery Ruins

Very little is left of the monastery complex that once sprawled across the hills north of the Trum-chu. It is still worth climbing up through the Tibetan town and taking a walk around what remains. The northern monastery predates the southern monastery (the oldest temple at the northern monastery was built in 1073), and it is alleged to have contained 108 buildings, like Ganden. It may once have housed some 3000 monks who concentrated on Tantric studies.

Aim for the white chörten, which is a reconstruction of a chörten that held the remains of Kunga Nyingpo, the founder of the Sakyapa order and the second Sakya abbot. There are three main complexes on this side of the river: the Labrang Shar, the Namjachu and the Rinche Gang. The Labrang Shar has some holy caves.

Ujay Lhakhang

This small monastery linked to Sakya is located in the village of Chongkhor Lam, around 5km along the road from Sakya to the Friendship Hwy. There's nothing special here, but it's a good place to aim for if you fancy an hour's walk.

Places to Stay

Hedonists beware – accommodation in Sakya cannot be described as luxurious, and there's not a shower to be found for several hundred square kilometres.

Sakya Guesthouse (☎ 824 2233) Beds Y15-20. This is the most popular place to stay in Sakya (look for the English sign saying 'Hotel'). The rooms are pretty basic with no electricity, but it's bearable if you have a sleeping bag, and there's a certain timeless feel about the place.

Grain Department Guesthouse (Liangshiju Zhaodaisuo) Beds around Y15. This is another place well worth checking out. There's a variety of rooms here arranged around a large courtyard. Most are pretty

grim, but there is one suite of three interconnected rooms (sleeping up to 12) that are by far the best rooms in town.

Finally, one place to avoid is the *Sakya Guesthouse* (there's no English sign). This decrepit fleapit is on its last legs and even the staff (if you can track them down) will recommend you go elsewhere.

Places to Eat

Sakya has a lot of restaurants, many set up by Sichuanese immigrants. The food, while relatively pricey, is excellent – it's some consolation for the guesthouse situation.

Sakya Restaurant & Teahouse Dishes Y10-15. This popular place with an English menu is just outside the Sakya Guesthouse. It has the standard selection of noodles and fried dishes and a cosy atmosphere.

Sakya Monastery Restaurant (☎ 824 2267) Dishes Y7-12. This Tibetan place is owned by the monastery and serves up good-value fried rice and thugpa.

The tiny *Sakya Restaurant and Teahouse* opposite the main gate to the monastery is a good place to stop for a cup of tea after you've made the rounds.

There are several *shops* about, where you can stock up on instant noodles, soft drinks and dry, crumbly biscuits.

Getting There & Away

There are minibuses every other day from Shigatse to Sakya (Y27), returning to Shigatse the following day. They leave from outside Tashilhunpo Monastery at around 8am. Buses from Sakya depart from the Sakya County Guesthouse.

Another option is to take a Lhatse-bound bus to the Sakya turn-off and then hitch the remaining 25km, although there aren't many vehicles on this road. The distance between Shigatse and the turn-off is 127km (kilometre marker 5028).

Very occasionally there are buses from Sakya to Lhatse (ask at the Sakya County Guesthouse), but you'll probably have to change transport at the Sakya turn-off. If you are hitching this way it's worth heading out early to catch the morning minibuses that run from Shigatse to Lhasa.

LHATSE
☎ 0892 • elevation 4050m

Approximately 150km south-west of Shigatse and some 30km west of the Sakya turn-off, Lhatse is a spread-out town lining the Friendship Hwy. It has some good restaurants, well-stocked shops and a few guesthouses. Most of the traffic here is en route to Zhangmu on the Nepali border, but some vehicles take the turn-off 6km down the road for Ali in western Tibet; see the Ngari (Western Tibet) chapter for details.

If you get stuck in Lhatse for a day or so (perhaps trying to hitch out of the place) you could visit the ruined **dzongs** at each end of town, although there's not much to see except the views of the plain below. At the western end of town is the small **Changmoche Monastery**. You can also hike 10km out to the Dongaba Hot Springs or visit Lhatse Chöde and Drampa Gyang Temple; see Around Lhatse for details.

Places to Stay

For those heading to western Tibet, Lhatse is your last chance for a hot shower. None of the hotels have functioning showers, but you can take one at the squeaky-clean Xiang La Room Shower, on the southern side of the Friendship Hwy near the post office. It's open from 8am to 11pm and costs Y10.

Lhatse Tibetan Farmers Adventure Hotel (☎ 832 2333) Beds in 4-bed/3-bed dorms from Y25/35, doubles Y50 per person. This is the best place to stay in town, with genial staff, cheerful flowerbeds and a small carpet factory on the upstairs balcony. Go out for dinner though – the restaurant here is not as good as the accommodation.

Lhatse Hotel (☎ 832 2208) Beds in 11-bed/4-bed dorms Y20/25, doubles Y100. This place has gone downhill in recent years. It has a range of rooms set around a huge courtyard, but the cheaper ones are grubby and the staff are unfriendly. The double rooms come equipped with a TV. You can make international calls at reception.

Meteorological Hotel (☎ 832 2236) Beds in 6-bed/4-bed/3-bed dorms Y25/35/40, doubles Y100. The gimmick of this Chinese-style hotel is that it posts the weather forecast on a board in the foyer. It has a string of rather smelly rooms off an endless green-and-white corridor.

There are a few cheaper guesthouses along the Friendship Hwy, such as the *Lazi Guesthouse*, but they aren't allowed to take foreigners.

Places to Eat

Lhatse Friendship Restaurant (*Lhatse Hotel Courtyard*) Breakfast Y15. There are two restaurants in the Lhatse Hotel and this Tibetan-style one is the best. Located in the main courtyard, it has an English menu (kind of), including a set breakfast with an omelette, bread and coffee.

Holy Land Restaurant (*Meteorological Hotel*) Dishes Y12-20. This restaurant on the main street is a good place to sit and watch the world go by outside. There's a Chinese and Western menu, including a rather bland section for vegetarians.

Chengdu Restaurant Dishes Y16-20. This place is expensive but the food is good; try the 'fish-resembling eggplant' (Y20). It consists of eggplant cooked with *yuxiang wei*, a tasty fish-flavoured sauce that draws on vinegar, soy sauce, garlic and ginger.

Lhatse has numerous other restaurants as it's a fairly busy truck stop. Many other *Chinese restaurants* line the south side of the street; wander in and take a look in the kitchen – no-one seems to mind.

Getting There & Away

Daily minibuses run between Shigatse and Lhatse. In Lhatse they circle for customers every morning 150m east of the Lhatse Hotel and depart when full. The cost is Y35. On rare occasions there is a bus to Sakya from Lhatse, but don't depend on catching it.

If you're headed westward without a hired Land Cruiser, to either the Nepali border or western Tibet, Lhatse is the end of the line for public transport. Almost all truck traffic stops here but hitching a lift out of town is notoriously difficult. Some hitchers find themselves stuck here for two or more days. One of the problems is the checkpoint 6km to the west, which scares off any prospective lift provider who doesn't have permission to carry foreigners. It's well worth walking for 1½ hours to the check-point and then looking for a lift a kilometre or two on the other side.

A ride from Lhatse to Zhangmu should cost around Y150, although this will probably require some determined bargaining. Those looking at hitching to Tingri or Shegar for the trek to Everest Base Camp will probably have to pay around Y70, but again this depends on how hard you bargain. It will also help if you get a travel permit in Shigatse for Lhatse, Shegar, Nyalam and Zhangmu.

For information on hitching from here out to Ali and Mt Kailash, see the Ngari (Western Tibet) chapter.

AROUND LHATSE
Dongaba Hot Springs

Tibetans come from far and wide to bathe in the healing waters of Dongaba Hot Springs (baths Y15 per person), which are said to cure a multitude of ills, especially skin irritations. There are a few baths in the complex, including private rooms for the sick and elderly. The largest pool is in a rectangular courtyard surrounded by veranda posts and reclining bathers so that it resembles a Roman bath. Watch out – the water is very hot and gets hotter in the middle. Foreigners are not allowed to stay overnight in the guesthouse here, but the manager can find you a room somewhere to change.

The hot springs are 10km east of Lhatse and within walking distance of the town. To get there, turn north off the Friendship Hwy at the town of Dongaba (kilometre marker 5041) and continue for 500m to the centre. There's a small shop here selling beer and soft drinks. It's a good idea to agree beforehand about including the springs in your itinerary if you want to visit by hired Land Cruiser.

Phuntsoling Monastery & Jonang Kumbum

Situated at the foot of a gargantuan sand dune, Phuntsoling Monastery (admission Y20) was once the central monastery of the Jonangpas. This Kagyu sect is especially known for the examination of the nature of emptiness undertaken at the monastery by its greatest scholar, Dolpopa Sherab Gyaltsen (1292–1361). He was one of the first proponents of the hard-to-grasp notion of *shentong*. Roughly, this is based on the idea that the Buddha-mind (which transcends all forms) is not ultimately empty, even though all forms are empty illusions.

Shentong has been debated among Buddhist philosophers for seven centuries. The Gelugpa school did not share Dolpopa's view – to the point where in the 17th century the fifth Dalai Lama suppressed the Jonangpa school and forcibly converted Phuntsoling into a Gelugpa institution.

You can visit the large **assembly hall**, which is dominated by a statue of Chenresig (Avalokiteshvara). Other statues include those of the 10th Panchen Lama, Tsongkhapa and the fifth Dalai Lama. The **inner sanctum** of the hall contains a statue of Akshobhya (Mikyöba), while **murals** on the roof tell the story of the life of Sakyamuni (Sakya Thukpa).

From Phuntsoling you can head south for a two-hour walk to the ruins of the **Jonang Kumbum**. Once 20m high, the chörten was built by Dolpopa in the 14th century and was the spiritual centre of the Jonangpas. It was said to be one of the best-preserved monuments in Tibet, resembling the Gyantse Kumbum, before it was destroyed during the Cultural Revolution.

The Phuntsoling Monastery can be visited on the way from Shigatse to Lhatse. Take the detour north of the Friendship Hwy, 17km west of the Gyading checkpoint at kilometre marker 4977. The monastery is 36km (about 1½ hours) north-west from here.

It's a 66km journey from Phuntsoling to Lhatse (2½ to three hours). The road follows a valley through charming villages and sometimes narrows to a precarious track between the river and the face of the cliff. About 55km from Phuntsoling (and 10km from Lhatse), you'll pass the ruins of **Lhatse Chöde** and **Drampa Gyang Temple**. The latter is one of Songtsen Gampo's demoness-subduing temples, and in this case it pinions the troublesome demoness's left hip; today there is little to see here. From the temple you hit the main road at kilometre marker 5052, just 1km east of Lhatse.

It's also possible to walk to Phuntsoling – the route is described in Victor Chan's *Tibet Handbook*.

SHEGAR
☎ 0892 • elevation 4050m

The turn-off to Shegar (also known as New Tingri, but not to be confused with Tingri) on the Friendship Hwy is where you buy your permit for the Qomolangma Nature Preserve. Inside the preserve are Everest Base Camp, Rongphu Monastery and Cho Oyu Base Camp. You can't miss the office (there's a huge sign over the highway), but you may need to knock on a few doors to find someone to sell you a permit. For prices, see Everest Region following. The checkpoint 5km west of Shegar is one of the more thorough on the highway, and your bags are likely to be searched.

Shegar itself, a 7km diversion north-west of the Friendship Hwy, is worth a visit for the ruins of **Shegar Dzong** (Crystal Fort), once the capital of the Tingri region. The remains of the dzong's defensive walls snake incredibly over the abrupt pinnacle that looms over the town. A kora trail up to the peak leads up from the western side of town. Morning light is best for taking photographs.

Also of interest here is **Shegar Chöde Monastery** *(admission Y10)*, a small Gelugpa institution at the foot of the mountain. If you climb up to the wall behind the monastery you can get a peek at the top of Everest far in the distance. Paths continue up from here around to the dzong.

Places to Stay & Eat

You can stay in Shegar, but most people en route to the border stay overnight in Tingri, which has views of Everest on clear days.

Kangjong Hotel Beds Y25. The rooms are basic but neat at this friendly Tibetan guesthouse right on the highway at the turn-off to Shegar town. The real attraction of the place is the *restaurant* and sitting area which offers wall-to-wall comfy sofas arranged around a warm stove. Good food

is available at around Y10 to Y15 per dish and you can sit back with a thermos of sweet tea.

Everest Family Hotel Dorm beds Y40. This place at the ticket office is clean but overpriced.

Qomolangma Shegar Guesthouse *(in Lhasa ☎ 0891-682 9313)* Dorm beds/ doubles from Y40/300. Across the river from the Kangjong is this ridiculously expensive attempt to capture passing tour groups for the night. Rooms are in varying states of disrepair and there's no hot water unless a tour group is staying.

QNP San Chen Guesthouse Singles/ doubles Y100/200. This new Chinese-American joint venture has clean rooms in the new red-and-white building across the river. With a bit of persuasion they'll drop the price to Y80 per person.

You can pick up peanuts and dry biscuits for your trekking snacks in the *shops* around the Kangjong Hotel.

Getting There & Away

There is no public transport to or from Shegar. A ride from Shegar to Lhatse should cost around Y70, and from Shegar to the Nepali border around Y150. It may be possible to hitch from the Friendship Hwy to Shegar, but the chances are you'll end up walking the 7km stretch of road. It's 6km from the Shegar turn-off to the Shegar checkpoint and another 6km to the Everest turn-off.

EVEREST REGION

For foreign travellers, Everest Base Camp has become the most popular trekking destination in Tibet, offering the chance to gaze on the stunning north face of the world's tallest peak, Mt Everest (8848m). The Tibetan approach to the mountain provides far better vistas than those on the Nepali side, and access to the mountain is a lot easier as there is also a road all the way up.

Everest's Tibetan name is generally rendered as Qomolangma, and some 27,000 sq km of territory around Everest's Tibetan face have been designated as the Qomolangma Nature Preserve. Planning of the project was cooperative and included local Tibetan organisations, the Chinese Academy of Sciences and The Mountain Institute of the USA. For details of the park, see the boxed text 'Qomolangma Nature Preserve' in the Trekking chapter.

The most satisfying way to get to Everest is to make the popular three- or four-day trek from the Friendship Hwy near Shegar, or from Tingri. (For detailed information on trekking in the region, see the Trekking chapter.) However, most people include Everest Base Camp in their itinerary for a Land Cruiser trip to the border. At the time of writing, a massive road reconstruction project was under way from Chay all the way to Base Camp, which will make the trip much easier than the rough ride it once was.

There are even whispers that a tourist-class hotel is in the pipeline. This doesn't mean that the region is exactly swarming with travellers, but it is also not realistic to expect that you will be the only one up there.

Whatever you do, don't attempt to walk to Base Camp directly after arriving in Tingri from the low altitudes of the Kathmandu Valley. Land Cruiser trips often reach Base Camp within two days of leaving Zhangmu, and the altitude gain of over 2600m in less than 30 hours leaves most people reeling from the effects of AMS (acute mountain sickness, also known as altitude sickness).

Finally, and just as importantly, do not be tempted by the enthusiasm of others to climb any higher than you feel comfortable. As Base Camp becomes more popular,

What's in a Name?

In 1849 the Great Trigonometrical Survey of India mapped the heights of peaks in the Himalaya range. The calculations were carried out from the Indian foothills of the Himalaya, and three years later the computed results showed a peak, known to the West as Peak XV, to be the highest mountain in the world. This came as a surprise, as until this time a mountain called Kanchenjunga near Sikkim was thought to be the peak whose head rose closest to the heavens. Peak XV was rather an ignominious name for the highest mountain in the world, and immediately a search began for its real name.

Western linguists working in Nepal and India reported various local names for the mountain. In Nepal, it was claimed, XV was known as Devadhunga (Abode of the Gods). German explorers, on the other hand, reported that the Tibetan name was Chingopamari. In 1862 the Royal Geographic Society opted for an alternative Nepali name for the mountain: Gaurisanka.

In the meantime, Andrew Waugh, surveyor general of India, embarked on a mission of his own: to have the mountain named after the head of the Great Trigonometrical Survey, Sir George Everest (actually pronounced eve-rest). He met with much opposition (including from Everest himself), largely because it was argued that a local name would be more appropriate. In 1865 the Royal Geographic Society decided to back the Everest contingent because of the uncertainties surrounding Gaurisanka (in 1902 it was determined that Gaurisanka was another peak, some 50km from Everest).

The Everest name stuck amid much controversy, not least due to the fact that there were probably no shortage of experts who knew the true Tibetan name for the mountain to be Chomolangma (or Qomolangma, as the Chinese have transliterated it). As early as 1733, the French produced a map on which Everest is indicated as Tschoumou Lancma.

Chomolangma can be interpreted as 'Goddess Mother of the Universe' ('Sagarmatha' in Nepali), or (more literally, if less poetically) 'Princess Cow'. According to Tibetan scriptures safeguarded at Rongphu Monastery Chomolangma is the name of the mountain while the goddess who dwells there is called Miyo Langsangma. She is one of a group of five well-known long-lived sisters called the Tsering Che Nga, Tibetan deities who predate Buddhism.

The Tibetans and Chinese have little regard for the Westernised name of the world's loftiest peak. Trekkers who make it up to Everest Base Camp have to make do with a posed photograph in front of a sign inscribed with the words 'Mt Qomolangma Base Camp'.

many travellers are starting to set their sights on higher camps. It is probably only a matter of time before some idiot decides to scale the peak itself and dies up there. Remember that unlike on the Nepali side, there is no rescue service up here in the shadow of Everest.

Permits

You need two permits to visit Everest Base Camp. The first is the usual PSB travel permit, available in Shigatse for Y50 (if you've hired a Land Cruiser the travel agency will arrange this one for you). The second is a park-entry permit for Qomolangma Nature Preserve that you must buy at an office by the turn-off to Shegar on the Friendship Hwy (see Shegar earlier in this chapter). It costs Y405 per vehicle, plus Y65 per passenger for a two-day pass. You can get a 10-day pass for the same price but you'll need to request it. A 15-day pass is an extra Y105 per person. Some Lhasa agencies include the price of both personal park entry and vehicle entry in their tour costs, others include just the vehicle fee and some agencies don't include anything, so check with your agency beforehand.

The Assault on Everest

There had been 13 assaults on Everest before Edmund Hillary and sherpa Tenzing Norgay finally reached the summit in John Hunt's major British expedition of 1953. Some of these attempts verged on insanity.

In 1934 Edmund Wilson, an eccentric ex–British army captain, hatched a plan to fly himself from Hendon direct to the Himalaya, crash land his Gypsy Moth halfway up Everest and then climb solo to the summit, despite having no previous mountaineering experience (and marginal flying expertise). Needless to say he failed spectacularly. When his plane was impounded by the British in India he trekked to Rongphu in disguise and made a solo bid for the summit. He disappeared somewhere above Camp III, and his body was later discovered by the mountaineer Eric Shipton at 6400m. Shipton read Wilson's diary until the entries abruptly finished on 31 May. A second solo effort was later attempted by a Canadian in disguise from the Tibet side. It was abandoned at 7150m.

From 1921 to 1938, all expeditions to Everest were British and were attempted from the north (Tibetan) side, along a route reconnoitred by John Noel – disguised as a Tibetan (with blue eyes) – in 1913. In all, the mountain claimed 14 lives. Perhaps the most famous early summit bid was by George Mallory and Andrew Irvine (then aged 22), who were last seen going strong above 7800m (26,000ft), before clouds obscured visibility. Their deaths remained a mystery until May 1999 when an American team found Mallory's body, reigniting theories that the pair may have reached the top two decades before Norgay and Hillary. The possibility, however slight, has become one of the most enduring mysteries of mountaineering. It was Mallory who, when asked why he wanted to climb Everest, famously quipped 'because it is there'.

With the conclusion of WWII and the collapse of the British Raj, the Himalaya became inaccessible. Tibet closed its doors to outsiders and, in 1951, the Chinese invasion clamped the doors shut even more tightly. In mountaineering terms, however, the Chinese takeover had the positive effect of shocking the hermit kingdom of Nepal into looking for powerful friends. The great peaks of the Himalaya suddenly became accessible from Nepal.

Much to their dismay, the British found that the mountain was no longer theirs alone. In 1951, Eric Shipton led a British reconnaissance expedition that explored the Nepali approaches to Everest and came to the conclusion that an assault via Nepal might indeed be met with success. In 1952, however, Nepal issued only one permit to climb Everest – to the Swiss. The Swiss, who together with the British had virtually invented mountaineering as a sport, were extremely able climbers, and British climbers secretly feared that the Swiss might mount a successful ascent on their first attempt; something that eight major British expeditions had failed to achieve. As it happened, the Swiss

Your passport and PSB permit will be scrutinised at the checkpoint 5km west of Shegar. The park permit is checked at the Chay checkpoint, 3km after the turn-off from the Friendship Hwy. Officials don't seem to be too worried about travellers leaving the Everest region, so you probably won't have to worry about the park-entry permit if you trek in from Tingri and leave via Chay.

Shegar to Rongphu

The Everest access road turns off the Friendship Hwy around 6km west of the Shegar checkpoint shortly after kilometre marker 5145. By the time you read this, the 63km drive along the new road should take around two or three hours.

About 3km from the Friendship Hwy you get to the village of Chay (4300m), where your entry permit is checked. From Chay, it is a winding drive up to Pang-la (5120m), which has a makeshift teashop. The views here are stupendous on a clear day, and feature a huge sweep of the Himalaya range including Makalu, Lhotse, Everest, Gyachung and Cho Oyu. A plaque on the pass shows you what's what. You can climb up a scree slope to the left for slightly wider views.

The Assault on Everest

climbed to 8595m on the south-east ridge – higher than any previous expedition – but failed to reach the summit.

The next British attempt was assigned for 1953. Preparations were particularly tense. It was generally felt that if this attempt were unsuccessful, any British hopes to be the first to reach the summit would be dashed. There was considerable backroom manoeuvring before the expedition set off. As a result, Eric Shipton, who had led three previous expeditions (including one in 1935), was dropped as team leader in favour of John Hunt, an army officer and keen Alpine mountaineer who was relatively unknown among British climbers.

Shipton's 1951 expedition had at the last minute accepted two New Zealand climbers. One of them was Edmund Hillary, a professional bee-keeper and a man of enormous determination. He was invited again to join Hunt's 1953 expedition. Also joining the 1953 expedition was Tenzing Norgay, a sherpa who had set out on his first Everest expedition at the age of 19 in 1935 and who had subsequently become infected with the dream of conquering the world's highest peak.

On 28 May 1953, Hillary and Norgay made a precarious camp at 8370m on a tiny platform of the south-east approach to the summit, while the other anxious members of the expedition waited below at various camps. The two men feasted that night on chicken noodle soup and dates. At 6.30 the next morning they set out.

Almost immediately they were in trouble, confronted with a vast, steep sweep of snow. It was the kind of obstacle that had turned back previous expeditions, but Norgay agreed with Hillary that it had to be risked. It was a gamble that paid off. The next major obstacle was a chimney-like fissure which the two men squirmed up painfully. Struggling onwards they suddenly found themselves just metres away from a snow-clad dome. At 11.30am, 29 May, they stepped up to the top of Mt Everest and stood at the closest point to the heavens it is possible to reach on foot.

By 2000, around 900 people had reached the peak of Everest (including George Mallory II, Mallory's grandson), while more than 160 climbers had died in the attempt. The first woman to reach the summit was Junko Tabei from Japan on 16 May 1975. The youngest person was 15-year-old sherpa Temba Tseri from Nepal, who reportedly reached the top in May 2001 after loosing five fingers to frostbite in a previous attempt. The oldest person to make the climb was Toshio Yamamoto at 63 years and 311 days. In May 1999 a National Geographic Society expedition recorded a global positioning system (GPS) reading at the top of Everest which pegged the height at a controversial 8850m – two metres higher than the 8848m accepted since 1954. Reports on the latest attempts on Everest are available at Ⓦ www.everestnews.com.

TSANG

The road descends past a couple of photogenic villages and ruins into the fertile Dzaka valley and the village of Tashi Dzom (also known as Peruche), where you can get lunch or a bed for the night. The dirt road then bumps up the wide valley passing the village of Pasum, which also offers accommodation (see the Trekking chapter for details). The next main village is Chödzom and from here the road turns south towards Rongphu. The first views of Everest appear half an hour before you arrive at Rongphu.

Rongphu Monastery
elevation 4980m
Although there were probably monastic settlements in the area for several hundred years, Rongphu Monastery (admission free) is the main Buddhist centre in the valley and once coordinated the activities of around one dozen smaller religious institutions, all of which are now ruined. It was established in 1902 by a Nyingmapa lama.

While not of great antiquity, Rongphu can at least lay claim to being the highest monastery in Tibet and thus the world. There were once 500 monks and nuns living here, but locals report that there are now only 20 nuns and 10 monks. The nuns and monks use the same prayer hall but have separate residences.

Renovation work has been ongoing at the monastery since 1983, and some of the interior murals are absolutely stunning. The monastery itself makes a fabulous photograph with Everest thrusting its head skyward in the background.

Monastery Guesthouse Dorm beds Y40. This place, arranged around a courtyard opposite the monastery, is the main traveller accommodation. Rooms are basic – avoid the ones with broken windows or you'll spend the whole night shivering. There's also a cosy **restaurant** here that quickly fills with travellers at the end of the day. Egg, meat, noodle and rice dishes are served to order for around Y10 each.

There are basic **rooms** in the monastery for Y25 per bed (ask at the guesthouse). **Camping** nearby costs Y10 per tent; there is water at the southern side of the monastery.

For detailed information on the trek between Rongphu Monastery and Everest Base Camp, see stage four of the trek called Friendship Highway to Everest Base Camp in the Trekking chapter.

Everest Base Camp
elevation 5200m
Endowed with springs, Everest Base Camp was first used by the 1924 British Everest expedition. The site has a couple of permanent structures – a tea tent, some incongruous recycling bins and usually some clusters of tents belonging to various expeditions. Clamber up the small hill festooned with prayer flags for great views of the star attraction, then have your photo taken at the Base Camp marker, which disappointingly does not even mention the word 'Everest'. It reads: 'Mt Qomolangma Base Camp' and the Chinese below indicates that it is 5200m above sea level.

The cold will soon drive you into the tea tent where, if you're lucky, you can have a cup of tea and a chat with the latest brave souls making the attempt on the summit. The highest post box in the world is also in here.

It's possible to walk on to the edge of the Rongphu Glacier across the gravel plain just 15 minutes away. There is a creek to ford along the way – try to cross it as high up as possible and in the early morning before water levels rise.

Getting There & Away
There is no public transport to Everest Base Camp. Most people include Everest as part of a 'package' of sights to visit in a hired Land Cruiser travelling between Lhasa and the Nepali border. Hiring a Land Cruiser in Lhasa for a round trip will cost almost as much – about Y5800. In Shigatse, a round trip to Everest costs Y3400 for three or four days. You'll need a minimum of one night at Rongphu; two nights is much better.

The Trekking chapter has information about the logistics of hiking in and out of the Everest region from near Shegar and from Tingri.

Not everyone wants to trek the entire distance, however, and it is possible to use a combination of trekking and hitching to get to Everest Base Camp. Up to 20 vehicles a day head up to Rongphu and while it's difficult to get a lift because most of them are Land Cruisers filled with tourists, you might be able to score a ride at least part of the way. Coming down from Rongphu, your best bet is to befriend a tour group with a spare seat at the monastery guesthouse.

TINGRI
elevation 4390m

Tingri, a huddle of Tibetan homes that overlook a sweeping plain bordered by the towering Himalaya, is where most travellers spend their last night in Tibet en route to Nepal, or their first night en route to Lhasa from Kathmandu. For newcomers from Kathmandu, the discomforts of the sudden altitude gain are likely to make it an unpleasant stay. There is little in the way of sights around Tingri, although the views of Everest and the muscular-looking massif of Cho Oyu more than compensate for this.

Ruins on the hill overlooking Tingri are all that remain of the **Tingri Dzong**. This is a fort that was not blown up by Red Guards, but rather destroyed in a Nepali invasion in the late 18th century. On the plains between Shegar and Tingri many more ruins that shared the same fate can be seen from the Friendship Hwy.

For detailed information on the trek between Everest Base Camp and Tingri, see Everest Base Camp to Tingri in the Trekking chapter.

Langkhor Monastery

If you've got time on your hands you could head out to Langkhor Monastery, which is about 20km south-west of Tingri. The monastery is associated with Padampa Sangye, an Indian ascetic who was an important figure in the second diffusion of Buddhism on the Tibetan plateau. There's not much to see here, but it's a good chance to hire a pony and cart for the bumpy ride out there. Most villagers have a cart and although it's not a comfortable 4½-hour return ride (bring some padding!) you'll get to see much more this way. The cost for a

pony, cart and driver is around Y50 to Y70; alternatively you could trek out on foot.

Tsamda Hot Springs

Ten kilometres west of Tingri, this small complex makes a pleasant stop and is a good place to spend the night (see Places to Stay & Eat). The single pool is pretty slimy and it's not exactly private (in fact it's in the middle of the guesthouse courtyard), but there probably won't be anyone else around and the water is a good temperature for soaking in. Baths cost Y10 per person. The springs are 1km off the Friendship Hwy, and are signposted in English near kilometre marker 5206.

Places to Stay & Eat

All accommodation, except the guesthouse at the hot springs, is on the Friendship Hwy. The town's interior decorators favour lurid, patterned wallpaper that may well give you psychedelic nightmares.

Tsamda Hot Spring Beds Y30. At the hot springs there are simple dorm rooms with dirt floors (watch where you drip), and a basic restaurant.

Everest View Hotel Beds Y20. Most budget travellers passing through in rented vehicles stay at the Everest View Hotel (or the 'Lao Dhengre Haho Everest Veo Hotel & Restaurant' as the sign cryptically advertises), which is a shabby little place arranged around a compound. Basic food is available.

Amdo Hotel Beds Y25. Nearby, this basic truck stop offers beds in cramped rooms. Hot showers are available in the evenings and cost Y10 for guests and Y15 for nonguests.

Everest Snow Leopard Hotel Dorm beds Y80, doubles/triples Y180/270. The nicest place by far is the Everest Snow Leopard Hotel, about 400m east of the other hotels. The cosy, all-brick rooms are spotlessly clean and there are views of Cho Oyu from most of the rooms. There's also a nice restaurant and sitting area, which doubles as reception. Dorm rates will slide to Y30 if you don't arrive in a flashy Land Cruiser.

Amdo Restaurant Dishes Y15. This friendly place serves up meat or vegie *bobies* (two chapatis with filling) and big fluffy pancakes.

There are several ***Chinese restaurants*** nearby which cater largely to the local army garrison. All the English menus are the same, with dishes starting at around Y20.

Getting There & Away

There is no public transport along this stretch of the Friendship Hwy. Hitching a lift with trucks bound for the border from Shigatse or Lhatse would be your best bet. You will have to pay for the lift. The sum is entirely negotiable, but expect around Y70 to Y100 to get to Zhangmu (around Y50 to Nyalam).

NYALAM

☎ 0892 • elevation 3750m

Nyalam is a one-street town with a vigilant checkpoint around 30km before the Nepali border. It has been steadily growing in size, and its facilities have improved over the past few years, no doubt as a result of the burgeoning trade opportunities with nearby Nepal.

From Nyalam the road drops like a stone off the Tibetan plateau into a mossy gorge of waterfalls and cascades. During the summer monsoons, the road submerges into a sea of cloud, no doubt one of the reasons why Nyalam means 'gateway to hell' in Tibetan.

The post office is at the top (southern) end of Nyalam and is open from 9.30am to 1pm and 4pm to 7pm. You can make international calls at a number of shops in town. There's nowhere to change money in Nyalam.

For those who want to use Nyalam as a base for treks, Gary McCue has a section on treks around Nyalam in his book *Trekking in Tibet – A Traveler's Guide*. One possible day hike takes you up the valley behind Nyalam for three or four hours to Dara-tso, a holy lake from where Shisha Pangma (the only 8000m-plus mountain planted squarely in Tibet) is visible.

In the town itself is the **Mani Tundu Temple**. It's often closed and there's not much to see, but it's a nice five-minute walk to the temple and there are usually a few pilgrims around. To get there take the road that branches off from the southern end of town.

Milarepa's Cave

The closest cultural sight to Nyalam is Milarepa's Cave *(admission Y10)* and **Nyalam Pelgye Ling**, the small temple built over it. Milarepa was a famous Buddhist mystic and composer of songs who lived in the late 11th and early 12th centuries. During his long meditation in this cave he renounced all luxuries and survived on a diet of local weeds (famously turning green as a result). Milarepa is credited with many magical feats in Tibetan literature; one was raising the ceiling of his cave with his bare hands. You can still see his handprints in the roof.

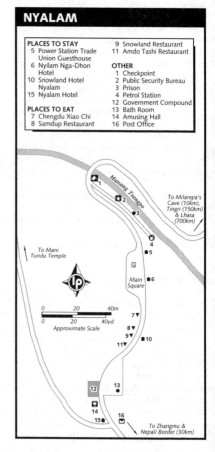

NYALAM

PLACES TO STAY	9 Snowland Restaurant
5 Power Station Trade Union Guesthouse	11 Amdo Tashi Restaurant
6 Nyilam Nga-Dhon Hotel	**OTHER**
10 Snowland Hotel Nyalam	1 Checkpoint
15 Nyalam Hotel	2 Public Security Bureau
	3 Prison
PLACES TO EAT	4 Petrol Station
7 Chengdu Xiao Chi	12 Government Compound
8 Samdup Restaurant	13 Bath Room
	14 Amusing Hall
	16 Post Office

The temple is 10km north of Nyalam, at Gangka village. There's a well-signposted car park on the Friendship Hwy. It takes about three hours to hike here from Nyalam.

Places to Stay

None of the guesthouses in town have showers, but you can have one at the Bath Room, opposite the government compound, for Y10. It's open from 8am to 11pm. It costs Y5 to park overnight on the east side of the main square – but on the west side they'll try to charge you Y20.

Nyilam Nga-Dhon Hotel (☎ 827 2113) Dorm beds/singles Y30/50. The best option in town is this place, which has a range of clean rooms. The hotel is a bit cramped, but the owners are friendly, and there's a clean toilet and washing block.

Snowland Hotel Nyalam (☎ 827 2111) Dorm beds/doubles Y25/30. Further up the road, this is the favourite pick of most tour groups, even though the hotel seems to be falling apart. It offers crumbling rooms up a rickety ladder.

Nyalam Hotel (☎ 827 2507) Dorm beds Y30, singles/doubles Y30/60. Despite the alluring sign there are no hot showers to be found here, only depressing box-like rooms with paper-thin walls.

Power Station Trade Union Guesthouse (☎ 827 2164) Dorm beds Y20. This place is not officially allowed to take foreigners, although the rooms are quite good value for the money. They back onto the river below. The toilet is pretty grim.

Places to Eat

Amdo Tashi Restaurant Dishes Y18. The main travellers' dive is straight across the road from the Snowland Hotel. There are two rooms, one with Western tables and one with Tibetan couches. The menu makes a similar split – you can get a bowl of ice cream or good *thanthuk* (Tibetan noodles).

Snowland Restaurant Vegetarian dishes Y15-20, meat dishes Y25-30. This is the classiest place for a final Chinese dinner before the hedonistic delights of Kathmandu. There are private booths and functioning lazy Susans.

Chengdu Xiao Chi Dishes Y15-25. There are several cheaper Chinese restaurants near the main square including this one with an English menu and slightly inflated prices (although they may offer to knock Y5 off the listed price).

Samdup Restaurant Thugpa Y15-25. This small and friendly Tibetan place has an English menu on the wall featuring mainly soup and thugpa, although you are invited to 'please say frankly on any request'.

You can get a beer at the *Amusing Hall* in the evening – it's next to the government compound, in the south end of town.

Getting There & Away

It's a stunning 30km journey from Nyalam to Zhangmu and you can even walk there if you are keen. There's a good chance you'll get a lift with a Land Cruiser heading down to Zhangmu to pick up a tour group somewhere along the route if you start flagging.

From Tingri you'll have to hitch a ride to Nyalam (expect to pay about Y50).

ZHANGMU

☎ 0892 • elevation 2300m

Zhangmu, also known as Khasa in Nepali and Dram in Tibetan, is a remarkable town that hugs the rim of a seemingly never-ending succession of hairpin bends down to the customs area at the border of China and Nepal. After Tibet, it all seems incredibly green and luxurious; the smells of curry and incense in the air are smells from the sub-continent, and the babbling sound of the fast-flowing streams that cut through the town is music to the ears.

Zhangmu is a typical border town, much larger than Nyalam, and has a restless, reckless feel to it. The population is a fascinating mix of Han, Tibetan and Nepali, the shops brim with goodies from India, Nepal and China, and in the curry shops Tibetans watch videos of Indian soap operas. Chinese officials strut around town with coiffured hair, microthin socks and jackets hanging off their shoulders like parading generals. Meanwhile, Indian traders squeeze their Tata trucks through the congested streets, sending Western tour groups running.

TSANG

There are nice views of the town from the back of the **Mani Lhakhang**, halfway up the town.

Information

Moneychangers deal openly and aggressively in front of the Zhangmu Hotel and will change any combination of Chinese yuan, US dollars or Nepali rupees. The Bank of China is halfway up the hill in the middle of town – it will change US dollars into yuan, but doesn't deal in Nepali rupees.

There are international telephone and fax facilities at the branch of the post office near the Gang Gyen Hotel. The main post office is further north.

The PSB (☎ 874 2264) is on the first floor of a ramshackle blue building about 20m north of the Gang Gyen Hotel. The officers won't give you an Alien Travel Permit to head north into Tibet unless you have a guide, a driver and the mysterious Tibetan Tourism Bureau (TTB) permit – effectively

making it impossible for independent travellers to come up from Nepal without a tour booked in Kathmandu. The checkpoint just north of town makes sure of this. The PSB cannot extend your visa.

Places to Stay

Zhangmu Hotel (☎ 874 2221, fax 874 2220) Dorm beds Y50, singles & doubles with private bathroom Y400. The main hotel in Zhangmu is right down in the south of town next to customs. As you might expect of the last tourist-class hotel in Tibet, it is expensive and apathetically run. It's also the only hotel in Tibet whose reception is on the top floor! While the double rooms are really very luxurious, hot water can be a bit dicey.

Gang Gyen Hotel (☎ 874 2188, fax 874 2413) Beds in 3-bed dorms Y50, doubles Y150. Most budget travellers sensibly give the Zhangmu Hotel a miss in favour of this place across the road. The dorms are nice and reasonably clean, although the communal bathrooms are pretty grim. Hot showers are available on the roof and are free for guests (Y8 for nonguests).

Sherpa Guesthouse (☎ 874 2098) Doubles Y30 per person. This place does not have a permit to take foreigners, but is willing to risk it if you are. There are simple but comfortable rooms and a pleasant restaurant.

Pema Hotel (☎ 874 2106, fax 874 2605) Dorm beds/doubles Y75/200. The Pema has neat, if overpriced, rooms with fantastic views over the valley. It's a bit of a trek from the border into the middle of town – look out for its pedestrian overpass.

Places to Eat

There is no shortage of restaurants in Zhangmu. Wander up the hill for an excellent selection of Chinese, Tibetan and Nepali cuisine – for anyone who has come in from other parts of Tibet, Zhangmu is paradise.

Gang Gyen Restaurant (*Ground floor, Gang Gyen Hotel*) Dishes from Y20. This hotel has a popular but pricey ground-floor restaurant that serves Nepali, Chinese and Tibetan mains, and Western breakfasts. Meat/vegie thalis go for Y75/55.

ZHANGMU

PLACES TO STAY & EAT	OTHER
3 Pema Hotel	1 Main Post Office
4 Sherpa Guesthouse	2 Bank of China
7 Tashi Delek Restaurant	5 Mani Lhakhang
8 Lhasa Tibetan Restaurant	6 Temple
10 Snowland Happy Livelihood Restaurant	9 Public Security Bureau
12 Qixingjiao Restaurant	11 Post Office Branch
13 Gang Gyen Hotel & Restaurant	15 Customs & Chinese Border
14 Zhangmu Hotel	

Qixingjiao Restaurant Dishes Y18-20. Next door to the Gang Gyen, this Chinese place is better value – try the excellent 'fish-resembling eggplant'.

Snowland Happy Livelihood Restaurant Breakfast Y15. Snowland opens early for naan-style bread, coffee and omelettes.

For Tibetan food try the *Lhasa Tibetan Restaurant* or the *Tashi Delek Restaurant*, both a short walk up the hill from the border.

Getting There & Away

To Kathmandu Access to Nepal is via the Friendship Bridge and Kodari, around 8km from Zhangmu. Customs opens at 9.30am. Traffic on the stretch of no-man's land between the two countries has increased over the last few years and it has now become quite easy to hitch a lift. You will probably have to pay – around Y20 should do the trick, but the amount depends on who is giving the lift, and on the condition of the road. Frequent landslides mean that many travellers find themselves scrambling over debris in the places where vehicles can't pass.

If you decide to walk, it takes a couple of hours to get down to the bridge. There are porters at both customs points who will carry your pack for a few rupees or Renminbi (RMB). Look out for short cuts down between the hairpin bends of the road. They save quite a bit of time if you find them, although they put a real strain on the knees.

It is possible to get a Nepali visa at the border for the same price as in Lhasa (you'll need a passport photo) although it is sensible to get one in Lhasa just in case.

There are a couple of hotels on the Nepali side. For those looking at continuing straight on to Kathmandu, there are a couple of buses a day from Kodari that leave whenever they are full. If you can't find a direct bus you'll have to change halfway at Barabise. The other option is to hire a vehicle. There are usually touts for vehicles to Kathmandu in front of the hotels on the Nepali side. The cost is around US$30, but this depends a lot on the condition of the road. If the buses can get through easily, the price of the cars is forced down. Most of the vehicles are private cars, and small ones at that; you will be hard pressed to fit more than three people into one, especially if you have big packs. Depending on the condition of the road, it should take around four to five hours from Kodari to Kathmandu.

Nepal is 2¼ hours behind Chinese time.

From Kathmandu For information on getting to Zhangmu from Kathmandu, see Friendship Highway (Nepal to Tibet) under Land in the Getting There & Away chapter. It's almost impossible to hitch from Zhangmu into the rest of Tibet. Some travellers have tried sneaking across the Zhangmu checkpoint before dawn but it's a long hike up there so you'd have to leave extremely early. And you'd still have to bluff your way across the other checkpoints on the Friendship Hwy.

Ngari (Western Tibet)

Ngari, the western region of Tibet, is one of the most remote and inaccessible parts of the country. Ngari is a real frontier – but the engine of Chinese development is chugging steadily across the wild plains of the nomads.

The trip from Lhasa is marked by stunning, if desolate, scenery, and sacred Mt Kailash (Tibetan: Kang Rinpoche) and Lake Manasarovar (Mapham yum-tso) are two of the most remote and legendary travel destinations in the world. You have to be a certain kind of person to undertake this journey – many of the pilgrims on the road have been planning it all their lives. The main attractions of what is likely to be a three-week trip are a mountain and a lake, but what a mountain and what a lake! And for the truly intrepid there are the otherworldly ruins of the ancient Guge kingdom at Tsaparang and Ngari's almost unknown prehistoric rock carvings near Rutok.

For those not overly fussed by the spiritual significance of Mt Kailash, going to one of the most isolated corners of the globe is likely to be as much an attraction as the destination itself.

Until recently, Western travellers were quite thin on the ground in Ngari – the area was largely the preserve of tour groups and the occasional intrepid traveller with a taste for adventure and plenty of time to spare. This situation, for good or for bad, is starting to change. Over the past few years, the Chinese have accelerated their massive infrastructure expansion program to develop the region. Travel in Ngari is still not what you'd call easy or comfortable, but improved roads, new bridges and telephone lines have made it more physically accessible. These days there's even a bus from Lhasa to Ali (Shiquanhe), something that would have been unthinkable just a few years ago.

That said, the Chinese authorities do their best to keep a tight rein on tourism by putting up as many hurdles as possible for travellers. Permits are scrupulously examined at the

Highlights

- Making the pilgrimage to one of the most mystical and remote corners of the world
- Joining the crowds at holy Mt Kailash for the Saga Dawa festival
- Visiting sacred Lake Manasarovar, a body of turquoise water bordered by snowy peaks
- Pitting yourself against the rigours of the long, dusty road
- Tunnelling through the mountain ruins of the ancient Guge kingdom at Tsaparang
- Spotting the outlines of prehistoric engravings in the cliffs near Rutok

many checkpoints, and permit requirements can change without warning. The instability in the region has not encouraged the Chinese to loosen their grip – just after research on this chapter was completed, all of Ngari was closed to foreigners as a result of the war in Afghanistan.

History

Most histories of Tibet begin with the kings of the Yarlung Valley region and their unification of central Tibet in the 7th century. But it is thought that the Shangshung kingdom of western Tibet probably ruled the Tibetan plateau for several centuries before this. According to some scholars, the Bön religion made its way into the rest of Tibet from here. The Shangshung kingdom may also have served as a conduit for Tibet's earliest contacts with Buddhism. For more on Bön, see the boxed text 'Bön' in the Kham (Eastern Tibet) chapter.

There is little material evidence of the Shangshung kingdom in modern Tibet. Khyunglung Monastery, on the Sutlej River near Tirthapuri Hot Springs, and ruins in its near vicinity are thought to mark the site of the old kingdom. If you have a particular

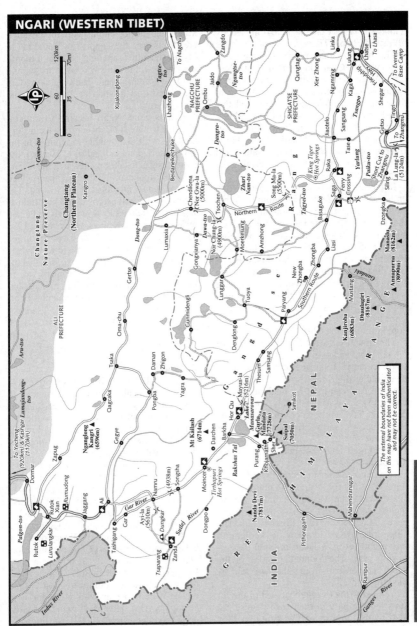

interest in this archaeological site and other remote monasteries in the area, bring a copy of Victor Chan's *Tibet Handbook*.

The next regional power to emerge in Ngari was the Guge kingdom in the 9th century. After the assassination of the anti-Buddhist Lhasa king Langdharma, one of the king's sons, Wosung, established this kingdom at Tsaparang, west of Lake Manasarovar and Mt Kailash. The Guge kingdom, via its contacts with India, led a Buddhist revival on the Tibetan plateau and was home to over 100 monasteries, most of them now in ruins.

In the late 16th century, the Jesuits took an interest in the remote kingdom of Guge. At their enclave in Goa, rumours reached the Jesuits of a kingdom whose religion strongly resembled Catholicism – probably a result of the monastic nature of Tibetan Buddhism. Speculation that this was the long-lost Christian civilisation of Prester John (a legendary Christian priest and king who was believed to have ruled over a kingdom in the Far East) soon sparked enthusiasm for an expedition to this faraway community of lost Christians.

The first Jesuit expedition to set out for the kingdom ended in failure with the death of its leader in 1603. A second expedition disguised as pilgrims and led by Father Antonio de Andrede in 1624, made its way to the head of the Mana Valley and looked down on Tibet only to be turned back by heavy snows, snow blindness and acute mountain sickness (AMS). A month later they returned and descended to the Guge kingdom.

If de Andrede had expected to find Christians waiting for him at Tsaparang, the Guge capital, he was disappointed. Nevertheless, he did meet with surprising tolerance and respect for the Christian faith. The Guge king agreed to allow de Andrede to return and set up a Jesuit mission the following year. The foundation stone of the first Christian church in Tibet was laid by the king himself.

Ironically, the evangelical zeal of the Jesuits led not only to their own demise but also to the demise of the kingdom they sought to convert. Lamas, outraged by their king's increasing enthusiasm for an alien creed, enlisted the support of Ladakhis in laying siege to Tsaparang. Within a month the city fell, the king was overthrown and the Jesuits imprisoned. The Guge kingdom foundered on Christian zeal and factional manoeuvring.

At this point, Ngari became so marginalised as to almost disappear from the history books – with one notable exception. In the late Victorian era, a handful of Western explorers began to take an interest in the legend of a holy mountain and a lake from which four of Asia's mightiest rivers flowed. The legend, which had percolated as far afield as Japan and Indonesia, was largely ridiculed by Western cartographers. However, in 1908 the Swedish explorer Sven Hedin returned from a journey that proved there was indeed such a mountain and such a lake, and that the remote part of Tibet they occupied was in fact the source of the Karnali (a major tributary of the Ganges), the Brahmaputra (Yarlung Tsangpo), the Indus (Senge Tsangpo) and the Sutlej (Langchen Tsangpo) Rivers. The mountain was Kailash and the lake, Manasarovar.

Permits

Western Tibet is a politically sensitive area and is periodically closed to foreigners. In 2001, the region was closed three times as a result of political protests on the Mt Kailash *kora* (ritual circumambulation circuit), Indian war games and as a response to the US strikes on Afghanistan. If regional conflicts continue it's unlikely that the area will be reopened – get current information before you make firm travel plans.

Even when the area is open, it's no easy matter to arrange a trip to Ngari. Officially, all foreigners must have a fistful of permits: an Alien Travel Permit, a military permit, a Tibet Tourism Bureau (TTB) permit, a foreign affairs permit… If you arrange a Land Cruiser trip in Lhasa the travel agency will organise all these permits for you (which means it can take up to a week for it to arrange a trip). However, many independent travellers, especially those hitching,

Planning a Land Cruiser Trip to Mt Kailash

Any pilgrimage worth its salt involves its fair share of trials and tribulations, but with careful planning it's possible to avoid many of the common pitfalls of arranging a trip to Mt Kailash.

Obviously, the first step is to draw up a proposed itinerary for the trip. This will allow the agency to give you a firm quote based on distance covered and number of days on the road. One point to consider carefully when drawing up an itinerary is the rate of altitude gain. Build in an extra day early on to acclimatise – after Lhatse nowhere is lower than 4500m.

Most basic itineraries take around 17 to 21 days, which allows for six days to get to Mt Kailash stopping en route at places such as Sakya Monastery, a couple of days around Lake Manasarovar to rest up and enjoy the lake, four days on the Mt Kailash *kora* (ritual circumambulation circuit) and four to five days to get back to Lhasa. A visit to Thöling Monastery or Tsaparang will add on at least three days, probably four. An itinerary that takes in both the northern and southern routes will eat up a minimum of three weeks. A final consideration if you are heading for Nepal is whether to take the short cut from Saga to Zhangmu.

Once you have planned your itinerary you can start to recruit travellers to share the costs of the trip. The noticeboards at Lhasa's budget hotels are the best places to post an advertisement. The final number of people in your group determines the type of vehicle you rent. Most groups of five or six take one Land Cruiser, and one truck to carry supplies, petrol and normally one passenger. Remember that you will have a guide as well. Groups of four may be able to hire just a Land Cruiser, although agencies are normally loathe to do this.

Andre Ticheler

cycling or catching the Ali bus, don't bother with them. The catch with applying for permits and doing the trip officially is that the authorities only give out permits to tour groups with a guide and Land Cruiser, and (for large groups) a truck to carry the fuel.

Those planning on doing the trip on their own will have no luck obtaining a permit from either the Lhasa or Shigatse Public Security Bureau (PSB) offices, and will be better off not drawing attention to themselves by trying.

There are checkpoints all along the road, but the main danger spots for individual travellers are Ali and Darchen, where there are usually a couple of English-speaking PSB officers with a special interest in foreigners. Fines for being caught without a permit are often negotiable, but can be anything from Y300 to Y1000.

At the time of research it was possible for individual travellers to get a permit for Mt Kailash, Manasarovar, Zanda and the Guge kingdom in Ali. The key, it seems, is to surrender yourself immediately to the local PSB officer. Here you will have to eat humble pie and pay a fine of Y300 yuan, but you should

receive in return a Y50 permit, making the rest of your trip delightfully legal. Even with the fine, you have got away with doing the trip a lot more cheaply than if you had hired a Land Cruiser. Be warned, however, that this could change at any time, so check with other travellers before you head off.

Finally, if you want to visit the main attractions in Ngari you're up for more permits and entrance fees. It costs Y320 to visit Tsaparang and Y100 for Thöling Monastery.

When to Go
May, June, and from mid-September to early October are probably the best times to head out to Ngari. Rates for Land Cruiser hire are cheapest in November. Drölma-la on the Mt Kailash kora is normally blocked with snow from late October or early November until early April.

What to Bring
Warm clothes are essential, as is a sleeping bag. A tent is very useful if you are hitching or trekking around the Mt Kailash area, although it can be a nuisance to cart around and you can get by without one.

You'll save your backside from the worst punishments of the road if you invest in a decent piece of foam mattress. A square big enough to sit on will cost about Y10 and you can get it cut to measure. If you're hitching, a face mask will help keep some of the dust out.

These days the towns along the northern route offer reasonable meals and even fresh vegetables at most of the overnight stops; however, these are few and far between. On the southern route you'll be staying in places where the options run to Chinese instant noodles and *tsampa* (a dough made of roasted-barley flour mixed with yak butter and tea).

It's well worth bringing along a few treats to ease you through the bare patches. Possibilities include dried or bottled fruit, peanuts, boiled eggs, sweets, chocolate bars and dehydrated food from home. For more culinary ideas, see Food in the Facts for the Visitor and the Trekking chapters.

The only places to change money in Ngari are the banks in Ali and Purang – and they will only change US dollars, not travellers cheques. Depending on the kind of trip you're doing, you'll need to budget for hitching costs, permits, fines and the steep entrance fees for the main attractions (see Permits earlier for details).

Travelling to Ngari

Most travellers approach Ngari from Lhasa, because it's the easiest place to organise permits and find travelling companions. Ngari can also be approached from Xinjiang and Nepal.

In 2001 a nonstop bus service started operating along the northern route between Lhasa and Ali. The only other motorised options are to hire a vehicle or to hitch.

Land Cruiser trips are the most popular way to get out to Mt Kailash. During the peak season (July, August and September) you'll probably find three or four trips being advertised on Lhasa's noticeboards at any one time. In 2001, all the private agencies operating in Lhasa were closed and only the government-run Family (Foreign) Independent Traveller (FIT) office was allowed to offer trips to the Mt Kailash area (see Travel Agencies under Information in the Lhasa chapter for contact details). The introduction of this monopoly has pushed up prices, but ask around in Lhasa, as the private agencies could reopen at any time.

Costs depend on a number of factors but usually come to about US$600 to US$700 per person for four people on a 21-day trip with a driver, a guide, their expenses, a Land Cruiser, permits and fuel. Usually if you have more than four people in your party you need a truck to carry supplies, which adds another US$2000 or so to the trip. Large groups take one truck and a number of Land Cruisers. Additional days or changes in the routing (for example, getting dropped off in Zhangmu) seem to add little to the cost.

You really need a minimum of a week to arrange a trip of this sort. For tips on planning, see the boxed texts 'Planning a Land Cruiser Trip to Mt Kailash' earlier in this chapter and 'Dealing with an Agency' in the Getting Around chapter.

Travellers planning on hitching out to Ngari should take the bus to Lhatse first. There's a checkpoint 6km west of Lhatse, but most hitchhikers just walk straight through it and onto the bridge, 2km further on. This is a good place to begin hitching, as a sharp corner in the road means that traffic has to slow before crossing the river. Some travellers have managed to get lifts all the way to Ali from this point, sometimes in Land Cruisers.

However, truck drivers are increasingly reluctant to give foreigners lifts and hitchhikers sometimes have to turn back. One traveller wrote of how he placed a stone on the roadside for every truck that passed him in the three days he waited for a lift. After three days he gave up and headed back to Lhasa to rent a Land Cruiser, leaving behind a sizeable roadside *chörten* (stupa). You need to be very flexible with your itinerary, carry plenty of supplies and, more importantly, have sufficient time (a minimum of three weeks) remaining on your visa.

SOUTHERN ROUTE

The southern route to Ngari really begins in Saga (Sajia), but there are two ways to approach Saga: You can come from Lhasa through Lhatse, or from Zhangmu on the Nepali border.

Lhatse to the Northern Turn-Off

Both the northern and southern routes follow the same road beyond Lhatse and on to the northern turn-off near Raka. For information on the places along the Lhasa-Lhatse road see the Tsang chapter.

From Lhatse onwards there is little in the way of food or accommodation. There are truck stops strategically situated a day's travel from each other, but all it takes is a breakdown (a frequent occurrence) and a delay of a few hours to fall completely out of sync with this arrangement.

Just 4km beyond Lhatse the paved road ends; from there it's dust and corrugations all the way to Ali. At the Lhatse checkpoint (6km after Lhatse), the road leaves the Friendship Hwy and bears west. It is approximately 240km from the checkpoint to the northern turn-off.

From the bridge across the Yarlung Tsangpo (Brahmaputra River), 2km after leaving the Friendship Hwy, the road soon

---

Travelling to Ngari

For those hitching, the northern route has the most traffic. If you are lucky enough to get a ride all the way to Ali, expect to pay from Y200 to Y500 depending on the condition of the road and the attitude at the checkpoints.

From Lhasa

There are two routes from Lhasa to Ngari: a southern route and a northern route. The northern route is considerably longer than the southern route: about 1700km to Ali versus 1200km.

Southern Route If your aim is Mt Kailash and Lake Manasarovar and you've hired a Land Cruiser, the southern route is the way to travel. Mt Kailash is about 870km from Lhasa on this route, which on a good run can be covered in four days, as opposed to six or seven (or more) on the northern route. There are now bridges over all the major rivers along this road, removing the difficult business of fording them. For hitchhikers, it's notoriously difficult to get a ride on the southern route (you are at the mercy of paying tourists who are generally not interested in freeloaders).

Northern Route Although there are no stellar attractions on the longer route, it is the road taken by the Lhasa-Ali bus and by most people hitching. The northern route is under constant repair, making it easier for trucks and buses to get through. There are also better facilities at the expanding towns along this route and it has the added advantage of taking you through Ali, 330km north-west of Mt Kailash, where you can arrange a permit for Mt Kailash and Lake Manasarovar.

From Xinjiang

Although it's a very hard road, the Xinjiang-Tibet Hwy route is increasingly popular with hitchhikers, cyclists and tour groups. It's now even possible to take a bus from Yecheng to Ali when road conditions allow. The route passes through the remote Aksai Chin region; with the unpredictability of breakdowns, it can take three days to a week or more to travel the 1100km from Yecheng to Ali.

From Nepal

If you're coming up from Kathmandu via the Friendship Hwy, a short cut to Saga cuts a day's travel off your trip. It is also possible to enter Ngari via a four-day trek from Simikot in the Humla region of western Nepal to Purang on the Chinese border near Mt Kailash. This route is open only to tour groups who trek in from Humla, which is a restricted region.

enters a surprisingly lush (during the summer at least) river valley, scattered with Tibetan villages. This is a beautiful area for photographs if your driver is amenable to the idea of stopping occasionally. **Lulung village**, 31km from Lhatse, has many buildings decorated with what looks like the red, white and blue of the French tricolour. These are actually the colours of the three bodhisattvas connected with the Sakya Monastery.

The road edges around the north side of a lake and climbs up to a pass. At kilometre marker 2085, 60km from Lhatse, the road passes through the very small town of **Kaga** (Kajia). The Tibetan town and an army base are to the right of the road. To the left, a little further on, there's a *truck stop* where you can get a huge bowl of noodles for Y7. At the time of writing a new *guesthouse* was under construction here. The town is next to the very picturesque **Ngamring-tso**. A turn-off runs round the east side of the lake to the larger settlement of Ngamring, visible on the north-east side of the lake and about 6km off the main route.

Within 10km of Kaga, 70km west of Lhatse, you'll pass the last trees for many days and soon after you'll also leave behind the last agricultural fields. Just beyond kilometre marker 2060, *mani* stones (stones with the mantra *'om mani padme hum'*, meaning 'hail to the jewel in the lotus' carved on them) and prayer flags mark the start of a path to a hilltop monastery overlooking the road from the north. The road then makes a zigzag ascent to the 4700m Kar-la before dropping down to Sangsang.

Sangsang, 122km west of Lhatse, is a larger town than Kaga. There are a couple of *guesthouses* at the entrance to town; expect to pay Y15 to Y25 for very basic accommodation. There are also some Chinese *shops* and the Tibetan *Shigatse Tan Menu* restaurant, whose walls are plastered with pin-ups of Communist stars such as Marx, Engels, Stalin and Mao. A small **nunnery** overlooks the town from the north.

From Sangsang the route passes through a succession of valleys and follows a gorge into the spectacular, wide ravine of the Raka Tsangpo. Emerging from this ravine it skirts around a lake and then crosses a flood plain, which is prone to flood damage during the monsoon. The route then climbs a couple of passes before dropping down past the tiny settlement of **Raka**, near kilometre marker 1912 and about 5km before the junction where the northern and southern routes split, 120km from Sangsang. There are a handful of Chinese *guesthouses* here where you can get a bowl of noodles or a room for the night (from Y15 to Y25). If you're taking the northern route this is the last truck stop for 240km and there may be a checkpoint here. Confusingly, many maps show Raka (or Raga) right at the crossroads; in fact the turn-off is marked only by a weather-worn sign in Tibetan and Chinese pointing to Ali.

Zhangmu to Saga

This short cut from Zhangmu on the Nepali border to Saga (Sajia) on the southern route to Ngari saves 250km (at least a day of travel) and is used by Land Cruiser groups that want to visit Ngari directly from Nepal.

See Nyalam and Zhangmu in the Tsang chapter for more details on the first part of this route, which follows the Friendship Hwy. Past Nyalam the road climbs to the 5120m Tong-la then drops down before climbing to the second high point of the double pass, the La Lung-la (5124m). Soon after the pass the short cut turns west off the Friendship Hwy, rounding some hills at the start of a vast plain. To the south there are views of **Shisha Pangma** (8012m), known to the Nepalese as Gosainthan, the only 8000m-plus mountain planted completely inside Tibet. The road passes just a few kilometres south of the huge lake, **Peiku-tso**, and provides access to the north base camp of the mountain.

The road, most of it very bad, continues across the plain, although stunning Himalayan views compensate for the discomfort. The route then follows a narrow gorge before climbing to a pass and dropping steeply down to a ferry crossing over the Yarlung Tsangpo. From here, it's not far from the crossing to Saga where you pick up the southern route.

Prayer flags are believed to purify the air and pacify the gods.

Chörten at Thöling Monastery in western Tibet

Chörtens near the Potala, Lhasa

Gyantse Kumbum, the largest chörten in Tibet

Mural at Lhakhang Marpo in western Tibet showing variations in Himalayan chörten types

Saga
elevation 4600m

From the northern turn-off it is 60km to Saga, which is also the junction for the short cut from Zhangmu on the Nepali border. The army town of Saga is the last town of any size on the southern route and it's your last chance to eat a lavish meal. There's a tough checkpoint at the east entrance to town. Turn left off the main road around the wall of the army compound to find the town's hotels.

Yak Hotel Dorm beds Y25. This Tibetan place has basic rooms with dirt floors and electricity in the evening.

Sheru Hotel Beds Y25. Next door, this friendly guesthouse also has simple rooms arranged around a large courtyard.

Kun Cheng Hotel Beds Y25. This place is run-down and rather whiffy, and doesn't have the atmosphere of its competition across the road.

Just down from the hotels there are a couple of excellent *Chinese restaurants* and *dumpling sellers*, and the last well-stocked *shops* en route west.

Zhongba

From Saga it is 145km to Zhongba. The road is good, and most Land Cruisers complete the trip in around 2½ hours. 'Old' Zhongba is a dusty village on the main road; these days it has been reduced to a ghost town with looming sand dunes threatening to bury it at any moment. 'New' Zhongba, 25km north-west, is a small town with a couple of shops, hotels and restaurants. It's 10km north of the main road and has little to recommend it.

There is a small **monastery** at the western end of Old Zhongba on a hill, but it's not worth a special stop. There's also a couple of basic guesthouses in town, but given the choice try to stay at Saga.

Tashi Hotel Beds Y20. On the eastern entrance to town, this place offers beds in a grimy room.

Hotel Kailash Dorm beds Y20. Better than the Tashi Hotel, this place in the middle of town is a good place to stop for lunch. It has tasty *thugpa* (Tibetan noodles) for Y5, or try a bowl of rice, yak yogurt and sugar.

Zhongba to Paryang

From Zhongba the southern road deteriorates and the kilometre markers disappear altogether. The section between Zhongba and Paryang is particularly prone to sand being swept down from the sand dunes on either side of the road. Many trucks get stuck briefly here – experienced drivers carry long poles that they wedge between both the twin rear wheels of their trucks for traction. You shouldn't have any real problems with this section of road if you are in a 4WD.

Paryang
elevation 4750m

Paryang is the next town of any significance. It's 110km on from Zhongba (and about five hours' drive from Saga). It is a squalid place, littered with bones and broken beer bottles and infested with dogs. The centre of town is graced with an enormous rubbish dump.

Tashi Hotel Dorm beds Y30. This is a friendly hotel with rudimentary dorm beds; it also offers meals.

Yak Hotel Dorm beds Y25. The Yak has basic dorm rooms with rather charming paintwork.

There are a few *restaurants* in town, and you can buy supplies from the nomad tents in the main square.

Paryang to Hor Qu

There is a checkpoint 16km west of Paryang and a tricky river crossing 47km later, but all the other major crossings now have bridges, which makes this long haul a much easier journey.

You climb over the Mayun-la (5216m), 130km west of Paryang, and descend to a grassy plain where you might see herds of *kyang* (wild ass). Mt Kailash comes into view approximately 90km after Mayun-la, just before the town of Hor Qu.

Hor Qu
elevation 4560m

Hor Qu is 40km from Darchen, the closest town to Mt Kailash. There's a military checkpoint in town and very limited dining options. You can spend the night at this

NGARI (WESTERN TIBET)

town on the Lake Manasarovar kora if you are running late (see the Trekking chapter for details on this walk).

Guesthouse Beds Y25. This unmarked guesthouse has fairly clean rooms with dirt floors and no electricity. The men's and women's toilets are behind any handy wall.

NORTHERN ROUTE

The northern route is the longer of the two routes from Lhasa to Ngari but is the more popular with hitchhikers because there's more traffic. The Chinese are developing the region, and new white-tiled buildings are being hastily constructed in all the towns along the way. Although it's no freeway, the road is at least maintained by teams of sweating road workers.

The first part of the northern route, like the southern route, follows the road from Lhatse to the turn-off near Raka (see Lhatse to the Northern Turn-Off earlier in this chapter). From Raka, there is basically nothing in the way of accommodation before Tsochen, 355km away. The stretch of 410km between the turn-off and the northern road proper, which links Ali to Nagchu, is often very hard going. The road conditions along this stretch can easily slow your progress down to between 15km/h and 25km/h. The one compensation for the shocking state of the road is the frequently breathtaking scenery. If you're travelling by Land Cruiser and camping, the possibilities for putting up a tent along the road are often excellent, and there's no shortage of grassy riverside spots with beautiful mountain views. Nomads' herds of goats and sheep are a common sight along this route.

King Tiger Hot Springs & Tagyel-tso

Only 21km north of the junction are the King Tiger Hot Springs, or the Tagyel Chutse, a collection of gushing geysers, bubbling hot springs, puffing steam outlets and miscellaneous smoking holes in the ground. They stretch from beside the road down to and across both sides of the fast flowing river that issues out of the lake. The bathhouse that was once here is now in

ruins, so you can't bathe, but the spurting springs, which reach heights of up to 15m, are well worth a look.

From the hot springs the road runs around the western side of a lake then through a wide valley, one of the stretches of flat terrain in Ngari where every driver seems to have been intent on finding his own new route. As a result, myriad different tracks fan out across the plain. From a low pass the route descends to a much larger lake, Tagyel-tso, the waters of which are a miraculous shade of the deepest blue imaginable.

North to Tsochen

For 25km the road runs along the eastern side of Tagyel-tso, mountain ranges closing it in on both sides, before passing two small truckers' ***guesthouses*** and climbing to the 5500m Song Ma-la. It then follows a long valley cut by a fast-flowing mountain stream and eventually descends to a bridge and checkpoint. Checking the paperwork of passing vehicles doesn't seem to be a priority at this checkpoint. From here the valley widens out before the route reaches Tsochen, the major outpost between the turn-off and the northern road proper.

Tsochen

Tsochen (Coqen or Cuoqin), 235km from the northern turn-off and 173km south of the northern road proper, is one of those miserable western Tibetan hybrids, a depressing combination of the ugliest of Chinese and the slummiest of Tibetan urban conglomerations. Like all the towns on the northern route, frantic construction is under way – there are new public phones on almost every building (where you may be able to make international calls) and a large post office is planned. But there's not much to write home about here. Getting in late and leaving early is definitely a good idea.

Plateau Hotel *(Gaoyuan Lüshe)* Beds Y20-30. This hotel offers basic accommodation. It's on the south side of Tsochen's main street, and is easily identified by the satellite dish and the more northern of the town's two telecommunications towers in its compound.

Tanug Hotel Beds Y40. On the right as you enter town, this government-run guesthouse has rooms over a karaoke bar that has loudspeakers cranked up until the early hours. If the road has exhausted you enough to sleep through this, the rooms are not bad – they are reasonably clean and have tiled floors and TVs.

The street between the two guesthouses is lined with *Chinese restaurants*. The food is tasty but expensive, as supplies have to be trucked out here. There are several *stores* with basic food supplies.

Tsochen to Gertse

From Tsochen to the junction of the northern road is a journey of about 175km (five hours). The route crosses the relatively insignificant Tsochen-la and then, 43km north of Tsochen, the more impressive 4900m **Nor Chung-la** (Small Wild Yak Pass) before descending to the turquoise waters of **Dawa-tso**. For the next 60km the route crosses from one attractive valley to another, sometimes connected by the river and gorge, at other times by passes.

The road crosses the **Nor Gwa-la** (Wild Yak Head Pass), another pass of nearly 5000m, 94km north of Tsochen, where there may be yak skulls entangled in the prayer flags among the mani stones. From the pass the route descends to a bridge, 109km from Tsochen, at **Chendiloma**, where there are a small *guesthouse* and a *teahouse*, and then drops down into another valley that continues most of the way to the northern road proper.

From around 10km before Chendiloma and for the next 50km the road runs right alongside a beautiful, small, snow-capped mountain range running north-south. The glaciers from the higher peaks often come down to what looks like a stone's throw west of the road. The valley narrows towards its northern end and the road suddenly pops out onto a wide plain before meeting the northern road proper (the one that links Amdo with Ali), just south of Dong-tso. So many different roads fan out across the plain at this point that it's difficult to pinpoint exactly where the roads meet, about 173km north of Tsochen. Some trucks travelling the northern road come this far to collect salt that is mined from a salt lake near the junction and take it back to Lhasa or Shigatse.

From the junction it's 84km (about two hours) west to Gertse, the road often forming a single lane. About 20km before Gertse, multiple trails fan out across the wide, empty plain until you reach the town. Hitching prospects are better from here – there's a lot more traffic once you hit the northern road.

Gertse

Gertse (Gaize) is a bleak and windy town and there are often thick clouds of dust blowing down the main street – a dust mask is an essential accessory for locals. There's a long line of chörtens and mani walls studded with yak and goat horns and draped with prayer flags stretching off to the north of the town.

In the main street you'll find a number of shops, the usual collection of rickety pool tables and, if your Land Cruiser or truck is on its last legs, some rudimentary repair places.

Government Guesthouse Beds Y40. This unmarked guesthouse is opposite the hospital at the eastern end of town. Leave your thoughts in the comment books that dangle on strings in the rooms.

Guesthouse Beds Y40. There's another unmarked guesthouse opposite the market offering slightly better rooms with TV.

Hengdu Restaurant Dishes Y15. Walking out of the dust into this place, opposite the basketball courts, is like entering another world. Neat waitresses in lime-green uniforms will seat you at a spotless table where you can listen to Western Muzak while you search your phrasebook for the names of Sichuan dishes to order.

You can stock up on fresh fruit and vegetables at the sleepy indoor *market*, which offers treats such as bananas, pears, bread and other supplies.

Gertse to Gegye

It's 368km from Gertse to Gegye, the next town of any size. Soon after leaving Gertse,

China's Gifts to Ngari

Chinese settlement has certainly brought a number of developments to Ngari, one of which is stacks of beer bottles. Ngari is simply too remote and the roads too terrible for anyone to contemplate returning empty beer bottles. As a result the whole region is being submerged under mountains of beer bottles, most of them broken. When a truck or Land Cruiser driver needs to add oil, transmission fluid, brake fluid or some other vital liquid to his vehicle he doesn't think, 'Where did I put the funnel?' No, he just reaches down and picks up the nearest beer bottle, expertly smashes the bottom off and has an instantly disposable funnel.

Then there's Chinese architecture, rapidly sweeping right across Tibet, elbowing traditional Tibetan design to one side and replacing it with bizarrely designed buildings heavily dependant on white lavatory tiles and bright blue tinted glass to get the message across.

Finally, we cannot forget Chinese entertainment. Karaoke bars and nightclubs are everywhere and no Tibetan Chinatown is complete without a string of brothels. In most towns they're cheerless affairs resembling hair salons; the shopfronts have a long mirrored wall (for powdering the nose) along one side and a couch along the other. Here the young workers wait, whiling away the hours watching TV, playing mah jong or, most often, knitting.

you'll pass a lake adorned with many prayer flags. **Oma-chu**, a small village, is 54km west of Gertse. For about 150km from Oma-chu to Tsaka and between Tsaka and Pongba, the route is regularly identified by red-and-white marker posts. In winter, when this road is often snow-covered, they are supposed to identify the route across the otherwise trackless plain. Fortunately the posts marking the new underground telephone cable (also red and white) head in generally the same direction.

After 42km the road passes the tiny **Oma-tso,** from where it's another 73km (about 4½ hours from Gertse) to **Tsaka**. This is a major salt-mining community and many hitchhikers find themselves dropped off here by a salt-laden truck. There's a *guesthouse* in the centre of town with beds for Y15 to Y30 and good thugpa for Y8. Expect to pay Y50 to Y100 for a lift to Ali, which you can negotiate at the truck depot behind the guesthouse.

Another route continues west from the turn-off to meet the Ali-Kashgar road just north of Palgon-tso. The Pongba road crosses a couple of passes and wide plains dotted with nomads' tents before descending to the town, 96km from the turn-off.

Pongba (Xiongba) is another rather dismal little place that's a wool-trading centre

for nomads in the region. Here you'll find a very basic truckers' *guesthouse* and a few *restaurants*.

The last stretch of road between Pongba and Ali is fairly good. An hour or so out of town the road enters a gorge and follows the Indus River to Gegye, 105km (two hours) from Pongba.

Gegye

The town of Gegye (Geji), nestled against a ridge, is a good place to stop for lunch or for the night. As you enter town, there is a road running off to the north that is resplendent with drains, footpaths and even a golden Chinese statue.

Shanghai Hotel Beds Y40. The rooms here are quite pleasant – if you can ignore the huge brown water stains on the walls – and have tiled floors, stoves and TVs.

The main road contains plenty of *shops* and the odd *restaurant* serving standard Chinese fare.

Gegye to Ali

Ali is just 112km (2½ hours) from Gegye; 30km before Gegye the road reaches the infant Indus River, not far from its birthplace north of Mt Kailash, and follows it all the way to Ali. At first it's a gently looping river, spreading out in multiple channels across the valley floor, but later it straightens out and the valley narrows.

Ali emerges like a bizarre mirage; from a distance it looks very large and modern and the shock is reinforced when you actually reach the town. It has clusters of modern-looking buildings, shops, neon signs, paved roads and hordes of taxis, just like Beijing. Here you will drive onto your first bitumen road since Lhatse and it's an amazing experience to glide smoothly into town after five or six days of bone-jarring bouncing around.

ALI

☎ 0897 • elevation 4280m

Ali, also known as Shiquanhe in Chinese and Senge Khabab (Town of the Lion) in Tibetan, is the capital of Ali prefecture. There is nothing much to see, but it is a good place to clean up, have some decent food, do some shopping and rest for a while before heading off to the real attractions of Ngari.

Ali is thoroughly Chinese. There are plenty of Tibetans wandering the streets, but, like you, they are probably visitors from further afield. The town is expanding rapidly, especially to the south of the river, and there's a big army presence. This is another centre for the white-tile-and-blue-glass school of architecture that is sweeping across Tibet. After the barren emptiness of the surrounding country, Ali, with its bright lights, video-game parlours, department stores and karaoke bars, comes as a real shock to the system.

Information

Ali has two banks, but only the Agricultural Bank of China, near the army post west of the roundabout, will change foreign currency (it won't change travellers cheques). There is an English-speaking teller here.

Ali also has two post offices. You can make international calls from the main post office near the roundabout, or from the card-operated yellow phones around town. A shop south of the roundabout offers an unreliable Internet service.

The PSB office is in the red-and-white building just west of the main intersection.

It's a very good idea to get a permit in Ali, or have your existing permit stamped here. See Permits earlier in this chapter for details.

The Ali PSB is also one of the few places in Tibet where you can extend your visa. The cost depends on your nationality. For a one-month extension Australians pay Y100, Japanese Y125, Americans Y125 and the French Y160.

Places to Stay

For most travellers, Ali offers the first chance to take a shower in many dusty days. Clean, hot, public showers (Y10) are available 150m east of the roundabout. For those staying at the Ying Hotel, the public showers at the hairdresser's next door are more convenient. They're open until 10pm and also cost Y10.

Mu Kun Sang Guest House (☎ 282 3055) Beds from Y30. This guesthouse, right on the roundabout, is pretty dismal. It's run-down, there are no toilets and it can be noisy. Climb the spiral stairs to the office.

Ying Hotel (☎ 282 1354) Dorm beds Y35, doubles Y300. The Ying is the pick of many budget travellers – it has a range of rooms, most with showers and toilets that don't work. The pit toilets are a long, cold walk out the back.

Shiquanhe Hotel (☎ 282 4966) Doubles from Y120, deluxe doubles with private bathroom Y688. Built on the site of the notoriously decrepit Ali Guesthouse, this new hotel has a range of clean Western-style rooms with TV.

Telecom Hotel (☎ 282 2998) Singles/doubles/suites Y380/400/460. This posh Chinese place has pleasant rooms opening off an atrium that has a central skylight. Check out the shoe-shining machine in the entrance to the foyer.

There are also cheaper *guesthouses* in town that aren't allowed to take foreigners, although you might get in during the low season.

Places to Eat

Ali has numerous restaurants; given the town's remote location, they are surprisingly good value for money. The best hunting

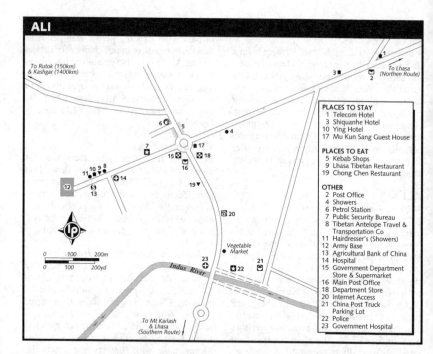

ALI

To Rutok (150km)
& Kashgar (1400km)

To Lhasa
(Northen Route)

Indus River

0   100   200m
0   100   200yd

Vegetable
Market

To Mt Kailash
& Lhasa
(Southern Route)

PLACES TO STAY
1 Telecom Hotel
3 Shiquanhe Hotel
10 Ying Hotel
17 Mu Kun Sang Guest House

PLACES TO EAT
5 Kebab Shops
9 Lhasa Tibetan Restaurant
19 Chong Chen Restaurant

OTHER
2 Post Office
4 Showers
6 Petrol Station
7 Public Security Bureau
8 Tibetan Antelope Travel &
   Transportation Co
11 Hairdresser's (Showers)
12 Army Base
13 Agricultural Bank of China
14 Hospital
15 Government Department
   Store & Supermarket
16 Main Post Office
18 Department Store
20 Internet Access
21 China Post Truck
   Parking Lot
22 Police
23 Government Hospital

ground is beside the roundabout marking the centre of town, and from there south towards the river. Sichuan fare is the standard cuisine and most places will let you pick and choose in the kitchen.

Chong Chen Restaurant Dishes Y5-10. This Chinese place, south of the roundabout between a large gate and a clinic, doesn't have a sign in English. It serves excellent fresh food from its spotless kitchen.

Lhasa Tibetan Restaurant This little tea-house, next to the Ying Hotel, is a rare Tibetan find. *Momos* (Tibetan dumplings) are five mao each.

North of the roundabout are some *kebab shops* with outdoor tables. They're a good place to have a cup of tea and watch the world go by. .

Shopping

It is not as if you are likely to leave Ali loaded down with souvenirs, but the town is a good place to stock up on some supplies,

especially if you are heading down to Mt Kailash. There are some small shops in Darchen, but prices are higher. In Ali there are several *department stores* and a host of *small shops* selling basic supplies, including instant noodles, biscuits, fruit, dried foods, sweets and drinks. The main *vegetable market* is near the river.

Getting There & Away

Bus The headlining news in travel to Ngari is the new bus from Lhasa to Ali. The Tibetan Antelope Travel and Transportation Co (☎ 282 2226, ⓔ ttt010406@sina.com) has its head office in Ali, east of the round-about on Xingxu Lu. There's also a branch in Lhasa next to the Ali Regional Office on Nyangdren Chang Lam (take Sera bus No 5 from Dekyi Shar Lam).

The 26-berth sleeper bus departs Lhasa every two or three days and runs nonstop along the northern route to Ali, returning the next day. Tickets are priced on a sliding scale – Y550 for a seat, Y650 for a sleeper in the bumpy rear, and up to Y800 for a sleeper in the front. Like all vehicles on the road in Ngari, the bus breaks down frequently, but it usually takes a minimum of 48 hours to make the trip. You can also arrange to board the bus in Shigatse or Lhatse for the same price. The bus stops outside the Sang Zhu Zi Hotel in Shigatse at midnight. Be aware that you must pay a deposit on your ticket in Lhasa.

The official status of the Ali bus is quite shaky – the company has permission to operate in Ali prefecture, but not Shigatse prefecture. This means that foreign passengers must get off the bus in Lhatse at 6am and sneak around the checkpoint on foot. How long the service will last is anyone's guess, but while it does it's a great cheap option for travel to Ali. Booking tickets two or three days in advance is essential.

Tibetan Antelope also offers a service from Ali to Yecheng twice a week (when road conditions allow). It costs Y350/450 for a seat/sleeper and takes 1½ days, but don't rely on this service running. At the time of writing this company was also planning to start a bus service from Ali to Mt Kailash in 2002.

Hitching Those hitching to Mt Kailash should check out the schedule of the China Post trucks at the post office near the roundabout, or at the truck parking lot, a block north of the river. They depart on alternate days and you'll pay Y100 for a ride to Darchen. Otherwise start hitching from the roundabout on the southern side of the river.

Expect to pay around Y500 for a lift to Lhasa, while a lift to Kashgar should cost about Y400. The kebab shops north of the roundabout are a good place to ask around for trucks headed that way.

Getting Around
Taxis are part of the 'mirage-in-the-desert' shock of arriving in Ali – the town is thronging with little Daihatsu Charades, just like Beijing. There seem to be hundreds of taxis in the town, ricocheting around like birds in a cage. None of them would survive 5km

beyond the city limits without falling apart on the potholes and corrugations or getting stuck in a sand drift (which raises the question of how they got here in the first place). Within the city limits there's a standard taxi fare of Y5, but the town is actually compact enough that you can walk anywhere.

ALI TO MT KAILASH
From Ali to Darchen, the only town in the near vicinity of the Mt Kailash kora, is a trip of around 330km. Providing there are no serious breakdowns and you do not spend too long languishing in a stream, there is no reason you can't complete the trip in a single day. A new bridge across the Gar River 113km from Ali means that you can now take the shorter road on the eastern bank of the river even when it's swollen with spring snowmelt.

However, after the road from Ali meets the river, for 100km or so there are still many streams to ford along the broad river valley. Most vehicles seem to get stuck in at least one of them. Deep ruts in the sand and gravel normally indicate where other vehicles have been bogged down. At Namru a road turns off west to climb over the 5610m Ayi-la to Thöling Monastery and Tsaparang. At Moincer (Mensi) there is a checkpoint, and a road peels off to Tirthapuri Hot Springs.

Mt Kailash comes into view on the left around 30 or 40 minutes before reaching Darchen. There is one last thing to be careful of: Just before Darchen there is a fairly deep river crossing. It comes up at the last minute before the town, around 6km or 7km after leaving the main road.

MT KAILASH
elevation 6714m
Throughout Asia exist stories of a great mountain, the navel of the world, from which flow four great rivers that give life to the areas they pass through. The myth originates in the Hindu epics, which speak of Mt Meru – home of the gods – as a vast column 84,000 leagues high, its summit kissing the heavens and its flanks composed of gold, crystal, ruby and lapis lazuli. These Hindu accounts placed Mt Meru somewhere in the

towering Himalaya but, with time, Meru increasingly came to be associated specifically with Mt Kailash. The confluence of the myth and the mountain is no coincidence. No-one has been to the summit to confirm whether or not the gods reside there (although some have come close), but Kailash does indeed lie at the centre of an area that is the key to the drainage system of the Tibetan plateau. Four of the great rivers of the Indian subcontinent originate here: the Karnali, which feeds into the Ganges (south); the Indus (north); the Sutlej (west); and the Brahmaputra (Yarlung Tsangpo, east).

Mt Kailash, at 6714m, is not the mightiest of the mountains in the region, but with its hulking shape – like the handle of a millstone, according to Tibetans – and its year-long snow-capped peak, it stands apart from the pack. Its four sheer walls match the cardinal points of the compass, and its southern face is famously marked by a long vertical cleft punctuated halfway down its traverse by a horizontal line of rock strata. This scarring resembles a swastika – a Buddhist symbol of spiritual strength – and is a feature that has contributed to Kailash's mythical status. The mountain is known in Tibetan as Kang Rinpoche, or 'Precious Jewel of Snow'.

Mt Kailash has long been an object of worship for four major religions. For the Hindus, it is the domain of Shiva, the Destroyer and Transformer. To the Buddhist faithful, Mt Kailash is the abode of Demchok (Sanskrit: Samvara), a wrathful manifestation of Sakyamuni (Sakya Thukpa) thought to be the equivalent of Hinduism's Shiva. The Jains of India also revere the mountain as the site at which the first of their saints was emancipated. And in the ancient Bön religion of Tibet, Kailash was the sacred Yungdrung Gutseg (Nine-Stacked-Swastika Mountain) upon which the Bönpo founder Shenrab alighted from heaven.

Mt Kailash has been a lodestone to pilgrims and adventurous travellers for centuries, but until recently, very few had set their eyes on the sacred mountain. This situation has begun to change in recent years. In May 2001 Spanish climbers even

gained permission to climb the peak, only to abandon their attempt in the face of international protests. (Reinhold Messner also gained permission to scale the peak in the 1980s, but abandoned his expedition when he got to the mountain in deference to the peak's sanctity.)

Mt Kailash is accessed via the small town of **Darchen** (elevation 4560m), which is the starting point of the kora. It is a forgettable little village strewn, as usual, with broken beer bottles and dotted around the outskirts with nomads' tents. Most travellers linger long enough to organise their kora and then get out.

The PSB is on the east side of town, just outside the compound of the Darchen Guesthouse. You will need to get your travel permit stamped here on arrival. Permits for the Mt Kailash kora (Y50) are available at a tent inside the hotel compound. For details of the kora, including information on hiring porters or yaks in Darchen, see the Trekking chapter.

Day Walks

If you've got extra time at Darchen, or you want to spend a day or two acclimatising before setting out on the Mt Kailash kora, you can find some interesting short walks in the area. The ridge to the north of the village obscures Mt Kailash, but an hour's walk up to the top of the ridge following the trail running to the north-west will offer fine views of the mountain. To the south

To the Land of Shiva

While out in Ngari you may well find bands of hundreds of shivering Indian pilgrims hauling themselves around Mt Kailash. An agreement between China and India allows a limited number of Indian pilgrims to make the pilgrimage to Lake Manasarovar and Mt Kailash each year. Hindus believe Mt Kailash to be the abode of Shiva and Lake Manasarovar to be a mental creation of Brahma. The trip is so important to Hindus that the quota is oversubscribed and places have to be determined by a lottery.

you will be able to see the twin lakes of Manasarovar and Rakshas.

You can also venture north of this ridge – walking 2½ hours to the north will take you to the **Gyangdrak Monastery**, largest of the Mt Kailash monasteries. Like the other monasteries, it was rebuilt after the depredations of the Cultural Revolution. The **Selung Monastery** is a two-hour walk to the west; a trail heads back to Darchen from here.

Places to Stay & Eat

Darchen Guesthouse Beds Y120. This is the only guesthouse in Darchen allowed to take foreigners, and you can't miss it because the road into the village leads straight through its central gate. Don't be confused by the sign beside the gate announcing that it's the Gangdishi Guesthouse. Foreigners are charged an extravagant price for the grubby facilities, although with determined bargaining you may be able to knock off Y20. The only saving grace is that at the time of writing, modern shower and toilet blocks were being built in the compound.

Deciding to *camp* at Darchen doesn't help, as you must set up your tent inside the ugly guesthouse compound, and you're charged the same price (Y120) as a bed for that dubious pleasure. A better idea is to walk for 1½ hours to Tarboche on the Mt Kailash kora and camp here for free.

In the low season some travellers have found cheaper, unofficial beds in Darchen.

There's a *Chinese restaurant* in the compound, but it's hard to find anyone to feed you. There are also a couple of Tibetan restaurants north of the compound, including the *Darchen Restaurant* offering decent noodles with fresh vegetables for Y8, or the cranky but warm *Lhasa Restaurant* outside the east gate.

In the high season there are *nomad traders* to the east of town offering a limited range of food supplies including sweets, biscuits, powdered milk and the ubiquitous instant noodles.

Getting There & Away

The town of Darchen, the starting point for the Mt Kailash kora, is 6km north of the main Ali-Paryang route and about 12km from Barkha, 107km north of Purang, 330km south-east of Ali and a lonely 1200km from Lhasa. See Ali to Mt Kailash and Southern Route, earlier in this chapter, for descriptions of the roads.

At the time of research, the Tibetan Antelope Travel & Transportation Co (☎ 282 2226, e ttt010406@sina.com), based in Ali, was planning to start a bus service from Ali to Mt Kailash in 2002.

LAKE MANASAROVAR

elevation 4560m

Lake Manasarovar, or Mapham Yum-tso (Victorious Lake) in Tibetan, is the most venerated of Tibet's many lakes. According to ancient Hindu and Buddhist cosmology the four great rivers of the Indian subcontinent, the Indus, Ganges, Sutlej and Brahmaputra, arise from Manasarovar. In reality, only the Sutlej River originates at the lake, although the headwaters of the other great rivers are in close proximity.

Manasarovar is linked to the smaller lake Rakshas Tal (also known as Lhanag-tso) by a channel called Ganga-chu. On rare occasions, water flows via this channel from Lake Manasarovar to Rakshas Tal; this is said to augur well for the Tibetan people. The channel had long been dry, but water has indeed been flowing between the two lakes in recent years. The two bodies of water are associated with the conjoined sun and moon, a powerful symbol of Tantric Buddhism. Sadly, the sacred landscape of the lake has been disturbed by the construction of a large mine dug by bulldozers on the isthmus between the two lakes.

Manasarovar has been circumambulated by Indian pilgrims at least since being extolled in the sacred Sanskrit literature called the *Puranas*, written around 1700 years ago. One Hindu interpretation has it that *manas* refers to the mind of the supreme god Brahma, the lake being its outward manifestation. Accordingly, Indian pilgrims bathe in the waters of the lake and circumambulate its circumference. Tibetans, who are not so keen on the bathing bit, generally just walk around it. It's not unusual to see

Kailash & Manasarovar Books

There are numerous books about Mt Kailash, Lake Manasarovar and the surrounding area, but the gold star for Kailash enthusiasm has to go to the Indian author Swami Pranavananda. His numerous stays in the region between 1928 and 1947 normally lasted two to six months but included two visits that lasted a year. Not only did he complete 23 *parikramas* (circuits of the holy mountain; the Hindu equivalent of a *kora*), he also did 25 circuits of Lake Manasarovar, including seven when it was completely frozen over, and visited the source of all four holy rivers. He also sailed on the holy lake, made many scientific measurements and in 1949 published his findings in *Kailas Manasarovar*. It was reprinted in India in 1983 and you should be able to find a copy in a Kathmandu bookshop.

Clearly, Kailash trekking has become much easier in the past 50 or 60 years. Under the heading 'Highway Robbers, Firearms and Guides' Pranavananda suggests firing two or three blank shots into the air after sunset to frighten off 'any robber lurking in the neighbourhood'. The Kailash chapters in German-born Lama Anagarika Govinda's *The Way of the White Clouds* (Rider, London, 1966) includes a classic account of the pilgrimage during a trip to Tibet in 1948.

Each year several hundred Indian pilgrims are allowed to visit Mt Kailash; the Indian government selects the lucky candidates by a lottery. Since the Chinese charge US$1000 per person, the pilgrimage is only open to wealthy Indians but they have plenty of guidebook possibilities. Kathmandu bookshops will probably have several titles on their shelves including *Kailash-Manasarovar – A Travelogue & Yatra Guide* by Dipti Sharad (Dipta Publications, Chennai, 1998). The author advises on everything from suitable supplies to how to ride a yak and even wags a warning finger at Indian gentlemen who may 'suffer from the wrong notion that the women in the group should be responsible for the cooking'.

Kathmandu bookshops may also have Sven Hedin's three-volume *Transhimalaya: Discoveries & Adventures in Tibet* (London, 1909–13). Volumes II and III cover Hedin's time in the Mt Kailash region. Charles Allen's *A Mountain in Tibet* investigates the hunt for the sources of the region's four great rivers. *The Sacred Mountain* by John Snelling reports on early Western explorers, as well as the colourful list of characters who turned up in the early 1980s, when the door to China and Tibet first creaked narrowly open. *Kailas – On Pilgrimage to the Sacred Mountain of Tibet*, by Kerry Moran with photos by Russell Johnson, is a beautifully photographed essay on Mt Kailash, Lake Manasarovar and the region's colourful pilgrims. *Walking to the Mountain* by Wendy Teasdill is a delightfully laid-back account of the author's lengthy pilgrimage to Mt Kailash, a far from easy task when she visited there in 1988.

naked Westerners throwing themselves into the lake to wash away the sins of a lifetime (and the dirt of the last week). Legend has it that the mother of the Buddha, Queen Maya, was bathed at Manasarovar by the gods before giving birth to her son.

Hindi poet Kalidasa once wrote that the waters of Lake Manasarovar are 'like pearls' and that to drink them erases the 'sins of a hundred lifetimes'. Be warned, however, that the sins of a hundred lifetimes tend to make their hasty exit by way of the nearest toilet. Make sure that you thoroughly purify Manasarovar's sacred waters before you drink them, however sacrilegious that may sound.

Most groups and individuals base themselves at picturesque Chiu Monastery, on the north-western shore of the lake, and use this small monastery as a base for day walks. For detailed information on the Lake Manasarovar kora and a map of the region, see the Trekking chapter.

Chiu Monastery

Thirty-three kilometres south of Darchen and 8km south of the main highway, Chiu Monastery *(admission free)* enjoys a fabulous location atop a craggy hill overlooking the sapphire blue Lake Manasarovar. The chapel here contains images of Sakyamuni

(Sakya Thukpa) and Guru Rinpoche. Climb up to the roof of the monastery for stunning views of the lake. The huge peak on the southern horizon is 7728m Gurla Mandata, near the border with Nepal.

There are hot springs behind the monastery, and a small glass-roofed **bathhouse** *(admission Y20)* close to the village. The water is channelled from the hot springs into individual cubicles via open ducts and it's barely lukewarm by the time you can get a few centimetres of water into the mouldy tiled tubs. Don't expect a pleasant soak, but if you need a wash this is a good spot. You can also do your laundry in the warm outflow around the back.

There are a couple of friendly, unmarked *guesthouses* near the bathhouse that offer dorm beds for around Y25, but food is scarce. You may have to content yourself with instant noodles. You can also *camp* by the lake. An Indian pilgrim *guesthouse* was under construction at the lake's shore at the time of writing.

Getting There & Around
You will have made it this far either by hitching or by hiring a Land Cruiser. There is no public transport and very little in the way of truck activity on the road between Darchen and the monastery. There may occasionally be trucks on the main Ali-Purang road, which is around 6km south of Darchen – be prepared for a long wait if you are hitching.

TIRTHAPURI HOT SPRINGS & KORA
On the banks of the Sutlej, only a few hours' drive north-west of Darchen, the Tirthapuri Hot Springs enjoy close associations with Guru Rinpoche. Pilgrims traditionally bathe here after the Mt Kailash kora.

It only takes about an hour to walk Tirthapuri's own short kora. Starting from the hot springs the trail climbs to a cremation point, an oval of fire-blackened rocks. From this point an alternative longer kora route climbs up to the very top of the ridge, rejoining the trail near the long mani wall. The regular kora trail continues past a hole where pilgrims dig 'sour' earth for medicinal purposes. Further along there's a 'sweet' earth hole. The trail reaches a miniature version of the Mt Kailash kora's Drölma-la, marked with mani stones and a large collection of yak horns and skulls. Below, prayer flags

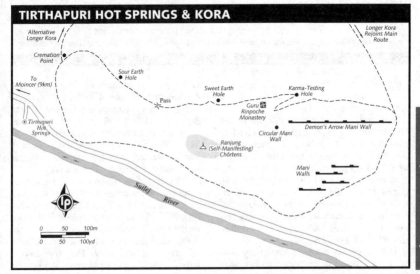

TIRTHAPURI HOT SPRINGS & KORA

Alternative Longer Kora

Longer Kora Rejoins Main Route

Cremation Point

To Moincer (9km)

Sour Earth Hole

Pass

Sweet Earth Hole

Karma-Testing Hole

Guru Rinpoche Monastery

Demon's Arrow Mani Wall

Tirthapuri Hot Springs

Circular Mani Wall

Ranjung (Self-Manifesting) Chörtens

Mani Walls

Sutlej River

0   50   100m
0   50   100yd

NGARI (WESTERN TIBET)

Pilgrimage

Pilgrimage is practised throughout the world, although as a devotional exercise it has been raised to a level of particular importance in Tibet. This may be because of the nomadic element in Tibetan society; it may also be that in a mountainous country with no roads and no wheeled vehicles, walking long distances became a fact of life, and by visiting sacred places en route pilgrims could combine walking with accumulating merit. To most Tibetans their natural landscape is imbued with a series of sacred visions and holy 'power places'; mountains can be perceived as mandala images, rocks assume spiritual dimensions, and the earth is imbued with healing powers.

The motivations for pilgrimage are many, but for the ordinary Tibetan it amounts to a means of accumulating merit *(sonam)* or good luck *(tashi)*. The lay practitioner might go on pilgrimage in the hope of winning a better rebirth, curing an illness, ending a spate of bad luck or simply because of a vow to take a pilgrimage if a bodhisattva granted a wish.

In Tibet there are countless sacred destinations, ranging from lakes and mountains to monasteries and caves that once served as meditational retreats for important yogis. Specific pilgrimages are often prescribed for specific ills; certain mountains, for example, expiate certain sins. A circumambulation of Mt Kailash offers the possibility of liberation within three lifetimes, while a circuit of Lake Manasarovar can result in spontaneous buddhahood. A circuit of Tsari in south-eastern Tibet can improve a pilgrim's chances of being reborn with special powers such as the ability to fly.

Pilgrimage is even more powerful in certain auspicious months; at certain times, circumambulations of Bönri are reckoned to be 700 million times more auspicious than those of other mountains.

The three foremost pilgrimage destinations of Tibet are all mountains: Mt Kailash, in western Tibet; Tapka Shelri and the Tsari valley in south-eastern Tibet; and Mt Labchi, east of Nyalam, in Tsang. Lakes such as Manasarovar, Yamdrok-tso, Nam-tso and Lhamo La-tso attract pilgrims partly because their sacred water is thought to hold great healing qualities. The cave hermitages of Drak Yerpa, Chimpuk and Sheldrak are particularly venerated by pilgrims for their associations with Guru Rinpoche.

Pilgrims often organise themselves into large groups, hire a truck and travel around the country visiting all the major sacred places in one go. Pilgrim guidebooks have existed for centuries to help travellers interpret the 24 'power places' of Tibet. Such guides even specify locations where you can urinate or fart without offending local spirits (and probably your fellow pilgrims).

Pilgrimage is not just a matter of walking to a sacred place and then going home. There are a number of activities that focus the concentration of the pilgrim. The act of *kora*, or circumambulating

---

hang right across the gorge and a series of rocky pinnacles are revered as *ranjung*, or self-manifesting chörtens.

The trail passes the **Guru Rinpoche Monastery**. Where the trail doubles back to enter the monastery there is a rock with a hole in it right below the solitary prayer wheel, which is a handy karma-testing station. Reach into the hole and pull out two stones. If both are white your karma is excellent; one white and one black means that it's OK; and if both are black you have serious karma problems. Perhaps another Kailash kora would help?

The monastery *dukhang* (assembly hall) is entered through an antechamber with vivid paintings of the Four Guardian Kings. A collection of comical-looking statues (the one of Jampa is particularly bad) overlooks the altar, while to the right side are stone footprints of Guru Rinpoche and his consort Yeshe Tsogyel. At one time the monastery was connected with the important Hemis Monastery in neighbouring Ladakh.

Outside the monastery a large circle of mani stones marks the spot where the gods danced in joy when Guru Rinpoche was enshrined at Tirthapuri. Beside it is a mani wall (a wall made of mani stones) over 200m long, the end result of a demon firing an arrow at the guru. He stopped the arrow's flight and transformed it into this

Pilgrimage

the object of devotion, is chief among these. Circuits of three, 13 or 108 koras are especially auspicious, with sunrise and sunset the most auspicious hours. Prostration *(chaktsal)* is a powerful way of showing devotion. Prostration follows a sequence: placing your hands in a *namaste* (prayer-like) position, touching your forehead, throat and heart, getting down into a half-prostration (as for Muslim prayer) and then lying full on the ground with the hands stretched out. The particularly devout carry out whole pilgrimages like this, stepping forward the length of their body after each prostration (often marking the spot with a small conch shell) and starting all over again. The hardcore even do their koras sideways, advancing one side step at a time!

Most pilgrims make offerings during the course of a pilgrimage. *Kathaks*, white ceremonial scarves, are given to lamas or holy statues as a token of respect. Offerings of yak butter or oil, fruit, *tsampa* (dough made with roasted-barley flour), seeds and money are all left at altars, and bowls of water and *chang* (barley beer) are replenished. Monks often act as moneychangers, converting Y10 notes into wads of one-mao notes, which makes limited funds go further.

Outside chapels, at holy mountain peaks, passes and bridges, you will see pilgrims throwing offerings of tsampa or printed prayers into the air (often with the cry *'sou, sou, sou!'*). Pilgrims also collect sacred rocks, herbs, earth and water from a holy site to take back home to those who couldn't make the pilgrimage, and deposit personal items, often leaving them hanging in a tree. Other activities in this spiritual assault course include adding stones to cairns, rubbing special healing rocks, and squeezing through narrow gaps in rocks as a method of sin detection. Many of these actions are accompanied by the visualisation of various deities and practices.

Koras usually include stops of particular spiritual significance, such as rock-carved syllables or painted buddha images. Many of these carvings are said to be 'self-arising; ie, not having been carved by a human hand. The Mt Kailash kora, for example, is a treasure trove of these, encompassing sky-burial sites, stones that have 'flown' from India, monasteries, bodhisattva footprints, and even at one point a lingam, or penis-print.

Other pilgrimages are carried out to visit a renowned holy man or teacher. Blessings from lamas, *trulkus* (reincarnated lamas) or *rinpoches* (highly esteemed lamas) are particularly valued, as are the possessions of famous holy men. According to Keith Dowman in his book *The Sacred Life of Tibet*, the underpants of one revered lama were cut up and then distributed among his eager followers!

Bradley Mayhew

wall. Finally the kora path drops back down to the riverside, passing a large collection of mani walls of various sizes on the way.

There are no facilities at the hot springs so you must be self-sufficient. Don't plan to wash away the dust of Ngari's roads here either; the springs simply gush down to the river, although pilgrims have dug a couple of very public bathing holes.

There is no public transport to Tirthapuri. The hot springs are 9km south of Moincer (Mensi), which in turn is 65km west of Darchen along the main road to Ali. There's a checkpoint at Moincer, which is the dormitory town for the coal mines 20km to the north-east.

GUGE KINGDOM

Thöling and neighbouring Tsaparang are the ruined former capitals of the ancient Guge kingdom of Ngari, accessed via the modern Chinese town of Zanda (also known as Thsada or Zhada). Tsaparang, in particular, is a truly amazing sight, in part because it is so little known. The 9th-century ruins are carved into the steep sides of an imposing ridge. Cave dwellings, stunning monastic buildings and a ruined palace are linked by twisting paths and secret tunnels that worm their way into the rock itself.

This barren landscape seems an unlikely place for a major civilisation to have developed; yet the Guge kingdom thrived as an important stop on the trade route between India and Tibet. By the 10th century it was a wealthy centre supporting several thousand people, and the great Guge king Yeshe Ö began to nurture an exchange of ideas between India and Tibet. Yeshe Ö sent the young monk Rinchen Zangpo to study in India; the monk returned 17 years later to become one of Tibet's greatest translators of Sanskrit texts, and a key figure in the revival of Buddhism across the Tibetan plateau. Rinchen Zangpo built 108 monasteries throughout western Tibet and Ladakh. The two most important were those at Tsaparang and Thöling. He also invited Kashmiri artists to paint the unique murals still visible today. It was partly at Rinchen Zangpo's behest that Atisha (Jowo-je), a renowned Bengali scholar and another pivotal character in the revival of Tibetan Buddhism, was invited to Tibet. Atisha spent some three years in Thöling before travelling on to central Tibet.

The kingdom fell into ruin just 50 years after the first Europeans to enter Tibet arrived in 1624 (for more information, see History earlier in this chapter).

Tsaparang is 21km east of the modern town of Zanda, and the Guge monastery at Thöling is now merely an adjunct to the town. The Chinese government has entangled these sites in an amazing amount of red tape, but they are a highlight of Ngari and well worth the three- or four-day detour from the Ali-Kailash road.

The stunning scenery in the area is an attraction in itself. In particular, the northern road from Ali into Zanda passes through incredible sand canyons and amazing eroded mountains, cut through by the Sutlej River on its way to the subcontinent.

Permits

Having done their best to destroy Thöling Monastery and Tsaparang, the Chinese now charge Western visitors to see what escaped their ravages. It's worth checking the latest situation in Ali or Lhasa before you set out as part of the fee for Tsaparang, theoretically, is supposed to be paid in Lhasa, another part of it at either the Ali or Darchen

PSB and yet another part of it at Tsaparang! You also need a separate permit (Y20) from the Zanda PSB to visit Thöling.

The PSB is just south of the Armed Forces Hotel in Zanda and you must register there on arrival in town. Make sure your permit is stamped in Ali or Darchen, otherwise you risk a fine here. If you're travelling with a guided tour you can usually leave it up to your guide to sort out all the paperwork.

Zanda
elevation 3650m

Zanda, the base for visits to the ancient Guge kingdom, has an incredible location. It's perched high above the Sutlej River against crumbling cliffs – a patch of vivid green among the unrelentingly barren canyons. There are even real trees, the first in hundreds of kilometres. Zanda is a major Chinese army post and there's a checkpoint at the bridge 5km before the entrance to town.

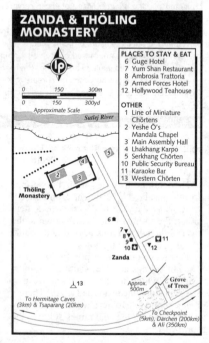

ZANDA & THÖLING MONASTERY

PLACES TO STAY & EAT
6 Guge Hotel
7 Yum Shan Restaurant
8 Ambrosia Trattoria
9 Armed Forces Hotel
12 Hollywood Teahouse

OTHER
1 Line of Miniature Chörtens
2 Yeshe Ö's Mandala Chapel
3 Main Assembly Hall
4 Lhakhang Karpo
5 Serkhang Chörten
10 Public Security Bureau
11 Karaoke Bar
13 Western Chörten

Guge Hotel Beds Y90. This hotel has well-kept rooms, by Tibetan standards, in the newer block. It even has TVs, which can be used to provide illumination if the lights in your room aren't working.

Armed Forces Hotel Beds from Y60. Although the beds have lumpy sand-filled pillows, the Armed Forces Hotel offers clean rooms and a slightly less horrible version of the Tibetan toilet-from-hell. There's no hope of running water except for a tap in the courtyard.

Ambrosia Trattoria Dishes Y20. The enticing name of this little dirt-floored place will draw you in like a magnet, but you'll get no closer to a spaghetti *matriciana* than the chopstick holder on the table – an old tomato-paste tin.

The Guge Hotel has a *restaurant* downstairs, while on the main street there's the Chinese *Yum Shan Restaurant*. The *Hollywood Teahouse* offers Tibetan dishes. There's also a *karaoke bar* a block behind the main street.

Thöling Monastery

Thöling Monastery *(admission Y80)*, founded by Rinchen Zangpo, was once Ngari's most important monastic complex. It was still functioning in 1966 when the Red Guards shut down operations. Unfortunately much of what survived the depredations of the Cultural Revolution looks likely to be destroyed in the current round of 'restorations'. Three main buildings survive within the monastery walls. You need to get a Y20 permit from the Zanda PSB (on top of the entrance fee) to visit Thöling.

Yeshe Ö's Mandala Chapel

The main building in the Thöling complex, Yeshe Ö's Mandala Chapel, was also known as the Golden Chapel and was built in the form of a three-dimensional representation of a Tibetan mandala. Before destruction during the Cultural Revolution, the square main hall had four secondary chapels at the centre of each wall. Figures of the deities were arrayed around the wall facing in towards a central image atop a lotus pedestal. All the images were destroyed, although many of the wall murals survived. At the time of writing this chapel was closed to visitors for renovations. When it reopens, visitors should be able to see the main hall, an open corridor with shrines and chapels facing in towards the centre. Again, the images in these rooms were all destroyed in the 1960s.

Main Assembly Hall

The dukhang has fine wall murals showing strong Kashmiri and Nepali influences. Scholarly opinion varies on whether these date from the 13th and 14th or 15th and 16th centuries. Bring a powerful light if you want to inspect these well-preserved murals of deities and their consorts. The main statues here are of the past, present and future buddhas, and there's also a footprint of Rinchen Zangpo.

Lhakhang Karpo

The blandly functional-looking exterior of the Lhakhang Karpo, or White Chapel, doesn't hint at the quality of the murals within. As with Yeshe Ö's Mandala Chapel, a great deal of restoration is taking place.

Outside the Monastery Walls

A few steps to the east of the monastery compound is the recently restored Serkhang chörten. An external stairway ascends the three levels of the chörten. It's unclear what resemblance the structure bears to the original Serkhang, which was totally destroyed. A similar chörten stands in total isolation just to the west of the town. To the north, between the monastic compound and the cliff face, which falls away to the Sutlej River below, are two long lines of miniature chörtens.

Tsaparang

Tsaparang *(admission Y320)* has been gracefully falling into ruin ever since its slide from prominence in the 17th century and is of great interest to experts on early Buddhist art. The ruins, which seem to grow organically out of the hills, make for a photogenically surreal landscape, but there are restrictions on photographing Tsaparang's foremost attraction: its early Tantric-inspired murals.

NGARI (WESTERN TIBET)

The ruins climb up the ridge through three distinct areas. At the bottom of the hill is the monastic area with the four best-preserved buildings. From there the trail to the top climbs through the residential quarters, where monks' cells were dug into the clay hillside. This area is mainly in ruins. Finally the route dives straight into the hill and through a tunnel before emerging in the palace citadel at the very top of the hill.

Although smaller and less impressive than the buildings at the bottom of the hill, some of the palace buildings are also in reasonable repair and the views are fantastic. There's a spooky collection of underground rooms that are all that remains of the winter palace. Because Tsaparang was already partially abandoned at the time of the Cultural Revolution the Chinese did not attack it with quite the same vandalistic fury that they vented upon other religious complexes in Tibet. However, when a little more survives it only makes it even more sadly evident

how much was destroyed. The latest caretaker, a keen artist, has placed his own sculptures in some of the honoured spaces once devoted to ancient images of the gods and goddesses.

Tsaparang is just 21km west of Zanda, and unless you're very lucky with hitching a ride, the only way you will be able to get there is with a rented vehicle or by walking. The road follows the south side of the fantastically eroded Sutlej River valley all the way from Zanda to Tsaparang. Many maps incorrectly show both centres on the north side of the river.

Chapel of the Prefect Just inside the entrance to the complex is a small building that was a private shrine for Tsaparang's prefect or regent. The caretaker has named it the 'Drölma Lhakhang' after his own sculpture of Drölma (Tara) displayed here. The wall murals date from the 16th century, by which time the style evinced in other Tsaparang murals was in decline. The main mural on the back wall shows Sakyamuni (Sakya Thukpa) flanked by Tsongkhapa and Atisha wearing the pointed head coverings typical of the period. Small figures of the Buddha's disciples stand beside his throne and many other miniature images crowd between the three large ones.

Lhakhang Karpo Slightly above the entrance the large Lhakhang Karpo, or White Chapel, has the oldest paintings at Tsaparang and is probably the most important chapel in Ngari. The murals of the chapel probably date back to the 15th or 16th century. Their influences, however, extend back to 10th-century Kashmiri Buddhist art, and for this reason are of particular interest to scholars of Buddhist art. Apart from Tsaparang, very little material evidence of early Kashmiri art remains.

The ceiling is beautifully painted as are the many thin columns that support it. The carvings and paintings of Sakyamuni (Sakya Thukpa) that top each column are particularly noteworthy and the paintings around the skylight are vivid. At one time 22 life-size statues lined the walls; six have

TSAPARANG

To Thöling (21km)

Ticket Office

P

Entrance

Lhakhang Karpo

Chapel of the Prefect

Lhakhang Marpo

Yamantaka Lhakhang

Monastic Quarters

0   50   100m
0   50   100yd
Approximate Scale

Tunnel

Very Steep Cliff

Summer Palace

Stairs to Winter Palace

Mandala (Demchok) Lhakhang

HANNAH LEVY

The rhythm of monastery life is marked by ritual, relaxation and sleep.

BRADLEY MAYHEW

BRADLEY MAYHEW

RICHARD I'ANSON

Motivations for pilgrimage are many. The ritual of prostration is a powerful way to show devotion; some pilgrims don wooden blocks to protect their hands.

disappeared completely and the remaining 10 are damaged. Even so, this chapel has fared better than most temples attacked during the Cultural Revolution. In addition the doors are flanked by two 5m-high guardian figures, red Tamdrin (Hayagriva) and blue Chana Dorje (Vajrapani). Again both are damaged, but even armless they hint at the lost marvels of the chapel.

The huge figure of Sakyamuni (Sakya Thukpa) that once stood in the recess, the Jowo Khang, at the back of the hall has been replaced by one of the caretaker's statues. On the side walls at the back there were once row after row of smaller figures of deities, each perched on its own small shelf. A few of these figures on the higher levels have survived intact.

Fortunately the destruction of the statues must have distracted attention from the chapel's magnificent murals which have survived in excellent condition.

Lhakhang Marpo Above the Lhakhang Karpo stands the equally large Lhakhang Marpo, or Red Chapel, which was built around 1470, perhaps 30 years earlier than the Lhakhang Karpo. The murals in this chapel were repainted around 1630, shortly before the fall of the Guge kingdom, so they are actually younger than those in the Lhakhang Karpo.

The original door to the chapel, with its series of concentric frames, has survived and is worth close inspection. Inside, many thin columns support the chapel roof, similar to those of the neighbouring Lhakhang Karpo. Although the wall murals have been damaged by vandalism and water leakage they remain so remarkably brilliant it's hard to contemplate that they are actually over three and a half centuries old.

The statues that once stood in the chapel were placed towards the centre of the hall, not around the edges, and although only the bases and damaged fragments remain, the crowded feel to the space, the intense colours and the eerie silence combine to give the chapel the feel of a Hollywood movie set. You almost expect Indiana Jones to come striding out from behind the wreckage. At the back of the hall there were once many small statues on individual shelves; a handful of them still have bodies but all the heads have gone.

Dorje Jigje Lhakhang The murals in the smaller chapel devoted to Dorje Jigje (Yamantaka), a few steps above the Lhakhang Marpo, are also painted red, and are almost solely devoted to wrathful deities. Like the Chapel of the Prefect near the entrance gate, the paintings here are of later origin and lower quality than the earlier paintings in the larger chapels. All the statues that once stood here were destroyed.

Summer Palace From the four chapels at the base of the hill, the path to the top climbs up through the monastic quarters and then ascends to the palace complex atop the hill via a tunnel. The Summer Palace, at the northern end of the hilltop, is well preserved with a balcony offering wonderful views over Tsaparang and out across the marvellously eroded valleys around the site. The Sutlej River valley is just to the north, while across the smaller valley just to the north-east is the ruined Lotang Lhakhang.

The most interesting of the palace buildings is the small but well-preserved Mandala (Demchok) Lhakhang, the red painted building in the centre of the hilltop ridge. The centrepiece of this small chapel was a wonderful three-dimensional mandala, only the base of which survived the desecrations of the Cultural Revolution.

Winter Palace Accessed by a steep and treacherous eroded staircase, the Winter Palace is an amazing ants' nest of rooms tunnelled into the clay below the Summer Palace. The rooms are 12m underground and the eastern rooms have windows that open out onto the cliff-face. There are seven dusty chambers, all empty, linked by a cramped corridor. Branching off from the stairs is a dim passage that provided vital access to water during sieges and served as an emergency escape route for the royal family. This tunnel once opened onto a hidden spring in the valley on the western side of the ridge.

The stairs to the Winter Palace lead down from between the Summer Palace and the Mandala (Demchok) Lhakhang. Don't come down here if you're prone to vertigo or claustrophobia.

Getting There & Away

There is no public transport to the Guge kingdom sites, so unless you have a rented Land Cruiser getting there can involve some tough hitching. Even with your own vehicle access is not easy; the roads to Zanda from the Darchen-Ali road are rough and go over some very high passes. In a rented truck or Land Cruiser it should be possible to make it to Zanda from either Ali or Mt Kailash in a single day, providing you get an early start.

To/From Darchen It's 65km from Darchen to Moincer (Mensi), the turn-off to Tirthapuri, and another 56km from there to the army base at Songsha, where there's a basic Tibetan restaurant. From there a road leaves the main Ali route and climbs to a pass after 15km, then over the next 80km zigzags down into a series of gorges and climbs up the other side before eventually making a long, winding and very rough descent down a fantastically eroded gully where the hills on both sides are worn into incredible shapes. Eventually this side valley debouches into the wider Sutlej River valley, and after crossing a bridge the road finally reaches the oasis-like town of Zanda, six or seven hours and 122km from Songsha.

To/From Ali Coming from Ali the road is equally tough going. The road to Zanda branches off the main road from Ali to Darchen (see Ali to Mt Kailash, earlier in this chapter) near Namru. It climbs a long ravine from the plain and then goes up and over a series of low passes and wide valleys before zigzagging its way up to the very high 5610m Ayi-la. From this high point the route drops down into a deep valley and crosses a number of other valleys before reaching the eerily eroded mud-walled canyon approaching Zanda. It's 130 winding and arduous kilometres from Namru to Zanda.

DUNGKAR

Caves with extensive wall paintings were discovered at this remote site in the early 1990s. The paintings of the Buddha are possibly the oldest in Ngari. Dungkar is approximately 40km north of Zanda, near the road to Namru.

RUTOK

The new Chinese town of Rutok Xian is a busy army post with a number of new buildings in the bizarre modern Chinese style of architecture popping up all over Tibet.

North of Rutok Xian the road runs around the eastern end of Palgon-tso before reaching a junction from where the Kashgar road continues north while another road turns off east to meet the northern route to Lhasa at Tsaka. Rutok is surrounded by extensively irrigated fields – this is one of the few areas of intensive agriculture in Ngari.

The old town of Rutok is about 10km off the main road from a turn-off about 5km south of Rutok Xian. This white-painted traditional Tibetan village huddles at the base of a hillock. Atop the hill is the red **Lhakhang Monastery**, flanked at both ends of the hill by the crumbling but still impressive ruins of **Rutok Dzong**. Clearly, at one time the whole eastern face of the hill was covered in buildings, which have now all fallen into decay. The monastery was destroyed during the Cultural Revolution, rebuilt in 1983–84 and now has just eight monks. You need a permit from the PSB in Rutok Xian to visit the monastery and ruins.

Ancient Petroglyphs

Prehistoric etchings depicting animals and symbols were discovered in 1985 at Lurulangkar, 12km from Rutok. They are closely connected to the prehistoric illustrations beside the Ali-Rutok road at Rumudong. See the boxed text 'Prehistoric Petroglyphs' for more information on these ancient rock carvings.

Places to Stay

There's a *guesthouse* in Rutok Xian where you can get a mouldy room from Y40 per person. There's no accommodation or any

Prehistoric Petroglyphs

In 1985 prehistoric rock carvings, or petroglyphs, were found at several sites in Rutok county. This was the first time such a find had been made in Tibet, although subsequently similar finds have been made at numerous other sites. Two of these sites are easily found; one of them is actually right by the roadside between Rutok and Ali, while the other is 12km west of the old town of Rutok. For more information on these carvings and many others in Tibet look for the book *Art of Tibetan Rock Paintings* by Li Yongxian & Huo Wei (Sichuan People's Publishing House, 1993). Unfortunately the book has no map showing the location of the sites.

Rumudong

The extensive collection of rock carvings at Rumudong is right beside the road about 50km south of the old Rutok turn-off, or about 75km north of Ali. There are kilometre markers every 5km along this road. Travelling north from Ali start looking on the east side of the road at kilometre marker 970; the petroglyphs would be at around 967. There are two distinct groups on the rock face right beside the road, just before it crosses a bridge to travel along a causeway over the marshy valley floor of the Maga Zangbu-chu.

The first, and more extensive, group also features a number of more recent carvings, some of them carved right over their ancient predecessors. The most impressive of the rock carvings features four extravagantly antlered deer racing across the rock and looking back at three leopards in hot pursuit. Also depicted are eagles, yaks, camels, goats, tigers, wild boars and human figures.

Lurulangkar

This collection of paintings is about 12km south-west of the old town of Rutok – follow the road along the river valley. The carvings here are relatively primitive compared to those at Rumudong. They are found beside the road, up to a height of 4m above the ground, and show a variety of pre-Buddhist symbols and animals, including eagles, dogs, yaks, deer and goats. Human figures are shown standing in isolation or riding on horses. There are a number of hunting scenes showing dogs pursuing deer and hunters shooting at them with bows and arrows.

---

other facilities at old Rutok but there is a pleasant grassy area to ***camp*** behind the hills, on the banks of the Kargye-tso.

Getting There & Away

It's about 130km from Ali to the new town of Rutok Xian; there's a checkpoint around 6km north of Ali. The turn-off to old Rutok is 5km south of the new town. Palgon-tso, where there's another checkpoint, is about 10km beyond Rutok Xian, on the road into Xinjiang.

XINJIANG TO ALI

The 1100km road from Yecheng (in southern Xinjiang) to Ali is not an easy ride, and the high passes along the way can be closed by snow during winter (December to February). Coming from Kashgar, you have to be particularly careful about altitude sickness as the initial rate of altitude gain is dramatic.

There are truck stops along the way, about a day's travel apart, where food and basic accommodation are available, but it's wise to bring as much food and water as you can carry. Breakdowns are a frequent occurrence and it can be a long, hungry wait between stops. It's good insurance to bring a tent as well, unless you fancy sleeping in the back of the truck in the case of a breakdown. The trip can take anything from three days to a week or more.

From Kashgar there are buses every half hour to Yecheng (Karghilik; Y23, five hours), and a bus makes the journey between Yecheng and Ali when road conditions allow. (For details, see Getting There & Away under Ali earlier in this chapter.)

NGARI (WESTERN TIBET)

If you're hitching from Yecheng to Ali, the truck stop 4km south-east of Yecheng is the best place to sniff out a lift. *Accommodation* is available here and trucks depart in the early morning. Expect to pay Y150 to Y500 for a lift, depending on the road conditions.

Yecheng to the Tibetan Border

Leaving Yecheng, there is a checkpoint south of the town, but it's possible to drive around it. The road climbs two passes (3150m and 4800m), then follows a narrow gorge to the truck stop at **Kudi**. Around 270km from Yecheng, K2 is visible across the Pakistan border. About 150km later you'll reach **Mazar** (3700m), which has some *shops* and *restaurants*. The road turns east from here and climbs over a couple of passes, fanning out across barren plains in between. Conditions improve around 60km before you reach the depressing little town of **Dahongliutan** (4200m), which offers basic food and a *guesthouse*.

From here the road turns south and around 23km beyond Dahongliutan you climb out of the flat valley of Xinjiang via the Jitai Daban pass (5050m), which marks the beginning of the remote region of Aksai Chin. For the next 170km road conditions are very bad and progress is slow. The construction of the road here, through a triangle of territory that India claimed as part of Ladakh, was a principal cause of the border war between India and China in 1962. The fact that the Chinese managed to build this road without India even realising that it was under construction is an indication of the utter isolation of the region. Finally you come to the edge of Aksai Chin and climb up to the Jieshan Daban pass (5200m), which has stunning views and which takes you over the border into Tibet. From here, Ali is around 420km away.

Tibetan Border to Ali

Road conditions don't get any better over the border. For the next 30km the road is muddy, rutted and desolate. Trucks frequently get stuck here and traffic can bank up in the summer months. The road climbs a 5050m pass where conditions improve, before heading down to the small town of **Sumzhi** which has basic *accommodation* and a *restaurant*. After crossing the last major pass (5250m) the road descends to the town of **Dormar** (4350m), 80km away, which has a few *restaurants*. It then skirts around the eastern end of **Palgon-tso** (4170m), where a checkpoint awaits the unwary. In mid-October this checkpoint moves to the east side of the lake. Soon afterwards the road arrives at **Rutok Xian**. Nearby are the old town of Rutok and ancient rock engravings (see Rutok and the boxed text 'Prehistoric Petroglyphs' earlier in this chapter for details). From here it is 130km south to Ali, passing a checkpoint 6km north of the city.

WESTERN NEPAL TO MT KAILASH

See Lonely Planet's *Trekking in the Nepal Himalaya* for details of the trek from Humla, a restricted region in the far west of Nepal, to Mt Kailash. This route is open only to tour groups who trek in from Humla and you will need a specially endorsed Chinese visa.

From the Nepali border at Sher, the road makes a long descent to a stream and then follows the Humla Karnali to the village of Khojarnath, 10km north.

Khojarnath
elevation 3790m

For those travelling up from Nepal, Khojarnath, 21km south of Purang, is the first large village over the border in Tibet. It boasts the **Korja Monastery** *(admission Y20)*, an important monastery of the Sakya order. This monastery escaped the worst excesses of the Cultural Revolution, and the damage it sustained is being repaired with financial assistance from German and Italian sponsors. The statues in the **assembly hall** show Guru Rinpoche, Rinchen Zangpo, Chenresig (Avalokiteshvara), Jampelyang (Manjushri), Chana Dorje (Vajrapani), Drölma (Green Tara) and Sakyamuni (Sakya Thukpa). The entrance to the assembly hall is flanked by statues of the Four Guardian Kings.

The **main hall**, large, empty and under restoration, is presided over by a figure of Jampa (Maitreya). Hanging from the ceiling are the stuffed carcasses of a yak, an Indian tiger, a snow leopard and a wolf.

Khojarnath to Purang

From Khojarnath the road passes **Kangtse**, presided over by a hilltop monastery to the west, and fords two rivers. Look for the Tibetan mills built along the banks. It then passes through two villages and eventually enters Purang, 21km north of Khojarnath, along a walled road lined with willow trees. Make the most of them, as you won't be seeing any more trees for a long time.

Purang
☎ 08060 • elevation 3800m

Purang (Taklakot to the Nepalis) is a large trading centre composed of a number of distinct settlements separated by the Humla Karnali River and tributaries. Nepali traders come up from the south-east, from the Humla district of western Nepal, following the same route as Western trekking groups, and cross the border to Sher in Tibet. The Nepalis also come in from the south-west,

from Darchula in the extreme west of Nepal. In Purang, they trade a variety of goods, including rice, carried up from Nepal in huge trains by goods-carrying goats. This Nepali rice is traded for Tibetan salt. Wool from the Tibetan plateau and Indian consumer goods are other important trading commodities.

Nepali traders and Western trekkers are not the only foreigners passing through Purang. This is also the arrival point in Tibet for the annual influx of Hindu pilgrims from India, intent on making a *parikrama* (the Hindu equivalent of a kora) of Mt Kailash, which devout Hindus consider the abode of Shiva.

Purang is a weird combination of the ultramodern mixed with the traditional Tibetan, and it's very spread out. The hill north-west of town is the site of a huge army base said to extend far into the mountain in a series of caves. It's even rumoured there are missiles here, aimed at New Delhi. There are hundreds of People's Liberation Army (PLA) soldiers in baggy green uniforms in the town.

Information Purang has a PSB building opposite the Peacock Hotel, where you need to register on arrival.

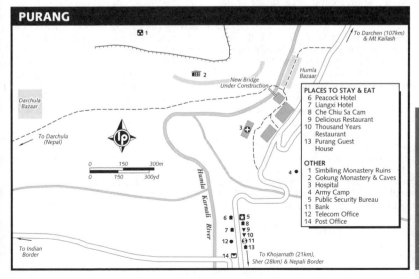

PURANG

To Darchen (107km)
& Mt Kailash

Humla
Bazaar

New Bridge
Under Construction

Darchula
Bazaar

To Darchula
(Nepal)

0   150   300m
0   150   300yd

Humla Karnali River

To Indian
Border

To Khojarnath (21km),
Sher (28km) & Nepali Border

PLACES TO STAY & EAT
6 Peacock Hotel
7 Liangxi Hotel
8 Che Chiu Sa Cam
9 Delicious Restaurant
10 Thousand Years
   Restaurant
13 Purang Guest
   House

OTHER
1 Simbiling Monastery Ruins
2 Gokung Monastery & Caves
3 Hospital
4 Army Camp
5 Public Security Bureau
11 Bank
12 Telecom Office
14 Post Office

NGARI (WESTERN TIBET)

There's a bank that will change US dollars in cash but not Nepali rupees or travellers cheques. Nepali rupees are accepted in Tibetan and Nepali shops in town. Nepali traders refer to yuan as 'suka'.

Purang also has an intermittently open post office and a telecom office where you can make overseas calls. Shops are dotted along the main street or there are the town's two busy bazaars.

Bazaars Purang has two bazaars, catering to Nepali traders. The riverside **Humla bazaar** has an extensive collection of shops dealing mainly in Chinese consumer goods such as clothes and household equipment. It takes its name from the Nepali Humla region to the south. At the time of writing, a vehicle bridge that will take the road over the river alongside the older footbridge was under construction here.

The **Darchula bazaar**, a 15-minute walk to the west, has lines of mud-walled buildings, some of them roofed with white canvas. There's a large trade in Tibetan wool in this bazaar as well as tinned food, cloth and necessities such as rice, sugar and flour. The focus of trade is with the Darchula district of Nepal, several days' walk to the south. Goods from India are also traded here.

Monasteries In the hills above the trail between the bazaars are caves, one containing the **Gokung Monastery**. Many of the caves have doors and windows and have been made into substantial dwellings.

Towering over the town from its hilltop position above the Darchula bazaar is the ruined **Simbiling Monastery**. In 1949 Swami Pranavananda described this monastery, which housed 170 monks, as the biggest monastery in the region. The Chinese shelled it during the Cultural Revolution and nothing remains apart from the crumbling walls. It's a steep and treacherous climb up to the monastery from the Darchula bazaar,

and officially you need a permit from the Purang PSB.

Places to Stay & Eat All the accommodation options are in the southern (Chinese) part of town.

Liangxi Hotel (☎ 2215) Doubles Y45 per person. This comfortable place is the best value in town, and has clean rooms with TV and outside toilets.

Peacock Hotel (☎ 2362) Beds Y100. With decent Western-style rooms, this place in the government compound is not bad. The toilets are inside and the dorm rooms have TV and carpet.

Purang Guest House (☎ 2140) Beds Y130. This guesthouse on the south side of town is scruffy and shamelessly tries to overcharge Western visitors. There is no running water, the electricity is erratic and the toilets at the rear of the compound are horrible to smell, see or use. Give it a miss.

There are a number of restaurants around the guesthouses, including the *Thousand Years Restaurant* and the *Delicious Restaurant*, both of which offer decent Chinese meals. You can breakfast on *baozi* (steamed dumplings) for Y2 at *Che Chiu Sa Cam*.

Getting There & Away Western trekkers arriving from Nepal usually arrange to be met at the border town of Sher for the 28km drive via Khojarnath to Purang.

From Purang it's 74km north to Chiu Monastery on the shores of Lake Manasarovar and another 33km from there to Darchen, starting point for the Mt Kailash kora. The road from Purang passes **Toyo**, where the Sikh invader Zorawar Singh was killed in 1841, before passing a number of small Tibetan settlements and fording several rivers en route to the Gurla-la (4590m). Just beyond the pass, Rakshas Tal and (on a clear day) Mt Kailash come into view. A few kilometres before reaching the village at Chiu Monastery you pass a gold mine.

Kham (Eastern Tibet)

Kham is a land apart from the rest of Tibet. Its climate, geography, flora, fauna and isolation all lend it a unique, almost magical atmosphere. Traditional life seems less disturbed here than in central Tibet. The stone villages and vertical prayer flags resemble those in Bhutan and the unusually shaped *chörtens* (stupas) seem more at home in Mustang. The scenery often resembles more the Swiss Alps or Rocky Mountains than the high Tibetan plateau. The Chinese presence remains pronounced, especially along the strategic Sichuan-Tibet Hwy, but the countryside still belongs to windswept Khampa nomads and bands of Bönpo pilgrims.

Kham gains much of its charm from its people. Khampa men, long regarded as both the most religious and most warlike of all Tibetans, can be seen swaggering along the streets of many settlements wearing red (from Chamdo) or black (from Derge) braids in their long hair and a *chuba* (long-sleeved sheepskin cloak) hanging off the right shoulder. Many wear broad-brimmed cowboy hats (fur-lined hats in winter) and big boots, and sport at least one gold tooth, an amulet around their neck and a knife by their side. Women traditionally wear elaborate coral and amber jewellery and arrange their hair into 108 braids. In the remote southern areas bordering India and Bhutan there are small communities of tribal Lhopas (literally 'southern people') and Monpas.

Geographically the region offers great variety, from subtropical low-lying jungle to the glaciated peaks of Namche Barwa (7756m) and the high grasslands of north-eastern Tibet. At its eastern end the headwaters of some of Asia's greatest rivers – the Mekong, Salween and Yangzi – tumble off the Tibetan plateau, carving a dramatic concertina landscape of deep gorges, microclimates and remote valleys.

For some travellers the attraction of the area lies in the spectacular scenery, a few remarkable monasteries and the alternative route in or out of Tibet. For others the lure

Highlights

- Hiking around the gorgeous alpine lake of Draksum-tso, with its fairy-tale island monastery
- Making a pilgrimage to the Lamaling Temple, with its lovely location
- Gazing open-mouthed at the magnificent scenery from Nyingtri to Pomi, passing from lush subtropical forest to alpine valleys over snowy passes
- Relaxing by the stunning turquoise lakes of Rawok-tso, fringed with alpine peaks
- Exploring the dramatic, towering and remote Riwoche Tsuglhakhang
- Visiting the 'mini-Potala' of Sok Tsanden Monastery

will be the region's very remoteness – this is very much travel through the blanks on the maps. Travel is restricted to Land Cruiser tours or illegal hitching.

There are two main routes through the region: the northern and southern roads. The southern road, a strategic military road constructed in 1954–55, plunges into subtropical south-eastern Tibet and then rises up over the gorges of Kham, making this one of the most unpredictable roads in Tibet. The northern road is a higher roller-coaster ride from the deep valleys near the Sichuan border to alpine pasturelands, all the time rising to the north-eastern plateau of Amdo.

The traditional Tibetan province of Kham incorporates modern-day eastern Tibet (the eastern part of the Tibetan Autonomous Region, or TAR), western Sichuan and north-west Yunnan. Basic information on travel in western Sichuan is provided at the end of this chapter. For more information see Lonely Planet's *South-West China*.

History

The area around Chamdo was one of the first settled in Tibet, as attested to by the

KHAM (EASTERN TIBET)

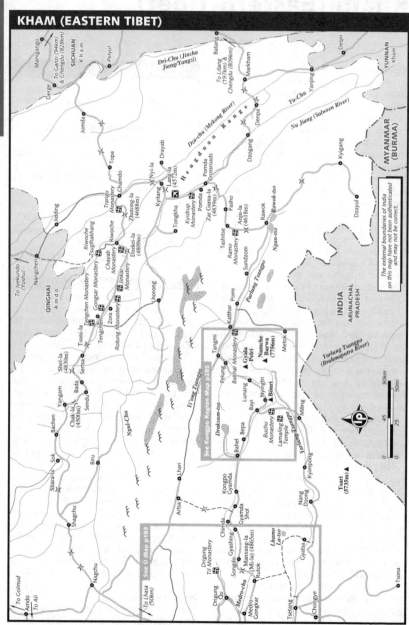

The external boundaries of India on this map have not been authenticated and may not be correct.

5000-year-old Neolithic remains at nearby Karo. Fossilised millet hints at a 5000-year tradition of agriculture in the region.

Kham was the home of many holy men including the founders of the Drigungpa and Karmapa schools. In 1070 many Buddhists fled persecution in central Tibet to Kham, where they set up influential monasteries, later returning to central Tibet to spearhead the so-called second diffusion of Buddhism in Tibet.

Lhasa's control over the region has waxed and waned over the centuries. Lhasa first gained control of Kham thanks to Mongol assistance, but most of the region has enjoyed political independence. Much of Kham until recently consisted of many small fiefdoms ruled by kings (Derge), lamas (Litang) or hereditary chieftains (Batang). Relations with China were generally restricted to those involving trade caravans, which carried bricks of Chinese tea in and pastoral products out.

Chinese warlords such as Zhao Erfeng and Liu Wenhui swept through eastern Kham (modern-day western Sichuan) in the late 19th and early 20th centuries to set up the Chinese province of Xikang (western Kham). Khampa rebellions occurred frequently, notably in 1918, 1928 and 1932, though not all were against the Chinese; in 1933 the Khampas tried to shake off Lhasa's nominal rule.

In 1950 Chamdo fell to the People's Liberation Army (PLA; see the boxed text 'The Fall of Chamdo' later in this chapter) and much of eastern Tibet was subsumed into China. In 1954 the eastern part of Kham was merged into Sichuan province and a program of land reforms was introduced, including the collectivisation of monasteries. Then in 1955 the Chinese tried to disarm the Khampas and settle nomads. The Kangding Rebellion erupted in the winter of 1955–56 and fighting spread to Litang, Zhongdian and Daocheng. As the PLA arrived, monasteries were bombed in Daocheng and Litang and the rebels fled into Chamdo and later to India and Nepal, to organise armed resistance from Mustang with CIA assistance.

Today eastern Tibet remains quite Sinicised in western Sichuan and along the Sichuan-Tibet Hwy, where there is a string of army bases, logging camps and even prisons, but off the highways Khampa life remains culturally strong.

Flora & Fauna

Warmer, wetter and more forested than anywhere else in Tibet, the region's wide vertical range creates a series of biological niches that hide Tibet's largest concentration of rare animal and plant species. Takins, red pandas, musk deer, gorals, long-tailed leaf monkeys, Himalayan tahrs, tragopans, pheasants and Himalayan monals all live in the tropical and subtropical regions along Tibet's south-eastern borderlands.

Eastern Tibet is also a botanical powerhouse, and attracted the attention of intrepid 19th- and 20th-century British plant hunters such as F Kingdon Ward. From May onwards the region is a riot of wildflowers, bursting with 190 species of rhododendrons, 110 types of gentianas and 120 species of primulas, not to mention rare flowers such as the blue poppy, which was discovered by the explorer (and spy) FM Bailey in the Rong-chu valley in 1913. Many of the rhododendrons and azaleas found in the West do indeed descend from samples taken from eastern Tibet. Pockets of ancient cypresses up to 2500 years old continue to thrive.

Logging is a serious problem in the temperate forests of eastern Tibet, though logging was formally banned in the Tibetan areas of Sichuan and Yunnan in 1998 after a series of devastating floods.

Climate

Eastern Tibet has a dramatically different climate from the rest of Tibet. The effects of the summer monsoon from Assam bring a lot of rain from early June to September. Snowfall generally starts in October.

The best times to travel are late March, April and early May, and September, October and early November. During other times the southern route is usually out of use for weeks at a time.

What to Bring

For a few ideas on items you'll need on any Land Cruiser trip, see the boxed text 'Dealing with an Agency' in the Getting Around chapter. Rain gear is essential for any time of year. Insect repellent can be useful for low-lying areas.

Shops are generally quite well stocked en route so you'll be able to load up every couple of days, but it's worth packing luxuries such as fruit, coffee and chocolate. When buying supplies, budget in an extra couple of days in case your trip is extended unavoidably.

Most importantly, pack plenty of time, route flexibility and a visa with at least a few days' validity remaining after the end of your planned trip.

Four Rivers, Six Ranges: The Khampa Resistance

By the late 1950s thousands of Khampa warriors had begun to rebel against Chinese rule and reforms. News of the armed rebellion filtered through to central Tibet but the Khampas' pleas for help fell on deaf ears. The Dalai Lama, keen to avoid conflict with the Chinese, asked the Khampas to disarm. Without organisation or cohesive leadership the rebellion was routed.

Yet a core of Khampa fighters managed to regroup in Lhoka, in southern Tibet, and in a rare moment of Khampa unity formed an organisation called Chizhi Gangdrung (Four Rivers, Six Ranges), the traditional local name for the Kham region. Soon 15,000 men were assembled, led by Gonbo Tashi, and a new flag was created.

The Khampas eventually attracted the attention of exiled Tibetan leaders in Kalimpong (India), as well as the Chinese Kuomintang (KMT or Nationalist Party; some Khampas were trained in Taiwan) and even the CIA, who liaised with the Tibetans through Thubten Norbu and later Gyalo Dhundup, both brothers of the Dalai Lama.

Before long, Tibetan leaders were liaising with CIA agents in Kolkata (Calcutta), arranging meetings through dead letter drops and secret messages. The first batch of six Khampa agents trekked over the border to Kalimpong, were driven to Bangladesh and then were flown to the Pacific island of Saipan, where they were trained to organise guerilla groups. Agents were later parachuted behind enemy lines into Samye and Litang.

In 1957, guerilla attacks were made on Chinese garrisons and road camps, and in 1958, 700 Chinese soldiers were killed by guerillas near Nyemo. The movement met with the Dalai Lama in southern Tibet when he fled Lhasa in 1959 as the CIA readied three plane loads of arms – enough for 2000 people.

The flight of the Dalai Lama to India marked a setback for the resistance and the focus switched to a base in Mustang, an ethnically Tibetan area in Nepal, where between 1960 and 1972 the Nepalis turned a blind eye to the movement. Between 1960 and 1962 over 150 Tibetans were sent to Colorado for training.

Yet the resistance was living on borrowed time. The Americans never had much confidence in the Tibetans and by the mid-1960s CIA funding had dried up. By 1972 the international political climate had changed; US president Richard Nixon's visit to China and the coronation of Nepal's pro-Chinese king had left the Khampas out on a limb. Moreover, the resistance was riddled with feuds – most of the Khampa rebels had always been fighting more for their local valley and monastery than for any national ideal. In 1973 the Nepalis demanded the closure of the Mustang base and the Dalai Lama asked the rebels to surrender. It was the end of the Khampa rebellion and the end of Tibetan armed resistance to the Chinese.

For more on the CIA's funding of Tibetan resistance guerilkas and the diplomatic wrangling behind the scenes, read *Orphans of the Cold War – America and the Tibetan Struggle for Freedom* by John Kenneth Knaus. Knaus, a 44-year veteran of the CIA, was personally involved in training Tibetan agents in Colorado. For a Tibetan perspective, try *Warriors of Tibet* by Jamyang Norbu, published by Wisdom Publications.

Permits

Eastern Tibet is officially forbidden to foreigners without a guide, private transport (normally a Land Cruiser) and a fistful of permits, including an Alien Travel Permit and a military permit. These can only be obtained by the travel agency arranging your trip.

Even with all requisite permits you may still have problems visiting Sok Tsanden and Riwoche Monasteries. Try to get these monasteries (not just the towns of Sok and Riwoche) specified by name on your permits. Places close to the disputed Indian border such as Namche Barwa and the Tsangpo gorges are almost impossible to get permits for; your agency will need military connections for these. Nervous guides often want to register your group with every county-level Public Security Bureau (PSB) office along your route, which can be a real pain.

If you decide to hitch through eastern Tibet you will have to be extremely cautious, especially in larger towns and county capitals. We weren't stopped at a single check post throughout eastern Tibet but maybe we were just lucky. The biggest problem with hitching is that you'll probably need to remain out of sight for large sections of the trip, so you may miss much of the scenery. Permits are most often checked in hotels so you'll dramatically increase your chances of not getting caught if you have a tent and are self-sufficient in food.

Permits are not required for anywhere in Sichuan or Yunnan provinces.

Itineraries

If you don't have much time, an eight- or nine-day Land Cruiser loop from Lhasa to Bayi and back could take in Draksum-tso, the Serkhym-la, Lamaling Temple, Lhamo La-tso, the Yarlung Valley, Samye and views of Yamdrok-tso (see the Ü chapter for details on the Yarlung Valley and Samye).

A more comprehensive 17-day loop to Chamdo and back could take in Draksum-tso, Bayi, Lamaling Temple, Serkhym-la, Lunang, Pomi, Rawok, Pomda, Chamdo, Riwoche, Tengchen, Sok Tsanden, Nagchu, Nam-tso and Lhasa. From Lhasa it's a good idea to travel anticlockwise so that if the road is closed around Tangmi you have less distance to backtrack. This kind of trip costs around Y15,000 from Lhasa, including transport, guide and permits. If you are travelling in May it's a good idea to have a back-up plan in case the Sichuan-Tibet Hwy is closed. Discuss an option with your agency and get a price quote for an alternative route back to Lhasa, perhaps via Miling and Tsetang.

A straight run from Lhasa to Chengdu takes about eight days nonstop (10 days on the northern route), though you are better off budgeting at least two weeks in a Land Cruiser, longer if hitching.

Lhasa to Deqin in Yunnan can be done in six or seven days, though again 10 days is better.

KONGPO GYAMDA
☎ 0894

There's little reason to stop in this modern town, unless you get a late start from Lhasa and need to spend the night. The nearby village of Gyamda Shol, 13km to the west of Kongpo Gyamda, was once an important stop on the Lhasa-Chamdo caravan trail, which branches north from here over the mountains into the Yi'ong Tsangpo valley.

The **Kathok Nunnery** in the hills to the north of town has a small community of nuns and a hermitage. A path leads up to the nunnery from the eastern outskirts. To kill time you could also walk up the hills bedecked in prayer flags to the south of town.

The PSB office is at the eastern end of town.

Places to Stay & Eat

Kongpo Gyamda is a decent place to spend the night.

Taizhao Hotel *(Taizhao Binguan)* Doubles with private bathroom Y100. Rooms here are comfortable and come with Western toilet. Running water is most reliable on the 3rd floor; hot water comes in thermoses only. Unfortunately the wrecked hotel courtyard doubles as the town's only public toilet.

Bank Hotel *(Yinhang Zhaodaisuo)* Doubles without bathroom Y60. Rooms are

KHAM (EASTERN TIBET)

Kongpo

The Kongpo region is culturally, ecologically and linguistically quite distinct from the rest of Tibet. A former kingdom of the early Yarlung kings and rival to Lhasa, Kongpo has for centuries been vilified by central Tibetan rulers as a land of incest and poison, where strangers are routinely drugged so that the locals can steal their souls. Along the road to Draksum-tso, look out for the tall 12-sided stone towers; these are referred to locally as *dudkhang* (demons' houses).

The traditional Kongpo costume features a round hat with an upturned rim of golden brocade for men (known as a *gyasha*) and a pretty pillbox hat with winged edges (known as a *dieu*) for women. Men wear brown woollen tunics, belted around the waist.

Logging, both legal and illegal, is a particularly pressing problem in Kongpo. Several prisons and work camps for political prisoners were built in this remote region during the Cultural Revolution and some still operate to this day.

passable and there's a toilet down the hall, though no shower.

Grain Department Guesthouse *(Liangshiju Zhaodaisuo)* Doubles Y60. Rooms are cheaper here than elsewhere but the guesthouse may not take foreigners.

The main street is lined with ***Sichuanese restaurants***.

Getting There & Away

Kongpo Gyamda is 277km from Lhasa, over the impressive 4865m Manxung-la (also known as the Mi-la). En route, in the upper Medro-chu valley, the road passes Rutok, which has a monastery and several Tibetan teahouses and is the trailhead for the trek to Lhamo La-tso (see Getting There & Away under Lhamo La-tso in the Ü chapter). Buses from Lhasa pass through Kongpo Gyamda on the way to Bayi (Y30) after a lunch stop in Songdo. Buses to Lhasa (Y50 to Y60) leave around 8am. If you are cycling you should be able to find accommodation in Songdo, 96km east of Kongpo Gyamda.

DRAKSUM-TSO
elevation 3540m

This beautiful alpine lake, also known as Bagsum-tso and Basong-tso (depending on the dialect), is a long day's drive from Lhasa and a worthy 41km detour off the Sichuan-Tibet Hwy. Apart from the sheer beauty of the lake and its surrounding 6000m-plus peaks, the site has strong connections to Gesar of Ling, the semimythical ruler of eastern Tibet, and Guru Rinpoche, the Indian sage, both of whom are said to have resided at the lake. Many pilgrimage sites are connected to the two.

The highlight of the lake is the magical **Tsodzong Monastery** (also spelled Tsomum Monastery), a small Nyingmapa chapel sited on a superbly photogenic island just off the southern shore. The island is an organic fusion of dozens of types of flora and a sprinkle of holy sights. Shout out and the gracious monk caretaker will ferry you across on a cable raft and show you around.

The monastery was founded by Sangye Lingpa in the 14th century. The main monastery building has statues of a wrathful and peaceful Guru Rinpoche and smaller statues of Sakyamuni (Sakya Thukpa), Chenresig (Avalokiteshvara) and Kongtsun Demo, a local protector. The statues were actually shot and then burned by Red Guards during the Cultural Revolution, before being restored by the famous local lama Dudjom Rinpoche and his son Chuni Rinpoche (now resident in Lamaling). In the corner of the monastery is what is said to be a stone hoofprint of Gesar's horse. The monastery entrance is flanked by ancient-looking male and female fertility symbols.

A small *kora* (ritual circumambulation circuit) path around the monastery passes many hard-to-discern holy sites, including a tree said to resemble a conch horn, a sky-burial site, a 'body print' of Gesar, an underground treasury of the Karmapa, a tiger print and a tree whose leaves bear magical symbols.

For the best short walks around the island walk west back along the road to a small pass which is decorated with prayer flags and rock paintings and ascend the hill to the north side of the road. You could also walk

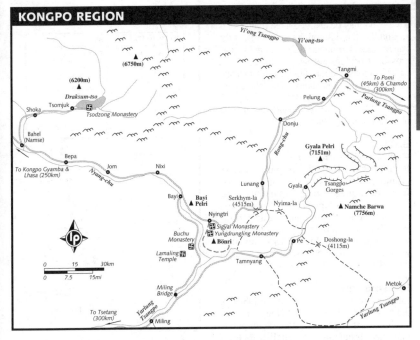

KONGPO REGION

a couple of hours east along the southern shore or even further to Tsomgo village for the best views of the mountains to the north. A two-day kora path rings the lake.

Road upgrading will soon lead to increased development on the lake, with plans for several hotels and even speedboats aimed at Chinese tourists, so get here soon. You may have to pay an entry fee of Y30 and possibly an extra Y5 fee to visit the island.

PSB officers at Tsodzong, Tsomjuk and possibly Bahel will want to see your travel permits. It's hard to visit Draksum-tso if you don't have a permit.

Places to Stay & Eat
Tourism officials haven't made it all that easy to visit the lake, and accommodation remains a problem.

Across from Tsodzong island, ***Draksum Lake Tourism Holiday Village*** (*Basong Hu Luyou Dujia Cun*) offers beds in comfortable rooms (no water) but will often demand

an outrageous Y100 per person. Management also tries to force foreigners to pay a fee of Y100 for camping anywhere around the lake. The PSB official at the hotel will scrutinise your travel permit so make sure all is in order. If you are camping and without travel permits it's best to get off the beaten track as fast as possible.

There is a second ***government guesthouse***, with similar prices, at Tsomjuk (Tsojom), at the mouth of the lake, but few people stay here.

Food at both hotels is grossly overpriced, so bring your own. Foreigners are not allowed to stay overnight at the monastery.

It is possible to stay at Bahel village, on the Sichuan-Tibet Hwy near the turn-off to Draksum-tso: ***Lhasa Gesar Drukhang*** has beds for Y15.

Getting There & Away
The road to Draksum-tso branches off the main highway at Bahel Bridge (also known

KHAM (EASTERN TIBET)

as Namse) and soon passes an entry gate, where you may be charged a fee if anyone is around. On the right, high on the cliff, is the Pangri Jokpa hermitage. After 15km the road crosses a bridge and swings to the right, passing Shoka and Jara villages and an abandoned military radio station. The lake comes into view 35km from Bahel at Tsomjuk (Lake's Mouth). The road continues another 6km to Tsodzong island.

BAYI

☎ 0894 • elevation 2990m

Bayi is a large Han Chinese military town of minor interest, except perhaps as a base from which to visit the surrounding sights or restock your supplies. 'Bayi' in Chinese means '1 August', the founding date of the PLA. Groups will probably need to register with the unfriendly local PSB – travellers without a permit should steer well clear of the town.

Information

Internet access is available at the lobby of the New Century Hotel and Hongdenglong Teahouse, though the latter's computers may have problems with English fonts. A third option is located above a bookshop on Xianggang Lu.

Several bathhouses around town offer hot showers for Y4 and are generally open until midnight.

Pelri Kora

At the eastern edge of town rises Bayi Pelri, a holy mountain connected to Guru Rinpoche, who fought demons on the hill and then conjured up the surrounding farmland from a vast lake. A delightful three-hour kora path rings the peak but finding the correct path can be tricky without the help of pilgrims. If you are walking on your own, it's easiest to follow the logging road that switchbacks up the hill, keeping to the left of the peak. Hidden off the road about halfway up is the tiny Geshigong Monastery. Atop a saddle on the north side of the hill is a forest of prayer flags surrounding a white chörten. From here the kora leads clearly around the back of Pelri, past several

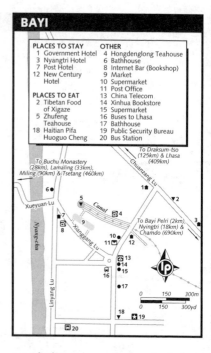

sacred sites where pilgrims hang hats, bowls and even miniature ladders, to several rock prints connected to Guru Rinpoche. The path continues through forest and eventually descends back down to the logging road.

Places to Stay

Post Hotel (Youzheng Dajiudian; ☎ *588 9718)* Doubles without/with private bathroom Y48/268. The old block of rooms out the back (ask in Chinese for the *putongjian*) is the only budget option in town. The plusher standard rooms come with hot showers and carpet and are worth a splurge, especially when discounted.

Nyangtri Hotel (Linzhi Binguan; ☎ *582 3040, 25 Shuangyong Lu)* Singles/doubles Y198/268. This is the choice of most party cadres and occasional tour groups.

New Century Hotel (Xin Shiji Dajiudian; ☎ *588 5468, Shuijingyuan Lu)* Doubles with private bathroom from Y188.

Places to Eat

There are a couple of Tibetan restaurants in the sea of Chinese snack bars, including the *Tibetan Food of Xigaze* and the *Niutou Zangcan*, which is recognisable from the murals around the door.

Haitian Pifa Huoguo Cheng Dishes from Y5. This was one Chinese restaurant we kept coming back to. Vegie dishes are cheap and tasty and the service is friendly.

Zhufeng Teahouse Beers Y12. This kitsch Chinese teahouse was built to resemble Lamaling Temple and is the most eye-catching building in town. It serves up expensive teas and beers.

Getting There & Away

It's unlikely that foreigners will use the bus station (travellers without permits should avoid the place like the plague), but there are daily buses to Lhasa (Y80 to Y100, six hours), Kongpo Gyamda (Y37), and Pomi (Y78, 6am). Minibuses to Miling (Y25) depart from the main bridge over the Nyang-chu. There are also frequent minibuses to Nyingtri (Y5). Buses to Nang Dzong (Chinese: Langxian; Y59) depart three times a week. The easiest place from which to catch a minibus to Lhasa (Y100) is the main square. Every five days there is a sleeper bus to Chengdu (Y400, four days); it travels via Lhasa and Golmud, not the Sichuan-Tibet Hwy.

Bayi is 409km from Lhasa and 239km from Pomi. The stretch of road between the Draksum-tso turn-off and Bayi, along the Nyang-chu valley, is one of the region's most beautiful.

AROUND BAYI
Buchu Monastery

Some 28km south of Bayi is the small but ancient Gelugpa monastery of Buchu. The original dates from the 7th century, when it was built at the command of King Songtsen Gampo as one of the demoness-subduing temples; it pins the demoness's right elbow (see the boxed text 'Demoness-Subduing Temples' in the special section 'The Jokhang'). The monastery is recognisable by its striking golden roof.

The entrance to the main chapel is flanked by unusual murals of several protector gods. The main hall has statues of a standing Guru Rinpoche (right) and Jampa (Maitreya) and there are two small statues of the protectors Dorje Lekpa and Kongtsun Demo. The inner sanctum has statues of a 1000-armed Chenresig (Avalokiteshvara) flanked by Songtsen Gampo. Behind these are the Indian translator Shantarakshita, Guru Rinpoche and King Trisong Detsen. Upstairs is a cheesy, modern 3-D mandala. Buchu is home to three lamas and five monks.

Lamaling Temple

About 1.5km south of Buchu a dirt road (impassable after heavy rain) branches west off the main road 4km up to the stunning Lamaling (Zangdrok Pelri) Temple. The monastery was until recently the seat of the exiled Dudjom Rinpoche (1904–87), the former head of the Nyingma order. It is now looked after by his son Chuni Rinpoche.

The octagonal main temple has been wonderfully restored (reconstruction began in 1989) and rises through four storeys, bringing to mind the Ütse of Samye Monastery. The building is draped in enormous prayer beads.

Above the main prayer hall is a kora path with four protector chapels in each corner. The chapel above this houses statues of Öpagme (Amitabha), flanked by Chenresig (Avalokiteshvara) and Chana Dorje (Vajrapani). The top-floor chapel contains a four-armed Chenresig as well as two statues of Jampelyang (Manjushri).

The other main building, to the right, is where most religious services are held, on the 10th, 15th and 25th days of each lunar month. The hall is dominated by a huge statue of Sakyamuni (Sakya Thukpa). Pilgrims circumambulate both this building and the main temple.

Behind this building, trails lead right to a small chörten. Another trail leads up the hillside for 40 minutes (follow the prayer flags) to Norbu Ri, where the original Lamaling Temple stood before it was destroyed in 1930 in an earthquake. The small chapel has a statue of Dorje Julut and an old photo of Dudjom Rinpoche. Look out for the Sakyamuni footprint above the door.

It's not possible to stay the night at Lamaling so you'll have to either visit as a day trip from Bayi or camp in the friendly village below.

Nyingtri

This two-street town (sometimes spelled Nyangtri; Linzhi in Chinese) is much smaller than Bayi, 18km away, but is actually the county capital. Travellers without permits have been stopped here, fined and sent back to Lhasa so don't hang around here if you are hitching.

Neche Goshog Monastery *(Neche Kushuk Monastery; admission Y5)* is a small Bön monastery 1km south-west of Nyingtri at the river confluence. The monastery is famous for its 2000-year-old juniper tree sacred to Bönpos.

En route between Bayi and Nyingtri look out for a group of 2500-year-old cypresses just north of the highway near Pagyi (Bajie) village. There is a small fee for entry to the nature reserve.

There are a couple of basic hotels in town but you'll find higher standards in Bayi.

Trade Company Guesthouse *(Maoyi Gongsi Zhaodaisuo)* Triples Y30 per bed. This noisy and smoky place is right on the

Bön

As a result of the historical predominance of Buddhism in Tibet, the Bön religion has been suppressed for centuries and has only recently started to attract the attention of scholars. Many Tibetans remain quite ignorant of Bön beliefs and your guide might refuse to even set foot in a Bön monastery. Yet Bön and Buddhism have influenced and interacted with each other for centuries, exchanging texts, traditions and rituals. In the words of Tibet scholar David Snellgrove, 'every Tibetan is a Bönpo at heart'.

The word 'Bön' has three main connotations. The first relates to the pre-Buddhist religion of Tibet, which was suppressed and supplanted by Buddhism in the 8th and 9th centuries. The second is the form of 'organised' Bön (Gyur Bön) systematised along Buddhist lines, which arose in the 11th century. Third, and linked to this, is a body of popular beliefs that involve the worship of local deities and spirit protectors. Bön was formally accepted by the Dalai Lama as one of the five schools of Tibetan Buddhism in 1998.

Bön has its deepest roots in the earliest religious beliefs of the Tibetan people. These centred on an animist faith shared by all central Asian peoples, and religious expression took the form of spells, talismans, oaths, incantations, ritual drumming and sacrifices. The rituals often revolved around an individual who mediated between humans and the spirit world.

The earliest form of Bön, sometimes referred to as Black Bön, also Dud Bön (the Bön of Devils) or Tsan Bön (the Bön of Spirits), was concerned with counteracting the effects of evil spirits through magical practices. Bönpo priests, or *shen*, were entrusted with the wellbeing and fertility of the living, with curing sicknesses and affecting the weather. A core component was control of the spirits, to ensure the safe passage of the soul into the next world. For centuries Bönpo priests controlled the complex burial rites of the Yarlung kings. Bön was the state religion of Tibet until the reign of Songtsen Gampo.

Bön is thought to have its geographical roots in the kingdom of Shang-Shung, in western Tibet, and its capital at Kyunglung (Valley of the Garuda). Bön's founding father was Shenrab Miwoche, also known as Tonpa Shenrab, the Teacher of Knowledge, who was born in the second millennium BC in the mystical land of Olma Lungring in Tajik (possibly the Mt Kailash area or even Persia). Buddhists often claim that Shenrab is merely a carbon copy of Sakyamuni (Sakya Thukpa), and certainly there are similarities. Biographies state that he was born a royal prince and ruled for 30 years before becoming an ascetic. His 10 wives bore him 10 children who formed the core of his religious disciples. Many of the tales of Shenrab deal with his protracted struggles with the demon king main road and really isn't up to much. There are hot showers (Y3) but the toilets are filthy.

County Guesthouse (Xian Zhaodaisuo) Dorm beds Y20. Down a side road at the only junction in town, this ramshackle compound offers equally basic rooms but at least it's quieter than the Trade Company.

Bönri

Bönri is the Bön religion's most sacred mountain, a sprawling massif where Bön founder Tonpa Shenrab fought and defeated his arch-rival Khyabpa Lagring. Bönpo pilgrims come from all over Tibet to circumambulate the mountain anticlockwise.

The full 60km kora takes two or three days, climbing to the 4500m Bönri-la on the second day. It's an excellent walk but foreigners will probably find it hard to get permits for the kora, even on an organised Land Cruiser trip. The kora passes many sites connected to Tonpa Shenrab as well as an ancient burial tumulus, a 9th-century stele and a cemetery for babies.

Perhaps the easiest Bön monastery to visit on the kora is **Yungdrungling Monastery**, 6km south of Nyingtri along a motorable road (take the left fork early on) and then 1.5km up a side valley. The main monastery has a series of gods that will be unfamiliar even to visitors who are *au fait*

Bön

Khyabpa Lagring. At one stage the demon seduces Shenrab's daughter, who bears him two sons. Khyabpa also kidnaps Shenrab's seven horses and takes them to his castle in Kongpo. En route to reclaim his horses, Shenrab carves a passage through mountains with an arrow and pauses at Mt Kailash to teach Bön rituals before finally defeating the demon on the slopes of Bönri. Tradition tells that Shenrab returned to Olma Lungring and died there aged 82.

Bön was first suppressed by the eighth Yarlung king, Drigum Tsenpo, and then by King Trisong Detsen. The Bön master Gyerpung Drenpa Namkha (a *gyerpung* is the Bön equivalent of a lama or guru) struggled with Trisong Detsen to protect the Bön faith until the king finally broke Shang-Shung's political power. After the founding of Samye Monastery, many Bön priests went into exile or converted to Buddhism, and many Bön texts were hidden.

The modern Bön religion is known as Yungdrung (Eternal Bön). A *yungdrung* is a swastika, Bön's most important symbol. ('Yungdrungling' means 'swastika park' and is a common name for Bön monasteries). *The Nine Ways of Bön* is the religion's major text. Bönpos still refer to Mt Kailash as Yungdrung Gutseg (Nine-Stacked-Swastika Mountain).

To the casual observer it's often hard to differentiate between Bönpo and Buddhist practice. It can be said that in many ways Bön shares the same goals as Buddhism but takes a different path. The word 'Bön' has come to carry the same connotation as the Buddhist term 'dharma' (Tibetan: *chö*). Shared concepts include those of samsara, karma and rebirth in the six states of existence. Even Bön monasteries, rituals and meditation practice are almost identical to Buddhist versions. Still, there are obvious differences: Bön has its own Kangyur, a canon made up of texts translated from the Shang-Shung language, and Bönpos turn prayer wheels and circumambulate monasteries anticlockwise. The main difference comes down to the source of religious authority: Bönpos see the arrival of Buddhism as a catastrophe, the supplanting of the truth by a false religion.

Bönpo iconography is unique. Tonpa Shenrab is the most common central image, depicted as either a monk or a deity. He shares Sakyamuni's *mudra* (hand gesture) of 'enlightenment', but holds the Bön sceptre, which consists of two swastikas joined by a column. Other gods include Satrid Ergang, who holds a swastika and mirror, Shenrab Wokar and his main emanation, Kuntu Zangpo, with a hook-like wand, and Sangpo Bumptri. Complementing these is a large number of local deities – potentially harmful male spirits known as *gekho* (the protectors of Bön) and their female counterparts, *drapla*. Welchen Gekho is the king of the gekho, and his consort Logbar Tsame is the queen of the dralpa.

with Buddhist iconography. The main prayer hall has some Bön publications in English from Solan in India's Himachel Pradesh. The ruins behind the monastery offer fine views over the valley, and there are some lovely ruined chörtens and water-driven prayer wheels.

Another easily visited Bön monastery is **Sigyal Monastery**, a two-hour hike from Nyingtri (alternatively, drive partway down the road to Yungdrungling and then hike an hour from there). Take a guide or ask villagers for directions. It's possible to hike to Sigyal from Nyingtri and then continue down to Yungdrungling, visiting both of the monasteries on a nice day trip.

NYINGTRI TO POMI

From Nyingtri the road switchbacks up the hillside, past the final sections of the Bönri kora path and up to the 4515m **Serkhym-la**. From the pass you can scramble up 100m to a former military camp, which gives dramatic views of Namche Barwa (7756m) and Gyala Pelri (7151m). A new Chinese military camp is visible to the north, so try not to be too conspicuous.

Lunang

From the Serkhym-la the road descends past gorgeous alpine valleys lined with rhododendron bushes into the Rong-chu valley and the logging town of **Lunang**. There are some lovely villages in the valley and fine views of Mt Kongpo Lapsen to the north.

Lunang has a PSB office, a bathhouse next door, and several decent restaurants. The valley is perfect for camping, but fixed accommodation is also available.

Nyingtri Lunang Hotel (Linzhi Lunang Binguan) Doubles with private bathroom Y40 per bed, quads Y20 per bed. This hotel is in the centre of town near the PSB office. There's a decent restaurant on the ground floor.

Pomi Tibetan Teahouse (Pomi Zangshi Chaguan) Beds Y10. At the southern end of town, look for this bright Tibetan building, which doubles as a teahouse. Upstairs rooms are basic but clean; there are no toilets.

The Tsangpo Gorges

Hidden deep behind the mountains south and east of the Sichuan-Tibet Hwy, the swollen Yarlung Tsangpo makes some dramatic U-turns and crashes over a series of dramatic falls, through what Chinese scientists claim is the world's deepest gorge. With 7756m Namche Barwa and 7151m Gyala Pelri towering over either side of the gorge, only 27km apart, the gorge records a depth of 5382m (almost three times the depth of the Grand Canyon), with a length of 496km. At one point the river narrows to a mere 20m, before bursting out into the Assamese plain as the vast Brahmaputra River.

The region remains one of the world's least explored areas, and is home to king cobras, leopards, red pandas, musk deer, monkeys, tigers, waterfalls and virgin forests.

One of the most remarkable visitors to the area was the Indian pundit Kinthup, who came to the region in 1880 with instructions from the British to release 500 marked logs into the Tsangpo, to confirm that the river did indeed flow into the Brahmaputra as suspected. Before he could even get to the gorges, Kinthup was sold into slavery by his companion, a lama who frittered away all the money on women and alcohol. Kinthup finally escaped, prepared the 500 logs and sent a letter to the British from Lhasa specifying a new date for the drop. Tragically, the letter was never received and the logs floated through India unnoticed. To add insult to injury, by the time Kinthup got to India, four years after setting off, the riddle of the Brahmaputra had already been solved and none of his superiors even believed his story.

Foreigners are currently not allowed in this strategic border area of the gorges, though a few specialised agencies are hoping to run trekking tours in the next few years. Chinese tourists already trek through the region from Pe and Gyatso.

Grain Guesthouse *(Liangshiju Zhao-daisuo)* Triples Y25 per bed, dorm beds Y10-15. Next door to the teahouse, above a restaurant, this is another decent option. Each of the triples has a TV.

Lunang to Pomi

From Lunang the road passes **Pelung**, home to communities of Monpa people. Not far from here the Rong-chu and the Parlung Tsangpo meet and flow away south-east into the Yarlung Tsangpo (Brahmaputra River). This marks the lowest part of the Sichuan-Tibet Hwy (around 1700m). The next 17km to Tangmi and the 10km after Tangmi rank as the most dangerous sections of road in Tibet. The hillsides are scarred by landslides and often hidden in subtropical fog. The numerous hot springs around here are testament to the region's geological instability.

At Tangmi the Yi'ong Tsangpo joins the valley. A poor-quality side road heads about 25km north-west up to the south-eastern end of **Yi'ong-tso**, a stunning but hard-to-reach lake. Tea is produced in this area.

As the main road heads up the Parlung Tsangpo valley, pine trees and settlements slowly return and the scenery becomes increasingly spectacular. This region is known in Tibetan as Powo. Some 64km from Tangmi is **Bakhar Monastery**, stunningly located on a river island. Cross the bridge, turn left and a footpath leads up to the monastery after about 20m. The site has a small community of both nuns and monks and a small but delightful kora path.

POMI

☎ 0894 • elevation 3000m

Formerly known as Tramo, this small county capital has well-stocked shops and several hotels and restaurants, making it a logical place to spend the night. In clear weather the surrounding scenery is stupendous.

Hedonists will love the bathhouse a short walk west of the Pomi Hotel (past the PSB), which offers hot showers for Y5 and even a hot tub and sauna out the back (Y68 per person, open until midnight).

Try to allow a morning to make the hour-long walk from Pomi to **Dodung Monastery**.

Tibet's Hidden Lands

The Pemako region south of Pomi is a *beyul* (or *pelyul*), one of 16 'hidden lands' scattered throughout the Himalaya that were rendered invisible by Guru Rinpoche to provide hidden retreats in times of danger. Guidebooks on how to get to the hidden lands were written by Guru Rinpoche as *terma* (concealed teachings), to be rediscovered at a suitable time (in this case the 17th century) by *terton* (treasure seekers).

Spiritual realisation is said to be easily attained in such places, and, in some cases, the beyul also act as sanctuaries providing protection in times of war or famine. Many Khampas fled to Pemako when the Chinese invaded eastern Tibet in the 1950s.

Turn left out of the Pomi Hotel and take the road bridge over the Parlung Tsangpo. On the far (southern) side take the right (west) fork and continue 30 minutes or so to a smaller second bridge and a collection of prayer flags and *mani* (prayer) walls. From here it's a short climb to the monastery. The main prayer hall is worth a visit; inside to the right look for a collection of *cham* (dance) masks and a huge snake (it's a fake). Upstairs are murals depicting the life story of two forms of Gesar, as well as Guru Rinpoche and Tsepame (Amitayus). A new prayer hall is being built behind the main complex. There are some lovely chörtens and mani walls nearby. The monastery has 30 monks and two lamas.

Places to Stay & Eat

Pomi Hotel *(Pomi Fandian)* Triples without/with private bathroom Y20/30 per bed, suites with private bathroom Y80. This is the officially sanctioned place for foreigners. The enormous suites come with two bedrooms and are pretty good value, though there's no hot water (you may even have to ask the staff to turn on the cold water). The ground-floor rooms are the cheapest and come with a communal toilet down the hall.

Traffic Hotel *(Jiaotong Luguan;* ☎ 542 2798) Singles Y60, triples with private bathroom Y40 per bed. This new hotel, next to the bus station in the west end of town, is probably the best-value option. Triples have an electric water heater for hot showers.

Grain Guesthouse Dorms Y10, doubles with private bathroom Y25-50. Located just east of the Pomi Hotel, this place is worth checking out.

The main street is lined with excellent *restaurants*.

Getting There & Away
Pomi is 160km from Lunang and 127km from Rawok. There is little public transport, though you might find seats in a shared jeep heading to Bayi.

RAWOK-TSO
The scenery east of Pomi is particularly beautiful. The road heads up the Parlung Tsangpo valley, passing a gorge and several stunning side valleys before you get your first magical views of the blue waters and sandy beaches of Ngan-tso. There are good camping and picnicking spots by the lake.

At the far end of the lake is the disappointing town of **Rawok**. (We saw a human skull lying ignored in the gutter of the main street during our visit!) The old town is worth a look. Take a right by the antenna of the telecom office into the medieval warren. From here you can work your way through to the large chörten, mani wall and small temple overlooking the lake in the southeast of town. The surrounding fields are full of wooden platforms for drying barley.

It's worth heading north of town and taking a side road south-east for around 7km to a second lake, Rawok-tso (both this lake and Ngan-tso are commonly referred to as Rawok-tso). The views here are sensational and it's a great place for a picnic. From Rawok town it's a 1½-hour hike or a short jeep trip, past a small hydroelectricity station. En route you'll see an anachronistic Chairman Mao propaganda slogan that says (in Chinese): 'We are concerned not only with smashing the old world but also with building a new one'.

The road from Rawok-tso continues past a check post into the border region of Dzayul

(Zayu), which is only about 20km from Myanmar (Burma). Foreigners are not allowed on this road and there are check posts.

Places to Stay & Eat
If the weather is clear then the best option is to camp around either of the two lakes. Otherwise there are two hotels in Rawok town.

Bus Station Hotel (*Keyunzhan Zhaodaisuo*) Dorm beds Y15. The pit toilet in the car park could well be the worst in Tibet (and that's saying something) but this is still the best option. And no, there's no bus station in Rawok.

Pingan Hotel (*Ping'an Zhaodaisuo*) Dorm beds Y15. This plywood dosshouse was occupied by road workers during our visit. Expect it to be noisy and lacking in privacy. The town's PSB is stationed here, which is just one more reason to avoid the place.

Rawok has several *restaurants* catering to the nearby army base. You'll find the Chinese restaurants on the left-hand side of the road; the Tibetan restaurants are on the right.

Getting There & Away
There's no public transport to Rawok so if you haven't organised a tour you'll have to hitch. Traffic is meagre at best.

RAWOK-TSO TO PASHO
From Rawok the road climbs north past nomad camps to the Anju-la (4618m), which marks a dramatic step up from the subtropical Parlung Tsangpo valley onto the arid high plateau. The pass also marks the watershed between the waters of the Brahmaputra, flowing into India, and the Salween, flowing into South-East Asia.

Around 13km from the pass on the left, near Guza village, is Ramo Monastery and a nearby ruined *dzong* (fort). There is another ruined dzong 26km further on at Tashitse. As the road descends, the landscape changes colour from arid khakis to rocky reds, reminiscent of south-west USA. About 7km before Pasho the asphalt road finally kicks in again and everyone breathes a collective sigh of relief.

PASHO
☎ 0895

Pasho (Chinese: Bashe), formerly known as Pema (Baima), is a pleasant town that makes for a good overnight stop.

Things to See & Do

On the north-western outskirts of town is **Neru Monastery**, a Gelugpa monastery destroyed during the Cultural Revolution, which is worth a quick look. The renovated central chapel holds the throne of the Pakhpala, a religious leader based in Chamdo, whose current incarnation is a government minister. It was the current Pakhpala who paid for the restoration of Neru Monastery. The back wall contains the funeral chörten of the monastery's last *trulku* (reincarnated lama). The back room has a large seated Jampa (Maitreya) statue made by craftsmen from Chamdo. You can reach the monastery by car from the western end of town or by foot over a bridge accessed from the centre of town.

A 45-minute walk along the main road east of town is **Dola Monastery**. The small main chapel is surrounded by chörtens and lovely old prayer wheels. A kora path leads up the mountainside to a plateau and then descends west to Pasho town, offering fine views of the arid valley. The leisurely half-day kora is chock-a-block with jovial pilgrims on the 15th and 16th days of the fifth lunar month, around the time of the Saga Dawa festival (see Special Events in the Facts for the Visitor chapter).

Places to Stay & Eat

Fukang Hotel (Fukang Zhaodaisuo; ☎ *456 2178)* Doubles Y30 per bed, triples Y15 per bed. This is the best option in town. The ground-floor triples are good value and the upper-floor doubles come with a sofa and desk. Toilets are shared but there are a useful washing area and lines for drying clothes. You can get a shower for Y5 in the large building by the nearby small roller-skating rink.

Post Office Hotel (Youdian Zhaodaisuo; ☎ *456 2378)* Dorm beds Y15. This place by the post office in the east of town has small rooms separated by wooden partitions, which make it a little noisy. There are cheaper dorm rooms above the post office.

Transport Centre Hotel (Keyun Zhongxin Zhaodaisuo) Dorm beds Y10-20, singles Y50, doubles with shared bathroom Y40 per bed. This compound doubles as a truck stop and depot for the *very* occasional bus. The clean doubles have proper mattresses, unlike the cheaper dorms. Showers (Y6) are made available to guests and the public here in the afternoon and evening until around midnight.

Tianlong Restaurant (Tianlong Fandian) Dishes from Y8. Between the Fukang and Transport Centre Hotels, this is probably the best restaurant in town, though there are plenty of snack bars along the main street.

The morning *fruit and vegetable market* on the main street is one of the few places in Tibet where you can buy pineapples and mangoes.

PASHO TO CHAMDO

From Pasho the road east passes picturesque villages and chörtens reminiscent of those in Ladakh. There is a stretch of road 32km from Pasho that is particularly susceptible to landslides, so check on road conditions before setting off. From here the road crosses the Ngul-chu (Nu Jiang or Salween River) and then starts an endless series of switchbacks up to the 4839m **Zar Gama-la**, marking the highest single altitude gain of any motorable pass in Tibet.

From the pass the road descends to a crossroads where the southern Sichuan-Tibet Hwy branches off to Markham (see Southern Route to Sichuan later in this chapter). There are a couple of *restaurants* here and there's very basic *accommodation* at a government truck stop for Y15 per bed.

Six kilometres from the crossroads is the lovely village and monastery of Pomda, set at the edge of a wide valley. The village has several wealthy houses that feature fine woodwork.

Pomda Monastery dates back 360 years but was destroyed in the Cultural Revolution and rebuilt in 1980. The main hall has excellent murals and statues of Sakyamuni

(Sakya Thukpa), flanked by Jampelyang (Manjushri) and Jampa (Maitreya), and Drölma (Tara). The inner sanctum features Tsongkhapa and his two disciples. There is also a protector chapel and a debating courtyard, as well as a huge mani wall and a mani *lhakhang* (chapel). The 75 monks are very friendly.

Another 13km brings you to Kyidrup Monastery. A further 10km from here a bridge gives access to a small yellow monastery across the river. The paved road picks up 20km away at Chamdo's airport, from where it's still 130km to Chamdo town. There's a *hotel* at the airport (see Getting There & Away under Chamdo, later, for details). At over 4300m, the airport is reckoned to be world's highest civilian airport.

Look out for an amazing-looking monastery across the river, 10km north of the airport. If you want to check it out you'll have to take the turn-off west to Lhorong (Luolong), a further 6km away. This road follows the former caravan trail to Lhasa.

Soon the main road descends into gorges, rises to the 4572m Lang-la and then descends dramatically to Kyitang (Gyitang) village. Before long you cross a ridge over the Nya-la to get views of the chocolate-coloured Dza-chu (Mekong River). Just before the pass, look for a series of hermit caves in the cliff face across the valley.

The road now parallels the Mekong, passing villages of contrasting purple mud-baked houses and green terracing. About 7km after the pass is a turn-off that leads 34km south-east along a dirt track to Drayab town and Endun Monastery.

CHAMDO
☎ 0895 • elevation 3600m
Chamdo (literally 'river confluence'; Chinese: Changdu), located at the strategic river junction of the Dza-chu and the Ngon-chu, is a surprisingly pleasant town. It is dominated by the hilltop Jampaling Monastery, below which huddle the Tibetan old town and the Chinese new town. Over 1000km from Lhasa and 1250km from Chengdu, the town is the major transport, administrative and trade centre of the Kham region.

Chamdo has had a troubled relationship with nearby China. The Chinese warlord Zhao Erfeng captured Chamdo in 1909 and ruled the region until the Tibetans recaptured it in 1917. Chamdo fell to Communist troops in 1950 (for more information, see the boxed text 'The Fall of Chamdo' later in this chapter).

Information
The PSB is just north of the Chamdo Hotel. If you have all the correct permits this can be a better place than Lhasa to get a visa extension, of up to 30 days. Internet access is available for Y5 per hour across from the Kangsheng Hotel.

Galden Jampaling Monastery
This active hilltop monastery (Chinese: Qiangbalin Si) of over 800 monks dominates Chamdo. The monastery was built between 1436 and 1444 by Jangsem Sherab Zangpo, a disciple of Tsongkhapa. It was destroyed in 1912 and then rebuilt in 1917, after the Tibetan army retook Chamdo.

Pilgrims continuously circumambulate the walled compound and it's worth following them on at least one circuit. Behind the monastery, to the north of town, trails lead up to a sky-burial site.

Visitors enter the monastery from the east side and a paved road leads up from the town below. The first building on the right is the impressive Dialectic College, behind which is a debating courtyard. Just to the left of the college is an entrance – go in here, take an immediate left up the stairs and then turn right at the top. This leads to a protector chapel packed with old Khampa weaponry.

Back outside, the monastery's enormous kitchen is well worth a look, but only men can go inside.

The main *dukhang* (assembly hall) is particularly impressive, especially when it is packed with hundreds of murmuring monks. This is probably the largest assembly of monks you will see in Tibet these days, outside festival times. The inner sanctum is dominated by Sakyamuni (Sakya Thukpa) and his two disciples.

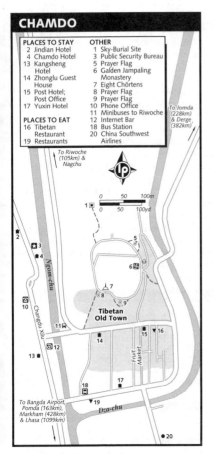

CHAMDO

PLACES TO STAY	OTHER
2 Jindian Hotel	1 Sky-Burial Site
4 Chamdo Hotel	3 Public Security Bureau
13 Kangsheng	5 Prayer Flag
Hotel	6 Galden Jampaling
14 Zhonglu Guest	Monastery
House	7 Eight Chörtens
15 Post Hotel;	8 Prayer Flag
Post Office	9 Prayer Flag
17 Yuxin Hotel	10 Phone Office
	11 Minibuses to Riwoche
PLACES TO EAT	12 Internet Bar
16 Tibetan	18 Bus Station
Restaurant	20 China Southwest
19 Restaurants	Airlines

To Jomda
(228km)
& Derge
(382km)

To Riwoche
(105km) &
Nagchu

0   50   100m
0   50   100yd

Ngom-chu

Changdu Xilu

Tibetan
Old Town

Fruit
Market

To Bangda Airport,
Pomda (163km),
Markham (428km)
& Lhasa (1099km)

Dza-chu

In the main courtyard is a *gönkhang* (protector chapel), full of protector gods such as bull-headed Dorje Jigje (Yamantaka), Palden Lhamo (Shri Devi) and Chögyel (Dharmaraja), plus lots of old armour.

Behind the gönkhang is the former residence of the Pakhpala. The southern part of the building holds the Tsenkhang, hidden around the back of the interior courtyard, which has a fantastic collection of protector masks stuck up on a series of pillars, along with a stuffed wolf and snake. The neighbouring Nanje Lhakhang and the northern Pakye Tsangkhang are being restored.

Old Town

Squeezed between the encroaching Chinese streets and piled up on the hillside around the monastery, the Tibetan old town is worth a wander. The main market street has been modernised but the surrounding warren of streets is interesting and there are lots of silver workshops around here.

Places to Stay & Eat

Chamdo has lots of hotels, and the local PSB seems surprisingly relaxed about where foreigners can stay.

Zhonglu Guest House (Zhonglu Zhaodaisuo) Rooms Y15-25 per bed. A good location and passable rooms make this the cheapest option, though it's one place where you might well get a visit from the PSB.

Jindian Hotel (Jindian Dajiudian; ☎ *482 4910)* Doubles with private bathroom Y30 per bed. More of a restaurant than hotel, this place has an inconvenient location in the north of town and grubby rooms.

Yuxin Hotel (Yuxin Binguan) Doubles and triples Y50 per person. Much better value, this hotel is hidden on the upper floors, above a restaurant, but has pleasant rooms with private bathroom and hot water. Some rooms are more spacious than others.

Post Hotel (Youzheng Binguan; ☎ *482 6925)* Doubles Y80-100. Another decent choice, right in the centre of town, this hotel is above the post office on the 3rd floor. Rooms are comfortable and clean.

Kangsheng Hotel (Kangsheng Binguan; ☎ *482 3168, Changdu Xilu)* Ordinary/ standard doubles Y80/160, triples Y105, suites Y280. The ordinary doubles are acceptable but the standard doubles are spartan and overpriced. Hot water is available in the evening.

Chamdo Hotel (Changdu Fandian; ☎ *482 5998, fax 482 1428, 22 Changdu Xilu)* Economy/standard doubles Y260/320, triples Y300. This is Chamdo's flagship hotel and, along with the Kangsheng, the officially sanctioned hotel for tourists. The ordinary rooms are comfortable and pretty good value, especially as discounts of 20% are normally available. Hot water is available from 8am to 11am and 8pm to 11pm.

The Fall of Chamdo

In spring 1950, Chamdo was in real trouble. Although there were still pockets of resistance at Derge and Markham, the Communist Chinese had taken control of Kham without even a fight. Chinese armies were moving in on Tibet from Xinjiang and Xikang (now Sichuan) provinces in a strategy masterminded by, among others, Deng Xiaoping.

The first skirmish between Chinese and Tibetan troops took place in May 1950 when the People's Liberation Army (PLA) attacked Dengo on the Dri-chu (Yangzi River). Then on 7 October 1950 the PLA moved in earnest, as 40,000 troops crossed the Dri-chu and attacked Chamdo from three directions: Jyekundo to the north, Derge to the east and Markham to the south.

As panic swept through Chamdo, the city responded to the military threat in characteristic Tibetan fashion with a frenzy of prayer and religious ritual. When the local Tibetan leader radioed the Tibetan government in Lhasa to warn of the Chinese invasion, he was coolly told that the government members couldn't be disturbed because they were 'on a picnic'. To this the Chamdo radio operator is said to have replied *'skyag pa'i gling kha!'*, or 'shit the picnic!'. It was to be the last ever communication between the Chamdo and Lhasa branches of the Tibetan government.

The city was evacuated (with the Chamdo government commandeering most of the town's horses) but the PLA was one step ahead. Chinese leaders know that speed is of the essence (the Chinese described the military operation as 'like a tiger trying to catch a fly') and had already cut the Tibetans off by taking Riwoche. The Tibetans surrendered without a shot on 19 October. The Tibetan troops were disarmed, given lectures on the benefits of socialism and then given money and sent home. It was the beginning of the end of an independent Tibet.

Getting There & Away

Air China Southwest Airlines operates a flight every Thursday to Lhasa (Y720) and three flights a week to Chengdu (Y750). The ticket office (☎ 482 1004) is on the southern edge of town and is open from 9am to noon daily. Staff will sell you a ticket without checking for permits but you might still be checked at the airport when you check in.

Bangda (Pomda) airport is 130km south of Chamdo. Airport buses (Y40) depart at 4pm the day before flights, requiring an overnight stay at the airport. Rooms at the *Airport Hotel* cost Y40 per bed in a quad, or Y120 per bed in a double with private bathroom.

Bus Officials at the bus station are suspicious of foreigners and enforce a whopping 100% official foreigner surcharge, which is curious as foreigners aren't even supposed to be in Chamdo without a tour! Buses run about once a week to Lhasa (Y240, three to four days), via Nagchu, overnighting in hotels en route. Sleeper buses run weekly nonstop to Chengdu (Y300, 60 hours). There are also weekly buses to Jomda (Jangda; Y55) where you can change for Derge. In general, permitless travellers are probably better off hitching. Occasional minibuses depart for Riwoche town (Y50).

Getting Around

Taxis cost a flat Y5 anywhere in town.

CHAMDO TO RIWOCHE

The northern highway to Nagchu passes a weir 5km outside Chamdo and then crosses the river near a series of chörtens and a large mani lhakhang. Kiss the tarmac a fond farewell here. Soon the road leaves the Mekong River and swings south, eventually climbing past the stunningly located Trangu Monastery, on a grassy plateau backed by a huge granite wall. The road continues to climb, through sections of 1500-year-old juniper forest, protected as a nature reserve since 1992. The road crosses the 4688m Zhutong-la before making a long descent into an alpine valley. The distance between Chamdo and Riwoche town is 105km.

RIWOCHE

It's important to realise that there are two places called Riwoche: Riwoche town (also known as Ratsaka in Tibetan and Leiwuqi Zhen in Chinese), which is the county capital on the main highway, and the village of Riwoche 29km north-west, which is home to the Riwoche Tsuglhakhang.

Riwoche town is of little interest in itself but you may well have to stay the night here if you want to visit the Riwoche Tsuglhakhang. Either way, you will need to go to the town's PSB to register and to get permission to visit the *tsuglhakhang* (literally 'grand temple').

Riwoche County Guesthouse *(Leiwujixian Canlubu Zhaodaisuo;* ☎ *450 2257)* Six-bed dorms Y15 per bed, four-bed dorms Y20-25 per bed. The rooms at this somewhat hard-to-find place are clean and comfortable, but the single outside toilet is an absolute horror. Look for the hotel at the eastern end of town above a restaurant. Access and parking are around the back. The PSB is nearby, on the opposite side of the street.

Post Hotel *(Youzheng Binguan)* Quads Y120. The only other real option is at the rowdy western end of town, but rooms are overpriced and can be noisy.

RIWOCHE TSUGLHAKHANG

From the western edge of Riwoche town a road branches north-west off the main highway and follows the river north, west and then north again. The 'road' rapidly degenerates into a mud pie after rain so check its condition before you set off. A couple of kilometres before Riwoche village the road crests a ridge and you get your first views of the amazing tsuglhakhang.

Founded in 1276 by Sangye On, who relocated to Kham after the death of his master Sangye Yarjon, the third leader of the Taglung order, Riwoche started as an off-shoot of Talung Monastery in Ü. Eventually, however, it grew to overshadow its parent monastery. It is still the more vibrant of the two and retains the characteristic red, white and black vertical stripes of the Taglung school.

Permits

The PSB in Riwoche town, located on the main street, requires foreigners to register and get permission to visit the tsuglhakhang, though it's far from certain that you actually need any such permission. To visit the upper floors of the temple you will definitely need to get permission (not to mention the keys) from the village PSB (which may well want to see proof that you registered with the town PSB). There is no entry or permit fee.

The Temple

The tsuglhakhang towers over Riwoche village, dwarfing the medieval-looking pilgrims who circumambulate the massive structure. You enter through huge doors on the eastern side into a breathtaking open inner courtyard.

The eye is immediately drawn to the huge beams and enormous statues lining the walls. The entry is flanked on the left by Zambala, the god of wealth, and eight chörtens, and to the right by two protector masks on a pillar. The left wall has statues of Öpagme (Amitabha), Tsepame (Amitayus), Guru Rinpoche (one peaceful and one smaller wrathful variety) and Sakyamuni (Sakya Thukpa). The west wall has a Sakyamuni, a funerary chörten, a second version of Sakyamuni, two abbots, and Sakyamuni with the two early Taglung lamas – Sangye Yarjon (1203–72) on the right and Sangye On to the left. Along the right wall is a white statue of Namse (Vairocana) in front of a mandala, and a gold chörten, a seated Jampa (Maitreya), Matrö Bodhisattva, a medicine buddha and finally two 1000-armed statues of Chenresig (Avalokiteshvara).

The upper floor is bare but has fine murals of several protector deities, Milarepa and Marpa, and the Kagyud lineage. There are statues of Guru Rinpoche, a 1000-armed Chenresig, Sakyamuni and Guru Rinpoche.

The top floor is where the real gems are kept. The most precious items are kept behind a locked grill, and include some lovely statues and an old saddle said to have belonged to Gesar of Ling. The main central

Flora or Fauna?

In summer you will see nomads and entrepreneurs camped in the high passes digging for a strange root known as a *yartse gompu* (*Cordiceps sinensis*) that locals claim is half-vegetable, half-caterpillar. It is in fact a fusion of a fungus and the caterpillar it has parasitised. The root is particularly valued in Tibetan and Chinese medicine and can fetch Y12 for a single root, making it one of the most expensive commodities in Tibet.

statues are of Sakyamuni and Panchuk Rinpoche. Look out for the very old statue of Dorje Chang (Vajradhara).

Monks' quarters and the grander residences of the abbot and rinpoche lie to the north. It's worth walking up the hillside a little to get overviews of the site. One track leads diagonally up the hillside to a high collection of prayer flags.

Places to Stay & Eat

At the time of research there was nowhere to stay in the village, though the local government was planning to build a guesthouse. There is one basic *Sichuanese restaurant* and a shop but you'd be wise to bring your own food.

Getting There & Away

There's little traffic and no public transport at all between Riwoche town and the tsuglhakhang (29km, 1½ hours by Land Cruiser). A terrible road does lead north to Nangchen and Jyekundo (Yushu) in Qinghai province but it's far from certain that even a Land Cruiser would make it through on this route, especially after rain. It's an adventurous trip and well worth a try if you're properly prepared, but it would be wise to come with a back-up plan.

RIWOCHE TO TENGCHEN

Back at Riwoche town the main highway west swings to the south and starts to climb, reaching **Chayab Monastery** after 17km. This small but charming monastery is surrounded by dozens of chörtens, thousands

of mani stones and a short kora path. High above the monastery is a sky-burial site.

The design of the main chapel is similar to that of Lamaling Temple but on a much smaller scale. Look for a photo of the current Takzham Rinpoche, the reincarnation of Takzham Nuden Dorje, an 18th-century terton who founded the monastery (and whose portrait is painted in the right-hand corner of the chapel). Monks will probably invite you for delicious yogurt and yak milk fresh from the surrounding nomadic encampments – leave a donation if they do. There are lovely camping sites nearby.

The ruins of Sibta Dzong lie a further 5km along the highway. After another 4km, the road passes a striking white marble mountain before it summits at the 4809m Dzekri-la. In summer many nomads camp here, employed in the lucrative search for medicinal roots (see the boxed text 'Flora or Fauna?').

The road descends through a series of impressive gorges until, 95km from Riwoche, you reach **Jinkar Monastery**, a small Gelugpa monastery of about 30 monks that is being restored. The monastery has a small enclosed garden called the Norbulingka where it might be possible to camp, with the monks' permission.

From the western end of the monastery a path leads for about 10 minutes past a chörten and through barley fields, down to the remarkable **Rotung Monastery**, a small Nyingmapa monastery of 50 monks surrounded on all sides by tens of thousands of votive carved mani stones. Pilgrims circumambulate the monastery from dawn to dusk and the surrounding village has a timeless, medieval atmosphere.

There are plenty of monasteries in the region to keep you busy, including Zora Monastery, 30km west of Rotung, Gongsar Monastery, high on a ridge 7km north-west of Zora, and another fine-looking monastery, 3km before you arrive in Tengchen. **Gongsar Monastery** is probably the most interesting of the three. It's a hard 45-minute climb from the road but the views from the ridge line are stunning. There are some small ruins and a two-storey chapel here; further up the hillside are more ruins.

TENGCHEN
☎ 0895 • elevation 4200m

Tengchen (Chinese: Dingqing) is an unremarkable but reasonably pleasant two-street town. It's possible to make calls at the town's telecom office. Both Tengchen and the surrounding region of Khyungpo are strong centres of the Bön religion. For more on Bön, see the boxed text 'Bön' earlier in this chapter.

Things to See

The main reason to stop here is to visit **Tengchen Monastery**, on a hillside 4km west of town. This interesting Bön monastery is actually made up of two separate institutions. The main building, founded in 1110, has an impressive assembly hall and upper-floor chapel. Bön deities here include Tonpa Shenrab and an amazing Palpa Phurbu, whose lower half consists of a ritual dagger.

To the east is the Ritro Lhakhang, built in 1180. The main chapel, the Serdung, contains three funerary chörtens (including that of Monlam Tai, the founder of the monastery) and another many-armed Palpa Phurbu. Another chapel displays a row of six Bön gods on a variety of mounts. There are fine views from the roof.

There are said to be **hot springs** in the valley that leads north of Tengchen, between the town and monastery.

Places to Stay & Eat

Pengsheng Hotel (Pengsheng Binguan; ☎ *459 2662)* Doubles Y100-120. Rooms in this private hotel in the eastern end of town are nice and clean but definitely overpriced. There's a public bathhouse just west of the hotel entrance that offers hot showers for Y5 (open 10am to 10pm).

Grain Department Guesthouse (Liangshiju Zhaodaisuo; ☎ *459 2141)* Quads Y20 per bed. This government guesthouse offers barracks-style accommodation. The rooms have a sofa and wooden floors and are passably serviceable, though a little grimy. The showers weren't working during our visit. Look for the red and white 'Hotel' sign just to the east of the lion statues of the Grain Department.

Government Guesthouse (Zhengfu Zhaodaisuo) Doubles Y30-40 per bed, triples Y15 per bed. This local-government guesthouse is another decent option. To get here take the north-west branch at the town's only junction; you'll find the guesthouse about 400m along on the right.

Minzheng Fuli Zhaodaisuo Beds Y15. This second government guesthouse is of a lower standard and not to be confused with the main government guesthouse.

There are several decent Chinese restaurants in town, including the *Dingqing Jiujia* in the centre of town, on the north side of the street.

TENGCHEN TO SOK

The 37km from Tengchen to the Tsuni-la launches you up into the highlands of north-eastern Tibet, offering fabulous views of nomad camps and yak herds made tiny by the huge range of snowy peaks to the south. The pass itself gives fine views westward to the Nyenchen Tanglha (Tangula) range. The road then drops to the lovely village and monastery of **Sertsa** and its neighbouring (and less charming) county capital. There are plenty of excellent camping spots around here. About 14km from Sertsa keep an eye out for the monastery across the valley perched dramatically on the face of a high ridge. At Sendu there are vistas south to one of Tibet's most beautiful chörtens.

Here the road swings north and starts to climb up to the stunning **Shel-la** (4830m), the highest and most dramatic pass along the northern route. At the start of the climb is a small *hotel*. There is also the option of barracks-like accommodation (Y10 to Y20 per bed) on the other side of the pass at the *County Government Guesthouse (Xianzheng Zhaodaisuo)* in Bada.

The road continues past the villages of Gubengda, Gyaruptang (Chinese: Jieruotang) and Wengdaka and then climbs yet again to the 4500m Chak-la, where you turn a corner for a dramatic view of one of the Salween's many tributaries. The road then makes a long descent to some scattered nomad camps, a chörten and then **Yangan** village, where there is a collection of basic

Tibetan guesthouses and *teahouses*. It's a good place to catch your breath and fill up on butter tea.

From here it's another 48km to **Bachen**, a scruffy town with three small *guesthouses* and several restaurants. At the western end of town there is a new monastery encircled by a kora of prayer flags. From Bachen it's 33km to Sok.

SOK

Sok's claim to fame is the impressive **Sok Tsanden Monastery**, set on an outcrop in the north-western suburbs. The monastery, founded by the Mongol leader Gushri Khan, brings to mind a miniature Potala.

The monastery was made off limits to foreigners in 2001 after tourists smuggled out a letter from the monks of Sok to the Dalai Lama. Local authorities remain sensitive to foreign visitors. If you want to visit the monastery, make sure that Sok Monastery (not just the town) is specifically written on your travel permits (we were refused entry to the monastery even though we had permits for Sok). You may have to get permission from the PSB in Nagchu, though even they may refer you to Lhasa.

There is also a nunnery on the hill to the north-east of town. If you decide to stay the night you could easily take some nice hikes in the vicinity.

The town has a public bathhouse open from 11am to 8pm Wednesday, Saturday and Sunday, though water supplies are unreliable. The PSB office is inside a compound in the east of town, not far from the main crossroads. There are several shops and a supermarket next to the post office in the west of town if you need to stock up on supplies, and a few places to stay.

Bus Station Hotel Triples Y25-30 per bed. This is definitely the best option in town. Rooms are clean and come with a heater, and there's a nice common seating area. The main drawback is the lack of any kind of bathroom.

Huopi Guesthouse (*Huopi Zhaodaisuo*) Beds Y25-30. The Huopi is on the corner of the main junction, just across from the Bus Station Hotel. Grubby rooms come without a bathroom, which is no particular loss as there's no water anyway.

Government Guesthouse Doubles Y50 per bed. Because of official paranoia in relation to foreigners, the government hotel charges foreigners over twice the local rate and will probably call the PSB as soon as you set foot in the compound. The rooms are poor and the place is best avoided.

SOK TO NAGCHU

South from Sok the road passes several small villages and their small monasteries and then a large chörten by the roadside. After the No 47 *daoban* (roadwork unit) the road rises to the gentle Shara-la and then descends past the turn-off to Biru.

Shagchu, 135km from Sok, is a truck stop with a good restaurant, the *Sichuan Zigong Fanguan*. From here it's 103km over high plateau grassland and a couple of gentle passes to Nagchu. You are now well and truly in the grasslands of northern Tibet.

NAGCHU

☎ 0896 • elevation 4500m

Nagchu (Chinese: Naqu) is one of the highest, coldest and most windswept towns in Tibet. Perched on the edge of the Changtang (northern plateau), it is a dismal town of mud and concrete, but is still an important pit stop on the road between Qinghai and Tibet. It's a literally breathtaking place: Oxygen levels here are only 60% of those at sea level, so be prepared for headaches and watch for the symptoms of altitude sickness. Bring extra clothes, even in summer.

Nagchu has a horse-racing festival from 10 to 16 August, when the town swells with up to 10,000 nomads and their tents from all over the Changtang. Accommodation can be very tight at this time.

On the western outskirts of town are Zhabten Monastery and Samtenling Nunnery. There are also a couple of markets in town where you might see the occasional northern nomad trading fleeces for pots and pans and other goods.

Foreigners are supposed to have permits for Nagchu, even though the town is officially open. Your permits will be checked by the reception staff at the Naqu Hotel but probably not the other hotels.

There are several bathhouses around town. The Western Hotel has public showers (Y5) and saunas (Y30 per person per hour).

Places to Stay

Naqu Hotel (Naqu Fandian; ☎ *382 2424)* Ordinary/standard doubles Y200/320, quads Y30 per bed. This is the officially designated tourist hotel, which means it will try to charge foreigners double the local rate. The spartan but essentially clean quads aren't a bad deal if you can get them at the local rate.

China Tibet Grassland Telecom Hotel (☎ *382 8888)* Doubles Y480, triples with shared bathroom Y280. This new hotel, opened in 2001, is the best of the mid-range places. The modern rooms are comfortable and the Tibetan-style murals in the lobby give the hotel some charm, a rare hotel commodity in this part of Tibet. The hotel is in the north-east of town, about 400m from the Naqu Hotel. Substantial discounts are often available.

Western Hotel (Xibu Binguan) Doubles with shared/private bathroom Y100/160, triples Y95, quads Y100. Next door to the Naqu Hotel, this place isn't supposed to take foreigners but will let you in if you just stay a night.

Bus Station Hotel Five-bed dorms Y16 per bed, doubles/triples Y50/ 60. This noisy but convenient option is by the bus station in the south of town.

There are several *snack bars* opposite the Naqu Hotel that serve up delicious *shaguoji* (chicken casserole) for around Y15.

Getting There & Away

The main bus station is in the south of town. A taxi from the centre costs Y10. Buses to Lhasa (Y63 to Y73, seven hours, 326km) depart between 8am and 9am. There are also weekly buses to Sok (Y55) and Bachen (Y65), irregular minibuses to Biru (Y60) and afternoon minibuses to Lhari (Jiali; Y25).

Sleeper buses run to Golmud for Y150, though most locals take a seat in a truck for Y80 to Y100.

NAGCHU TO LHASA

The road south of Nagchu is the Qinghai-Tibet Hwy (Tso-Bö Lam in Tibetan), the busiest and most strategic highway in Tibet. The highland scenery along the road swings from completely dismal in bad weather to breathtakingly beautiful in good light.

Past a couple of truck stops, the road crosses the Goluk Bridge, 109km from Nagchu, and climbs to the Chokse-la, where Tibetans throw into the air the paper prayers they bought at Nagchu bus station. Just after the pass, 128km from Nagchu and 40km from Damxung, is the Chörten Rango, a line of eight chörtens that commemorate the eight main events in the life of Sakyamuni (Sakya Thukpa).

Damxung is the turn-off for Nam-tso and is a good place to get lunch (see Nam-tso in the Ü chapter for details).

About 18km south of Damxung a side road branches off east towards Reting Monastery, while the main highway continues south to Yangpachen, Tsurphu Monastery and Lhasa. See the Ü chapter for more details on these monasteries.

NORTHERN ROUTE TO SICHUAN

This is one of two main routes along the Sichuan-Tibet Hwy linking the Tibetan areas of eastern Tibet with Chengdu. Longer than the southern route, the northern route extends from Chamdo via Derge and Ganzi, converging with the southern route at Kangding and continuing into China proper. It is described here from west to east. For detailed information on Chengdu see Gateway Cities in the Getting There & Away chapter.

Chamdo to Derge

From Chamdo it's 228km to Jomda (Jiangda) via Topa and several high passes, and then a further 111km to Derge, crossing the Dri-chu (Jinsha Jiang, or Yangzi River) at the border with Sichuan. If you are hitching along this route you'll have to be careful at Jomda (where there are a guesthouse and a PSB office) and at the check post at the bridge over the Dri-chu (though checks are usually fairly cursory here). The occasional minibus runs between Jomda, Derge and Chamdo, but you will probably have to change rides in Jomda.

Derge
☎ 0836 • elevation 4000m

Resting in a valley between the Tibetan border and the Trola (Chola) range to the east, Derge forms the cultural heartland of Kham. While the Chinese influence is evident and growing rapidly in the town, the old town and surrounding villages are very much Tibetan.

There are many historically important monasteries in the valleys south of Derge, namely at Pelpung (Chinese: Babang), Dzongsar, Pewar (Baiya), Kathok and Pelyul (Baiyu). For details on these monasteries and treks in the area see Lonely Planet's *South-West China* guidebook or visit the Web site ⓦ www.khamaid.org.

Bakong Scripture Printing Press & Monastery

At the heart of Derge is the 18th-century Bakong Scripture Printing Press and Monastery *(admission Y35)*. The press houses more than 217,000 engraved blocks of Tibetan scriptures from all the Tibetan Buddhist orders (including Bön), making up an estimated 70% of Tibet's literary heritage. Texts include ancient works on astronomy, geography, music, medicine and Buddhist classics, including two of the most important Tibetan sutras. A history of Indian Buddhism comprising 555 woodblock plates is the only surviving copy in the world (it is written in Hindi, Sanskrit and Tibetan).

Within the monastery, dozens of workers hand-produce over 2500 prints to order each day, as ink, paper and blocks fly through the workers' hands at lightning speed. Upstairs is an older crowd of printers who produce larger and more complex prints of Tibetan gods on paper or coloured cloth.

You can also examine storage chambers, paper-cutting rooms and the main hall of the monastery itself. Protecting the monastery from fire and earthquake is the guardian goddess Drölma (Tara). There are some nice murals in the two ground-floor chapels, so

bring a torch. You can get a close-up look at the workers who carve the printing blocks (in relief) in the administrative building across from the monastery.

Admission to the monastery includes an English-language brochure and an obligatory guide. Photography is not allowed.

To reach the printing house, turn left out of the bus station and right over the bridge. Continue up this road to the south-east of town and to the monastery's front door. The monastery is closed from noon to 2pm.

Other Things to See Just uphill behind the printing house, the large Sakyapa **Gonchen Monastery** is well worth a look. Restored during the 1980s, the three inner sanctums are dedicated to Guru Rinpoche, Sakyamuni (Sakya Thukpa) and Jampa (Maitreya).

Also worth seeking out is the Tangtong Gyelpo Chapel (Tangyel Lhakhang) – as you head uphill to the printing press look out for the small alley leading to the right. For an introduction to the remarkable Tangtong Gyelpo, see the boxed text 'Tangtong Gyelpo' in the Facts about Tibet chapter.

Places to Stay & Eat Only one place in town is open to foreigners.

Derge Hotel (Dege Binguan; ☎ 822 2167). Doubles/triples Y35/30 per bed. Rooms here are clean but damp. Renovation work may soon bring some mid-range rooms.

There are a number of point-and-choose *restaurants* around town but none really stand out.

Getting There & Away Buses to Ganzi (Y61) and Kangding (Y163, two days) leave at 7am. There may also be seats on the bus from Pelyul (Baiyu) to Ganzi, which passes through about lunch time. The ticket office sells tickets for next-day buses between 3.30pm and 5pm. If you're travelling from east to west, note that individuals are officially forbidden from travelling into the TAR without travel permits. The occasional sleeper bus trundles through to and from Chamdo but rarely has empty berths. There is occasional transport west to Jomda, just over the Tibetan border.

Derge to Ganzi

East of Derge the road winds through deep gorges and pretty Tibetan villages before ascending to the wild and craggy scenery of the 4916m Tro-la. From the pass, the road descends to the crossroads of Manigango.

About 13km before you reach Manigango is **Yilhun La-tso** (*Xinlu Hai; admission Y20*), a stunning, holy alpine lake bordered by chörtens and dozens of rock carvings. The lake is backed by the huge glaciers of 6018m Trola Peak (Que'er Shan) and it's possible to walk an hour or two up the left (east) side of the lakeshore for glacier views. The lake has many great places to camp, though you need to guard against the mosquitoes. To get here you'll have to hitch to the turn-off where there's a bridge and trail 1km to the lake.

A 50km detour north from Manigango could take you to **Dzogchen Monastery** (Zhuqing Si), the home of the Dzogchen school. The monastery and *shedra* (Buddhist college) have a stunning location at the foot of a glacial valley. It's possible to stay at the college for Y15, though you'll need a sleeping bag and your own food. There are a couple of well-stocked shops in the village 1km below the valley. Several important high Nyingmapa lamas, now exiled abroad, originally came from nearby valleys.

If you want to use Manigango as a base to visit Yilhun La-tso or Dzogchen Monastery there is one guesthouse, *Manigango Guesthouse*, where beds cost Y15. This truck stop by the river has decent rooms and a restaurant where most buses stop for lunch. There are several Muslim *noodle restaurants* and shops at the crossroads.

Around 65km south-east of Manigango, near the village of Rongbatsa, are the circular walls of **Dargye Monastery**. Set against white-capped mountains, the monastery is a pleasant and relaxing place to rest for a day or two. A local lama named Gyalten Rinpoche is said to operate an excellent *guesthouse* nearby (Y35 to Y100 per person). You could also try the monastery itself. The nearby hot springs, although more lukewarm than hot, may be the only bathroom you get for some time.

From the monastery it's a two-hour walk north along the Nya-chu (Yalong River) to **Hadhi Nunnery**, home to around 60 nuns who operate a basic shop and are happy to receive short-term guests.

A further 15km along, on the north side of the river, is the Gelugpa **Beri Monastery**. There are several other monasteries in the pretty village of Beri.

Ganzi

The noisy market town of Ganzi (also spelled Kandze and Garze) sits in a valley at 3400m, surrounded by the sleeping giants of the Trola (Chola) range, and is a natural place to break your trip. The gorgeous surrounding countryside is peppered with Tibetan villages and resurgent monasteries.

Things to See & Do Over 540 years old, **Garze Monastery** is just north of the town's Tibetan quarter and is the region's largest monastery, with over 500 monks. Encased in the walls of the main prayer hall are hundreds of small golden Sakyamuni (Sakya Thukpa) statues. In a smaller hall just west of the main hall is an impressive statue of Jampa (Maitreya), dressed in silk.

To find the monastery, turn left out of the bus station and head north for about 10 minutes until you reach the Tibetan neighbourhood. A kora path winds clockwise around and above the monastery. To follow it take one of the roads to the left when you reach the Tibetan quarter and look for a huge chörten and then a hall of prayer wheels, from where the path winds uphill.

Den Monastery in the southern part of town is smaller but older and much more atmospheric. The inner chapel is surrounded by three pilgrimage paths and houses fierce statues of the protector god Nagpo Chenpo (Mahakala). Upstairs are several Mao slogans left over from the Cultural Revolution and a small printing press.

For a nice half-day walk head south from the bus station over the Nya-chu (Yalong River). The right fork leads through barley fields for 20 minutes to **Dongtong Monastery** (Dontok Monastery) and the new but impressive **Dingkhor chörten**. The left fork

Mandalas

The mandala (Tibetan: *kyilkhor*, literally 'circle') is a fascinating concept, as well as often being quite a beautiful artistic creation in itself. In a sense you might think of a mandala as being like a three-dimensional picture. What on the surface appears to be a plain two-dimensional design emerges, with the right visual approach, as a three-dimensional picture. Mandalas can take the form of paintings, patterns of sand, three-dimensional models or even whole monasteries, as in the case of Samye.

In the case of the two-dimensional mandala, the correct visual approach can be achieved only through meditation. The mandala is associated with Tantric Buddhism and is chiefly used in a ritual known as *sadhana*, or 'means for attainment'. According to this ritual, the adept meditates on, invokes and identifies with a specific deity, before dissolving into emptiness and re-emerging as the deity itself. The process, in so far as it uses the mandala as an aid, involves a remarkable feat of imaginative concentration.

A typical mandala features a central deity surrounded by four or eight other deities who are aspects of the central figure. These surrounding deities are often accompanied by a consort. There may be several circles of these deities, totalling several hundred deities in all. These deities and all other elements of the mandala have to be visualised as the three-dimensional world of the central deity and even as a representation of the universe. One ritual calls for the adept to visualise 722 deities with enough clarity to be able to see the whites of their eyes and hold this visualisation for four hours.

The ultimate aim of mandala visualisation, however, is to enter the three-dimensional world of the mandala and to merge with the deity at the centre of that world.

leads to Pongo Monastery after about an hour or so.

Ganzi has the region's best antique shops and many general stores selling Tibetan goods.

Places to Stay & Eat Ganzi has a number of sleeping and eating options.

Hongyueliang Hotel (☎ 752 2676) Doubles & triples Y20 per bed. Formerly the Post Office Hotel, this is the most convenient option. To find it, turn left out of the bus station, cross the main intersection, and continue on for about a block. It's on the left. Look for the hotel's telephone number on the blue, yellow and red sign. Unfortunately the toilets are grim and the no-prisoners karaoke kicks in nightly. There's a public hot shower (Y3) in a nearby building.

Kangba Hotel (Kangba Binguan; ☎ 752 3214) Beds Y25, suites with private bathroom Y120. The Kangba in the east end of town is a quieter government-run option.

Golden Yak Hotel (Jinmaoniu Jiudian) Doubles Y50 per person. This hotel is above the bus station (there's no English sign). Decent doubles come with private

bathroom with hot water, and there are some cheaper rooms.

Some small restaurants are located around the main intersection, just north of the bus station. The *Muslim restaurants* in a row just east of here double as video bars and offer good noodles if you can stand the ear-shattering sounds of kung fu.

The best restaurant in town is the *Ganzi Si Xinfu Fandian*, a block east of the intersection and recognisable by its purple sign. The sweet red pepper and pork (tianqing chaorou) is a treat.

Getting There & Away Buses to Ganzi (Y104, 12 hours) leave Kangding daily at 6.50am and 7.30am. From Ganzi, a bus leaves each morning at 6.30am for Kangding. A rather decrepit bus leaves Ganzi at 8.30am for Derge (Y60, 10 hours) and often continues to Pelyul (Baiyu).

You can also head north from Ganzi to Yushu (Jyekundo) in Qinghai via Serxu. Buses to Serxu originate in Kangding every day or two, stop overnight in Daofu and pause in Ganzi at around about 10am before resuming their drive.

This sand mandala will be swept away in a week or so; its dismantling represents impermanence.

The Wheel of Life is most commonly seen at monastery entrances.

To reach Beri and Dargye Monasteries, catch the morning bus to Derge or one of the sporadic local buses heading west.

Ganzi to Tagong

Several bustling towns en route from Ganzi to Tagong offer impressive monasteries and at least some basic accommodation. The Khampa houses in this region, built from wood and stone, are particularly elegant.

About 20km from Ganzi the road rises to a high pass before dropping down past the lake and monastery of Kasuo Lake.

Luhuo (Drango) is a newly rebuilt town about 90km from Ganzi and has the large Drango Monastery. A further 72km along is **Daofu**, with a hillside monastery and a huge chörten dedicated to the Panchen Lama.

Bamei (Garthar) is a lunch stop about 78km from Daofu; there's a pretty series of chörtens in the south of town. Just 8km north-east of town, along the road to Danba, is the Garthar Chöde Monastery (Chinese: Haiyuan Si), built by the seventh Dalai Lama. Bamei is famous as the birthplace of the 11th Dalai Lama.

From Bamei the road enters the Tagong grasslands, a vast expanse of lovely green meadows surrounded by snowcapped peaks and dotted with Tibetan herders and tents.

Tagong

In the midst of the grasslands is the vibrant Tibetan community of Tagong, an excellent place to spend a day or so exploring.

At the north end of town, **Tagong Monastery** (*admission Y10*) blends Han Chinese and Tibetan styles and appears to have survived the ravages of time amazingly well, though two of the three main halls have been rebuilt recently. The holiest statue in the far right building is a replica of Lhasa's Jowo Sakyamuni Buddha, said to have been carved in situ when the original passed through en route to Lhasa in the 7th century. Note also the beautiful 1000-armed Chenresig (Avalokiteshvara) in the building to the left. Make sure you visit the stunning

Wheel of Life

The Wheel of Life (Tibetan: Sipa Khorlo) is an aid to realising the delusion of the mind; a complex pictorial representation of how desire chains us to *samsara*, the endless cycle of birth, death and rebirth.

The wheel is held in the mouth of Yama, the Lord of Death. The inner circle of interdependent desire shows a cockerel (representing desire or attachment) biting a pig (ignorance or delusion) biting a snake (hatred or anger). A second ring is divided into figures ascending through the realms on the left and descending on the right.

The six inner sectors of the wheel symbolise the six realms of rebirth – gods, battling demigods, and humans (the upper realms), and hungry ghosts, hell and animals (the lower realms). All beings are reborn through this cycle dependent upon their karma. The Buddha is depicted outside the wheel, symbolising his release into a state of nirvana.

At the bottom of the wheel are hot and cold hells, where Yama holds a mirror that reflects one's lifetime. A demon to the side holds a scale with black and white pebbles, weighing up the good and bad deeds of one's lifetime.

The hungry spirits are recognisable by their huge stomachs, thin needle-like necks and tiny mouths, which cause them insatiable hunger and thirst. In each realm the Buddha attempts to convey his teachings (the dharma), offering hope to each realm.

The 12 outer segments depict the so-called '12 links of dependent origination', the 12 interlinked, codependent and causal experiences of life that perpetuate the cycle of samsara. The 12 images (whose order may vary) are of a blind woman (representing ignorance), a potter (unconscious will), a monkey (consciousness), men in a boat (self-consciousness), a house (the five senses), lovers (contact), a man with an arrow in his eye (feeling), a drinking scene (desire), a figure grasping fruit from a tree (greed), pregnancy, birth and death (a man carrying a corpse to a sky burial).

collection of over 100 chörtens behind the monastery; finish off a visit with a clockwise kora of the site.

The velvety hills around Tagong, topped with prayer flags and chörtens, offer views of the rolling grasslands and the stunning 5820m pyramid peak of Zhare Lhatse (Haizi Shan). Take a walk up to the hill above town, which is topped by a chörten surrounded by votive rags, amulets and beads left by pilgrims.

The grasslands are also the stage for an annual horse-racing festival, held at the beginning of the eighth lunar month (mid-July to August) and attended by thousands of local Tibetan herders.

A 20-minute walk west of town, over the river, leads to the shedra, which has a large collection of Buddhist rock carvings in the plain below.

Places to Stay & Eat The best option is the two-storey building diagonally opposite the monastery entrance – look for the English sign that says 'Tibetan Food and Butter Tea'. A karaoke pitstop for Chinese tourists during the day, the ornately decorated Tibetan-style room moonlights as a *guesthouse* in the evening, with Tibetan-style beds for Y20. Privacy and traffic noise can be a problem during the day, but things do quieten down at night.

Tagong Hotel (Tagong Lüshe) Beds Y10. This ramshackle hotel has acceptable rooms. To find it head 50m south down the main street, away from the monastery, and it's on your right in a government compound.

Along the main street you will find a number of small *restaurants* and *noodle shops*.

Getting There & Away Buses to Tagong run daily from Kangding (Y27, three hours) at 7.20am. If you're heading to Ganzi, you can pick up the same bus the next day at about 10am as it passes through town. A bus heading north to Luhuo also passes through Tagong around 9.30am or 10am.

Afternoon buses returning to Kangding can be flagged down in Tagong. You can also catch a minibus or shared taxi (Y20) to take you to the Xinduqiao crossroads, from where there are buses through to Kangding and Litang.

Kangding
☎ 0836 • elevation 2560m

Kangding (Tibetan: Dardo or Dartsedo) is nestled in a steep river valley at the confluence of the Zheduo and Yala Rivers, known in Tibetan as the Dar-chu and the Tse-chu. (The 'do' of the town's Tibetan name means 'river confluence').

Arriving in Kangding, there is a tangible sense that you've reached the border of the Chinese and Tibetan worlds. The town has been a trade centre between the two cultures for centuries with the exchange of yak hides, wool, herbs, and, especially, bricks of tea from Ya'an wrapped in yak hide. It also served as an important staging post on the road to Lhasa, as indeed it does today as western Sichuan's largest town. Kangding was historically the capital of the local Tibetan kingdom of Chakla (or Chala) and later, from 1939 to 1951, the capital of the short-lived province of Xikang, when it was controlled by the opium-dealing warlord Liu Wenhui. Today Kangding is largely Chinese.

Information The PSB (☎ 281 1415 ext 6035) is on the 4th floor of a building five minutes' walk south-east of the Black Tent Hotel. It processes visa extensions quickly and painlessly Monday to Friday.

The post and telecom office is next to the river on Yanhe Xilu. The Bank of China is next door but does not change money.

Several places around town offer Internet access for around Y3 per hour, especially around the Paoma Hotel.

Things to See & Do There are several monasteries in and around Kangding. Just behind the Black Tent Hotel, the **Ngachu Monastery** (Anjue Si) is a fairly quiet temple built in 1654. It is home to around 20 monks and a newly built Jampa Chapel.

The **Nanwu Monastery** in the western part of town is the most active monastery in the area and has around 80 lamas in residence. To reach it, walk south along the main road and follow its bend to the left for

2km, cross the bridge at the southern end of town and go another 300m. Next to a walled Han Chinese cemetery you will find a dirt path leading uphill alongside a stream that leads right to the monastery.

Next to Nanwu is **Dorje Drak Monastery** (Jin'gang Si), which is also worth a visit.

In town, the **market** on Dong Dajie is worth a look. You can also head up Paoma Shan for excellent views of Kangding and, if you're lucky, Mt Minya Konka (7556m). Take particular care when wandering around Paoma Shan and try to avoid hiking on your own. A British tourist was murdered here in the spring of 2000.

Zhuanshanjie, the festival whose name means 'walking around the mountain', takes place on Paoma Shan on the eighth day of the fourth lunar month to commemorate the birthday of Sakyamuni (Sakya Thukpa). White and blue Tibetan tents cover the hillside and there's plenty of wrestling and horse racing, with visitors from all over western Sichuan.

Places to Stay If you're only staying a night in Kangding, it's convenient to stay in the east of town near the bus station, although most guesthouses and attractions are over the river on the west side of town.

Black Tent Hotel (Hei Zhanpeng Zhuse) Triples Y17-27 per bed, doubles Y42 per bed. Next to Ngachu Monastery, this clean and sociable place has a teahouse on the ground floor and is the spot to meet other travellers. Washing facilities are limited to a basin and heated water, though showers are planned.

Kangding Hotel (☎ 282 3153) Triples Y36 per bed. Once the best in town, this chaotic place now has weary-looking rooms. Hot water comes on at night with the karaoke.

Taining Hotel (☎ 282 4530) Triples Y30 per bed, six-bed dorms Y20 per bed. This friendly place just south of the bus station has clean and pleasant rooms, though traffic noise can be a problem. Hot showers are down the hall.

Paoma Hotel (☎ 283 3110) Quads with private bathroom Y70 per bed, doubles with private bathroom Y240. Beds in quads are half price if you have a student card.

Places to Eat For a rousing cup of yak-butter tea, try the *teahouse* adjacent to the Black Tent Hotel.

Jixiang Fandian The friendly owners here have an English menu and serve fantastic local cuisine at good prices. Try the potato pancake (Y5) or the fish with black-bean sauce (Y18).

Taining Hotel Dishes Y8-20. The restaurant on the ground floor is pretty fancy but has surprisingly reasonable prices.

Getting There & Away The completion of the Erlang Shan (Two-Wolf Mountain) tunnel has cut the ride to Chengdu down to a comfortable eight hours. Buses leave hourly for Chengdu from 8am to 4pm (Y98). If you are heading to the Traffic Hotel make sure your bus is bound for the Xinnanmen station.

From Chengdu, early-morning buses for Kangding depart from the Xinnanmen station, though you won't be allowed on them until you have bought insurance. The 4pm sleeper will dump you in Kangding in the middle of the night.

Going west from Kangding, there are daily buses at 6.50am for Litang (Y78, seven hours), at 6.40am for Ganzi (Y103, 12 hours), at 7.50am for Batang (Y134, 11 hours) and at 7am for Derge (Y162, two days). Local minibuses run to Yajiang, Daofu and Luohu.

SOUTHERN ROUTE TO SICHUAN
Pomda to Batang
The southern road to Sichuan and Yunnan branches off from the truck-stop junction near Pomda (Pomda Crossroads). The road continues along the Yu-chu, a tributary of the Salween River, for 107km to **Dzogang** (Chinese: Yougong; also known as Wamda in Tibetan). It then continues 158km to Markham, en route crossing the 5008m Dongdo-la, dropping to stunning scenery around Denpa, rising again to the Joba-la, dropping again to cross the Dza-chu (Mekong River) at Druka and then rising

over yet another pass before finally dropping down to Markham (phew!). There is a basic *guesthouse* in Dzogang. Transport along this stretch of the road is particularly infrequent.

Markham, traditionally known as Garthog Dzong, is where permitless hitchhikers from Sichuan and Yunnan commonly get caught by the vigilant PSB. Try to avoid the town's main road, where there is a check post. Coming from the east, head for the road to the north of town that connects with the main highway. Markham has the *County Guesthouse*.

At Markham the road splits. The southern branch runs 112km over a pass to Yanjing (Salt Well) and the border with Yunnan, continuing on to Deqin. Yanjing used to be Tibet's major source of salt, once an essential commodity in these parts. Coming from Yunnan you will have to keep a low profile at Foshan, about 10km before Yanjing. There are some hot springs here. The north branch from Markham is the main road to Sichuan and continues 100km or so to Batang, crossing the Dri-chu (Jinsha Jiang) into Sichuan at Zhubalong.

Batang
☎ 0836 • elevation 2700m
Lying 32km from the Tibetan border and 5½ bumpy hours down a dirt track from Litang, low-lying Batang is the closest town to Tibet that is open to foreigners. Many travellers try to sneak into Tibet from here, so, unsurprisingly, the local PSB is a little suspicious of foreigners.

Transport Hotel (Keyun Fandian) Beds Y10-15. This place has dilapidated rooms, lumpy beds and grotty common toilets down the hall. Take a left out of the bus station and the hotel is in the first courtyard on the left.

Jinhui Hotel (Jinhui Binguan; ☎ 562 2700) Dorm beds Y10-20, doubles without/ with private bathroom Y50/70. This clean hotel is a better option. From the bus station continue into town and take the first right after the huge, hard-to-miss golden bird; it's a block down on the left.

Public transport picks up again in Batang. One bus heads east from Batang daily at 6.30am, stopping in Litang (Y60, 5½ hours) and Kangding (Y140, 13 hours) en route to Chengdu. Before reaching Kangding, this bus overnights in Yajiang where there is an unpleasant *hotel* in the bus compound. There's a better option in town, with doubles for Y50; to find it, go right out of the station, take the stairs up on the left until you reach a main road and stay to the right when the road forks. The hotel is on the left.

Litang
☎ 0836 • elevation 4680m
Surrounded by snowcapped peaks and resting on open grassland, Litang is a pleasant and friendly place to hang out for a couple of days. A horse-racing festival from 1 to 7 August sees the town swell with Tibetan visitors.

If you find yourself suffering from altitude sickness and can't get out of town, there is a local remedy consisting of medicated pills and rehydration drinks. The woman running the Xianhe Hotel may be able to help you out.

The post office is on the main north-south street. Next door is the telecom office, which has an Internet service for Y5 per hour, open until midnight.

Things to See At the northern end of town is **Litang Chöde Monastery**, built for the third Dalai Lama. Inside is a statue of Sakyamuni (Sakya Thukpa) that is believed to have been carried from Lhasa by foot. Tibetan homes lead up to the monastery and you are likely to encounter friendly monks en route who may offer to give you a tour.

On the eastern edge of Litang is a newly erected chörten, around which active worshippers seem to be perpetually circling, reciting mantras and spinning prayer wheels.

Places to Stay & Eat Litang has decent food and lodging, making it a fine place to break a trip for a day or more.

Xianhe Hotel (Xianhe Binguan) Beds Y25. Rooms here are impeccably clean and have fresh sheets and electric blankets – a great deal. Toilets are across the courtyard and washing facilities consist of basins and all the boiling water you can stand. The hotel is not easily spotted. Take a left out of the bus station and head about 350m east into town; it's on the right-hand side of the road. The Chinese-only sign over the entrance has a painting of a bird.

Litang Guest House *(Litang Zhao-daisuo;* ☎ *532 3089)* Dorm beds Y25. This slightly grotty place is on the same side of the road as the Xianhe, but further east.

High City Hotel *(Gaocheng Binguan)* Beds Y10. There seems be an abundance of rooms (or at least keys) here, but the conditions are something of a mystery to us as staff were unable to unlock the doors when we last visited. If the state of the reception is anything to go by, you should give it a miss.

Litang has countless small ***restaurants***, the majority of which are on the south side of the main road running east-west or over the road from the High City Hotel.

Getting There & Away Litang's bus station is a chaotic place so double-check all times and prices. At the time of writing buses were leaving Litang for Kangding daily at 8.30am. One or two Kangding-bound buses also pass through each day from Batang and Xiangcheng. Buses for Batang (Y60, 5½ hours) depart Litang daily at 7am and 7.30am.

An alternative route to Yunnan runs south from Litang, through 400km of spectacular scenery to Zhongdian. Buses run to Xiangcheng (Y60, five hours) at 7am but after this you'll have to hitch. For details of this route and the nearby Yading Nature Reserve, see Lonely Planet's *South-West China*.

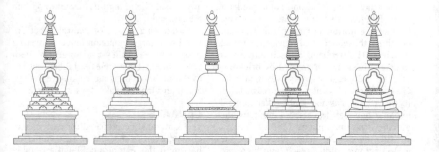

Trekking

A country as vast and mountainous as Tibet offers almost unlimited potential for walkers. From the frigid high northern plains to the steamy jungles of the south-east, Tibet is a land of rich cultural and ecological contrasts. The remoteness of Tibet combined with these climatic extremes poses special challenges for trekkers, as well as unique rewards. There are few places left in the world where you can walk for days, witnessing an ancient and sophisticated culture, without having the experience marred by the dross of modern civilisation.

Most trekking is conducted in the centre of the region in the vicinity of the major towns and highways. Cities such as Lhasa and Shigatse provide bases from which to equip and launch treks. The trailheads of four of the seven treks covered in this chapter can be reached by public transport.

Highlights

- Treading the old pilgrim trail from Ganden to Samye, a test of physical mettle as much as a spiritual feat
- Hiking from Shalu to Nartang, a great introduction to trekking in Tibet and a window on the ancient art of pilgrimage
- Circumambulating Mt Kailash – not just a walk around a mountain but a quest for deeper glimmerings of the self
- Stretching the imagination as well as the legs while peering into the lucid waters of sacred Lake Manasarovar
- Adventuring in the shadow of Everest, for spectacular scenery, rigorous exercise and the opportunity to come close to Tibetan culture

Facts about Trekking

HISTORY

In the 17th century Jesuit priests intent on spreading Christianity trekked over the mountains of western Tibet. In the late 19th and early 20th centuries a slew of spies, explorers and scholars, often in caravans, covered great distances on foot in their attempts to reach the Holy City, Lhasa.

Most never made it, and some paid for their Tibetan adventure with their lives. One such unfortunate person was Dutreuil de Rhins, the leader of a French expedition, who in 1891, after being refused permission to enter Lhasa, was murdered by brigands. One of the greatest treks was made by George Roerich's central Asiatic expedition in the 1920s. During their archaeological explorations they traversed a great swathe of Tibet's northern plains.

Still, there were many places that the early explorers didn't reach, and there are still many new frontiers in Tibet beckoning the experienced, well-equipped trekker.

GEOGRAPHY

For all its attractions, Tibet is a formidable place where even day walks involve survival skills and generous portions of determination. As it's situated on the highest plateau on earth and crisscrossed by the world's highest mountains, nothing comes easily and careful preparation is all important. Even on the most popular treks, which can involve several days of travel without any outside help, high passes up to 5300m are crossed.

Eastern and much of central Tibet are laced with large mountain ranges, towering passes and deep valleys and gorges. Western and northern Tibet are even higher, but between the mountains are expansive valleys and plains that can take days to traverse.

CLIMATE

Trekkers must be prepared for extremes in climate even in the middle of summer. A hot sunny day can turn cold and miserable in a matter of minutes, especially at higher elevations. Night temperatures at 4500m and above routinely fall below freezing even in July and August! At other times of the year it gets colder. In midwinter in north-western Tibet, minimum temperatures reach minus 40°C. Yet Tibet is a study in contrasts, and in the summer months a scorching sun and hot blustery winds can make even the hardiest walker scurry for any available shade. Between the two extremes the Tibetan climate is ideal for walking – cool and dry – but always be prepared for the worst.

ECOLOGY & ENVIRONMENT

Trekking responsibly in Tibet is a matter for special consideration (see also the boxed text 'Responsible Trekking' later in this chapter). The beautiful but fragile alpine biomes of the upland regions of Tibet deserve the utmost respect. For instance, a fire can scar the landscape for centuries. In recent years, the environment of Tibet has suffered tremendously. Forests are being decimated, wildlife eradicated and economically important plants depleted. In such a context it is imperative that trekkers make their way lightly and leave nothing but the proverbial footprints behind. Stay off fragile slopes and try not to tread on plants. Follow the Tibetan ethos, killing not even the

smallest of insects. In the long term this approach will buy trekkers respect from Tibetans and will help guarantee that later visitors enjoy the most pristine environment possible.

In the arid climate of much of Tibet water takes on a special significance and is highly regarded in Tibetan traditional beliefs. The *lu* (water spirits) guard the wellbeing of the community and are thought to be very dangerous if transgressed. For these reasons Tibetans tend to treat water reverently. Their traditional practices resemble those adopted by the ecotrek movement. For example, toilets are never constructed where they could contaminate water sources, and the washing of clothes in rivers and streams is restricted. In both traditional and modern terms, the aim is the same: to avoid the introduction of foreign substances into water sources.

FLORA & FAUNA

The mountain slopes of Tibet are home to many dozens of plants and flowers, but you should resist the temptation to pick them. There really is no need as many of the most useful plants are readily available as medicines, incense and condiments in the city markets. If you are interested in identifying Tibetan medicinal plants check out *Tibetan Medical Thangkas Of The Four Medical Tantras*, a lavish coffee-table book available in most Lhasa bookshops. Also see *Flowers of the Himalaya* by Oleg Polunin & Adam Stainton for some examples of Tibetan flora.

The more remote valleys and mountains are home to a rich variety of wildlife (see Flora and Fauna in the Facts about Tibet chapter). If you are lucky you might see the Himalayan black bear or perhaps the giant Tibetan brown bear searching for food in the alpine meadows. Snow leopards in the craggy heights and the common spotted leopard in eastern Tibet are occasionally spotted by alert trekkers.

Less daunting but no less spectacular are the ungulates of Tibet, which include several species of deer, wild yaks, antelopes, gazelles, blue sheep and the argali, the largest species of wild sheep in the world. Smaller mammals, a panoply of birds, and

---

Trekking Disclaimer

! ● Although the authors and publisher have done their utmost to ensure the accuracy of all information in this guide, they cannot accept any responsibility for any loss, injury or inconvenience sustained by people using this book. They cannot guarantee that the tracks and routes described here have not become impassable for any reason in the interval between research and publication.

The fact that a trip or area is described in this guidebook does not mean that it is safe for you and your trekking party. You are ultimately responsible for judging your own capabilities in the light of the conditions you encounter.

numerous reptiles and amphibians can be seen while trekking. Generally, large predatory animals are not attracted to camp sites and stay well away from humans. Still, do not court trouble by discarding food scraps near your camp – you would be extending a welcome to the local rodent population.

PEOPLE & SOCIETY

Tibetans are fun-loving by nature, as well as being a devoutly religious people. With a little effort and goodwill it should be possible to break down cultural barriers and even to make friends. In most out-of-the-way places trekkers can quickly become the centre of attention, and sometimes just a smile may lead to dinner invitations and offers of places to stay. If you really detest being the star of the show, don't camp in villages; if you do, don't expect Western notions of privacy to prevail.

As in much of Asia, nudity and open displays of affection are frowned upon. Try to dress modestly, which is pretty easy in such a rugged environment. You are better off covering up in the intense solar radiation of Tibet with light-coloured, lightweight clothing. Be especially vigilant at monasteries – these are not places for immodest Western fashions. As a rule, don't wear shorts or short dresses, especially in villages and at religious sites. For more information on cultural considerations see Society & Conduct in the Facts about Tibet chapter.

Tibetans tend to be very informal but with elders and religious figures a certain amount of deference is called for. And don't forget the value of a good joke in buiding bridges with people, even if it's at your own expense. If you ask directions be prepared to be sent in the direction you are walking no matter where you are trying to go. To avoid this age-old travellers' trap be prepared to patiently and repeatedly explain what your travel goals are and, if in doubt, ask someone else.

If you have any religious sentiments your trek probably qualifies as a pilgrimage, in which case, you will usually receive better treatment than if you are 'just going someplace'. Another helpful hint: If all else fails try a song and dance. Even the most amateur of efforts are met with great approval.

Facts for the Trekker

PLANNING
Maps

There are many commercially available maps covering Tibet, but very few are detailed enough to be more than a general guide for trekkers. The Chinese government produces small-scale topographical and administrative maps, but these are not for sale to the general public. The US-based Defense Mapping Agency Aerospace Center produces a series of charts covering Tibet in the 1:1,000,000, 1:500,000 and 1:250,000 scales (though the last can be hard to find). The most useful of the American 1:500,000 references for trekking in Tibet are:

H-10A – Lhasa region, Ganden to Samye, Tsurphu to Yangpachen
H-9A – Kailash and Manasarovar
H-9B – Shigatse region, Shalu to Nartang, Everest region

Soviet topographical maps in the 1:200,000 scale can now be consulted in many large university library map rooms. However, most libraries will not permit you to photocopy them because of international copyright laws. Buying them is also a problem because the Russian government only sells complete sets for each country – there are over 8000 for the PRC, probably costing more than your entire trip to Tibet!

The Swiss company Karto-Atelier (W www.karto-atelier.com) produces a 1:50,000 Mt Kailash trekking map.

For details of places to buy maps, see Maps under Planning in the Facts for the Visitor chapter.

What to Bring

There is a great deal to see while trekking and you will be revitalised by the natural surroundings, but you must be prepared for extremes in weather and terrain. The time of year you choose to walk will dictate the equipment you will need.

Clothing & Footwear As a minimum, you will need basic warm clothing including a hat, scarf, gloves, down jacket, long underwear, warm absorbent socks, all-weather shell and sun hat, in addition to comfortable well-made pants and shirts. Women may want to add a long skirt to their clothing list.

If you attempt winter trekking you will need more substantial mountaineering clothing. Many people opt for synthetic-pile clothing, but also consider wool, which has proven itself in the mountains of Tibet for centuries. One of your most important assets will be a pair of strong, well-fitting hiking boots. And remember to break them in before starting the trek!

Equipment Three essential items are a tent, a sleeping bag and a backpacking stove. There are no restaurants in remote areas of Tibet and provisions are hard to come by, so you will probably end up cooking all your own food. Count on camping because, except in certain villages on the main trekking routes, it can be difficult to find places to sleep. Invest in a good tent that can handle big storms and heavy winds. A warm sleeping bag is a must. Manufacturers tend to overrate the effectiveness of their bags so always buy a warmer one than you think you'll need – you can unzip it if you get too hot.

You will also need a strong, comfortable backpack large enough to carry all your gear and supplies. To save a lot of misery test the backpack on day hikes to be certain it fits and is properly adjusted.

Nonessentials include a Walkman, a journal, and elaborate camera gear. Basics, however, must include water containers with at least a 2L capacity, a system for water purification, a torch (flashlight), compass, pocketknife, first-aid kit, waterproof matches, sewing kit, cup, shrill whistle and walking stick or ski pole. This last item acts as a walking aid and, most importantly, for

defence against dog attacks. Tibetan dogs can be particularly large and brutal and roam at will in nearly every village and herders' camp. Bring your walking stick or pole with you from home, or purchase a shovel handle in Lhasa. They can be found at hardware stores on Lingkhor Chang Lam.

Petrol for camping stoves is widely available in towns and cities but is of fairly poor quality. To prevent your stove from getting gummed up you will have to clean it regularly. Kerosene (*meiyou* in Chinese) can also be obtained in cities. In Lhasa you will find kerosene vendors on Dekyi Shar Lam opposite the road to Ramoche.

For details on buying and hiring trekking gear in Tibet, see Shopping in the Lhasa chapter.

Physical Preparation

Before embarking on a trek make sure you are up to the challenge of high-altitude walking through rugged country. Test your capabilities by going on day walks in the hills around Lhasa and Shigatse. Try a hike to the top of a small mountain such as Bumpa Ri, on the other side of the Kyi-chu from Lhasa.

TREKKING AGENCIES

There is now a plethora of tourist agencies in Lhasa, some of which can arrange treks. Let the buyer beware, for the standard of service fluctuates wildly and may bear no correspondence to the amount you pay. In general, standards of service and reliability are much lower than in Kathmandu. Shop around carefully and compare the services and attitudes of at least several agencies. Kickbacks and shady dealings are part of everyday business but with some luck they won't ruin your trip.

The main advantage of going with an agency is that it takes care of all the red tape and deals with officials. Most agencies offer a full-package trek including transport to and from the trailhead, guide, cook, yaks or burros to carry the equipment, mess tent and cooking equipment. The package will probably not include tents to sleep in, at least any up to the task of trekking in Tibet.

Make sure the agency spells out exactly what is included in the price it is quoting, you and be prepared to provide all your own personal equipment.

It is a very good idea to sign a written contract with the tourist agency you intend to travel with. However, as none of the Lhasa companies seem to have contracts at hand you may find yourself drafting up one. If so, be certain to include details of the service you are paying for and money-back guarantees should your operator fail to deliver what has been agreed to. For the standard contents of tour contracts have a look at the brochures of adventure-travel companies in your home country.

None of the Lhasa-based agencies listed below can be unconditionally recommended, but all have run at least some successful treks. Prices vary according to group size and location but none are cheap. Costs per person tend to be lower in bigger groups. For treks in remote and border areas expect to wait at least four days for the permits to be sorted out. If you feel you have been cheated by your agent you may find help with Jigme, director of marketing and promotion for the Tibet Tourism Bureau (☎ 0891-683 4315, fax 683 4632) in Lhasa. This government organisation is in charge of training tour guides and monitoring the performance of all companies running treks and tours.

Tibetan Agencies

Holyland Adventure (☎ 0891-683 6652, fax 683 4472, ⓔ holyland@public.ls.xz.cn) 215 Dekyi Nub Lam. US$90 per day. Two blocks west of the Lhasa Hotel and just east of the Xinhua Bookstore, this long-established company is managed by the congenial Thupten Gendun and arranges treks just about anywhere.

Shigatse Travels (☎ 0891-633 0489, fax 633 0482, ⓔ amdo@public.ls.xz.cn) 2nd floor, Yak Hotel, 100 Dekyi Lam Shar. US$90 per day. Managed by Dorje Tashi, who works closely with the foreign tour operators, this company offers lots of tours but has limited experience in trekking.

Tibet International Sports Travel (☎ 0891-633 4082, fax 633 4855, ⓔ tist@public.ls.xz.cn) 4th floor, Himalaya Hotel, 6 Lingkhor Shar Lam. US$100 per day. This is the oldest agency specialising in trekking. Under the able management of Dawa, the director of sales, it is a contractor for several international travel companies.

Tibet Kada Group Potala Folk Service (☎ 0891-634 2032, fax 633 1357, ⓔ kadata@public.ls.xz.cn) 23 Chingdröl Shar Lam. US$80 per day. This company is managed by a Tibetan named Jimmy. He and his staff have substantial trekking experience, and seem willing to please.

Tibet Yungdru Adventure (☎ 0891-633 6642, fax 633 6496, ⓔ tny@public.ls.xz.cn) 3rd floor, New Century Hotel, 155 Dekyi Lam Shar. US$120 per day. A main focus of the managing director Thupten is trekking in the more remote regions of Tibet.

Kathmandu Agencies

If you want to organise your Tibet trek from Kathmandu here's a list of some of the most qualified agencies:

Arniko Travels (☎ 01-421684, fax 414594, ⓔ arnikotv@ccsl.com.np) PO 469, Baluwatar
Dharma Adventures (☎ 01-430499, fax 421053, ⓔ info@shivatours.com) PO Box 5385, Gairidhara
Great Escapes (☎ 01-418951, fax 411533, ⓔ grt@greatpc.mos.com.np) PO 9523, Baluwatar
Malla Treks (☎ 01-410089, fax 423143, ⓔ tsedo@mallatrk.mos.com.np) PO Box 5227, Lekhnath Marg
Mountain Travel Nepal (☎ 01-411225, fax 414075, ⓔ info@tigermountain.com.np) PO Box 170, Lazimpat

Western Agencies

A few Western companies offer fixed-departure treks in Tibet. These tours can be joined in your home country or abroad, usually in Kathmandu. Prices are higher than treks organised in Tibet or even Kathmandu, but they take the hassle out of organising a trek and are useful if you have the money but only a couple of weeks.

A standard trek organised at home will include a Western leader, a local leader, porters, a cook and so on. All your practical needs will be taken care of and you will be free to enjoy the trekking itself.

For a list of some Western companies that can organise treks in Tibet, see Organised Tours in the Getting There & Away chapter.

DOCUMENTS

Officially, individuals are not permitted to trek in Tibet and must join an organised group. Trekking, as with all travel in Tibet apart from that around Lhasa, requires a travel permit (for more information see Travel Permits under Visas & Documents in the Facts for the Visitor chapter).

That said, a number of trekkers opt to go it alone, in the true spirit of independent travel, and many succeed. If you are caught by the security police without the right documents be friendly but firm in your conviction that you did not know any better. You will probably be let off with a small fine, unless either you or the police lose their cool. It is unusual to be asked for any documentation while on a trek.

Trekkers heading from Ganden to Samye without a travel permit will face a problem after their trek is finished when they take the ferry over to the Tsetang side. Trekkers in the Mt Kailash region face the same permit regulations as other travellers – see the Ngari (Western Tibet) chapter for details. At the time of research Shigatse Public Security Bureau (PSB) was issuing travel permits covering Everest Base Camp. Make sure you get one if you are trekking in the Everest region; if you are stopped at least you'll have something to show. At the time of research there were no permit checks anywhere on the Tsurphu-Yangpachen or Shalu-Nartang treks but the trailhead at Tsurphu is often patrolled by police. Travel permits are not needed for Ganden, but at Tingri, Everest Base Camp, Tsurphu, Yangpachen and Shalu the authorities are within their rights to ask for one.

HEALTH

To maintain your health in such a difficult high-elevation environment you need to take special precautions. With a little preparation and good sense your trekking experience will be one of the highlights of your trip to Tibet. Bring a first-aid kit with all the basics and perhaps some extras as well (see Health in the Facts for the Visitor chapter). Tibet is not the place to wander alone – always trek with companions. If anything goes wrong you

will need others to depend on. In case of a real emergency you may require medical and evacuation insurance, which should be purchased before leaving home. For detailed information see *Medicine for Mountaineering*, published by Mountaineers Books.

The most common trekking health problem is sunburn. In serious instances (when accompanied by heat exhaustion), sunburn can require hospitalisation, but fortunately it is preventable. Wear loose-fitting clothes that cover your arms, legs and neck, and choose a wide-brimmed hat like the ones Tibetans wear. There are many fancy and expensive sunscreen lotions on the market but the most effective and cheapest is zinc oxide ointment. Bring it from home because you probably won't find it in Tibet.

Subfreezing temperatures mean there is a risk of hypothermia even in summer. Make sure you have the right clothing and an outer shell that protects against rain, snow and wind. Remember that exposed plains and ridges are prone to extremely high winds and this significantly adds to the cold. For example, on a 5000m pass in central Tibet in July, the absolute minimum temperature is roughly minus 4°C, but regularly occurring 70km/h winds plunge the wind-chill factor or apparent temperature to minus 20°C.

Trekkers are particularly at risk from acute mountain sickness (AMS; also known as altitude sickness). For information on this vital subject see Health in the Facts for the Visitor chapter.

TREKKING WITH CHILDREN

It is not a good idea to take very young children on high-altitude treks because they might not acclimatise well. Older children who are properly trained and acclimatised can make great trekking partners but don't become demoralised when you see that they are faster than you! Ensure that your kids are fully clad and wearing good sunglasses to protect their sensitive eyes and skin.

GUIDES & PACK ANIMALS

The rugged terrain, long distances and high elevations of Tibet make most people think

TREKKING

twice about carrying their own gear. In villages and nomad camps along the main trekking routes it is often possible to hire yaks to do the dirty work for you. Even on less travelled routes you might find help.

You will need to know some Tibetan to negotiate what you want and how much you are willing to pay. Be prepared for a good session of bargaining, and don't set out until you and the Tibetans working for you are perfectly clear about what's been agreed on. To avoid misunderstandings, spell out the amount of time you expect from your helpers and the exact amount you intend to pay. Your mule skinner or yak driver will also serve as your guide, an important asset on the unmarked trails of Tibet. Consider

just hiring a guide if you don't want or can't get pack animals – this could save you a lot of frustrating hours looking for the route.

Guides can also share their knowledge of the natural history and culture of the place, greatly adding to your experience. Even large trekking companies depend on local guides to make their trips work.

FOOD
You should be self-sufficient in food because there isn't much to eat on the trail. In most villages there is little or no food surplus and thus probably nothing to buy. But don't worry: In Lhasa there are now thousands of stalls and stores selling a huge variety of foodstuffs making well-balanced,

Responsible Trekking

Tibet is one of the great unspoiled wildernesses left on earth. Please consider the following tips when trekking and help preserve the unique ecology and beauty of this fragile region.

Fires & Cooking
Building fires is not an option. Wood is nonexistent in much of Tibet and where there are trees and bushes they are often scarce resources needed by locals. Cook on a lightweight kerosene, petrol, alcohol or Shellite (white gas) stove and avoid those powered by disposable butane gas canisters.

If you are trekking with a guide and porters, supply stoves for the whole team. In alpine areas, ensure that all members are outfitted with enough clothing so that fires are not needed for warmth.

Rubbish
Carry out all your rubbish. Don't overlook easily forgotten items such as silver paper, orange peel, cigarette butts and plastic wrappers. Empty packaging weighs very little and should be stored in a dedicated rubbish bag. Gain good karma by carrying out rubbish left by others.

Never bury your rubbish: Digging disturbs soil and groundcover and encourages erosion. Buried rubbish will more than likely be dug up by animals, who may be injured or poisoned by it. Moreover, it may take years to decompose, especially at Tibet's high altitudes.

Minimise the waste you must carry out by taking minimal packaging and taking no more than you will need. If you can't buy in bulk, unpack small-portion packages and combine their contents in one container before your trek. Take reusable containers, zip-lock bags or stuff sacks.

In Tibet it is not a good idea to burn plastic and other garbage as this is believed to irritate mountain spirits and affronts the sensibilities of more traditional Tibetans.

Sanitary napkins, tampons and condoms should also be carried out despite the inconvenience. They burn and decompose poorly.

Toilets
Where there is a toilet, please use it. Where there is none, human waste should be left on the surface of the ground away from trails and habitations to decompose. Aridity, cold and high ultraviolet exposure renders wastes into innocuous compounds relatively quickly.

tasty meals possible on the trail. Even in Shigatse and the smaller cities there are many foods suitable for trekking.

Vacuum-packed red meat and poultry, and packaged dried meat and fish are readily found in Lhasa. Many kinds of packaged and bulk dried fruits are sold throughout the city. The newest and tastiest varieties are figs and pineapples, which make a great trail mix when combined with peanuts and walnuts. You can even find almonds and pistachios imported from the US.

Soybean- and dairy-milk powders can be used with several kinds of prepackaged cereals. Pickled and dried vegetables are good for dressing up soups and stir-fries. On the Barkhor are stalls selling Indian pickles and curry powders. Lightweight vegetables such as bok choy and carrots can do wonders for macaroni and instant noodles, both of which are readily available.

Cooking mediums include butter, margarine, vegetable oil and sesame oil. Butter can be preserved for long treks or old butter made more palatable by turning it into ghee (boil for about 20 minutes and strain). For those with a sweet tooth all kinds of biscuits and sweets are sold in Lhasa and the larger towns. Decent-quality Chinese chocolate and Western chocolate are available in Lhasa.

DRINKS

As wonderfully cold and clear as much of the water in Tibet is, do not assume that it's

Responsible Trekking

If you are in a large trekking group dig a privy pit. Be sure to build it far from any water source or marshy ground and carefully rehabilitate the area when you leave camp. Pieces of turf, rocks and soil removed from the hole can be used to cap it. Also be certain that the latrine is not near *mani* (prayer) walls, shrines or any other sacred structures. Encourage all party members, including porters, to use the site.

Washing

Don't use detergents or toothpaste in or near watercourses, even if they are biodegradable. For personal washing, use biodegradable soap and a water container (or even a lightweight, portable basin) at least 50m away from the watercourse. Widely disperse the waste water to allow the soil to filter it fully before it finally makes it back to the watercourse.

Wash cooking utensils 50m from watercourses using a scourer, sand or snow instead of detergent.

Erosion

Hillsides and mountain slopes, especially at high altitudes, are prone to erosion. It is important to stick to existing tracks and avoid short cuts that bypass a switchback. If you blaze a new trail straight down a slope it will turn into a watercourse with the next heavy rainfall and eventually cause soil loss and deep scarring.

If a well-used track passes through a mud patch, walk through the mud: Walking around the edge will increase the size of the patch.

Avoid removing the plant life that keeps topsoil in place.

Cultural Considerations

Seek permission to camp from landowners. They will usually be happy to grant permission if asked, but may be confrontational if not.

Wildlife Conservation

Do not engage in or encourage hunting. This extends to not buying souvenirs and other items made from endangered species.

Overview of Treks

trek	no of days	distance (km)	passes	description
Ganden to Samye	4 to 5	80	Shug-la (5250m), Chitu-la (5100m)	Medium to difficult – the most popular trek in Tibet, connecting two of Tibet's most important monasteries
Tsurphu to Yangpachen	3 to 4	55	Lasar-la (5300m)	Medium to difficult – gives a good insight into the lives of Tibet's seminomadic herders
Shalu to Nartang	2 to 3	40	Showa-la (4200m), Char-la (4600m)	Moderate – easy access and relatively low passes make this a good beginners' trek
Friendship Hwy to Everest Base Camp	3 to 4	105	Geu-la (5170m) or Pang-la (5200m)	Difficult – but if you get tired you can always hitch part of the way
Everest Base Camp to Tingri	3 to 4	60	Nam-la (5250m)	Difficult – an excellent way to trek into or out of Everest and avoid the road
Mt Kailash Kora	3	52	Drölma-la (5630m)	Difficult – one of Tibet's most holy pilgrimage treks
Lake Manasarovar Kora	4 to 5	110	4680m	Difficult – a most sacred and beautiful lake, with a shore dotted with monasteries.

safe to drink. Livestock contaminate many water sources and Tibetans do not always live up to their cultural ideals. Giardia is common in Tibet and can slow your trek down to a crawl.

To protect your health you should treat all water before drinking by using chemical or filtration methods, or by boiling it for at least 10 minutes. For added protection more than one method can be used in tandem. If you plan to rely on chemical purification bring your supply from home so that you know how to use it. For more information see Health in the Facts for the Visitor chapter.

Follow Tibetan tradition and eliminate the monotony of drinking plain water by downing as much tea as you can. You can buy Chinese green tea in virtually every city and town in Tibet.

Consider staying clear of *chang* (Tibetan barley beer), which is made with untreated water, but give yak-butter tea a try. More like a soup than a tea, it helps fortify you against

the cold and replenishes the body's salts. If you are offered tea, have it served in your own cup as per tradition – this eliminates the risk of drinking from used cups.

Routes

Detailed descriptions of seven popular treks are given here. They offer fantastic walking, superb scenery and, with the exception of Lake Manasarovar (Tibetan: Mapham yum-tso) and Mt Kailash (Kang Rinpoche), are close to Lhasa or the Friendship Hwy. Walking times given are just that; they don't include breaks, nature stops or any other off-your-feet activities. On average, plan to walk five or seven hours at most in a day interspersed with frequent short rests. You will also need time to set up camp, cook and just plain enjoy yourself.

The trek stages can be used as a daily itinerary, but remember to plan ahead to avoid spending the night at the highest point reached in the day.

The directions 'right' and 'left' given in the descriptions of routes always correspond with the direction of travel.

GANDEN TO SAMYE

The Trek at a Glance

Duration 4 to 5 days
Distance 80km
Standard Medium to difficult
Start Ganden
Finish Samye
Highest Point Shug-la (5250m)
Nearest Large Towns Lhasa and Tsetang
Accommodation Camping
Public Transport Some buses
Summary This demanding trek crosses two passes over 5000m and begins less than 50km from Lhasa. A four- or five-day trek via Shug-la and Chitu-la connects two of Tibet's most important monasteries. It has emerged as the most popular in the Ü region.

This trek has much to offer: lakes, beautiful alpine forests and meadows, as well as two centres of Tibetan religious culture. With so much to offer, its popularity is understandable, but you should not underestimate the trek. Only those with experience hiking and camping in high-elevation wildernesses should attempt this trek alone. Otherwise it makes good sense to join an organised tour.

The best time for the trek is from mid-May to mid-October. The summer months can be wet but the mountains are at their greenest and wildflowers spangle the alpine meadows. Barring heavy snow, it is also possible for those with a lot of trekking experience and the right gear to do this trek in the colder months. If you are coming straight from Lhasa you will need to spend a couple of nights at Ganden Monastery (4500m) to acclimatise.

Public buses run between Lhasa and Ganden, and between Lhasa and the Samye ferry crossing. For information on these, see Ganden Monastery in the Lhasa chapter and Samye Monastery in the Ü chapter.

Stage 1: Ganden to Yama Do
5–6 hours • 17km • 450m descent • 300m ascent

The trek begins from the parking lot at the base of Ganden Monastery, traversing south along the ridge to reach the first village, Hepu, after about three hours. Leave the parking lot and look for the well-trodden trail heading south along the side of Angkor Ri, the highest point on the Ganden *kora* (ritual circumambulation circuit). The trail gradually ascends for 1½ hours before reaching a saddle. Near the saddle the trail comes close to the top of the ridge marked by cairns. The saddle itself is marked by a *lapse* (cairn) 2m tall and 3m in diameter.

From the saddle look west down the Kyichu valley to Lhasa. Traversing the west side of the ridge from the saddle, the trail reaches a spur surmounted by a cairn after 30 minutes. The trail now descends towards Hepu village. Twenty minutes from the spur is a spring. From here it is a further 30 minutes to the village.

There are around 30 houses in Hepu and it is possible for trekkers to *camp* or find *accommodation* among the friendly locals.

If carrying your gear up the pass beyond Hepu is not a pleasant thought, you might be able to rent yaks to do the work for you. Villagers charge around Y50 per yak per day, plus the salary of the yak herder, which is also approximately Y50 per day. You will also have to pay half-charges for the time it takes the yaks and herder to return home. Usually herders feed themselves and provide their own camping gear, but make all this clear before you set out. Intimately familiar with the environment, these people know how to make themselves at home on the trail. A yak can carry two or three backpacks, depending on their weight. Yak herders will load the beasts lightly to maximise their income and save wear and tear on the animals.

Finding a person willing to accompany your party all the way to Samye is not easy. You may have to settle for the summit of the first or second pass, which is a big help. If you don't get yaks all the way you might find others further along at a herders' camp

TREKKING

TREKKING

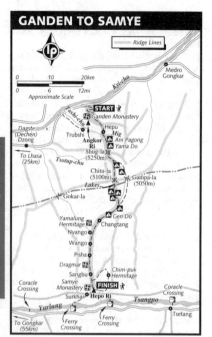

GANDEN TO SAMYE

Ridge Lines

0   10   20km
0   6   12mi
Approximate Scale

Medro
Gongkar

Kyi-chu

START — Ganden Monastery

Hepu
Mig
Trubshi   Ani Pagong
Angkor   Yama Do
Ri
Shug-la
(5250m)

Dagste
(Dechen)
Dzong

To Lhasa
(25km)

Tsotup-chu

Chitu-la
(5100m)   Gampa-la
Lakes   (5050m)

Gokar-la

Yamalung   Gen Do
Hermitage   Changtang
Nyango
Wango
Pisha
Dragmar
Chim-puk
Sangbu   Hermitage
Coracle   Samye   FINISH
Crossing   Monastery
Surkhar   Hepo Ri   Tsangpo
Yarlung   Coracle
Crossing

To Gongkar   Ferry   Ferry   Tsetang
(55km)   Crossing   Crossing

but this not a sure bet. It you have no luck in Hepu try down valley in the nearby village of Trubshi.

From Hepu the trail climbs towards the Shug-la, 3½ hours away. Look for a red-and-yellow masonry structure and white incense hearths at the edge of the village. This is the shrine of Hepu's *yul lha* (local protecting deity), the Divine White Yak. Go east from here and look for the bridge crossing the Tashi-chu Mig stream, which runs below the village. Outside of the summer months you can also easily ford this stream to the west bank. Head down the valley for a few minutes to the confluence with another stream. Round the inner side of the confluence and head upstream along the east bank. You are now following the watercourse originating from the Shug-la. Near the confluence are good *camping grounds*.

One hour from Hepu you reach Ani Pagong, a narrow, craggy bottleneck in the valley. A small nunnery used to be above the trail. From Ani Pagong the trail steadily climbs for one hour through marshy meadows to Yama Do.

Yama Do offers extensive *camping grounds* suitable for larger groups. Consider spending the night here as it is still a long way to the pass. Above Yama Do the valley's watercourse splits into three branches. Follow the central or south branch, not the south-east or south-west branches. The route leaves the flank of the valley and follows the valley bottom.

Beyond Yama Do the trail becomes indistinct but it is a straight shot upwards to the pass. Thirty minutes from Yama Do are two single-tent *camp sites*, the last good ones until the other side of the pass, at least five hours away.

Stage 2: Yama Do to Tsotup-chu Valley
5–7 hours • 10km • 1000m ascent • 450m descent

One hour past Yama Do leave the valley floor and ascend a shelf on the east (left) side of the valley to avoid a steep gully that forms around the stream. In another 45 minutes you enter a wet alpine basin studded with tussock grass. Because of the unsuitable terrain you should only consider camping here in an emergency.

The Shug-la is at least 1¼ hours from the basin. Remain on the east side of the valley as it bends to the left. You have to negotiate boulders and lumpy ground along the final steep climb to the pass. The Shug-la (5250m) cannot be seen until you're virtually on top of it. It is marked by a large cairn covered in prayer flags and yak horns.

The route continues over the Shug-la and descends sharply through a boulder field, losing 200m of elevation. Be on the lookout for a clear trail marked by cairns on the left side of the boulder field. This trail traverses the ridge in a south-easterly direction paralleling the valley below. Do not head directly down to the valley from the pass unless you have good reason. It is a long steep descent and once at the bottom you would have to go back up the valley to complete the trek. Retreat down the valley for a bolt hole back to the Lhasa-Ganden Hwy, a long day of walking away.

The trail gradually descends to reach the valley floor, 1½ hours from the pass. Cross the large stream, the Tsotup-chu, which flows through the valley. During heavy summer rains take special care to find a safe ford. The pastures in the area support large herds of yaks, goats and sheep, and during the trekking season herders are often camped here. This is an ideal place to *camp* and meet the *drokpas* (nomads). It is a two- to 2½-hour walk from the stream ford to the second pass, the Chitu-la, and at least 1¼ more hours to the first camping place.

An alternative route to Samye via the Gampa-la (5050m) follows the main branch of the Tsotup-chu past a couple of lakes to the pass. South of the Gampa-la the trail plunges into a gorge crisscrossing the stream that flows down from it. These fords may pose problems during summer rains or when completely frozen. See Gary McCue's *Trekking in Tibet – A Traveler's Guide* for details of this route.

Stage 3: Tsotup-chu Valley to Herders' Camps
5 hours • 14km • 300m ascent • 400m descent

From the Tsotup-chu ford, the main water course flows from the south-east and a minor tributary enters from the south-west. Follow this tributary, which quickly disappears underground, steeply upwards for 30 minutes until you reach a large basin. Stay on the west (right) side of the basin and turn into the first side valley opening on the right. Follow this broad valley which soon arcs south to the Chitu-la. The pass can be seen in the distance, a rocky rampart at the head of the valley. At first, stay on the west (right) side of the valley; there is a small trail. As you approach the pass the trail switches to the east side of the valley. If you miss the trail just look for the easiest route up. The terrain is not particularly difficult.

The Chitu-la (5100m) is topped by several cairns. Also on the summit is a small glacial cairn. Move to the west side of the pass to find the trail down and to circum-

vent a sheer rock wall on its south flank. A short but steep descent will bring you into a basin with three small lakes. The trail skirts the west side of the lakes. It takes 45 minutes to reach the south end of the basin. Drop down from the basin on the west side of the stream and in 30 minutes you will hit the first place to set up *camp*. Herders have carved out level places for their tents here.

Below the herders' highest camp the valley is squeezed in by vertical rock walls, forcing you to pick your way through the rock-strewn valley floor. There is no trail in this gorge and the descent is very steep. In about 20 minutes cross over to the west (right) side of the widening valley to recover the trail. In 10 more minutes you will come to a flat and a seasonal herders' camp on the east side of the valley, good for *camping*. At the lower end of the flat return to the west side of the valley. The trail again disappears as it enters a scrub willow and rosebush forest but there is only one way to go to get to Samye and that is downstream.

In 15 minutes, when a tributary valley enters from the right, cross to the east side of the valley. Fifteen minutes further, you will reach another seasonal herders' camp inhabited for only a short time each year. Another 15 minutes beyond this camp hop back to the west bank to avoid a cliff hugging the opposite side of the stream. Pass through a large meadow and ford the stream back to the east bank. From this point the trail remains on the east side of the valley for several hours.

Camping places, some of which are adequate for large groups, are numerous. Soon the trail crosses the stream draining the valley coming from the Gampa-la. During times of heavy summer rain you might not be able to ford this stream. If so, you will have no alternative but to wait for the water to subside.

Stages 4 & 5: Herders' Camps to Samye Monastery
10 hours • 39km • 1200m descent

The trail is now wide and easy to follow as it traces a course down the east side of the valley. Walk through the thickening scrub forest for one hour and you will come to another stream entering from the east side of the main valley. Look for a small wood-and-stone bridge 200m above the confluence. The valley now bends to the right and the trail enters the thickest and tallest part of the scrub forest. The right combination of elevation, moisture and aspect create a verdant environment, while just a few kilometres away desert conditions prevail.

The next three-hour stretch of the trail is among the most delightful of the entire trek. According to local woodcutters more than 15 types of trees and shrubs are found here, some growing 6m tall. Fragrant junipers grow on exposed southern slopes while rhododendrons prefer the shadier slopes. The rhododendrons begin blooming in early May and by the end of the month the forest is ablaze with pink and white blossoms.

The trail winds through a series of meadows. In one hour look for a ruined stone structure at a place known as Gen Do. Nearby is a shrine to the protector of the area, the ancient goddess Dorje Yudronma. Just past the shrine cross a small tributary stream. In one hour the forest rapidly thins and Changtang, the first permanent village since Hepu, pops up. Named after the northern plains of Tibet, its inhabitants are predominantly engaged in animal husbandry just like their northern counterparts. Although the villagers are friendly enough the village is infested with fierce dogs, which fortunately are usually tied up.

Look south to the distant mountains; this is the range on the far side of the Yarlung Tsangpo valley. Forty-five minutes down the valley is the turn-off for the Yamalung Hermitage. Look for a field of small cairns to the right of the trail pointing towards a bridge over the valley stream. It is nearly a one-hour steep climb to the hermitage. Group members not interested in making the climb can wait near the bridge with the group's gear. Yamalung (also called Emalung) is where Guru Rinpoche is said to have meditated and received empowerment from the long-life deity Tsepame (Amitayus).

The hermitage consists of several small temples, and a few meditators live here.

Below the temple complex is a sacred spring and an old relief carving in stone of Guru Rinpoche, King Trisong Detsen and the Indian scholar Shantarakshita, all of whom lived in the 8th century. The cave Guru Rinpoche meditated in is enshrined by the Drup Pug Mara Titsang Temple. Inside are the footprint and handprint of the saint said to have been created when he magically expanded the size of the cave.

From the turn-off to Yamalung the trail becomes a motorable track and the valley much wider. In 15 minutes you will reach a bridge; the trail now remains on the west (right) side of the valley all the way to Samye, a 3½-hour walk away. Twenty minutes from the bridge you will come to the village of Nyango with its substantially built stone houses. A big tributary stream, entering from the north-west, joins the Samye valley here. The old trade route from Lhasa to Samye via the Gokar-la follows this valley. In the lower half of Nyango are four small shops selling soda, cigarettes and, maybe, basic food supplies such as instant noodles. If you are looking for a place to doss down ask the shopkeepers; they might oblige you.

Half an hour past Nyango is the village of Wango and an hour beyond it, the hamlet of Pisha. En route there are several meadows in which you can set up *camp*.

From the lower end of Pisha, a hill can be seen in the middle of the mouth of the Samye valley. This is Hepo Ri, one of Tibet's most sacred mountains (see Samye Monastery in the Ü chapter). The entire lower Samye valley can be seen from Pisha: a tapestry of fields, woods and villages. Pisha is the last place that water can be conveniently drawn from the river. From here on in the trail only intersects irrigation ditches.

Fifteen minutes past Pisha a ridge spur called Dragmar meets the trail. On the summit is the partially rebuilt palace where King Trisong Detsen is said to have been born. Formerly a lavish temple it now stands empty. Below, just off the road, is a small red-and-white temple enshrining the stump of an ancient tree. Legend has it that a red-and-white sandalwood tree grew here, nourished by the buried placenta of Trisong Detsen. During the Cultural Revolution the tree was chopped down.

Twenty minutes further down the trail is Sangbu village, from where there are good views of the golden spires of Samye. The route follows the jeep track direct to Samye along the margin of woods and desert: It takes about one hour. Use the shiny temple roof as your beacon. The closer you get to Samye the hotter the valley can become; in May and June it can even be fiery hot. If the heat gets too much, flee to the stands of willows and poplars not far from the road. The gilt roofs get ever brighter as you approach the monastery. You will reach Samye 10 minutes after passing inside the monastery's perimeter wall.

If you can't catch a lift you are in for about a two-hour walk from Samye to the ferry crossing. One day's walk down the Yarlung Tsangpo valley at Tsetang, or six hours upstream from Samye, are alternative ferry crossings using traditional Tibetan leather coracles. If you don't have a travel permit for Samye, authorities can be eluded at these other crossings but the route is through extremely harsh sand-dune country. It is probably better to give them a miss unless your party is prepared for full-blown desert conditions.

TSURPHU TO YANGPACHEN

The Trek at a Glance

Duration 3 to 4 days
Distance 55km
Standard Medium to difficult
Start Tsurphu Monastery
Finish Yangpachen Monastery
Highest Point Lasar-la (5300m)
Nearest Large Town Lhasa
Accommodation Camping
Public Transport Pilgrim buses
Summary The Tsurphu to Yangpachen trek is an excellent choice for those who want to get a close look at the lifestyle of the *drokpas* (nomads). Although they have permanent winter homes they spend much of the year camping with their animals.

Beginning at Tsurphu Monastery, this rugged walk crosses several alpine valleys before emerging into the broad and windswept Yangpachen valley. This is a high-elevation trek exceeding 4400m for the duration. Combining alpine tundra and sweeping mountain panoramas with visits to monasteries and a nunnery, this trek nicely balances cultural and wilderness activities.

The best time for this walk is from mid-April to mid-October. Summer months can be rainy but be prepared for snow at any time. Plan on at least three days for this walk. As you will be in nomad country, beware of vicious dogs, some of which take a sadistic pride in chasing hapless foreigners. Fuel and food are not available so come prepared. There are few permanent settlements along the way and the inhabitants are often away from home, so don't count on these places to provide accommodation. Your only option on this trek is to be fully self-sufficient.

Minibuses leave the Barkhor in Lhasa daily between 7am and 8am for Tsurphu (Y15, 2½ hours). Minibuses to Yangpachen (Y25, three hours) depart from the office of the Civil Aviation Authority of China (CAAC) in Lhasa. Lhasa-Nagchu minibuses also pass through Yangpachen.

Tsurphu Monastery (4500m) is a good place to spend a couple of nights acclimatising. Two kilometres downstream from Tsurphu, beside the Karmapa's summer palace, is a small copse that is ideal for *camping*. Some of the area's herders spend a lot of time at the monastery so this is a good place to start looking for guides and yaks. However, Tsurphu is often crawling with police; if it is, you'd better head up valley before letting your plans be known.

Stage 1: Tsurphu Monastery to Leten

3½–4 hours • 11km • 500m ascent

The trek begins at Tsurphu, heading west or up the valley. Follow the kora trail 20 minutes west to a walled copse of old trees with a brook. This garden-like wood is used by the monks in the summer so ask permission before you set up camp. The trees here are the last you will see until after finishing the trek. Just above the copse, the valley splits: Follow the north-west branch and remain on the north side of the stream.

Forty-five minutes of walking through a rocky chasm on a well-graded trail brings you to Shupshading, a herders' camp on a shelf above the trail. If you are looking for yaks to carry your equipment try asking the herders here. The valley remains narrow above Shupshading and is often engulfed with ice left over from the winter. After 30 minutes cross a seasonal stream coming from the north-west (right). Soon the trail switches over to the south (left) side of the valley. Forty-five minutes onwards the trail forks. The left branch switchbacks up the ridge south of the valley and then traverses west into the drokpa settlement of Leten (5000m). Although you want to go here take the right fork that follows the valley floor – this is a more straightforward route to Leten, about 1½ hours away.

Leten is divided by the stream running through it. Several families live here permanently, braving the severe climate with their livestock. Leten is the last chance to find yaks and a guide, both of which are

highly recommended because the route to and from the Lasar-la is not easy to find.

Spend one or preferably two days in Leten acclimatising.

Stage 2: Leten to Bartso
5–6 hours • 15km • 300m ascent • 600m descent

It is about a three-hour walk from Leten to the Lasar-la. Head for the northern half of the settlement (assuming you aren't already there). The route climbs steeply up the north side of the Leten valley, reaching the highest house. Bear north-west into a steep side valley. As you ascend, a reddish knob of rock looms up ahead. Angle to the north, or right, of this formation and leave the valley by climbing to the top of a spur marked by three cairns. It is a 45-minute walk to here from Leten. This spur, called Damchen Nyingtri, is holy to the god ruling the environs.

As per Buddhist tradition, stay to the left of the cairns crowning Damchen Nyingtri and descend sharply into a narrow valley. Once on the valley bottom, cross to the east (right) side of the stream and strike out north (up the valley). In 15 minutes the valley forks: Follow the north (right) branch. Cross back to the left side of the stream as the terrain here is easier to traipse over. Walk up the widening valley through arctic-like mounds of tundra for one hour, following a minor trail. Then, as the valley turns west, look for a cairn on the opposite bank of the stream.

Using this cairn as a marker bear north-west over an inclined plain. This plain parallels the valley floor before the two merge. Continue ascending as the plain opens wider in the direction of the pass. There is no clear trail but favour the west side of the plain; the east side spills down into another valley system. The Lasar-la (5300m) is a broad gap at the highest point in the plain and is heralded by cairns lining the final approach.

From the Lasar-la there is a steep descent into a north-running valley. A trail can be found on the east (right) side of this valley. In a few minutes the grade levels out and the trail crosses the stream bed and continues down the west side of the valley. There

TSURPHU TO YANGPACHEN

To Damshung (50km)

Nyenchen Tangiha Range

Qinghai-Tibet Hwy

Ridge Lines

Yangpachen

Yangpachen Valley

Tolung-chu

Yangpachen Monastery
FINISH

0   7.5   15km
0   4.5   9mi
Approximate Scale

To Shigatse

Ngangkar

Brize

Dechen

Nyango-chu

Dorje Ling Nunnery

Mang

Tajung

Bartso

Lasar-la (5300m)

Damchen Nyingtri

START

To Lhasa (35km)

Leten
Shupshading   Tsurphu
Monastery

Karmapa Lingka

are many possible *camp sites* between the Lasar-la and Bartso.

As the trail descends you peer into the expansive Yangpachen valley, a broad plain laced with streams that opens up in front of the Nyenchen Tanglha (Tangula) range to the north. This range is part of the trans-Himalaya, which circumscribes the plateau, dividing southern Tibet from the Changtang.

The valley is covered in hummocks but there is a trail that avoids the ups and downs of these mounds of turf and earth. About one hour from the pass a break in the ridge running along the east side of the valley comes into view. The break coincides with a big west bend in the valley. As soon as you spot this interruption in the ridge line, ford the stream and traverse up to the right into a side valley. Heading north, the valley soon gives way to a plain paved with big plates of tundra.

There are superb views of the surrounding mountains along this stretch of the walk. In the north is Brize, a heavily glaciated peak enclosing the south side of the Yangpachen valley, and to the west is a distinctive pinnacle called Tarze. Brize, meaning 'female-yak herder', and Tarze, 'horse keeper', are two of many topographical features in a mythical society ruled by the mountain god Nyenchen Tanglha. These two mountains make convenient landmarks as you go against the grain by heading north over a series of drainage systems that run from east to west.

In one hour the trail intersects an east-west valley at the settlement of Bartso. This drokpa village of five homes with its permanent sources of water is a good place to *camp*. The slopes around the village are still covered in juniper. In the 1960s and '70s huge amounts of this valuable bush were extracted from the region and trucked to Lhasa to feed the hearths of the new provincial city.

Stage 3: Bartso to Dorje Ling Nunnery
3½–4 hours • 15km • 150m ascent • 150m descent

Look north-west from Bartso to the opposite side of the valley. Clearly visible, a wide trail winds up from the valley to the top of the ridge. Ford the valley stream and make for this trail, a 25-minute walk over marshy ground from Bartso. It takes another 30 minutes to reach the summit of the ridge. From the top you will see a saddle north of an intervening valley. On the far side of this saddle is the Dorje Ling Nunnery, still more than 2½ hours away.

Views of Nyenchen Tanglha, the 7111m mountain that gives its name to the range, are fantastic from here. This huge massif has a distinctive flat summit. Nyenchen Tanglha is the holiest mountain in central Tibet and is said to be inhabited by a god of the same name. Envisioned as a regal white warrior on a white horse, the god's half-smile, half grimace symbolises the benevolent and destructive sides of his personality.

From the saddle, drop down to the valley in 25 minutes to the village of Tajung. Stay to the left of the 14 whitewashed houses and ford the stream below it. Bear north-east into the parting in the ridge and after a few minutes cross a low saddle. Continue going north-east in the direction of Brize until a large dip appears in the hills to the west 40 minutes from Tajung. Leave the trail going towards Brize and head to the right of the dip cross-country. Traverse to the right of the low point in the ridge, remaining high enough to avoid the highest part of the east-west ridge looming up ahead. If you have gained enough height, you will see a group of white houses at the base of a hill to the north-west. The Dorje Ling Nunnery is just downstream of here.

A 25-minute traverse will bring you to a stream at the base of the ridge aligned east to west. A broad trail appears on the north bank of the stream. Follow it to the top of the ridge. From this point you'll have good views of the village just upstream of Dorje Ling Nunnery. The nunnery, which is out of view, sits at the bottom of a rock outcrop visible from the ridge top.

During the winter you can strike out across a swamp that fills the valley to go directly to Dorje Ling, reaching it in just 30 minutes. Otherwise you will have to take the long way around and skirt the north edge of the swamp to reach the north side of the Dorje Ling valley. This longer route requires at least one hour of hiking. There is a motorable road on the far side of the valley and the nunnery is only 10 minutes down from here.

The centrepiece of this friendly nunnery is a red *lhakhang* (chapel) in the midst of a group of little white houses. The lhakhang is simply decorated, reflecting the modest means of the 52 nuns who call this place home. A concerted effort is under way to build a house for all of them. The nuns are happy to show visitors around and donations are welcome. Without them reconstruction and maintenance of the nunnery is not possible. Good *camping* is found in the meadows around Dorje Ling.

Stage 4: Dorje Ling Nunnery to Yangpachen Monastery
3½–4½ hours • 14km • mostly level

From Dorje Ling follow the motorable road west, or downstream. In 15 minutes the road crosses to the south bank of the valley watercourse and soon forks. Take the right fork over the small concrete bridge and continue down the east bank of the stream along the track. Forty-five minutes from Dorje Ling the valley drains into the spacious Yangpachen valley. Stay on the same track, which turns into a motorable road as it runs north paralleling the course of the Nyango-chu, which drains the upper Yangpachen valley. The road stays close to the east bank of the river, skirting meadows that afford fantastic *camping* and encompassing views of the trans-Himalaya.

Once entering the Nyango drainage area it is an easy two hours' walk to a steel bridge spanning the river. Cross the bridge to join the northern road to Shigatse. Walk north on the road for 15 minutes, suddenly coming to Yangpachen Monastery, at the end of a line of cliffs. Perched on top of a small hill on the left side of the road, the monastery overlooks a broad sweep of trans-Himalaya peaks. There are several trails leading from the road to the monastery, but beware of the pack of dogs loitering around the grounds. The monastery was

home to 115 monks, but many of them have fled to Rumtek Monastery in Sikkim. Yangpachen is headed by Shamar Rinpoche, a leading lama of the Kagyupa order, who is based in India. If you're interested in seeing what Nyenchen Tanglha looks like check out the mural in the inner vestibule of the main assembly hall. It depicts the god in several of his wrathful animal manifestations. Donations are expected should you want to visit the chapels.

From Yangpachen Monastery it is a 15km road journey to Yangpachen. If your luck holds you should be able to hitch there. The hot-springs complex (admission Y20) on the western outskirts of Yangpachen is great to ease your aching limbs. From here there are many minibuses back to Lhasa (three hours).

SHALU TO NARTANG

The Trek at a Glance

Duration 2 to 3 days
Distance 40km
Standard Medium
Start Shalu
Finish Nartang
Highest Point Char-la (4600m)
Nearest Large Town Shigatse
Accommodation Camping
Public Transport Yes
Summary This two- or three-day walk is a good opportunity to get a feel for trekking in Tibet. The two passes en route, Showa-la and Char-la, are not particularly high or difficult and the trailheads are easily accessible from Shigatse.

This trek begins at the historic Shalu Monastery (see the Tsang chapter for more information) and traverses west over a couple of small ranges to Ngor Monastery. From Ngor it is a downhill slog to Nartang Monastery. The route passes through several villages as well as uninhabited dry canyons. It is about a 10-hour walk to Ngor from Shalu, which is best divided into two days, and another seven hours from there to Nartang. Finding guides and burros (yaks are not an option) to carry your gear is not easy but you can try in Shalu. If you can get local support go for it, because the route is not always easy to discern – in the canyons the trail tends to peter out.

The optimal walking season is from the beginning of April to the end of October. In the summer months (June, July and August) the trail can be sizzling hot, and in other months cold and windy, so be prepared! One advantage of hiking in the summer months is that this region gets less rainfall than the Ü region.

For information on getting to Shalu, see Shalu Monastery in the Tsang chapter. Lhatse-Shigatse minibuses travel the Friendship Hwy and pass near Nartang.

Stage 1: Shalu Monastery to Upper Lungsang

5½–6 hours • 14km • 250m ascent • 200m descent

From Shalu Monastery walk the motorable road south (up the valley). It is about three hours to the first pass, Showa-la. Thirty minutes from Shalu you will pass by the Ripuk Hermitage set on a hillside on the west side of the valley. If you wish to visit, cut across the fields and head directly up to the hermitage – the way is not difficult and there are several trails leading up to it.

Forty-five minutes from Shalu the road forks: Take the south (right) fork. In the south, a conical-shaped hill and a village at its base can be made out. If you struck out in Shalu, stay on the road to this village, called Phunup, about one hour's walk away, to look for a guide and pack animals. Otherwise, there is a short cut that saves 2km of walking. A few minutes from the fork in the road look for the base of a long red ridge. Leave the road and skirt the base of this ridge, going in a southerly direction. First cross a flood plain to reach a rectangular red shrine, and beyond it enter a plain bounded in the south by the red ridge.

Gradually the trail climbs to a small white ridge blocking the route to the south. As you approach you will see white cairns marking its summit. Look for the trail that ascends to the cairns, a one-hour walk from

the fork in the road. From the ridge's summit, Phunup village is to the left and the Showa-la is to the west. The pass is the obvious low point in the range at least one hour away. The trail descends gradually to enter the stream bed coming from the Showa-la 30 minutes from the cairns. If you came via Phunup, your route will converge with the main trail here.

The climb to the pass and the descent on the other side are through heavily eroded, waterless ravines and slopes, or badlands. Bring plenty of drinking water. From the stream bed the trail soon climbs back up the right side of the valley only to drop back in and out of the stream bed in quick succession. Don't make the mistake of walking up the stream bed for you would soon encounter ledges and other difficult terrain. After twice briefly dropping into the narrow stream bed be alert for a trail carving a route up the right slope. The trail climbs steeply to a group of ruins and then winds around to the pass in 30 minutes.

From the Showa-la (4200m), the second pass, Char-la, can be seen in the range of hills west of an intervening valley. It is the dip in the crest of the range. The easy-to-follow trail descends from the pass along the south (left) side of a ravine. In one hour you will reach the valley floor. Leave the trail when it crosses a small rise marked with cairns and continue west towards a distant group of trees. Cross over the sandy north-south running valley intersecting a road. Shigatse is about three hours north from here along this road.

The valley watercourse is dry except during summer flash floods. West of it is a poplar and willow copse, the only bit of shade in the area. Consider stopping here for lunch and a rest. From the copse you enter a side valley continuing in a westerly direction towards the Char-la. In a few minutes you will reach the village of Manitinga, on the southern margin of the valley, and pick up the main cart track going up the valley. The track passes through the village of Lower Lungsang and, one hour from the copse, crosses to the south side of the valley. You can glimpse the Char-la from here,

TREKKING

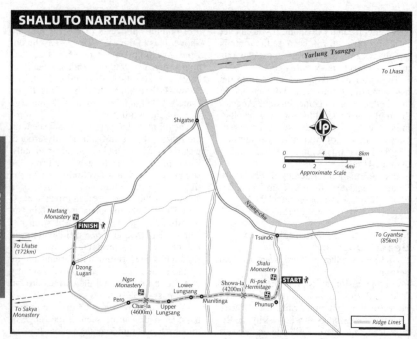

SHALU TO NARTANG

Yarlung Tsangpo

To Lhasa

Shigatse

0   4   8km
0   2   4mi
Approximate Scale

Nartang
Monastery
FINISH

To Lhatse
(172km)

Nyang-chu

Tsunde

To Gyantse
(85km)

Dzong
Lugari

Shalu
Monastery

Ngor
Monastery

Lower
Lungsang

Showa-la
(4200m)

Ri-puk
Hermitage   **START**

To Sakya
Monastery

Pero

Char-la
(4600m)

Upper
Lungsang

Manitinga

Phunup

Ridge Lines

which for most of the trek is hidden behind
the folds in the mountains.

In 30 minutes you will reach Upper
Lungsang. There is a fine old wood here
ideal for *camping* and resting.

Stage 2: Upper Lungsang to Ngor Monastery

3½–4 hours • 8km • 550m ascent

From Upper Lungsang cross back to the
north side of the valley. The cart track does
not extend past the village and the trail up to
the pass may be difficult to find in places. If
you are in doubt try to hire a local person to
show you the way. It is at least 2½ hours
from Upper Lungsang to the Char-la. At
first, the trail skirts the edge of a gravel
wash. However, in 15 minutes a series of
livestock tracks climb out of the stream bed
and onto an eroded shelf that forms above it.

The terrain becomes more rugged and a
gorge forms below the trail. There is a side
stream and small reservoir 45 minutes

above Upper Lungsang. This is the last convenient place to collect water until over the
pass. From the reservoir the trail descends
back to the stream bed but quickly exits the
opposite side of the valley.

Look for a series of switchbacks on the
south (left) side of the gorge and follow
them upwards. Fifteen minutes onwards the
trail crosses a gully, and then another gully
in 15 more minutes. The final leg to the pass
is cross-country over a steep slope of raw
expanses of rock. From the second gully
the Char-la can be reached in 45 minutes of
steep uphill walking. At one time this trail
was well maintained and formed a main
trade link between Shalu and Sakya Monasteries, but it has fallen into disrepair.

Eventually, cairns on the summit ridge
come into focus. The pass is the obvious
notch in the ridge line. From the Char-la
(4600m), mountain ranges stretch west
across the horizon and Ngor Monastery is
visible below. Ngor is a 45-minute downhill

ramble from the pass. The route from the Char-la descends the south (left) side of a ravine that forms below it. Several trails cross the stream that flows from the pass and provide access to Ngor, but the first trail is the quickest route – it climbs the right side of the ravine and traverses directly to the monastery. Consider camping near Ngor (ask the monastery for permission and the best place to camp) and saving the last five hours of walking for the next day, when you're rested.

The Sakya master Ngorchen Kunga Sangpo founded Ngor Monastery in 1429, giving rise to the Ngorpa suborder, a distinctive school of Buddhist thought. Once an important centre of learning, Ngor used to boast four monastic estates and 18 residential units inhabited by about 340 monks. Only a small fraction of the monastery has been rebuilt. The most eye-catching feature is a beautiful row of *chörtens* (stupas) at the lower end of the complex dedicated to the eight victorious forms of the Buddha. The largest structure is the assembly hall called the Gonshung; the outer walls of its gallery are painted in vertical red, white and blue stripes, a characteristic decorative technique used by the Sakya order. The three colours represent the Rigsum Gonpo, the three most important bodhisattvas. The present head of Ngor, Luding Khenpo, resides in northern India.

Stage 3: Ngor Monastery to Nartang Monastery
5 hours • 18km • 300m descent
From Ngor a motorable road runs down the valley. Fifteen minutes from the monastery is the sizable village of Pero. Ninety minutes from Ngor the valley and road bend to the north while the old trade route to Sakya continues west over a saddle. Thirty minutes further there is a copse at the edge of the flood plain that is good for fair-weather *camping*.

The road now swings to the west side of the wide alluvial valley and 30 minutes past the copse is the village of Dzong Lugari. The road exits the north side of the village and extends north-east for 10km before joining the Lhatse-Shigatse Hwy 10km

south-west of Shigatse. The trail to Nartang Monastery, however, splits from the road on the northern outskirts of Dzong Lugari and heads north. From Dzong Lugari it is at least a two-hour hike across a broad valley to Nartang.

The trail to Nartang crosses a small stream and an electric utility line. The track tends to merge with a welter of agricultural trails and if you miss it simply continue walking north. Soon the massive ramparts that surrounded the Nartang Monastery come into view. Just before arriving, cross the Lhatse-Shigatse Hwy 14km west of Shigatse. Donations are expected if you want to visit the chapels and famous printing presses at the monastery. For your physical needs you will find several shops selling soft drinks and noodle soup on the roadside. It should be pretty easy to catch a ride from here to Shigatse.

FRIENDSHIP HIGHWAY TO EVEREST BASE CAMP

The Trek at a Glance

Duration 3 to 4 days
Distance 70km
Standard Medium to difficult
Start Friendship Hwy, kilometre marker 5145
Finish Rongphu Monastery or Tingri
Highest Point Geu-la (5170m) or Pang-la (5200m)
Nearest Large Town Shigatse
Accommodation Camping and small lodges
Public Transport No
Summary With the attraction of the highest mountain in the world, the trek to the Everest Base Camp has become one of the most popular in Tibet – although in recent years increasing numbers of people are driving there instead of walking. Featuring spectacular views of the Himalaya from stark desert valleys, this is an unforgettable adventure for those who are not afraid to use their own two feet.

This trek and the trek from Everest Base Camp to Tingri (detailed later in this chapter) can be walked in the direction opposite the one described. One tiny advantage of doing it in the opposite direction is that you may not have to pay the fee of Y65 for entry to the Qomolangma Nature Preserve. It is also possible to hitch or hire a Land Cruiser into Everest Base Camp and then trek out to Tingri. If you get tired of trekking in along the road you can always try to get a lift part of the way. Land Cruisers ply the route in summer and there are also plenty of pony carts if you want a brief respite from carrying your bag.

The trekking season in the Everest region extends from April to late October. This is a difficult high-elevation walk beginning at 4400m and attaining altitudes of nearly 5300m, so careful preparation and the right gear are imperative. Subfreezing temperatures occur even in the summer at higher elevations and, conversely, hot gusty winds in May and June can make walking a sweaty experience. For very well-equipped and seasoned walkers, winter treks to Everest Base Camp are often possible. Thanks to the rain shadow created by Mt Everest (Qomolangma) and its lofty neighbours, even the monsoon months are relatively dry in the region.

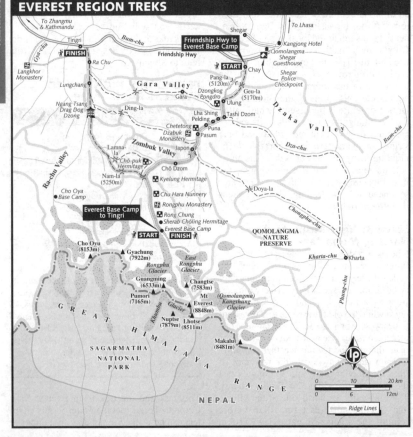

EVEREST REGION TREKS

It is a very good idea to travel with a tent and stove despite there being a couple of restaurants and lodges on the route. These facilities are few and far between and the service rudimentary. The only way to ensure privacy and comfort and to have the potential to trek out from Everest Base Camp via an alternative route is to have your home and hearth in your pack.

The trek begins at kilometre marker 5145 on the highway to Nepal, 6km west of the Shegar police checkpoint and 12km west of the nearest accommodation at the Shegar turn-off. The route to Everest Base Camp leaves the highway and goes south to the village of Chay and then over the Geu-la into the Dzaka valley. Mt Everest is at the head of the monastery-filled Dzaka valley.

If you are coming directly from Nepal be ready to spend as much as one week at 4400m before attempting the trek. One possibility is to walk 2km north of the highway and camp in the meadows on the banks of the Bum-chu for a couple of days. A fine spot directly north of the turn-off to Chay has chörtens and a ruined stone bridge, the only traces left of a village abandoned long ago.

There is no public transport in the region but it shouldn't be too difficult to get a lift along the Friendship Hwy to either the turn-off to Everest (kilometre marker 5145) or Tingri. Hired Land Cruisers can go all the way to Everest Base Camp.

For more information on the Everest region, including Everest Base Camp, see Everest Region in the Tsang chapter.

Stage 1: Kilometre Marker 5145 to beyond the Geu-la

4½–5 hours • 15km • 650m ascent • 300m descent

Six kilometres west of the Shegar police checkpoint, a small, unmarked road heads south to the village of Chay. After one hour it reaches the Qomolangma Nature Preserve checkpoint on the outskirts of Chay. Individuals must pay Y65 (Y105 for 15 days) to enter the preserve and are given a pass that has a set of regulations printed in English and Chinese. Visitors are appropriately instructed to behave modestly, not purchase

cultural relics, leave plants and animals alone and not to litter. The money raised supposedly goes to management of the preserve.

There are no restaurants or lodges in Chay but it's pretty easy to find a local family willing to put you up for the night. Burros can be hired to carry your gear to the top of the Geu-la for around Y50 each. You might also find someone willing to haul your stuff all the way to Tashi Dzom in the Dzaka valley, a long day's walk, but expect to pay as much as Y100. Watch out for hidden charges – negotiate exactly what you will pay before setting out.

From Chay there are two passes that cross the range south of the village and drop into the Dzaka valley. The pass furthest west is the Pang-la and is the way the road goes. The shortest and nicest walk is via the eastern pass, the Geu-la. The two routes meet a couple of hours south of the crest.

Follow the road out of Chay for 10 minutes and turn right onto a wide trail. This trail climbs directly up the valley, avoiding the switchbacks in the road. The trail soon fades out across rocky ground but keep heading south towards the switchbacks etched in the side of the ridge. The route crosses the road twice and remains on the west (right) side of the valley. Climb steadily, paralleling the road that is visible traversing the ridge to the right. The route keeps to the valley floor, intersecting an older disused road several times. One hour from Chay you'll reach a small, seasonal herders' camp and the valley's small watercourse; this is the last reliable source of water until well over the other side of the pass.

From the camp angle over to the left side of the valley towards the series of switchbacks cut into the slope. Twenty minutes from the herders' camp is the base of the Geu-la. Look for the trail in a gully below the switchbacks and follow it up. The trail climbs steeply crossing over the road twice. If you want to walk via the Pang-la, pursue the road west (right). The route to the Geu-la ascends directly above the road, reaching the crest of the ridge 1½ hours from the herders' camp. It is 30 minutes from here to the pass. Once on top, follow the crest

Détente

Since the 1980s persistent accounts of unfriendly villagers, petty theft and stone throwing have come out of the Everest region. Such incidents have soured relations between the local Tibetans and foreigners, and have led to a drop in the numbers of trekkers coming to this area. While there are no excuses for bad behaviour there are historical factors contributing to these antisocial episodes.

Under the Chinese, the entire religious and civic infrastructure of the region was destroyed and never satisfactorily restored, creating many hardships in a high, dry and poor area. In the early 1980s travellers and climbers started appearing in ever greater numbers, and the majority of them spent little or no money locally. This marginalisation of the locals created ill will that continues to this day. While the locals are not anti-foreigner, they are clamouring for a piece of the action. It can only be hoped that Qomolangma Nature Preserve, with its grand promises of bettering lives, will give the people of the area a piece of the economic pie, but as of yet there is little sign of this.

With some goodwill and understanding on your part you should be able to pull off a trip without any grief from the locals. A realisation is dawning among Tibetans that working with tourists rather than repelling them is the best long-term strategy. Encourage this new attitude by patronising local services and businesses as much as possible.

John Vincent Bellezza

south-west and look for a well-defined trail marked with cairns that leaves the ridge line to traverse the south side of the slope over to the pass.

The Geu-la (5170m) is festooned with prayer flags and cairns and presides over a dramatic view of the Himalaya. Before you is a 150km cross section of the Himalaya. To the south is Makalu and the unmistakable black pyramidal form of Everest, and in the south-west is Cho Oyu, the big snowy massif, with Shisha Pangma in the far west. Barren brown and purple mountains in the foreground flank the Dzaka valley. In the neighbourhood of the Geu-la, blue and white gentians bloom in late May, and a little further down, purple irises enliven the windswept meadows.

From the pass you can reach the Dzaka valley in 4½ hours. At first the descent is steep but in 30 minutes you reach a high valley floor along a well-trodden path. There is a stream and grassy *camp sites* here.

Stage 2: Base of the Geu-la to Upper Dzaka Valley

5½–6 hours • 20km • 100m ascent • 300m descent

Skip over the stream to the right side of the valley and continue downhill. The valley

soon turns to the west (right) and in 50 minutes crosses back to the left bank of the stream. A five-minute walk from the ford delivers you back to the road coming from the Pang-la. The road is now your constant companion all the way to Everest Base Camp.

Head downhill and in a few minutes you will see the first of three short-cut trails at the top end of a slew of switchbacks. At the bottom of the switchbacks the valley squeezes through a gorge before opening back up to reveal the first village, 1½ hours from the pass. Just before the village the road crosses over to the right side of the valley. Except during heavy summer rains, the stream draining the valley is but a trickle. Thirty minutes further on another valley joins the road from the right. Near the confluence at the hamlet of Ulung, the road crosses to the right of the joined valleys.

In 20 minutes you will reach extensive ruins stretching 2km down the valley. Called Dzongkog Pongdro, this is all that is left of an ancient fortified settlement. Below the ruins the road jumps over to the left side of the valley. In 30 minutes the big Gara valley enters from the west. Forty more minutes of walking and the road joins the Dzaka valley at the town of Tashi Dzom (the name means 'auspicious meeting place' or 'plentiful good luck'), the headquarters of the local township or region. If you go left at the road junction or down the valley you will eventually reach Arun, Kharta and the east face of Everest. See Gary McCue's *Trekking in Tibet – A Traveler's Guide* for details of further treks in this region.

At the junction of the road from the pass and the Dzaka valley road is a small **shop** and **inn** that sells drinks including beer and tea, as well as biscuits and rice and noodle dishes. Beds in common rooms go for Y25 each. The bedding is reasonably clean and the proprietors seem helpful and willing to please, but there's little privacy as the two large rooms have no doors. There's also a hideously noisy video hall across the road – bring earplugs. There is little in the way of hospitality or foreign-language skills taught locally, so expect nothing but the basics.

If you are looking for yaks or burros to save your back, start at Tashi Dzom and work your way up the valley. Chances are you will receive offers, but weigh your choices very carefully. Some locals might try to take advantage of you and quote exorbitant prices. Stick to your guns but expect to pay around Y50 per person per day. If you don't find animals and can't carry your pack, consider hitching rather than suffering.

The road to Everest goes up the valley from Tashi Dzom, a long two-day walk away. Engulfed by the enormity of the valley, the road passes through barley, pea and mustard fields spreading out in all directions. Twenty minutes out of Tashi Dzom the road splits; take the left or main branch. The right branch serves the nearby villages of Lha Shing and Rephel. Lha Shing was named after sacred ancient trees that grew on the slopes above the village, the last of which died 30 or 40 years ago. Rephel hosts the small Rabshi Monastery.

The trail reaches the hamlet of Pelding, 30 minutes beyond Rephel, and in another 45 minutes, Puna. Fifteen minutes past Puna, a rocky spur juts into the valley; this is the site of Chetetong, the ruined pre-Communist centre of power in the region.

Traditionally, the Dzaka valley upstream of Tashi Dzom was known as Phadrug and was affiliated with the fortress at Shegar.

Forty-five minutes up the valley the road cuts through Pasum, the administrative centre for the upper Dzaka valley.

Pasum Pembah Teahouse-Hotel has beds for Y25 to Y35. In the middle of the village, this well-run shop, restaurant and hotel approaches the quality of service found in the smaller trekking lodges of Nepal. The restaurant serves eggs, *momos* (dumplings), vegetables, mutton, rice and noodles for Y10 to Y20. The man who runs the place knows some English.

Stage 3: Upper Dzaka Valley to Chö Dzom

3–3½ hours • 15km • 200m ascent • 250m descent

In the hill behind Pasum is the tiny monastery of Dzabuk, where a few monks reside. Twenty minutes further along, the valley completes a big bend to the south. On the road, a small concrete bridge spans a stream that comes from a valley in the west. This valley leads towards Tingri via the Ding-la, two days' walking away.

In 45 minutes the road passes the mouth of a valley leading east. Up this side valley via the Doya-la is a three- or four-day route to Kharta. Thirty minutes past this confluence you reach the village of Japon. Fifteen minutes further a recently built concrete bridge crosses to the east (left) side of the Dza-chu (also known in its upper reaches as the Rongphu-chu).

The valley now arcs to the west and is carpeted in lush meadows. One hour from the bridge is the uppermost agricultural village in the Dzaka valley, Chö Dzom. Operating out of the local school grounds are a *lodge*, *teahouse* and small *shop*. Beds here cost Y20. If you are camping move up the valley at least 30 minutes to skip being the village's feature entertainment for the evening. It is still a long day's walk from Chö Dzom to Everest Base Camp.

Out of Chö Dzom the road ascends a small slope and a trail diverges to the left. The road remains in the valley bottom, while the trail

TREKKING

crosses an inclined plain, reuniting with the road in 1¾ hours. The trail, a shorter walk, follows a south-west trajectory, turning south where it meets the road. Ninety minutes from Chö Dzom, look to the right, up the mouth of the Zombuk valley – the pass at its head, the Lamna-la, leads to Tingri. Also on the west side of the Dzaka valley, 20 minutes onwards, are the remnants of Chöpuk Hermitage nestled in an escarpment.

Stage 4: Chö Dzom to Everest Base Camp
5 hours • 20km • 500m ascent

After the trail merges with the road, sheer rock slopes close in around the valley. After a few minutes' walk, the valley leading to the Nam-la, the southernmost route to the plains of Tingri, is visible. In 20 minutes a bridge crosses over the Dza-chu, accessing the valleys to the passes. Just above the bridge, a big tributary originating from the Gyachung massif flows into the Dza-chu.

It is still about 2½ hours to Rongphu and 4½ hours to Everest Base Camp. Twenty minutes further is a small spring and place to *camp* on the left side of the road. Another 30 minutes upstream, perched in a side valley to the left of the road, are the ruins of Kyelung Hermitage. Beyond here a wide, cairn-studded pilgrims' trail splits off the road, a less dusty walking option.

A stone chörten called the Khumbu Chörten is 30 minutes up the trail. Forty-five minutes later the exquisite form of Mt Everest comes into view for the first time since you surmounted the Geu-la. The trail continues to ascend for 20 minutes and then drops into a deep stream bed. East of the trail, where the stream emerges from the defile, are the crumbling walls of the remains of the Chu Hara Nunnery. Up from the stream, the trail meets the road and wends its way through a cluster of morainal hills, reaching Rongphu Monastery in 30 minutes. At the last bend in the road the monastery suddenly comes into view with Mt Everest as the all-encompassing backdrop. (For detailed information on the monastery, see Rongphu Monastery in the Tsang chapter.)

It's about a two-hour walk from Rongphu Monastery to Everest Base Camp. (Vehicles do the trip in around 15 minutes.) The walk is fairly straightforward; the mountain climbs only 220m over about 8km.

Qomolangma Nature Preserve

The Qomolangma Nature Preserve (QNP) was established in 1989 by the government of the Tibetan Autonomous Region to conserve the natural and cultural heritage of the Mt Everest region.

The preserve covers over 34,000 sq km. Bordering Nepal's Sagarmatha, Langtang and Makalu-Barun National Parks and their buffer zones, it is the only protected area to straddle both sides of the Himalaya. QNP's park managers hold regular exchanges with Nepal's to share experiences and promote conservation cooperation across political boundaries.

More than 7000 foreign tourists visit the QNP each year, and numbers are growing. The goal of the QNP is to encourage tourism and generate local benefits and employment while protecting the environment. Fees for entry to core preserve areas are invested in maintaining access roads and controlling litter at major mountaineering and trekking camps.

Funding for various environmental and economic-development activities comes from national and regional governments. QNP also collaborates with a number of international organisations. The Mountain Institute is one such organisation; it supports QNP in conserving local environment and culture and improving village livelihoods through its multi-year Qomolangma Conservation Project (QCP).

For more information on the project, visit the Mountain Institute's Web site (**w** www.mountain .org), or contact Brian Peniston (**e** bpeniston@mountain.org), senior program manager, Asian regional office, PO Box 2785, Tangal, Kathmandu, Nepal. In the USA, you can contact the Mountain Institute at 245 Newman Ave, Harrisonburg, VA 22801, or call ☎ 540-437 0468.

Above Rongphu the valley expands into a large glacial outwash plain. There is a short cut from behind the big chörten at the monastery that cuts through a meadow and then past a superbly photogenic complex of ruins called **Rong Chung**. Until the Communist takeover this was a thriving meditation retreat. Permission to rebuild has not yet been granted. From Rong Chung the trail descends from the shelf to meet the road at a sacred spring.

The road climbs up through a jumble of boulders and glacial debris favouring the left side of the valley. Passing the recently rebuilt **Sherab Chöling Hermitage** (signposted as the Guru Rinpoche Cave of the Pamasambawa), the road runs into the terminal moraine of the Rongphu Glacier, mounds of stone and silt barricading the valley. You may see herds of deer and yaks on the hillsides.

It is still 30 minutes from here to Base Camp. The road snakes through the moraine to reach a sandy plain, with Everest Base Camp at its far edge.

Be aware that expeditions further from Base Camp are only for those very experienced in trekking and mountaineering. It is all too easy easy, once you have reached Base Camp, to succumb to the temptation to push just a little further. Do not do it without adequate preparation. At the very least, spend a couple of days acclimatising in the Rongphu area and doing day hikes to higher altitudes.

For highly fit and prepared groups it is possible to trek beyond Base Camp as far as Camp III. Including time for acclimatisation, you would need to allow at least one week for this trek. The route skirts the Rongphu Glacier until Camp I and then meets the East Rongphu Glacier at Camp II. This glacier must be crossed in order to reach Camp III (6340m). For information on reaching the advanced camps, see Gary McCue's *Trekking in Tibet – A Traveler's Guide*.

From Everest Base Camp you can either walk or hitch back to the Shegar-Nepal Hwy. For details on how to walk to Tingri, see Everest Base Camp to Tingri following.

EVEREST BASE CAMP TO TINGRI

The Trek at a Glance

Duration 3 to 4 days
Distance 60km
Standard Medium to difficult
Start Everest Base Camp
Finish Tingri
Highest Point Nam-la (5250m)
Nearest Large Town Shigatse
Accommodation Camping
Public Transport No
Summary If you walked into Everest Base Camp from the highway near Shegar and are looking for an alternative exit route consider the trek to Tingri. This is a three- or four-day walk through remote country where it is essential to be absolutely self-sufficient. You may be able to buy some basic foodstuffs at the small shop at the Rongphu Monastery.

The route passes through an isolated valley on the way up to the Nam-la and enters a region used by herders and their livestock. Following the Ra-chu valley, the route swings north to the plains of Tingri. It is possible to do this trek in the opposite direction.

The trek via the Nam-la is the fastest route from Everest Base Camp to Tingri, but if you are short on supplies or not so well equipped consider one of the alternative passes covered in Gary McCue's *Trekking in Tibet – A Traveler's Guide*. The longer routes may be preferable because they follow more of the main road, reaching villages where supplies might be bought – but don't count on finding much. Once you leave Rongphu Monastery there are no permanent settlements until well in reach of Tingri, three days away. Such an untravelled route is great for those who are up to a wilderness experience but is best missed by everyone else. Don't chance this trip unless you are really ready.

There is no public transport in the region but it shouldn't be too difficult to get a lift along the Friendship Hwy to either the turn-off to Everest (kilometre marker 5145) or Tingri. Hired Land Cruisers can go all the way to Everest Base Camp.

For more information on the Everest region, including Everest Base Camp, see Everest Region in the Tsang chapter.

Stage 1: Everest Base Camp to beyond the Nam-la
9½ hours • 27km • 450m ascent • 520m descent

The route to the Nam-la retraces the route taken to reach Everest Base Camp as far as the bridge over the Dza-chu, two or more hours down the valley from the Rongphu Monastery (for details, see stage four of the previous trek). A trail angles down a steep embankment from the road to the bridge. Cross the bridge and look for the trail along the west bank of the river. Soon the trail ascends the embankment and emerges onto a shelf above the Dza-chu. In a few minutes the trail climbs further and traverses around the base of a slope into the mouth of a side valley. It takes 30 minutes to reach the mouth of this valley from the road.

While the majority of the Dzaka valley is dry and barren, this side valley is relatively luxuriant, hosting a variety of plants and shrubs and plenty of freshwater. This is a nice place to *camp* or take a long lunch break. The valley bends to the left as the trail to Nam-la leaves the valley floor and climbs past a corral onto a plain abutting the north (right) side of the valley. The route to the pass now bears west all the way to the summit, paralleling the valley floor. It is at least a 3½-hour hike to the pass.

As you begin your ascent towards the pass there is a saddle in the ridge bounding the north side of the valley – this is the most direct route to the Zombuk valley. Walk close to the ridge enclosing the north side of the valley. Past the corral there is no trail. The route clambers over rock-strewn shrubby terrain and then over big plates of tundra that fit together like a giant jigsaw puzzle. One hour from the corral, a steep slope blocks the view to the west. It takes 10 minutes to climb over this onto another broad tundra-covered pitch. In 10 more minutes you can see the head of the valley; however, the Nam-la is out of sight, tucked behind the folds in the ridge.

The route gradually levels out and in 15 minutes descends into a marshy side valley. There is a small stream in this valley, the last place you can count on for water until well beyond the pass. Look for a small corral on the far side of the side valley and bear to the left of it. Continue walking up for 10 minutes before gradually descending into the main valley floor in another 15 minutes.

Remain on the right side of the valley, taking the trail that steeply climbs towards the pass. The trail remains clear for 40 minutes until it is absorbed by the tussock grass of the valley floor. The pass is near where the ridge south of the valley bends around to the west. It is still 40 minutes from here to the Nam-la over alpine meadows, but the terrain is now much more open and the gradient less steep.

Proceed west, looking out for the lowest point on the horizon. The Nam-la (5250m) is a very broad summit simply delineating the parting of drainage basins over a vast plain. There are a few small cairns on top, seen only when you are upon them. To the west, across a wide, wet downhill slope is a small valley bottom and the Ra-chu valley far beyond that. North of the Nam-la, with only a small summit in between, is the Lamna-la coming from the Zombuk valley.

Descend from the pass in a westerly direction over tussock grasses and tundra for one hour, and cross the cart track coming from the Lamna-la. If the time is right you may see gazelles during your descent. From the cart track descend a precipitous slope into the valley floor. There are both springs and a stream in this swampy valley of grasses and wildflowers, a tributary of the Ra-chu. Great *camp sites* are found on the drier margins of the valley. It is at least a five-hour trek from here to the first village, Lungchang.

Stage 2: Base of Nam-la to Lungchang
5–6 hours • 21km • 200m descent

Do not follow the valley down and northward. It is easier to walk west to the ridge next to the valley and pick up the cart track. You can see the cart track cutting across the

Tents dwarfed by Shisha Pangma (8012m), the only 8000m-plus mountain planted squarely in Tibet

Proof that it *is* possible to cycle to Everest Base Camp

Rongphu Glacier and Mt Everest: You might prefer to rent a Land Cruiser.

There's no shortage of tent space on the plains between Lhasa and Amdo.

Samye Monastery marks the end of the Ganden to Samye trek, the most popular trek in Ü.

ridge from a group of corrals on the west side of the valley. The track goes all the way to Tingri, making route-finding easy.

By tracing a north-west trajectory over the ridge the track avoids the swampy valley floor. Follow the cart track for 20 minutes, coming to a junction marked by a cairn. The foot trail to Lamna-la leaves the road here and goes east to intersect the valley. Leave the cart track and take the trail bearing north-west – this is a short cut that rejoins the main track in 15 minutes.

The short cut descends to cross the cart track and then merges with it after a switchback. Back in the valley bottom the track stays on the south (left) side of the valley, crossing a small stream coming from the south. This unbridged crossing may pose problems during heavy summer rains, in which case try to ford it in the early morning when the volume of water is lower.

The track angles across the middle of the stony valley and is very wide and straight, like a runway used by bush planes. In 30 minutes the track returns to the left side of the valley. Fifteen minutes further, it passes through a narrow constriction in the valley formed by a series of orange cliffs. Beyond the cliffs the valley turns north (right) and retains this bearing all the way to Tingri. A few minutes after emerging through the bottleneck look for a continuation of the track on the north bank of the stream. During summer rains it's best to carefully select a ford in the area a little downstream of the track crossing.

The view to the north is now dominated by the blue or purple Tsebu Mountains. Tingri is in front of these mountains, south of the Bum-chu. The mostly sandy track unfolds along the east (right) bank of the stream for 45 minutes. It then ascends above the bank and traverses the side of a ridge with the stream running through a narrow channel directly below. Look south to see the glittering white Cho Oyu massif. In 30 minutes descend into the widening valley floor. In 10 more minutes cross a small side valley.

The track unrolls across a level shelf above the stream for 30 minutes before climbing over a small ridge that circumvents the gorge forming below. Just up-

stream of the gorge, the stream you've been following from the base of the pass flows into the much higher-volume main branch of the Ra-chu which originates from the flanks of Cho Oyu. The summit of the ridge is marked with a cairn and prayer flags and takes 10 minutes to reach from the shelf.

From the summit the track descends to cross a side valley before ranging across a long, barren stretch of valley. In the distance you can see two rocky knobs at the end of the long east ridge line. It takes about one hour to reach the knobs. On top of them are the disintegrating walls of the long-abandoned fort known as Ngang Tsang Drag Dog Dzong. Thirty minutes after passing beneath the ramparts of the ancient fort you reach Lungchang, the first permanent settlement since Rongphu.

The cubicle two-storey houses of Lungchang are impeccably whitewashed and decorated with red, blue and white stripes near their roof lines. Blocks of dung are neatly stacked on the roofs between prayer-flag masts. At the north end of the village, in one of the houses, is a small *lodge* and *shop* marked by a sign that reads 'Leg Jang'. Simple meals and beds are usually available here or with other families in the village. It is still 3½ hours from Tingri and the highway.

Stage 3: Lungchang to Tingri
3½ hours • 12km • 150m descent
From Lungchang, you can see several low-lying hills in the mouth of the Ra-chu valley: Tingri is at the foot of the northernmost of these. From Lungchang the track moves towards the middle of the valley, following a bluff along the edge of the Ra-chu. In 1½ hours it reaches the outskirts of the village Ra Chu. Before the village, at a white shrine, the track splits; the right, or main, branch goes to Tingri via Ra Chu village, while the left fork jogs west and then north over wide pastures to Tingri. The left fork is the shorter route to Tingri and is a more pleasant walk. The lower part of the Ra-chu valley is green during the warmer half of the year; extensive meadows support flocks of goats and sheep. The homes of the shepherds dot the edges of the huge expanse of turf.

TREKKING

Fifteen minutes south of Ra Chu village you will pass ruins on the slopes bounding the east side of the valley – look back to see Everest pop up from behind the anterior ranges. The two tracks that split near Ra Chu are reunited 45 minutes beyond the village.

Thirty minutes further, you reach a bridge over the Ra-chu, which allows you to access the south side of Tingri. You can cross the Ra-chu here and pass through the village to the highway or remain on the right bank and cross the new highway bridge. It is only 15 minutes to the highway. If you stay on the right bank there is an irrigation ditch to cross below the shoulder of the highway.

For information on Tingri, see the Tsang chapter. If you decide to trek into Everest from Tingri by reversing the direction in this trek description it is usually possible to hire yaks, guides and even pony carts in Tingri, though if you want to keep a low profile it might be better to organise this in Ra Chu.

MT KAILASH KORA

The Trek at a Glance

Duration 3 days
Distance 52km
Standard Medium to difficult
Start Darchen
Finish Darchen
Highest Point Drölma-la (5630m)
Nearest Large Town Ali
Accommodation Camping and monastery guesthouses
Public Transport No, but see Mt Kailash in the Ngari (Western Tibet) chapter for relevant information
Summary The 52km circuit or kora of Mt Kailash (6714m) is one of the most important pilgrimages in Asia. A religious sanctuary since pre-Buddhist times, a trek here wonderfully integrates the spiritual, cultural and physical dimensions of a trip to Tibet, which explains its growing attraction. The well-trodden track around the sacred mountain passes through verdant alpine valleys linked by a lofty pass, the Drölma-la. Being able to meet pilgrims from across Tibet and other countries is one of the many allures of this walk.

The Kailash trekking season runs from mid-May to mid-October, but trekkers should be prepared for changeable weather at any time. See the Ngari (Western Tibet) chapter for an introduction to Mt Kailash and the kora, as well as for further information on Darchen, the shabby little town where the walk starts and finishes. Snow may be encountered on the Drölma-la at any time of year and the temperature will often drop below freezing at night. The pass tends to be snowed in from early November to early April.

Darchen PSB requires all foreigners to buy a permit for Y50 for the Kailash and Manasarovar region, even if you already have one from Lhasa. Some travellers have apparently been fined for spending the night at Manasarovar before heading to Darchen to buy the permit. Check with your tour agency, or with the PSB at Darchen or Ali. Having paid Y50 to start the Kailash kora, there's a checkpoint at the end where you have to pay another Y50 to finish it!

If you have a heavy load it is worth considering hiring a porter or yaks; the Darchen guesthouses can help make arrangements and store gear while you are on the kora. Porters are usually friendly young guys who know the circuit well and typically cost Y50 per day, perhaps less if you make arrangements yourself in town. If you hire yaks and yak drivers, count on about Y50 per yak and another Y35 for each handler; yaks are skittish creatures requiring expert management. Allow a few days to arrange the yaks.

Instant noodles and a very limited range of other supplies are available at the shops in Darchen. A wider range is available in Ali to the north and Purang to the south.

If you do not have a tent the accommodation possibilities on the kora are very limited. There are primitive *guesthouses* associated with the Dira-puk and Zutul-puk Monasteries, but they only have a half-dozen rooms each. During the Indian pilgrimage season (June to early September), it may be possible to get a bed in the tents that are erected for the pilgrims near the two monasteries. Very limited food may also be available at the guesthouses. If at all possible you should bring a tent since there

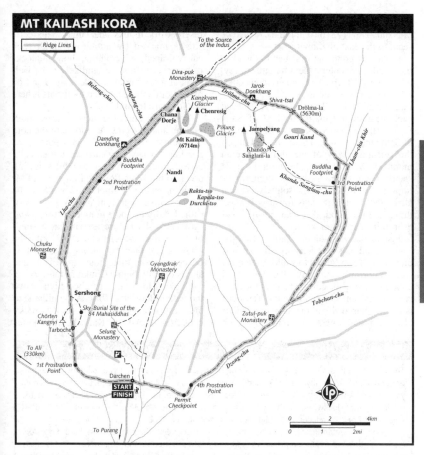

MT KAILASH KORA

Ridge Lines

To the Source of the Indus

Belung-chu

Dunglung-chu

Dira-puk Monastery

Drölma-chu

Jarok Donkhang

Shiva-tsal

Drölma-la (5630m)

Kangkyam Glacier

Chana Dorje ▲ Chenresig

Damding Donkhang

Pölung Glacier

▲ Jampelyang

Gouri Kund

Buddha Footprint

Mt Kailash (6714m)

Khando Sanglam-la

Buddha Footprint

2nd Prostration Point

Nandi ▲

Khando Sanglam-chu

3rd Prostration Point

Lham-chu Khir

Chuku Monastery

Rakta-tso Kapala-tso Durchi-tso

Lha-chu

Gyangdrak Monastery

Sershong

Sky-Burial Site of the 84 Mahasiddhas

Tobchan-chu

Chörten Kangnyi

Tarboche

Selung Monastery

Zutul-puk Monastery

To Ali (330km)

1st Prostration Point

Darchen

Dzong-chu

START FINISH

4th Prostration Point

Permit Checkpoint

To Purang

0   2   4km
0   1   2mi

LP

TREKKING

is no guarantee you will find a room free or a bed available in a pilgrim tent. If you are equipped for camping, however, there are wonderful grassy *camp sites* all around the kora and there is certainly no shortage of water. Fuel for cooking is another matter. There is no wood and even yak dung is in short supply.

Stage 1: Darchen to Dira-puk Monastery
6 hours • 20km • 200m ascent
The Mt Kailash kora trail quickly leaves grubby Darchen behind, heading west along the base of the east-west ridge, which blocks off views of the holy mountain. The vast Barkha plain spreads out to the south, Gurla Mandata (7728m) rises to the southeast, Api and other peaks in Nepal to the south and the twin, sharp humps of Kamet (7756m) in India off to the south-west. Only 4km from Darchen the trail climbs up over the south-west end of the ridge to reach a cairn at 4730m after about an hour's walk. It's bedecked with prayer flags and marks the first views of the mountain's southern or sapphire face and a *chaktsal gang*, the first of the kora's four prostration

points. From here the more rounded profile of Nanda Devi (7816m) in India can also be seen, to the east of Kamet.

From this point the trail bends round to the north and enters the Lha-chu valley, where the tall Tarboche flagpole soon comes into view. It's about an hour's walk to the flagpole at 4750m. The flagpole is replaced each year at the major festival of Saga Dawa. The festival marks the enlightenment of Sakyamuni (Sakya Thukpa), and falls on the full-moon day of the fourth Tibetan month (in May or June). How the flagpole stands when it is re-erected is of enormous importance. If it stands absolutely vertical all is well, but if it leans towards Kailash things are not good; if it leans away, however, things are even worse.

Just to the west of the Tarboche is the 'two-legged' Chörten Kangnyi. It's an auspicious act for pilgrims to walk through the small chörten's archway. The kora trail continues along the eastern bank of the Lha-chu, but a short climb above the Tarboche is the sky-burial site of the 84 *mahasiddhas* (Tantric practitioners who reached a high

level of awareness), revered as it was once reserved for monks and lamas. This eerie site is marked by numerous small rock cairns draped with clothing, shoes and locks of hair, but visitors are unlikely to be welcome if a sky burial is under way. The first of the kora's three Buddha footprints is here but it's hard to find.

You can continue across this small plateau and descend back down to the kora trail and the river, in the area known as Sershong. The valley narrows dramatically at Sershong, with majestic hills falling down to the swift-flowing Lha-chu and Mt Kailash appearing impressively above the eastern ridge. The trail passes a series of ruined chörtens and a number of long *mani* (prayer) walls before arriving at a small bridge across the Lha-chu at 4710m. The bridge is less than an hour's walk from Tarboche, or about three hours from Darchen, and is directly below Chuku Monastery.

Chuku Monastery, perched high above the valley floor at 4820m on the hillside to the west, blends secretively into its rocky background. All the Kailash monasteries

Which Way, How Many Days, How Many Times, How Many Rivers?

These are the important questions for walking the 52km circuit – a *kora* if your pilgrimage is a Buddhist one, a *parikrama* if you're on a Hindu circuit – of Asia's most holy mountain. Buddhist or Hindu, you should be walking the mountain in a clockwise direction, but if you meet walkers coming the other way (anticlockwise), don't be surprised; they're followers of Bön, the ancient pre-Buddhist religion of Tibet – a religion that still thrives in remote parts of Tibet, particularly in the east.

If you're a Tibetan Buddhist you'll probably plan to complete the circuit in one hard day's slog. Achieving this feat requires a pre-dawn start and a late-afternoon return to Darchen. Occasionally Westerners emulate this feat – Tyrolean Reinhold Messner recorded a time of 12 hours, slightly faster than the average Tibetan walker. Hindu pilgrims, with the odd ritual immersion in an icy cold lake to endure along the way, typically take three days, overnighting in encampments set up for them close to the Dira-puk and Zutul-puk Monasteries. Independent Western visitors usually aim for a three-day circuit as well, staying at the monastery guesthouses at the same locations. Western trekking groups typically do the circuit in three or four days, as a longer circuit allows time for side trips and excursions such as visits to the Kailash north-face glaciers.

Eschewing the normal high-speed one-day circuit, some very enthusiastic Tibetans make the walk much more difficult by prostrating themselves the entire way. They lie down at full length with their arms stretched over their heads, then stand up, place their feet where their hands ended up and repeat the process. Count on around three weeks to complete a prostration kora.

How many times around the mountain? Well, at least once to wipe out the sins of a lifetime, although even that small achievement requires the right attitude predeparture and perhaps a couple were wrecked during the Cultural Revolution and the Chuku (or Nyenri) Monastery was the first to be rebuilt. It takes about 20 minutes to climb from the river bank up to this hillside monastery, which was founded in the 13th century by Götsangpa Gompo Pel, a Kagyupa-order master. In the monastery's *dukhang* (assembly hall), look up to the skylight for the mirror angled to perfectly frame a fine view of Mt Kailash. In a glass case over the altar there's a highly revered marble statue called Chuku Opame (originally from India and reputed to talk!) and a conch shell inlaid with silver. Beside the altar there's a copper pot and elephant tusks, as found in temples in Bhutan.

From the Chuku bridge there are alternative trails along the east and west banks of the river. The trail along the east bank is the regular pilgrim route but the west-side trail offers better views of the west face of Mt Kailash. Either way it's about another three hours to Dira-puk Monastery. Trekking groups generally take the west-side trail since there are some fine grassy *camp sites* on the river banks at Damding Donkhang

(4890m), about an hour before the monastery. The west or ruby face of Kailash makes a dramatic backdrop to this camp site and in the early morning Tibetan pilgrims can be seen striding resolutely past on the other side of the river, already well into their one-day circuit.

At points along the trail the west and north faces of the mountain can be seen together. The steep hillsides on both sides of the valley make this one of the most impressive stretches of the walk. Golden *piya* (marmots) regularly pop up out of their holes to peer worriedly at passing walkers. Many of the formations along this stretch have mythical connections, a number of them related to Tibet's legendary hero Gesar of Ling. The second prostration point is also encountered on the east side of the valley, followed by the second Buddha footprint.

Dira-puk Monastery, which was rebuilt in 1985, looks across to the north or gold face of Kailash from the hillside north of the Lha-chu. Walkers who have followed the Lha-chu's east-bank trail will have to cross the river to reach the monastery and

TREKKING

of checks of your current sin status at the 'sin-testing stones' on the ascent to the Drölma-la. Tibetans look upon three circuits as a much more satisfactory starting point and 13 as the real minimum. Like gold status for frequent fliers, completing 13 circuits also allows access to high-status detours like the short cut over the Khando Sanglam-la or a visit to an inner kora *(nangkor)* on the south side of the mountain. Real walkers should aim for 108 circuits, which guarantees instant nirvana and a clean sin slate for all your lifetimes. Economisers should note that koras completed during a full moon are better than ordinary ones; ditto for koras during the Tibetan Year of the Horse.

And the rivers? Well it's a geographic quirk that four of the subcontinent's most important rivers all have their birth close to the base of Mt Kailash. The mighty Indus flows off to the north-west through Ladakh and the Pakistani-held portion of Kashmir before turning south and flowing through the whole length of Pakistan and eventually emptying into the Arabian Sea to the east of Karachi. The Sutlej River heads off to the west, flowing through the Indian states of Himachal Pradesh and Punjab then turning south-west into Pakistan and finally joining the Indus near Multan. Meanwhile, the Humla Karnali heads straight off to the south, cutting its way right across the Himalaya through western Nepal then turning east and, as the Ghaghara or Gogra, joining the mighty Ganges River just before Patna. Finally, the Yarlung Tsangpo flows eastward all the way across Tibet before bending south around the easternmost end of the Himalaya and, as the Brahmaputra River, flowing through India and down into Bangladesh. The Ganges and Brahmaputra both empty into the Bay of Bengal in an extensive delta system between Kolkata (Calcutta) and Dhaka, 2500km east of the Indus' arrival at the Arabian Sea.

its guesthouse, at the base of the hill below. West-bank walkers may also get their feet wet since they have to cross the Belung-chu and Dunglung-chu, tributaries of the Lha-chu, before they reach the monastery.

The monastery takes its name from the female-yak-horn *(dira)* cave *(puk)* where Götsangpa meditated. Buddhists say it was Götsangpa who first discovered the kora route around Mt Kailash and that he was led here by a yak that turned out to be the lion-faced goddess Dakini (Khadroma) who guards the Khando Sanglam-la. The main image in the dukhang is of Chenresig (Avalokiteshvara), flanked by images of the Buddha and a fearsome protector deity.

From the monastery there are superb views of the impressive north face of Mt Kailash. Three lesser mountains are arrayed in front of Kailash: Chana Dorje (Vajrapani) to the west, Jampelyang (Manjushri) to the east and Chenresig (Avalokiteshvara) in the centre. The Kangkyam Glacier descends from the north face of Mt Kailash between Chana Dorje and Chenresig and it takes a round trip of a couple of hours to walk up to the glacier and back. Hindu pilgrims usually camp near the monastery, while independent walkers often overnight in the monastery's rather basic guesthouse, where a grubby mattress on the dirt floor will cost Y25.

Stage 2: Dira-puk Monastery to Zutul-puk Monastery

6–7 hours • 18km • 550m ascent • 600m descent

The Lha-chu flows down the valley running north from Dira-puk. Swami Pranavananda followed this valley up to the source of the Indus River, a two- to three-day walk. Kora walkers, on the other hand, head off to the east, crossing the Lha-chu by a bridge and starting the long ascent up the Drölma-chu valley that will eventually lead to the Drölma-la. The route climbs on to a moraine and soon meets the trail from the east bank of the Lha-chu.

Less than an hour along this route some trekking groups *camp* on the meadow at Jarok Donkhang (5210m). Camping here makes the ascent to the Drölma-la on the following day a much easier task. It is not wise to camp any higher than Jarok Don-khang because of the risk of problems with acclimatisation.

Another glacier descends from the eastern ridge off the north face of Mt Kailash, down the Pölung valley between Chenresig (Aval-okiteshvara) and Jampelyang (Manjushri). This glacier can also be reached in a round trip of a couple of hours from this camp site. You can follow the glacial stream that runs down the middle of the valley to merge with

The Faces & Rivers of Mt Kailash

It's easy to confuse the mystical Mt Kailash, the Mt Meru of legend reaching from the lowest hell to the highest heaven, with the real one. From the legendary Mt Kailash a river flows into the legendary Lake Manasarovar, from which flow four separate rivers in the four cardinal directions. In reality there may not be any rivers flowing from Manasarovar, but four real rivers do flow from the mountain in, more or less, the cardinal directions. And Kailash really does have four distinct faces – composed, according to legend, of lapis lazuli, ruby, gold and crystal.

direction	face	mythical river	real river
south	lapis lazuli	Mabja Kambab (River from the Peacock Mouth)	Karnali
west	ruby	Langchan Kambab (River from the Elephant's Mouth)	Sutlej
north	gold	Seng-ge Kambab (River from the Lion's Mouth)	Indus
east	crystal	Tamchog Kambab (River from the Horse's Mouth)	Yarlung Tsangpo (Brahmaputra)

Milarepa versus Naro Bönchung

All around the Mt Kailash kora there's evidence of the long-running contest for supremacy between Milarepa, the Buddhist poet-saint, and Naro Bönchung, the Bön master. In every encounter it was Milarepa who came out the victor, but despite this he still agreed to a final, winner-takes-all duel, a straightforward race to the top of the mountain. Mounting his magic drum Naro Bönchung immediately set out to fly to the summit, but despite his acolytes' urging Milarepa didn't even bother getting out of bed. Finally, as the first rays of dawn revealed that Naro Bönchung was about to reach the top, Milarepa rose from his bed and was carried by a ray of light directly to the top. Shocked by this defeat his opponent tumbled off his drum, which skittered down the south face of the mountain, gouging the long slash marking Mt Kailash to this day. Hindu pilgrims call it the 'stairway to heaven'. Gracious in victory, Milarepa decreed that Bön followers could continue to make their customary anticlockwise circuits of Mt Kailash, and awarded nearby Bönri as their own holy mountain.

the Drölma-chu or avoid losing altitude from the camp site by terracing around the side of Jampelyang.

From here to the Drölma-la there is a constant parade of interesting points along the trail. Only a short distance above Jarok Donkhang is Shiva-tsal (5330m), a rocky expanse dotted with stone cairns draped with items of clothing. Pilgrims are supposed to undergo a symbolic death at this point, leaving their old life behind along with an item of clothing to represent it. A drop of blood or a lock of hair might be even better. If you really do decide to drop dead at this point this is a very meritorious place to die. Right by the trail at the end of the Shiva-tsal is a red footprint of Milarepa.

Nearby a trail branches off to the southeast, leading over the snow-covered Khando Sanglam-la, a short cut to the east side of Mt Kailash which bypasses the normal route over the Drölma-la. Don't be tempted to take this route – only on your auspicious 13th kora is the pass open to you and intruders are likely to find themselves face to face with the pass's protector, the fearsome lion-faced goddess Dakini (Khadroma).

Climbing beyond Shiva-tsal the trail reaches the sin-testing stone of Bardo Trang. A narrow passage squeezes beneath the flat stone and pilgrims are supposed to measure their sinfulness by wriggling under the stone. Fat or thin you may find yourself stuck under the rock if your sin quota is too high, and in that case the sin-washing power

of a Kailash kora may not be sufficient to clean up your karma. High above the trail is a large mirror rock; it looks red to ordinary people, white to bodhisattvas and black to sinners. A little further along, the much more convoluted passage under the Dikpa Karnak awaits those in need of a second opinion. Other points of interest along this stretch include a stack of stones marking where Milarepa and Naro Bönchung engaged in one of their contests of saintly one-upmanship. The stone of the triumphant Milarepa tops the pile.

Finally the trail turns to the east for the final ascent to the 5630m Drölma-la. Look south for your last glimpse of the north face of Mt Kailash. A small glacial trickle halfway up presents your last sin-washing opportunity before the top. Allow about an hour for the 200m climb to the wide and rocky pass, festooned with an enormous number of prayer flags strung from the Drölma Do (Drölma's Rock). Pilgrims perform a circumambulation, pasting money onto the rock with butter, stooping to pass under the lines of prayer flags, and chanting the Tibetan pass-crossing mantra, 'ki ki so so, lha gyalo' ('ki ki so so' being the empowerment and happiness invocation, 'lha gyalo' meaning 'the gods are victorious'). Naturally there's a tale associated with this revered rock. When Götsangpa, who pioneered the kora for the Buddhists, wandered into the valley of Dakini (Khadroma), he was led back to the correct route by 21

TREKKING

wolves who were, of course, merely 21 emanations of Drölma (Tara), the goddess of mercy and protectress of the pass. Reaching the pass the 21 wolves merged into one and then merged into the great boulder. To this day Drölma helps worthy pilgrims on the difficult ascent – it did seem easier than you expected didn't it?

Weather permitting, most pilgrims and trekkers pause at the pass for a rest and refreshments before starting the steep descent. Almost immediately, Gouri Kund (5608m; one of its Tibetan names translates as 'Lake of Compassion') comes into view below. Hindu pilgrims are supposed to immerse themselves in the lake's green waters, breaking the ice if necessary. Tibetans, as is well known, have no truck with all this bathing nonsense. It takes about an hour to make the long 400m descent across generally barren and rocky ground before reaching the grassy banks of the Lham-chu Khir. There's the remains of a stone hut where the trail meets the river, leaning up against a huge rock topped by the kora's third Buddha footprint.

As in the Lha-chu valley on the western side of Mt Kailash, there are routes along both sides of the river. The east-bank trail presents better views and less marshy ground, but it requires a lot of boulder-hopping and wading back across the river at some point. If you opt for that side keep an eye on the river level, which may become uncomfortably deep further south during the wetter months. Not far south a valley comes down from the Khando Sanglam-la to join the main trail. This valley provides the only glimpse of Mt Kailash's eastern or crystal face; the kora's third prostration point is at the valley mouth.

Trekking groups may decide to camp on the grassy west banks of the river somewhere along this stretch but walkers without tents will probably press on to the guesthouse at Zutul-puk Monastery (4790m). The monastery is about two hours' walk along the valley. By this point the river has changed name to the Dzong-chu, which translates as 'Fortress River'.

The miracle (zutul) cave (puk) that gives the monastery its name is at the back of the main hall. Milarepa is said to have meditated in this cave, which was also the site of yet another confrontation between the Buddhist poet-saint and Naro Bönchung. Needing shelter from the rain they agreed to jointly construct a cave, but when Milarepa casually put the roof in place, without waiting for Naro Bönchung to make the walls, it was yet another easy victory for Buddhism. Milarepa then decided the roof was too high and went outside and pressed it down with his foot, leaving a footprint. Back inside he realised he'd pushed it too far, but some more shoving from below adjusted things to his satisfaction. His hand and head prints can be seen on the cave ceiling but the monastery roof covers the footprint atop the cave.

The monastery **guesthouse** is primitive, but probably in slightly better shape than the one at Dira-puk. The cost per bed is typically Y30.

Stage 3: Zutul-puk Monastery to Darchen
3–4 hours • 14km • 150m descent
The final day's walk only takes three to four hours and starts with the easy stroll down to where the river emerges onto the Barkha plain. The valley narrows and at times its sides look like something from the American south-west or the Australian outback, except for the prayer flags fluttering across the river.

Prostration Points & Footprints

Really serious pilgrims may make the kora in continuous prostrations but even the least dedicated will prostrate themselves at the four major prostration points (chaktsal gang). If you want to join them, quickly touch your joined hands to forehead, mouth and heart then stretch full length with your arms extended. The kora is also dotted with important shabje (footprints). The Buddha's are the most important of course, but you may also come across indications that Milarepa and other notables have set foot on the trail.

Where the trail emerges onto the plain, close to the fourth prostration point (4610m), there's a permit checkpoint where Westerners are charged another Y50 for their efforts. Gurla Mandata once more provides a backdrop to the lake Rakshas Tal (Lhanag-tso; 4573m). There's a rough road from here back to Darchen, but it's less than an hour's walk, passing many mani walls embellished with yak skulls en route.

LAKE MANASAROVAR KORA

The Trek at a Glance

Duration 4 to 5 days
Distance 110km
Standard Medium
Start Chiu Monastery
Finish Chiu Monastery
Highest Point 4680m
Nearest Large Town Ali
Accommodation Camping
Public Transport No
Summary Tucked away in the extreme south-west corner of Tibet near Mt Kailash, Lake Manasarovar (Mapham yum-tso; 4560m) is one of the country's most sacred and beautiful lakes. Just 20km from Mt Kailash across the Barkha plain, Manasarovar can be circumambulated in four or five days. Five of the original eight monasteries in the area have been partially rebuilt.

Few Western travellers undertake the Lake Manasarovar kora. One of the main problems is the marshiness of the ground around the lake, and there are also many streams to ford, some of which become quite deep in the summer months. But those who do may be rewarded. The lake represents the female or wisdom aspect of enlightenment, and is a symbol of good fortune and fertility. While Mt Kailash stands fully revealed, the depths of Lake Manasarovar are hidden from view to all but the greatest of adepts.

The best place to start the Lake Manasarovar circuit is at the north-west corner near Chiu Monastery. The road from Kailash comes within 1km of here. Chiu (Little Bird) Monastery sits astride a crag

overlooking the lake and enshrines a cave said to have been used by Guru Rinpoche at the end of his life. The fantastic view from the top of the monastery helps put the trek in perspective – there are not many treks of this duration where the entire route is visible from the starting point.

The kora, save for a spell on the north side, follows the lakeshore. The route alternates between sandy, gravelly and marshy ground. Manasarovar is often a gem-like cobalt colour but during storms it can turn into a churning black sea. High elevation lends it a radiance unmatched by lower lakes and its fresh waters are as clear as can be.

At the base of the monastery are two small shops selling basic foods. Nearby, at the edge of the Ganga-chu, are hot springs great for washing. Some of the eroded stone walls in the vicinity are part of a pre-Buddhist archaeological site. (For more information on Chiu, see the Ngari (Western Tibet) chapter.)

Don't expect to find many supplies locally; bring everything you need. May, June and September are the best months to visit. July and August are also good months but in some years they are very wet and hordes of gnats infest the shores. A tent and stove are required on this trek and be prepared for any kind of weather any time. Strong winds often hit in the afternoons so plan on doing most of your walking in the morning.

As there is little public transport in western Tibet, you will have made it this far either by hitching or by hiring a Land Cruiser. If you are hitching you should be aware of the permit restrictions in this region. See the Ngari (Western Tibet) chapter for details.

Stage 1: Chiu Monastery to Hor Qu

7½–8 hours • 30km • 120m ascent • 120m descent

As per Buddhist tradition, head in a clockwise direction from Chiu, travelling east along the north shore. You will pass mani stones nearly 2m tall. The trail soon leaves the waterline and ascends over the top of a red escarpment for two hours. The cliffs below are sprinkled with caves that have

TREKKING

TREKKING

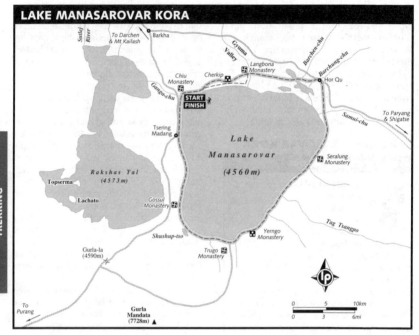

LAKE MANASAROVAR KORA

been used by religious practitioners for centuries. Some of these caves have been converted into permanent homes. From the grass-capped, rolling top of the escarpment the route descends into a small vale where you can see the ruins of Cherkip Monastery; at this point you're a little over two hours from Chiu Monastery.

From Cherkip it is faster to follow the trail east over the headlands to Langbona Monastery, a 90-minute walk. There is also a lakeshore route past more caves and cliffs. When the escarpment ends look for the trail going north along the Gyuma valley to Langbona on the west bank of the Gyuma-chu.

East of Langbona the route traverses a marshy plain to the settlement of Hor Qu, four hours away. There are *camp sites* along the watercourses before Hor Qu so this does not have to be a long day.

Look for a series of tracks heading towards the distant margin of the plain. Under no circumstances return to the edge of the

lake from Langbona. The swamps along this part of the lakeshore give way to several lakes that flow into Manasarovar, effectively blocking the route to all but birds and fish.

Hor Qu is the administrative centre of the area and there are several shops here that sell beer, soda, instant noodles and other basics. There is a *guesthouse* in Hor Qu used by Indian pilgrims; beds here cost Y25.

Stage 2: Hor Qu to Seralung Monastery
3 hours • 13km • level

The trail from Hor Qu leaves the settlement in a south-westerly direction, avoiding the extensive swamps abutting the lake. A little south of Hor Qu you cross the bridge over the Samui-chu – the main road east initially follows this valley. South of the swampy tracts, the trail rejoins the lakeshore along a stone beach. Look out for white-and-black polished stones, sacred to both Buddhists and Hindus.

The route is squeezed between the water and a cliff, before a side valley and Seralung Monastery appear. Some of the monastery's religious property thrown into Lake Manasarovar during the Cultural Revolution has been recovered. The monastery was rebuilt in the mid-1980s. The valley here is a good place to *camp*.

Stage 3: Seralung Monastery to Trugo Monastery
7 hours • 27km • level

At first the route south of Seralung stays near the lakeshore, but in about one hour the mountains retreat and a plain forms next to Manasarovar. The trail moves inland about 1km and crosses the bridge over the Tag Tsangpo about three hours from Seralung. Up this valley are extensive hot springs and geysers as well as Bön and Buddhist sites.

About three hours from the Tag Tsangpo bridge you will round the south side of Manasarovar and reach the ruined Yerngo Monastery situated in a broad plain. This is spacious country, ideal for those looking for secluded camp sites. South of the plain the massive flanks of the Gurla Mandata (7728m) massif rise up to a heavily glaciated summit. In Buddhist tradition, Gurla Mandata (Tibetan: Menmo Nanyi) is the dwelling place of the goddess of wisdom, Saraswati. However, in the older Bön tradition the mountain is the home of the Queen of the Dralha, an important class of ancient warrior deities.

You will reach Trugo Monastery after another hour. Trugo is the only monastery at either Kailash or Manasarovar belonging to the Gelugpa order. Trugo (Bathing Head) is so named because of its importance as a place for ritual bathing. Kailash seems to embrace the lake from this angle, lending credence to ancient myths that speak of the two representing a god and goddess in union. Large by local standards, Trugo has both a *shop* and *hostel* and is a fine place to take a day or two off to enjoy the atmosphere. You can get a bed here for about Y30.

Stages 4 & 5: Trugo Monastery to Chiu Monastery
9–10 hours • 40km • level

From Trugo a motorable track shoots over the range of hills south-west of the lake to join the Purang-Darchen road, but the kora route stays near the lakeshore. Eventually, swampy ground gives way to sandy expanses near the south-west corner of Manasarovar. The trail passes between the lake and the much smaller Shushup-tso along a narrow sand and gravel bridge. You'll round the west side of the lake two hours from Trugo; continue walking along the beach for two more hours to Gossul Monastery.

Gossul Monastery sits on top of a cliff and is best known as the place where the great Kagyupa saint Götsangpa meditated. On the lakeshore below the monastery are a couple of caves used by pilgrims to camp. Retreat caves are found on the circuit around the monastery. The kora follows the lakeshore to the Tsering Madang valley three hours away. You can crash out in the *guesthouse* here unless the authorities have been coming down particularly hard on individual travellers. From here it is two more hours back to Chiu along the beach.

TREKKING

Language

The two principal languages of Tibet are Tibetan and (Mandarin) Chinese. The importance of Chinese is an unfortunate reality in Tibet, and all Tibetans undertaking higher studies do so in Chinese. In fact, in urban Tibet (the countryside is another matter) almost all Tibetans speak Chinese. Nevertheless, even if you have studied or picked up some Chinese in China, it is worth trying to get a few phrases of Tibetan together. It will be much appreciated by Tibetans you encounter on your travels.

Chinese and Tibetan have very little in common linguistically. They use different sentence structures, and the tonal element in Tibetan is far less crucial to conveying meaning than it is in Chinese. Also, unlike the dialects of China (and Japanese, Korean and Vietnamese), Tibetan does not use and never has used Chinese characters for its written language.

Tibetan

Tibetan is classed as belonging to the Tibeto-Burman family of languages. It differs in many ways from Chinese, having a different written language and a different grammar, and being nontonal. Lhasa dialect, which is the standard form of Tibetan, does employ a system of rising and falling tones, but the differences are subtle and meaning is made clear by context. Beginners need not worry about it.

Grammar

Like Chinese, Tibetan has no articles (a, the) and doesn't use plurals. Here the similarity ends, however. Tibetan differs from European and Chinese languages in employing a subject-object-verb sentence structure. Thus, where in English we would say *I* (subject) *see* (verb) *John* (object), in Tibetan the sentence is rendered *nga*, 'I' (subject) *John* (object) *thong gi duk*, 'see' (verb). In another marked difference with

Chinese, Tibetan has tenses and conjugates its verbs with particles. There's also a fairly complicated system of prepositions (in, on, at, etc) in Tibetan.

If all this makes Tibetan sound extremely difficult to pick up on the road, don't fret; providing you relax a little, it's fairly easy to get together a basic repertoire of phrases that will win you friends and help to get things done.

Written Language

The Tibetan script was developed during the reign of Songtsen Gampo in the 7th century. It was founded on Indian models and comprises 30 basic letters (each of which may be written in three different styles depending on the context in which a text is to be used), including the vowel 'a', and four extra vowel signs for 'e', 'i', 'o' and 'u'. This 7th-century Tibetan script was based on the language that was spoken in Tibet at the time, and spellings have never been revised since. This means that, as a result of significant changes in spoken Tibetan over the last 12 centuries, written Tibetan and spoken Tibetan are very different, and the development of a transliteration system for speakers of European languages is a formidable task.

There is no commonly accepted Romanisation system for Tibetan. Some academic texts use a Romanisation system that is based on written Tibetan, but for those who have not studied the written language of Tibet the results are usually unintelligible. The alternative is to base the Romanisation system on contemporary Lhasa dialect. This is what most writers on the subject of Tibet generally do, and already certain standards have begun to emerge. Most guides and histories, for example, use the same spellings for cities and towns (Lhasa, Shigatse, Gyantse etc) and for major geographical features. In the case of less well known Tibetan place names, however, there's a lot of disagreement in English sources.

In this book we've tried not to introduce new complexities to the various spellings available and have generally chosen the most widely used term. In cases where there is wide disagreement, we have chosen the spelling that's easiest to pronounce.

Naturally, the best way to approach these difficulties is to work through a phrasebook with a native speaker or with a tape. Lonely Planet publishes a useful *Tibetan phrasebook*, which includes sections on trekking, visiting temples and handicrafts.

Pronunciation

Like all foreign languages Tibetan has its fair share of tricky sounds. There are quite a few consonant clusters, and Tibetan is a language (like Korean and Thai) that makes an important distinction between aspirated and non-aspirated consonants.

Vowels The following pronunciation guide is based on standard British pronunciation.

a	as in 'father'
ay	as in 'play'
e	as in 'met'
ee	as in 'meet'
i	as in 'begin'
o	as in 'slow'
oo	as in 'soon'
ö	similar to the 'u' in 'put'
u	as the 'oo' in 'woo'
ü	similar to the 'u' in 'flute'

Consonants With the exception of the consonants listed below, Tibetan consonants should be pronounced as in English. Where a consonant is followed by an 'h', it means that the consonant is aspirated (accompanied by a puff of air). An English example might be 'kettle', where the 'k' is aspirated and the 'tt' is nonaspirated. The distinction is fairly important, but in simple Tibetan the context should make it clear what you are talking about, even if you get the sounds muddled up a bit.

ky	as the 'kie' in 'Kiev'
ng	as the 'ng' in 'sing'
r	like a slightly trilled Spanish 'r'
ts	as the 'ts' in 'bits'

Useful Phrases

Hello.
  tashi dele བཀྲ་ཤིས་བདེ་ལེགས

Goodbye.
(when staying)
  kale phe གལེ་ཞེབས

Goodbye.
(when leaving)
  kale shoo གལེ་བཞུགས

Thank you.
  thoo jaychay ཐུགས་རྗེ་ཆེ

Yes, OK.
  la ong ལགས་འོང་

Sorry.
  gonda དགོངས་དག

I want ...
  nga la ... go ང་ལ ... དགོས

Do you speak English?
  injeeke shing gi yö pe? དབྱིན་ཇི་སྐད་ཤེས་ཀྱི་ཡོད་པས

I don't understand.
  ha ko ma song ཧ་གོ་མ་སོང་

I understand.
  ha ko song ཧ་གོ་སོང་

How much?
  ka tsö ray? ག་ཚོད་རེད

It's expensive.
  gong chenpo ray གོང་ཆེན་པོ་རེད

What's your name?
  kerang gi ming la karey zer gi yö?
  ཁྱེད་རང་གི་མིང་ལ་ག་རེ་ཟེར་གྱི་ཡོད

My name is ... – and yours?
  ngai ming-la ... sa, a- ni kerang-gi ming-la karey zer gi yö?
  ངའི་མིང་ལ ...་ས། ཨ་ནི། ཁྱེད་རང་གི་མིང་ལ་ག་རེ་ཟེར་གྱི་ཡོད

Is it OK to take a photo?
  par gyabna digiy-rebay?
  པར་བརྒྱབ་ན་འགྲིག་གི་རེད་པས

Where are you from?
  kerang lung-pa ka-ne yin?
  ཁྱེད་རང་ལུང་པ་ག་ནས་ཡིན

I'm from ...
  nga ... ne yin ང ...་ནས་ཡིན

Australia
  ausitaliya ཨོསི་ཏྲ་ལི་ཡ

Canada
  canada ཁེ་ན་ཏ

France
  farensi ཕ་རན་སི

Germany
jarman འཇར་མན་
New Zealand
shinshilen ནེ་ཏུ་ཛོ་ལཎཊ་
UK
injee lungpa དབྱིན་ཇི་ལུང་པ་
USA
amerika ཨ་མི་རི་ཀ་

Accommodation

Where is ...?
... kaba du? ... ག་པར་འདུག
a guesthouse/inn
dhön khang མགྲོན་ཁང་
a hotel
dru-khang འགྲུལ་ཁང་

Do you have a room?
kang mi yöpe?
ཁང་མིག་ཡོད་པས
How much is it for one night?
tsen chik la katsö ray?
མཚན་གཅིག་ལ་གཚོད་རེད
I'd like to stay with a Tibetan family.
nga phöbe mi-tsang nyamdo dendö yö
ང་བོད་པའི་མི་ཚང་མཉམ་དུ་བསྡད་འདོད་ཡོད
I need some hot water.
nga la chu tsapo go
ང་ལ་ཆུ་ཚ་པོ་དགོས
boiling water
chu körma
ཆུ་འཁོལ་མ

Getting Around

Where is the bus going?
mota diy kaba drugiy ray?
མོ་ཊ་འདི་ག་པར་འགྲོ་གི་རེད
Will it go to ...?
diy...-la drugiy rebay?
འདི་ ... ལ་འགྲོ་གི་རེད་པས
Is this bus going to (Ganden Monastery)?
mota di (ganden gompa) drugiy rebay?
མོ་ཊ་འདི་དགའ་ལྡན་དགོན་པ་ཚུ་ འགྲོ་གི་རེད་པས
I want to go to ...
nga ... la drondö yö
ང ... ལ་འགྲོ་འདོད་ཡོད
Can I get there on foot?
phagay gompa gyab-nay leb thub-kiy rebay?
ཕ་གིར་གོམ་པ་བརྒྱབ་ནས་སླེབས་ཐུབ་ཀྱི་རེད་པས

Signs – Tibetan

Danger
nyen-ka ཉེན་ཁ
Entrance
zu-sa འཛུལ་ས
Exit
donsa ཐོན་ས
Stop
kah kag ཁ་བཀག
Open
ko-chay སྒོ་ཕྱེ
Closed
ko-gyab སྒོ་བརྒྱབ
No Photographs
pa gyab michok པར་བརྒྱབ་མི་ཆོག
No Smoking
tama ten michok ཐ་མག་འཐེན་མི་ཆོག
Toilets
sang cho གསང་སྤྱོད

What time do we leave?
ngatso chutsö katsö la dro-gi yin?
ང་ཚོ་ཆུ་ཚོད་ག་ཚོད་ལ་འགྲོ་གྱི་ཡིན
What time do we arrive?
ngatso chutsö katsö la lep-gi ray?
ང་ཚོ་ཆུ་ཚོད་ག་ཚོད་ལ་སླེབ་ཀྱི་རེད
What time is the ... bus?
mota ... chutsö katsay-la drogiy ray?
མོ་ཊ་ ... ཆུ་ཚོད་གཚོད་ལ་འགྲོ་གི་རེད

next
jema-te རྗེས་མ་དེ་
first
tangpo-te དང་པོ་དེ་
last
thama-te མཐའ་མ་དེ་
airport
nam-tang གནམ་ཐང་
bus
basay/ འབབ་སེ་
mota/ མོ་ཊ་
lamkhor ཧྣངས་འཁོར་
bicycle
kanggari ཀང་སྒ་རིལ་

Where can I hire a bicycle?
kanggari kaba ragi ray?
ཀང་སྒ་རིལ་གཡར་ས་ག་པར་ཡོད་རེད

How much per day?
nyima chik-la gong katsö ray?
ཉིན་མ་གཅིག་ལ་གོང་ག་ཚོད་རེད།
Where is the ...?
... kaba yo ray?
... ག་པར་ཡོད་རེད།
I'm looking for ...
... ka-bah yö-may
... ག་བར་ཡོད་མེད་བལྟ་གི་ཡོད།

right
yeba གཡས་པ
left
yönba གཡོན་པ
straight ahead
shar gya ཤར་རྒྱག
north
chang བྱང་
south
lo ལྷོ་
east
shar ཤར་
west
nub ནུབ
porter
dopo khur khen དོ་པོ་ཁུར་མཁན
pack animals
kel semchen/ ཁལ་སེམས་ཅན་
kelma ཁལ་མ
yak
ya གཡག

Geographical Terms
road/trail
lam ལམ
mountain
ri རི་
cave
puk/trapoo བྲག་ཕུག
pass
la ལ
river
chu/tsangpo ཆུ་གཙང་པོ
valley
loong shon ལུང་གཤོང་
lake
tso མཚོ
hot spring
chu-tsen ཆུ་ཚན

Help!
rog nangda! རོགས་གནང་དང་།
Fire!
may bahgi! མེ་འབར་གྱིས།
Thief!
kuma du! རྐུ་མ་འདུག
I'm ill.
nga nagidu ང་ན་གི་འདུག
It's an emergency.
za dagpo ray! ཛ་དྲག་པོ་རེད།
Go away!
phah gyuk! ཕར་རྒྱུགས།
hospital
menkang སྨན་ཁང་
diarrhoea
troko shewa གྲོད་ཁོག་བཤལ་བ
fever
tsawa ཚ་བ

Call a doctor!
amchi kay tongda!
ཨེམ་ཆི་སྐད་གཏོང་དང་།
Call the police!
korsung-wa kay tongda!
སྐོར་སྲུང་བ་སྐད་གཏོང་དང་།
I'm lost.
nga lamga lasha
ང་ལམ་ཀ་བརྫུགས་ཤག
Where are the toilets?
sangchö kabah yöray?
གསང་སྤྱོད་ག་པར་ཡོད་རེད།

Time
What's the time?
chutsö katsö ray?
ཆུ་ཚོད་ག་ཚོད་རེད།
... hour ... minute
... chutsö ... karma
... ཆུ་ཚོད་ ...སྐར་མ

When?
kadü? ག་དུས
now
thanda ད་ལྟ
today
thiring དེ་རིང
tomorrow
sangnyi སང་ཉིན

yesterday
  kesa   ཁ་སང་
morning
  shogay   ཞོགས་ཀས་
afternoon
  nying gung gyab la   ཕྱི་དྲོ་ཉིན་གུང་རྒྱབ་ལ་
evening/night
  gonta   དགོང་དག་

Numbers

1	*chik*	གཅིག་
2	*nyi*	གཉིས་
3	*sum*	གསུམ་
4	*shi*	བཞི་
5	*nga*	ལྔ་
6	*dug*	དྲུག་
7	*dün*	བདུན་
8	*gye*	བརྒྱད་
9	*gu*	དགུ་
10	*chu*	བཅུ་
11	*chu chik*	བཅུ་གཅིག་
12	*chu nyi*	བཅུ་གཉིས་
13	*chok sum*	བཅུ་གསུམ་
14	*chub shi*	བཅུ་བཞི་
15	*chö nga*	བཅོ་ལྔ་
16	*chu dug*	བཅུ་དྲུག་
17	*chu dun*	བཅུ་བདུན་
18	*chö gye*	བཅོ་བརྒྱད་
19	*chu gu*	བཅུ་དགུ་
20	*nyi shu*	ཉི་ཤུ་ ཅུ་
21	*nyi shu tsa chik*	ཉི་ཤུ་རྩ་གཅིག་
30	*sum chu*	སུམ་བཅུ་ སོ་
40	*shib chu*	བཞི་བཅུ་ ཞེ་
50	*nga chu*	ལྔ་བཅུ་ ང་
60	*dug chu*	དྲུག་བཅུ་ རེ་
70	*dün chu*	བདུན་བཅུ་ དོན་
80	*gye chu*	བརྒྱད་བཅུ་ ཀྱ་
90	*gub chu*	དགུ་བཅུ་གོ་
100	*gya*	གཅིག་བརྒྱ་
200	*ngi gya*	ཉིས་བརྒྱ་
1000	*chik tong*	ཆིག་སྟོང་

one million
  saya-chig/   ས་ཡ་གཅིག་
  bum chu   འབུམ་བཅུ་

Chinese

Travellers going from China into Tibet or from Tibet onwards into China are well advised to pick up a Chinese phrasebook such as Lonely Planet's *Mandarin Chinese phrasebook*. It should help you through most of your travel needs, in both Tibet and China.

Pinyin

The standard form of Romanisation for Mandarin adopted by China is known as pinyin. It means literally 'spell the sounds', and once you get used to the idiosyncracies of its spellings it is a very accurate way of representing the sounds of Mandarin. The pronunciation of pinyin spellings are by no means obvious to speakers of European languages, however, and need to be memorised. There's no way of knowing, for example, that a pinyin **x** is pronounced like an English 's' or that **zh** is pronounced like a 'j'

Pronunciation

The dialects of China are tonal, which means that variations in vocal pitch within words are used to determine their meaning. When learning Mandarin Chinese, the standard example given to demonstrate the principle of its four tones is *ma*, which variously means 'mother', 'hemp' (yeah, as in 'dope'), 'horse' or 'scold' (see the boxed text 'Tones – Mandarin Chinese' below).

To use a Mandarin phrasebook effectively, you need to internalise the pronunciation of pinyin. The best way, naturally, is to learn pinyin with a native speaker or with a tape. Failing this, the following guidelines should help get you started.

Vowels Pronunciation of Mandarin vowels can be fairly tricky for English speakers. In some instances they change depending on

---

Tones – Mandarin Chinese

high tone: *mā*, 'mother'
rising tone: *má*, 'hemp' or 'numb'
falling-rising tone: *mǎ*, 'horse'
falling tone: *mà*, 'scold' or 'swear'

the consonant that precedes them, and in other cases they are sounds that are not used in English.

The following vowel sounds follow standard British pronunciation.

a	as in 'father'
ai	as the 'y' in 'fly'
ao	as the 'ow' in 'cow'
e	as the 'ur' in 'blur'
ei	as the 'ay' in 'way'
i	as the 'ee' in 'meet' when preceded by **j**, **q**, **x** or **y**
i	as the 'e' in 'her' when preceded by other consonants
ian	as in 'yen'
iao	as in the exclamation 'yow!'
ie	as the 'ere' in 'here'
o	as in 'or'
ou	as the 'oa' in 'boat'
u	as in 'flute' after **j**, **q**, **x** or **y**
u	as the 'oo' in 'woo' when preceded by other consonants
ü	as in German or as the 'u' in 'flute'
ui	as in 'way'
uo	as in 'war'

Consonants Don't assume that consonants are pronounced as they are in English or in other European languages. One point worth noting briefly is that some consonants have the same pronunciation. This is not a redundancy. While **q** and **c**, for example, have the same pronunciation, the value of the following vowel changes depending on which is used. Thus **ci** is pronounced 'tser', while **qi** is pronounced 'tsee'. There are three such pairs of consonants: **c** and **q**, **j** and **z**, and **s** and **x**.

c	as the 'ts' in 'bits'
ch	as the 'ch' in 'church'
j	as the 'ds' in 'suds'
h	as the guttural 'ch' in Scottish *loch*
q	as the 'ts' in 'bits'
r	somewhere between an English 'r' and the 's' in 'pleasure'
s	as in 'sock'
sh	as in 'shack'
x	as the 's' in 'sock'
z	as the 'ds' in 'suds'
zh	as the 'j' in 'judge'

Greetings & Civilities

Hello.
  nǐ hǎo　　　　你好
Goodbye.
  zàijiàn　　　　再见
Thank you.
  xièxie　　　　谢ゼ谢谢
You're welcome.
  búkèqi　　　　不客气
I'm sorry.
  duìbùqǐ　　　　对不起

Small Talk

No. (don't have)
  méi yǒu　　　　没有
No. (not so)
  búshì　　　　不是
It doesn't matter.
  méishì　　　　没事
I want ...
  wǒ yào ...　　　　我要...
No, I don't want it.
  búyào　　　　不要

Language Difficulties

I understand.
  wǒ tīngdedǒng　　　　我听得懂
I don't understand.
  wǒ tīngbudǒng　　　　我听不懂
Do you understand?
  dǒng ma?　　　　懂吗?
Could you speak more slowly please?
  qīng nǐ shuō màn　　　　请你说慢
  yīdiǎn, hǎo ma?　　　　一点，好n吗彝?

Toilets

Men/Women　　　　男/女
toilet (restroom)
  cèsuǒ　　　　厕所
toilet paper
  wèishēng zhǐ　　　　卫生纸
bathroom (washroom)
  xǐshǒu jiān　　　　洗手间

Visas & Documents

passport
  hùzhào　　　　护照
visa
  qiānzhèng　　　　签证
visa extension
  yáncháng qiānzhèng　　　　延长签证

Public Security Bureau
gōng'ān jú 公接安局
Foreign Affairs Branch
wài shì kē 外蝬事科

Money

How much is it?
dūoshăo qián? 多少钱?
Is there anything cheaper?
yŏu piányi yìdiăn de ma? 有便宜一点的吗?
That's too expensive.
tài guìle 太贵了
Bank of China
zhōngguó yínháng 中国银行
change money
huàn qián 换钱

Getting Around

I want to go to ...
wŏ yào qù ... 我潠要去 ...
I want to get off.
wŏ yào xiàchē 我要下车
What time does it depart/arrive?
jĭdiăn kāi/dào? 几点开/到?
How long does the trip take?
zhècì lŭxíng yào huā duōcháng shíjiān? 这次旅行要花多长时间?
buy a ticket
măi piào 买票
one ticket
yìzhāng piào 一张票
two tickets
liăngzhāng piào 两张票
microbus taxi
miànbāo chē, miàndī 面包车, 面的
airport
fēijīchăng 飞机场
Civil Aviation Authority of China (CAAC) office
zhōngguó mínháng 中国民航
shòupiào chù 售票处
one-way ticket
dānchéng piào 单程票
return ticket
láihuí piào 来回票
bus
gōnggòng qìchē 公共汽车

When is the first bus?
tóubān qìchē jĭdiăn kāi? 头班汽车几点开?
When is the last bus?
mòbān qìchē jĭdiăn kāi? 末班汽车几点开?
When is the next bus?
xià yìbān qìchē jĭdiăn kāi? 下一班汽车几点开?

bicycle
zìxíngchē 自行车
I want to hire a bicycle.
wŏ yào zū yíliàng zìxíngchē 我要租一辆自行车
How much is it per day?
yìtiăn duōshăo qián? 一天多少钱?
How much is it per hour?
yíge xiăo shí duōshăo qián? 一个小时多少钱?

Directions

Where is the ...?
... zài năli? ... 在哪里?
I'm lost.
wŏ mílùle 我迷路了
Turn right.
yòu zhuăn 右转
Turn left.
zuŏ zhuăn 左转
Go straight ahead.
yìzhí zŏu 一直走
Turn around.
wàng huí zŏu 往回走
map
dìtú 地图

Accommodation

hotel
lŭguăn 旅馆
hostel
zhāodàisuŏ/lŭshè 招待所/旅社
tourist hotel
bīnguăn/fàndiàn/jiŭdiàn 宾馆/饭店/酒店
dormitory
duōrénfáng 多人房
single room
dānrénfáng 单人房

twin room
  shuāngrénfáng　双人房
bed
  chuángwèi　床位

Time

What's the time?
  jǐ diǎn?　几迪点点？
... hour ... minute
  ... diǎn ... fēn　... 点 ... 分
3.05
  sān diǎn wǔ fēn　3点5分
now
  xiànzài　现在
today
  jīntiān　今天
tomorrow
  míngtiān　明天
yesterday
  zuótiān　昨天
Wait a moment.
  děng yī xià　等一下

Health

hospital
  yīyuàn　医院
pharmacy
  yàodiàn　药店
diarrhoea
  lādùzi　拉肚子
fever
  fāshāo　发烧
flu
  liúgǎn　流感
giardia
  āmībā fùxiè　阿米巴腹泻
hepatitis
  gānyàn　肝炎
rabies
  kuángquǎnbìng　狂犬病
tetanus
  pòshāngfēng　破伤风
anti-diarrhoea
medicine
  zhǐxièyào　止泻药
aspirin
  āsīpīlín　阿斯匹林
antibiotics
  kàngjūnsù　抗菌素
condom
  bìyùn tào　避孕套

Emergencies – Chinese	
Help!	
jiùmìng a!	救命啊
Fire!	
huǒ zāi!	火灾
Thief!	
xiǎo tōu!	小偷
I'm ill.	
wǒ shēng bìng	我生病
emergency	
jǐnjí qíngkuàng	紧急情况
police	
jǐngchá	警察
foreign affairs police	
wàishì jǐngchá	外事警察

tampon
  wèishēng mián tiáo　卫生棉条
sanitary napkin (Kotex)
  wèishēng mián　卫生棉
sunscreen (UV) lotion
  fáng shài yóu　防晒油
mosquito coils
  wénxiāng　蚊香

Numbers

0	*líng*	零
1	*yī, yāo*	一, 幺
2	*èr, liǎng*	二, 两
3	*sān*	三
4	*sì*	四
5	*wǔ*	五
6	*liù*	六
7	*qī*	七
8	*bā*	八
9	*jiǔ*	九
10	*shí*	十
11	*shíyī*	十一
12	*shí'èr*	十二
20	*èrshí*	二十
21	*èrshíyī*	二十一
100	*yìbǎi*	一百
200	*liǎngbǎi*	两百
1000	*yìqiān*	一千
2000	*liǎngqiān*	两千
10,000	*yíwàn*	一万
20,000	*liǎngwàn*	两万
100,000	*shíwàn*	十万
200,000	*èrshíwàn*	二十万

LANGUAGE

Food & Drinks

I don't want MSG.
wǒ bú yào wèijīng 我不要味精
I'm vegetarian.
wǒ chī sù 我吃素
not too spicy
bú yào tài là 不要太辣
(cooked) together
yíkuàir 一块儿
steamed white rice
mǐfàn 米饭
steamed meat buns
bāozi 包子
boiled dumplings
jiǎozi 饺子
fried rice with vegetables
shūcài chǎofàn 蔬菜炒饭
fried rice with beef
niúròusī chǎofàn 牛肉丝炒饭
fried rice with egg
jīdàn chǎofàn 鸡蛋炒饭
fried noodles with vegetables
shūcài chǎomiàn 蔬菜炒面
beef noodles in a soup
niúròu miàn 牛肉面
spicy chicken with peanuts
gōngbào jīdīng 宫爆鸡丁
sweet and sour pork fillets
tángcù lǐjī/ 糖醋里脊
double-cooked fatty pork
huíguō ròu 回數锅肉
'wooden ear' mushrooms and pork
mùěr ròu 木耳肉
'fish-resembling' eggplant
yúxiāng qiézi 鱼香茄子
red-cooked eggplant
hóngshāo qiézi 红烧茄子
fried green beans
chǎo biǎndòu 炒扁豆
fried vegetables
sùchǎo sùcài 素炒素菜
egg and tomato
fānqié chǎodàn 番茄炒蛋
spicy tofu
málà dòufu 麻辣豆腐
egg soup
dànhuā tāng 蛋花汤
wonton soup
húndùn tāng 馄饨汤

Muslim noodles
lāmiàn 拉面

Muslim noodles and beef
gànbàn miàn 干拌面
noodles, tofu and vegetables in soup
dàlǔmiàn 大卤面
fried noodle squares
chǎopàozhàng 炒疙炮涨

beer
píjiǔ 啤酒
milk
niúnǎi 牛奶
mineral water
kuàng quán shu 矿泉水
boiled water
kāi shuǐ 开水
tea
chá 茶
Muslim tea
(in Muslim restaurants)
bābǎo wǎnzi 八宝琬子
hot
rède 热的
ice cold
bīngde 冰的

Gazetteer

Ali
ཨ་མདོ 狮泉
Chamdo
ཆབ་མདོ 昌都
Chongye
འཕྱོངས་རྒྱས 阴结
Chusul
ཆུ་ཤུལ 曲水
Damxung
འདམ་གཞུང 当雄
Drepung Monastery
འབྲས་སྤུང 哲蚌寺
Drigung
འབྲི་གུང
Everest, Mt (Qomolangma)
ཇོ་མོ་གླང་རི 珠峰
Ganden Monastery
དགའ་ལྡན 甘丹寺
Gegye
དགེ་རྒྱས 革吉
Gertse
སྒེར་རྩེ 改则

Golmud		格尔木
Gongkar	གོང་དཀར་	贡嘎
Gongkar airport		贡嘎机场
Gyantse	རྒྱལ་རྩེ་	江孜
Gyatsa		加查
Hor Qu		霍尔区
Jokhang, the	ཇོ་ཁང་	大昭寺
Kailash, Mt		神山
Kangding		康定
Kashgar		喀什
Lhasa	ལྷ་ས་	拉萨
Lhatse	ལྷ་རྩེ་	拉孜
Lhundrub	ལྷུན་གྲུབ་	林周
Litang	ལི་ཐང་	理塘
Manasarovar, Lake	མཚོ་མ་ཕམ་	圣湖（马旁雍错）
Markam	རྨར་ཁམས་	芒康
Medro Gungkar	བསམ་ཡིད་དགོན་པ་	墨竹工卡
Mindroling Monastery	སྨིན་གྲོལ་གླིང་དགོན་པ་	敏珠林寺
Nam-tso	གནམ་མཚོ་	纳木错
Nangartse		浪卡子
Naqu	ནག་ཆུ་	那曲
Norbulingka, the	ནོར་བུ་གླིང་ཁ་	罗布林卡
Nyalam	གཉའ་ལམ་	聂拉木
Nyingchi		林芝
Paryang		帕羊
Pongba		雄巴
Potala, the	པོ་ཏ་ལ་	布达拉宫
Purang	སྤུ་ཧྲེང་	普兰
Rongphu Monastery		绒布寺
Sakya	ས་སྐྱ་	萨迦
Samding Monastery	བསམ་སྡིང་དགོན་པ་	桑顶寺
Samye Monastery	བསམ་ཡིད་དགོན་པ་	桑耶寺
Sangsang		桑桑
Sera Monastery	སེར་ར་དགོན་པ་	色拉寺
Shegar	ཤེལ་དཀར་	新定日
Shigatse	གཞིས་ཀ་རྩེ་	日喀则
Tingri	དིང་རི་	定日
Trandruk Monastery		昌珠寺
Tsang	གཙང་	
Tsaparang	རྩ་ཧྲེང་	札达
Tsetang	རྩེ་ཐང་	泽当
Tsochen	མཚོ་ཆེན་	措勤
Tsomei	མཚོ་སྨད་	指美
Tsona	མཚོ་སྣ་	错那
Tsurphu Monastery	མཚུར་ཕུ་དགོན་པ་	
Ü	དབུས་	
Yamdrok-tso	ཡར་འབྲོག་མཚོ་	羊卓雍错
Yatung	ཡར་དུང་	亚东
Yumbulagang	ཡུམ་བུ་བླ་སྒང་	雍布拉康
Zhangmu	ཞམ་མོ་	樟木
Zhongba		仲巴

Glossary

For ease of reference, this glossary is divided into two sections. The first section, Who's Who, provides succinct descriptions of some of the deities, historical figures and other people mentioned in this book. The second section covers general terms used.

Who's Who

Many of the terms in this section are of Sanskrit origin. Entries in parentheses indicate the Sanskrit equivalent of each Tibetan term. (An exception is Sakyamuni (Sakya Thukpa), in which case the Sanskrit 'Sakyamuni' is commonly used in Tibet.) For more information on who's who in Tibet, see the special section 'Important Figures of Tibetan Buddhism' earlier in this book.

Akshobhya – see *Mikyöba*
Amitabha – see *Öpagme*
Amitayus – see *Tsepame*
Atisha (Jowo-je) – Buddhist scholar from contemporary Bengal. His arrival in Tibet at the invitation of the king of Guge, in western Tibet, was a catalyst in the 11th-century revival of Buddhism on the high plateau.
Avalokiteshvara – see *Chenresig*

Bhrikuti – the Nepali consort of King Songtsen Gampo, an early Tibetan king

Chana Dorje (Vajrapani) – the wrathful Bodhisattva of Energy whose name means 'thunderbolt in hand'
Chenresig (Avalokiteshvara) – an embodiment of compassionate bodhisattvahood and the patron saint of Tibet. The *Dalai Lamas* are considered to be manifestations of this deity.
Chögyel (Dharmaraja) – *Gelugpa* protector deity, blue and with the head of a bull
Chökyong (Lokpalas) – the Four Guardian Kings
Citipati – dancing skeletons, often seen in protector chapels

Dalai Lamas – The 14 (so far) manifestations of *Chenresig* (Avalokiteshvara), who, as spiritual heads of the *Gelugpa* order, ruled over Tibet from 1642 until 1959. The honorific title means 'ocean of wisdom' and was bestowed by the Mongolian Altyn Khan. The present (14th) Dalai Lama resides in Dharamsala, India.
Dorje Chang (Vajradhara) – one of the five Dhyani *buddhas*, recognisable by his crossed arms holding a bell and thunderbolt
Dorje Jigje (Yamantaka) – a meditational deity who comes in various aspects. The Red and Black aspects are probably the most common.
Dorje Lekpa – Dzogchen deity, recognisable by his green round hat
Drölma (Tara) – a female meditational deity who is a manifestation of the enlightened mind of all *buddhas*. She is sometimes referred to as the mother of all *buddhas*, and has many aspects, but is most often seen as Green Tara or as Drölkar (White Tara).
Dromtönpa – 11th-century disciple of *Atisha* (Jowo-je) who founded the *Kadampa* order and Reting Monastery

Ekajati (Tsechigma) – deity with one eye, one tooth and one breast, associated with the *Dzogchen* movement

Gesar – a legendary king and the name of an epic concerning his fabulous exploits. The king's empire is known as Ling, and thus the stories, usually sung and told by professional bards, are also known as the *Stories of Ling*.
Guru Rinpoche – credited with having suppressed demons and other malevolent forces in order to introduce Buddhism into Tibet during the 8th century. In the *Nyingmapa* order he is revered as the Second Buddha.

Hayagriva – see *Tamdrin*

Jamchen Chöde – disciple of *Tsongkhapa* and founder of Sera Monastery; also known as Sakya Yeshe

Jampa (Maitreya) – the Buddha of Loving Kindness; also the Future Buddha, the fifth of the 1000 *buddhas* who will descend to earth (*Sakyamuni* or Sakya Thukpa was the fourth)
Jampelyang (Manjushri) – the Bodhisattva of Insight. He is usually depicted holding a sword, which symbolises discriminative awareness, in one hand, and a book, which symbolises his mastery of all knowledge, in the other.
Jamyang Chöje – founder of Drepung Monastery
Je Rinpoche – an honorific title used for *Tsongkhapa*, founder of the *Gelugpa* order
Jowo-je – see *Atisha*
Jowo Sakyamuni – the most revered image of *Sakyamuni* (Sakya Thukpa) in Tibet. It depicts the Historical Buddha at the age of 12 and is kept in the Jokhang in Lhasa.

Karmapa – a lineage of spiritual leaders of the *Karma Kagyupa*. They are also known as the Black Hats, and there have been 17 so far.
Khadroma (Dakini) – literally 'sky dancer'; a fierce, lower-ranking *Tantric* goddess, often depicted as red

Langdharma – the 9th-century Tibetan king accused of having persecuted Buddhism

Maitreya – see *Jampa*
Manjushri – see *Jampelyang*
Marpa – an ascetic of the 11th century whose disciple, *Milarepa*, founded the *Kagyupa* order
Mikyöba (Akshobhya) – the Buddha of the State of Perfected Consciousness, or Perfect Cognition; literally 'unchanging', 'the 'immutable one'
Milarepa – 11th-century disciple of *Marpa* and founder of the *Kagyupa* order; renowned for his songs

Namri Songtsen – 6th-century Tibetan king, father of *Songtsen Gampo*
Namse (Vairocana) – Buddha of Enlightened Consciousness
Namtöse (Vaishravana) – the Guardian of the North, one of the Lokpalas or Four Guardian Kings

Nechung – protector deity of Tibet and the *Dalai Lamas*. Nechung is manifested in the State Oracle, who is traditionally installed at Nechung Monastery, near Drepung, Lhasa.
Nyentri Tsenpo – legendary first king of Tibet

Öpagme (Amitabha) – the Buddha of Perfected Perception; literally 'boundless light'

Palden Lhamo (Shri Devi) – special protector of Lhasa, the *Dalai Lama* and the *Gelugpa* order; the female counterpart of Nagpo Chenpo (Mahakala)
Panchen Lama – literally 'guru and great teacher'. The Panchen Lama lineage is associated with Tashilhunpo Monastery, Shigatse, and goes back to the 17th century. The Panchen Lama is a manifestation of *Öpagme* (Amitabha).
Pehar – oracle and protector of the Buddhist state, depicted with six arms, wearing a round hat and riding a snow lion

Rahulla – Dzogchen deity with nine heads, eyes all over his body, a mouth in his belly and the lower half of a serpent (coiled on the dead body of ego)
Ralpachen – 9th-century king whose assassination marked the end of the Yarlung Valley dynasty

Sakya Pandita – literally the 'scholar from Sakya'; former abbot of Sakya Monastery who established the priest-patron system with the Mongols; also known as Kunga Gyaltsen
Sakyamuni – literally the 'sage of Sakya'; the founder of Buddhism, the Historical Buddha; known in Tibetan as Sakya Thukpa. See also *Siddhartha Gautama* and *buddha*.
Samvara – a wrathful manifestation of *Sakyamuni* (Sakya Thukpa)
Shantarakshita – Indian scholar of the 8th century and first abbot of Samye Monastery
Shenrab – mythical founder of the *Bön* faith
Shiromo – *Bönpo* name for *Sakyamuni* (Sakya Thukpa)
Shri Devi – see *Palden Lhamo*

Siddhartha Gautama – the personal name of the Historical Buddha; see also *Sakyamuni* (Sakya Thukpa)

Songtsen Gampo – the 7th-century king associated with the introduction of Buddhism to Tibet

Tamdrin (Hayagriva) – literally 'horse necked'; a wrathful meditational deity and manifestation of *Avalokiteshvara*, usually associated with the *Nyingmapa* order

Tara – see *Drölma*

Tenzin Gyatso – the 14th and current *Dalai Lama*

Terdak Lingpa – founder of Mindroling Monastery

Trisong Detsen – 8th-century Tibetan king; founder of Samye Monastery

Tsepame (Amitayus) – a meditational deity associated with longevity; literally 'limitless life'. Tsepame is often featured in a trinity with *Drölma* (Tara) and Vijaya.

Tseringma – protector goddess of Mt Everest, depicted riding a snow lion

Tsongkhapa – 14th-century founder of the *Gelugpa* order and Ganden Monastery

Vairocana – see *Namse*
Vaishravana – see *Namtöse*
Vajradhara – see *Dorje Chang*
Vajrapani – see *Chana Dorje*

Wencheng – Chinese consort of King *Songtsen Gampo*

Yama – Lord of Death, who resides in *sky burial* sites

Yamantaka – see *Dorje Jigje*

Yeshe Tsogyel – female consort of *Guru Rinpoche* and one-time wife of King *Trisong Detsen*

General Terms

Ambans – Chinese representatives of the Manchu Qing dynasty posted in Lhasa from the early 19th century until the Chinese republican overthrow of the Qing in 1911

Amdo – a traditional province of Tibet, now Qinghai province

AMS – acute mountain sickness; often referred to as altitude sickness

ani – Tibetan for 'nun', as in 'ani gompa' (nunnery)

arhat – literally 'worthy one'. The arhat is neither a *buddha* nor a *bodhisattva*, but one who has become free of the *Wheel of Life* and is free of hatred and all delusions.

Bardo – as detailed in *The Tibetan Book of the Dead*, this term refers to the intermediate stages between death and rebirth.

Barkhor – an intermediate circumambulation circuit, or *kora*, but most often specifically the intermediate circuit around the *Jokhang* temple of Lhasa

binguan – Chinese term for guesthouse or hotel

Black Hat – strictly speaking, this refers to the black hat embellished with gold that was presented to the second *Karmapa* of the *Karma Kagyupa* order of Tsurphu Monastery by a Mongol prince, and worn ceremoniously by all subsequent incarnations of the Karmapa. By extension the black hat represents the Karma Kagyupa order.

Bö – Tibetans' name for their own land, sometimes written 'Bod' or 'Po'

Bodhgaya – the place in contemporary Bihar, India, where *Sakyamuni* (Sakya Thukpa), the Historical Buddha, attained enlightenment

bodhisattva – literally 'enlightenment hero'. The bodhisattva voluntarily does not take the step to *nirvana*, being motivated to stay within the *Wheel of Life* by compassion for all sentient beings.

Bön – the indigenous religion of Tibet and the Himalayan borderlands. In its ancient form its main components were royal burial rites, the cult of indigenous deities and magical practices. In the 11th century, Bön was systemised along Buddhist lines and it is this form that survives today.

Bönpo – a practitioner of *Bön*

buddha – literally 'awakened one', a being who through spiritual training has broken free of all illusion and karmic consequences and is 'enlightened'; most often specifically the Historical Buddha, *Sakyamuni* (Sakya Thukpa)

Büton – suborder of Tibetan Buddhism based on the teachings of Büton Rinchen Drup, the 14th-century compiler of the major Buddhist texts; associated with Shalu Monastery, near Shigatse

CAAC – Civil Aviation Authority of China
cairn – a mound of stones erected as a marker
chakje – handprint
chaktsal – Tibetan for the ritual of prostration
chaktsal gang – prostration point
cham – a ritual dance carried out by monks and *lamas*, usually at festivals. All participants except the central *lama* are masked.
chang – Tibetan barley beer
Changtang – vast plains of northern Tibet extending into Xinjiang and Qinghai; the largest and highest plateau in the world
chö – see *dharma*
chömay – butter lamp
chörten – Tibetan for 'stupa'; usually used as reliquary for the cremated remains of important *lamas*
chu – river, stream, brook etc
chuba – long-sleeved sheepskin cloak
CITS – China International Travel Service
CTS – China Travel Service

darchok – string of prayer flags
dharma – 'chö' in Tibetan, and sometimes translated as 'law', this very broad term covers the truths expounded by *Sakyamuni* (Sakya Thukpa), the Buddhist teachings, the Buddhist path, and the Buddhist goal of *nirvana*. In effect it is the 'law' that must be understood, followed and achieved in order for one to be a Buddhist.
dorje – literally 'diamond' or 'thunderbolt'; a metaphor for the indestructible, indivisible nature of buddhahood; also a *Tantric* hand-held sceptre symbolising 'skilful means'
drokpa – Tibetan for 'nomad'
dukhang – Tibetan for 'assembly hall'
dukkha – *Sanskrit* for 'suffering', the essential condition of all life
dürtro – sky-burial site; see also *sky burial*
dzo – domesticated cross between a bull and a female yak

Dzogchen – the Great Perfection teachings associated with the *Nyingmapa* order
dzong – fort

Eightfold Path – one of the *Four Noble Truths* taught by *Sakyamuni* (Sakya Thukpa); the path that must be taken to achieve enlightenment and liberation from the *Wheel of Life*

FIT office – Family (or Foreign) and Independent Traveller office
Four Noble Truths – as stated in the first speech given by *Sakyamuni* (Sakya Thukpa) after he achieved enlightenment, the Four Noble Truths are the truth that all life is suffering; the truth that suffering originates in desire; the truth that desire may be extinguished; and the truth that there is a path to this end.

Ganden – the *pure land* of *Jampa* (Maitreya), and the seat of the *Gelugpa* order; 'Tushita' in *Sanskrit*
Garuda – mythological bird associated with Hinduism. In Tibetan *Tantric* Buddhism it is seen as a wrathful force that transforms malevolent influences.
gau – an amulet or 'portable shrine' worn around the neck, containing the image of an important spiritual figure, usually the *Dalai Lama*
Gelugpa – major order of Tibetan Buddhism, associated with the *Dalai Lamas*, the *Panchen Lamas* and Drepung, Sera, Ganden and Tashilhunpo Monasteries. The order was founded by *Tsongkhapa* in the 14th century, and is sometimes known as the Yellow Hats.
geshe – title awarded on completion of the highest level of study (something like a doctorate) that monks may undertake after completing their full indoctrinal vows; usually associated with the *Gelugpa* order
gompa – Tibetan for 'monastery'
gönkhang – protector chapel
Guge – a 9th-century kingdom of western Tibet
guru – *Sanskrit* term for 'spiritual teacher', literally 'heavy'. The Tibetan equivalent is *lama*.

Hinayana – also called Theravada, this is a major school of Buddhism. It follows the original teachings of the Historical Buddha, *Sakyamuni* (Sakya Thukpa), and places less importance on the compassionate *bodhisattva* ideal and more on individual enlightenment. See also *Mahayana*.

Jokhang – situated in Lhasa, this is the most sacred and one of the most ancient of Tibet's temples. It is also known as the *Tsuglhakhang*.

Kadampa – order of Tibetan Buddhism based on the teachings of the Indian scholar *Atisha* (Jowo-je). The school was a major influence on the *Gelugpa* order.

Kagyupa – order of Tibetan Buddhism that traces its lineage back through *Milarepa* and *Marpa* and eventually to the Indian *mahasiddhas*. It is divided into numerous suborders, the most famous of which is the *Karma Kagyupa*, or the *Karmapa*.

kangtsang – monastic residential quarters

Kangyur – the Tibetan Buddhist canon. The complement of the Kangyur is the *Tengyur*.

karma – action and its consequences, the psychic 'imprint' that action leaves on the mind and that continues into further rebirths. The term is found in both Hinduism and Buddhism, and may be likened to the law of cause and effect.

Karma Kagyupa – suborder of the *Kagyupa* order, established by Gampopa and Dusum Khyenpa in the 12th century

Kashag – Tibetan for the cabinet of the *Gelugpa* lamaist government

kathak – prayer scarf; used as a ritual offering or as a gift

Kham – traditional eastern Tibetan province; much of it is now part of western Sichuan and north-western Yunnan

Khampa – a person from *Kham*

khenpo – Tibetan term for 'abbot'

kora – ritual circumambulation circuit; pilgrimage circuit

kumbum – literally '100,000 images', this is a *chörten* that contains statuary and paintings. The most famous in Tibet is the Gyantse Kumbum in *Tsang*.

la – Tibetan for 'mountain pass'

lama – literally 'unsurpassed', Tibetan equivalent of *guru*; a title bestowed on monks of particularly high spiritual attainment.

lamaism – term used by early Western writers on the subject of Tibet to describe Tibetan Buddhism; also used by the Chinese in the term 'lamajiao', literally 'lama religion'

lamrim – the stages on the path to enlightenment; a graduated approach to enlightenment as expounded by *Tsongkhapa*. Lamrim is associated with the *Gelugpa* order.

lapse – see *cairn*

lha – Tibetan term for 'life spirit'. It may also be present in inanimate objects such as lakes, mountains and trees.

lhakhang – Tibetan term for 'chapel'

ling – Tibetan term usually associated with lesser, outlying temples

lingkhor – an outer pilgrimage circuit; famously, the outer pilgrimage of Lhasa

Losar – Tibetan New Year

lu – 'road' in Chinese; see also *naga*

lungta – prayer flag

mahasiddha – literally 'of great spiritual accomplishment'. A mahasiddha is a *Tantric* practitioner who has reached a high level of awareness; there are 84 famous mahasiddhas. The Tibetan term is 'drubchen'.

Mahayana – the other major school of Buddhism along with *Hinayana*. Mahayana emphasises compassion and the altruism of the *bodhisattva* who remains on the *Wheel of Life* for the sake of all sentient beings.

mandala – a circular representation of the three-dimensional world of a meditational deity; used as a meditational device. The Tibetan term is 'kyilkhor'.

mani – prayer

mani lhakhang – small chapel housing a single large prayer wheel

mani stone – a stone with the mantra *'om mani padme hum'* ('hail to the jewel in the lotus') carved on it

mani wall – a wall made with *mani stones*

mantra – literally 'protection of the mind'. This is one of the *Tantric* devices used to achieve identity with a meditational deity and break through the world of illusion; a series of syllables recited as the pure sound made by an enlightened being.

mara – literally 'evil influences'. Mara stands between us and enlightenment.

meditational deity – a deified manifestation of the enlightened mind with which, according to *Tantric* ritual, the adept seeks union and thus experience of enlightenment

momo – Tibetan dumpling

Mönlam – a major Lhasa festival established by *Tsongkhapa*

Mt Meru – the sacred mountain at the centre of the universe; also known as Sumeru

naga – water spirits that may take the form of serpents or semi-humans. The latter can be seen in images of the naga kings. The Tibetan term is 'lu'.

nangkhor – inner circumambulation circuit, usually within the interior of a temple or monastic assembly hall, and taking in various chapels en route

Newari – the people of the Nepali Buddhist kingdoms in the Kathmandu Valley

Ngari – ancient name for the province of western Tibet; later incorporated into *Ütsang*

nirvana – literally 'beyond sorrow'. Nirvana is an end to desire and suffering, and an end to the cycle of rebirth.

Norbulingka – the summer palace of the *Dalai Lamas* in Lhasa

Nyingmapa – the earliest order of Tibetan Buddhism, based largely on the Buddhism brought to Tibet by *Guru Rinpoche*

'om mani padme hum' – this mantra means 'hail to the jewel in the lotus' and is associated with *Chenresig* (Avalokiteshvara), patron deity of Tibet.

oracle – in Tibetan Buddhism an oracle serves as a medium for protective deities, as in the State Oracle of Nechung Monastery near Drepung, Lhasa. The State Oracle was consulted on all important matters of state.

Pandita – a title conferred on great scholars of Buddhism, as in the Sakya Pandita

parikrama – the Hindu equivalent of a *kora*

PLA – People's Liberation Army (Chinese army)

PRC – People's Republic of China

protector deities – deities who can manifest themselves in either male or female forms and serve to protect Buddhist teachings and followers. They may be either wrathful aspects of enlightened beings or worldly powers who have been tamed by *Tantric* masters.

PSB – Public Security Bureau. The Chinese term is 'gonganju'.

puk – Tibetan for 'cave'

pure lands – otherworldly realms that are the domains of *buddhas*. They are realms completely free of suffering, and in the popular Buddhist imagination are probably something like the Christian heaven.

Qiang – proto-Tibetan tribes that troubled the borders of the Chinese empire

Qomolangma – Tibetan name for Mt Everest as transliterated by the Chinese; also spelt 'Chomolangma'

Qu – Chinese term for an administrative district, as in Shannan Qu (around Tsetang)

ranjung – self-manifesting or self-arising. For example, a rock spire could be a ranjung *chörten*.

rebirth – a condition of the *Wheel of Life*; all beings experience limitless rebirths until they achieve enlightenment.

regent – a representative of an incarnate *lama* who presides over a monastic community during the *lama's* minority. Regents came to play an important political role in the *Gelugpa* lamaist government.

ri – Tibetan for 'mountain'

Rigsum Gonpo – trinity of *bodhisattvas* consisting of *Chenresig* (Avalokiteshvara), *Jampelyang* (Manjushri) and *Chana Dorje* (Vajrapani)

Rinpoche – literally 'high in esteem', a title bestowed on highly revered *lamas*. Such *lamas* are usually incarnate but need not be.

ritrö – hermitage

RMB – acronym for Renminbi or 'people's money', the currency of China

rogyapas – the 'body-breakers' who prepare bodies for *sky burial*

sadhu – an Indian ascetic who has renounced all attachments

364 Glossary

Saga Dawa – festival held at the full moon of the fourth lunar month to celebrate the enlightenment of *Sakyamuni* (Sakya Thukpa)
Sakyapa – Tibetan Buddhist order associated with Sakya Monastery and founded in the 11th century; also known as the Red Hats
samsara – the cycle of birth, death and *rebirth*
Samye – the first Buddhist monastery in Tibet, founded by King *Trisong Detsen* in the 8th century
sang – incense
Sangha – community of Buddhist monks or nuns
sangkang – pot-bellied incense burners
Sanskrit – ancient language of India, with a complex grammar and rich vocabulary; a classical mode of expression with the status that Latin had in earlier Western society
self-arising – thought to have been created naturally by itself (ie, not by humans); often applied to rock carvings. See also *ranjung*.
shabje – footprint
Shambhala – the mythical great northern paradise, near the Kunlun mountains. The modern era consists of 32 kings of Shambhala. We are in the reign of the 29th king at present. There will be a terrible war in the reign of the 32nd king, followed by a great period of peace and enlightenment.
Shangshung – ancient kingdom of western Tibet and place of origin of the *Bön* faith
shedra – Buddhist college
sky burial – Tibetan funerary practice of chopping up the corpses of the dead in designated high places *(dürtro)* and leaving them for the birds
stupa – see *chörten*
sutra – Buddhist scriptures that record the teachings of the Historical Buddha, *Sakyamuni* (Sakya Thukpa)

Tantra – scriptures and oral lineages associated with *Tantric* Buddhism
Tantric – of Tantric Buddhism, a movement combining mysticism with Buddhist scripture
TAR – Tibetan Autonomous Region
Tengyur – a Tibetan Buddhist canonical text that collects together commentaries on the teachings of *Sakyamuni* (Sakya Thukpa)

terma – 'discovered' or 'revealed' teachings; teachings that have been hidden until the world is ready to receive them
terton – discoverer of *terma*
thamzing – 'struggle sessions', a misconceived Chinese tool for changing the ideological orientation of individuals; ultimately a coercive tool that encouraged deceit under the threat of torture
thangka – a Tibetan religious painting usually framed by a silk brocade
Theravada – see *Hinayana*
thugpa – traditional Tibetan noodle dish
torma – offerings of sculptured *tsampa* cakes
trapa – Tibetan for 'monk'
tratsang – monastic college
Tripa – the post of abbot at Ganden Monastery; head of the *Gelugpa* order
trulku – incarnate *lama*
tsampa – roasted-barley flour, traditional staple of the Tibetan people
Tsang – traditional province to the west of *Ü*, with Shigatse as its capital
tsangpo – large river
tso – Tibetan for 'lake'
tsuglhakhang – literally 'grand temple', but often specifically the *Jokhang* of Lhasa
TTB – Tibetan Tourism Bureau

Ü – traditional province to the east of *Tsang*, with Lhasa as its capital
Ütsang – the area comprising the provinces of *Ü* and *Tsang*, also incorporating *Ngari*, or western Tibet; effectively central Tibet, the political, historical and agricultural heartland of Tibet

Vajrayana – literally the 'diamond vehicle', a branch of *Mahayana* Buddhism that finds a more direct route to bodhisattvahood through identification with meditational deities

Wheel of Life – this term refers to the cyclic nature of existence and the six realms where *rebirth* take place. The Wheel of Life is often depicted in monasteries.

yabyum – *Tantric* sexual union, symbolising the mental union of female insight and male compassion. Fierce deities are often depicted in yabyum with their consorts.

yidam – see *meditational deity*; may also have the function of being a personal protector deity that looks over an individual or family

yogin – 'yoga' in *Sanskrit* refers to a 'union' with the fundamental nature of reality. For Tibetan Buddhists this can be achieved through meditative techniques and through identification with a meditational deity. A yogin is an adept of such techniques.

yuan – unit of Chinese currency

zhaodaisuo – Chinese for 'guesthouse', usually a basic hostel

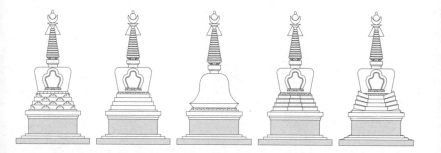

Thanks

Thanks to readers of the last edition who wrote to us with anecdotes and helpful hints:

Scott Ackiss, Jerry Alder, A Alexander, Lael Ambrose, G DeLois Anders, Raymond Ang, Matt Apfel, John Atkinson, Muneeza Aumir, Oded Barer, Roy Barton, Ounout Beeck, Jeff Bell, Betty Bellis, Jeremy Bernstein, Carol Bishop, Rebecca Blackwell, Lawrence Blieberg, Pamela Bode, Michael Boehm, A Bompy, John Bower, Graeme Brock, Claire Brondex, James Buchanan-Dunlop, Alice Buchtova, Peter Buechel, LE Butler, Pieter Buyck, Janet Cain, Dwight Call, Juan Carlos Picena, EA Carswell, Anne Carter, Flaminia Chapman, Max G Chapman, Dudu Cohen, Diana Cole, Nick Conway, Steve Davey, Frank de Groot, Anne-Mai Do Chi, Barbara Dombrowski, Eshed Doni, Gudrun Droop, B Dubois, Tomek Dudek, Elaine Duffy, Laurent-Jan Dullaart, Mark Duncan, James Dunn, Bruce Edwards, Robin Edwards, Troy Etulain, Brooks Evans, Ferdinand Fellinger, Linda & Jim Franklin, Margaret Gardner, Paul W Gioffi, Anne Girardet, Marie Goodwin, Brigitte Graeser, Jolanda Griens, Rolf Gross, Jez Gunnell, Martin Haase, Jacob Hak, Flora Hanitijo, Ron Harding, Stephanie Harrison, James Hatcher, Alex & Suzanne Hayes, Loona Hazarika, Dr Silke Heidrich, Bob Hoffman, Kathryn Howley, Mike & Nadine Hudson, Raimo Huebner, Laura Hughes, Robert H Jacoby, Volkmar E Janicke, Marjon Janmaat, Derek Jennings, Vladimir Jiras, Barnaby Joll, Stephen Jones, Tim Kangro, Robert Kelman, Dudi Kenig, Simone Klik, Rachael Knapp, Alex Koh Wei Hiong, Jan Kok, Lt Col Nilesh Korgaokar, Edward J Kormondy, Peter Krebs, Marie Kvamme, Peter van der Lans, S Latza, Richard Leavitt, Min Lee, Hans & Esther Leeuw, Karen Lefere, J Lester, Saskia Lieshout, Viridian Light-Hart, Franke Lutz, Margaret Macdonald, Fabio Maino, Iain Masterton, Dann Matts, Dave McFarlane, Jim McHugh, Clare Mercer, Csaba Mikusi, Rachel Miles, Dies van & Ruud Mil-Vogel, Ryo Miyanami, Gavin Moey, Dennis Mogerman, Judy Moore, Vincenzo Morelli, Dieter Neujahr, Nomi & Uri Nir, Joe Osentoski, Adam John Patterson, Manibrata Paul, Julio Penalva-Puig, Pelle Petersson, Bernard Phelps, Barbara Prevel, Wolfgang Rabitsch, Helen Ranger, Michelle Renbaum, Jonathon ED Richmond, Geja Rijsman-van den Akker, Claus Rislin, Susanne Ritz, Guy Rubin, Albert Sant, Alan Savage, Kelvin Schafli, Harry Schneider, Brett Schuppan, Penny Schwartz, Eugene Semb, Andrew Sewell, Dan Shingleton, Diana Silbergeld, Zsolt Sipeki, Steven Slutry, Donald Smith, Sandy Smith, Vanessa Smith Hilburn, Saskya Speer, Lea Stogdale, Johanna Surla, Eliav & Lihi Tal, Mark Thomas, Rene Tielkemeijer, Jennifer Tombaugh, Marion Trommsdorff, Lars van der Bruggen, Sietsche van Gunst, Ingrid van Klingeren, Stephen VanWyck, Daniel Vetter, Christine Veulemans, Ricard Vilata, Jerry Vinal, Frank & Karin Weeber, Frederic Wehowski, Susan Werner, Cliff Wheeler, Jan Willem Roks, Kirsten Wilson, Jon Wyler, Tian Yi, Jeff Young, Ondrej Zapletal, Walter Ziermann, Maike Ziesemer, Arianne de & Richard Zwart

Index

Text

A

accommodation 102-3
activities, see entries on specific
    activities
acute mountain sickness 88-90
agriculture 40-1
air travel 108-13
    table of major routes 112
    to/from Australia 111-12
    to/from continental Europe
        111
    to/from Hong Kong 112
    to/from major Chinese cities
        118-19
    to/from Nepal 118
    to/from New Zealand 111-12
    to/from North America 111
    to/from South-East Asia 112
    to/from the UK 109-11
Aksai Chin 276
Ali 260-1, 261-3, 275-6, **262**
altitude sickness 88-90
Amitabha 48
Amitayus 48
AMS, see acute mountain
    sickness
Ani Sangkhung Nunnery 154
Anjue Si, see Ngachu
    Monastery
Anti–British Imperialists Museum
    219
architecture 38-9
    Chinese styles 260
arts 35-40
    books on 79-80
    petroglyphs 275
Arun 333
autorickshaw travel 129
Avalokiteshvara 49

B

Babang, see Pelpung
Bachen 300
Baiya, see Pewar
Baiyu, see Pelyul
Bajie, see Pagyi
Bakhar Monastery 291
Bakong Monastery 302

Bakong Scripture Printing
    Press 302
Bamei 305
bargaining 74
Barkhor area 138-40, **139**
Bartso 325
Bashe, see Pasho
Batang 307, 308
Bayi 286-7, **286**
Beri 303
Beri Monastery 303
beyul 291
bicycle travel 101, 125-8, 168-9,
        see also road travel to/from
        Tibet
bird-watching 30-1
bodhisattvas 49-50
Bön 57-8, 288-9
Bönri 289-90
books 76-80, 87,
        see also literature
    Buddhism 37, 80
    fiction 80
    flora 311
    for children 80
    guidebooks 77
    health 87
    Lake Manasarovar 266
    medicinal plants 311
    Mt Kailash 266
    rock art 275
    Tibetan resistance 282
    travel 77-8
Brize 325
Buchu Monastery 142, 287
Buddha, the 45-7, 48
buddhas 48-9
Buddhism 12-13, 43-57, see
        also monkhood, see also
        Panchen Lama, see also
        Dalai Lama, see also
        Dalai Lamas
    basic concepts 46-7
    books on 37, 80
    Gelugpa order 56-7
    important figures 48-52,
        358-60
    Kagyupa order 56
    literature 37
    music 36-7
    Nyingmapa order 54-6
    Red Hats 57

    reincarnation 14
    Sakyapa order 56, 236
    symbols 55
    Wheel of Life 305
    Yellow Hats 57
bus travel 124
business hours 98-9

C

camping 102
carpet making 40
Chagpo Ri 152
Chakrasamvara 51
cham 35-6
Chamdo 293, 294-6, 301, **295**
Chana Dorje 50
chang 106
Changdu, see Chamdo
Changtang Nature Preserve 32
Changtang village 322
Chay 243, 331
Chayab Monastery 298
Chendiloma 259
Chengdu 117-18
Chenresig 49
Cherkip Monastery 346
Chetetong 333
children
    travelling with 96, 109, 315
    books for 80
Chim-puk hermitage 202-3, 268
China International Travel
    Service 114-15
China Travel Service 115
Chingwa Tagtse Dzong 210
Chiu Monastery 266-7, 345
Chö Dzom 333
Chöding hermitage 175
Chödzom 244
Chökorgye Monastery 211
Chongye 210
Chongye valley 209-10, **206**
Chö-puk hermitage 334
Chörten Rango 301
chörtens 38-9
Christianity 18
Chu Hara Nunnery 334
Chuku Monastery 340-1
cinema 80-2
CITS, see China International
    Travel Service

climate 28, 310-11
clothing
    for travellers 63-4
    for trekkers 313
    traditional Tibetan 42-3
consulates, see embassies &
    consulates
Coqen, see Tsochen
costs 73
courses 101-2
CTS, see China Travel Service
cultural considerations, see
        also responsible tourism
    etiquette 43
    for gay travellers 95
    for lesbian travellers 95
    for trekkers 317, 332
    for women travellers 95
    photography 83-4
    sky burial 42
    tipping & bargaining 74
    visiting monasteries &
        temples 134
Cuoqin, see Tsochen
customs 71
cycling, see bicycle travel

D

Daden Ritrö hermitage 177
Dagtse Dzong 180
Dahongliutan 276
Dalai Lama (the present) 20,
    25-7
    books by & about 79, 80
    illegality of material on 71, 98
Dalai Lamas 16-26, 51, see
    also Potala, the, see also
    Norbulingka
Damding Donkhang 341
Damxung 189, 301
Danba 305
dance 35-6
Dangxiong, see Damxung
Daofu 305
Darchen 264, 265, 338
Dardo, see Kangding
Dargye Monastery 303
Dartsedo, see Kangding
David-Neel, Alexandra 95
Dawa-tso 259
Demchok 51
demoness-subduing temples
    142
Den Monastery 303
departure tax 109
Derge 301, 302, 303

Dingboche Monastery 198
Dingqing, see Tengchen
Dipamkara 48
Dira-puk Monastery 338-9,
    341-2
disabled travellers 96, 109
documents 66-70, see also
    travel permits
Dodung Monastery 291
Dola Monastery 293
Dongaba Hot Springs 239
Dongtong Monastery 303
Dontok Monastery,
    see Dongtong Monastery
Dorje Drak Monastery (Ü) 197
Dorje Drak Monastery (Kham)
    307
Dorje Jigje 50
Dorje Ling Nunnery 325-6
Drak Yerpa 189-90, 268
Draksum-tso 284-6
Dram, see Zhangmu
drama 35-6
Drampa Gyang Temple 239
Dranang Monastery 197-8
Drango, see Luhuo
Dratang Monastery, see
    Dranang Monastery
Drayub 294
Drepung Monastery 169-72,
    172
Drigung Qu 193, 194-5
Drigung Til Monastery 193,
    194-5
drinks 105-6, 317-9
Drölma 49-50
Drölma Lhakhang 180-1
Drubthub Nunnery 152
Dungkar 274
Dzabuk Monastery 333
Dzayul 292
Dzogang 307
Dzogchen Monastery 303
Dzong Lugari 329
Dzongkog Pongdro 332
Dzongsar Monastery
    (Kham) 302
Dzongsar Monastery (Ü) 194

E

ecology 28-9, see also
    environmental issues
economy 33
education 35
electricity 84
email access 76-7

embassies & consulates 70-1
    Nepali consulate in Lhasa 134
Endun Monastery 294
entertainment 106
environmental issues 28-9,
    311, 316-17, 332
    endangered species 31-2
    in Qomolangma Nature
        Preserve 334
    logging 281
    national preserves 32
    rubbish (trash) 260
    Yamdrok-tso hydroelectricity
        project 213
Everest Base Camp 244, 335,
        see also Mt Everest
    trekking from Friendship
        Hwy to 329-35
    trekking to Tingri from 335-8

F

fauna 30-1, 281, 311-12
    Cordiceps sinensis 298
    in national preserves 32
fax services 76
festivals 99-101
    Saga Dawa 340
    Zhuanshanjie 307
films 80-2
flora 29-30, 281, 311-12
    Cordiceps sinensis 298
    in national preserves 32
food 103-5
    for good health 87
    for trekkers 316-17
Four Noble Truths, the 46-7
Friendship Hwy 120, 232

G

Gaize, see Gertse
Galden Jampaling Monastery
    294-5
Ganden Monastery 177-80
    trekking to Samye
        Monastery from 319-23
Gangpo Ri 206
Ganzi 303-5
Garthar, see Bamei
Garthar Chöde Monastery 305
Garthog Dzong, see Markham
Garze, see Ganzi
Garze Monastery 303
gay travellers 95
Gegye 259-60, 260-1
Geji, see Gegye
geography 27-8

geology 28
Gertse 259-60
Gesar Ling 152
Geshigong Monastery 286
gift giving 43
Gokung Monastery 278
Golmud 120-1
Gonchen Monastery 302
Gongkar 168, 196-7
Gongkar Chöde Monastery 196-7
Gongsar Monastery 298
Gossul Monastery 347
Gouri Kund 344
government 32-3
Gubengda 299
Guge kingdom 269-74
Gurla Mandata 347
Guru Rinpoche 51
Guru Rinpoche Monastery 268
Guza 292
Gyangdrak Monastery 265
Gyantse 216-22, **217**
Gyantse Dzong 219
Gyantse Kumbum 218-19
Gyaruptang 299
Gyatsa 211
Gyeling Tsokpa 198
Gyüme 153-4

H
Hadhi Nunnery 303
Haiyuan Si, see Garthar Chöde Monastery
handicrafts 40
Hayagriva 50
health 84-95
    books on 87
    for trekkers 315
    insurance 69, 87
    traditional medicine 157, 298, 311
Hepo Ri 202, 322
Hepu 319
highlights 59-61
hiking, see trekking
Hinduism 264
history 11-27
    books on 78-9
    fall of Chamdo 296
    important figures in Tibetan 51-2
    Khampa resistance 282

Sakyapa reign 236
Younghusband expedition 220-1
hitching 43, 128-9
Hor Qu 257-8, 346
horse-racing festivals 100
hotels, see accommodation

I
immunisations 84-7
industry 33
insurance 69, 87
Internet access 76-7
Internet resources 76

J
Jampa 49
Jampaling Kumbum 198
Jampelyang 49
Japon 333
Jara 286
Jarok Donkhang 342
Jiangda, see Jomda
Jieruotang, see Gyaruptang
Jin'gang Si, see Dorje Drak Monastery (Kham)
Jinkar Monastery 298
Jokhang, the 141-7, **143**
Jomda 301
Jonang Kumbum 239-40

K
Kaga 256
Kailash, see Mt Kailash
Kajia, see Kaga
Kandze, see Ganzi
Kangchen Monastery 233
Kangding 306-7
Kangtse 277
karaoke 106
karma 46
Karmapa 185
Karmashar Temple 154
Kashgar 275
Kathmandu 115-17
Kathok Monastery 302
Kathok Nunnery 283
Katsel Monastery 142, 194
Kham 279-309, **280**
Khampa resistance 282
Kharta 333
Khasa, see Zhangmu
Khojamath 276-7
King Tiger Hot Springs 258
Kodari 249

Kongpo region 284, **285**
Kongpo Gyamda 283-4
koras 133, 268-9
Korja Monastery 276
Kudi 276
Kunde Ling 152
Kyidrup Monastery 294

L
Labrang Monastery 121
Lake Manasarovar 265-7, 345-7
Lamaling Temple 287-8
Land Cruiser rental 125-8
Land Cruiser travel 125, 126, 130, see also road travel to/ from Tibet
Langbona Monastery 346
Langkhor Monastery 245
Langtang Monastery 191-2
language 58, 348-57
    courses 101-2
    glossary 358-65
    signs in Chinese 159
    Tibetan script 37
laundry services 84
legal matters 98
Leiwuqi Zhen, see Riwoche town
lesbian travellers 95
Leten 323-4
Lha Shing 333
Lhakhang Monastery 274
lhamo 36
Lhamo La-tso 210-11
Lhasa 131-81, **136-7**, **139**, **170**
    accommodation 158-61
    airport 168, 196-7
    entertainment 163-4
    places to eat 161-3
    shopping 164-6
    travel to/from 166-8
    travel within 168-9
Lhatse 238-9, 255-6
Lhatse Chöde 239
Lho Rigsum Lhakhang 154
Lhundrub 191
Lhundrub Dzong 192
Lhundrub valley 190-2
Lingkhor 133
Linzhi, see Nyingtri
Linzhou, see Lhundrub
Litang 308-9
Litang Chöde Monastery 308
literature 37, see also books
Lower Tantric College 153-4
Luhuo 305

Bold indicates maps.

Lukhang 153
Lulung 256
Lunang 290-1
Lungchang 337
Lurulangkar 275

M

magazines 82
Mahakala 50
Maitreya 49
Manasarovar, see Lake
    Manasarovar
mandalas 201, 304
Mani Tundu Temple 246
Manigango 303
Manitinga 327
Manjushri 49
Mapham Yum-tso, see Lake
    Manasarovar
maps 62-3, 312
Markham 308
Marmedze 48
Mazar 276
measures & weights 84
media 82
meditation courses 102
Medro Gungkar 193, 194
Mensi, see Moincer
Meru Nyingba Monastery 140
Meru Sarpa Monastery 154
Milarepa 52
Milarepa's Cave 246-7
Mindroling Monastery 198-9
minibus travel 124-5, 129
mining 33
Moincer 263
monasteries 176, see also
    monkhood
  design 38
  etiquette of visiting 134
money 71-4
monkhood 26, 41, 176, see
    also monasteries
mountain biking, see bicycle
    travel
mountaineering 101
Mt Everest 240-5
  trekking in region of 329-35
Mt Kailash 253, 263-5, 338-45
  pilgrimage to 268
  trekking around 338-45
Mt Labchi 268
Mt Meru 342, see also Mt
    Kailash
music 36-7
Muslim quarter, Lhasa 155

N

Nagchu 300-1
Nagpo Chenpo 50
Nalendra Monastery 191
Namseling Manor 204
Nam-tso 186-9
Nangartse 213
Nanwu Monastery 306
Naqu, see Nagchu
Nartang Monastery 233
  trekking from Shalu
      Monastery to 326-9
national preserves 32
  Changtang Nature Preserve 32
  Qomolangma Nature
      Preserve 32, 332, 334
Neche Goshog Monastery 288
Neche Kushuk Monastery, see
    Neche Goshog Monastery
Nechung Monastery 172-3
Nechung oracle 173
Neru Monastery 293
New Tingri, see Shegar
newspapers 82
Ngachö Monastery 204
Ngachu Monastery 306
Ngamring-tso 256
Ngang Tsang Drag Dog
    Dzong 337
Ngari 250-78, **251**
Ngor Monastery 326-7, 329
nirvana 47
Nisu Monastery 192
Noble Eightfold Path, the 47
nomads 30-1, 40-1, 188
Norbulingka 155-7, **155**
Nyalam 246-7, **246**
Nyalam Pelgye Ling 246-7
Nyango 322
Nyangtri, see Nyingtri
Nyenchen Tanglha 325
Nyenri Monastery, see Chuku
    Monastery
Nyingtri 288-9, 290

O

Oma-chu 260
Oma-tso 260
Öpagme 48
opera 36
organisations 96-7

P

Pabonka Monastery 176-7
Pagyi 288
painting 39-40

Palden Lhamo 51
Palha Lupuk 152
Panchen Lamas 228-9
Pangri Jokpa hermitage 286
Parma Ri 152
Paryang 257
Pasho 292, 293
Pasum 244, 333
pedicabs 129
Peiku-tso 256
Pelding 333
Pelkor Chöde Monastery 217-18
Pelpung 302
Pelung 291
Pelyul 302
Pemako 291
people 34-5, 188, 312
  books on 79
permits, see travel permits
Pero 329
Peruche 244
petroglyphs 275
Pewar 302
Phadrug 333
Phenpo valley,
    see Lhundrub valley
Phongdo 193
photography 82-3
Phuntsoling Monastery 239-40
pilgrimage 264, 268-9
pilgrimage circuits, see koras
Pisha 322
places to stay, see
    accommodation
planning 61-5
  climatic considerations 28,
      310-11
  for trekkers 312-13
  suggested itineraries 59-61
police, see Public Security
    Bureau
politics 32-3
Pomda 307
Pomda Monastery 293-4
Pomi 290, 291-2
Pongba 260
population 34-5
postal services 74
Potala, the 140, 148-52, **150**
Powo 291
prayer flags 44
prayer wheels 44
prostration 344
PSB, see Public Security Bureau
public holidays 99
Public Security Bureau 26,
    98-101

Puna 333
Purang 277-8, **277**

Q

Qomolangma, *see* Mt Everest
Qomolangma Nature Preserve
32, 332, 334

R

Ra Chu 337-8
Rabshi Monastery 333
radio 82
Raga, *see* Raka
Raka 256
Rakshas Tal 345
Ralung Monastery 215
Ramo Monastery 292
Ramoche Temple 153
Ratö Monastery 181
Ratsaka, *see* Riwoche town
Rawok 292
Rawok-tso 292
Rechung-puk Monastery 209
Red Hats 57
rebirth 46
reincarnation 14
religion 43-58, *see also* entries
on specific religions
rental vehicles 125-8, 167-8
Rephel 333
resources for travellers 96-7
responsible tourism 65, *see*
also cultural considerations
Dalai Lama materials 26, 71,
98
etiquette 43, 134
in Everest region 332, 334
photography 83-4
sky burial 42
when trekking 311, 312,
316-17, 332, 334
Reting Monastery 192-3
Riwo Dechen Monastery 210-11
Riwoche town 297-8
Riwoche Tsuglhakhang 297-8
Riwoche village 297-8
road travel to/from Tibet 119-23
Friendship Hwy 120, 232-3,
249, 255
Qinghai-Tibet Hwy 120-1
Sichuan-Tibet Hwy 121-2,
301-9
Sikkim to/from Tibet 123

Xinjiang-Tibet Hwy 122-3,
255, 275-6
Yunnan-Tibet Hwy 122
road travel within Tibet 125-8
Rong Chung ruins 335
Rongbatsa 303
Rongphu Glacier 335
Rongphu Monastery 243-4, 334
Rotung Monastery 298
Rumudong 275
Rutok 274-5
Rutok Dzong 274
Rutok Xian 274-5

S

safe travel 97-8
carrying money 73
in monasteries 26
road hazards 128
when trekking 88-90
Saga 256, 257
Sakya 234-7, **235**
Sakya Monastery 234-7
Sakya Thukpa 45-7, 48
Sakyamuni 45-7, 48
Samdeling Nunnery 177
Samding Nunnery 213-5
Samtenling Nunnery 193, 300
Samye mandala 201
Samye Monastery 199-204, **200**
Sanga Monastery 180
Sang-ngag Zimche Nunnery 204
Sangsang 256
sculpture 40
Selung Monastery 265
Senge Khabab, *see* Ali
senior travellers 96
Sera Monastery 173-6, **174**
Seralung Monastery 347
Sertsa 299
Sha Monastery 194
Shagchu 300
Shalu Monastery 233-4
trekking to Nartang
Monastery from 326-9
Shalung Nunnery 194
Shar Nunnery 192
Shegar 240, 243-4, 330, 331
Shegar Chöde Monastery 240
Shegar Dzong 240
Sheldrak Cave 207
Sheldrak hermitage 268
Sherab Chöling Hermitage 335
Shide Tratsang 155
Shigatse 223-33, **224**
Shigatse Dzong 228-9

Shiquanhe, *see* Ali
Shisha Pangma 256, 332
Shoka 286
shopping 106-7
Shri Devi 51
Shupshading 324
Sichuan 301-7
Sigyal Monastery 290
Sili Gotsang hermitage 192
Simbiling Monastery 278
sky burials 42
society 40-3, 312
Sok 299, 300
Sok Tsanden Monastery 300
Songtsen Gampo 11-12, 51-2
sport 106
statuary 40
student cards 69
stupas, *see* chörtens
swastikas 44

T

Ta'ersi Monastery 121
Tagong 305-6
Tagong Monstery 305
Tagyel-tso 258
Talung Monastery 192, 215
Tamdrin 50
Tangboche Monastery 209-10
Tangtong Gyelpo 16
Tangtong Gyelpo Chapel 302
Tapka Shelri 268
Tara 49-50
Tashi Chöling hermitage 177
Tashi Dor Monastery 187
Tashi Dzom 244, 332-3
Tashilhunpo Monastery 225-8,
226
taxes 74
departure tax 109
taxis 129-30
telephone services 74-5
television 82
temple etiquette 134
Tengchen 299
Tengchen Monastery 299
Tengye Ling 154
thangkas 39-40
Thöling Monastery 271, **270**
Thsada, *see* Zanda
Tibet Museum 158
Tibet Tourism Bureau 65
Tibetan Traditional Hospital 157
Tidrum Monastery 193-4
Tidrum Nunnery 195-6
time 83

Bold indicates maps.

Tingri 245-6
  trekking from Everest Base
    Camp to 335-8
tipping 74
Tirthapuri Hot Springs 267-9,
  267
toilets 84, 85, 316-17
tourist offices 65
tours 125, 129-30, see
    also travel agencies
  Chengdu-based operators 117
  Kathmandu-based operators
    116
  international-based operators
    113-15
Toyo 278
tractor travel 129
traditional life 40-3, 188, see
    also monkhood
  books about 79
  medicines 157
train travel 123
Tramo, see Pomi
Trandruk Monastery 142, 207
Trangu Monastery 296
travel agencies 125, see also tours
  Lhasa-based agencies 135
  trekking agencies 313-14
travel permits 68-9, 98-101, 315
trekking 101, 310-47
  agencies 313-14
  equipment 164-5, 312-13
  safety 88-90
  supplies 105, 163
trekking routes 318
  Bönri kora 289
  Damxung to Nam-tso 187
  Dranang valley 198
  Everest Base Camp to Tingri
    335-8, **330**
  Friendship Hwy to Everest
    Base Camp 329-35, **330**
  Ganden to Samye 319-23, **320**
  Humla to Mt Kailash 276
  Lake Manasarovar kora
    345-7, **346**
  Lhasa to Drak Yerpa
    hermitage 190-1
  Mt Kailash kora 338-45, **339**
  Rutok to Lhamo-La-tso 211
  Samye Monastery to
    Chim-puk hermitage 202-3

Sangri to Lhamo La-tso 211
Shalu to Nartang 326-9, **328**
Tashi Chöling hermitage to
    Samdeling Nunnery 177
to/from Nepal 123
Tsurphu to Yangpachen
    323-6, **324**
Trisong Detsen 52
Trugo Monastery 347
Tsaka 260
Tsamda Hot Springs 245
Tsang 212-49, **214-5**
Tsaparang 271-4, **272**
Tsechen 222
Tsepak Lhakhang 153
Tsepame 48
Tsetang 204-5, **205**
Tsetang Monastery 204
Tsochen 258-9
Tsodzong Monastery 284
Tsome Ling 154
Tsomum Monastery, see
    Tsodzong Monastery
Tsongkhapa 51
Tsurphu Monastery 184-6, 323
  trekking to Yangpachen
    Monastery from 323-6
TTB, see Tibet Tourism Bureau

Ü 182-211; **183**
Una Monastery 194

vaccinations 84-7
Vajrapani 50
vehicle rental, see rental
    vehicles
video systems 82
video, tips for filming 82-3
visas 66-8

Wamda, see Dzogang
Wango 322
water, safety for drinking 87-8,
    317-19
weaving 40
weights & measures 84
Wengdaka 299
Wheel of Life 305

women travellers 95
  health 94
woodcarving 40
work 102

Xiongba, see Pongba

yak-butter tea 105
yaks 30-1
Yama Do 319-20, 320-1
Yamalung hermitage 203, 322
Yamantaka 50
Yamdrok-tso 212-16, **216**
Yangan 299
Yangpachen Monastery 326
  trekking from Tsurphu
    Monastery to 323-6
Yarlung Tsangpo gorges 290
Yarlung valley 206-9, **206**
Yecheng 275-6
Yellow Hats 57
Yerngo Monastery 347
Yerpa Drubde Monastery 189
Yilhun La-tso 303
Yi'ong-tso 291
Yougong, see Dzogang
Younghusband, Francis 220-1
Yumbulagang 208-9
Yungdrungling Monastery
    (Tsang) 222-3
Yungdrungling Monastery
    (Kham) 289

Zanda 270-1, **270**
Zayu, see Dzayul
Zhabten Monastery 300
Zhada, see Zanda
Zhangmu 247-8, 256, **248**
Zhongba 257
Zhuanshanjie (festival) 307
Zhubalong 308
Zhuqing Si, see Dzogchen
    Monastery
Zora Monastery 298
Zutul-puk Monastery 338-9, 344

X

Y

Z

U

V

W

Boxed Text

Air Travel Glossary 110
Alexandra David-Neel 95
Assault on Everest, The 242-3
Basic Buddhist Concepts 46-7
Bayonets to Gyantse 220-1
Bön 288-9
China's Gifts to Ngari 260
Christian Missionaries in Early
    Tibet 18
Dealing with an Agency 125
Demoness-Subduing Temples 142
Détente 332
Down the Drain 213
Faces & Rivers of Mt Kailash,
    The 342
Fall from Grace (or Full of
    Shit?), A 85
Fall of Chamdo, The 296
Flora or Fauna? 298
Highs & Lows of Tibetan
    Travel 59
Kailash & Manasarovar
    Books 266
Karmapa Connection, The 185
Kilometre Markers along the
    Friendship Highway 232-3
Kilometre Markers along the
    Yarlung Tsangpo 196

Kongpo 284
Latest Word, The 68
Lhasa Signs in Chinese 159
Lhasa's Pilgrim Circuits 133
Mandalas 304
Milarepa versus Naro
    Bönchung 343
Mission Impossible 123
Monasteries in Tibet 176
Monastery Layout 38
Mythology of the Yarlung
    Valley 208
Nechung Oracle, The 173
Nomads 188
Overview of Treks 318
Panchen Lamas, The 228-9
Pilgrimage 268-9
Planning a Land Cruiser Trip to
    Mt Kailash 253
Prehistoric Petroglyphs 275
Priests & Patrons: The Reign of
    the Sakyapas 236
Prostration Points & Footprints
    344
Qomolangma Nature Preserve
    334
Red Hats versus Yellow Hats 57
Reincarnation Lineages 14

Religious Symbols in Tibetan
    Buddhism 55
Responsible Trekking 316-17
Sacred Items & Symbols 44-5
Samye Mandala, The 201
Sky Burial 42
Tangtong Gyelpo 16
Tibet Chic 81
Tibet in Exile 32
Tibet's Hidden Lands 291
Tibetan Medicine 157
Tibetan Tasters 121
To the Land of Shiva 264
Travelling to Ngari 254-5
Trekking Disclaimer 311
Undercover Monks 26
Visas for Hong Kong &
    Macau 66
Visiting Monasteries &
    Temples 134
What's in a Name? 241
Which Way, How Many Days,
    How Many Times, How
    Many Rivers? 341-2
World of a Monk, The 41
Yak-Butter Tea 105
Yakety-Yak 30-1

MAP LEGEND

CITY ROUTES

Highway	Sealed Highway	====	Unsealed Road
Road	Primary Road		One-Way Street
Road	Secondary Road		Pedestrian Street
Street	Street		Stepped Street
Lane	Lane	)===	Tunnel
	Roadblocks		Footbridge

HYDROGRAPHY

	River, Creek		Dry Lake, Salt Lake
	Canal		Spring/Watering Hole
	Lake, Tank		Waterfalls

REGIONAL ROUTES

	Sealed Highway
	Primary Road
	Secondary Road
	Minor Road

TRANSPORT ROUTES & STATIONS

	Train		Cable Car, Chairlift
	Metro		Ferry
	Tramway		Path in Park
	Bus Route		Walking Trail
	Monorail		Walking Trail/Kora

BOUNDARIES

	International
	State
	Disputed
	Fortified Wall

AREA FEATURES

	Building		National Park
	Park, Garden		Market
	Beach		Cemetery
	Campus		Urban

MAP SYMBOLS

CAPITAL	National Capital	Bus Terminal, Stop	Jain Temple		Ruin
CAPITAL	State Capital	Camping Ground	Lighthouse		Shopping Centre
City	City, Large Town	Cathedral, Church	Lookout		Stately Home
Town	Town	Cave	Monument		Chörten
Village	Village	Checkpoint	Mountain, Hill		Swimming Pool
	Place to Stay	Cinema	Mountain Range		Taxi
	Place to Eat	Dzong	Museum, Gallery		Transport (General)
	Point of Interest	Embassy, Consulate	Parking Area		Telephone
	Airfield, Airport	Ferry Terminal	Pass		Theatre
	Bank	Golf Course	Petrol/Gas Station		Toilet
	Bird Sanctuary	Gompa	Public Security Bureau		Tomb
	Border Crossing	Hindu Temple	Post Office		Tourist Information
	Bön Monastery/Temple	Hospital	Prayer Wheel		Trailhead
	Buddhist Monastery/ Nunnery/Temple	Internet Cafe	Pub, Bar		Zoo

Note: Not all symbols displayed above appear in this book.

LONELY PLANET OFFICES

Australia
Locked Bag 1, Footscray, Victoria 3011
☎ 03 8379 8000 fax 03 8379 8111
email: talk2us@lonelyplanet.com.au

USA
150 Linden St, Oakland, CA 94607
☎ 510 893 8555 TOLL FREE: 800 275 8555
fax 510 893 8572
email: info@lonelyplanet.com

UK
10a Spring Place, London NW5 3BH
☎ 020 7428 4800 fax 020 7428 4828
email: go@lonelyplanet.co.uk

France
1 rue du Dahomey, 75011 Paris
☎ 01 55 25 33 00 fax 01 55 25 33 01
email: bip@lonelyplanet.fr
www.lonelyplanet.fr

World Wide Web: www.lonelyplanet.com *or* AOL keyword: lp
Lonely Planet Images: lpi@lonelyplanet.com.au